Microsoft Outlook 2013
Inside Out

Jim Boyce

Published with the authorization of Microsoft Corporation by:
O'Reilly Media, Inc.
1005 Gravenstein Highway North
Sebastopol, California 95472

ISBN: 978-0-7356-7127-0

1 2 3 4 5 6 7 8 9 LSI 8 7 6 5 4 3

Printed and bound in the United States of America.

Microsoft Press books are available through booksellers and distributors worldwide. If you need support related to this book, email Microsoft Press Book Support at *mspinput@micro-soft.com*. Please tell us what you think of this book at *http://www.microsoft.com/learning/booksurvey*.

Acquisitions and Development Editor: Kenyon Brown

Production Editor: Rachel Steely

Editorial Production: Zyg Group, LLC

Technical Reviewer: Vincent Averello

Copyeditor: Nicole LeClerc

Indexer: BIM Publishing Services, Inc.

Cover Design: Twist Creative • Seattle

Cover Composition: Ellie Volckhausen

Illustrator: Rebecca Demarest

Contents at a glance

Part 6: Security and backup

Part 7: Customizing Outlook and using advanced features

Table of contents

Part 4: Managing your calendar and tasks

Part 5: Collaboration

Part 7: Customizing Outlook and using advanced features

Introduction

Welcome to *Microsoft Outlook 2013 Inside Out*. If you are a typical computer user, you probably spend at least some portion of your day in Outlook reading and creating email messages, managing your calendar, and using Outlook's other features for contacts and tasks. A growing number of people spend 60–80% of their time in Outlook. With Outlook being such a big part of your day, you likely are looking for a resource to help you make the most of Outlook. That's where *Microsoft Outlook 2013 Inside Out* comes in.

This book is intended to not only help you learn to use all of Outlook's features, but also use them *effectively*. By gaining new skills and optimizing the time you spend in Outlook, you'll be more productive and no doubt more satisfied with the application.

Who this book is for

Understanding all of the Outlook 2013 features and putting them to work is the focus of *Microsoft Outlook 2013 Inside Out*. Rather than providing just the how-to content for people who want to learn to use Outlook, *Microsoft Outlook 2013 Inside Out* also explores collaboration topics, server-side issues and administration, customized deployment, and higher-level topics geared toward the experienced user and administrator. So you get the best of both worlds: a solid explanation of Outlook's features and how to make the most of them, as well as deeper knowledge about Outlook customization, collaboration, and management.

This book makes some assumptions about the reader. You should be familiar with your Windows operating system, whether Windows 7 or Windows 8. You should be comfortable working with a computer and have a good understanding of how to work with menus, dialog boxes, and other aspects of the user interface. In short, *Microsoft Outlook 2013 Inside Out* assumes that you're an experienced computer user who wants a comprehensive look at what Outlook 2013 can do, how to put the application to work for you, and how to manage Outlook.

How this book is organized

Microsoft Outlook 2013 Inside Out offers a structured, logical approach to all aspects of using and managing Outlook 2013. Each chapter focuses on a specific aspect of Outlook 2013.

Part I, "Getting started with Outlook 2013," provides an overview of Outlook and the new features in Outlook 2013, as well as features that have been removed from or are deprecated in the new edition. You learn how to control the way Outlook starts, set up various types of accounts, and use the new interface. In addition, you learn about color categories and how to use them effectively in Outlook.

Part II, "Working with email," covers the most common tasks people perform in Outlook—managing their email. This part of the book starts with basic email tasks and then moves on to more complex features such as text formatting, using tables, working with graphics, and using signatures. Part II also covers how to secure your email and system with digital signatures, encryption, junk email filtering, and digital rights management. You learn in detail how to manage your email using rules, alerts, and automatic responses, as well as how to find and organize your email using features such as Search Folders, Outlook folders, and more.

Part III, "Working with contacts and address books," offers a comprehensive look at address books and contacts in Outlook. In addition to these foundational topics, Part III explains the new features in Outlook for integrating social networking services such as Facebook, LinkedIn, and SharePoint to provide a unified look at your contacts and their online information.

Part IV, "Managing your calendar and tasks," provides detailed guidance for using Outlook's Calendar folder and related features to manage your schedule, set up and conduct meetings, and schedule and manage resources such as meeting rooms. Part IV also explains how to use the Tasks folder and its features to manage your tasks and projects, including how to assign tasks to others.

Part V, "Collaboration," is the place to go to learn how to integrate Outlook with other collaboration tools such as Lync and SharePoint. In addition, Part V explains how to use the delegation features in Outlook that enable an administrative assistant to manage your calendar and other items in Outlook, as well as how to share your calendar with others.

Part VI, "Security and backup," explores a broad range of security-related topics that will help you secure your system and Outlook data. You learn about virus protection and how to control the Outlook antivirus features, as well as how to archive and back up your data.

Part VII, "Customizing Outlook and using advanced features," moves into more advanced Outlook topics, starting with a solid overview of the ways you can customize the Outlook interface to suit the way you work and streamline common tasks. Part VII also explains how to create custom views to help you organize and analyze the information stored in Outlook. You'll find additional customization- and development-related topics in Part VII, including how to create and use templates and custom forms, create macros and begin to program Outlook using Visual Basic for Applications (VBA), use Group Policy to customize Outlook deployment and configuration, and access your Outlook data without using Outlook.

Features and conventions used in this book

This book uses special text and design conventions to make it easier for you to find the information you need.

Text conventions

Convention	Meaning
Abbreviated commands for navigating the ribbon	For your convenience, this book uses abbreviated commands. For example, "Click Home, Insert, Insert Cells" means that you should click the Home tab on the ribbon, click the Insert button, and then finally click the Insert Cells command.
Boldface type	**Boldface** indicates text that you type.
Initial Capital Letters	The first letters of the names of tabs, dialog boxes, dialog box elements, and commands are capitalized—for example, the Save As dialog box.
Italicized type	*Italicized* type indicates new terms.
Plus sign (+) in text	Keyboard shortcuts are indicated by a plus sign (+) separating key names. For example, Ctrl+Alt+Delete means that you press the Ctrl, Alt, and Delete keys at the same time.

Design conventions

INSIDE OUT   This statement illustrates an example of an "Inside Out" heading

These are the book's signature tips. In these tips, you get the straight scoop on what's going on with the software—inside information about why a feature works the way it does. You'll also find handy workarounds to deal with software problems.

Sidebar

Sidebars provide helpful hints, timesaving tricks, or alternative procedures related to the task being discussed.

TROUBLESHOOTING

This statement illustrates an example of a "Troubleshooting" problem statement

Look for these sidebars to find solutions to common problems you might encounter. Troubleshooting sidebars appear next to related information in the chapters. You can also use "Index to Troubleshooting Topics" at the back of the book to look up problems by topic.

Cross-references point you to locations in the book that offer additional information about the topic being discussed.

CAUTION

Cautions identify potential problems that you should look out for when you're completing a task or that you must address before you can complete a task.

Note

Notes offer additional information related to the task being discussed.

Acknowledgments

I have written many books for Microsoft Press and O'Reilly over the years, and it has always been a great experience. The great people at both organizations have made the experience what it is. I want to first thank Kenyon Brown for the opportunity to work on this series again, and for his great advice on content and direction. I also want to thank Rob Tidrow for stepping in to help with authoring. Rob has been a joy to work with over the many years I've known him, and I hope we have the opportunity to work together again in the future.

Many other people have contributed to this book as well, and it would not be possible without them. So I would also like to thank technical reviewer Vince Averello, copy editor Nicole LeClerc, and production editors Rachel Steely and Kristen Borg for their hard work and efforts.

Jim Boyce
July 2013

Support and feedback

The following sections provide information on errata, book support, feedback, and contact information.

Errata

We've made every effort to ensure the accuracy of this book and its companion content. Any errors that have been reported since this book was published are listed on our Microsoft Press site at oreilly.com:

http://aka.ms/Outlook2013IO/errata

If you find an error that is not already listed, you can report it to us through the same page.

If you need additional support, email Microsoft Press Book Support at

mspinput@microsoft.com

Please note that product support for Microsoft software is not offered through the addresses above.

We want to hear from you

At Microsoft Press, your satisfaction is our top priority, and your feedback is our most valuable asset. Please tell us what you think of this book at

http://www.microsoft.com/learning/booksurvey

The survey is short, and we read every one of your comments and ideas. Thanks in advance for your input!

Stay in touch

Let's keep the conversation going! We're on Twitter at

http://twitter.com/MicrosoftPress

PART I

Getting started with Outlook 2013

What's new in Outlook 2013?

A s you might expect, Microsoft has made some significant changes to the latest edition of its Office applications, and Outlook 2013 is no exception. For example, all of the Microsoft Office apps sport a new, streamlined interface in the same style as the new Windows 8 user interface. Other changes go much deeper than the interface, however. For example, Microsoft Outlook 2013 builds on the social networking features in Outlook 2010 to enable you to integrate contacts from several different social networking sites (such as Facebook) and to view social networking content from those sites within Outlook. Other changes include improved ActiveSync support, new calendar and email features, changes for Microsoft Exchange Server users, and more.

If you're an experienced Outlook user, one of your first questions might be, "What's new in Outlook 2013?" That's what this chapter is all about. While not every little change to or nuance of the new Outlook 2013 interface or the new and improved features is covered here, this chapter offers a broad overview of the new features in Outlook 2013 to help you get up to speed quickly. Let's start with the most obvious: the user interface.

A new look

The most obvious change to Outlook 2013 is the new, streamlined user interface. With the introduction of the new Windows 8–style user interface, Microsoft has introduced a new design philosophy for Windows applications. These applications have fewer interface elements, giving the applications a cleaner, less cluttered look. But while Outlook 2013 has a more simplified interface, it doesn't have the spartan look of a Windows 8–style app. For example, Outlook 2013 still has a title bar, the ribbon, and other interface elements you've come to expect in a Windows app. Figures 1-1 and 1-2 contrast the new Outlook 2013 with the Windows 8 Mail app to give you a feel for the difference.

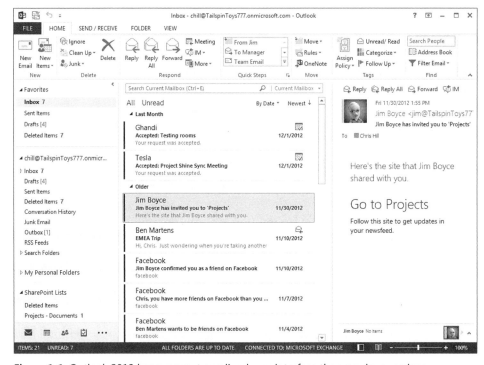

Figure 1-1 Outlook 2013 has a more streamlined user interface than previous versions.

Admittedly, the new interface might take you some time to get used to, but having used Outlook 2013 since the technical preview was released, I can tell you that it's a short learning curve. Spend a day or so with the app, and you'll feel as comfortable using it as you did the previous versions.

Chapter 1

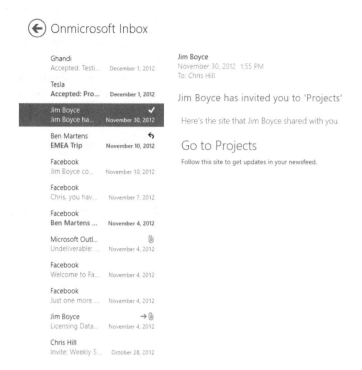

Figure 1-2 The Windows 8–style Mail app's interface is much more simplified than the Outlook 2013 interface.

Note
Office apps still run on the Windows desktop, even on a Windows 8 computer. This includes the Windows RT versions of the Office 2013 apps that run on the Microsoft Surface RT. Whether you run Office 2013 on a Windows 7 or Windows 8 computer, the apps will look and function the same. Only the way you start your Office apps will be different between these two platforms; these differences are noted in Chapter 2, "Starting Outlook."

> **Note**
>
> There is currently no version of Outlook 2013 for devices running Windows 8 RT (such as the Microsoft Surface RT). However, the Windows 8 Mail app does enable you to connect to Exchange Server, Microsoft Office 365, and other mail services. If you're looking for an email option for a Windows RT device, the Mail app makes a serviceable alternative to Outlook on those devices. Also, an RT version of Outlook might be available by the time you read this.

New ways to work in Outlook

Outlook 2013 introduces a handful of changes that give you new ways to work in Outlook. For example, as Figure 1-3 shows, you can compose a message reply right in the Reading Pane, rather than having to open the message reply in a new window. You can also pop out the message into its own window for editing by clicking Pop Out at the top of the Reading Pane.

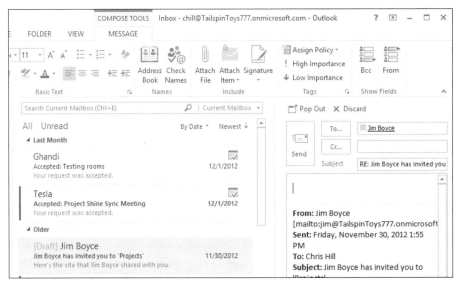

Figure 1-3 Outlook 2013 enables you to compose replies within the Reading Pane.

Composing replies inline is just one of the new ways you can work in Outlook 2013. Other new ways include the following:

- Use the blue vertical bar at the left edge of a message header to mark the message as either read or unread.

- Use the icons at the right edge of the message header to view reply status, flag a message, or delete a message.

- Hover the mouse on a calendar item to see a pop-up preview (see Figure 1-4).

- Minimize the Folder Pane (previously called the Navigation Pane), and then click All Folders in the Folder Pane to temporarily open a folder list where you can select another folder to view.

- Use the Zoom slider in the status bar to change the text zoom for the message displayed in the Reading Pane.

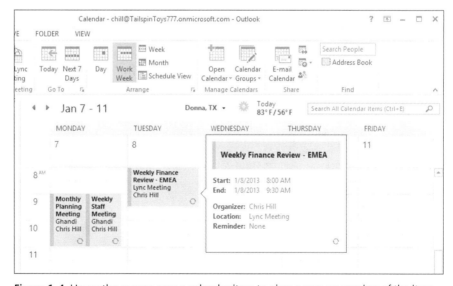

Figure 1-4 Hover the mouse over a calendar item to view a pop-up preview of the item.

Email changes

Outlook 2013 incorporates some changes for working with email and email accounts. For example, you can compose replies inline in the Reading Pane, rather than in a separate message window. Also, Outlook 2013 now runs a spelling checker on the text you type in a message's Subject field. That's a small but important change for ensuring your messages are polished and professional.

Another new email-related feature is the capability to warn you when you might have forgotten to add an attachment to a message. For example, if your message contains the word *attached*, Outlook will warn you with a dialog box before sending the message if no file is attached to the message.

Several other email-related changes in Outlook 2013 are more global in nature. These changes are described in other sections of this chapter.

The People Hub and social networking

Outlook 2013 integrates social networking features, enabling you to connect social networking accounts with Outlook. Doing so allows you to view contact information from contacts stored in those social networking accounts (such as your Facebook friends, for example). Social networking integration also enables you to view updates about your social contacts within Outlook.

The Contacts folder still exists in Outlook 2013, but it's now referred to as the People Hub, with the default view now named People. As Figure 1-5 shows, the People Hub brings together information from your contact items, as well as information for those contacts from social networking sites. In this example, the contact includes information from a Facebook account.

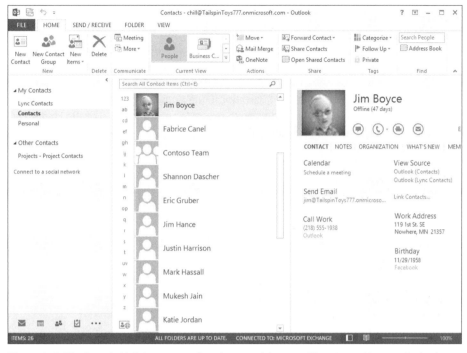

Figure 1-5 The People Hub integrates data from social networking sites with your Outlook contacts.

Outlook 2013 includes built-in support for Facebook, LinkedIn, and Microsoft SharePoint accounts, which means you can view contact information and social networking update feeds for your contacts from those services.

> **Note**
> After you add a social networking account to Outlook, the app uses the email address associated with a contact item to pull information from the social networking account, where applicable. For example, Outlook won't pull down all of your Facebook friends to the Contacts folder if you add your Facebook account. Instead, when you add a contact to Outlook, Outlook checks your Facebook contacts for one that has the same email address as the address you added for the Outlook contact. If it finds a match, it pulls down the other data for that contact from Facebook.

Folder Pane changes

The Navigation Pane in previous versions of Outlook has been renamed the Folder Pane in Outlook 2013. The Folder Pane provides all of the same features as the Navigation Pane, but it naturally has a new streamlined look to match the rest of the new Outlook 2013 interface. For example, if you choose the Compact Navigation option for the Folder Pane, the various Outlook folders are represented at the bottom of the Folder Pane by small icons, as shown in Figure 1-6.

Figure 1-6 The Folder Pane (shown here both in normal and minimized states) provides the same features as the Navigation Pane from previous versions of Outlook.

As in previous versions, you can minimize the Folder Pane to give you more space to show message headers, message content, and so on. When minimized, the Folder Pane displays as a narrow vertical bar. You can click All Folders to temporarily expand the Folder Pane to select a different folder. When in minimized view, the Folder Pane shows the icons for the primary Outlook folders as small icons arranged vertically rather than horizontally.

The Weather Bar

The Weather Bar is a new addition to the default Calendar folder views. As Figure 1-7 illustrates, the Weather Bar shows the current temperature and next day's weather for a selected location. When you hover the mouse on the weather data, Outlook shows a pop-up window with additional weather information for the selected location. You can add multiple locations and choose between them using the drop-down button to the left of the weather data.

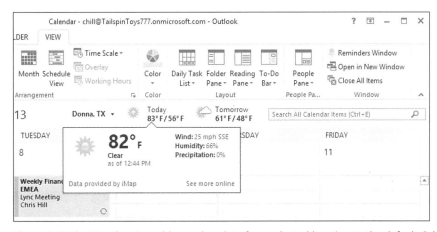

Figure 1-7 The Weather Bar adds weather data for a selected location to the default Calendar folder views.

Exchange ActiveSync support

Outlook 2013 improves support for additional email services through built-in Exchange ActiveSync (EAS) support. This feature enables you to connect Outlook 2013 to Outlook.com (Hotmail), Office 365, and other email services that use ActiveSync, without the need for a separate connector or add-on. EAS also enables mobile devices to connect to these types of email services.

Quick Peek preview

Outlook 2013 adds a couple of new features to help you view information from the Folder Pane without opening the folder where the data resides. As shown previously in Figure 1-4, you can hover the mouse on a calendar item to view a pop-up preview of that item. In addition, you can preview your calendar by hovering the mouse on the Calendar icon in the Folder Pane. By default, the Quick Peek preview shows any items scheduled for the current day. You can also click a date in the preview to show the calendar items for that day, as shown in Figure 1-8. Calendar preview enables you to view upcoming calendar items without switching away from the current folder.

Figure 1-8 You can preview your schedule, favorite contacts, and tasks from the Folder Pane.

The People and Tasks icons in the Folder Pane also provide Quick Peek previews. Hover the mouse on the People icon to view the contacts that you have added to your Favorites list. Hover the mouse on the Tasks icon to see a list of active tasks.

Cached Exchange Mode

Outlook 2013 implements a couple of new features to improve offline caching for Exchange Server accounts (including Outlook.com and Office 365 accounts). The new Sync Slider feature lets you configure the amount of data that is synchronized to the local offline store (.ost) file. By default, when Cached Exchange Mode is enabled for the account, Outlook will download 12 months' worth of data and automatically remove (but not delete from the account) any data that is older than 12 months. However, as shown in Figure 1-9, you can use the slider to increase or decrease the amount of data that Outlook caches. This can be particularly useful if you have a relatively large mailbox but not a lot of local storage space to hold the cache (such as on a tablet with a smaller solid state drive).

Figure 1-9 Use the Sync Slider on the Change Account dialog box to specify how much data to cache locally.

If the data you want isn't cached locally, you can still view it. For example, if you have configured your account to show only one month of data, but there are messages in your Inbox that are three months old, you can retrieve and view those older messages by clicking the link labeled Click Here to view more on Microsoft Exchange than appears at the bottom of the messages list.

Outlook also uses a new feature called Exchange Fast Access to improve the synchronization experience for users in situations where syncing messages might take a noticeable amount of time, such as on initial mailbox setup, when returning from vacation (with lots of messages waiting), and similar situations. Exchange Fast Access shows the user's updated calendar and most recent messages while it continues to synchronize the other data in the background.

IMAP

Outlook 2013 incorporates some changes in the way it supports IMAP accounts. For example, Outlook 2013 notifies you when you receive a new email message from an IMAP account. The synchronization experience is also improved, with synchronization happening in the background (messages appear more quickly than if an entire sync had to take place before your messages were displayed).

In addition, the IMAP folders appear in the Folder Pane much like they do for an Exchange Server account. Outlook shows nonroaming, local folders with the text This Computer Only next to the folder name to indicate that the folder is local rather than a part of your IMAP account's folder structure (see Figure 1-10).

Figure 1-10 Local folders for IMAP accounts are identified in the Folder Pane.

OST compression

By default, when you add an Exchange Server account that uses an offline .ost file, Outlook creates a compressed .ost file for the account. The compressed .ost file can be up to 40 percent smaller than a noncompressed .ost file. You can use group policy and the Do Not Create New OST File On upgrade policy to prevent Outlook from using a compressed .ost file. The default size for the compressed .ost file is also configurable.

> **Note**
>
> An uncompressed .ost file can be as much as 80 percent larger than the user's corresponding mailbox size on the server because of differences between the data format on the server and the local data format.

Apps for Outlook

Apps for Outlook are add-in apps available from the Microsoft Office Store that provide specific add-on functionality to Outlook 2013. For example, the Twitter by PowerInbox app lets you follow, tweet, and direct messages to other Twitter users from Outlook. Exchange Server administrators can also deploy apps for their users (this requires Exchange Server 2013).

Site mailboxes

Site mailboxes are a collaboration feature that relies on Exchange Server 2013 and SharePoint 2013 to provide access to a shared mailbox through a common interface. A site mailbox comprises SharePoint owners and members, shared storage through an Exchange Server 2013 mailbox for messages, and a SharePoint 2013 site for documents. While the messages reside in Exchange Server, they are exposed in Outlook and in SharePoint, enabling site members to access the messages from either application.

Features deprecated or removed from Outlook

Several Outlook features have been either deprecated or removed altogether in Outlook 2013. An example of a deprecated feature is the Notes folder, which still exists but for which Outlook 2013 provides fewer configuration settings. Table 1-1 provides an overview of deprecated or removed features for Outlook 2013.

TABLE 1-1 Deprecated or removed features for Outlook 2013

Feature	Change type	Change description
Outlook Meeting Workspaces	Removed	The capability to create Meeting Workspaces is removed to provide a simpler ribbon experience.
Outlook Exchange Classic Offline	Removed	Offline mode is removed in favor of Cached Exchange Mode and EAS.
/CleanFreeBusy switch	Removed	This startup switch is removed because of the removal of the Public Folder Free/Busy feature.
Command Bars Object Model	Removed	This object model has been removed because command bars are not used in Outlook 2013.
Outlook Direct Booking	Removed	This feature is superseded by the Exchange Availability service and free/busy for resources.
Import/Export to applications	Changed	Some file types and data sources are no longer supported for import/export with Outlook 2013.

Feature	Change type	Change description
Journal	Removed	Journal and automatic journaling are removed.
Link Collection	Removed	The Link Collection object model is removed and functionality is no longer available in the user interface.
Notes customization	Changed	Outlook 2013 provides fewer options for configuring notes.
Legacy contact linking	Removed	The capability to link Outlook items to contacts, which was designed to support the Activities tab (also removed), is removed and replaced by the Outlook Social Connector and New Person Card.
Outlook Activities tab	Removed	These features are implemented by the Outlook Social Connector and People Pane.
Outlook Mobile Service	Removed	The capability to send and receive text messages is removed from Outlook 2013.
Suggested Contacts	Removed	On clean installations, this folder is not created, nor are contacts suggested. On an upgrade, the existing data is retained and is used for linking, aggregation, and searching, but contacts are not suggested.
Office.com Calendar publishing	Removed	The capability to publish calendars to Office.com for sharing is removed. Calendars can be shared from Exchange Server and through services such as Outlook.com/Hotmail.
Outlook/Exchange deliver to .pst file	Removed	Exchange accounts no longer have the capability to deliver new messages to a .pst file.
Dial-up/VPN options	Removed	Dial-up and VPN options are removed from Outlook because they are supported through the Windows operating system.
Public Folder Free/Busy	Removed	This feature is replaced by the Exchange Availability Service.
User Datagram Protocol (UDP)	Removed	This feature is replaced by an asynchronous notification method.
AutoPreview	Removed	The feature is removed, but it is still possible to configure a view to show a preview of one, two, or three lines of a message.
Outlook search through Windows shell	Removed	Outlook items do not appear in searches from the Windows shell (such as from the Start menu). To find Outlook 2013 items, search within Outlook.

I N most cases, starting Microsoft Outlook 2013 is as simple as double-clicking an icon, choosing an item from the Start menu, or double-clicking a tile on the Windows 8 Start screen. However, there are some optional ways to start Outlook that either simplify how you start Outlook or cause Outlook to function in certain ways. For example, you can use command-line switches to have Outlook open specific types of items (such as a new message window) on startup.

This chapter explores the options you have for starting Outlook and describes the command-line switches you can use to control Outlook's startup behavior.

Standard methods for starting Outlook

You have several methods to start Outlook, some of which depend on the version of Windows running on your PC.

Normal startup

When you install Outlook 2013, the options that become available for starting Outlook depend on whether your PC is running Windows 7 or Windows 8.

When you install Microsoft Office on a Windows 7 PC, Setup adds shortcuts to the Start menu for your Office apps. You can start Outlook 2013 by choosing Start, All Programs, Microsoft Office 2013, Outlook 2013 (see Figure 2-1).

Figure 2-1 Setup creates shortcuts in the Start menu when you install Office 2013 on a Windows 7 PC.

On a Windows 8 device, Setup places tiles for the Office apps on the Start screen, as shown in Figure 2-2. To start an Office app on a Windows 8 device, just tap the app's tile on the Start screen. Office 2013 apps run on the desktop rather than as Windows 8–style apps, so the app will open on the desktop.

> **Note**
>
> Windows 8 RT devices include copies of Word, Excel, PowerPoint, and OneNote. Currently, the other Office 2013 apps are not provided for Windows 8 RT devices.

Figure 2-2 Setup adds tiles to the Windows 8 Start screen when you install Office 2013 on a Windows 8 device.

Creating shortcuts

The Windows 7 Start menu and the Windows 8 Start screen work just fine for starting Office apps such as Outlook, but depending on how you work in Windows, you might prefer to create shortcuts for Outlook and some of your other Office apps to make them accessible from the desktop or taskbar. That way, you don't have to open the Start menu or Start screen to start the apps. The following sections explain how to create these types of shortcuts.

Pinning Outlook to the Start menu and taskbar (Windows 7)

Windows 7 enables you to *pin* programs to the Start menu and Windows taskbar, making the programs easily accessible. You can then simply click the program's icon on the Start menu or taskbar to open the program. To pin Outlook to the Windows 7 Start menu or taskbar, click Start, All Programs, Microsoft Office, and then right-click Microsoft Outlook 2013 and choose Pin To Start Menu or Pin To Taskbar.

Pinning Outlook to the Start screen and taskbar (Windows 8)

Windows 8, similar to Windows 7, enables you to pin app shortcuts to the Start screen or taskbar. By default, Setup pins the Office 2013 app tiles to the Start screen, but if your PC has been customized, those tiles might no longer be located on the Start screen. If that's the case, you can easily put them back on the Start screen. To do so, follow these steps:

1. Open the Start screen.

2. Open the charms (press Windows logo key+C).

3. Click Search.

4. Locate the Office apps, which are all listed under the Microsoft Office 2013 group.

5. Right-click the app you want to pin to the Start screen (or drag down on it to select it), and click or tap Pin To Start (see Figure 2-3).

Figure 2-3 You can easily pin apps to the Start screen in Windows 8.

You can also pin apps to the Windows 8 taskbar, which makes the apps easily accessible from the Windows 8 desktop. To pin an app to the taskbar, locate the app on the Start screen or All Apps search results (as described in the previous example), select the app, and click or tap Pin To Taskbar. Figure 2-4 shows the Outlook 2013 shortcut pinned to the Windows 8 taskbar.

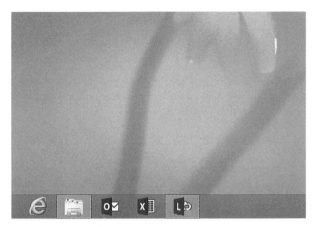

Figure 2-4 A selection of Office 2013 app shortcuts pinned to the Windows 8 taskbar.

Specifying an Outlook profile

Outlook uses a *profile* to store account settings and configure Outlook for your email servers, directory services, address books, data files, and other settings. You can configure Outlook to prompt you to choose a profile (if multiple profiles exist) or have it use a specific one by default. Figure 2-5 shows Outlook prompting to choose a profile.

Figure 2-5 Outlook 2013 prompts you to choose a profile at startup.

To use an existing profile, simply select it in the drop-down list in the Choose Profile dialog box and then click OK. Click New to create a new profile (this is covered in Chapter 3,
"Setting up accounts in Outlook"). Click Options in the Choose Profile dialog box to display
the option Set As Default Profile. Select this option to specify the selected profile as the
default profile, which will appear in the drop-down list by default in subsequent Outlook
2013 sessions. For example, if you maintain separate personal and work profiles, and your
personal profile always appears in the drop-down list, but you want the work profile to
show up by default instead, select your work profile and then choose Set As Default Profile
to make the work profile the default.

**For an in-depth discussion of creating and configuring profiles, see the section "Creating and
using Outlook profiles" in Chapter 3. The details of configuring service providers (such as for
Exchange Server) are also covered in Chapter 3.**

If you prefer to have Outlook start with a specific profile without prompting you, follow
these steps:

1. In the Control Panel, open the Mail applet.

2. In the Mail Setup dialog box, click Show Profiles.

3. Select the option Always Use This Profile.

4. Choose the desired profile from the drop-down list, and then click OK.

Safe Mode startup

Safe Mode is a startup mode available in Outlook 2013 and the other Office system applications. Safe Mode makes it possible for Office system applications to recover automatically
from specific errors during startup, such as a problem with an add-in or a corrupt registry
setting. Safe Mode allows Outlook 2013 to detect the problem and either correct it or
bypass it by isolating the source.

In certain situations, you might want to force Outlook 2013 into Safe Mode when it would
otherwise start normally—for example, if you want to prevent add-ins or customized toolbars or command bars from loading. To start Outlook 2013 (or any other Office system
application) in Safe Mode, hold down the Ctrl key and start the program. Outlook 2013
detects the Ctrl key and asks whether you want to start Outlook 2013 in Safe Mode. Click
Yes to start in Safe Mode or No to start normally (see Figure 2-6).

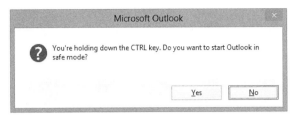

Figure 2-6 Outlook detects if you hold down the Ctrl key when starting the app and asks if you want to start in Safe Mode.

See the section "Using startup switches" in this chapter to learn how to use Safe Mode switches as an alternative to holding down the Ctrl key when starting Outlook.

If Outlook is running in Safe Mode and you want to view and/or enable a disabled add-in, click File, Options and then click Add-Ins in the left pane of the Outlook Options dialog box. Near the bottom of the dialog box, choose Disabled Items from the Manage drop-down list, and then click Go. Outlook displays the Disabled Items dialog box, which lists the disabled items and lets you enable them (see Figure 2-7). Given that Outlook disabled the items for a reason, you should generally re-enable them only if you know that they will not cause a problem.

Figure 2-7 Use the Disabled Items dialog box to view and manage disabled items.

If you start an application in Safe Mode, you cannot perform certain actions in the application. The following is a summary of these actions (not all of which apply to Outlook 2013):

- Templates can't be saved.

- The last used webpage is not loaded (Microsoft FrontPage).

- Customized toolbars and command bars are not opened. Customizations that you make in Safe Mode can't be changed.

- The AutoCorrect list isn't loaded, and changes that you make to AutoCorrect in Safe Mode cannot be saved.

- Recovered documents are not opened automatically.

- No smart tags are loaded, and new smart tags can't be saved.

- Command-line options other than /a and /n are ignored.

- You can't save files to the alternate startup directory.

- You can't save preferences.

- Additional features and programs (such as add-ins) are not loaded automatically.

To start Outlook 2013 normally, simply shut down the program and start it again without pressing the Ctrl key.

Starting Outlook automatically

If you're like most Microsoft Office system users, you work in Outlook 2013 a majority of the time. Because Outlook 2013 is such an important aspect of your workday, you might want it to start automatically when you log on to your computer, saving you the trouble of starting it later. Although you have a few options for starting Outlook 2013 automatically, the best solution is to place a shortcut to Outlook 2013 in your Startup folder.

To start Outlook 2013 automatically when you start Windows, simply drag the Outlook icon from the Start menu or Quick Launch bar to the Startup folder in the Start menu.

INSIDE OUT   Create a new Outlook 2013 shortcut

If you have no Outlook 2013 icon on the desktop, you can use the Outlook 2013 executable to create a shortcut. Open Windows Explorer and browse to the folder \Program Files (x86)\Microsoft Office\Office15 (or \Program Files\Microsoft Office\Office15, depending on your version of Windows and Office). Create a shortcut to the executable Outlook.exe. Right-click the Outlook.exe file, and then choose Create Shortcut. Windows asks whether you want to create a shortcut on the desktop. Click Yes to create the shortcut.

INSIDE OUT   Change the Outlook shortcut properties

If you want to change the way Outlook 2013 starts from the shortcut in your Startup folder (for example, so you can add command switches), you need only change the shortcut's properties. For details, see the section "Changing the Outlook shortcut" in this chapter.

Using startup switches

Outlook 2013 supports a number of command-line switches that modify the way the program starts and functions. Although you can issue the Outlook.exe command with switches from a command prompt, it's generally more useful to specify switches through a shortcut, particularly if you want to use the same set of switches more than once. Table 2-1 lists some of the startup switches that you can use to modify the way Outlook 2013 starts and functions.

For an explanation of how to modify a shortcut to add command-line switches, see the section "Changing the Outlook shortcut" in this chapter. See "Command-Line Switches for Microsoft Outlook 2013" in the Outlook Help content for a complete list of switches.

TABLE 2-1 Startup switches and their uses

Switch	Use
/a <filename>	Opens a message form with the attachment specified by <filename>
/c ipm.appointment	Opens the appointment form by itself
/c ipm.contact	Opens the contact form by itself
/c ipm.note	Opens the message form by itself
/c ipm.stickynote	Opens the note form by itself
/c ipm.task	Opens the task form by itself
/c <class>	Creates an item using the message class specified by <class>
/CheckClient	Performs a check to see whether Outlook 2013 is the default application for email, calendar, and contacts
/CleanReminders	Regenerates reminders
/Safe	Starts Outlook without the Reading Pane or toolbar customizations and with native and COM add-ins disabled
/safe:1	Starts Outlook with the Reading Pane off
/safe:3	Starts Outlook with native and COM add-ins disabled

Changing the Outlook shortcut

Let's assume that you've created a shortcut to Outlook 2013 on your Quick Launch bar or in another location so that you can start Outlook 2013 quickly. Why change the shortcut? By adding switches to the command that starts Outlook 2013, you can customize the way that the application starts and functions for the current session. You can also control the Outlook 2013 startup window state (normal, minimized, or maximized) through the short-cut's properties. For example, you might want Outlook 2013 to start automatically when you log on, but you want it to start minimized. In this situation, you would create a shortcut to Outlook 2013 in your Startup folder and then modify the shortcut so that Outlook 2013 starts minimized.

> **Note**
>
> You cannot add switches to the Outlook icon that is pinned to the Windows 7 Start menu, Windows 8 Start screen, or Windows taskbar. Instead, you must create a shortcut on the desktop or in another folder and modify the settings there.

To change the properties for a shortcut, locate the shortcut, right-click its icon, and then choose Properties. You should see a Properties page similar to the one shown in Figure 2-8.

Figure 2-8 A typical Properties page for an Outlook 2013 shortcut.

The following list summarizes the options on the Shortcut tab of the Properties page:

- **Target Type**   This read-only property specifies the type for the shortcut's target, which in the example shown in Figure 2-8 is Application.

- **Target Location**   This read-only property specifies the directory location of the target executable.

- **Target**   This property specifies the command to execute when the shortcut is executed. The default Outlook 2013 command is "C:\Program Files (x86)\Microsoft Office\Office15\Outlook.exe". The path could vary if you have installed Office in a different folder. The path to the executable must be enclosed in quotation marks, and any additional switches must be added to the right, outside the quotation marks. See the section "Using startup switches" to learn about additional switches that you can use to start Outlook 2013.

- **Start In**   This property specifies the startup directory for the application.

- **Shortcut Key**   Use this property to assign a shortcut key to the shortcut, which allows you to start Outlook 2013 by pressing the key combination. Simply click in the Shortcut Key box, and then press the keystroke to assign it to the shortcut.

- **Run**   Use this property to specify the startup window state for Outlook 2013. You can choose Normal Window, Minimized, or Maximized.

- **Comment**   Use this property to specify an optional comment. The comment appears in the shortcut's tooltip when you position the mouse pointer over the shortcut's icon. For example, if you use the Run As Different User option, you might include mention of that in the Comment box to help you distinguish this shortcut from another that starts Outlook 2013 in the default context.

- **Open File Location**   Click this button to open the folder containing the Outlook.exe executable file.

- **Change Icon**   Click this button to change the icon assigned to the shortcut. By default, the icon comes from the Outlook.exe executable, which contains other icons that you can assign to the shortcut. You also can use other .ico, .exe, and .dll files to assign icons. You'll find several additional icons in Moricons.dll and Shell32.dll, both located in the %SystemRoot%\System32 folder.

Chapter 2

- **Advanced**   Click this button to access the following options:

  - **Run In Separate Memory Space**   This option is selected by default and can't be changed for Outlook 2013. It provides crash protection for other applications and for the operating system.

  - **Run As Administrator**   Select this option to run Outlook 2013 in the administrator user context.

When you're satisfied with the shortcut's properties, click OK to close the Properties dialog box.

Creating shortcuts to start new Outlook items

In some cases, you might want to create new Outlook 2013 items directly from the Start menu, the taskbar, or a shortcut icon without first opening the Outlook program window. For example, perhaps you would like an icon that starts a new email message and another icon that starts a new appointment item. With Outlook 2013, you can access these items right from the Start menu without any additional setup. Just click Start, hover the mouse over Outlook 2013 (or click the Expand button at the right of the menu), and choose the type of item that you want to create from the cascading menu that appears. If Outlook is pinned to the taskbar in Windows 7, you can also right-click the Outlook icon in the taskbar and, from the Tasks section of the menu, choose the type of Outlook item to create.

You can also create a shortcut to a mailto: item on the desktop or on the Quick Launch bar to make it easy to create a new email message. Here's how to create the shortcut:

1. Right-click the desktop, and then choose New, Shortcut.

2. In the Create Shortcut dialog box, type **mailto:** as the item to start, and then click Next.

3. Type **New Mail Message** as the shortcut name, and then click Finish.

4. Drag the shortcut to the Quick Launch bar to make it quickly accessible without minimizing all applications.

When you double-click the shortcut, Outlook 2013 starts and prompts you for a profile unless a default profile has been set. However, only the new message form appears—the rest of Outlook 2013 stays hidden, running in the background.

You can use the Target property of an Outlook 2013 shortcut to create other types of Outlook 2013 items. Refer to the section "Changing the Outlook shortcut" to learn how to create an Outlook 2013 shortcut. See Table 2-1 for the switches that open specific Outlook 2013 forms. For example, the following two shortcuts start a new message and a new appointment, respectively:

```
"C:\Program Files (x86)\Microsoft Office\Office15\Outlook.exe" /c ipm.note
"C:\Program Files (x86)\Microsoft Office\Office15\Outlook.exe" /c ipm.appointment
```

> **Note**
>
> You can use the */a* switch to open a new message form with an attachment. The following example starts a new message and attaches the file named **Picture.jpg**:
>
> ```
> "C:\Program Files (x86)\Microsoft Office\Office15\Outlook.exe" /a Picture.jpg
> ```

Choosing a startup view

When you start Outlook 2013, it defaults to using the Inbox view, but you might prefer to use a different view or folder as the initial view. For example, if you use Outlook 2013 primarily for scheduling, you'll probably want Outlook 2013 to start in the Calendar folder. If you use Outlook 2013 mainly to manage contacts, you'll probably want it to start in the Contacts folder.

To specify the view that should appear when Outlook 2013 starts, follow these steps:

1. Start Outlook 2013, click the File tab, and then click Options.

2. Click Advanced to display the Advanced Options page, as shown in Figure 2-9.

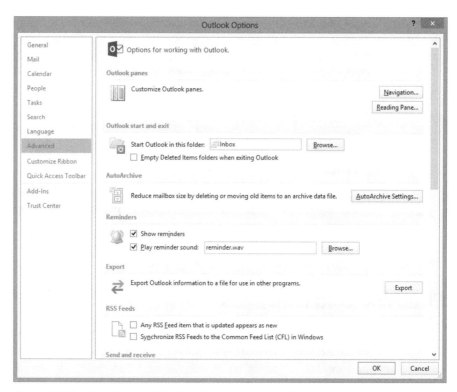

Figure 2-9 Use the Advanced Options dialog box to specify the Startup view.

3. Under Outlook Start And Exit, click Browse, select the folder that you want Outlook 2013 to open at startup, and click OK.

4. Click OK, and then close the dialog box.

If you switch Outlook 2013 to a different default folder and then want to restore Outlook Today as your default view, you can follow the preceding steps to restore Outlook Today as the default.

Simply select Outlook Today in the drop-down list or follow these steps with the Outlook Today window open:

1. Start Outlook 2013, and then open the Outlook Today view.

2. Click Customize Outlook Today at the top of the Outlook Today window.

3. In the resulting pane, select When Starting Go Directly To Outlook Today, and then click Save Changes.

Setting up accounts in Outlook

THE previous two chapters provided an overview of what's new in Microsoft Outlook 2013 and explained the options you have for starting Outlook. The next step is to understand how to add accounts to Outlook so you can begin using it productively. In order to add accounts to Outlook, you need to understand a few basics, including how Outlook stores data, how it stores your accounts and settings, and the types of accounts with which you can use Outlook. This chapter explains these topics.

How Outlook stores data

Like almost every app, Outlook helps you manage data. Outlook's data consists primarily of email messages, meetings and appointments, contacts, and tasks.

If your Outlook 2013 folders aren't stored as individual folders on your system's hard disk, where are they? The answer to that question depends on how you configure Outlook 2013. As in earlier versions of Outlook, you can use a set of personal folders to store Outlook 2013 data. Outlook 2013 uses the .pst extension for a set of personal folders.

You can use multiple .pst files, adding additional personal folders to your Outlook 2013 configuration, as shown in Figure 3-1. For example, you might want to create another set of folders to separate your personal information from work-related data. You can add personal folders to your Outlook 2013 configuration simply by adding another .pst file to your profile.

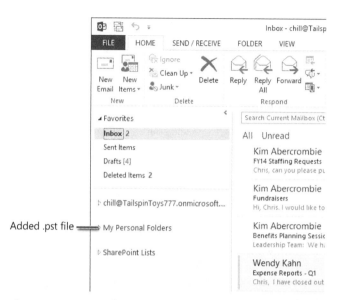

Added .pst file

Figure 3-1 You can add multiple sets of folders to your Outlook 2013 configuration.

If you are using an Exchange Server or Exchange ActiveSync account (such as for Office 365), Outlook uses an *offline folder file* to store the data for that account. The offline file has an .ost file extension. The .ost file acts as a cached copy of the data stored in your Exchange Server mailbox. When you're working offline (not connected to your Exchange Server mailbox), changes that you make to contacts, messages, and other Outlook 2013 items and folders occur in the offline store. When you go online again, Outlook 2013 synchronizes the changes between the offline store and your Exchange Server store. For example, if you've deleted messages from your offline store, Outlook 2013 deletes those same messages from your online store when you synchronize the folders. Any new messages in your Inbox on the server are added to the local cache in the .ost file. Synchronization is a two-way process, providing the most up-to-date copy of your data in both locations, ensuring that changes made in each are reflected in the other.

> To learn how to access your Exchange Server mailbox without using Outlook, see Chapter 30, "Accessing your mailboxes without Outlook."

Outlook 2013 always works from the copy of your mailbox that is cached locally on your computer through a feature called Cached Exchange Mode. Outlook 2013 automatically handles synchronization between your offline cache and the mailbox stored on the server. With Cached Exchange Mode, you don't need to worry about synchronizing the two— Outlook 2013 detects when the server is available and updates your locally cached copy automatically.

When you create an Outlook 2013 storage file, Outlook 2013 defaults to a specific location for the file. The default location is the AppData\Local\Microsoft\Outlook folder of your user profile. For example, if your user name is jim, the default location is C:\Users\Jim\AppData\ Local\Microsoft\Outlook.

INSIDE OUT   Find your data store

If you're not sure where your Outlook data files are, open Outlook and click File, Account Settings, Account Settings, and then click the Data Files tab. This tab lists the data files associated with your current Outlook profile, as well as their location on disk.

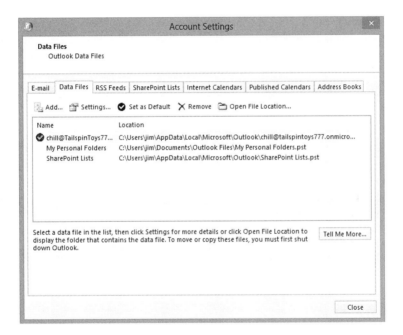

Now that you have an understanding of where Outlook stores your data, let's look at the types of accounts you can use with Outlook.

Creating and using Outlook profiles

In Outlook 2013, *profiles* store the configuration of email accounts, data files, and other settings that you use in a given Outlook 2013 session. For example, your profile might include an Exchange Server account, an Internet mail account, and a set of personal folders.

Chapter 3

Outlook 2013 either prompts you to select a profile at startup or selects one automatically, depending on how you've configured it.

In most cases, you'll probably use only one profile and you'll configure Outlook 2013 to select it automatically. In some situations, however, multiple profiles can be useful. For example, you might prefer to keep your work and personal data completely separate on your notebook computer because of privacy concerns or office policies. In this situation, you maintain two profiles: one for your work data and a second for your personal data. You then configure Outlook 2013 to prompt you to choose a profile at startup. The profile controls which set of data files and configuration settings are used for that specific session. For example, when you're working at the office, you use the office profile, and when you're using the computer at home, you use the personal profile.

It's important to understand that Outlook 2013 profiles have no relationship to the other types of profiles that you'll find in a Microsoft Windows operating system, which include hardware profiles and user profiles. *Hardware profiles* store hardware settings and allow you to switch between different hardware configurations without reconfiguring your system. *User profiles* store the unique working environment (desktop, documents, and so on) that you see when you log on to your computer. Outlook 2013 profiles, in contrast, apply only to your Outlook data.

> **Note**
>
> Unless otherwise noted, the term *profile* in this book refers to an Outlook 2013 profile.

Each profile can contain multiple accounts and data files, which means that you can work with different email servers at one time and use multiple sets of data files (such as a set of personal folders, or .pst files). The following list describes the items stored in an Outlook 2013 profile:

- **Email accounts and data files** Your profile might include an Exchange Server account, two POP3 email accounts, two .pst files, and a directory service account. When these accounts are in a single profile, you can use all of them in the same Outlook 2013 session.

- **RSS feeds** The profile stores the list of Really Simple Syndication (RSS) feeds that you have configured in Outlook. You don't need to open the profile to add a feed; instead, you can simply subscribe to it and allow Outlook to add the feed to your profile for you.

- **SharePoint lists** SharePoint lists (such as calendars and task lists) that you have connected to Outlook appear in your profile. You add these from the SharePoint site, rather than from Outlook.

- **Internet calendars**   You can add Internet calendars to Outlook from your profile and view those calendars alongside your own.

- **Published calendars**   The profile lists the calendars that you have published to Office Online or other online calendar servers. You can change the account and other settings for the published calendar from the profile.

- **Delivery settings**   The profile specifies the store to which Outlook 2013 should deliver new mail when it arrives. You also can specify the order in which Outlook 2013 processes accounts.

- **Address settings**   You can specify which address book Outlook 2013 displays first, where Outlook 2013 should store personal addresses, and the order of the address books that Outlook 2013 uses to check email addresses when the profile includes multiple address books.

   For detailed information about configuring and using address books in Outlook 2013, see Chapter 13, "Managing address books and contact groups."

The first time you run Outlook 2013, it creates a profile named Outlook even if you don't add any email accounts to the profile. If you do add an email account, Outlook 2013 uses the name that you specify in the account settings as the name for the profile.

As mentioned earlier, you can use multiple profiles. The following sections explain how to create new profiles, copy existing profiles to new profiles, and perform related operations.

Creating profiles

You don't have to be in Outlook 2013 to create a profile—in fact, you *can't* create one in Outlook 2013. You can create profiles through Control Panel. In addition to specifying a profile name, you can also (optionally) add email and other services to the profile. You can create a profile from scratch or copy an existing profile to create a new one.

Creating a profile from scratch

When you have no existing Outlook profile or no profile that contains the accounts or settings you need, you must create a profile from scratch.

Follow these steps to create a new profile:

1.   Open the Mail item from Control Panel.

2.   In the Mail Setup dialog box, shown in Figure 3-2, click Show Profiles. If no profiles exist, the Mail dialog box appears; continue with step 3.

Figure 3-2 You access the current profile's settings as well as other profiles in the Mail Setup dialog box.

3.   Click Add, specify a name for the profile in the New Profile dialog box, and then click OK.

4.   The Add New Account Wizard starts. Add accounts and other services to the profile. Enter requested data, such as an email address and password. To create a new profile without adding any services (useful if you are not using Outlook 2013 for email), click Cancel, and then click OK. In this situation, Outlook 2013 automatically creates a set of personal folders (a .pst file) to store your Outlook 2013 data.

Copying a profile

In addition to creating profiles from scratch, you can create a profile by copying an existing one. When you copy a profile, Outlook 2013 copies all the settings from the existing profile to the new one, including accounts and data files.

Follow these steps to copy an existing profile:

1.   Open the Mail item from Control Panel.

2.   In the Mail Setup dialog box, click Show Profiles.

3.   Select the existing profile that you want to use as the basis for the new profile, and then click Copy.

4.   In the Copy Profile dialog box, specify a name for the new profile and click OK.

Modifying or removing a profile

You can modify a profile at any time to add or remove services. You can also remove a profile altogether if you no longer need it.

Follow these steps to modify or remove an existing profile:

1. Open the Mail item from Control Panel.

2. In the Mail Setup dialog box, click Show Profiles.

3. Select the profile to be modified or removed.

4. Click Remove if you want to remove the profile, or click Properties to modify the profile settings.

Using profiles

After you create one or more profiles, you can use them in Outlook. The following sections explain the options you have for using profiles in Outlook.

Setting a default profile

You can configure Outlook 2013 either to use a specific profile automatically or to prompt you to select a profile at startup. If you use the same profile most of the time, you can configure Outlook to start automatically with that profile.

Follow these steps to specify the default profile and use it automatically when Outlook 2013 starts:

1. Open the Mail item from Control Panel.

2. In the Mail Setup dialog box, click Show Profiles.

3. In the Mail dialog box, on the General tab, select Always Use This Profile, as shown in Figure 3-3. In the drop-down list, select the default profile that you want Outlook 2013 to use.

Figure 3-3 You can specify a default profile on the General tab.

4. Click OK.

Choosing a profile

If you work with multiple profiles and switch profiles relatively often, you'll probably want to configure Outlook 2013 to prompt you to choose a profile at startup. This saves you the trouble of changing the default profile each time you want to switch. For example, assume that you use one profile for your personal accounts and another for your work accounts. Have Outlook 2013 prompt you for the profile when the program starts, rather than configuring the settings each time to specify the default profile.

Follow these steps to configure Outlook 2013 to prompt you to choose a profile:

1. Open the Mail item from Control Panel.

2. In the Mail Setup dialog box, click Show Profiles.

3. In the Mail dialog box, select Always Use This Profile, select the profile that you want Outlook 2013 to display as the initial selection in the list, and then select Prompt For A Profile To Be Used.

4. Click OK.

INSIDE OUT   Set the initial profile

You probably noticed in step 3 of the preceding procedure that you enabled an option and then immediately disabled it by selecting Prompt For A Profile To Be Used. In effect, you've accomplished two tasks: setting the default profile and also configuring Outlook 2013 to prompt you for a profile. In the drop-down list, select the profile that you use most often, which saves you the step of selecting it when prompted at startup.

Adding Outlook accounts to a profile

Outlook 2013 supports a selection of account types. The following sections describe these account types and explain how to add and configure each type in Outlook. First, let's start with an overview of the types of accounts you can use in Outlook.

An overview of account types

A *messaging protocol* is a mechanism that messaging servers and applications use to transfer messages. Being able to use a specific email service requires that your application support the same protocols the server uses. To configure Outlook 2013 as a messaging client, you need to understand the various protocols supported by Outlook 2013 and the types of servers that employ each type. The following sections provide a brief overview of these protocols.

SMTP/POP3

Simple Mail Transport Protocol (SMTP) is a standards-based protocol used for transferring messages and is the primary mechanism that Internet-based and intranet-based email servers use to transfer messages. It's also the mechanism that Outlook 2013 uses to connect to a mail server to send messages for an Internet account. SMTP is the protocol used by an Internet email account for outgoing messages.

SMTP operates by default on TCP port 25. When you configure an Internet-based email account, the port on which the server is listening for SMTP determines the outgoing mail server setting. Unless your email server uses a different port, you can use the default port value of 25. If you want to use Outlook 2013 for an existing Internet mail account, confirm the SMTP server name and port settings with your ISP.

Chapter 3

POP3 is a standards-based protocol that clients can use to retrieve messages from any mail server that supports it. Outlook 2013 uses this protocol when retrieving messages from an Internet-based or intranet-based mail server that supports POP3 mailboxes. Nearly all ISP-based mail servers support POP3.

POP3 operates on TCP port 110 by default. Unless your server uses a nonstandard port configuration, you can leave the port setting as is when defining a POP3 mail account.

To learn how to set up an Internet email account for an SMTP/POP3 server, including setting port numbers, see the section "Adding POP3 accounts."

IMAP

Like POP3, IMAP is a standards-based protocol that enables message transfer. However, IMAP offers some significant differences from POP3. For example, POP3 is primarily designed as an offline protocol, which means that you retrieve your messages from a server and download them to your local message store (such as your local Outlook 2013 folders). IMAP is designed primarily as an online protocol, which allows a remote user to manipulate messages and message folders on the server without downloading them. This is particularly helpful for users who need to access the same remote mailbox from multiple locations, such as home and work, using different computers. Because the messages remain on the server, IMAP eliminates the need for message synchronization.

INSIDE OUT Keep POP3 messages on the server

IMAP by default leaves your messages on the server. If needed, you can configure a POP3 account in Outlook 2013 to leave a copy of messages on the server, allowing you to retrieve those messages later from another computer. (To learn how to configure a POP3 account, see the section "Adding POP3 accounts.") IMAP offers other advantages over POP3 as well. For example, with IMAP, you can search for messages on the server using a variety of message attributes, such as sender, message size, or message header. IMAP also offers better support for attachments because it can separate attachments from the header and text portion of a message. This is particularly useful with multipart Multipurpose Internet Mail Extensions (MIME) messages, allowing you to read a message without downloading the attachments so that you can decide which attachments you want to retrieve. With POP3, the entire message must be downloaded.

Security is another advantage of IMAP because it uses a challenge-response mechanism to authenticate the user for mailbox access. This prevents the user's password from being transmitted as clear text across the network, as it is with POP3.

IMAP support allows you to use Outlook 2013 as a client to an IMAP-compliant email server. Although IMAP provides for server-side storage and the ability to create additional mail folders on the server, it does not offer some of the same features as Exchange Server, or even POP3. Even with these limitations, however, IMAP serves as a flexible protocol and generally surpasses POP3 in capability.

Exchange Server

Exchange Server is a Microsoft unified messaging solution that supports the types of data you find in Outlook, such as email, contacts, calendars, tasks, and so on. Some of the key advantages of Exchange Server compared to other messaging systems include group scheduling, resource scheduling (rooms and devices), collaboration through public folders, SharePoint integration, and PBX/voice integration.

Exchange Server actually uses a large number of discrete protocols to function, including the protocols previously discussed. For example, Exchange Server uses SMTP for message transfer. It also supports both POP3 and IMAP for client access. However, in most situations, you'll use the Exchange Server native client support rather than POP3 or IMAP because of its greater range of features.

Exchange ActiveSync

Exchange ActiveSync (EAS) is another protocol supported by Exchange Server. It was originally implemented by Microsoft in 2002 for mobile devices such as cell phones. Microsoft has improved and expanded EAS over the ensuing years, and EAS now supports a much broader range of devices including Windows Phone, iPads and iPhones, Android devices, and of course a variety of tablets.

EAS is significant in that it is the protocol used by Office 365 and Outlook.com for client access. Because Outlook 2013 natively supports EAS, you can access your Office 365 or Outlook.com account using Outlook, your cell phone, and your tablet, all for a relatively seamless experience.

Adding POP3 accounts

Many Internet-based email servers use SMTP and POP3 to allow subscribers to send and receive messages across the Internet. (A few exceptions use IMAP; still other services use HTTP. Some, like Google mail, give you an option of which protocol to use. These other protocols are covered later in this chapter.) If you have an account with a local ISP or other service provider that offers POP3 accounts, or if your office server is a non–Microsoft Exchange Server system that supports only POP3, you can add a POP3 account to Outlook 2013 to access that server.

Chapter 3

INSIDE OUT Configure multiple accounts in one profile

You can configure multiple email accounts in a single Outlook 2013 profile, giving you access to multiple servers to send and receive messages.

Follow these steps to add a POP3 email account to Outlook 2013:

1. With Outlook 2013 open, click File, Add Account.

2. To use the automatic discovery feature to obtain your server configuration information automatically from your existing email server, on the Auto Account Setup page, shown in Figure 3-4, specify the following information:

   ○ **Your Name**   Specify your name as you want it to appear in the From box of messages you send.

   ○ **E-mail Address**   Enter your email address in the form *<user>@<domain.tld>*, where *<user>* is your user account name and *<domain.tld>* is the name of your email domain.

   ○ **Password/Retype Password**   Type your password in the Password field, and then confirm the password in the Retype Password field.

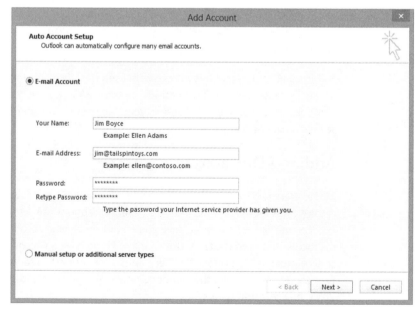

Figure 3-4 Use the Auto Account Setup page to configure the email server settings automatically.

3. Enter your name, email address, and password (twice) for your email account, and then click Next. Outlook 2013 will try to connect to your email server and obtain configuration information via an encrypted connection. If Outlook is able to identify your account settings, the process is complete (although you might get a security alert dialog box), and you can skip the remaining steps.

4. If your email server doesn't support encrypted connections, this attempt will fail, and you will be prompted to try an unencrypted connection.

5. If this attempt doesn't complete, you will be prompted to verify the email address and click Retry.

6. If this attempt doesn't complete, the Problem Connecting To Server dialog box will display, indicating that you will need to configure the settings manually—the Change Account Settings check box will be selected automatically. Click Next to continue.

7. In the Choose Service dialog box, select POP or IMAP, and then click Next.

8. On the POP and IMAP Account Settings page, shown in Figure 3-5, configure the following settings:

   ○ **Your Name**   Specify your name as you want it to appear in the From box of messages that others receive from you.

   ○ **E-mail Address**   Specify the email address for your account in the form *<account>*@*<domain>*—for example, *chill@tailspintoys.com*.

   ○ **Account Type**   In the Server Information area, select the Account Type (in this case, POP3) of the email server.

   ○ **Incoming Mail Server**   Specify the IP address or Domain Name System (DNS) name of the mail server that processes your incoming mail. This is the server where your POP3 mailbox is located and from which your incoming mail is downloaded. Often, your mail server will use the host name *mail* and your mail server's domain name. So an example of a mail server DNS name might be *mail.tailspintoys.com*. However, this isn't a rule, so check with your ISP or network administrator for the correct mail server host name.

   ○ **Outgoing Mail Server (SMTP)**   Specify the IP address or DNS name of the mail server that you use to send outgoing mail. In many cases, this is the same server as the one specified for incoming mail, but it can be different. Some organizations and many ISPs separate incoming and outgoing mail services onto different servers for load balancing, security, or other reasons.

Chapter 3

> **Note**
>
> Many mail servers will not allow outgoing mail unless you authenticate on the server. See the section "Configuring outgoing server settings for Internet accounts" for details.

○ **User Name**   Specify the user account on the server that you must use to log on to your mailbox to retrieve your messages. In some cases, you should not include the domain portion of your email address. For example, if your address is *chill@tailspintoys.com*, your user name is *chill*. However, some mail servers require the full email address as the user name to log on.

○ **Password**   Specify the password for the user account entered in the User Name box.

○ **Remember Password**   Select this option to have Outlook 2013 maintain the password for this account in your local password cache, eliminating the need for you to enter the password each time you want to retrieve your mail. Clear this check box to prevent other users from downloading your mail while you are away from your computer. If the check box is cleared, Outlook 2013 prompts you for the password for each session.

○ **Require Logon Using Secure Password Authentication (SPA)**   Select this option if your server uses SPA to authenticate your access to the server.

○ **New Outlook Data File**   Choose this option to have Outlook 2013 create a new .pst file to contain your data for the new account.

○ **Existing Outlook Data File**   Choose this option if you want to use an existing .pst file to store mail and other items for this account.

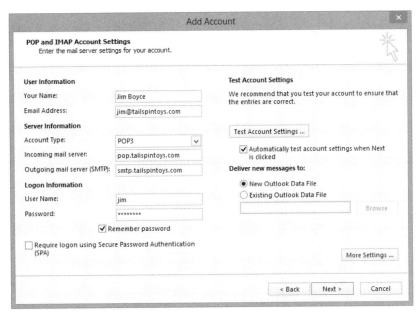

Figure 3-5 Use the POP and IMAP Account Settings page to configure the account settings.

9. Click More Settings to display the Internet E-mail Settings dialog box, shown in Figure 3-6. You can configure these settings based on the information in the following sections.

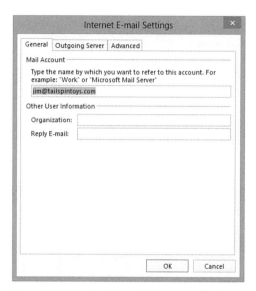

Figure 3-6 Use the General tab to specify the account name, organization, and reply email details.

Configuring general settings for Internet accounts

Use the General tab of the Internet E-mail Settings dialog box (shown in Figure 3-6) to change the account name that is displayed in Outlook 2013 and to specify organization and reply address information as follows:

- **Mail Account**   Specify the name of the account as you want it to appear in the Outlook 2013 account list. This name has no bearing on the server name or your account name. Use the name to differentiate one account from another—for example, you might have a couple of accounts named Work and Personal.

- **Organization**   Specify the group or organization name that you want to associate with the account.

- **Reply E-mail**   Specify an email address that you want others to use when replying to messages that you send with this account. For example, you might redirect replies to another mail server address if you are in the process of changing ISPs or mail servers. Enter the address in its full form—**chill@tailspintoys.com**, for example. Leave this option blank if you want users to reply to the email address that you specified in the E-mail Address box for the account.

Configuring outgoing server settings for Internet accounts

Use the Outgoing Server tab, shown in Figure 3-7, to configure a handful of settings for the SMTP server that handles the account's outgoing messages. Although in most cases you won't need to modify these settings, you will have to do so if your server requires you to authenticate to send outgoing messages. Some ISPs use authentication as a means of allowing mail relay from their clients outside their local subnets. This allows authorized users to relay mail and prevents unauthorized relay or unauthorized users from sending spam through the server.

Figure 3-7 Use the Outgoing Server tab to configure authentication and other options for your SMTP server.

The Outgoing Server tab contains the following options:

- **My Outgoing Server (SMTP) Requires Authentication**   Select this option if the SMTP mail server that processes your outgoing mail requires authentication. Connections that don't provide valid credentials are rejected. Selecting this option makes several other options on the tab available.

- **Use Same Settings As My Incoming Mail Server**   Select this option if the SMTP server credentials are the same as your POP3 (incoming) server credentials.

- **Log On Using**   Select this option if the SMTP server requires a different set of credentials from those required by your POP3 server. You should specify a valid account name on the SMTP server in the User Name box as well as a password for that account. In general, you will have to change this setting only if your SMTP and POP3 servers are separate physical servers.

- **Remember Password**   Select this check box to have Outlook 2013 save your password from session to session. Clear the check box if you want Outlook 2013 to prompt you for a password each time.

- **Require Secure Password Authentication (SPA)**   Select this check box if your server uses SPA to authenticate your access to the server.

- **Log On To Incoming Mail Server Before Sending Mail**   Select this option to have Outlook 2013 log on to the POP3 server before sending outgoing messages. Use this option if the outgoing and incoming mail servers are the same server and if the server is configured to require authentication to send messages.

Configuring advanced settings for POP3 accounts

Although you won't normally need to configure settings on the Advanced tab for an Internet account, the settings can be useful in some situations. You can use the following options on the Advanced tab, shown in Figure 3-8, to specify the SMTP and POP3 ports for the server, along with time-outs and these other settings:

- **Incoming Server (POP3)**   Specify the Transmission Control Protocol (TCP) port used by the POP3 server. The default port is 110. Specifying a nonstandard port works only if the server is listening for POP3 traffic on the specified port.

- **Outgoing Server (SMTP)**   Specify the TCP port used by the SMTP server for outgoing mail. The default port is 25. Specifying a nonstandard port works only if the server is listening for SMTP traffic on the specified port.

- **Use The Following Type Of Encrypted Connection**   If your server requires an encrypted connection, use this drop-down list to select the correct type of encryption method: SSL, TLS, Auto, or None. Select SSL if the server requires the use of a Secure Sockets Layer (SSL) connection, TLS if it requires Transport Layer Security (TLS), and Auto if you want Outlook 2013 to negotiate encryption automatically with the mail server. With rare exceptions, public POP3 and SMTP mail servers do not require SSL connections.

- **Server Timeouts**   Use this control to change the period of time that Outlook 2013 will wait for a connection to the server.

- **Leave A Copy Of Messages On The Server**   Select this check box to retain a copy of all messages on the server, downloading a copy of the message to Outlook 2013. This is a useful feature if you want to access the same POP3 account from different computers and want to be able to access your messages from each one. Clear this check box if you want Outlook 2013 to download your messages and then delete them from the server. Some servers impose a storage limit, making it impractical to leave all your messages on the server.

- **Remove From Server After *n* Days**   Select this check box to have Outlook 2013 delete messages from the server a specified number of days after they are down-loaded to your system.

- **Remove From Server When Deleted From "Deleted Items"**   Select this option to have Outlook 2013 delete messages from the server when you delete the down-loaded copies from your local Deleted Items folder.

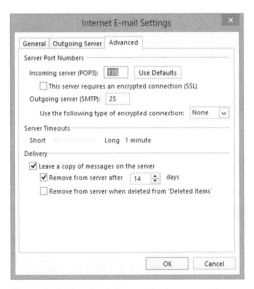

Figure 3-8 Use the Advanced tab to specify nonstandard TCP ports for the server.

Adding IMAP accounts

Outlook 2013's support for IMAP means that you can use Outlook 2013 to send and receive messages through IMAP servers as well as through the other mail server types that Outlook 2013 supports.

For more information about IMAP and its differences from POP3, see the section "IMAP" in Chapter 1.

Configuring an IMAP account is a lot like configuring a POP3 account. The main difference is that you select IMAP as the account type rather than POP3 when you add the account.

Chapter 3

You can refer to the preceding section on creating POP3 accounts, "Adding POP3 accounts," for a description of the procedure to follow when adding an IMAP account.

One setting you might want to review or change for an IMAP account as opposed to a POP3 account is the root folder path. This setting is located on the Advanced tab of the account's Internet E-mail Settings dialog box (Figure 3-9). Specify the path to the specific folder in your mailbox folder structure that you want to use as the root for your mailbox. If you aren't sure what path to enter, leave this option blank to use the default path provided by the account.

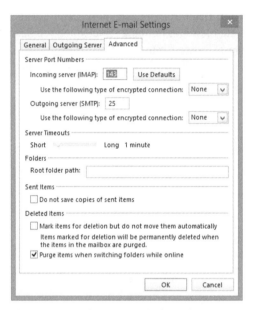

Figure 3-9 Use the Advanced tab to change settings for the IMAP account.

Adding an Exchange account

Outlook 2013 makes a great client for Exchange Server or a service built on Exchange Server, such as Office 365. Of all the services supported by Outlook 2013, Exchange Server offers the broadest range of functionality, providing excellent support for collaboration, information sharing, group scheduling, and more.

Setting up an Exchange Server account in Outlook 2013 isn't difficult, but it does involve several steps, as follows:

1. If you are running Outlook 2013 for the first time, in the Outlook 2013 Startup Wizard, go to the Choose E-mail Service page. To reach this page if you have run Outlook 2013 previously and your profile already includes a mail account, open the Mail item from Control Panel, select the profile, and then choose Properties. Click

E-mail Accounts, and then click New on the E-mail tab in the Account Settings dialog box. If Outlook 2013 is already open, click File, Add Account.

2. The Auto Account Setup page, shown in Figure 3-10, gives you a place to specify your name, email address, and password. If AutoDiscover is configured properly for your Exchange Server environment, you can enter your name, email address, and password as it is set on the server, click Next, and have Outlook 2013 determine the necessary settings to connect to your server. However, the following steps assume that you are not able to use AutoDiscover and must configure the account manually.

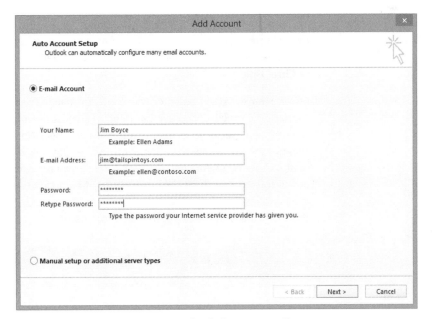

Figure 3-10 Use this page to enter details for your email account.

> **Note**
>
> AutoDiscover requires that your computer be able to resolve the AutoDiscover host in your domain. For example, if your computer resides in the *tailspintoys.com* domain, your computer must be able to resolve *autodiscover.tailspintoys.com* to the servers on the *tailspintoys.com* network that are providing AutoDiscover services. For more details on AutoDiscover, see the Exchange Server documentation.

3. If you don't want to use AutoDiscover, choose Manual Setup Or Additional Server Types, and then click Next.

4. Choose Microsoft Exchange Or Compatible Service, and then click Next.

5. On the Server Settings page, shown in Figure 3-11, specify the following information:

❍ **Server** Specify the NetBIOS or DNS name of the computer running Exchange Server, or its Internet Protocol (IP) address. You don't have to include a double backslash (\\) before the server name.

❍ **Use Cached Exchange Mode** Select this check box to have Outlook 2013 create a locally cached copy of your entire Exchange Server mailbox on your local computer. Outlook 2013 creates an offline folder store (.ost) file in which to store the mailbox and works from that cached copy, handling synchronization issues automatically.

❍ **User Name** Specify the name of your mailbox on the server. You can specify your logon account name or mailbox name. For example, you might use **chill** or **Chris Hill**.

❍ **Check Name** After you enter your logon or mailbox name, click Check Name to check the specified account information against the information on the server. If you specify your logon name, clicking Check Name automatically changes the user name to your mailbox name. Outlook 2013 indicates a successful check by underlining the user name. If you are connecting to the server using Outlook Anywhere (RPC over HTTP), do not click Check Name—you must configure the connection first because Outlook 2013 must be able to communicate with the server to check your name.

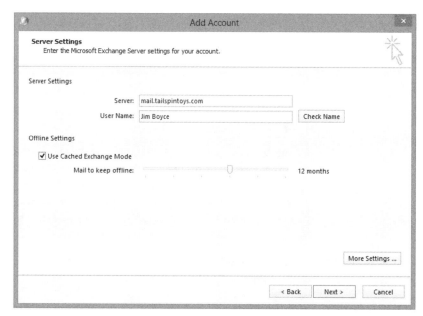

Figure 3-11 Configure basic Exchange Server settings on the Server Settings page.

6. Click More Settings to open the Microsoft Exchange dialog box, and then use the information in the following sections to configure additional settings if needed. Then click OK to close the Microsoft Exchange dialog box. Click Next, and then click Finish.

Configuring general properties

You use the General tab in the Microsoft Exchange dialog box to configure the account name. This name has no bearing on the Exchange Server name or your account name. For example, you might name the account Office Email, Work Account, or Microsoft Exchange Server.

Configuring advanced properties

You use the Advanced tab in the Microsoft Exchange dialog box, shown in Figure 3-12, to configure additional mailboxes to open, as well as security and offline processing settings. Why use additional mailboxes? You might own two mailboxes on the server and need access to both of them. For example, if you are the system administrator, you probably need to manage your own account as well as the Administrator account; or perhaps you've been delegated as an assistant for a set of mailboxes and need to access them to manage someone's schedule (discussed in Chapter 21, "Delegating responsibilities to an assistant"). The Advanced tab is where you add mailboxes that you own or for which you've been granted delegate access.

Figure 3-12 Use the Advanced tab to configure additional mailboxes, Cached Exchange Mode, and offline file settings.

The options on the Advanced tab are as follows:

- **Open These Additional Mailboxes**   This option defines the set of mailboxes you want Outlook 2013 to open. These can be mailboxes that you own or for which you've been granted delegate access.

- **Use Cached Exchange Mode**   This option has Outlook 2013 create and work from a locally cached copy of your mailbox. This setting corresponds to the Use Cached Exchange Mode setting on the Exchange Server Settings page of the E-mail Accounts Wizard.

- **Download Shared Folders**   Select this option if you want Outlook 2013 to download the contents of shared folders, such as other users' Inbox or Calendar folders made available to you through delegate permissions or Microsoft SharePoint folders.

- **Download Public Folder Favorites**   Select this check box if you want Outlook 2013 to cache the public folders that you have added to the Favorites folder in the Public Folders branch. Before selecting this check box, consider how much replication traffic you will experience if the folders in your Favorites folder contain a large number of posts and are very active.

- **Outlook Data File Settings**   You can use this option to set up an .ost file to use as your data cache while working offline.

Configuring security properties

The following settings on the Security tab of the Microsoft Exchange dialog box, shown in Figure 3-13, control whether Outlook 2013 encrypts data between the client and the server and how authentication is handled:

- **Encrypt Data Between Microsoft Outlook And Microsoft Exchange**   This setting determines whether Outlook 2013 uses encryption to secure transmission between your system and the server. Select this check box to enable encryption for greater security.

- **Always Prompt For Logon Credentials**   Select this check box if you want Outlook 2013 to prompt you for your logon credentials each time it needs to connect to the server. This is useful if you are concerned that others who have access to your computer might be accessing your mailbox.

- **Logon Network Security**   This setting specifies the type of authentication to use when connecting to Exchange Server. The Password Authentication option causes Exchange Server to use Microsoft Windows NT LAN Manager (NTLM) challenge/

response to authenticate on the server using your current logon account credentials. Kerberos Password Authentication is the default authentication mechanism for
Microsoft Windows 2000 Server and later domains. You can choose either of these
or choose the Negotiate Authentication option to have Outlook 2013 attempt both.
Alternatively, you can choose Insert A Smart Card to use a smart card to log on
to Exchange.

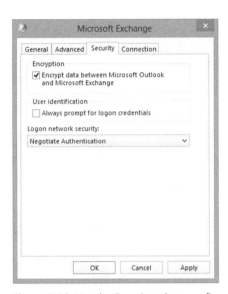

Figure 3-13 Use the Security tab to configure security settings.

Configuring connection properties

The Connection tab in the Microsoft Exchange dialog box, shown in Figure 3-14, allows
you to configure Outlook 2013 to connect to Exchange Server using HTTP. The capability to use HTTP to connect to a remote computer running Exchange Server provides an
additional connection option for users of Outlook 2013 and can drastically reduce administrative overhead. Administrators do not need to provide virtual private network (VPN)
access to the network or configure VPN client software for users to access the computer
running Exchange Server from remote locations. HTTP access also provides native access
to the computer running Exchange Server as an alternative to Outlook Web Access (OWA)
for users.

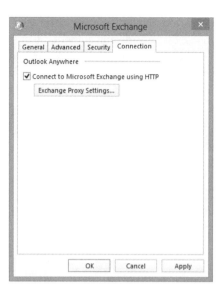

Figure 3-14 Use the Connection tab to configure Outlook to use HTTP to connect to Exchange Server.

The Connect To Microsoft Exchange Using HTTP check box, if selected, causes Outlook 2013 to connect to the computer running Exchange Server using the HTTP protocol. To configure additional settings, click Exchange Proxy Settings to open the Microsoft Exchange Proxy Settings dialog box, shown in Figure 3-15.

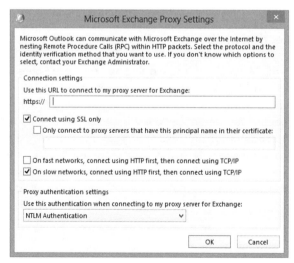

Figure 3-15 Specify settings for the HTTP connection in the Microsoft Exchange Proxy Settings dialog box.

Configure settings in this dialog box using the following list as a guide:

- **Use This URL To Connect To My Proxy Server For Exchange**   This option specifies the URL that serves as the access point for the server. The default is *<server>*/RPC, where *<server>* is the web address of the front-end server running Exchange Server. An example is *httpmail.boyce.us/rpc*. Omit the *https://* prefix.

- **Connect Using SSL Only**   Select this check box to connect to the server using SSL. Note that Outlook 2013 changes the URL prefix to *https://* for the URL. (See the preceding option.)

- **Only Connect To Proxy Servers That Have This Principal Name In Their Certificate**   This option specifies the principal name for the remote proxy server for SSL authentication.

- **On Fast Networks, Connect Using HTTP First, Then Connect Using TCP/IP**   With this setting, when Outlook 2013 senses a fast connection to the server, it attempts HTTP first and then resorts to TCP/IP if HTTP fails.

- **On Slow Networks, Connect Using HTTP First, Then Connect Using TCP/IP**   With this setting, when Outlook 2013 senses a slow connection to the server, it attempts HTTP first and then resorts to TCP/IP if HTTP fails.

- **Use This Authentication When Connecting To My Proxy Server For Exchange**   Select the authentication method to use to authenticate on the remote computer running Exchange Server. Choose the type of authentication required by the front-end server.

Verifying connection status

After you have finished configuring Outlook 2013 to use RPC over HTTP to connect to your computer running Exchange Server, you can verify the type of connection that it is using. To do this, hold down the Ctrl key, right-click the Outlook 2013 icon in the system tray, and then choose Connection Status to open the Outlook Connection Status dialog box, shown in Figure 3-16.

Chapter 3

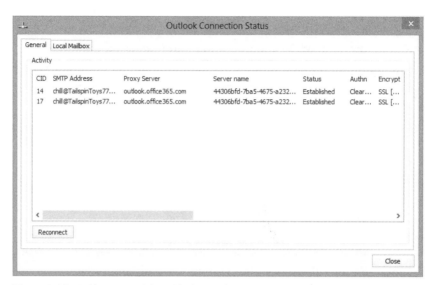

Figure 3-16 Verify connectivity with the Outlook Connection Status dialog box.

Testing AutoConfiguration

Outlook 2013 supports automatic account configuration, which means that Outlook 2013 can attempt to determine your account settings automatically. With Exchange Server 2010, Outlook 2013 relies on being able to identify and communicate with the AutoDiscover host for your domain, such as *autodiscover.tailspintoys.com*. This host corresponds to a virtual server hosted on the computer(s) running Exchange Server.

To be able to resolve the fully qualified AutoDiscover host name, your client must be pointed to a DNS server that hosts the records for the AutoDiscover host or that can forward a query to the appropriate DNS server(s).

After your client is configured appropriately to resolve the AutoDiscover host, you can use a feature in Outlook 2013 to test the capability to discover account information. If you are having difficulties viewing free/busy information or using the Out of Office Assistant, the inability of the client to contact the AutoDiscover host could be the problem.

To test the connection, create an Outlook 2013 profile, with or without a valid email account. Then, start Outlook 2013, hold down the Ctrl key, and right-click the Outlook 2013 icon in the system tray. Choose Test E-mail AutoConfiguration to open the Test E-mail AutoConfiguration dialog box, shown in Figure 3-17.

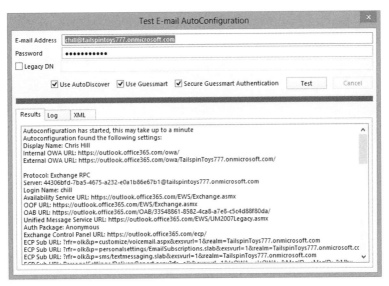

Figure 3-17 Use the Test E-mail AutoConfiguration dialog box to test AutoDiscover functionality.

Type the email address for your Exchange Server account in the E-mail Address field, type your email account password in the Password field, and then click Test. If AutoConfiguration succeeds, the dialog box will display information similar to that shown in Figure 3-18. If AutoConfiguration fails, the dialog box will display an error message indicating that it was unable to determine the correct settings. If you receive the error, verify that the client is configured for the appropriate DNS server(s) and retest.

Adding Outlook.com and Hotmail accounts

Outlook 2013 provides native support for both Outlook.com and Hotmail accounts, and it can automatically discover and configure settings for both types of accounts. To add either an Outlook.com or a Hotmail account to Outlook 2013, click File; click Add Account; enter your name, email address, and password in the fields provided in the Add Account dialog box; and click Next. Outlook will automatically configure settings as necessary for the account.

Configuring Outlook for Office 365

As with Outlook.com and Hotmail, Outlook 2013 natively supports Office 365 and can automatically configure your account in Outlook to connect to your Office 365 mailbox. However, before you connect with Outlook you must first connect to your Office 365 mailbox at least once with Outlook Anywhere. To do so, sign in to your Office 365 sign-in page, and then click Outlook at the top of the page to open your mailbox. Log off, and then add the account in Outlook, allowing Outlook to use AutoDiscover to determine the appropriate settings for your account.

Working in and configuring Outlook

I F you've used earlier versions of Outlook, you'll find that the interface in Microsoft Outlook 2013 has both changed and stayed the same. Many elements are the same or similar in previous versions, such as the presence of the ribbon throughout the application. There are also differences, such as the "flatter," simplified look of the interface. In any case, if you're new to Outlook 2013 entirely, you need to become familiar with its interface, which is the main focus of this chapter.

This chapter examines standard elements of the interface, including the ribbon, toolbars, the Folder Pane, the Folder List, and the Reading Pane. You'll also learn how to use multiple Outlook 2013 windows and views, and navigate your way through the Outlook 2013 interface. In short, this chapter takes you on a guided tour of the Outlook 2013 interface to help you understand how to work in and navigate through Outlook's views.

Using the Folder Pane

The Folder Pane appears on the left in the Outlook 2013 window and contains shortcuts to the standard Outlook 2013 folders as well as shortcuts to folders you've created and other important data folders, as shown in Figure 4-1. Just click an icon in the Folder Pane to open that folder or item. The Folder Pane gives you quick access not only to Outlook 2013 folders but also to all your data.

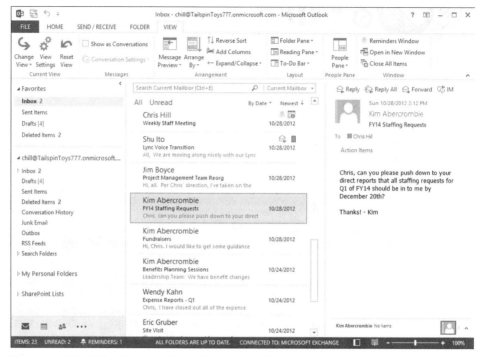

Figure 4-1 The Folder Pane provides quick access to all Outlook 2013 data and other frequently used resources and folders.

For a detailed discussion of the Folder Pane, including how to create your own groups and shortcuts, see the section "Customizing the Folder Pane" in Chapter 26.

> **Note**
>
> You can create new shortcuts in any of the existing Shortcuts groups in the Folder Pane, and you can also create your own groups.

Outlook 2013 offers two options for viewing the list of available folders. As Figure 4-1 shows, you can use the Compact Navigation option to view the list of folders as small icons and open a given folder by clicking its icon. The other option displays the folders as text across the bottom of the window, just above the status bar, and you can open a folder by clicking its text.

> **Note**
> To change between normal and compact view, click the ellipsis at the right of the folder
> list, choose Navigation Options, and either select or clear the Compact Navigation
> check box.

Using objects in the Folder Pane

Most of the time, you'll probably just click an icon in the Folder Pane to open its associated folder. However, you can also right-click an object and use the resulting shortcut menu to perform various tasks with the selected object. For example, you might right-click the Calendar icon and then choose Open In New Window to open a second window showing the calendar's contents. To view a different folder, simply click the folder's button in the Navigation Bar at the bottom of the Folder Pane. The content of the upper portion of the Folder Pane changes according to the folder that you select. For example, the Folder Pane shows your mail folders if you click the Mail icon.

Controlling the appearance of the Folder Pane

Outlook 2013 shows a selection of view buttons for standard folders in the Folder Pane. If you don't use certain folders very often, however, you might prefer to remove them from the Folder Pane to make room for other view buttons. For example, if you never use the Notes folder, you can remove that button from the Folder Pane and use the Folder List to access that folder when needed.

In Outlook 2013, you can't specifically remove a folder from the Folder Pane, but you can change the order and the number of items displayed, which has the same effect. For example, if you don't want to see the Tasks folder, you might make it fourth on the priority list and then only show three items, which effectively removes Tasks from the list.

To change the buttons displayed in the Folder Pane, click the ellipsis in the lower-right section of the Folder Pane, and then choose Navigation Options to open the dialog box shown in Figure 4-2. Use the Move Up and Move Down buttons to change the order, and then use the Maximum Number Of Visible Items box at the top of the dialog box to control how many of the items will be shown.

Chapter 4

Figure 4-2 Use the Navigation Options dialog box to control what items appear in the Folder List menu.

> **Note**
>
> If you seldom use the Folder Pane, you can close it or minimize it to make room on the screen for the Folder List or other data. Simply click the View tab, click Folder Pane, and then choose Off or Minimize to alter the display.

Using the Reading Pane

The Reading Pane allows you to preview Outlook 2013 items without opening them. For example, you can preview an email message in the Reading Pane simply by clicking the message header. To turn the Reading Pane on or off, click the View tab, click Reading Pane, and then choose Right, Bottom, or Off.

To some degree, the way that the Reading Pane functions depends on how you configure it. For example, you can set up the Reading Pane to mark messages as read after they've been previewed for a specified length of time. To configure the Reading Pane, click File, Options; click Mail in the left pane of the Outlook Options dialog box; and then click Reading Pane. Select options based on the following list:

- **Mark Items As Read When Viewed In The Reading Pane** Select this option to have messages marked as read when they've been previewed for the time specified by the following option.

- **Wait *n* Seconds Before Marking Item As Read** Specify the number of seconds that a message must be displayed in the Reading Pane before it is marked as read.

- **Mark Item As Read When Selection Changes** Select this option to have the message in the Reading Pane marked as read when you select another message.

- **Single Key Reading Using Spacebar** Selecting this option allows you to use the Spacebar to move through your list of messages to preview them. Press Shift+Spacebar to move up the list. You also can use the Up Arrow and Down Arrow keys to move up and down the message list.

The Reading Pane in Outlook 2013 offers some additional features, which include the following:

- You can compose replies to messages in the Reading Pane without needing to open the reply in a separate window.

- In a message, you can double-click an address in the Reading Pane to view details for the address.

- The Reading Pane header displays the message's attachments. You can double-click an attachment to open it, or you can right-click the attachment and choose other tasks on the shortcut menu (such as saving the attachment).

- The Reading Pane displays Accept and Decline buttons so that you can accept or decline a meeting request in the Reading Pane without opening the request.

- When a meeting invitation is selected, the Reading Pane shows a snippet of your calendar with the proposed meeting and the adjacent items to help you determine if you can attend the meeting (see Figure 4-3).

Chapter 4

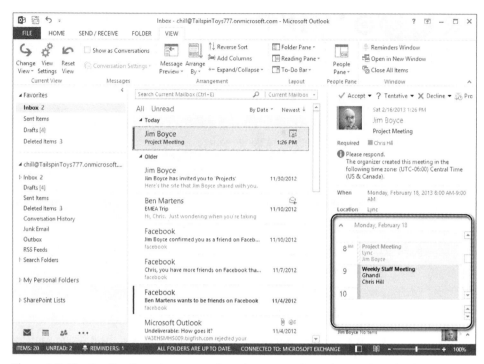

Figure 4-3 The Reading Pane shows a preview of a proposed meeting on the calendar.

Using the To-Do Bar

The To-Do Bar enables you to view items for your Calendar, People (Contacts), and Tasks folder, and you can specify which of these items appear in the To-Do Bar. The To-Do Bar appears at the right side of the Outlook window (see Figure 4-4). The visibility of the To-Do Bar is set on a folder-by-folder basis, so for example you can have it displayed in your Calendar folder but not in your Inbox.

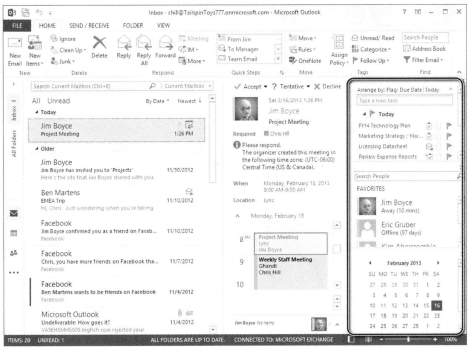

Figure 4-4 The To-Do Bar shows tasks, contacts, and the calendar.

Using the People Pane

The People Pane is another optional element of Outlook 2013 that you can turn on or off. The People Pane shows a list of the people associated with a selected item, and it gives you the ability to view information about those people. For example, if you have the People Pane displayed for your mail folders, when you select a message, the People Pane shows an icon for each person addressed in the email (including you). Each icon shows presence information (available, busy, and so on) and enables you to open chat, voice, and video conversations or create a new email to that person. Clicking a person's icon changes the view of the People Pane to show social updates (such as from SharePoint or Facebook), emails received from that person, meetings you have scheduled with the person, and attachments the person has sent you.

> **Note**
>
> To turn the People Pane on or off, click the View tab, click People Pane, and choose the desired state.

> **Note**
>
> To view social updates in the People Pane, you must configure corresponding social networking accounts in Outlook. See Chapter 15, "Social networking and Outlook," to learn more.

Using the ribbon

Outlook implements the full Microsoft Office ribbon interface to give you access to commands, options, and tools in Outlook 2013. The ribbon is shown in Figure 4-5.

Figure 4-5 The ribbon provides quick access to context-sensitive commands and features.

The ribbon places features onto individual *tabs*, each of which comprises tools with related functions. For example, all the tools that relate to inserting items into a new message are located together on the Insert tab of the new message form.

Each ribbon tab is divided into *groups*, and each group organizes the features for a specific function. On the Message tab of the new message form, for example, the Basic Text group organizes the tools you use to format text in the message.

The ribbon operates in the context of the currently selected folder. For example, when you have the Inbox open, the tabs and commands in the ribbon apply primarily to the Inbox. When the Inbox is open, for instance, the New group on the Home tab shows a New E-mail button that, when clicked, starts a new email message. Likewise, when the Calendar folder is open, the buttons displayed are New Appointment and New Meeting. Other tabs and commands change as well, such as the commands on the View menu, which show view choices for the selected folder.

You'll see at least four tabs in the ribbon regardless of which folder is open, and the Search tab appears when you click in the Search box. These tabs include the following:

- **Home** This tab is the place to go to create new items and access the most common commands for items in the selected folder. For the Inbox, for example, the Home tab contains commands for replying to messages, creating and using Quick Steps, moving messages, and performing other common email tasks.

- **Send/Receive** Use this tab to synchronize folders (send/receive email, for example), show send/receive status, and set connection and download preferences.

- **Folder** Use this tab to access folder-specific tasks such as setting permission for a folder, cleaning up the folder, recovering deleted items, and so on.

- **View** Use the View tab to access various views for the current folder, create and manage views, and set options for the various interface panes (such as the Folder Pane).

- **Search** This tab appears only when you click in the Search box, and it offers options that you can use to define your search criteria and access search options and other tools.

In addition to these tabs, Outlook will show other tabs as appropriate. For example, when you click an appointment in the calendar, Outlook displays the Calendar Tools/ Appointment tab, which includes commands that are specific to the appointment. If you click a meeting, Outlook shows the Calendar Tools/Meeting tab. The important point is that these tabs are context-sensitive and apply to the selected item.

Using the Quick Access Toolbar

Outlook, like other Office applications, provides a Quick Access Toolbar that, as its name implies, gives you quick access to commonly used commands and options (see Figure 4-6). By default, the Quick Access Toolbar contains only two commands: Send/Receive All Folders and Undo. To use one of these commands, just click its button. If you want to move the toolbar below the ribbon instead of above it, click the small arrow button at the right of the toolbar and choose Show Below The Ribbon. Click the button again and choose Show Above The Ribbon to move it back to its default location.

Figure 4-6 Use the Quick Access Toolbar to access common commands.

> **Note**
> As you might expect, you can customize the ribbon to your liking. See Chapter 26, "Customizing the Outlook interface," for details on customizing the ribbon and the Quick Access Toolbar.

Using the Backstage view

You use the Microsoft Office Backstage view in Outlook (see Figure 4-7) to access account settings, open files, print, set up Out of Office replies, clean up the mailbox, and access rules and alerts.

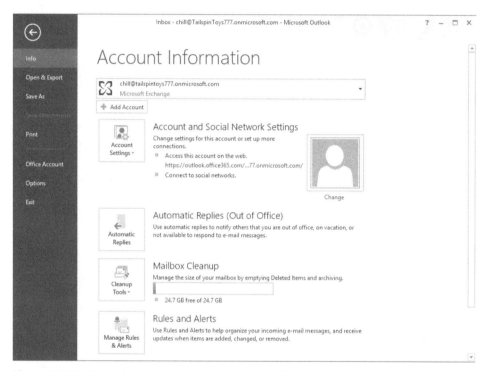

Figure 4-7 Use the Backstage view to access account settings and other general Outlook options and commands.

The Backstage view is fairly self-explanatory. Individual items are covered where applicable throughout this book. To return to your Outlook folders, just click the Back button at the top left.

Using other Outlook features

In addition to the various folders and views described in this chapter, Outlook 2013 incorporates several other standard components in its interface. The following sections explain these features and how to use them effectively.

> **Note**
>
> This book assumes that you're familiar with your operating system and comfortable using menus. Therefore, neither the Outlook 2013 ribbon nor its individual tabs are discussed in this book, except for specific tabs and commands where applicable.

Using multiple Outlook windows

Although Outlook 2013 opens in a single window, it supports the use of multiple windows, which can be extremely useful. For example, you might want to keep your Inbox open while you also browse through your schedule. Or perhaps you want to copy items from one folder to another by dragging and dropping them. Whatever the case, it's easy to use multiple windows in Outlook 2013.

When you right-click a folder in the Folder Pane, the shortcut menu for that folder contains the Open In New Window command. Choose this command to open the selected folder in a new window, keeping the existing folder open in the current window. You also can open a folder from the Folder List (discussed next) in a new window. Simply right-click a folder, and then choose Open In New Window to open that folder in a new window.

Using the Folder List

When you need to switch between folders, you'll probably use the Folder Pane most of the time. But the Folder Pane doesn't include shortcuts to all your folders by default, and adding those shortcuts can clutter the pane, especially if you have multiple data stores. Fortunately, Outlook 2013 provides another quick way to navigate your folders: the Folder List.

Click the Folder List button in the Folder Pane to display the Folder List, as shown in Figure 4-8. In the list, click the folder that you want to open.

Chapter 4

Figure 4-8 Use the Folder List to browse and select other folders.

Using the status bar

The status bar appears at the bottom of the Outlook 2013 window, as shown in Figure 4-9, and presents information about the current folder and selected items, such as the number of items in the folder. It can also include other status information, such as the progress of folder synchronization and connection status for Exchange Server.

Figure 4-9 The status bar provides useful information, such as the number of items in the selected folder and the current connection status to the server.

You can customize the status bar to control what information appears in it. To do so, just right-click the status bar to display a pop-up menu with available items. Items that have a check mark by them appear on the status bar, and those without a check mark do not. Just put a check mark by the ones you want displayed (see Figure 4-10).

Figure 4-10 You can customize the status bar.

Using the InfoBar

The InfoBar is the banner near the top of an open email message, appointment, contact, or task. It tells you whether a message has been replied to or forwarded, along with the online status of a contact who is using instant messaging, and so on. The InfoBar in a message form, for example, displays the From, To, Cc, and other fields. In Outlook 2013, the InfoBar resides in the Reading Pane, as shown in Figure 4-11.

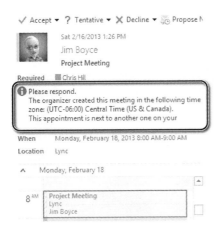

Figure 4-11 The InfoBar appears in the Reading Pane as well as in message and appointment forms.

Chapter 4

Some of the fields in the InfoBar simply display information, but others lead to more details. For example, you can double-click a name in the InfoBar to view the associated address and other contact information, or you can double-click attachments to open them. If the InfoBar displays a message that you replied to or that you forwarded, click that message and choose Find Related Messages to search for messages in the same conversation as the selected message.

Creating and using categories

O NE of the primary functions of Microsoft Outlook 2013 is to help you organize your data, whether that data is a collection of contacts, a task list, your schedule, or a month's worth of messages. To make this easier, you can use Outlook 2013 categories. A *category* is a combination of words or phrases and colors that you assign to Outlook 2013 items as a means of organizing them. For example, you might assign the category Personal to a message from a family member to differentiate that message from your work-related messages and then customize the Inbox view to exclude personal items. Outlook 2013 incorporates color with categories, making it easy to identify categories at a glance.

This chapter explains how categories work in Outlook 2013 and shows you how to work with color categories, add categories, assign categories to Outlook 2013 items, and use categories to arrange, display, and search through Outlook 2013 data.

Understanding categories

If you've used a personal finance or checkbook program, you're probably familiar with categories. In these programs, you can assign a category to each check, deposit, or other transaction and then view all transactions for a specific category, perhaps printing them in a report for tax purposes. For example, you might use categories to keep track of business expenses and separate them by certain criteria, such as reimbursement policy or tax deductions.

Outlook 2013 categories perform essentially the same function: you can assign categories to Outlook 2013 items and manipulate the data based on those categories. For example, you might use categories to assign Outlook 2013 items such as messages and tasks to a specific project. You could then locate all items related to that project quickly. Alternatively, you might use categories to differentiate personal contacts from business contacts. Whatever your need for organization, categories offer a handy and efficient way to achieve your goal.

> **Note**
> Outlook 2013 combines colors with categories, giving you the ability to see category assignments at a glance. As you'll learn later in this chapter, you can still use categories without colors, simply by assigning the color None to the category.

What can you do with categories? First, with the integration of color with categories, you can tell instantly what category is assigned to a given item. For example, say you create a rule that assigns the Red category to all messages from a particular contact. You can then tell at a glance—without doing anything else—which messages are from that person. Or perhaps you assign the Red category to business messages and Green to personal. Whatever the case, color categories are a great means for visually identifying specific types of messages.

> **Note**
> You can use conditional formatting to display items in certain colors when they meet criteria like sender, subject, and so on without assigning a category to the items. Alternatively, you can use rules to assign categories automatically, which essentially gives you both automatic formatting and category options at the same time.

After you assign a category to each relevant Outlook 2013 item, you can sort, search, and organize your data according to the category. Figure 5-1, for example, shows the Advanced Find dialog box after a search for all Outlook 2013 items assigned to the category Toy Show. Figure 5-2 shows the Contacts folder organized by category, displaying all contacts who are involved in the toy show. The ability to search by category makes it easy to find all the items associated with a specific project, contract, issue, or general category.

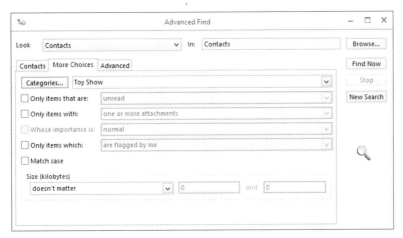

Figure 5-1 Use the Advanced Find dialog box to search for all items in a given category.

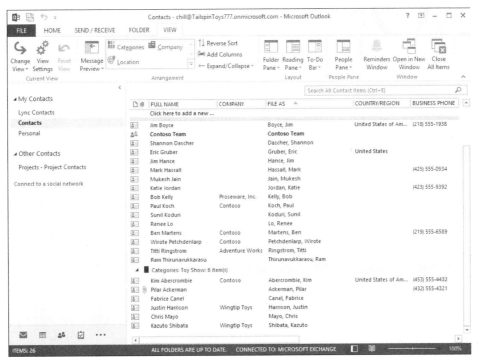

Figure 5-2 You can group contacts by category to list all contacts involved in a particular event or project.

> **Note**
>
> You can perform a search for items based on their categories easily using the ribbon. Just click in the Search box, which causes the Search tab to appear in the ribbon. Then, click Categorized from the Refine group and choose the categories for which to search.

Categories are useful only if you apply them consistently. After you become disciplined in using categories and begin to assign them out of habit (or with rules), you'll wonder how you ever organized your day without them.

CAUTION

> The Master Category List in versions of Outlook prior to Outlook 2007 has been removed. Categories listed in the Master Category List but not assigned to any items are not imported when you upgrade to Outlook 2013.

Customizing your category list

Before you assign categories to Outlook 2013 items, you should go through the category list and add the categories that you need or tailor the existing categories to suit your needs. To determine which categories to add, spend some time thinking about how you intend to use them, including which colors you want to apply to specific categories. Although you can always add and modify categories later, creating the majority up front not only saves time but also helps you organize your thoughts and plan the use of categories more effectively.

Follow these steps when you're ready to create categories:

1. Open the Color Categories dialog box, shown in Figure 5-3, by selecting any item in Outlook 2013 and clicking Categorize, All Categories from the Home tab of the ribbon or by right-clicking an item and choosing Categorize, All Categories on the shortcut menu.

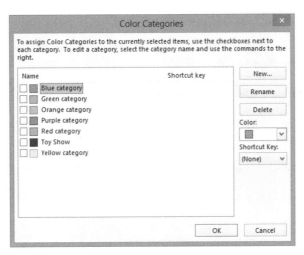

Figure 5-3 You can add a new category in the Color Categories dialog box.

2. Click New to open the Add New Category dialog box.

3. Type the new category name in the Name field, select a color in the Color drop-down list, optionally specify a shortcut key, and then click OK.

> **Note**
>
> Select None in the Color drop-down list if you want a text-only category.

4. Repeat steps 2 and 3 to add other categories as desired, and then click OK to close the Color Categories dialog box.

> **Note**
>
> When you create a new category, Outlook 2013 automatically adds the category to the selected item. You must clear the category if you don't want it assigned to the selected item. For information about creating new categories while you are assigning categories to an item, see the next section, "Assigning categories to Outlook items."

The categories that you add to your category list depend entirely on the types of tasks that you perform with Outlook 2013, your type of business or organization, and your preferences. The following list suggests ways to categorize business-related data:

Chapter 5

- Track items by project type or project name.

- Organize contacts by their type (for example, managers, assistants, technical experts, and financial advisors).

- Keep track of departmental assignments.

- Track different types of documents (for example, drafts, works in progress, and final versions).

- Track contacts by sales potential (for example, 30-day or 60-day).

Organize items by priority. The following list offers suggestions for categorizing personal data:

- Use color to identify critical or urgent issues.

- Organize personal contacts by type (friends, family, insurance agents, legal advisors, and medical contacts, for starters).

- Track items by area of interest.

- Organize items for hobbies.

- Track items related to vacation or other activities.

Assigning categories to Outlook items

Assigning categories to items is easy. You can assign multiple categories to each item if needed. For example, a particular contact might be involved in more than one project, so you might assign a category for each project to that contact. If you have a task that must be performed for multiple projects, you might assign those project categories to the task.

Outlook 2013 will display multiple colors for an item, depending on its type and location. For example, if you assign the Red, Blue, and Green categories to an email message, Outlook 2013 displays each of those three color indicators in the message header, as shown in Figure 5-4. You can resize the Categories column if you want Outlook 2013 to show indicators for all the assigned categories.

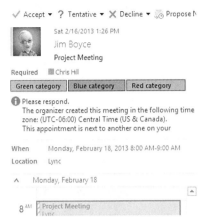

Figure 5-4 Outlook 2013 can show multiple color categories in the message header to indicate multiple categories.

In the Calendar view, Outlook 2013 displays the item using the last color you assigned and places as many color indicators as it can in the item label. So if you add the Blue, Green, and Red categories, Outlook 2013 colors the item as Red and puts Blue and Green indicators in the item for the Day and Week views. In the Month view, you see only the last color assigned.

> **Note**
> If you assign multiple categories to an item at the same time from the Color Categories dialog box, Outlook isn't consistent about which category it uses to display the item. For example, it doesn't always use the last one you selected. If you want to have the item appear using a specific color, assign the categories individually, choosing the desired color as the last one.

To learn how to assign categories to existing items, see the next section, "Assigning categories to existing Outlook items."

Chapter 5

Follow these steps to assign categories to a new item:

1. Open the folder in which you want to create the item, and then click New.

2. Click Categorize in the Tags group on the ribbon. You'll find the Tags group on the first tab of the ribbon, but the tab name changes depending on the type of item that you are working with (Message, Appointment, Event, and so on).

3. Select a single category on the shortcut menu, or click All Categories, and in the Color Categories dialog box, select all the categories that pertain to the item. If you need to add a category, simply click New, type a name, and click OK.

4. Click OK to close the Color Categories dialog box and continue creating the item.

As you can see in step 3, you can create a category on the fly when you're assigning categories to an item. However, a drawback to creating categories on the fly is that you might not enter the category names consistently. As a result, you could end up with a category being given more than one name. As you might expect, Outlook 2013 treats category names literally, so any difference between two names, however minor, makes those categories different. Searching for one won't turn up items assigned to the other.

Assigning categories to existing Outlook items

Often you will want to add categories to existing Outlook 2013 items. For example, you will likely want to categorize email messages after they arrive. The easiest way to assign a category to an existing item is to right-click the item, choose Categorize, and then choose a category from the shortcut menu, as shown in Figure 5-5. You can use this method for any of the Outlook 2013 items.

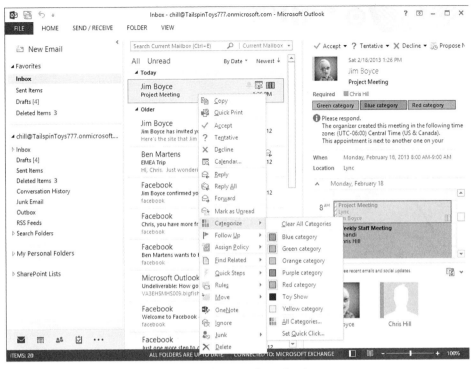

Figure 5-5 Right-click and choose a color category from the shortcut menu.

Assigning a Quick Click category

Outlook 2013 offers the capability to assign a category quickly, with a single click. In message folders, you can add the Categories column to the view and then click the Categories column to assign a Quick Click category.

Follow these steps to specify the Quick Click category:

1. Click Categorize in the Tags group on the ribbon, and then choose Set Quick Click to open the Set Quick Click dialog box, shown in Figure 5-6.

Figure 5-6 Use the Set Quick Click dialog box to specify the Quick Click category.

2. Select a category, and then click OK.

Assigning categories automatically

You can assign categories easily when you create an item, but you might prefer to simplify the process for items that will be assigned to the same category (or set of categories). For example, if you frequently create email messages that have specific category assignments, you could bypass the steps involved in adding the categories to each new message. You can accomplish this by using an email template.

For a detailed discussion of templates, see Chapter 25, "Creating and using templates."

You can use templates for other Outlook 2013 items as well. Simply create the template, assign categories to it as needed, and then save it with a name that will help you easily identify the category assignments or the function of the template. When you need to create a message with that specific set of category assignments, you can create it from the template rather than from scratch. Because the category assignments are stored in the template, new items created from the template are assigned those categories. Using templates to assign categories not only saves you the time involved in adding categories individually, but also ensures that the category assignments are consistent. (For example, you won't misspell a name or forget to add a category.)

A more likely possibility is that you want to add categories to email messages when they arrive. You can create a rule to assign one or more categories to messages when they arrive or even when you send them. For example, let's say you subscribe to six newsletters and you want Outlook 2013 to highlight them in the Inbox with the Green category. A great way to do that is to assign the color category to the messages based on the recipient address or other unique characteristics of the messages.

To learn how to create and manage rules in Outlook 2013, see Chapter 11, "Using rules, alerts, and automatic responses."

Modifying categories and category assignments

At some point, you'll want to recategorize Outlook 2013 items—that is, you'll want to add, remove, or modify their category assignments. For example, when one project ends and another begins, some of your contacts will move to a different project, and you'll want to change the categories assigned to the contact items. Perhaps you've added some new categories to organize your data further and want to assign those categories to existing items, or perhaps you made a mistake when you created an item or assigned categories to it, and now you need to make changes. Whatever the case, changing categories and category assignments is easy.

Changing existing categories

For one reason or another, you might need to change a category name. You might have misspelled the name of the category when you created it, or you might want to change the wording a little. For example, you might delete the category Foes and create a new one named Friends to replace it (assuming that your friends are not really foes). You can also change existing categories in Outlook 2013. When you change a category, all items assigned to that category are updated.

For example, assume that you have created a category named Dallas Toy Show and made the category red. You open the Inbox and assign the category to several messages. Then you open the calendar and assign the category to a few meetings. A week later, you dis-cover that the toy show is moving to Seattle. So you open the Color Categories dialog box, rename the category Seattle Toy Show, and change the color to blue. When you look in the Inbox, all the messages with that assigned category now show the new name and color. Likewise, the appointments in the calendar also show the new name and color.

If you need to change a category globally rather than add one, see the section "Changing category assignments of multiple items at one time."

Earlier in this chapter, you learned how to create new categories. Changing a category is much like adding a new one.

Follow these steps to change a category:

1. In Outlook 2013, select any item, and then click Categorize and choose All Categories.

2. In the Color Categories dialog box, click a category to select it.

3. Click Rename, and then type a new name for the category.

4. If you want, select a new color in the Color drop-down list.

5. Click OK to close the Color Categories dialog box.

Chapter 5

Changing category assignments

You can assign categories to an item at any time, adding and removing the categories you want. To change the categories assigned to a specific item, follow these steps:

1. In Outlook 2013, locate the item for which you want to change the category assignment.

2. Select the item and then click Categorize in the Tags group on the ribbon, or right-click the item and choose Categorize on the shortcut menu.

3. Select a new category in the drop-down list, or choose All Categories to open the Color Categories dialog box, and then assign or remove multiple categories.

Changing category assignments of multiple items at one time

In some cases, you'll want to change the category assignments of several items at one time. For example, assume that you've assigned the category Seattle Toy Show to 50 messages in your Inbox. Now you want to clear the categories on all those messages. You could change the messages one at a time, or you could hold down Ctrl, select each message, and then change the category. But for a larger number of items, there is an easier way—the trick is to use a view organized by category. To do this, perform the following steps:

1. Open the folder containing the items whose categories you want to change.

2. Click the View tab, click Change View, and choose List.

3. In the List view, click the Categories tab to organize the view by category.

4. Locate the items under the category that you want to change.

5. If the category that you want to assign to the items has not been assigned yet to any items, assign the category to one item. That item should now show up in the view under its category.

6. Click the category you are changing and drag it to the target category.

> **Note**
> There is no List view for mail folders. You can instead create a Table view that groups by category, and then use the preceding steps to change categories.

An important point to understand when using this method to change categories is that Outlook 2013 assigns the target category (the one on which you drop the items) exclusively to the items. For example, assume that you have several items with Red, Blue, and Green category assignments. You drag those items to the Yellow category. All the items now have *only* the Yellow category. The other categories are removed.

If you want to assign categories to a group of items, you have a couple of different methods to use. If the number of items is relatively small, hold down the Ctrl key, select each item, and then right-click an item and choose Categorize, followed by a category selection. Or choose All Categories to assign multiple new categories.

> **Note**
>
> A list view usually works best when you need to select multiple items.

If you need to change a lot of items, first organize the view by category (to do this, click the View tab on the ribbon, click Change View, choose List, and click the Categories column). Then right-click the category whose items you want to change, choose Categorize, and then choose a new category (or choose All Categories to modify multiple categories). Outlook 2013 displays a warning message informing you that the action will be applied to all items in the selected category. Click OK to continue with the change.

Organizing data with categories

Now that you've created your personal category list and faithfully assigned categories to all your data in Outlook 2013, how do you put those categories to work for you? Searching for items with given categories is a good example of how you can use categories to organize and sort your data: by specifying those categories in the Advanced Find dialog box, you can compile a list of items to which those categories have been assigned.

You also can sort items by category. To do so, follow these steps:

1. Open the folder containing the items that you want to sort. If the Categories field isn't displayed, right-click the column bar, and then choose Field Chooser.

2. Drag the Categories field to the column bar, and then close the Field Chooser dialog box.

3. Right-click the Categories column, and then choose Group By This Field.

> **Note**
>
> To clear groupings, right-click the Categories column in the Group By box and choose Don't Group By This Field.

Chapter 5

Viewing selected categories only

In many situations, it's beneficial to be able to restrict a view to show only selected categories. For example, perhaps you want to view all messages that have the Toy Show and Travel Required categories. Whatever the case, you can use a couple of methods to view only items with specific category assignments.

First, you can use a custom, filtered view to filter only those items that fit your criteria. Follow these steps to customize a view to show selected categories:

1. Open the Outlook 2013 folder that contains the items you want to view.

2. On the View tab of the ribbon, click View Settings in the Current View group.

3. In the Advanced View Settings dialog box, click Filter.

4. In the Filter dialog box, click the More Choices tab, as shown in Figure 5-7.

Figure 5-7 Use the More Choices tab in the Filter dialog box to create a custom view.

5. On the More Choices tab, click Categories, select the categories that you want to view, and then click OK.

6. Click OK in the Filter dialog box, and then click OK in the Customize View dialog box to view the filtered view.

See the section "Creating and using custom views" in Chapter 26, "Customizing the Outlook interface," to learn more about working with custom views.

Another way to view items with only selected categories, provided you are working with a mail folder, is a Search Folder. You can create a new Search Folder that shows only messages in the desired categories. Follow these steps to create the Search Folder:

7. Right-click Search Folders in the Folder List (Folder Pane), and then choose New Search Folder.

8. In the New Search Folder dialog box, shown in Figure 5-8, scroll to the bottom of the list, select Create A Custom Search Folder, and then click Choose.

Figure 5-8 Create a custom Search Folder in the New Search Folder dialog box.

9. In the Custom Search Folder dialog box, shown in Figure 5-9, type a name for the Search Folder in the Name field.

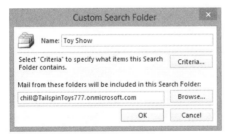

Figure 5-9 Specify properties in the Custom Search Folder dialog box.

10. Click Criteria to open the Search Folder Criteria dialog box, and then click More Choices.

11. Click Categories, and then select the categories to include in the Search Folder.

12. Click OK twice to return to the Custom Search Folder dialog box.

Chapter 5

13. Click Browse, select the folders to be included in the search, and then click OK.

14. Click OK in the Custom Search Folder dialog box, and then click OK to close the New Search Folder dialog box.

See the section "Finding and organizing messages with Search Folders" in Chapter 9, "Managing your email," to learn more about creating and using Search Folders.

Using categories effectively

The addition of color categories in Outlook 2013 makes categories even more useful and extends the ways that you can use categories to manage your schedule, messages, and other items in Outlook 2013. Like most Outlook 2013 features, categories are not useful in and of themselves—it's how you use them that makes them useful. Here are several tips for using categories effectively:

- **Create your categories first**   By creating your category list up front before you start assigning categories, you force yourself to take the time to think about what categories you need and how you will use them. What makes sense for someone else might not fit your needs, and vice versa. This doesn't mean that you can't add categories after the fact or change the way that you use categories, but some planning up front will help ensure that you get the most out of categorization.

- **Use categories in combination with folders to organize messages**   Categories offer an excellent means for you to organize your Outlook 2013 data. Some people use folders to organize their messages; others use categories exclusively to manage their messages, keeping everything in the Inbox but assigning categories so that they can identify messages quickly. The best approach falls in between these two options, with a combination of folders and categories. Use categories to classify messages, but also use folders to organize those messages. For example, you might create a folder named Toy Show to store all messages relating to the upcoming toy show and then use categories to further classify messages in that folder.

- **Use Search Folders in combination with categories**   After you have categorized your messages, you can use Search Folders to locate all messages with specified categories quickly. Search Folders give you the benefit of potentially searching all your message folders for specific items, enabling you to locate all items with a specific category quickly, regardless of where they are stored. Take some time to consider which Search Folders will best suit your needs, and then create them.

- **Rely on colors to help you visually identify items**   Although you can create categories with no color, color will help you tell at a glance that a given message, appointment, or other item fits a specific category. For example, you might color all your important meetings in red, personal appointments in green, and optional appointments or meetings in yellow. The ability to tell at a glance what an item is will help improve your productivity and effectiveness.

- **Assign color categories to messages using rules**   Although you can certainly assign colors to messages manually, you should also take advantage of rules to assign categories for you automatically. For example, you might categorize messages from specific senders so that you can identify them easily in your Inbox, or use categories to identify messages from mailing lists, friends, and so on.

- **Identify your most commonly used category**   Determine which category you use the most, and define that category as your Quick Click category. You can then assign that category with a single click of the mouse.

CHAPTER 6

Basic email tasks

O F all the features in Microsoft Outlook 2013, messaging is probably the most frequently used. Even if you use Outlook 2013 primarily for contact management or scheduling, chances are good that you also rely heavily on Outlook 2013 email and other messaging capabilities. Because many of the Outlook 2013 key features make extensive use of messaging for workgroup collaboration and scheduling, understanding messaging is critical to using the program effectively.

This chapter provides an in-depth look at a wide range of topics related to sending and receiving messages with Outlook 2013. You'll learn the fundamentals—working with message forms, addressing, replying, and forwarding—and you'll also explore other, more advanced topics. For example, this chapter explains how to control when your messages are sent, how to save a copy of sent messages in specific folders, and how to work with attachments.

Working with messages

This section of the chapter offers a primer to bring you up to speed on Outlook 2013 basic messaging capabilities. It focuses on topics that relate to all types of email accounts. The Inbox is the place to start learning about Outlook 2013, so launch the program and open the Inbox folder. The next section explains how to work with message forms.

> **Note**
> If you haven't added email accounts to your profile, see Chapter 3, "Setting up accounts in Outlook," to learn how to configure various types of email accounts in Outlook.

Opening a standard message form

You can begin a new message in Outlook 2013 by using any one of these methods:

- With any mail folder open, choose New Email from the New group on the Home tab of the ribbon.

- Click the New Items button and choose E-mail Message.

- With any mail folder open (such as the Inbox), press Ctrl+N.

When you begin a new message, Outlook 2013 displays the Untitled Message form, shown in Figure 6-1.

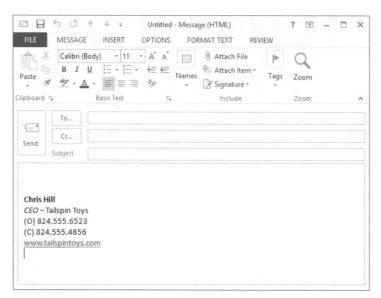

Figure 6-1 You use this standard message form to compose email messages.

Addressing messages

The Outlook 2013 address books make it easy to address messages. When you want to send a message to someone whose address is stored in your Contacts folder or in an address list on your server, you can click in the To box on the message form and type the recipient's name—you don't have to type the entire address. When you send the message, Outlook 2013 checks the name, locates the correct address, and adds it to the message. If multiple addresses match the name you specify, Outlook 2013 shows all the matches and prompts you to select the appropriate one. If you want to send a message to someone whose address isn't in any of your address books, you need to type the full address in the To box.

For more information about Outlook 2013 address books, see Chapter 13, "Managing address books and contact groups."

> **Note**
>
> Outlook 2013 can check the names and addresses of message recipients before you send the message. To perform this action, enter the names in the To box and either click the Check Names button on the ribbon or press Ctrl+K.

To open the address book, click an address book button (To, Cc, or Bcc) beside an address box on the message form. Outlook 2013 opens the Select Names dialog box (see Figure 6-2), which you can use to address the message.

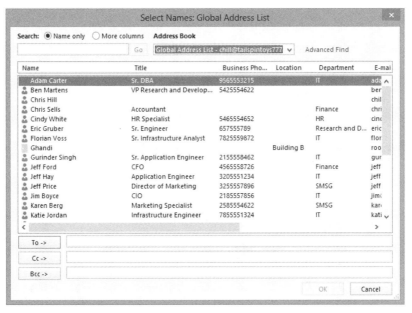

Figure 6-2 In the Select Names dialog box, you can select addresses from the address book.

Follow these steps to select addresses in this dialog box and add them to your message:

1. In the Address Book drop-down list, select the address list you want to view.

2. Select a name from the list, and click To, Cc, or Bcc to add the selected address to the specified address box.

3. Continue this process to add more recipients if necessary. Click OK when you're satisfied with the list.

> **Note**
>
> You can include multiple recipients in each address box on the message form. If you're typing the addresses yourself, separate them with a semicolon.

Including carbon copies and blind carbon copies

You can direct a single message to multiple recipients by including multiple addresses in the To box on the message form or by using the Cc (carbon copy) and Bcc (blind carbon copy) boxes. The Cc box appears by default on message forms, but the Bcc box does not. To display the Bcc box, on the Options tab on the ribbon, in the Show Fields group, choose Bcc. You use the Cc and Bcc boxes the same way you use the To box: Type a name or address in the box, or click the Address Book icon beside the box to open the address book.

> **Note**
>
> The term *carbon copy* is slowly being replaced by *courtesy copy*. I remember the days of carbon paper (do an online search if you don't know what that is). The two terms mean the same thing: a copy sent to someone for informational purposes.

INSIDE OUT   Hide addresses when necessary

The names contained in the To and Cc boxes of your message are visible to all recipients of the message. If you're using a contact group or server-side distribution list, Outlook 2013 converts the names on the list to individual addresses, exposing those addresses to the recipients. If you want to hide the names of one or more recipients, or you don't want distribution lists exposed, place those names in the Bcc (blind carbon copy) box.

Copying someone on all messages

In some situations, you might want every outgoing message to be copied to a particular person. For example, maybe you manage a small staff and want all employees' outgoing messages copied to you. Or perhaps you want to send a copy of all your outgoing messages to yourself at a separate email account.

Rules that you create with the Outlook 2013 Rules Wizard can process outgoing messages as well as incoming ones. One way to ensure that a recipient is copied on all outgoing messages is to add a rule that automatically adds the recipient to the messages' Cc field. Follow these steps to do so:

1. On the Home tab on the ribbon, click Rules in the Move group and choose Manage Rules and Alerts to begin creating the rule.

2. Click New Rule, select Apply Rule On Messages I Send in the Start From A Blank Rule group, and then click Next.

3. Click Next again without choosing any conditions to cause the rule to be used for all messages. Click Yes in the warning dialog box to confirm that you want the rule applied to all messages.

4. Select the action Cc The Message To People Or Public Group, and then click the underlined link in the Rule Description box and select the addresses where you want to send the carbon copies. These addresses can be from any of your address lists in the address book, or you can type in specific addresses.

5. Click Next, set exceptions as needed, and then click Next.

6. Supply a Name for the rule, verify that the Turn On This Rule check box is selected, ensure that you are satisfied with the rule settings, and then click Finish. Click OK to close the Rules And Alerts dialog box.

For more details about working with message rules, see Chapter 11, "Using rules, alerts, and automatic responses."

> **Note**
> Outlook might display a dialog box informing you that the rule you are creating is client-side only. For information on client-side rules, see the section "Creating and using rules" in Chapter 11.

Unfortunately, Outlook 2013 doesn't offer a Bcc action for the rule. The add-on Always BCC for Outlook 2013, available at *http://www.sperrysoftware.com/Outlook/Always-BCC.asp*, enables you to add a Bcc recipient automatically.

Using templates and custom forms for addressing

A rule is handy for copying all messages—or only certain messages—to one or more people, as explained in the preceding section. Contact groups and server-side distribution lists are handy for addressing a message to a group of people without entering the address for each person.

If you regularly send the same message to the same people but want to specify some in the To field, others in the Cc field, and still others in the Bcc field, contact groups and rules won't do the trick. Instead, you can use a template or a custom form to send the message. You create the form or template ahead of time with the addresses in the desired fields; you then open that item, complete it, and send it on its way. Use the following steps to create and use a template for this purpose:

1. In Outlook 2013, start a new message.

2. Enter the email or distribution list addresses as needed in the To, Cc, and Bcc fields.

3. Enter any other information that remains the same each time you send the message, such as subject or boilerplate text in the body of the message.

4. Click File and then click Save As.

5. Choose Outlook Template from the Save As Type drop-down list.

6. Enter a name in the File Name field, and if you want to use a location other than your Templates folder, choose a path for the template.

7. Click Save to save the template.

8. Close the message form and click No if prompted to save changes.

9. When it's time to create the message, click New Items on the Home tab of the ribbon, choose More Items, and select Choose Form to open the Choose Form dialog box (see Figure 6-3).

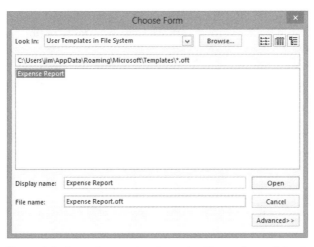

Figure 6-3 Open the template from the Choose Form dialog box.

10. Choose User Templates In File System from the Look In drop-down list, choose the template that you created in step 7, and click Open.

11. Add any other recipients of message content and click Send to send the message.

> **Note**
>
> If you use the default Templates folder for your templates, you don't have to browse for them when you choose the User Templates In File System option.

See Chapter 25, "Creating and using templates," for more information on using templates in Outlook 2013, and Chapter 27, "Designing and using custom forms," for details on creating and using custom forms.

Specifying message priority and sensitivity

By default, new messages have their priority set to Normal. You might want to change the priority to High for important or time-sensitive messages, or to Low for non-work-related mail or other messages that have relatively less importance. Outlook 2013 displays an icon in the Importance column of the recipient's Inbox to indicate High or Low priority. (For messages with Normal priority, no icon is displayed.)

The easiest way to set message priority is by using the Message tab on the ribbon in the message form. In the Tags group, click the High Importance button (which has an exclamation point icon) to specify High priority. Click the Low Importance button (which has a down arrow icon) to specify Low priority. To set the priority back to Normal, click the selected priority again to remove the highlight around the button (see Figure 6-4).

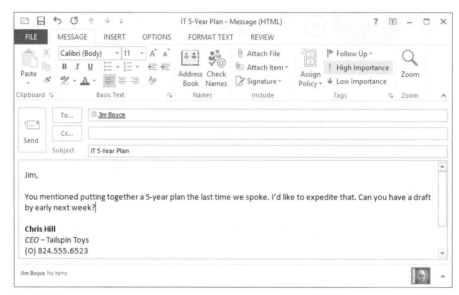

Figure 6-4 Outlook 2013 highlights the appropriate priority button to provide a visual indicator of the message's priority.

You also can specify a message's sensitivity by choosing a Normal (the default), Personal, Private, or Confidential sensitivity level. Setting sensitivity adds a tag to the message that displays the sensitivity level that you selected. This helps the recipient see at a glance how you want the message to be treated. To set sensitivity, on the Options tab on the ribbon, click the small Message Options button in the lower-right corner of the More Options group and select the sensitivity level from the Sensitivity drop-down list.

> ### Note
> You can also use Information Rights Management (IRM) with Microsoft Exchange Server to control the actions that recipients can take with messages. For example, you can allow recipients to read a message but not forward, print, or reply to the message.

Saving a message to send later

Although you can create some messages in a matter of seconds, others can take considerably longer—particularly if you're using formatting or special features, or if you're composing a lengthy message. Outlook 2013 automatically creates a draft of messages that you are composing. If you are composing a reply, Outlook adds [Draft] at the left of the message header, as shown in Figure 6-5. If you click away from that message to select another before you finish drafting the reply, the [Draft] text remains on the message header as a reminder that you haven't sent the message yet. If you create a new message, Outlook simply puts a copy of the message in the Drafts folder automatically.

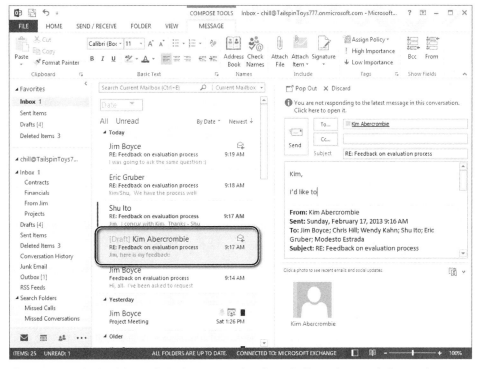

Figure 6-5 Outlook adds [Draft] in the message header to indicate that a reply has not been sent yet.

You can also save a copy of a message to the Drafts folder yourself at any time. Click File and choose Save in the message form to have Outlook 2013 save the message to the Drafts folder. When you're ready to work on the message again, open the Drafts folder and double-click the message to open it.

> **Note**
> You can click File and choose Save As to save a message in one of several formats outside your Outlook 2013 folders in your Windows file system (such as your Documents folder).

Setting sending options

You can configure various options that affect how Outlook 2013 sends email messages. To set these options, in the main Outlook window, click File, Options, and then click Mail in the left pane (see Figure 6-6). Scroll down to find the Send Messages group of settings.

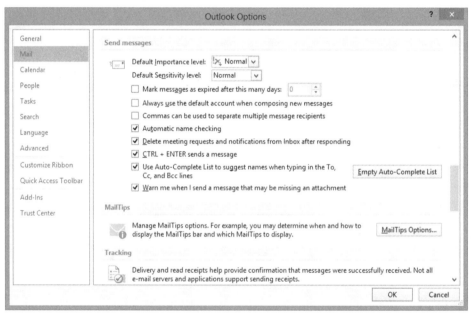

Figure 6-6 You can choose options for sending messages on the Mail page of the Outlook Options dialog box.

You can modify the following settings in the Send Messages group:

- **Default Importance Level** This option sets the default importance or priority level for all new messages. When you compose a message, you can override this setting by clicking the High Importance button or the Low Importance button on the ribbon in the message form, or by clicking Message Options on the Options tab of the message form's ribbon and setting the priority in the Properties dialog box. The default setting is Normal.

- **Default Sensitivity Level**   This option sets the default sensitivity level for all new messages. When you compose a message, you can override this setting by clicking Message Options on the ribbon and setting the sensitivity level in the Properties dialog box. The default setting is Normal.

- **Mark Messages As Expired After This Many Days**   This option causes the messages to expire after the specified number of days. The message appears in strikethrough in the recipient's mailbox at that time. (This setting does not necessarily work with every email client.)

- **Always Use The Default Account When Composing New Messages**   This option directs Outlook to always use the default email account to compose new messages when there are multiple email accounts configured in Outlook.

- **Commas Can Be Used To Separate Multiple Message Recipients**   If this check box is selected, you can use commas as well as semicolons in the To, Cc, and Bcc boxes of a message form to separate addresses.

- **Automatic Name Checking**   Select this check box to have Outlook 2013 attempt to match names to email addresses. Verified addresses are underlined, and those for which Outlook 2013 finds multiple matches are underscored by a red wavy line. When multiple matches exist and you've used a particular address before, Outlook 2013 underscores the name with a green dashed line to indicate that other choices are available.

- **Delete Meeting Requests And Notifications From Inbox After Responding**   Select this check box to have Outlook 2013 delete a meeting request from your Inbox when you respond to the request. If you accept the meeting, Outlook 2013 enters the meeting in your calendar. Clear this check box if you want to retain the meeting request in your Inbox.

- **Use Auto-Complete List To Suggest Names When Typing In The To, Cc, And Bcc Lines**   When this check box is selected, Outlook 2013 completes addresses as you type them in the To, Cc, and Bcc lines of the message form. Clear this check box to turn off this automatic completion.

- **Empty Auto-Complete List**   Click this button to empty the Auto-Complete List.

Chapter 6

- **Ctrl+Enter Sends A Message**   When this check box is selected, Outlook 2013 accepts Ctrl+Enter as the equivalent of clicking the Send button when composing a message.

- **Warn Me When I Send A Message That May Be Missing An Attachment**   This option causes Outlook to use certain criteria to try to determine if your email should contain an attachment (such as the word "attached" present in the body of the message). If there is no attachment, Outlook displays a warning dialog box prior to sending the message, giving you the option of cancelling the send operation and adding an attachment.

Other options in the Outlook Options dialog box are explained in other parts of this book, including in the following sections.

Controlling when messages are sent

To specify when Outlook 2013 should send messages, click File, Options, and click Advanced in the left pane to locate the Send Immediately When Connected option in the Send And Receive group. With this option selected, Outlook 2013 sends messages as soon as you click Send (provided that Outlook 2013 is online). If Outlook 2013 is offline, the messages go into the Outbox until you process them with a send/receive operation (which is also what happens if you do not select this option).

Requesting delivery and read receipts

You can request a *delivery receipt* or a *read receipt* for any message. Both types of receipts are messages that are delivered back to you after you send your message. A delivery receipt indicates the date and time your message was delivered to the recipient's mailbox. A read receipt indicates the date and time the recipient opened the message.

Specifying that you want a delivery receipt or read receipt for a message doesn't guarantee that you'll get one. The recipient's mail server or mail client might not support delivery and read receipts. The recipient might have configured the email client to reject requests for receipts automatically, or the recipient might answer No when prompted to send a receipt. If you receive a receipt, it's a good indication that the message was delivered or read. If you don't receive a receipt, however, don't assume that the message wasn't delivered or read. A message receipt serves only as a positive notification, not a negative one.

To request receipts for a message you're composing, click the Options tab on the message ribbon. You'll find the delivery and read receipt options in the Tracking group (see Figure 6-7).

Figure 6-7 Use the options in the Tracking group on the ribbon to request a delivery receipt, a read receipt, or both.

Using message tracking and receipts options

You can set options to determine how Outlook 2013 handles delivery and read receipts by default. In the main Outlook window, click File, Options, and click Mail in the left pane. Scroll down to the Tracking group, shown in Figure 6-8, in which you'll find the options discussed in this section.

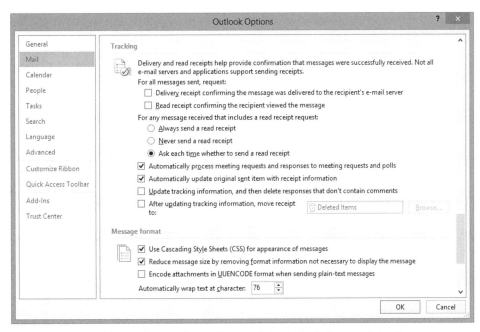

Figure 6-8 Set tracking options on the Mail page of the Outlook Options dialog box.

The following options control how Outlook 2013 requests read receipts and how the receipts are processed after they are received:

- **Automatically Process Meeting Requests And Responses To Meeting Requests And Polls**   Select this check box to have Outlook 2013 process all message receipt requests and responses when they arrive.

- **After Updating Tracking Information, Move Receipt To**   Select this check box to have Outlook 2013 move receipts from the Inbox to the specified folder.

- **Read Receipt Confirming The Recipient Viewed The Message**   Select this check box to have Outlook 2013 request a read receipt for each message you send. When you compose a message, you can override this setting; to do so, click the Options button in the Options group of the message ribbon.

- **Delivery Receipt Confirming The Message Was Delivered To The Recipient's E-mail Server**   Select this check box to have Outlook 2013 request a delivery receipt for each message you send.

The following three options in the Tracking group let you control how Outlook 2013 responds to requests from others for read receipts on messages that you receive and apply to Internet mail accounts only:

- **Always Send A Read Receipt**   When this option is selected, Outlook 2013 always sends a read receipt to any senders who request one. Outlook 2013 generates the read receipt when you open the message.

- **Never Send A Read Receipt**   Select this option to prevent Outlook 2013 from sending read receipts to senders who request them. Outlook 2013 will not prompt you regarding receipts.

- **Ask Each Time Whether To Send A Read Receipt**   Selecting this option enables you to control, on a message-by-message basis, whether Outlook 2013 sends read receipts. When you open a message for which the sender has requested a read receipt, Outlook 2013 prompts you to authorize the receipt. If you click Yes, Outlook 2013 generates and sends the receipt. If you click No, Outlook 2013 doesn't create or send a receipt.

> **Note**
> If selected, the Update Tracking Information, And Then Delete Responses That Don't Contain Comments check box causes Outlook 2013 to process voting and meeting requests and then delete them if they contain no comments.

See the section "Voting in Outlook" in Chapter 7, "Advanced email tasks," to learn more about voting. See Chapter 16, "Scheduling appointments," to learn about the Calendar and scheduling meetings.

Replying to messages

When you reply to a message, Outlook 2013 sends your reply to the person who sent you the message. Replying to a message is simple: Select the message in the Inbox, and then click the Reply button on the Home tab on the ribbon, right-click the message and choose Reply, or press Ctrl+R. Outlook 2013 opens a message form and, depending on how you have configured Outlook 2013 for replies, it can also include the original message content in various formats.

If the message to which you're replying was originally sent to multiple recipients and you want to send your reply to all of them, click Reply All, right-click and choose Reply All, or press Ctrl+Shift+R.

For more information about message replies, see the section "Using other reply and forward-ing options" in this chapter.

> **Note**
>
> When you use Reply All, Outlook 2013 places all the addresses in the To box. If you don't want the recipients list to be visible, use the Bcc box to send blind carbon copies. To do this, click Reply All, highlight the addresses in the To box, and cut them. Then click in the Bcc box and paste the addresses there.

Forwarding messages

In addition to replying to a message, you can forward the message to one or more recipi-ents. To forward a message, select the message header in the message folder (the Inbox or another one), and then click Forward in the Respond group on the Home tab of the ribbon or press Ctrl+F. Outlook 2013 opens a new message form and either incorporates the origi-nal message in the body of the current one or attaches it to the new message.

If you forward a single message, Outlook 2013 forwards the original message in the body of your new message by default, and you can add your own comments. If you prefer, however, you can configure Outlook 2013 to forward messages as attachments instead of including them in the body of your messages.

> **Note**
>
> If you select multiple messages and click Forward, Outlook 2013 sends the messages as attachments instead of including them in the body of your message.

Chapter 6

If you want to forward a single message as an attachment without reconfiguring the default behavior of Outlook, you can do so easily. Just click the message to select it, click the More button in the Respond group of the Home tab, and then choose Forward As Attachment.

Using other reply and forwarding options

You can change how Outlook 2013 handles and formats message replies and forwarded messages. These options are found in the Replies And Forwards group on the Mail page of the Outlook Options dialog box, as shown in Figure 6-9.

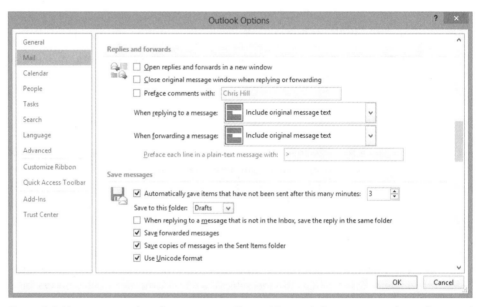

Figure 6-9 You can set options for message replies and forwarded messages on the Mail page of the Outlook Options dialog box.

To open this dialog box, click File, Options, and then click Mail. You can then view or set the following options in the Replies And Forwards group that affect replies and forwards:

- **Open Replies And Forwards In A New Window**   Select this check box to have Outlook 2013 open replies and forwards in a separate window rather than opening them in the Reading Pane.

- **Close Original Message Window When Replying Or Forwarding**   Select this check box to have Outlook 2013 close the message form when you click Reply or Forward. Clear this check box to have Outlook 2013 leave the message form open.

If you frequently forward the same message with different comments to different recipients, it's useful to have Outlook 2013 leave the message open so that you don't have to open it again to perform the next forward.

- **Preface Comments With**   Select this check box and enter a name or other text in the associated box. Outlook 2013 will add the specified text to mark your typed comments in the body of a message that you are replying to or forwarding.

- **When Replying To A Message**   Use this drop-down list to specify how Outlook 2013 handles the original message text when you reply to a message. You can choose to have Outlook 2013 generate a clean reply without the current message text, include the text without changes, or include but indent the text, for example. Note that you can either include the original message text in the body of your reply or add it to the message as an attachment.

- **When Forwarding A Message**   Use this drop-down list to specify how Outlook 2013 handles the original message text when you forward a message. You can, for example, include the message in the body of the forwarded message or add it as an attachment.

For more details on replying to and forwarding messages, see the sections "Replying to messages" and "Forwarding messages" earlier in this chapter.

Deleting messages

When you delete messages from any folder other than the Deleted Items folder, the messages are moved to the Deleted Items folder. You can then recover the messages by moving them to other folders, if needed. When Outlook 2013 deletes messages from the Deleted Items folder, however, those messages are deleted from Outlook 2013 permanently.

You can set Outlook 2013 to delete all messages from the Deleted Items folder automatically whenever you exit the program, which helps keep the size of your message store manageable. However, it also means that unless you recover a deleted message before you exit Outlook 2013, that message is irretrievably lost. If you seldom have to recover deleted files, this might not be a problem for you.

To change what happens to items in the Deleted Items folder when you exit Outlook 2013, click File, Options, and then click Advanced in the left pane. Select or clear Empty Deleted Items Folders When Exiting Outlook, and then click OK.

Undeleting messages

Exchange Server mailboxes have a retention period, defined by the Exchange Server administrator, that causes deleted items to be retained for a certain period of time after you have deleted them permanently from your Deleted Items folder. To recover a deleted item, in the Folder Pane, click any folder in your Exchange Server mailbox, and then click the Folder tab on the ribbon. Click Recover Deleted Items from the Clean Up group to open the Recover Deleted Items dialog box (see Figure 6-10). Click the item that you want to recover and click Recover Selected Items.

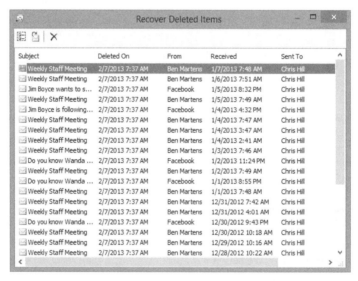

Figure 6-10 You can undelete items from an Exchange Server mailbox if they have not aged past the retention period.

Unfortunately, there is no way to recover permanently deleted items from non–Exchange Server accounts.

Controlling synchronization and send/receive times

Outlook 2013 uses send and receive groups (or *send/receive groups*) to control when messages are sent and received for specific email accounts. You can also use send/receive groups to define the types of items that Outlook 2013 synchronizes. *Synchronization* is the process in which Outlook 2013 synchronizes the local copy of your folders with your

Exchange Server message store. For example, assume that while you were working offline, you created several new email messages and scheduled a few events. You connect to the computer running Exchange Server and perform a synchronization. Outlook 2013 uploads to your computer the changes you made locally and also downloads changes from the server to your local store, such as downloading messages that have been delivered to your Inbox on the server.

Send/receive groups enable you to be flexible in controlling which functions Outlook 2013 performs for synchronization. For example, you can set up a send/receive group for your Exchange Server account that synchronizes only your Inbox, not your other folders, for those times when you simply want to perform a quick check of your mail.

Send/receive groups also are handy for helping you manage different types of accounts. For example, if you integrate your personal and work email into a single profile, you can use send/receive groups to control when each type of mail is processed. You might create one send/receive group for your personal accounts and another for your work accounts. You can also use send/receive groups to limit network traffic to certain times of the day. For example, if your organization limits Internet connectivity to specific times, you could use send/receive groups to schedule your Internet accounts to synchronize during the allowed times.

Think of send/receive groups as a way to collect various accounts into groups and assign to each group specific send/receive and synchronization behavior. You can create multiple send/receive groups, and you can include the same account in multiple groups if needed.

Setting up send/receive groups

To set up or modify send/receive groups in Outlook 2013, click the Send/Receive tab on the ribbon, click Send/Receive Groups, and then click Define Send/Receive Groups. Outlook 2013 displays the Send/Receive Groups dialog box, as shown in Figure 6-11. By default, Outlook 2013 sets up one group named All Accounts and configures it to send and receive when online and offline. You can modify or remove that group, add others, and configure other send/receive behavior in the Send/Receive Groups dialog box.

Figure 6-11 You can specify send/receive actions in the Send/Receive Groups dialog box.

When you select a group from the Group Name list, Outlook 2013 displays the following associated settings in the Setting For Group area of the dialog box:

- **Include This Group In Send/Receive (F9)**   Select this check box to have Outlook 2013 process accounts in the selected group when you click Send/Receive on the message form toolbar or press F9. Outlook 2013 provides this option for both online and offline behavior.

- **Schedule An Automatic Send/Receive Every *n* Minutes**   Select this check box to have Outlook 2013 check the accounts in the selected group every *n* minutes (the default is 30 minutes). Outlook 2013 provides this option for both online and offline behavior.

- **Perform An Automatic Send/Receive When Exiting**   Select this check box to have Outlook 2013 process the accounts in the selected group when you exit Outlook 2013 from an online session.

Creating new groups

Although you could modify the All Accounts group to process only selected accounts, it's better to create other groups as needed and leave All Accounts as is for those times when you want to process all your email accounts together.

Follow these steps to create a new group:

1. In Outlook 2013, click the Send/Receive tab on the ribbon, and then click Send/ Receive Groups, Define Send/Receive Groups.

2. Click New, type the name of the group as you want it to appear on the Send/Receive submenu, and click OK. Outlook 2013 displays the Send/Receive Settings dialog box, shown in Figure 6-12.

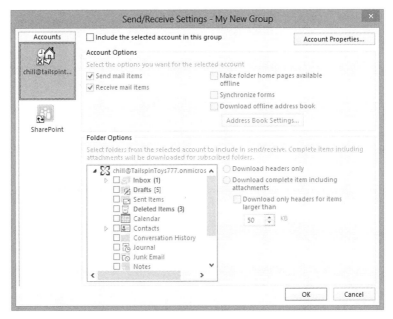

Figure 6-12 You can configure account processing in the Send/Receive Settings dialog box.

3. In the Accounts bar on the left, click the account you want to configure. By default, all accounts in the group are excluded from synchronization, as indicated by the red *X* on the account icon.

4. Select the Include The Selected Account In This Group check box to activate the remaining options in the dialog box and to have the account included when you process messages for the selected group.

5. In the Select Folders From The Selected Account To Include In Send/Receive list, select the check box beside each folder that you want Outlook 2013 to synchronize when processing this group.

6. Select other settings, using the following list as a guide:

   ○ **Send Mail Items**   Select this check box to have Outlook 2013 send outgoing mail for this account when a send/receive action occurs for the group.

   ○ **Receive Mail Items**   Select this check box to have Outlook 2013 retrieve incoming mail for this account when a send/receive action occurs for the group.

   ○ **Make Folder Home Pages Available Offline**   Select this check box to have Outlook 2013 cache folder home pages offline so that they are available to you any time.

   ○ **Synchronize Forms**   Select this check box to have Outlook 2013 synchronize changes to forms that have been made locally as well as changes that have been made on the server.

   ○ **Download Offline Address Book**   When this check box is selected, Outlook 2013 updates the offline address book when a send/receive action occurs for the group.

   ○ **Get Folder Unread Count**   This option is for IMAP accounts only; you can select it to have Outlook 2013 get the number of unread messages from the server.

7. If you need to apply filters or message size limits, do so. Otherwise, click OK, and then click Close to close the Send/Receive Groups dialog box.

> **For information on how to apply message size limits, see the section "Limiting message size" in this chapter.**

Other options for the send/receive group are explained in the following sections.

Modifying existing groups

You can modify existing send/receive groups in much the same way you create new ones. Click the Send/Receive tab on the ribbon, and then click Send/Receive Groups, Define Send/Receive Groups. Select the group you want to modify and click Edit. The settings that you can modify are the same as those discussed in the preceding section.

Limiting message size

You can also use the Send/Receive Settings dialog box to specify a limit on message size for messages downloaded from the Inbox of the selected account. This provides an easy way to control large messages that arrive in your mailbox. Instead of downloading messages that are larger than the specified limit, Outlook 2013 downloads only the headers. You can then mark the messages for download or deletion, or you can simply double-click the message to download and open it.

> **Note**
> Specifying a message size limit in the Send/Receive Settings dialog box doesn't affect the size of messages that you can receive on the server. It simply directs Outlook 2013 to process them differently.

Follow these steps to specify a message size limit for an account:

1. Open the Send/Receive Groups dialog box as described previously.

2. Select a group to modify and click Edit.

3. From the Accounts bar, select the account containing the folder for which you want to set a message size limit.

4. Select a folder, as shown in Figure 6-13 (not available for POP3 accounts).

Figure 6-13 Select a folder and then set its parameters in the Send/Receive Settings dialog box.

5. Specify the criteria that you want to use to limit message download based on the following option list, and click OK:

   ○ **Download Headers Only** Download only the message header, not the message body or attachments.

   ○ **Download Complete Item Including Attachments** Download the entire message, including the message body and attachments.

   ○ **Download Only Headers For Items Larger Than** Download only headers for messages over the specified size.

Scheduling send/receive synchronization

You can schedule synchronization for each send/receive group separately, giving you quite a bit of control over when Outlook 2013 processes your Inbox, Outbox, and other folders for synchronization. You can configure Outlook 2013 to process each send/receive group on a periodic basis and to process specific groups when you exit Outlook 2013. For example, you might schedule the All Accounts group to synchronize only when you exit Outlook 2013, even if you scheduled a handful of other groups to process messages more frequently during the day. Because you can create as many groups as needed and can place the same account in multiple groups, you have a good deal of flexibility in determining when each account is processed.

Simplify with Cached Exchange Mode

If you use an Exchange Server account, configure the account to use Cached Exchange Mode (keep a local copy of the mailbox) and avoid the issue of synchronization altogether. With Cached Exchange Mode enabled, Outlook 2013 handles synchronization on the fly, adjusting to online or offline status as needed.

For a discussion of Cached Exchange Mode, see Chapter 3.

Configuring send/receive schedules

Follow these steps to configure synchronization for each send/receive group:

1. Open the Send/Receive Settings dialog box.

2. In the Send/Receive Groups dialog box, select the group for which you want to modify the schedule.

3. In the Setting For Group area, select Schedule An Automatic Send/Receive Every *n* Minutes, and then specify the number of minutes that should elapse between send/receive events for the selected group. Set this option for both online and offline behavior.

4. If you want the group to be processed when you exit Outlook 2013, select Perform An Automatic Send/Receive When Exiting.

You can use a combination of scheduled and manually initiated send/receive events to process messages and accounts. For example, you can specify in the Send/Receive Group dialog box that a given group (such as All Accounts) must be included when you click Send/Receive or press F9 and then configure other accounts to process as scheduled. Thus, some accounts might process only when you manually initiate the send/receive event, and others might process only by automatic execution. In addition, you can provide an overlap so that a specific account processes manually as well as by schedule—simply include the account in multiple groups with the appropriate settings for each group.

Disabling scheduled send/receive processing

On occasion, you might want to disable scheduled send/receive events altogether. For example, assume that you're working offline and don't have a connection through which you can check your accounts. In that situation, you can turn off scheduled send/receive processing until a connection can be reestablished.

To disable scheduled send/receive processing, click Send/Receive Groups on the ribbon and choose Disable Scheduled Send/Receive. Select this command again to enable the scheduled processing.

Configuring other messaging options

This section of the chapter provides an explanation of additional options in Outlook 2013 that control messaging features and tasks. You can specify how you want to be notified when new mail arrives, configure how Outlook 2013 connects for email accounts that use dial-up networking, and control the formatting of Internet and international email messages.

Setting up notification of new mail

You might not spend a lot of time in Outlook 2013 during the day if you're busy working with other applications. However, you might want Outlook 2013 to notify you when you receive new messages. Outlook 2013 offers several desktop alert features to provide you with notification of the arrival of new messages. These options and additional notification options are located in the Message Arrival group on the Mail page of the Outlook Options dialog box (see Figure 6-14):

- **Play A Sound**   Select this option to have Outlook 2013 play a sound when a new message arrives. By using the Change System Sounds option in Control Panel, you can change the New Mail Notification sound to use a .wav file of your choosing.

- **Briefly Change The Mouse Pointer**   Select this option to have Outlook 2013 briefly change the pointer to a mail symbol when a new message arrives.

- **Show An Envelope Icon In The Taskbar**   Select this option to have Outlook 2013 place an envelope icon in the system tray when new mail arrives. You can double-click the envelope icon to open your mail. The icon disappears from the tray after you have read the messages.

- **Display A Desktop Alert**   Enable this option to have Outlook 2013 display a pop-up window on the desktop when a new message arrives.

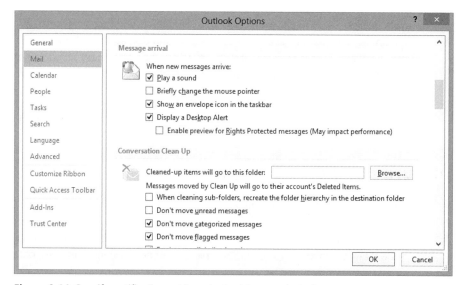

Figure 6-14 Specify notification settings in the Message Arrival group.

Note

Outlook 2013 can display a desktop alert for new messages that arrive for any account, not just for the default Inbox.

Using message alerts

If you enable the Display A Desktop Alert option, Outlook 2013 displays the alert for each new message. If you receive a lot of mail during the day, that's more than you need. Instead, you probably want Outlook 2013 to alert you only when you receive certain messages, such as those from people in your Contacts folder, from a specific sender, or with certain words in the subject line. So instead of enabling this option globally, you might prefer to create a rule that causes the alert to be displayed when the rule fires.

You can use two rule actions to generate alerts:

- **Display A Desktop Alert**   This action causes Outlook 2013 to display a desktop alert when the rule fires. The alert persists on the desktop for the period of time you have set for the alert on the Mail page of the Outlook Options dialog box.

- **Display A Specific Message In The New Item Alert Window**   With this action, you can specify a message that appears in the New Mail Alerts window (see Figure 6-15). The window persists on the desktop until you close it.

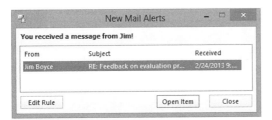

Figure 6-15 The New Mail Alerts window displays text you specify.

Which action you use depends on whether you want a custom message to appear for the alert and whether you want the alert to persist until you close it or to appear and then go away. To create an alert rule using one (or both) of these actions, create the rule as you would any other and select the alert action that you want to use.

> ## Note
> To create a rule that displays a New Mail Alert, you can use the rule template Display Mail From Someone In The New Item Alert Window.

For more details about working with message rules, see Chapter 11.

If you create an alert rule that uses the Display A Desktop Alert action, it's likely that you will not want Outlook 2013 to display an alert for all messages. Open the Mail page of the Outlook Options dialog box as described previously, and then clear the Display A Desktop Alert option. If you use the Display A Specific Message In The New Item Alert Window rule, you might want to leave desktop alerts enabled, which causes Outlook 2013 to display a desktop alert for all messages and to display the New Item Alerts window for those messages that fire the rule.

> **Note**
>
> If enabled, the Enable Preview For Rights Protected Messages option in the Message Arrival group causes Outlook to display a preview of rights-protected content (that is, content that is restricted in some way, such as preventing printing or forwarding).

If you have an Exchange Server account, you also have the option of sending alerts to your mobile device when you receive messages. See Chapter 11 for details on how to set up mobile alerts.

Managing messages and attachments

Using the Outlook 2013 email features effectively requires more than understanding how to send and receive messages. This section of the chapter helps you get your messages and attachments under control.

Saving messages automatically

You can configure Outlook 2013 to save messages automatically in several ways—for example, saving the current message periodically or saving a copy of forwarded messages. You'll find the following options on the Mail page of the Outlook Options dialog box (see Figure 6-16).

- **Automatically Save Items That Have Not Been Sent After This Many Minutes**   Use this check box to have Outlook 2013 save unsent messages in the Drafts folder. Outlook 2013 by default saves unsent messages to the Drafts folder every three minutes. Clear this check box if you don't want unsent messages saved in this folder.

- **Save To This Folder**   Specify the folder in which you want Outlook 2013 to save unsent items. The default location is the Drafts folder.

- **When Replying To A Message That Is Not In The Inbox, Save The Reply In The Same Folder**   With this check box selected, Outlook 2013 saves a copy of sent items to the Sent Items folder if the message originates from the Inbox (a new message, reply, or forward). If the message originates from a folder other than the Inbox—such as a reply to a message stored in a different folder—Outlook 2013 saves the reply in the same folder as the original. If this option is cleared, Outlook 2013 saves all sent items in the Sent Items folder.

> **Note**
>
> You can also use rules to control where Outlook 2013 places messages. For more information on creating and using rules, see Chapter 11.

- **Save Forwarded Messages**   Select this check box to save a copy of all messages that you forward. Messages are saved in either the Sent Items folder or the originating folder, depending on how you set the previous option.

- **Save Copies of Messages In The Sent Items Folder**   Select this option to have Outlook save a copy of all new messages and replies that you send in the Sent Items folder (see the following section).

- **Use Unicode Format**   Select this option to have Outlook store the saved messages in Unicode format.

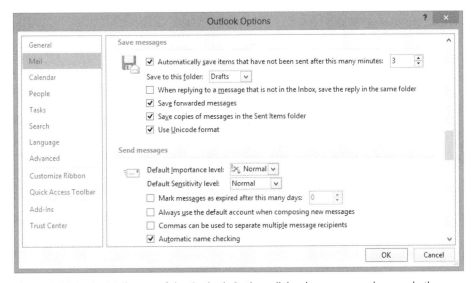

Figure 6-16 In the Mail page of the Outlook Options dialog box, you can choose whether Outlook 2013 automatically saves unsent messages.

Retaining a copy of sent messages

Keeping track of the messages you send can often be critical, particularly in a work setting. Fortunately, with Outlook 2013, you can automatically retain a copy of each message you send, providing a record of when and to whom you sent the message.

By default, Outlook 2013 stores a copy of each sent message in the Sent Items folder. You can open this folder and sort the items to locate messages based on any message criteria. You can view, forward, move, and otherwise manage the contents of Sent Items just as you can with other folders.

If you allow Outlook 2013 to save a copy of messages in the Sent Items folder, over time the sheer volume of messages can overwhelm your system. You should therefore implement a means—whether manual or automatic—to archive or clear out the contents of the Sent Items folder. With the manual method, all you need to do is move or delete messages from the folder as your needs dictate.

If you want to automate the archival process, you can do so. For details on how to archive messages from any folder automatically, see Chapter 9, "Managing your email," for tips on organizing and archiving your email.

You'll find the Save Copies Of Messages In The Sent Items Folder option on the Mail page of the Outlook Options dialog box, as described in the previous section. Select this option to have Outlook store copies of sent items in that folder.

INSIDE OUT   Override default message-saving settings

If you need to change the Outlook 2013 behavior for a single message, you can override the setting. To choose the folder in which you want to save a message, with the message form open, on the Options tab, in the More Options group, click Save Sent Item To, click Other Folder, and then select the folder in which Outlook 2013 should save the message. If you normally save sent messages but do not want to keep a copy of this message, choose Do Not Save from the menu.

Working with attachments

It's a sure bet that some of the messages you receive include attachments such as documents, pictures, or applications. Outlook 2013 has an attachment preview feature that enables you to preview many types of files that you receive in email. In general, you can work with these attachments in Outlook 2013 without saving them separately to disk, although you can do so if needed.

Previewing attachments

Attachment preview is a feature of Outlook 2013 that enables you to view the contents of files sent to you in email. You can preview some attachments in the Reading Pane. Outlook 2013 comes with previewers for a variety of file types, including Office applications, webpages, and Microsoft Windows Media Player files, as well as images and text files. Some vendors also make additional file previewers available for download at their websites.

To preview a file attachment, follow these steps:

1. In Outlook 2013, with the message selected, click the attachment in the Reading Pane.

2. If the attachment type has a preview handler registered, Outlook 2013 displays a preview of the attachment (see Figure 6-17). If there is no preview handler for the attachment file type, Outlook 2013 displays a message indicating this. To view a file for which there is no previewer installed, save the file to disk and open it with the appropriate application.

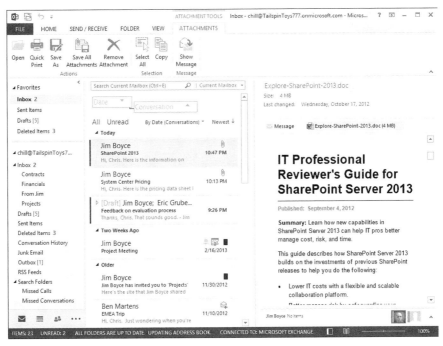

Figure 6-17 Outlook 2013 can preview an attachment in the Reading Pane.

There are limitations on attachment preview, including the following:

- You can preview attachments in HTML and plain text messages, but not those in rich text messages (because of the way the attachments are embedded in rich text messages).

- For security reasons, active content (such as macros, scripts, and ActiveX controls) in the attached files is disabled.

You can configure how attachment previews are handled using the Trust Center dialog box. To choose attachment-previewing options, follow these steps:

1. With Outlook 2013 open, click File, Options, Trust Center, and click Trust Center Settings.

2. In the Trust Center dialog box, select Attachment Handling.

3. To enable sending replies with edited attachments, select Add Properties To Attachments To Enable Reply With Changes.

4. If you do not want to be able to preview attachments, select Turn Off Attachment Preview.

5. To manage individual previewers, click Attachment And Document Previewers to open the File Previewing Options dialog box (see Figure 6-18). Select all the previewers that you want enabled and clear the check box of any previewer you want to disable. Click OK.

6. When you are satisfied with the attachment previewing configuration, click OK to close the Trust Center dialog box.

Figure 6-18 Enable or disable individual previewers.

Viewing attachments

You might want to view an attachment in the application in which it was created, perhaps to display content that is disabled by the previewer. There are three ways to open a file in the external application directly from Outlook 2013:

- Right-click the attachment, in either the Reading Pane or the open message, and choose Open.

- Double-click the attachment, in either the Reading Pane or the open message.

- In either case, if the attachment is an Office document that originated outside your network (and the associated application is installed), Outlook 2013 opens the document using Protected View. Protected View uses a rights-limited sandbox instance of the application to reduce the potential for virus infection from the attachment. Editing and other features are disabled, but you can view the document. To edit the document, click the Enable Editing button on the application's InfoBar. If the document came from inside your network, such as from another mailbox in your same Exchange Server environment, it does not use Protected View but simply opens the document for editing (or in read-only mode, depending on the document).

  For non-Office applications, Outlook either simply opens the document in its associated application or displays the Open With dialog box.

Saving attachments to disk

In many instances, it's necessary to save attachments to disk. For example, you might receive a self-extracting executable containing a program that you need to install. In that case, the best option is to save the file to disk and install it from there.

> **CAUTION !**
>
> It's important to have antivirus protection installed on your computer to protect against viruses from a variety of potential sources, including email attachments. Saving an attachment to disk before opening it enables the antivirus application on your computer to scan the file before you open it. Make sure your antivirus solution is configured to scan files as soon as they are added to disk when they are accessed so you don't have to manually scan them each time.

You can save attachments using either of these methods:

- If you're using the Reading Pane, right-click the attachment in the message and choose Save As.

- Click File, Save Attachments if you want to save one or more attachments or if the Reading Pane is not available. You can also do this by right-clicking an attachment and choosing Save All Attachments. This option is handy when you want to save all attachments.

Saving messages to a file

Although Outlook 2013 maintains your messages in your stored folders, occasionally you might need to save a message to a file. For example, you might want to archive a single message or a selection of messages outside Outlook 2013 or save a message to include as an attachment in another document. You can save a single message to a file or combine several messages into a single file.

To save one or more messages, open the Outlook 2013 folder in which the messages reside, and then select the message headers. Click File, Save As, and then specify the path, file name, and file format. Click Save to save the message.

When you save a single message, Outlook 2013 gives you the option of saving it in one of the following formats:

- **Text Only**   Save the message as a text file, losing any formatting in the original message.

- **Outlook Template**   Save the message as an Outlook 2013 template that you can use to create other messages.

- **Outlook Message Format**   Save the message in MSG format, retaining all formatting and attachments within the message file.

- **Outlook Message Format–Unicode**   Save the message in MSG format with the Unicode character set.

- **HTML**   Save the message in HTML format, storing the images in a folder that you can view with a web browser.

- **MHT Files**   Save the message in MIME HTML (MHT) format as a single file with all its resources (such as images).

When you save a selection of messages, you can store the messages only in a text file, and Outlook 2013 combines the body of the selected messages in that text file. You can then concatenate the various messages (that is, join them sequentially) into a single text file. You might use this capability, for example, to create a message thread from a selection of messages.

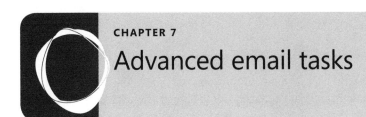

Advanced email tasks

A s email has become a more important part of many people's day, the content of email messages has become more complex. Whereas text was once adequate, an email message is now likely to contain many other things: a table, clip art, a photograph, or a link to a website. Similarly, the overall look of an email message has evolved with the use of text formatting and stationery.

In this chapter, you'll discover how to add more than just plain text to your messages by working with graphics, hyperlinks, files, attachments, and electronic business cards. As this chapter explains, you can also spruce up your messages by using themes or stationery, allowing you to apply a customized look to your messages. Microsoft Outlook 2013 provides a choice of themes and stationery, or you can create your own. You'll also learn how to attach a text signature or an electronic business card automatically to each message you send, use proofing tools, control when messages are delivered, and use the voting features in Outlook with a Microsoft Exchange Server account.

Formatting text in messages

The majority of your messages might consist of text without any special formatting, but you can use formatted text and other elements to create rich text and multimedia messages. For example, you might want to use character or paragraph formatting for emphasis, add graphics, or insert hyperlinks to websites or other resources. The following sections explain how to accomplish these tasks.

Formatting text in messages is easy, particularly if you're comfortable with Microsoft Word. Even if you're not, you should have little trouble adding some interest to your messages with character, paragraph, and other formatting.

Outlook 2013 uses a native email editor with a rich palette of tools for you to use in creating and formatting messages. For example, you can apply paragraph formatting to indent some paragraphs but not others, create bulleted and numbered lists, and apply special color and font formatting. These options are simple to use. Understanding the underlying format in which your messages are sent, however, requires a little more exploration. Outlook 2013 supports three formats for email messages:

- **HTML format**   Lets you create multimedia messages that can be viewed directly in a web browser or an email client that supports HTML.

- **Rich Text Format**   Lets you add paragraph and character formatting and embed graphics and other nontext media into your message. By default, Rich Text Format (RTF) messages are converted to HTML when sent to an Internet address, but you can configure Outlook to convert them to plain text instead or leave them in RTF.

> **Note**
>
> You can specify how Outlook 2013 handles RTF messages sent to the Internet by clicking File, Options. On the Mail page, scroll down to find the Message Format group of options. From the drop-down list labeled When Sending Messages In Rich Text Format To Internet Recipients, select the format that you prefer. You can choose to have Outlook 2013 send messages as HTML, plain text, or rich text.

- **Plain text format**   Doesn't allow any special formatting, but it offers the broadest client support—every email client can read plain text messages.

By default, Outlook 2013 uses HTML as the format for sending messages. HTML format lets you create multimedia messages that can be viewed directly in a web browser and an email client. Depending on the capabilities of the recipient's email client, however, you might need to use a different format. Most current email clients support HTML.

> **Note**
>
> Using HTML format for messages doesn't mean that you need to understand HTML to create a multimedia message. Outlook 2013 takes care of creating the underlying HTML code for you.

INSIDE OUT   Compose HTML messages outside of Outlook

Outlook provides lots of features for composing content-rich messages in HTML format, including tables, graphics, and much more. In some situations, however, you might find it easier to use a different application to create very complex HTML messages, but you still need to send them in Outlook. In this case, use an HTML editor to create and format the message, and then simply copy the content from the HTML editor into a new, blank message in Outlook.

The ribbon on the new message form provides many options for formatting messages. To choose the format for the current message, on the Format Text tab, in the Format group, select Plain Text, HTML, or Rich Text. To set the default message format for all new messages, click File, Options, click Mail in the left pane, and then select the desired format from the Compose Messages In This Format drop-down list (see Figure 7-1).

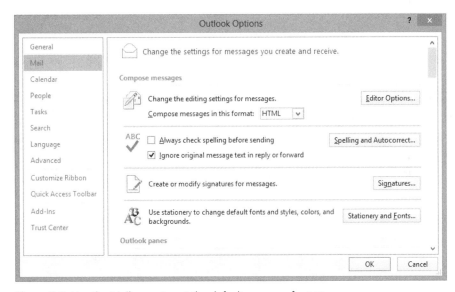

Figure 7-1 Use the Mail page to set the default message format.

On the Mail page of the Outlook Options dialog box, you can click Stationery And Fonts to display the Signatures And Stationery dialog box, as shown in Figure 7-2. Use the options in this dialog box to control which fonts Outlook 2013 uses for specific tasks, such as composing new messages, replying to or forwarding a message, and composing or reading plain text messages. You can specify the font as well as the font size, color, and other font characteristics. You can also select Pick A New Color When Replying Or Forwarding to have Outlook 2013 choose a color that has not yet been used in that message for text that you add to a message when replying or forwarding it. This is useful when you are replying inline to someone else's message and want your text to be easily distinguishable.

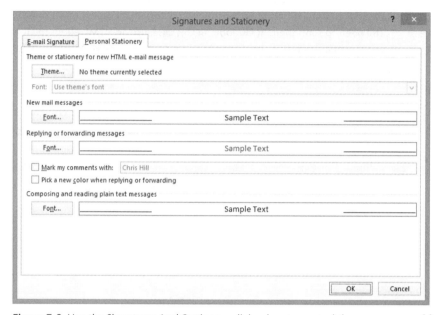

Figure 7-2 Use the Signatures And Stationery dialog box to control the appearance of fonts in Outlook 2013 for specific tasks.

For more information about stationery, see the section "Customizing the appearance of your messages" later in this chapter.

Outlook 2013 has a number of text-formatting controls that are distributed over a number of groups on multiple tabs. The most commonly used formatting commands are on the Message tab, in the Basic Text group for convenient access, as shown in Figure 7-3. You can specify the font face, size, color, style (bold, italic, or underline), and highlight. Settings for bulleted and numbered lists are also available in this group.

Figure 7-3 Use the Basic Text group on the Message tab for common text formatting options.

INSIDE OUT   The appearance of the ribbon changes

The exact appearance of the ribbon varies depending on the width of the message window. A command might have an icon with a text label in full screen appear as just an icon when the window is narrower, and then disappear altogether when the window is narrower still. If a particular command is not immediately apparent, you should resize the window to see whether the command becomes visible.

When you select some text in your message, a transparent mini toolbar pops up next to your mouse pointer, as shown in Figure 7-4. If you move the mouse pointer over the toolbar, it becomes opaque, and you can choose formatting options to apply to the highlighted text.

Figure 7-4 The mini toolbar gives you immediate access to the most commonly used text formatting options.

Extensive text formatting capabilities are provided on the Format Text tab, shown in Figure 7-5, which has font and paragraph formatting as well as style-related options. In addition to the options found in the Basic Text group on the Message tab, you can apply character formatting such as strikethrough, subscript, and superscript. Finer paragraph control is provided with options such as line spacing, borders, and background shading. More complex multilevel lists are also available on this tab. In addition, you can sort text using the Sort option in the Paragraph group.

Figure 7-5 The Format Text tab has a wide range of text formatting options.

Several special text options like WordArt and Drop Cap are available on the Insert tab, in the Text group, as shown in Figure 7-6. You can also insert Quick Parts (prewritten sections of text), text boxes, or the date and time (with optional automatic update).

Figure 7-6 The Insert tab has text options that provide special effects.

Themes are configured on the Options tab, in the Themes group, as shown in Figure 7-7, where you can select a theme or change individual parts of your current theme.

Figure 7-7 Use the Options tab to choose and configure a theme.

Formatting lists

Outlook 2013 provides three types of lists: bulleted, numbered, and multilevel. Although each type of list looks different, the basic procedures used to create them are the same. Each type of list has a library of preconfigured styles, and you can define your own list styles if you want. All three types of lists are available in the Paragraph group on the Format Text tab; bulleted and numbered lists are also found on the Message tab, in the Basic Text group.

To format a bulleted list, follow these steps:

1. With the message open, select the text that you want formatted as a list.

2. On the Format Text tab, in the Paragraph group, select Bullets. To select a different style for the list, click the arrow next to Bullets, and then select a style from the library.

3. If you want to change the text to a different level, click Multilevel List, select Change List Level, and then choose the new level from the menu. Alternatively, simply press Tab with the cursor in the paragraph.

4. To create a new style for the list, click the arrow beside the Bullet button, and then select Define New Bullet to display the Define New Bullet dialog box, shown in Figure 7-8. Click Symbol, Picture, or Font, select the new bullet character in the resulting dialog box, and then click OK. Click OK again to close the Define New Bullet dialog box.

Figure 7-8 Choose the new bullet style in the Define New Bullet dialog box.

Numbered lists are created in much the same way as bulleted lists, letting you choose the number style (Roman, Arabic, and so on) and related options. Multilevel lists have many additional options that you can configure, as shown in Figure 7-9, allowing you to create highly customized lists if needed.

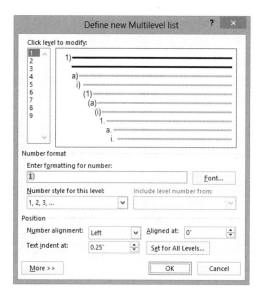

Figure 7-9 You can modify many options for multilevel lists in the Define New Multilevel List dialog box.

Options on the Format Text tab

You can access only a portion of the text formatting options in the Basic Text group on the Message tab. A number of other options are available on the Format Text tab, including the following:

- **Character Formatting** Additional character styles include strikethrough, subscript, and superscript.

- **Shading** This option lets you apply a color to the background of the selected text.

- **Borders And Shading** You can choose options for adding borders, gridlines, and shading to selected paragraphs.

- **Line Spacing** You can set the spacing between lines and paragraphs. You can also open the Paragraph dialog box, which has settings for indentation, line breaks, and page breaks, as well as control over text flow that occurs over page breaks (widow/orphan control, keeping lines together, and so on).

- **Sort** With this option, you can order the selected paragraphs based on the criteria that you specify in the Sort Text dialog box.

- **Show/Hide** You can toggle the display of normally hidden formatting characters such as paragraph marks.

Working with styles

Outlook 2013 lets you choose from a gallery of styles to format text easily using a number of predefined looks. Each theme has its own complete set of font styles created based on the colors and fonts that you specify for the theme. You can also define your own custom style sets if you prefer to use styles that are not defined by the current theme. A *style set* is a working set of font styles used for messages: normal, heading, title, and so on.

The Styles gallery, shown in Figure 7-10, displays the most commonly used styles, giving you an easy way to format the text in your message. When you define custom styles, they are also displayed in the Styles gallery.

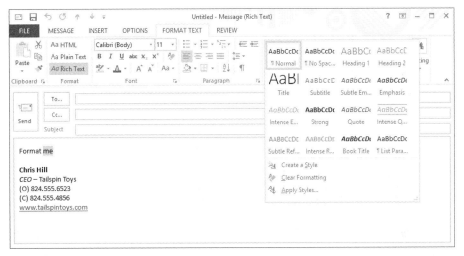

Figure 7-10 The Styles gallery has a number of predefined styles for a variety of uses.

To apply a style using the Styles gallery, follow these steps:

1. With a message open, select the text that you want to format.

2. On the Format Text tab, in the Styles group, click Styles to display the Styles gallery.

> **Note**
> If the ribbon is wide enough, a selection of styles will be displayed instead of the Styles button. In this case, click More to view the Quick Styles gallery.

3. Point to a style for which you would like to see a Live Preview of the style applied to the selected text. Then, select the style that you want to apply when you are satisfied with the results.

You can create new styles that will be available in the Styles gallery. To create a new style, first format some text as you want the new style to appear. Next, on the Format Text tab, in the Styles group, click Styles, and then click Create A Style. The Create New Style From Formatting dialog box displays, and you can give the style a name here. You can also click Modify to change the style if you want.

To remove a style from the Styles gallery, right-click the style in the gallery, and then choose Remove From Style Gallery. The deletion is immediate, without a confirmation message box, but you can undo it using the Undo command (note that you must use the Undo command immediately, though—if you move on, it will be too late).

To display the complete list of styles, on the Format Text tab, in the Styles group, click the Styles button at the lower-right corner of the group to open the Styles dialog box. You can format your message in the same way as with the Styles gallery, by selecting some text and then choosing the style to apply from the Styles dialog box.

You can create new styles and examine the formatting of text in messages by using the Style Inspector from the Styles window. The complete set of styles can be configured by clicking Manage Styles and using the Manage Styles dialog box. (Approximately 300 styles are available.) To configure options for the Styles window, click Options.

> **Note**
>
> When you change the theme, custom fonts are not changed unless they use a theme color—in which case, the color is updated. You can reset font styles by reapplying a style set.

You can change the fonts and colors used to determine the current Styles gallery. To change these options, on the Format Text tab, in the Styles group, click Change Styles, and then select one of the following options:

- **Style Set** This setting specifies the fonts used for the Quick Styles. You can choose from several options or create your own style set from the existing message (saved as a Word 2013 template).

- **Colors** You can select a set of theme colors to use for the font color set or create a custom set of theme colors.

- **Fonts**   This option lets you pick a font set from an existing theme or create your own font set by selecting a body font and a heading font.

- **Paragraph Spacing**   Choose from a selection of predefined paragraph spacing settings or create your own with settings for line spacing and spacing before and after paragraphs.

- **Set As Default**   Choosing this option sets the current configuration (theme, style set, and any customized settings except background) as the default for new messages.

Using style sets

A style set consists of a number of font styles, initially created from the theme settings, but customizable after that. Style sets can be created, saved, and applied independent of theme-related font changes and will override theme settings.

To work with style sets, with a new message open, on the Format Text tab, in the Styles group, click Change Styles, and then click Style Set. You can then choose from the following actions:

- To apply a style set, select the style set from the menu.

- To set the font styles back to the new message default, choose Reset To The Default Style Set.

- To create a new style set, select Save As A New Style Set. The Save As A New Style Set dialog box will display, allowing you to name the style set.

Creating a custom style set

To customize font styles, follow these steps:

1. Type some text, and then format it as you want the updated style text to appear. (In this example, you will change the Title style.) Select the text, and on the Format Text tab, in the Styles group, click More.

2. In the Styles gallery, right-click Title, and then choose Update Title To Match Selection.

3. Repeat steps 1 and 2 for each font style you want to define.

4. When you have finished customizing the font styles, delete all the text in your message. (This leaves the styles you created intact but creates the new message without unwanted text content.)

5. To save the style set that you created, on the Format Text tab, in the Styles group, click Change Styles, Style Set, Save As A New Style Set.

6. In the Save As A New Style Set dialog box, specify a file name for the style set, and then click Save. The style set is saved as a Word 2013 template file.

Using tables

Using Outlook 2013, you can add a variety of tables to your email messages easily. You can use a Word 2013 table for textual information or a Microsoft Excel 2013 spreadsheet with its support for mathematical operations. You can apply a style to your table easily by selecting it from the visual gallery of built-in and custom styles.

Inserting a table in a message

You can add a table to your email quickly with one of several methods provided by Outlook 2013. To insert a table in a message, follow these steps:

1. With a message open, position the insertion point where you want the table to appear. (You can nest tables by setting the insertion point inside a table cell.)

2. On the Insert tab, in the Tables group, click Table to display the Insert Table menu. You can create a table using one of the following methods:

   ○ To draw a table, use the mini-table grid on the Insert Table menu. As you move your mouse over the table grid on the menu, you get a preview of the table in the body of your message, as shown in Figure 7-11. Click the lower-right cell of the desired table grid to insert it in the message.

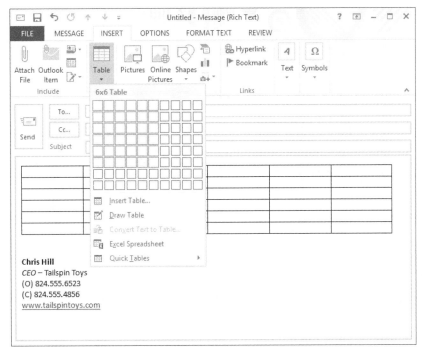

Figure 7-11 You can preview a table before you insert it in your message.

   ❍ Select Insert Table on the Insert Table menu to open the Insert Table dialog
      box, shown in Figure 7-12, and specify the table size and AutoFit behavior.
      Selecting the Remember Dimensions For New Tables check box makes these
      settings the default for new tables.

Figure 7-12 You choose the settings for a new table in the Insert Table dialog box.

○ Selecting Draw Table lets you draw a single table cell in the message window. If needed, you can then split the cell or add cells to the table. When you finish editing the table, you can double-click anywhere else in your message to return to editing the text.

○ Selecting Excel Spreadsheet creates an Excel 2013 table in the message and displays the Excel 2013 commands on the ribbon. When you finish editing the spreadsheet, you can click anywhere else in your message to return to editing the text.

○ Selecting Quick Tables displays a gallery that lets you select a previously saved table design. Outlook 2013 does not have any Quick Tables by default, so this option is usable only after you have created some Quick Tables of your own.

For information about creating Quick Tables, see the section "Working with Quick Tables" later in this chapter.

Working with tables

When you select a table in an email message, the ribbon displays two additional Table Tools tabs. The Design tab lets you control visual style effects and configure settings such as header rows. The Layout tab has commands that let you add and remove table cells and work with cell properties.

INSIDE OUT   Limitations on styling Excel 2013 spreadsheets

Although Excel 2013 tables provide a lot of additional functionality, you are limited in your ability to do page layout on an Excel 2013 object in your message. Neither of the Table Tools tabs (Design and Layout), which contain commands used to apply styles to tables, is available when an Excel 2013 object is selected. If you want to use the tools in Outlook 2013 to format your tables, you can create an Excel spreadsheet with your data and then copy the completed information to an appropriately sized Outlook 2013 table. You can then apply the Outlook 2013 built-in styling effects to the table.

On the Design tab, shown in Figure 7-13, specify the table style, colors, borders, and options, such as whether a header row is used, as described here:

- **Table Style Options**   You can apply specific effects to individual rows and columns, such as Header Row, Total Row, First Column, or Last Column. You can also choose to have rows, columns, or both banded in alternating colors for readability.

- **Table Styles**   You can select a visual table style from the built-in gallery, modify the current style, or create a new table style. Shading and border effects can be applied to a selection of cells.

- **Borders**   This group contains commands to format the Line Style, Line Weight, and Pen Color. You can draw a new table or erase existing table cells and content. You can also click the dialog box launcher to display the Borders And Shading dialog box and configure these options.

Figure 7-13 You can apply a variety of style options to a table by using the Design tab commands.

You can use the commands on the Layout tab, shown in Figure 7-14, to insert and delete cells and configure how the data is displayed inside table cells.

Figure 7-14 Use the Layout tab to manage cells and format the information they contain.

The Layout tab contains these command groups:

- **Table**   You can select all or part of the table, view gridlines (or turn them off), and display the Table Properties dialog box.

- **Draw**   You can use this group to draw and erase table elements.

- **Rows & Columns**   You can insert and delete rows and columns using these commands. Click the Insert Cells dialog box launcher to specify the direction to shift existing cells when inserting new ones.

- **Merge** These commands let you merge cells, split cells, or split the table into multiple tables.

- **Cell Size** You can specify the size of individual cells, distribute rows or cells evenly, or choose AutoFit. Click the dialog box launcher to display the Table Properties dialog box, and then set the size, alignment, text wrapping options, and margins for the cell.

- **Alignment** You can choose from nine preset alignment options (Align Top Left, Align Top Right, Align Center, Align Bottom Right, and so on) for the selected table text. Text can be written from left to right, top to bottom, or bottom to top using the Text Direction command. Cell margins for the entire table can be set here as well.

- **Data** You can sort the table information, convert the table to text, or insert a formula using these commands. To have the header row repeat on tables that span multiple pages, select the header row in the table, and then click Repeat Header Rows.

Working with Quick Tables

The Quick Tables gallery is your personal gallery of tables that you can insert quickly into your messages. This can be simply an empty table formatted exactly the way that you want or a complete table with not only a custom look but data as well. Once you have customized the appearance of a table, you can save it as a Quick Table so that you can re-create the format and style of frequently used tables easily.

To create a Quick Table, follow these steps:

1. Insert a table into a message, format it, and then enter any content that you want to be contained in your Quick Table (headings, for example).

2. Select the table (or part of it), and on the Insert tab, in the Table group, click Table, choose Quick Tables, and then click Save Selection To Quick Tables Gallery.

3. In the Create New Building Block dialog box, give the table a name, and then click OK. The Quick Table is now listed in the Quick Tables gallery for easy use. If you want the table to appear in a different gallery, such as Text Box or Quick Parts, select the gallery name from the Gallery drop-down list. (Some galleries are available only in the Building Blocks Organizer, shown in Figure 7-15.) You can assign a category to the table in the Category drop-down list. (This category is visible only in the Building Blocks Organizer.) The Options drop-down list selections have no effect on Quick Tables.

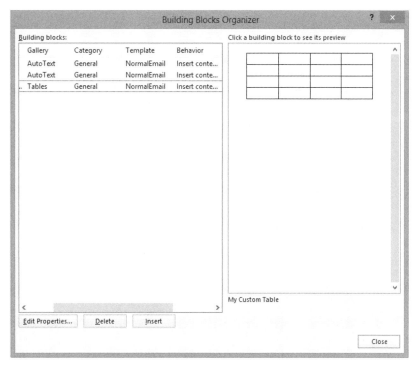

Figure 7-15 Use the Building Blocks Organizer to remove a Quick Table.

To remove a Quick Table from the gallery, on the Insert tab, click Table, Quick Tables, right-click the table, and then choose Organize And Delete to open the Building Blocks Organizer (see Figure 7-15). Select the table you want to remove, click Delete, click Yes, and then click Close.

INSIDE OUT   Add the Building Blocks Organizer to the Quick Access Toolbar

You can manage the entire range of building blocks, such as Quick Tables, Quick Parts, text boxes, and so on, in the Building Blocks Organizer. It is also the only way to insert Quick Tables that have been added to custom galleries. If you use the Building Blocks Organizer often, you might want to add an icon to the Quick Access Toolbar to give you quicker access. To add the Building Blocks Organizer to the Quick Access Toolbar, follow these steps:

1. With a new message open, right-click the Quick Access Toolbar and choose Customize Quick Access Toolbar.

2. In the Choose Commands From drop-down list, select Commands Not In The Ribbon. Select Building Blocks Organizer, click Add, and then click OK.

Using special text features

Outlook 2013 includes a number of text options and text objects that you can insert into your email messages. If you repeatedly type the same text in multiple messages, for example, you can save the text for reuse. You can apply decorative text effects such as drop caps and WordArt as well. These options are available on the Insert tab, in the Text group.

Quick Parts

Quick Parts are chunks of reusable content (text, graphics, and so on) that you can insert into a message with a click of your mouse. You can create a Quick Part for anything that you commonly have to enter into a message, such as contact information, directions and a map, and so on.

To save a Quick Part, follow these steps:

1. Create a message with the content that you want to reuse, and then select the content.

2. On the Insert tab, in the Text group, click Quick Parts, and then select Save Selection To Quick Part Gallery. You can select a gallery in the Gallery drop-down list. (Remember that some galleries are available only in the Building Blocks Organizer.) You can assign a category to the table in the Category drop-down list. By default, a Quick Part is inserted in its own paragraph; if you want to insert the Quick Part without inserting a line break first, select Content Only from the Options drop-down list.

Once you have saved the Quick Part, using it is easy. To use the Quick Part, on the Insert tab, in the Text group, click Quick Parts, and then select the Quick Part from the gallery.

Drop cap

You can use a drop cap to create a special look at the beginning of a paragraph. When you select a drop cap, Outlook 2013 creates a small text box and inserts a single, specially formatted character. (This character is still treated like part of the paragraph, not as a separate text box.) To create a drop cap, follow these steps:

1. Open the message, and then position the insertion point in the paragraph that should get the drop cap.

2. On the Insert tab, in the Text group, click Drop Cap. Figure 7-16 shows the result.

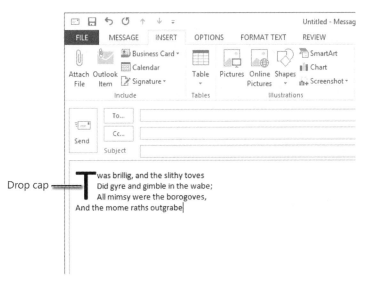

Figure 7-16 You can add drop caps to your messages quickly.

3. Select Dropped or In Margin to create a drop cap. To format the drop cap, choose Drop Cap Options.

4. In the Drop Cap dialog box, you can specify the position, font, number of lines to drop, and distance from text. When you have finished, click OK.

Date and time

To insert the date and time in a message, follow these steps:

1. With a message open, on the Insert tab, in the Text group, click Date & Time.

2. In the Date & Time dialog box, select the format you want in the Available Formats list. Select the Update Automatically check box if you want the time to be updated to the current time automatically, and then click OK.

Some of the options in the Text group operate more like objects than text. Options such as WordArt are inserted by creating an object; a tab is then added to the ribbon for related WordArt commands. In contrast to normal text, you can move such objects to any location in the message (in the same way that you can position a graphic) for layout purposes.

Text box

Use a text box to insert text inside a box at any location in the message. To create a text box, follow these steps:

1. With a message open, on the Insert tab, in the Text group, click Text Box, and then select Draw Text Box.

2. The Drawing Tools Format tab will display, as shown in Figure 7-17, allowing you to style the box (shape, shadows, colors, and so on) and specify layout options (text wrapping, layering, and grouping).

Figure 7-17 Use the Drawing Tools Format tab to apply styles to a text box.

3. Enter your text in the text box. This text can be formatted in the usual ways using the tools on the Format Text tab.

4. To move the text box, you can drag it with the mouse or select it and use the arrow keys on the keyboard to move it.

5. To rotate the text box, click the rotate handle at the top of the box and move the mouse left or right.

WordArt

WordArt is highly formatted text inside a text box. The text typically has three-dimensional (3-D) shading, special edge bevels, curved paths, or other complex features. Figure 7-18 shows some examples of WordArt, along with the Drawing Tools Format tab, which you can use to modify the WordArt layout. To create WordArt, follow these steps:

1. With a message open, on the Insert tab, in the Text group, click WordArt.

2. Select a beginning style for your WordArt from the gallery.

3. Outlook inserts a text box with some sample text in the box using the selected style. Type your text in the text box.

To format your WordArt, click the WordArt object to display the Drawing Tools Format tab, shown in Figure 7-18, and then apply the desired effects to your WordArt. When you have finished, click outside the WordArt box to return to editing the rest of your message.

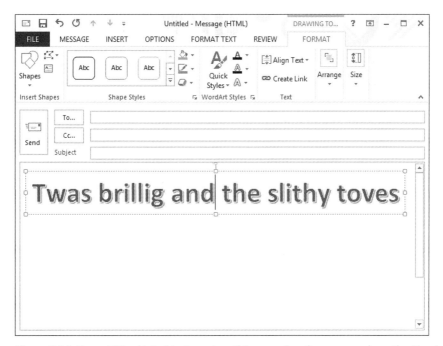

Figure 7-18 Format WordArt objects such as this one using the commands on the Drawing Tools Format tab.

Object

The last option in the Text group of the Insert tab is Object, which lets you insert an object such as a bitmap, a portion of an Excel workbook, or a PowerPoint slide (among other items) in your message. You can use an existing object or create a new one. To insert an object, with a message open, on the Insert tab, in the Text group, click Object. In the Object dialog box, select the object type or file name, and then click OK.

Including illustrations in messages

Outlook 2013 provides a variety of illustration types that you can use to enhance your email. You can add pictures, clip art, shapes, charts, and SmartArt. You control page layout, so you can place illustrations in any location in your message and then format them in a number of ways, including adding borders, shadows, and 3-D effects. (Exact options vary between illustration types.) You can wrap your text around illustrations in several styles and even layer text and graphics on top of each other, using transparency effects to make everything visible.

Each type of illustration has one or more groups of commands specific to it, providing the controls needed for that kind of illustration. They also share a number of groups of commands on the ribbon and operate in much the same way. You will examine the process of inserting a picture in some detail in the next section, including descriptions of the common commands. Following that, you will learn the differences between the other types of illustration.

Your ability to insert graphics in a message depends in part on which message format you use. You can insert embedded graphics when using HTML (the default) or RTF, with minor differences in layout options. You can't insert embedded graphics in a message that uses plain text format.

INSIDE OUT   Attach graphics files to plain text messages

Although you can't insert embedded graphics in a plain text message, you can attach a graphic (or other) file to a plain text message. To attach a graphic to a plain text message, follow these steps:

1.   In the message form, on the Insert tab, in the Include group, click Attach File.

2.   In the Insert File dialog box, locate the file that you want to attach, and then click Insert.

Inserting a picture from a file

Follow these steps to insert a picture in a message:

1.   On the Insert tab, in the Illustrations group, click Pictures to display the Insert Picture dialog box.

2.   In the Insert Picture dialog box, select the graphics file to insert in the message, and then click Insert. (To insert a link to the image, click the arrow next to Insert, and then select Link To File or Insert And Link.)

3.   In the message, when the picture is selected, Outlook 2013 displays the Picture Tools Format tab with tools used to format the picture, as shown in Figure 7-19.

Figure 7-19 You can adjust the appearance of the picture, as well as format how the picture is displayed in the email message.

To adjust the appearance of the picture, under Picture Tools, click the Format tab, and then in the Adjust group use the appropriate tools, as follows:

○ **Remove Background**   Use a mask to remove parts of the picture, such as the extra scenery around a group of people.

○ **Corrections**   You can increase or decrease the brightness or contrast, or sharpen or soften the image, by selecting a thumbnail on the menu.

○ **Color**   You can apply different color saturations and color tone to the picture, as well as recolor using various accent colors.

○ **Artistic Effects**   You can apply one of several artistic effects such as chalk, pencil, and other effects to the picture.

○ **Compress Pictures**   Outlook 2013 can compress the images in your email messages to minimize message size. When you select Compress Picture, you are given the option of compressing one picture or all the images in the message. In the Compress Pictures dialog box, you can set the automatic compression option, choose whether to delete cropped areas of images, and determine the picture quality.

○ **Change Picture**   This option lets you replace the current image while keeping the object formatting and size settings intact.

○ **Reset Picture**   You can reset the picture to the original image, discarding all changes that you have made.

4. You can customize how the picture appears in the message by using the options in the Picture Styles group, as described here:

○ **Quick Styles**   You can choose from a number of framing and perspective options to set the overall look of the picture.

○ **Picture Border**   You can add an optional border around the graphic, with a specified pixel width and pattern, and using the colors from your theme or custom colors. To configure additional border settings, choose More Lines on the

Weight menu to display the Format Picture pane, shown in Figure 7-20, and then configure the Line settings.

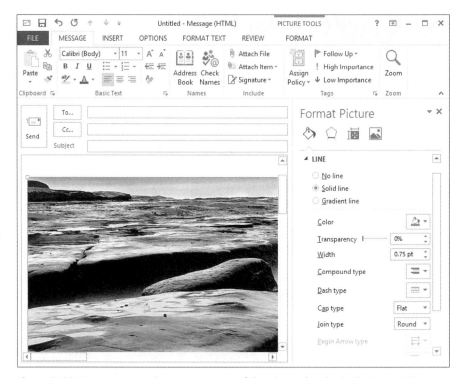

Figure 7-20 You can customize many aspects of the picture border in the Format Picture pane.

○ **Picture Effects** You can apply a number of effects to a picture to produce just the look you want for your message. The available effects are Shadow, Reflection, Glow, Soft Edges, Bevel, and 3-D Rotation. The Preset option has some preconfigured effects from which you can choose.

○ **Convert The SmartArt Graphic** This option changes the selected picture to a SmartArt graphic to apply SmartArt properties to the graphic and make it easy to manipulate and format the graphic using SmartArt shapes and properties.

5. You can specify how you want the image aligned in the message and how text will flow with the graphic using the options in the Arrange group. The commands operate as described here:

○ **Bring Forward/Send Backward**   These options specify which layer the picture is in.

○ **Wrap Text**   You can choose how the text wraps relative to the picture, selecting from having the image in line with text, behind text, or in front of text, or having the text only at the top and bottom of the picture or wrapped around a square. To drag a picture to a new location in the message, you must first select it and then choose either Behind Text or In Front Of Text.

○ **Selection Pane**   Click to open the Selection And Visibility pane, where you can select pictures in the email.

○ **Align**   You can line up multiple pictures (or other objects) by selecting them (using Shift-click) and then clicking Align. You can choose to align the edges or centers of the selected objects.

○ **Group**   This command is unavailable when you are working with pictures.

○ **Rotate**   You can change the orientation of the picture by selecting Rotate Right 90°, Rotate Left 90°, Flip Vertical, or Flip Horizontal. To have finer control over image orientation, choose More Rotation Options on the Rotate menu to open the Size dialog box, and then set the exact degree of rotation. (You can also resize and crop images in the Size dialog box.)

6.   The picture can be resized and cropped with the settings in the Size group. To crop the image, select Crop, and then drag the cropping handles on the image. To resize the image, enter the new size in the Shape Height and Shape Width fields. (If Outlook 2013 is configured to constrain the aspect ratio of pictures, you need to enter only one of these options, not both.)

7.   If you want to set Alternate Text (which is displayed in place of the picture for recipients whose email clients don't show graphics), right-click the picture, and then choose Format Picture on the shortcut menu. In the Format Picture dialog box, select Alt Text in the left pane. Enter your text in the Title box, and then click Close.

8.   To add a hyperlink to the picture, right-click the picture, and then choose Hyperlink on the shortcut menu. (For detailed instructions on working with hyperlinks, see the section "Working with hyperlinks.")

Some, but not all, of the formatting and graphical effects are cumulative, and you might have to experiment to get exactly the effect you want.

Inserting shapes

Outlook 2013 includes a library of shapes (previously called AutoShapes) from which you can select just the right one to illustrate your words. Shape types include lines, basic shapes (square, cylinder, and so on), arrows, flowchart objects, callouts, stars, and banners.

To insert a shape into a message, follow these steps:

1. With a message open, on the Insert tab, in the Illustrations group, select Shapes.

2. Choose a shape from the Shapes gallery.

3. Click and drag across the message where you want to create the shape.

4. With the shape selected, the Drawing Tools Format tab will display, as shown in Figure 7-21.

Figure 7-21 You can work with shapes using the commands on the Drawing Tools Format tab.

This tab provides you with the following options for formatting the shape:

○   **Insert Shapes**   You can select a shape to create, edit a shape, or edit text with the commands in this group.

○   **Shape Styles**   This group provides a Quick Styles gallery of frame and fill effects, shape fill, shape outline, and shape changing effects. You can also apply a range of special effects such as shadows, reflection, and 3-D rotation.

○   **WordArt Style**   This group includes commands for formatting WordArt objects.

○   **Text**   Use these controls to align text in a text box and create a link between two text boxes so that text flows between them (see Figure 7-22).

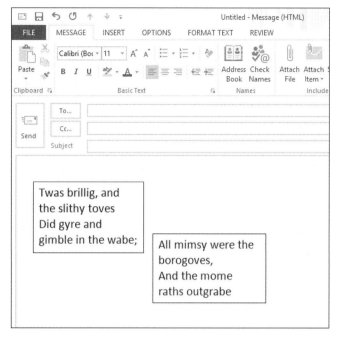

Figure 7-22 You can link text boxes so that the text flows between them.

○ **Arrange**   This group controls how the shape is aligned in the message and how text flows with the graphic. You can move the shape to the front or back layer, control text wrapping, align multiple shapes, group shapes together, and control rotation of the shape.

○ **Size**   This group lets you set the shape height and shape width.

INSIDE OUT   Insert a new drawing

To insert a blank drawing, with a message open, on the Insert tab, in the Illustrations group, click Shapes, and then click New Drawing Canvas. This will insert a blank drawing object in your message; you can draw in this object using the drawing tools built into Outlook 2013.

Inserting a chart

When you choose a chart as the illustration type to insert, the Insert Chart dialog box opens, allowing you to select the type of chart that you want to use. When you click OK, an Excel 2013 workbook is opened with a small amount of data entered. After you have entered your data, simply close the Excel window to update the chart and return to Outlook 2013. On the ribbon, under Chart Tools, there are three tabs with quite a few commands allowing you fine control over the appearance of your chart, as described in the following sections.

Chart Tools Design tab

The Chart Tools Design tab contains groups of commands that let you choose the type, style, and layout of the chart as well as the data it contains, as shown in Figure 7-23.

Figure 7-23 You can control the style and data for your chart using the Chart Tools Design tab.

The Design tab has these groups:

- **Type**   You can select the chart type (pie, bar, area, and so on) and save the current chart as a template.

- **Data**   This group has commands that let you manipulate your data in Excel 2013.

- **Chart Layouts**   You can choose from the Quick Layout gallery using various arrangements of the chart, legend, title, and other text.

- **Chart Styles**   This group consists of a Quick Styles gallery with a selection of colors, outlines, and effects.

Chart Tools Layout tab

When you click a chart in a message, Outlook displays some layout tools beside the chart, as shown in Figure 7-24. You can use these tools to change the text wrapping for the chart, add chart elements such as legends, choose a style and color scheme, and apply a filter to the chart data.

Figure 7-24 You can control the display of data and labels, as well as other layout options.

When you click a chart to select it, Outlook shows four buttons:

- **Layout Options**   Specify how text wraps around the chart, position and alignment, size, and other layout options for the chart.

- **Chart Elements**   Specify which chart elements are included, such as axes, titles, data labels, error bars, legends, and so on.

- **Chart Styles**   Choose a display style and a color scheme.

- **Chart Filters**   Specify which data items are included in the chart.

Chart Tools Format tab

The Chart Tools Format tab, shown in Figure 7-25, provides you with additional tools that you can use to customize the appearance of your charts. You can control colors, styles, effects, and the page layout of your chart using these commands.

Figure 7-25 You can customize the appearance of your chart with the commands on the Chart Tools Format tab.

The Format tab contains these groups:

- **Current Selection**   You can select a chart element and format the selection with this group.

- **Insert Shapes**   You can insert additional shapes in the chart.

- **Shape Styles**   This group provides a Quick Styles gallery with frame and fill effects, shape fill, shape outline, and shape effects options.

- **WordArt Styles**   These commands control the text used in text labels, axes, titles, and legends. (WordArt commands are available only if a suitable chart component is selected.)

- **Arrange**   This group contains the text wrapping, layering, and alignment commands. (This group is not available if your message is in RTF format.)

- **Size**   This group specifies the shape height and shape width.

Inserting SmartArt

SmartArt is a type of reusable object designed as a means of displaying complex information in an easy-to-understand graphical format. Outlook 2013 includes a gallery of SmartArt graphics in formats that represent things such as a list, a hierarchy (like an organizational chart), a process (like a flowchart), or a relationship (such as a Venn diagram).

To insert a SmartArt graphic into a message, follow these steps:

1. With a message open, on the Insert tab, in the Illustrations group, select SmartArt.

2. In the Choose A SmartArt Graphic dialog box, shown in Figure 7-26, select a SmartArt graphic, and then click OK.

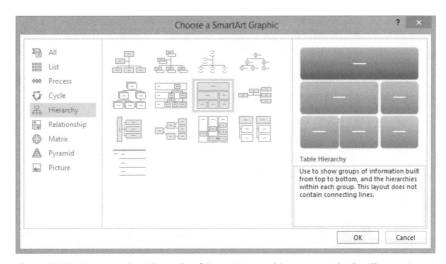

Figure 7-26 You can select the style of SmartArt graphic you want in the Choose A SmartArt Graphic dialog box.

Once the SmartArt graphic is inserted in the message, you can add text and format the graphic. The two SmartArt Tools tabs are described in the following sections.

SmartArt Tools Design tab

The SmartArt Tools Design tab, shown in Figure 7-27, contains groups of commands that let you work with the SmartArt content, adding and customizing shapes and changing layout and styles.

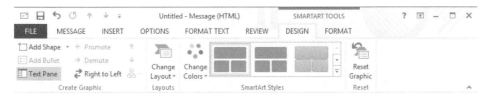

Figure 7-27 You can work with the graphics components and layout of SmartArt using the SmartArt Tools Design tab.

The groups available on the Design tab are as follows:

- **Create Graphic**   You can add a shape, bullet, or text pane to the SmartArt graphic and manipulate the text layout inside the SmartArt shapes with this set of controls.

- **Layouts**   This group lets you change the SmartArt type either from the gallery or in the Choose A SmartArt Graphic dialog box.

- **SmartArt Styles**   You can change the colors used in the SmartArt and the effects used in the SmartArt style.

- **Reset**   The Reset Graphic command lets you quickly remove all custom formatting from the selected object.

SmartArt Tools Format tab

The SmartArt Tools Format tab, shown in Figure 7-28, has the commands that you need to style the SmartArt and control its placement in the message.

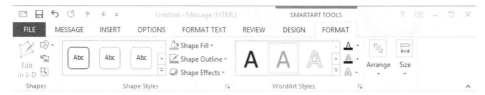

Figure 7-28 You can change the appearance of the SmartArt text, frame, and background using the SmartArt Tools Format tab.

The groups available on the Format tab are as follows:

- **Shapes**   You can choose the shapes to use as SmartArt elements and then resize those shapes.

- **Shape Styles**   This group provides frame and fill effects, shape fill, shape outline, and shape changing effects.

- **WordArt Styles**   You can format the text used in SmartArt objects, selecting a style from the gallery, text fill, text outline, and text effects. Each of these options has additional menu selections for fine-grained control over text format.

- **Arrange**   This group contains the text wrapping, layering, and alignment commands.

- **Size**   This group lets you specify the shape height and shape width.

Using symbols in a message

A few other options are available on the Insert tab for you to use in your email messages. You can also insert math equations, symbols (such as © or ™), and horizontal lines used for visual separation.

Inserting an equation

To insert an equation in a message, follow these steps:

1. On the Insert tab, in the Symbols group, click Equation to create an empty equation box in your message.

2. Use the commands on the Equation Tools Design tab, shown in Figure 7-29, to create the equation, as follows:

    ○ **Tools**   You can specify how the equation is displayed: Linear is one-dimensional for easy editing, whereas Professional is two-dimensional for display. (These two commands are unavailable until you have entered some data in the equation.) You can enter plain text by clicking Normal Text. Clicking Equation displays the Equation gallery and lets you save new equations to it. Click the dialog box launcher to view the Equation Options dialog box.

    ○ **Symbols**   To add a symbol to the equation, click the symbol. (Click the More arrow to display the entire gallery.)

    ○ **Structures**   You can insert a number of mathematical structures into your equation easily by selecting a structure from the Structures group. You can choose a structure from these sets: Fraction, Script, Radical, Integral, Large Operator, Bracket, Function, Accent, Limit And Log, Operator, and Matrix. Each set has a number of selections, including many commonly used options.

Figure 7-29 You can use the Equation Tools Design tab to complete your equation.

Inserting a symbol

On the Insert tab, in the Symbols group, click Symbol. Select the symbol from the display of commonly used symbols, or click More Symbols to open the Symbol dialog box. In the Symbol dialog box, select the symbol, click Insert, and then click Close. (You can insert multiple symbols by clicking Insert after selecting one, then selecting the next symbol and clicking Insert again, and so on.)

Inserting a horizontal line

On the Insert tab, in the Symbols group, click Horizontal Line. Outlook 2013 will insert a line at the insertion point location. To format the line, right-click it, and then choose Format Horizontal Line. In the Format Horizontal Line dialog box, shown in Figure 7-30, you can set the size, color, and alignment of the line. (Outlook 2013 uses the most recent settings in this dialog box when you create new lines.)

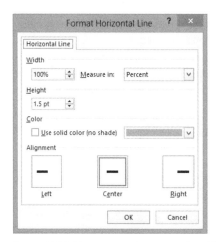

Figure 7-30 You can set the properties of horizontal lines in the Format Horizontal Line dialog box.

Working with hyperlinks

You can insert hyperlinks to websites, email addresses, network shares, and other items in a message easily. When you type certain kinds of text in a message, Outlook 2013 automatically converts the text to a hyperlink, requiring no special action from you. For example, if you type an email address, an Internet URL, or a Universal Naming Convention (UNC) path to a share, Outlook 2013 converts the text to a hyperlink. To indicate the hyperlink, Outlook 2013 underlines it and changes the font color.

When the recipient of your message clicks the hyperlink, the resulting action depends on the type of hyperlink. With an Internet URL, for example, the recipient can go to the specified website. With a UNC path, the remote share opens when the recipient clicks the hyperlink. This is a great way to point the recipient to a shared resource on your computer or another computer on the network.

INSIDE OUT   Follow a hyperlink

You can't follow (open) a hyperlink in a message that you're composing by just clicking the hyperlink. This action is restricted to allow you to click the hyperlink text and edit it. To follow a hyperlink in a message that you're composing, hold down the Ctrl key and click the hyperlink.

Inserting hyperlinks

You have another option for inserting a hyperlink in a message:

1. Position the insertion point where you want to insert the hyperlink.

2. On the Insert tab, in the Links group, click Hyperlink to display the Insert Hyperlink dialog box, as shown in Figure 7-31. (If you select text to use for the link, that text is inserted automatically in the Text To Display box.)

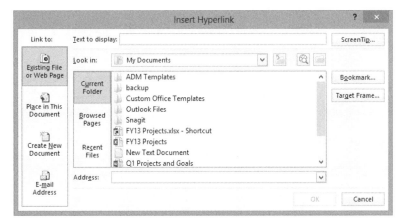

Figure 7-31 Use the Insert Hyperlink dialog box to insert a hyperlink and configure link settings.

The options displayed in the Insert Hyperlink dialog box vary according to the type of hyperlink you're inserting, as explained in the following sections.

Inserting hyperlinks to files or webpages

To insert a hyperlink to a file or webpage, select Existing File Or Web Page in the Link To bar. Then provide the following information in the Insert Hyperlink dialog box:

- **Text To Display**   In this box, type the text that will serve as the hyperlink in the message. Outlook 2013 underlines this text and changes its color to indicate the hyperlink.

- **Look In**   In this area, choose the location that contains the data to which you want to link. You can choose from these options:

  - **Current Folder**   If you are linking to a file, select Current Folder, and then use this drop-down list to locate and select the file on the local computer or on the network.

  - **Browsed Pages**   To insert a hyperlink to a page that you've recently viewed in your web browser, click Browsed Pages. The document list in the dialog box changes to show a list of recently browsed pages from Microsoft Internet Explorer.

  - **Recent Files**   If you want to insert a hyperlink to a file that you've used recently, click Recent Files to view a list of most recently used files in the document list of the dialog box.

- **Address**   Type the local path, the Internet URL, or the UNC path to the file or website in this box.

- **ScreenTip**   Click this button to define an optional ScreenTip that appears when the recipient's mouse pointer pauses over the hyperlink.

- **Bookmark**   Click this button to select an existing bookmark in the specified document. When the recipient clicks the hyperlink, the document opens at the bookmark location.

- **Target Frame**   Click this button to specify the browser frame in which you want the hyperlink to appear. For example, choose New Window if you want the hyperlink to open in a new window on the recipient's computer.

TROUBLESHOOTING

Recipients of your messages can't access linked files

If you're setting up a hyperlink to a local file, bear in mind that the recipient probably won't be able to access the file using the file's local path. For example, linking to C:\ Docs\Policies.doc would cause the recipient's system to try to open that path on that system. You can use this method to point the recipient to a document on his or her own computer. However, if you want to point the recipient to a document on your computer, you must either specify a UNC path to the document or specify a URL (which requires that your computer function as a web server).

The form of the UNC path you specify depends on the operating system of the recipient. For the deep hyperlink to work properly, the recipient must be using Windows 2000 or later.

Inserting a hyperlink to a place in the current message

If you click Place In This Document in the Link To bar, the Insert Hyperlink dialog box changes, as shown in Figure 7-32. The Select A Place In This Document area shows the available locations in the open document: headings, bookmarks, and the top of the document. Select the location to which you want to link, provide other information as necessary (the text to display in the hyperlink, for example, or perhaps a ScreenTip), and then click OK.

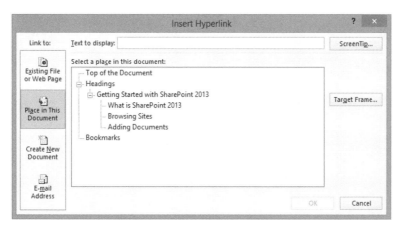

Figure 7-32 You can link easily to a location in the current document.

Note

This method is commonly used when you have opened a document in Word 2013 and are inserting a hyperlink in that document rather than in a separate email message.

Inserting a hyperlink to a new document

If you select Create New Document in the Link To bar of the Insert Hyperlink dialog box, you can specify the path to a new document and choose to either edit the document now or insert the hyperlink for later editing. You'll most often use this method for inserting hyperlinks in a Word 2013 document rather than in an email message.

Inserting a hyperlink to an email address

If you select E-mail Address in the Link To bar, you can insert an email address as a hyperlink in a message easily. When recipients click the hyperlink, their email programs will open a new email message addressed to the person you have specified in the hyperlink. Although you can simply type the email address in the message and let Outlook 2013 convert it to a *mailto:* link, you might prefer to use the Insert Hyperlink dialog box instead. As Figure 7-33 shows, you can use this dialog box to enter an email address or select from a list of email addresses that you have recently used on your system and to specify the subject for the message.

> **Note**
> The main reason to use the Insert Hyperlink dialog box to insert an email link is to enable you to specify the subject of the message automatically.

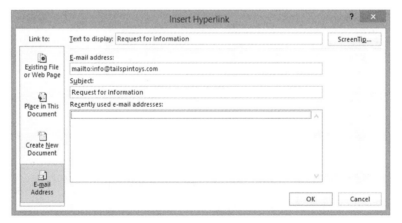

Figure 7-33 You can insert a *mailto:* hyperlink in your email message.

You can use the hyperlink's context menu to select, edit, and open the hyperlink, as well as copy it to the Clipboard. Just right-click the hyperlink and choose the appropriate option from the context menu.

Chapter 7

Removing a hyperlink

To remove a hyperlink, right-click the hyperlink, and then choose Remove Hyperlink from the context menu. Outlook 2013 retains the underlying text but removes the hyperlink.

Inserting bookmarks

A *bookmark* is an internal reference used to locate a specific place in a document and link to it by name. When you insert a bookmark in Outlook 2013, it is then available in the Insert Hyperlink dialog box as a linkable location. This is particularly useful if you have a lengthy email message, or one with sections or illustrations that you want the reader to be able to find quickly. To insert a bookmark in a message, follow these steps:

1. With a message open, select the text (or picture, chart, and so on) that you want the bookmark to reference. On the Insert tab, in the Links group, click Bookmark.

2. In the Bookmark dialog box, shown in Figure 7-34, enter a name in the Bookmark Name box, click Add, and then click OK. (Bookmark names cannot include spaces.)

Figure 7-34 You can manage bookmarks using the Bookmark dialog box.

To remove a bookmark, on the Insert tab, in the Links group, click Bookmark. Select the bookmark that you want to remove, click Delete, and then click Close.

Including other items in a message

You might also want to include things such as files and other Outlook 2013 items in your mail messages at times. Outlook 2013 makes it easy for you to insert a calendar, a business card, or another item in your email message.

Attaching files

To attach a file to a message, follow these steps:

1. Position your insertion point where you want to insert the file, and on the Insert tab, in the Include group, select Attach File to open the Insert File dialog box.

2. Locate and select the file to insert, and then click Insert.

Alternatively, you can click the paper clip icon on the toolbar to insert a file as an attachment, or you can simply drag the file into the message window.

Inserting files in the body of a message

Occasionally, you'll want to insert a file in the body of a message rather than attaching it to the message. For example, you might want to include a text file, a Word 2013 document, or another document as part of the message. To insert a file in the body of the message, you can use the steps described in the preceding section for attaching a file, with one difference: In step 2, click the button next to Insert, and then click Insert As Text.

INSIDE OUT   Use the Clipboard to insert a file

In some cases, you'll find it easier to use the Clipboard to insert a file in a message, particularly if the file is already open in another window. (Just select the file, and then copy and paste or cut and paste it into the message.) You can also use the Clipboard when you need to insert only a portion of a file, such as a few paragraphs from a document.

Including an Outlook 2013 item

You might want to include other Outlook 2013 items, such as messages and tasks, in a message you are sending. To include another Outlook 2013 item, follow these steps:

1. While creating a message, on the Insert tab, in the Include group, click Outlook Item.

2. In the Insert Item dialog box, shown in Figure 7-35, locate and select the item or items that you want to include.

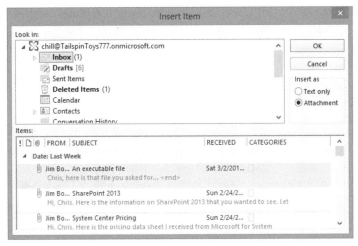

Figure 7-35 Select the Outlook 2013 items to include in a message in the Insert Item dialog box.

3. Select Attachment or Text Only, and then click OK.

> **Note**
> If the message is in RTF format, you also have the option to insert a shortcut to the item in the message.

Attaching a business card to a message

With Outlook 2013, you can send a copy of a contact item in vCard format, a standard format for exchanging contact information. This allows the recipient to import the contact data into a contact management program, assuming that the recipient's program supports the vCard standard (as most do).

You can send a vCard by email from the Contacts folder without first opening a message. To do this, perform the following steps:

1. In Outlook 2013, open the Contacts folder, and then select the contact item that you want to send.

2. Click the Home tab, and in the Share group, click Forward Contact and choose As A Business Card. Outlook 2013 inserts the vCard into the message.

3. Complete the message as you normally would, and then click Send.

You can also include a business card in a message from the new message form. On the Insert tab, in the Include group, click Business Card. If the contact is displayed in the recently used contacts list on the menu, you can select the contact. Otherwise, choose Other Business Cards to open the Insert Business Card dialog box, and then select a name from the complete Contacts list.

INSIDE OUT   Send data as an Outlook item

If you know that the recipient uses Outlook, in the Share group on the Home tab, click Forward Contact and choose As An Outlook Contact to send the contact data as an Outlook 2013 contact item. Outlook users can also use vCard attachments.

For more details on using and sharing vCards, see the section "Sharing contacts" in Chapter 14, "Working with contacts."

Including a calendar

Outlook 2013 makes it easy for you to share part of your calendar with others by simply inserting a calendar in a message. You can choose the range of items to send from a single day to the entire calendar, or you can specify a range of dates. You also have control over what level of detail to include, whether your availability only, limited details (availability and subject only), or full details. You can also control the formatting and whether to include items marked private or attachments to items. To send a calendar in email, follow these steps:

1. While composing a message, on the Insert tab, in the Include group, click Calendar to open the Send A Calendar Via E-mail dialog box, shown in Figure 7-36. Outlook will prompt you to switch to HTML if the message is currently plain text or RTF.

Figure 7-36 You can select the information that you want to include when sending a calendar via email.

2. Choose the Calendar, Date Range, and Detail level, and other parameters for the calendar. Click OK. Figure 7-37 shows a calendar inserted in a message.

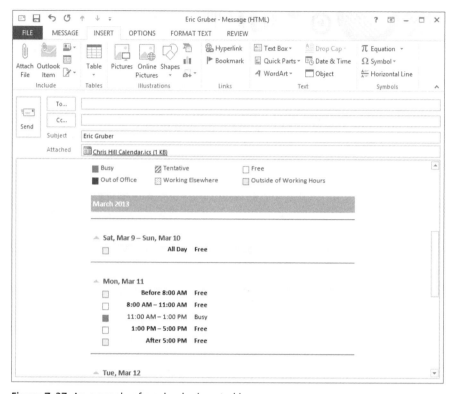

Figure 7-37 An example of a calendar inserted in a message.

See Chapter 22, "Sharing calendars," for more information about sharing your calendar using Outlook 2013.

> **Note**
>
> We will discuss the use of signatures in the section "Using signatures."

Customizing the appearance of your messages

By default, Outlook 2013 uses no background or special font characteristics for messages. However, it does support the use of themes and, to a lesser degree, stationery, so you can customize the look of your messages. Outlook 2013 has two types of themes as well as stationery, each of which functions a bit differently from the others. It helps to understand the differences between these options before you get started using them.

Understanding how Outlook formats messages

The appearance of an Outlook 2013 email message is the result of a complex behind-the-scenes interaction among a number of settings. A single message is likely to draw some of its formatting information from several different sources. While much of the process of determining how a given message looks is invisible to you, it helps to understand what goes into formatting an email message before you start working with these settings.

Office themes

Themes apply a single, customizable look to your messages (and other elements of your business, since they can be shared across Microsoft Office 2013 applications) by combining several settings to create a specific look. Themes make it easy for you to create and implement a unified look and feel for all of your Office documents.

A theme has a set of font faces, coordinated colors, and graphical effects that are combined to create a palette of styles that provides a unified look for all the elements of your messages. Each portion of a theme can use built-in or custom settings that you create, giving you an endless number of combinations to work with. The components of a theme are as follows:

- **Colors**   A set of colors is applied consistently across all the graphical elements in your email. You can use built-in color sets or create your own.

- **Fonts**   Two fonts—one for body text and another for heading text—are used as the basis for the gallery of font styles used by that theme. Outlook 2013 has a number of built-in theme fonts, or you can create a custom set.

- **Effects**   An effect is a particular look for graphical objects created by using different values for lines, fills, and 3-D effects to create varying results. Effects are selected from a built-in gallery. You cannot create custom effects.

- **Page color**   The page background can be a solid color, gradient, pattern, texture, or picture, or it can be left blank.

> ## Note
> Although you can save a theme that includes a background set by using the Page Color command, the background is not applied when you use that theme in Outlook 2013. To set a default background, you must use stationery or an older theme, or apply the background separately.

Office themes are created in Outlook 2013, Word 2013, Excel 2013, and PowerPoint 2013. (Microsoft PowerPoint 2013 has the widest range of theme creation options.) In Outlook 2013, you create and apply these themes within an email message. Themes are stored as .thmx files under your user profile.

Stationery

Stationery creates a customized look for your email using a background image and font formatting. With most of the Office System document formatting moving to themes, stationery is mostly an older feature with only a background image and a few font styles, but it is the simplest way to get a background into new messages by default. Stationery is stored as HTML files in C:\Program Files\Common Files\Microsoft shared\Stationery, with supporting graphics in an associated folder. If you create or modify stationery using Word 2013, graphics and any other files that you use in the stationery are saved in a subfolder of the directory where you save the template.

> **Note**
> To use themes or stationery, you must use RTF or HTML format for the message.

Style sets

Outlook 2013 creates a style set by applying the theme colors to the body and heading fonts to configure the actual font styles. You can customize the display of the fonts in a message and save it as a custom style set. Style sets are saved as Word 2013 templates.

Outlook 2013 combines these settings to configure the exact look of each message that you create. When you create a new message, the collective default settings for new messages that you have configured are applied, as described in Table 7-1. Backgrounds can come from older themes or stationery, while font and graphical styling information comes from the currently saved default settings (which is usually a theme). If you have customized font styles, those are loaded from the template that you created.

TABLE 7-1 Message style components

Component	Controlled by	To set
Backgrounds	Stationery or older theme	Choose File, Options, Mail, and then select Stationery And Fonts. On the Personal Stationery tab, under Theme Or Stationery To Use For New HTML Messages, choose Theme, and then select a theme.
Colors, fonts, and effects	Office themes	When composing a message, on the Options tab, in the Themes group, click one of the Themes options.
Custom font styles	Style set	When composing a message, on the Format Text tab, in the Styles group, click Change Styles, and then choose Style Set.

Using themes to customize your messages

You can select a theme from the Themes gallery, shown in Figure 7-38, which displays built-in Office themes and custom themes that you create.

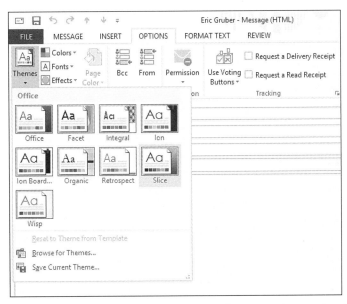

Figure 7-38 You can select a theme or save the current theme using the Themes command.

To select a theme, with a message open, on the Options tab, in the Themes group, click Theme, and then select a theme from the Themes gallery.

You can also choose Reset To Theme From Template, which causes new Outlook 2013 messages to use the Office theme that is the default for new messages.

If you have additional themes saved locally, you can select Browse For Themes to find them on your hard disk or in a network location. You can also choose Save Current Theme to save the current theme as a custom theme.

Colors

You can choose a set of colors to use for the text and other style options, or you can create a new set of custom colors. To select a color, with a message open, on the Options tab, in the Themes group, click Color. Select a set of theme colors in the Colors gallery, as shown in Figure 7-39.

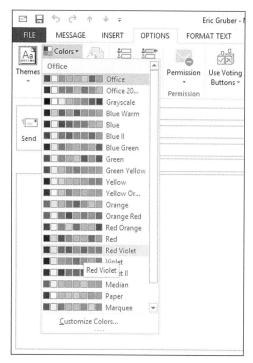

Figure 7-39 You can select a set of colors for your theme using the Colors gallery.

To create a new set of theme colors, follow these steps:

1. With a message open, on the Options tab, in the Themes group, click Color, and then click Create New Theme Colors.

2. In the Create New Theme Colors dialog box, shown in Figure 7-40, select the colors that you want, enter a name for the theme colors in the Name box, and then click Save. You can then select the theme colors from the Colors gallery.

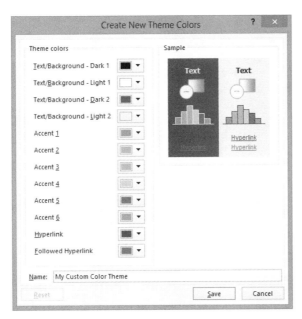

Figure 7-40 You can select a set of colors for your theme in the Create New Theme Colors dialog box.

Fonts

Themes use two font selections, in combination with colors and other settings, to create a range of Quick Styles for the fonts in your message. You choose a font for the headings and a font for the body text, and Outlook 2013 does the rest. You can control the font styles more precisely by saving stationery or saving a message form, or using the options on the ribbon, on the Format Text tab, in the Style group.

To select fonts, with a message open, on the Options tab, in the Themes group, click Fonts. Select a font pair from the Fonts gallery, as shown in Figure 7-41.

Figure 7-41 You can select the theme fonts in the Fonts gallery.

If you want to choose two specific fonts rather than a preset pair, follow these steps:

1. On the Fonts menu, choose Customize Fonts.

2. In the Create New Theme Fonts dialog box, shown in Figure 7-42, select a heading font and a body font. Give the theme fonts a name, and then click Save.

Figure 7-42 You can select one font for the body text of your messages and another for the headings in the Create New Theme Fonts dialog box.

Effects

Outlook 2013 themes use effects for creating a particular look in the graphical elements (such as SmartArt and charts) that you insert in your email. Effects vary in the weight of the lines they use and the opacity, glow, and texture of the surfaces on the objects that Outlook 2013 creates. The Effects gallery provides previews of the effects, but you should try out various effects on an email message with some graphical elements in it to see the effects in action.

To select an effect for your messages, open a message, and on the Options tab, in the Themes group, click Effects, and then select an effect in the Effects gallery, as shown in Figure 7-43.

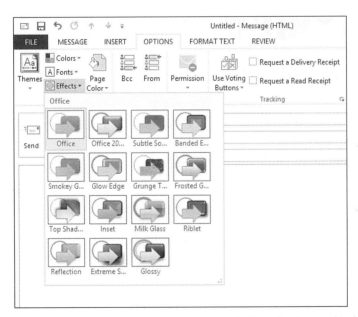

Figure 7-43 You can choose from a number of effects for the graphical elements of your messages.

Page color

The Page Color option allows you to select a background for the email message that you are composing. Outlook 2013 lets you choose from colors, gradients, textures, patterns, and pictures for your message background.

To select a page color, in Outlook 2013, with a new, blank email message open, on the Options tab, in the Themes group, select Page Color and do one of the following:

- To use a color that is displayed on the Page Colors menu, click the color. The Theme Colors area displays the theme colors on the top line and light-to-dark variations of each color in a vertical bar below the color. You can also choose a standard Video Graphics Array (VGA) color or no color.

- If you want to choose a different solid color, click More Colors to open the Colors dialog box. Select the color that you want to use, and then click OK.

- Select Fill Effects to use a gradient, texture, pattern, or picture as the message background. The Fill Effects dialog box has several tabs:

  - **Gradient**   The Gradient tab, shown in Figure 7-44, gives you several options to create a shaded background. Choose the number of colors to use, and then select the colors in the Color 1 and Color 2 drop-down lists. Choose a shading style, and then click a variant. The Sample area gives you a preview of the current settings. When you have finished, click OK.

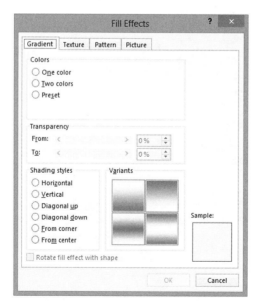

Figure 7-44 You can create your own shaded background on the Gradient tab in the Fill Effects dialog box.

○ **Texture**   This tab has a selection of small images that are tiled on the message background. Select a texture you like, or click Other Texture to select a different graphics file to use as the texture.

○ **Pattern**   This tab has a number of patterns to select from and lets you set the Foreground and Background colors to configure the final look of the pattern.

○ **Picture**   On this tab, you can choose a picture to use as the background by clicking Select Picture and locating the image you want to use.

INSIDE OUT   Use a background image automatically on new messages

Although you can add a background image to an email message using the Page Color command in the Theme group on the Options tab, a saved theme will not load the background image in an email message. You can use existing stationery, however, or an older theme to apply a background image to your new email messages by default. The only way to choose your own background image for email messages is by creating new stationery, which allows you to apply a background and font styles to new messages.

Creating a custom theme

You can create a customized theme that you can share across your Office System documents. To create your own theme, follow these steps:

1. On the Options tab, in the Themes group, click Colors, and then select a set of colors to use.

2. On the Options tab, in the Themes group, click Fonts, and then select a pair of fonts to use.

3. On the Options tab, in the Themes group, click Effects, and then select a style of effects to use.

4. Once you are satisfied with the configuration of the theme, save it so that you can apply it easily later. To save the theme, on the Options tab, in the Themes group, click Themes, and then click Save Current Theme. Name the theme, and then click Save.

Note
Outlook 2013 saves custom themes to *<profile>*\AppData\Roaming\Microsoft\Templates\Document Themes.

When you load this theme, it will set the message colors, fonts, and effects, but not the background settings. To save the background, you must create either stationery or a form. If you want to configure the theme settings as well as the background image, save a form. If you want to specify only the background image and font styles that you manually format, create stationery.

Using stationery to customize your messages

With Outlook 2013 stationery, you use a set of characteristics that define the font style, color, and background image for messages. In effect, stationery can give your messages a certain look and feel, as shown in Figure 7-45. Stationery provides more limited customization than themes, and Outlook 2013 uses stationery very little. There are several built-in stationery options, although the only way to use them is to assign them as the default message format. In addition, you cannot create new stationery or customize existing stationery directly in Outlook 2013; you must use another program such as Word 2013.

Figure 7-45 Stationery gives your messages a customized look.

You can assign a default stationery to be used in all your messages. To do so, follow these steps:

1. In Outlook 2013, click File, Options, and then select Mail in the left pane of the Outlook Options dialog box.

2. On the Mail page, click Stationery And Fonts to display the Signatures And Stationery dialog box.

3. On the Personal Stationery tab of the Signatures And Stationery dialog box, click Theme.

4. In the Theme Or Stationery dialog box, shown in Figure 7-46, choose the default stationery in the Choose A Theme list, and then click OK. If you have default stationery selected and no longer want your messages to use any stationery, follow the same procedure, but set the default stationery to No Theme.

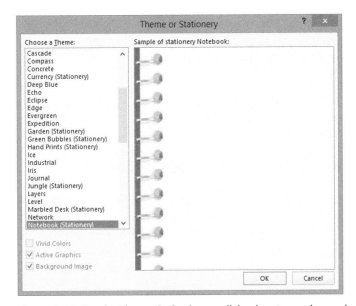

Figure 7-46 Use the Theme Or Stationery dialog box to preview and select stationery.

5. If you want to use fonts that are different from those in the stationery you just chose, in the Signatures And Stationery dialog box, in the Font drop-down list, under Theme Or Stationery For New HTML E-mail Message, select either Use My Font When Replying And Forwarding Messages or Always Use My Fonts.

6. In the Signatures And Stationery dialog box, click the Font button for each font you want to customize, configure the options in the Font dialog box, and then click OK.

7. When you have finished setting the new message defaults, click OK to close the Signatures And Stationery dialog box.

INSIDE OUT   Create new stationery

You can create new stationery in Word 2013 to use with Outlook 2013. To do this, create a new document in Word 2013, select the picture that you want to use as a background, and then format any font style that you want to use with Outlook 2013. Save the file as HTML in the C:\Program Files\Common Files\Microsoft shared\Stationery folder. You can then choose this stationery as the default for new messages in the Signatures And Stationery dialog box.

Using signatures

Outlook 2013 supports two types of signatures that you can add automatically (or manually) to outgoing messages: standard signatures and digital signatures. This chapter focuses on standard signatures, which can include text and graphics, depending on the mail format you choose.

To learn about digital signatures, which allow you to authenticate your identity and encrypt messages, see the section "Protecting messages with digital signatures" in Chapter 8, "Security and data protection."

Understanding message signatures

Outlook 2013 can add a signature automatically to your outgoing messages. You can specify different signatures for new messages and for replies or forwards. Signatures can include both text and graphics, as well as vCard attachments. Both rich text and HTML formats support inserting business cards and graphics in messages. If your signature contains graphics and you start a new message using plain text format, the graphics are removed, although any text defined by the signature remains. When you start a message using plain text format, business cards are attached, but they are not included in the body of the message.

Why use signatures? Many people use a signature to include their contact information in each message. Still others use a signature to include a favorite quote or other information in the message. In many cases, companies have a policy that all outgoing messages contain a legal disclaimer at the bottom of the message, and they can implement these disclaimers through signatures. Regardless of the type of information you want to include, creating and using signatures is easy.

INSIDE OUT   Use multiple signatures

You can create a unique signature for each email account, and you can use one signature for new messages and a different one when you reply to or forward a message. When you send a message, Outlook 2013 appends the appropriate signature to the outgoing message.

Defining signatures

If you want to include a graphic in a signature, check before you start to ensure that you already have that graphic on your computer or that it's available on the network.

Follow these steps to create a signature:

1. In Outlook 2013, click File, Options, and then select the Mail page.

2. Click Signatures to open the Signatures And Stationery dialog box, and then, on the E-mail Signature tab, click New.

3. In the New Signature dialog box, specify a name for the signature as it will appear in Outlook 2013, and then click OK.

4. In the Signatures And Stationery dialog box, click the signature that you just created in the Select Signature To Edit list.

5. In the Edit Signature area, type the text that you want to include in the signature, and then use the toolbar to format the text, as shown in Figure 7-47.

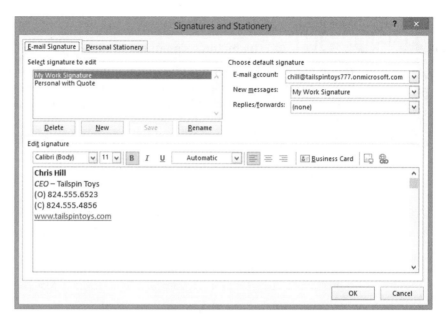

Figure 7-47 Format the text of your signature in the Edit Signature area of the Signatures And Stationery dialog box.

◯ To attach a vCard from an Outlook 2013 contact item, click Business Card. In the Insert Business Card dialog box, select the contact item, and then click OK.

◯ To insert a picture, click the Picture icon. In the Insert Picture dialog box, select the picture, and then click Insert.

◯ To insert a hyperlink, click the Hyperlink icon. In the Insert Hyperlink dialog box, select the location to link to, type the text to display (if needed), and then click Insert.

6. When you have finished with the signature, click Save.

7. Create other signatures if desired, and then click OK to close the Signatures And Stationery dialog box.

Adding signatures to messages

The signature that Outlook 2013 adds to new messages and the signature it adds to replies and forwards don't have to be the same. To set up different signatures for these different kinds of messages, click File, Options, select the Mail page, and then click Signatures.

In the Choose Default Signature area, select an account in the E-mail Account drop-down list. Select a signature in the New Messages drop-down list and, if desired, one in the Replies/Forwards drop-down list.

Chapter 7

INSIDE OUT   Specify the default message format

Keep in mind that the signature data that Outlook 2013 adds to the message depends on the message format specified on the Options tab. Set the message format to HTML or rich text if you want to create or edit signatures that contain graphics.

Other than letting you specify the signature for new messages or for replies and forwards, Outlook 2013 does not give you a way to control which signature is attached to a given message. For example, if you want to use different signatures for personal and business messages, you must switch signatures manually. However, Outlook 2013 does store signature options separately for each account, so you can control signatures to some degree just by sending messages through a specific account.

You can change the signature when composing a message. On the Insert tab, in the Include group, click Signature, and then select the signature on the menu. If you want a new signature, choose Signatures on the menu to open the Signatures And Stationery dialog box, and then create a new signature to use.

Backing up your signatures

You should back up your signatures when you finish creating them and after you add a significant number of new ones. Signatures are stored in <profile>\AppData\Roaming\Microsoft\Signatures as a set of files (text, HTML, and rich text) and a corresponding folder of files containing pictures, Extensible Markup Language (XML) files, and theme data.

There is no provision for backing up your signatures inside Outlook 2013. To back up your signatures, you should back up the contents of <profile>\AppData\Roaming\Microsoft\Signatures.

Using the proofing and research tools

From the old standby spelling and grammar checkers to research and translation tools, Outlook 2013 has a number of tools to help you get your message across clearly and professionally. You can perform searches across a wide variety of sources, from electronic reference books to websites. A number of research options are installed by default, and you can add more to customize your searches.

Adding the translator service

When you install Office 2013, the translator service might not get added by default. If not, you can easily add it:

1. Open a new email message, click the Review tab, and click Research.

2. In the Research pane, click Research Options.

3. In the Research Options dialog box, click Add Services.

4. In the Address text box, type **http://www.microsofttranslator.com/officetrans/ register.asmx**, and then click Add.

5. In the resulting Microsoft Translator Setup dialog box, click Continue.

6. Click Install.

Using the proofing tools

On the Review tab, in the Proofing group, you'll find these options:

- **Spelling & Grammar**   This option performs a spelling and grammar check in accordance with the current configuration.

- **Research**   This option performs a search across the sources you select. You can choose categories to search (for example, All Reference Books) or individual data sources.

See the section "Configuring research options" later in this chapter for details on customizing the services used for searches.

- **Thesaurus**   You can select English, French, or Spanish as the thesaurus language in the drop-down list.

- **Word Count**   Click to display the statistics for the message, including the number of words, lines, paragraphs, pages, and characters. You can choose to include the contents of footnotes, endnotes, and text boxes in the statistics.

- **Translate**   The translation features in Outlook 2013 let you translate small amounts of text between a number of common languages. Outlook gives you three options for translation: Send the text to an online site for translation, show a translation in the Research pane using local and online resources, or display a small translation window when you hover the mouse pointer over a word. The following three items describe these features:

  ○ **Translate Item**   Send the selected text to the Microsoft Translator website and view the translation in the resulting webpage (see Figure 7-48).

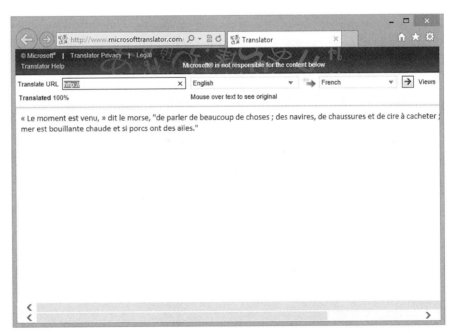

Figure 7-48 A selection of text can be translated using the Microsoft Translator website.

  ○ **Translate Selected Text**   Show in the Research pane a translation of the selected text (see Figure 7-49).

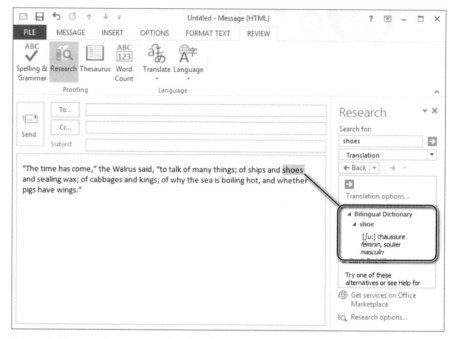

Figure 7-49 A word can be translated in the Research pane.

○ **Mini Translator**   Selecting this option causes Outlook 2013 to display a
   ScreenTip with a brief translation of a word when you point to the word with
   the mouse, as shown in Figure 7-50.

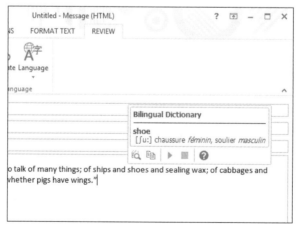

Figure 7-50 The Mini Translator gives you a quick translation of an individual word.

- **Choose Translation Language**   Click this option to specify the language for the Translate Item and Mini Translator options. To set the translation languages for the Research pane, choose languages using the From and To drop-down lists.

Setting the proofing language

When Outlook proofs your message for spelling and grammar, it does so using a specific language. For example, checking the spelling of a French email using the English language would probably result in most of the words being marked as incorrectly spelled. For that reason, you need to specify the proofing language that you want Outlook to use. To do so, on the Review tab, click Language, Set Proofing Language. In the resulting Language dialog box, choose the language used by the majority of the message. You can use the Detect Language Automatically option to allow Outlook to detect the language automatically for any given word or phrase. If Outlook is having problems proofing a selection of text because it is incorrectly identifying the language, select the text, click Language, Set Proofing Language, choose a specific language from the list, and click OK.

Configuring research options

The list of services that Outlook 2013 uses when doing various forms of research can be customized to meet your individual needs. To configure the reference books and research sites that Outlook 2013 searches, on the Message tab, in the Proofing group, click Research. In the Research pane, select Research Options. You can select from the following options:

- **Services**   Activate services and resources that are installed by selecting the check box in the Services list. To deactivate a service, clear its check box.

- **Add Services**   To add more services, select Add Services, and then select the provider in the Advertised Services list. To add a new provider, enter the location of the service in the Address box.

- **Update/Remove**   To manage installed services, select Update/Remove to display the Update Or Remove Services dialog box. To update a service, select it in the Currently Installed Services, Grouped By Provider list, and then click Update to reinstall the provider for that service. To remove a service, select the provider in the list, and then click Remove. (You cannot remove installed options such as dictionaries and thesauruses.) Click Close when you have finished updating services.

- **Parental Control**   If you want to provide filtered access to research services, click Parental Control to open the Parental Control dialog box. You can then choose Turn On Content Filtering To Make Services Block Offensive Results. You can also opt to Allow Users To Search Only The Services That Can Block Offensive Results. In addition, these settings can be protected with a password.

> **Note**
>
> You must be logged on with an account that has administrative permissions for parental controls to configure Parental Control settings.
>
> The parental controls provided by Outlook are separate from the parental controls provided in Windows. With the Windows options, you can set time limits for using the computer; control access to games based on rating, content, or title; and allow or block specific programs. You should also check out Family Safety at Windows Live (*http://www.home.live.com*) to learn how you can use it to limit searches, control web browsing and chat, view Internet activity reports, and much more.

Controlling when messages are delivered

When a message is sent, it is delivered immediately by default. You can, however, delay message delivery until a specified time for an individual message. Delayed delivery is not specific to Exchange Server accounts, but the feature goes hand in hand with message expiration (covered next), so it bears discussing here.

To place a message in the Outbox but have it delivered after a certain point, click the More Options button in the More Options group on the Options tab to open the Properties dialog box. Select the Do Not Deliver Before check box, and then set the date and time using the drop-down lists. Click Close, then complete the message and click Send. The message will not be sent until after the specified time.

> **Note**
>
> If there is enough room on the ribbon, Outlook displays a Delay Delivery button that, when clicked, opens the Properties dialog box, where you can enter the delivery date and time.

Setting messages to expire

Just as you can delay the delivery of a message, you can also set a message to expire. The message expires and is removed from the recipient's mailbox after a specified period of time whether or not it has been read. You might want to have a message expire if its contents become outdated after a certain amount of time, or if you want to ensure that the message is deleted. To set this option, open the Properties dialog box by clicking Message Options on the Options tab, select the Expires After check box, and then set a date and time. The message will no longer be available to the recipient after that time.

> **Note**
> The capability to set a message to expire is not a security feature; it simply causes the message to be deleted after the specified period. Use Information Rights Management (IRM), which is covered in Chapter 8, to prevent messages from being forwarded, copied, or printed.

Recalling a sent message before it is read

You might want to recall a message for a number of reasons. For example, perhaps the message contains a mistake or is now obsolete. You can recall a message that you have sent so long as the recipient has not read it and the message is still stored on a computer running Exchange Server. Messages sent to recipients using other mail servers cannot be recalled.

To recall a sent message, double-click the message in the Sent Items folder to open it. Click Actions in the Move group on the ribbon, and then click Recall This Message to open the dialog box shown in Figure 7-51. Select whether you want to simply delete all unread copies of the message or delete them and replace them with another message. You can also receive a response reporting the success or failure of each recall attempt.

CAUTION

> For a number of reasons, unread messages often cannot be recalled. You should always take the time to verify the content of a message before sending it.

Figure 7-51 This dialog box is displayed when you attempt to recall a message.

Voting in Outlook

The Outlook 2013 voting feature is useful when you want to solicit input from a group of message recipients. Perhaps you are looking for approval on a proposal, you are holding an informal election in your organization, or you just want to get the group's input on an issue.

You can use Outlook's voting feature with non–Exchange Server accounts as well as with Exchange Server accounts.

> **Note**
>
> The voting feature supported by Outlook is certainly useful, but it isn't a substitute for a formal approval process. If you have Microsoft SharePoint deployed in your organization, consider using workflows in SharePoint to automate approval processes for documents and other items.

With the voting feature, you solicit and tally votes from the group. Outlook 2013 provides predefined voting responses, but you can also create your own. In this section, you'll learn how to include voting buttons in messages, tally returned votes, and configure voting options.

Here's how voting works in general: You create a message containing the question or document on which the group will be voting. Next, you add voting buttons to the message. Then you send the message. Recipients cast their vote by clicking the appropriate button. Outlook 2013 prompts recipients to confirm their votes and then sends the replies back to you.

Sending a message for a vote

Sending a message for a vote is simple. In fact, so long as you want to use one of the Outlook 2013 default sets of voting options, the process takes only a few clicks.

Using the default voting responses

Use the following steps to create a message and add voting buttons to it:

1. Start Outlook 2013, and then open a new message or open an existing message from your Drafts folder.

2. On the Options tab, in the More Options group, click Message Options to open the Properties dialog box.

3. In the Voting And Tracking Options area, select the Use Voting Buttons check box. In the drop-down list, select the group of voting buttons that you want to include, as shown in Figure 7-52.

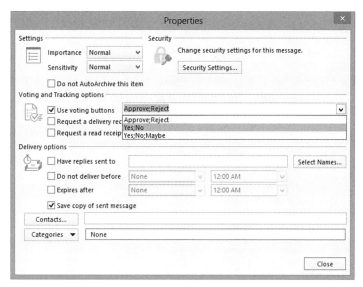

Figure 7-52 Select the voting buttons that you want to include using the Properties dialog box.

4. Click Close.

5. Edit your message. Include any message attachments, if needed.

6. Click Send to send the message.

Using custom responses

Outlook 2013 doesn't limit you to the default sets of voting options (such as Accept/Reject). You can create your own set that includes the responses that you need for any situation. For example, suppose that you're planning a company appreciation banquet and you need to finalize the menu. You want to give everyone a choice of entree and collect those responses for the caterer. What better way to do that than electronically, through Outlook 2013?

Here's how:

1. Compose your message.

2. On the Options tab, in the More Options group, click Message Options to open the Properties dialog box.

3. Select the Use Voting Buttons check box.

4. Click the text field in the Use Voting Buttons drop-down list. Delete the existing text. Type your custom vote options separated by semicolons, as shown in Figure 7-53.

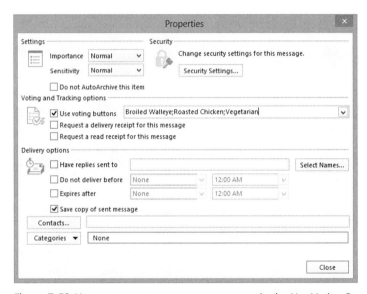

Figure 7-53 You can create custom vote responses in the Use Voting Buttons text field.

5. Click Close.

6. Make any final adjustments to the message as needed.

7. Click Send.

Casting your vote

When you receive a message that includes voting buttons, Outlook 2013 displays a message in the InfoBar to indicate that you can vote. Click the InfoBar and then choose an item, as shown in Figure 7-54.

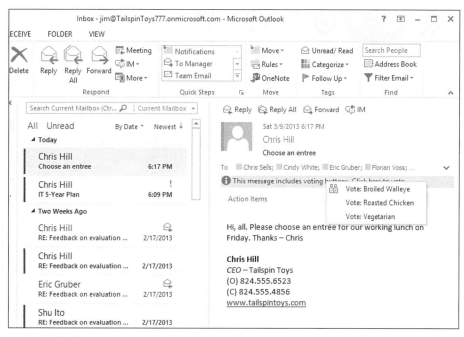

Figure 7-54 The Reading Pane shows a message prompting you to vote.

Voting is easy—just select an option to cast your vote. Outlook 2013 displays a simple dialog box asking whether you want to send the vote now or edit your response. To send the message without modification, select Send The Response Now. To cast your vote and open the message as a reply so that you can include text in your response, select Edit The Response Before Sending.

> **Note**
>
> Outlook 2013 changes the prompt in the InfoBar to indicate that you responded to the voting request, removing your ability to click the InfoBar link and vote again.

When you cast a vote, Outlook 2013 changes the subject of the message to include your vote. For example, if the original subject is Choose An Entree and you click the Roasted Chicken option, the subject of the reply returned to the sender is Roasted Chicken: Choose An Entree.

Viewing and sorting votes

Votes come back to you in the form of messages. You can view the vote summary in a few ways. If the Reading Pane is displayed, you can click the message header, click the summary message in the InfoBar, and then choose View Voting Responses, as shown in Figure 7-55. Alternatively, you can open the Sent Items folder, open the original message, and then click the Tracking button in the Show group on the ribbon. Both methods display the Tracking results, as shown in Figure 7-56.

Figure 7-55 Click the summary message in the InfoBar to display the Tracking page.

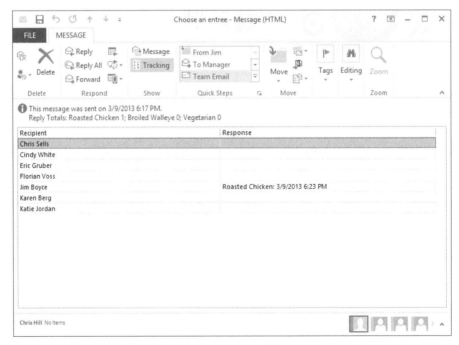

Figure 7-56 Open the message from the Sent Items folder as an alternative way to access the Tracking page.

The Tracking page summarizes the votes, with individual responses displayed one per line. The responses are also totaled in the InfoBar. If you want a printout of the vote responses, print the messages with the Tracking page visible.

Unfortunately, Outlook 2013 doesn't give you a way to sort the vote tally. You can, however, copy the data to Excel 2013 to sort it.

To copy voting data to Excel 2013, follow these steps:

1. Select the rows that you want to copy. (Select a row, and then hold down the Shift key to select contiguous responses, or hold down the Ctrl key to select noncontiguous ones.)

2. Press Ctrl+C to copy the data to the Clipboard.

3. Start Excel.

4. Select a cell in the worksheet and then press Ctrl+V to paste the data.

5. Choose Data, Sort to open the Sort dialog box, and then click OK to accept the default settings and sort the spreadsheet.

Setting options for voting

You can set options in Outlook 2013 to configure how it handles voting. To configure these settings, follow these steps:

1. Start Outlook 2013, and then click File, Options.

2. Click Mail in the left pane.

3. Scroll down to the Tracking group, shown in Figure 7-57.

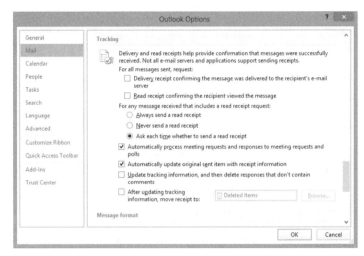

Figure 7-57 Use the Tracking group to configure voting options.

The Tracking group includes the following options that relate to voting:

○ **Automatically Process Meeting Requests And Responses To Meeting Requests And Polls** Outlook 2013 processes and tallies responses when they arrive. If you clear this check box, you must open each response to have Outlook 2013 tally it.

○ **Update Tracking Information, And Then Delete Responses That Don't Contain Comments** Outlook 2013 deletes voting responses that have no additional comments added to them.

4. Select the options that you want to use, and then click OK to close the Outlook Options dialog box.

TROUBLESHOOTING

Votes aren't being tallied automatically

The Outlook 2013 capability to tally votes automatically, without the user having to open each message, might not be apparent at first. Even on a completely idle system, Outlook 2013 can take several minutes to process the messages. If you need to process the responses more quickly, select all the responses, right-click the selection, and then choose Open Selected Items to open them all at once. Keep in mind, however, that you'll end up with an open message form for each response, which you'll then have to close.

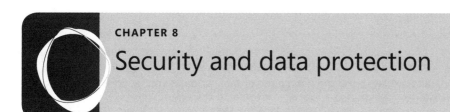

CHAPTER 8

Security and data protection

MICROSOFT Outlook 2013 includes features that can help protect your system from computer viruses and malicious programs, prevent others from using email to impersonate you, and prevent the interception of sensitive messages. Some of these features—such as the capability to block specific types of attachments—were first introduced in Outlook 2002. Other security features—such as the capability to block external images in HTML-based messages—were introduced in Outlook 2003. The latter feature enables Outlook to block HTML messages sent by spammers to identify valid recipient addresses. These messaging security features were extended and enhanced in Outlook 2007 and are also present in Outlook 2013.

This chapter begins with a look at the settings you can use to control HTML content. Because HTML messages can contain malicious scripts or even HTML code that can easily affect your system, the capability to handle these messages securely in Outlook 2013 is extremely important.

This chapter also discusses the use of both digital signatures and encryption. You can use a digital signature to authenticate your messages, proving to the recipient that a message indeed came from you, not from someone trying to impersonate you. Outlook 2013 enables you to encrypt outgoing messages to prevent them from being intercepted by unintended recipients; you can also read encrypted messages sent to you by others. In this chapter, you'll learn how to obtain and install certificates to send encrypted messages and how to share keys with others so that you can exchange encrypted messages.

Configuring HTML message handling

Spammers are always looking for new methods to identify valid email addresses. Knowing that a given address actually reaches someone is one step in helping spammers maintain their lists. If a particular address doesn't generate a response in some way, it's more likely to be removed from the list.

One way that spammers identify valid addresses is through the use of *web beacons*. Spammers often send HTML messages that contain links to external content, such as pictures or sound clips. When you display the message, your mail program retrieves the remote data to display it, and the remote server then validates your address. These external elements are the web beacons.

> **Note**
> Nonspammers also frequently include external content in messages to reduce the size of the message. So external content isn't a bad thing per se (depending on how it is used).

Since Outlook 2003, Outlook blocks external content from HTML messages by default, displaying a red *X* in place of the missing content. The result is that these web beacons no longer work because the external content is not accessed when the message is displayed. Messages that fit criteria for the Safe Recipients and Safe Senders lists are treated as exceptions—the external content for these messages is not blocked (unless you configure Outlook to do so).

> **Note**
> You can rest the mouse pointer on a blocked image to view the descriptive alternate text (if any) for the image.

When you preview in the Reading Pane an image for which Outlook 2013 has blocked external content, Outlook 2013 displays a message in the InfoBar indicating that the blocking occurred (see Figure 8-1). You can click the InfoBar and choose Download Pictures to view the external content. Outlook 2013 then downloads and displays the content in the Reading Pane. The same is true if you open a message; Outlook 2013 displays a warning message telling you that the content was blocked (see Figure 8-2). You can click the warning message and choose Download Pictures to download and view the content. Because Outlook 2013 blocks external content for messages in this way, you can take advantage of content blocking without using the Reading Pane.

If you edit, forward, or reply to a message containing blocked content (from an open message or a message displayed in the Reading Pane), Outlook 2013 displays a warning dialog box indicating that the external content will be downloaded if you continue. You can click OK to download the content and continue with the reply or forward, click No to tell Outlook 2013 to forward the content as text without downloading the content, or click Cancel to not open the message or download the content (see Figure 8-3). Thus, you can reply to or forward a message without downloading the external content.

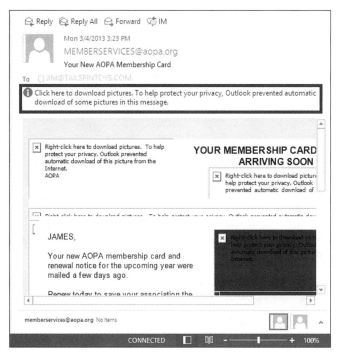

Figure 8-1 Click the InfoBar in the Reading Pane to view external content for a selected message.

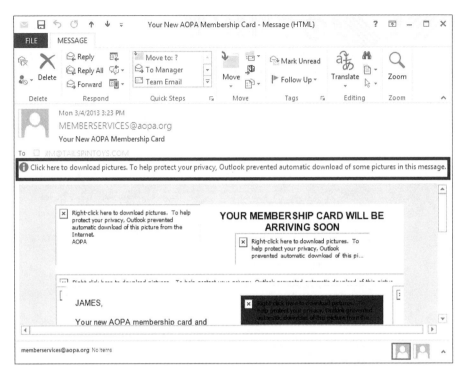

Figure 8-2 You can access blocked content when you open a message by clicking the InfoBar and selecting Download Pictures.

Figure 8-3 You can forward or reply to a message with blocked content without downloading the content.

Outlook 2013 provides a few options to control the way content blocking works. To configure these options, click File, Options, Trust Center, Trust Center Settings, and then click the Automatic Download page. Figure 8-4 shows the resulting Automatic Download settings page.

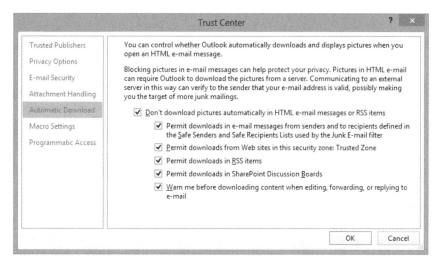

Figure 8-4 Configure content blocking with the Automatic Download settings page.

Configure content blocking using the following options:

- **Don't Download Pictures Automatically In HTML E-mail Or RSS Items**   Select this check box to allow Outlook 2013 to block external picture content with the exception of messages that fit the Safe Senders and Safe Recipients lists. When selected, this check box enables the five check boxes below it to refine content blocking further.

- **Permit Downloads In E-mail Messages From Senders And To Recipients Defined In The Safe Senders And Safe Recipients List Used By The Junk E-mail Filter**   Select this check box to allow Outlook to download content if the message is from a sender in your Safe Senders list or is addressed to a recipient in your Safe Recipients list.

- **Permit Downloads From Web Sites In This Security Zone: Trusted Zone**   Select this check box to allow external content from sites in the Trusted Sites zone in Microsoft Internet Explorer.

- **Permit Downloads In RSS Items**   Select this check box to allow external content included in Really Simple Syndication (RSS) feeds.

Chapter 8

- **Permit Downloads In SharePoint Discussion Boards** Select this check box to allow external content included in SharePoint discussion boards.

- **Warn Me Before Downloading Content When Editing, Forwarding, Or Replying To E-mail** Select this check box to receive a warning about external content when you edit, reply to, or forward a message for which external content has been blocked.

To take advantage of the exceptions for external content, you must add the message's originating address to the Safe Senders list, add the recipient address to the Safe Recipients list, or add the remote domain to the Trusted Sites zone in Internet Options (in the Windows Security Center).

For more details on configuring the Safe Recipients and Safe Senders lists, see the section "Enabling and configuring junk email filtering" in Chapter 10, "Managing junk email."

Protecting messages with digital signatures

Outlook 2013 supports the use of *digital signatures* to sign messages and validate their authenticity. For example, you can sign a sensitive message digitally so that the recipient can know with relative certainty that the message came from you and that no one is impersonating you by using your email address. This section of the chapter explains digital certificates and signatures and how to use them in Outlook 2013.

Understanding digital certificates and signatures

A *digital certificate* is the mechanism that makes digital signatures possible. Depending on its assigned purpose, you can use a digital certificate for a variety of tasks, including the following:

- Verifying your identity as the sender of an email message

- Encrypting data communications between computers—between a client and a server, for example

- Encrypting email messages to prevent easy interception

- Signing drivers and executable files to authenticate their origin

A digital certificate binds the identity of the certificate's owner to a pair of keys, one public and one private. At a minimum, a certificate contains the following information:

- The owner's public key

- The owner's name or alias

- A certificate expiration date

- A certificate serial number

- The name of the certificate issuer

- The digital signature of the issuer

The certificate can also include other identifying information, such as the owner's email address, postal address, country, or gender.

The two keys are the aspects of the certificate that enable authentication and encryption. The private key resides on your computer and is a large unique number. The certificate contains the public key, which you must give to recipients to whom you want to send authenticated or encrypted messages.

Think of it as having a "read content key" and a "create content key": one key (the private key) lets you create encrypted content, and the other key (the public key) lets others read the content encrypted with the private key.

Outlook 2013 uses slightly different methods for authenticating messages with digital signatures and for encrypting messages, as you'll see later in the chapter. Before you begin either task, however, you must first obtain a certificate.

Obtaining a digital certificate

Digital certificates are issued by certification authorities (CAs). In most cases, you obtain your email certificate from a public CA such as VeriSign or Thawte. However, systems based on Windows servers running Certificate Services can function as CAs, providing certificates to clients who request them. Check with your system administrator to determine whether your enterprise includes a CA. If it doesn't, you need to obtain your certificate from a public CA, usually at a minimal cost. Certificates are typically good for one year and must be renewed at the end of that period.

If you need to obtain your certificate from a public CA, point your web browser to a CA website, such as *http://www.verisign.com*. Follow the instructions provided by the site to obtain a certificate for signing and encrypting your email (see Figure 8-5, for example). The certificate might not be issued immediately; instead, the CA might send you an email message containing a URL that links to a page where you can retrieve the certificate. When you connect to that page, the CA installs the certificate on your system.

> **Note**
>
> Alternatively, in the Trust Center, click E-mail Security, and then click Get A Digital ID to display a page from the Microsoft website that includes links to several CAs. Select a vendor under Available Digital IDs and click the link to its website to obtain a certificate.

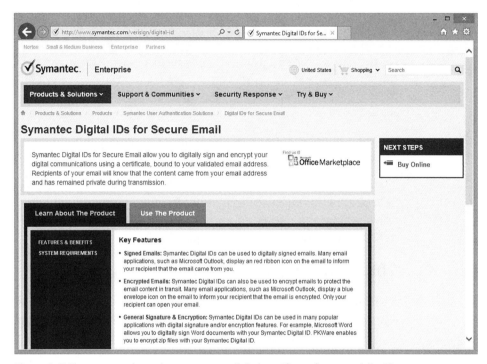

Figure 8-5 You can use the web to request a digital certificate from a public CA.

If you're obtaining a certificate from a CA on your network, the method that you use depends on whether the network includes an enterprise CA or a stand-alone CA.

If you're using Windows 7 or Windows 8 as a domain client on a network with an enterprise CA, follow these steps to request a certificate:

1. On Windows 7, click the Windows button, and then, in the Start Search box, type **MMC** and click OK. On Windows 8, open the Start screen and type **MMC**, and then click MMC when it appears on the Start screen.

2. In the Microsoft Management Console (MMC), choose File, Add/Remove Snap-in.

3. In the Add Standalone Snap-in dialog box, select Certificates, and then click Add.

4. In the Certificates Snap-in dialog box, select My User Account, and then click Finish.

5. Click OK to return to the MMC.

6. Expand the Certificates–Current User branch.

7. Expand the Personal branch, right-click Certificates, and choose All Tasks, Request New Certificate. You can also right-click the Personal branch and choose All Tasks, Request New Certificate.

8. Follow the prompts provided by the Certificate Request Wizard and the enterprise CA to request your certificate. The certificate should install automatically.

To request a certificate from a stand-alone CA on your network (or if your computer is part of a workgroup), point your web browser to *http://<server>/certsrv*, where *<server>* is the name or Internet Protocol (IP) address of the CA. The CA provides a webpage with a form that you must fill out to request the certificate (see Figure 8-6). Follow the CA prompts to request and obtain the certificate. The site includes a link that you can click to install the certificate.

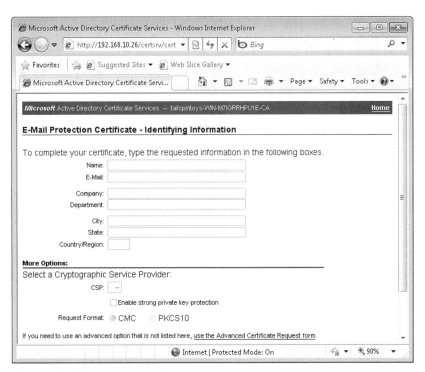

Figure 8-6 A Windows-based CA presents a web form that you can use to request a certificate.

Copying a certificate to another computer

You can copy your certificate from one computer to another, which means that you can use it on more than one system. The process is simple: You first export (back up) your certificate to a file, and then you import the certificate into the other system. The following sections explain how to export and import certificates.

> **Note**
>
> As you use the Certificate Import Wizard and the Certificate Export Wizard (discussed in the following sections), you might discover that they don't precisely match the descriptions presented here. Their appearance and operation might vary slightly, depending on the operating system you're running and the version of Internet Explorer you're using.

Backing up your certificate

Whether you obtained your certificate from a public CA or from a CA on your network, you should back it up in case your system suffers a drive failure or the certificate is lost or corrupted. You also should have a backup of the certificate so that you can export it to any other computers you use on a regular basis, such as a notebook computer or your home computer. In short, you need the certificate on every computer from which you plan to digitally sign or encrypt messages. To back up your certificate, you can use Outlook 2013, Internet Explorer, or the Certificates console. Each method offers the same capabilities; you can use any one of them.

Follow these steps to use Outlook 2013 to back up your certificate to a file:

1. In Outlook 2013, click File, Options, Trust Center, Trust Center Settings, and then click E-mail Security in the left pane.

2. Click Import/Export to display the Import/Export Digital ID dialog box, shown in Figure 8-7.

Figure 8-7 You can export certificates in the Import/Export Digital ID dialog box.

3. Select the Export Your Digital ID To A File option. Click Select, choose the certificate to be exported, and click OK.

4. Click Browse and specify the path and file name for the certificate file.

5. Enter and confirm a password.

6. If you plan to use the certificate on a system with Internet Explorer 4, select the Microsoft Internet Explorer 4.0 Compatible (Low-Security) check box. If you use Internet Explorer 5 or later, clear this check box.

7. If you want to remove this digital ID from this computer, select the check box next to Delete Digital ID From System.

8. Click OK to export the file. The Exporting Your Private Exchange Key dialog box is displayed. Click OK to complete the export process.

If you want to use either Internet Explorer or the Certificates console to back up a certificate, use the Certificate Export Wizard, as follows:

1. If you're using Internet Explorer, begin by choosing Tools, Internet Options. Click the Content tab, and then click Certificates. In the Certificates dialog box, shown in Figure 8-8, select the certificate that you want to back up and click Export to start the wizard. If you're using the Certificates console, begin by opening the console and expanding Certificates–Current User/Personal/Certificates. Right-click the certificate that you want to export, and then choose All Tasks, Export to start the wizard.

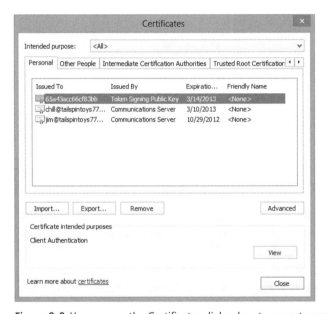

Figure 8-8 You can use the Certificates dialog box to export a certificate.

2. In the Certificate Export Wizard, click Next.

3. On the wizard page shown in Figure 8-9, select Yes, Export The Private Key, and then click Next.

Figure 8-9 The Certificate Export Wizard enables you to export the private key.

4. Select Personal Information Exchange; if other options are selected, clear them unless needed. (If you need to include all certificates in the certification path, remove the private key on export, or export all extended properties, and then select that option.) Click Next.

5. Specify and confirm a password to protect the private key and click Next.

6. Specify a path and file name for the certificate and click Next.

7. Review your selections and click Finish.

TROUBLESHOOTING

You can't export the private key

To use a certificate on a different computer, you must be able to export the private key. If the option to export the private key is unavailable when you run the Certificate Export Wizard, it means that the private key is marked as not exportable. Exportability is an option you choose when you request the certificate. If you request a certificate through a local CA, you must select the Advanced Request option to request a certificate with an exportable private key. If you imported the certificate from a file, you might not have selected the option to make the private key exportable during the import. If you still have the original certificate file, you can import it again—this time selecting the option that will enable you to export the private key.

Installing your certificate from a backup

You can install (or reinstall) a certificate from a backup copy of the certificate file by using Outlook 2013, Internet Explorer, or the Certificates console. You must import the certificate to your computer from the backup file.

The following procedure assumes that you're installing the certificate using Outlook 2013:

1. Click File, Options, Trust Center, Trust Center Settings, and then click E-mail Security.

2. Click Import/Export to display the Import/Export Digital ID dialog box, shown in Figure 8-7.

3. In the Import Existing Digital ID From A File section, click Browse to locate the file containing the backup of the certificate.

4. In the Password box, type the password associated with the certificate file.

5. In the Digital ID Name box, type a name by which you want the certificate to be shown. Typically, you'll enter your name, mailbox name, or email address, but you can enter anything you want.

6. Click OK to import the certificate.

You can also import a certificate to your computer from a backup file using either Internet Explorer or the Certificates console, as explained here:

1. If you're using Internet Explorer, begin by choosing Tools, Internet Options. Click the Content tab, click Certificates, and then click Import to start the Certificate Import Wizard. If you're using the Certificates console, begin by opening the console. Right-click Certificates–Current User/Personal, and then click All Tasks, Import to start the wizard.

2. In the Certificate Import Wizard, click Next.

3. Browse and select the file to import, and then click Open. (If you don't see your certificate file, check the types of certificates shown in the Open dialog box by clicking the drop-down list to the right of the file name field.) After your certificate is selected in the File To Import dialog box, click Next.

4. If the certificate was stored with a password, you are prompted to enter the password. Provide the associated password and click Next.

5. Select the Automatically Select The Certificate Store Based On The Type Of Certificate option and click Next.

6. Click Finish.

Signing messages

Now that you have a certificate on your system, you're ready to start digitally signing your outgoing messages so that recipients can verify your identity. When you send a digitally signed message, Outlook 2013 sends the original message and an encrypted copy of the message with your digital signature. The recipient's email application compares the two versions of the message to determine whether they are the same. If they are, no one has tampered with the message. The digital signature also enables the recipient to verify that the message is from you.

> **Note**
> Because signing your email requires Outlook 2013 to send two copies of the message (the unencrypted message and the encrypted copy), the signed email message is larger.

Understanding S/MIME and clear-text options

Secure/Multipurpose Internet Mail Extensions (S/MIME), an Internet standard, is the mechanism in Outlook 2013 that enables you to digitally sign and encrypt messages. The email client handles the encryption and decryption required for both functions.

Users with email clients that don't support S/MIME can't read digitally signed messages unless you send the message as clear text (unencrypted). Without S/MIME support, the recipient is also unable to verify the authenticity of the message or verify that the message hasn't been altered. Without S/MIME, then, digital signatures are relatively useless.

However, Outlook 2013 does offer you the option of sending a digitally signed message as clear text to recipients who lack S/MIME support. If you need to send the same digitally signed message to multiple recipients—some of whom have S/MIME-capable email clients and some of whom do not—digitally signing the message allows those with S/MIME support to authenticate it, and including the clear-text message allows the others to at least read it.

The following section explains how to send a digitally signed message, including how to send the message in clear text for those recipients who require it.

Adding your digital signature

Follow these steps to sign an outgoing message digitally:

1. Compose the message in Outlook 2013.

2. On the Options tab, in the More Options group, click the Message Options button (in the lower-right corner) to open the Message Options dialog box.

3. Click Security Settings to open the Security Properties dialog box, as shown in Figure 8-10.

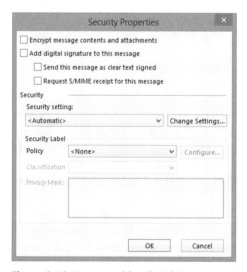

Figure 8-10 You can add a digital signature using the Security Properties dialog box.

4. Select Add Digital Signature To This Message, and then select other check boxes as indicated here:

    ○ **Send This Message As Clear Text Signed**   Select this check box to include a clear-text copy of the message for recipients who don't have S/MIME-capable email applications. Clear this check box to prevent the message from being read by mail clients that don't support S/MIME.

    ○ **Request S/MIME Receipt For This Message**   Select this check box to request a secure receipt to verify that the recipient has validated your digital signature. When the message has been received and saved, and your signature is verified (even if the recipient doesn't read the message), you receive a return receipt. No receipt is sent if your signature is not verified.

5. If necessary, select security settings in the Security Setting drop-down list. (If you have not yet configured your security options, you can do so by clicking Change Settings.)

    For details on security option configuration, see the section "Creating and using security profiles."

6. Click OK to add the digital signature to the message.

> **Note**
> If you send a lot of digitally signed messages, you'll want to configure your security options to include a digital signature by default; see the following section for details. In addition, you might want to add a button to the toolbar to let you quickly sign the message without using a dialog box.

For details about how to add a button to the toolbar to enable you to quickly sign messages, see the Troubleshooting sidebar "You need a faster way to sign a message digitally."

Setting global security options

To save time, you can configure your security settings to apply globally to all messages, changing settings only as needed for certain messages. In Outlook 2013, click File, Options, Trust Center, Trust Center Settings, and then click E-mail Security. On the E-mail Security page, shown in Figure 8-11, you can set security options using the following list as a guide.

Chapter 8

- **Encrypt Contents And Attachments For Outgoing Messages**   If most of the messages that you send need to be encrypted, select this check box to encrypt all outgoing messages by default. You can override encryption for a specific message by changing the message's properties when you compose it. Clear this check box if the majority of your outgoing messages do not need to be encrypted.

  > For information about encryption, see the section "Encrypting messages."

- **Add Digital Signature To Outgoing Messages**   If most of your messages need to be signed, select this check box to sign all outgoing messages digitally by default. Clear this check box if most of your messages do not need to be signed; you will be able to sign specific messages digitally as needed when you compose them.

- **Send Clear Text Signed Message When Sending Signed Messages**   If you need to send digitally signed messages to recipients who do not have S/MIME capability, select this check box to send clear-text digitally signed messages by default. You can override this option for individual messages when you compose them. In most cases, you can clear this check box because most email clients support S/MIME.

- **Request S/MIME Receipt For All S/MIME Signed Messages**   Select this check box to request a secure receipt for all S/MIME messages by default. You can override the setting for individual messages when you compose them. A secure receipt indicates that your message has been received and the signature verified. No receipt is returned if the signature is not verified.

- **Settings**   Select this option to configure more-advanced security settings and create additional security setting groups. For details, see the following section, "Creating and using security profiles."

- **Publish To GAL**   Click this button to publish your certificates to the Global Address List (GAL), making them available to other Microsoft Exchange Server users in your organization who might need to send you encrypted messages. This is an alternative to sending the other users a copy of your certificate. This option is only available with Exchange Server–based accounts (including Office 365).

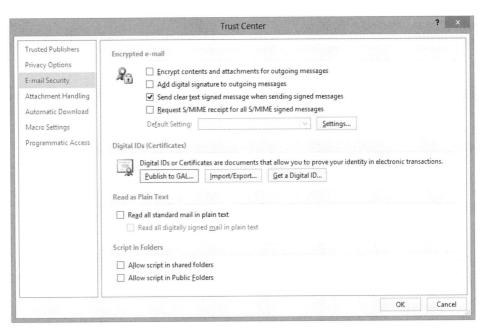

Figure 8-11 Use the E-mail Security page of the Trust Center to configure options for digital signing and encryption.

Creating and using security profiles

Although in most cases you need only one set of Outlook 2013 security settings, you can create and use multiple security profiles. For example, you might send most of your secure messages to other Exchange Server users and only occasionally send secure messages to Internet recipients. In that situation, you might maintain two sets of security settings: one that uses Exchange Server security and another that uses S/MIME, each with different certificates and hash algorithms (the method used to secure the data).

You can configure security profiles using the Change Security Settings dialog box, which you access through the Settings button on the E-mail Security page of the Trust Center dialog box. One of your security profiles acts as the default, but you can select a different security profile any time it's needed.

Follow these steps to create and manage your security profiles:

1. In Outlook 2013, click File, Options, Trust Center, Trust Center Settings, and then click E-mail Security.

2. Click Settings to display the Change Security Settings dialog box, shown in Figure 8-12. Set the options described in the following list as needed. If you are creating a new set of settings, start by clicking New prior to changing settings because selecting New clears all other setting values.

   ○ **Security Settings Name**   Specify the name for the security profile that should appear in the Default Setting drop-down list on the Security tab.

   ○ **Cryptographic Format**   In this drop-down list, select the secure message format for your messages. The default is S/MIME, but you also can select Exchange Server Security. Use S/MIME if you're sending secure messages to Internet recipients. You can use either S/MIME or Exchange Server Security when sending secure messages to recipients on your computer running Exchange Server.

   ○ **Default Security Setting For This Cryptographic Message Format**   Select this check box to make the specified security settings the default settings for the message format you selected in the Cryptography Format drop-down list.

   ○ **Default Security Setting For All Cryptographic Messages**   Select this check box to make the specified security settings the default settings for all secure messages for both S/MIME and Exchange Server security.

   ○ **Security Labels**   Click to configure security labels, which display security information about a specific message and restrict which recipients can open, forward, or send that message.

   ○ **New**   Click to create a new set of security settings.

   ○ **Delete**   Click to delete the currently selected group of security settings.

   ○ **Signing Certificate**   This read-only information indicates the certificate being used to sign your outgoing messages digitally. Click Choose if you want to choose a different certificate. Once you choose a signing certificate, all the fields in the Certificates And Algorithms area are populated automatically.

   You assign the default signing and encryption certificates through the global security settings in Outlook 2013; for information, see the section "Setting global security options."

❍ **Hash Algorithm**   Use this drop-down list to change the hash algorithm used to encrypt messages. Hash algorithm options include MD5, SHA1, SHA256, SHA384, and SHA512. For more information on these hashing algorithms, see the article "Cryptographic Services" at *http://msdn.microsoft.com/en-us/ library/92f9ye3s.aspx.*

❍ **Encryption Certificate**   This read-only information indicates the certificate being used to encrypt your outgoing messages. Click Choose if you want to specify a different certificate.

❍ **Encryption Algorithm**   Use this drop-down list to change the encryption algorithm used to encrypt messages. The encryption algorithm is the mathematical method used to encrypt the data.

❍ **Send These Certificates With Signed Messages**   Select this check box to include your certificate with outgoing messages. Doing so allows recipients to send encrypted messages to you.

3.   Click OK to close the Change Security Settings dialog box.

Figure 8-12 Configure your security profiles in the Change Security Settings dialog box.

4.   In the Default Setting drop-down list on the E-mail Security page, select the security profile you want to use by default and then click OK.

TROUBLESHOOTING

You need a faster way to sign a message digitally

If you don't send a lot of digitally signed messages, you might not mind going through all the steps for getting to the Security Properties dialog box to sign a message that you compose. However, if you frequently send digitally signed messages but don't want to configure Outlook 2013 to sign all messages by default, all the clicking involved in signing the message can be onerous. To sign your messages digitally faster, consider adding a toolbar button that lets you toggle a digital signature with a single click by following these steps:

1. Open the Inbox folder in Outlook 2013.

2. Click New E-mail to display the message form for a new message.

3. In the message form, choose the Customize Quick Access Toolbar drop-down list (at the end of the Quick Access Toolbar) and click More Commands.

4. In the Choose Commands From drop-down list, select All Commands.

5. In the All Commands list, shown in Figure 8-13, select Digitally Sign Message, click Add, and then click OK to close the dialog box. The Digitally Sign Message icon will be added to the end of the Quick Access Toolbar. If you later want to switch security profiles, you can select the profile that you want to use in the Default Setting drop-down list on the E-mail Security page in the Trust Center dialog box.

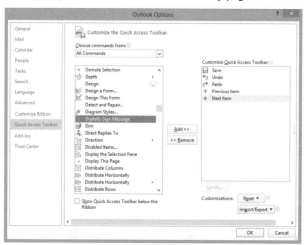

Figure 8-13 Use the Outlook Options dialog box to add the Digitally Sign Message command to the toolbar.

6. Close the message form.

Now whenever you need to digitally sign or encrypt a message, you can click the appropriate button on the Quick Access Toolbar when you compose the message.

Reading signed messages

When you receive a digitally signed message, the Inbox displays a Secure Message icon in place of the standard envelope icon (see Figure 8-14) and shows a Signature button in the Reading Pane. The message form also includes a Signature button (see Figure 8-15). You can click the Signature button in either the Reading Pane or the form to display information about the certificate.

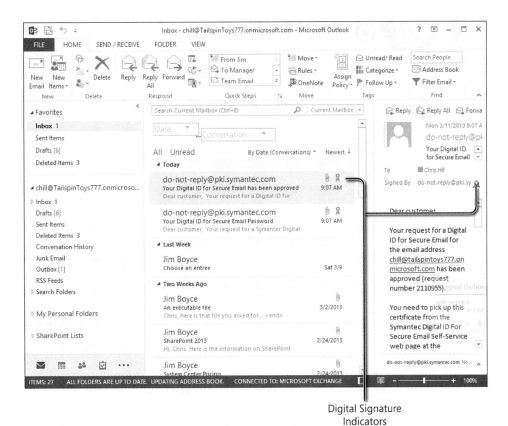

Digital Signature
Indicators

Figure 8-14 Outlook 2013 displays a different icon in the Inbox for secure messages.

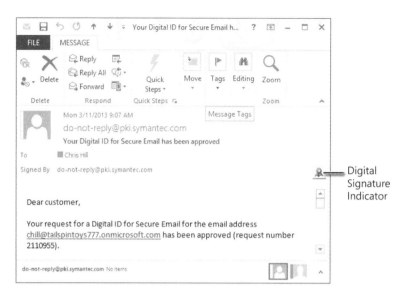

Digital
Signature
Indicator

Figure 8-15 Click the Signature button on the message form to view information about the certificate.

Because Outlook 2013 supports S/MIME, you can view and read a digitally signed message without taking any special action. How Outlook 2013 treats the message, however, depends on the trust relationship of the associated certificate. If there are problems with the certificate, you'll see a message to that effect in the Reading Pane header. You can click the Signature button to view more information about the certificate and optionally change its trust.

There is no danger per se in opening a message with an invalid certificate. However, you should verify that the message really came from the person listed as the sender and is not a forged message.

Changing certificate trust relationships

To have Outlook 2013 authenticate a signed message and treat it as being from a trusted sender, you must add the certificate to your list of trusted certificates. An alternative is to configure Outlook 2013 to inherit trust for a certificate from the certificate's issuer. For example, assume that you have a CA in your enterprise. Instead of configuring each sender's certificate to be trusted explicitly, you can configure Outlook 2013 to inherit trust from the issuing CA—in other words, Outlook 2013 will trust implicitly all certificates issued by that CA.

Follow these steps to configure the trust relationship for a certificate:

1. In Outlook 2013, select the signed message. Click the Digital Signature button to view the Digital Signature dialog box (see Figure 8-16). The dialog box varies depending on whether the signature is valid (trusted) or invalid (not trusted).

Figure 8-16 Use the Digital Signature dialog box to view the status and properties of the digital signature.

2. Click Details, and in the Message Security Properties dialog box, click the Signer line, and then click Edit Trust to display the Trust tab of the View Certificate dialog box, as shown in Figure 8-17.

Figure 8-17 Use the Trust tab to configure the trust relationship for the certificate.

3. Select one of the following options:

- ❍ **Inherit Trust From Issuer**   Select this option to inherit the trust relationship from the issuing CA. For detailed information, see the following section, "Configuring CA trust."

- ❍ **Explicitly Trust This Certificate**   Select this option to trust explicitly the certificate associated with the message if you are certain of the authenticity of the message and the validity of the sender's certificate.

- ❍ **Explicitly Don't Trust This Certificate**   Select this option to distrust explicitly the certificate associated with the message. Any other messages that you receive with the same certificate will generate an error message in Outlook 2013 when you attempt to view them.

4. Click OK, click Close to close the Message Security Properties dialog box, and click Close again to close the Digital Signature dialog box.

For information on viewing a certificate's other properties and configuring Outlook 2013 to validate certificates, see the section "Viewing and validating a digital signature."

Configuring CA trust

Although you might not realize it, your computer system by default includes certificates from several public CAs (typically VeriSign, Thawte, Equifax, GTE, or several others), which were installed when you installed your operating system. By default, Outlook 2013 and other applications trust certificates issued by those CAs without requiring you to trust explicitly each certificate issued by the CA.

The easiest way to view these certificates is through Internet Explorer, as follows:

1. In Internet Explorer, choose Tools, Internet Options, and then click the Content tab. Alternatively, open the Internet Options item from Control Panel.

2. Click Certificates to open the Certificates dialog box (see Figure 8-18). Click the Trusted Root Certification Authorities tab, which contains a list of the certificates.

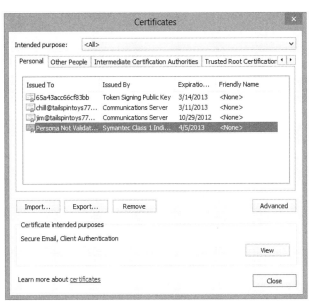

Figure 8-18 You can view a list of certificates in the Certificates dialog box in Internet Explorer.

If you have a personal certificate issued by a specific CA, the issuer's certificate is installed on your computer. Messages you receive that are signed with certificates issued by the same CA inherit trust from the issuer without requiring the installation of any additional certificates. If you have not yet obtained the CA certificate from your enterprise CA, you need to add that CA's certificate to your system before certificates issued by that CA will be trusted.

Follow these steps to connect to a Windows-based enterprise CA to obtain the CA's certificate and install it on your system:

1. Point your web browser to *http://<*machine*>/certsrv*, where *<machine>* is the name or IP address of the CA.

2. After the page loads, select Download A CA Certificate, Certificate Chain, Or CRL.

3. Select Download CA Certificate, and then choose to Open (at this point, you could also save it to your computer if you want to save the certificate file for later use).

4. Click Install Certificate to install the CA's certificate on your system. This will start the Certificate Import Wizard. Click Next.

5. In the Certificate Store dialog box, select Automatically Select The Certificate Store Based Upon The Type Of Certificate. Click Next and then click Finish to add the CA certificate. You will be notified that the import was successful and you will have to click OK twice to close the dialog boxes.

The procedure just outlined assumes that the CA administrator has not customized the certificate request pages for the CA. If the pages have been customized, the actual process you must follow could be slightly different from the one described here.

> **Note**
>
> If you prefer, you can download the CA certificate instead of installing it through the browser. Use this alternative when you need to install the CA certificate on more than one computer and must have the certificate as a file.

Configuring CA trust for multiple computers

The process described in the preceding section is useful when configuring CA trust for a small number of computers, but it can be impractical with a large number of computers. In these situations, you can turn to Group Policy to configure CA trust in a wider area such as an organizational unit (OU), a domain, or an entire site.

You can create a certificate trust list (CTL), which is a signed list of root CA certificates that are considered trusted, and deploy that CTL through Group Policy. This solution requires that you are running the Active Directory Domain Services (AD DS) with desktop clients running Microsoft Windows XP or later as domain members.

> **Note**
>
> The steps in this section for creating and deploying a CTL are for Windows Server 2008. If you are running Windows Server 2003, open the AD Users And Computers console and create a new Group Policy Object (GPO) or edit an existing GPO. In the Group Policy Editor, expand the branch User Configuration\Windows Settings\Security Settings\Public Key Policies\Enterprise Trust, right-click Enterprise Trust, and choose New, Certificate Trust List to start the Certificate Trust List Wizard.

Follow these steps on Windows Server 2008 to create and deploy the CTL:

1. Log on to a domain controller and open the Group Policy Management console.

2. Create a new GPO or edit an existing GPO at the necessary container in AD DS, such as an OU. Select the GPO and in the right pane click More Actions, Edit.

3. In the Group Policy Management Editor, expand the branch User Configuration\
Policies\Windows Settings\Security Settings\Public Key Policies\Enterprise Trust.

4. Right-click Enterprise Trust and choose New, Certificate Trust List to start the Certificate Trust List Wizard.

5. Click Next, and then specify a name and valid duration for the CTL (both optional), as shown in Figure 8-19. Select one or more purposes for the CTL in the Designate Purposes list (in this example, choose Secure Email), and then click Next.

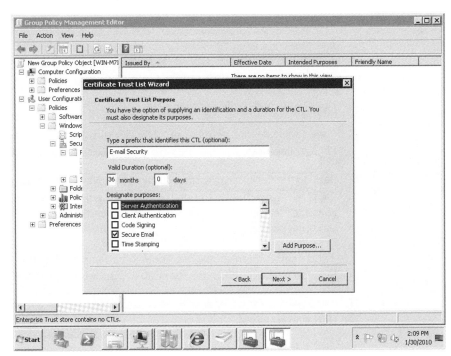

Figure 8-19 Select a purpose for the CTL and other properties, such as a friendly name for easy identification.

6. On the Certificates In The CTL page (see Figure 8-20), click Add From Store to add certificates to the list from the server's certificate store. Choose one or more certificates and click OK.

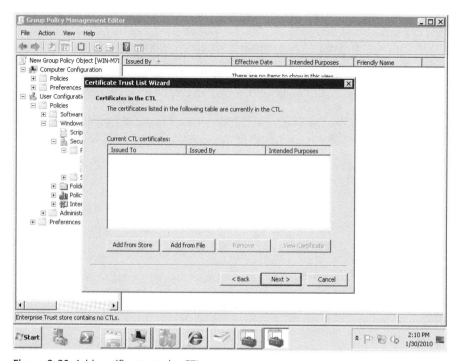

Figure 8-20 Add certificates to the CTL.

7. If the certificates are stored in an X.509 file, Microsoft Serialized Certificate Store, or PKCS #7 certificate file, click Add From File, select the file, and click Open.

8. Back on the Certificates In The CTL page, click Next. On the Signature Certificate page, select a certificate to sign the CTL. The certificate must be stored in the local computer certificate store instead of the user certificate store. Click Next after you select the certificate.

9. If you want, you can choose the Add A Timestamp To The Data option and specify a timestamp service URL if one is available. Otherwise, click Next.

10. If you want, enter a friendly name and description for the CTL to help identify it, click Next, and click Finish.

Viewing and validating a digital signature

You can view the certificate associated with a signed message to obtain information about the issuer, the person to whom the certificate is issued, and other matters.

To do so, follow these steps:

1. Open the message and click the Digital Signature button in either the Reading Pane or the message form, and then click Details to display the Message Security Properties dialog box, which provides information about the certificate's validity in the Description box.

2. Click Signer in the list to view additional signature information in the Description box, such as when the message was signed (see Figure 8-21).

Figure 8-21 The Description box offers information about the validity of the certificate.

3. Click View Details to open the Signature dialog box, shown in Figure 8-22, which displays even more detail about the signature.

Chapter 8

Figure 8-22 Use the Signature dialog box to view additional properties of the signature and to access the certificate.

4. On the General tab of the Signature dialog box, click View Certificate to display information about the certificate, including issuer, certification path, and trust mode.

5. Click OK, click Close to close the Message Security Properties dialog box, and click Close again to close the Digital Signature dialog box.

The CA uses a certificate revocation list (CRL) to indicate the validity of certificates. If you don't have a current CRL on your system, Outlook 2013 can treat the certificate as trusted, but it can't validate the certificate and will indicate this when you view the signature.

You can locate the path to the CRL by examining the certificate's properties as follows:

1. Click the Signature button for the message, either in the Reading Pane or in the message form, and then click Details.

2. In the Message Security Properties dialog box, click Signer and then click View Details.

3. On the General tab of the Signature dialog box, click View Certificate and then click the Details tab (see Figure 8-23).

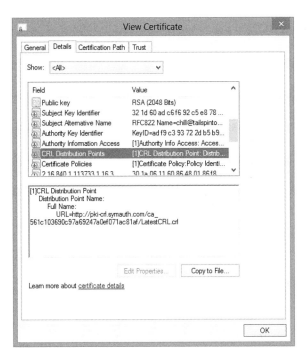

Figure 8-23 Use the Details tab to view the CRL path for the certificate.

4. Scroll through the list to find and select CRL Distribution Points.

5. Scroll through the list in the lower half of the dialog box to locate the URL for the CRL.

When you know the URL for the CRL, you can point your browser to the site to download and install the CRL. If a CA in your enterprise issued the certificate, you can obtain the CRL from the CA.

To obtain and install the CRL, follow these steps:

1. Point your browser to *http://*<machine>*/certsrv*, where <*machine*> is the name or IP address of the server.

2. Select the Retrieve The CA Certificate Or Certificate Revocation List option and click Next.

3. Click Download Latest Certificate Revocation List and save the file to disk.

4. After downloading the file, locate and right-click the file, and then choose Install CRL to install the current list.

Encrypting messages

You can encrypt messages to prevent them from being read by unauthorized persons. Of course, it is true that with significant amounts of computing power and time, any encryption scheme can probably be broken. However, the chances of someone investing those resources in your email are pretty remote. So you can be assured that the email encryption that Outlook 2013 provides offers a relatively safe means of protecting sensitive messages against interception.

Before you can encrypt messages, you must have a certificate for that purpose installed on your computer. Typically, certificates issued for digital signing can also be used for encrypting email messages.

For detailed information on obtaining a personal certificate from a commercial CA or from an enterprise or stand-alone CA on your network, see the section "Obtaining a digital certificate."

Getting ready for encryption

After you've obtained a certificate and installed it on your system, encrypting messages is a simple task. Getting to that point, however, depends in part on whether you're sending messages to an Exchange Server recipient on your network or to an Internet recipient.

Swapping certificates

Before you can send an encrypted message to an Internet recipient, you must have a copy of the recipient's public key certificate. To read the message, the recipient must have a copy of your public key certificate, which means you first need to swap public certificates.

> **Note**
>
> When you are sending encrypted messages to an Exchange Server recipient, you don't need to swap certificates. Exchange Server takes care of the problem for you.

The easiest way to swap certificates is to send a digitally signed message to the recipient and have the recipient send you a signed message in return, as outlined here:

1. In Outlook 2013, click File, Options, Trust Center, Trust Center Settings, and then click the E-mail Security link.

2. Click Settings to display the Change Security Settings dialog box.

3. Verify that you've selected S/MIME in the Cryptography Format drop-down list.

4. Select the Send These Certificates With Signed Messages option and click OK.

5. Click OK to close the Trust Center dialog box.

6. Compose the message and digitally sign it. Outlook 2013 will include the certificates with the message.

When you receive a signed message from someone with whom you're exchanging certificates, you must add the person to your Contacts folder to add the certificate by following these steps:

1. Open the message, right-click the sender's name, and then choose Add To Outlook Contacts. If the Reading Pane is displayed, you can right-click the sender's name in the pane and choose Add To Outlook Contacts.

2. Outlook 2013 displays the contact form. Fill in additional information for the contact as needed, and then save the contact.

3. Open the Contacts folder and display a view other than the People view, and then open the contact you just saved.

4. Click the Certificates button (in the Show group of the Contact tab). You should see the sender's certificate listed (see Figure 8-24), and you can view the certificate's properties by selecting it and clicking Properties. If no certificate is listed, contact the sender and ask for another digitally signed message.

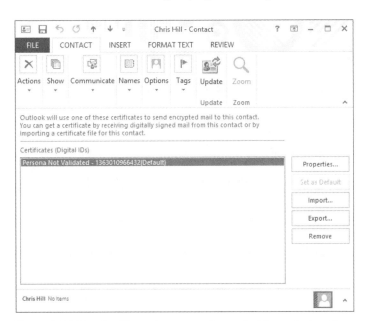

Figure 8-24 The Certificates button on the contact form displays the sender's certificate.

5. Click Save & Close to save the contact item and the certificate.

Obtaining a recipient's public key from a public CA

As an alternative to receiving a signed message with a certificate from another person, you might be able to obtain the person's certificate from the issuing CA. The process for downloading a public key varies by CA. In general, however, you enter the person's email address in a form to locate the certificate, and the form provides instructions for downloading the certificate. You should have no trouble obtaining the public key after you locate the certificate on the CA (there is a link to download the public key certificate from the CA to a file on your computer).

Save the public key to disk, and then follow these steps to install the key:

1. Open the Contacts folder in Outlook 2013, and choose a view other than People.

2. Locate the contact for whom you downloaded the public key.

3. Open the contact item, and then click Certificates.

4. Click Import. Browse to and select the certificate file obtained from the CA and click Open.

5. Click Save & Close to save the contact changes.

Sending encrypted messages

When you have everything set up for sending and receiving encrypted messages, it's simple to send one. Just do the following:

1. Open Outlook 2013 and compose the message.

2. On the Options tab, click the Message Options button in the lower-right section of the More Options group to display the Message Options dialog box, and then click Security Settings.

3. Select Encrypt Message Contents And Attachments, and then click OK.

4. Click Close, and then send the message as you normally would.

5. If the message is protected by Exchange Server security, you can send it in one of three ways, depending on your system's security level:

   ❍ If the security level is set to Medium (the default), Outlook 2013 displays a message informing you of your security setting. Click OK to send the message.

- ◯ If the security level is set to Low, Outlook 2013 sends the message immediately, without any special action on your part.

- ◯ If the security level is set to High, type your password to send the message.

> **Note**
>
> To make it easier to encrypt a message, you can add the Encrypt command to the Quick Access Toolbar in the message form. For details about the process involved in doing this, see the Troubleshooting sidebar "You need a faster way to sign a message digitally."

Reading encrypted messages

When you receive an encrypted message, you can read it as you would any other message, assuming that you have the sender's certificate. Double-click the message to open it. Note that Outlook 2013 uses an icon with a lock instead of the standard envelope icon to identify encrypted messages.

> **Note**
>
> You can't preview encrypted messages in the Reading Pane. Also, the ability to read encrypted messages requires an S/MIME-capable mail client. Keep this in mind when sending encrypted messages to other users who might not have Outlook 2013 or another S/MIME-capable client.
>
> You can verify and modify the trust for a certificate when you read a message signed by that certificate. For information on viewing and changing the trust for a certificate, see the section "Changing certificate trust relationships."

Protecting data with Information Rights Management

In response to market demands for a system with which companies can protect proprietary and sensitive information, Microsoft has developed an umbrella of technologies called Information Rights Management (IRM). Outlook 2013 incorporates IRM, enabling you to send messages that prevent the recipient from forwarding, copying from, or printing the message. The recipient can view the message, but the features for accomplishing these other tasks are unavailable.

Chapter 8

Microsoft has reduced the available options for using IRM in Outlook 2013. With Outlook 2010, you can leverage a free Microsoft-hosted IRM service to send and receive IRM-protected email, using your Windows Live ID as the credentials to authenticate your identity. In Outlook 2013, that capability has been removed and you cannot use the free Microsoft IRM service. Instead, you need to rely on IRM capabilities provided by your Exchange Server provider (whether an on-premise Exchange environment, Office 365, or a service hosted by another provider). In addition, while you can continue to use Microsoft's free service in Office 2010, it's certain that the service will eventually be retired.

However, using the capabilities provided by your Exchange service provider offers more flexibility because the IRM administrator can configure company-specific IRM policies, which are then available to users. For example, the administrator might create a policy template requiring that only users within the company domain can open all email messages protected by the policy. You can create any number of templates to suit the company's data rights needs for the range of Office system applications and document types.

Not everyone who receives an IRM-protected message will be running Outlook 2003 or later, so Microsoft has developed the Rights Management Add-On for Internet Explorer, which enables these users to view the messages in Internet Explorer. Without this add-on, recipients cannot view IRM-protected messages. With the add-on, recipients can view the messages, but the capability to forward, copy, or print the message is disabled, just as it is in Outlook 2013.

Using IRM in Outlook 2013

Assuming your Exchange Server provider or administrator has configured IRM, using IRM to send and receive protected emails is relatively easy. To protect a message, follow these steps:

1. Open a new email form by starting a new message, and then in the message window, click the Options tab.

2. Click the arrow below the Permission button on the ribbon and choose Connect To Digital Rights Management Servers And Get Templates (see Figure 8-25).

Figure 8-25 If no permission templates are already downloaded, Outlook enables you to connect to the digital rights management server to download permission templates.

3. After Outlook retrieves the available IRM templates, click Permission again choose the permission template that you want to apply to the message (see Figure 8-26).

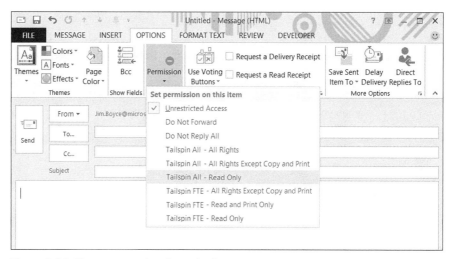

Figure 8-26 Choose a template from the list.

Chapter 8

4. After you choose the permission level, Outlook adds a description of the permission level in the message's header, as shown in Figure 8-27.

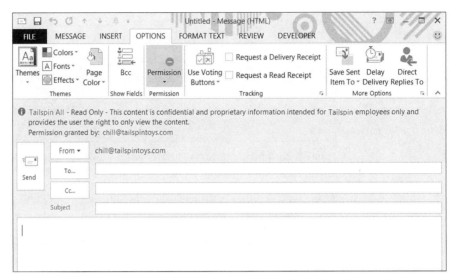

Figure 8-27 Outlook adds a summary of the permission level in the message window.

5. Complete the message as you normally would, and then click Send to send it.

When you receive a rights-protected email, there isn't anything special you need to do to read the email. You can preview and open the message to read it just as you would with an unprotected email.

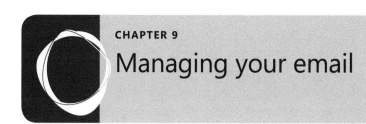

CHAPTER 9

Managing your email

Wᴵᵀᴴᴼᵁᵀ some means of organizing and filtering email, most people would be inundated with messages, many of which are absolutely useless. Fortunately, the Microsoft Outlook 2013 junk email filters can take care of most of, if not all, the useless messages. For the rest, you can use several Outlook 2013 features to help you organize messages, locate specific messages, and otherwise gain control of your Inbox and other folders.

This chapter shows you how to customize your message folder views, which will help you organize your messages. You'll also learn about the Outlook 2013 Search Folders, which give you a great way to locate messages based on conditions that you specify and to organize messages without adding other folders to your mailbox. This chapter also explains how to use categories and custom views to organize your messages.

Using Conversation view

Outlook 2013 includes features for working with message threads, also called *conversations*. A message conversation comprises the original message and all of the replies that result from the original message. Outlook 2013 offers a Conversation view that organizes all the messages in a conversation into an expandable/collapsible branch (see Figure 9-1).

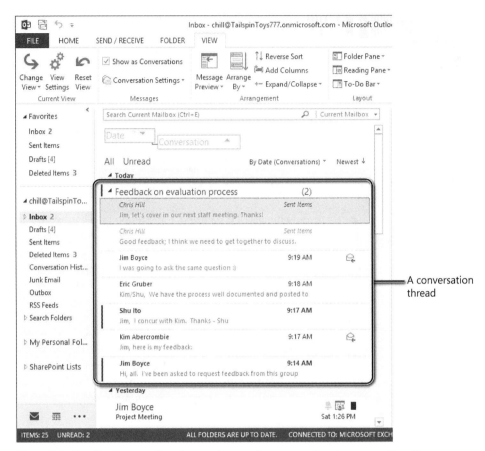

Figure 9-1 Use the Conversation view to show and manage related messages together.

The messages in a conversation need not be in the same folder. In fact, Conversation view works much like a Search Folder (discussed later in this chapter) in that it locates and displays the related messages regardless of where they are located. So, for example, it shows your replies from the Sent Items folder, any replies in your Inbox, and any replies that you have filed in other folders.

If you are using a different view and want to switch to Conversation view, click the View tab on the ribbon and click Show As Conversations in the Messages group. You'll also find a handful of options under the Conversation Settings drop-down list, including the following:

- **Show Messages From Other Folders**   Select this option to have Outlook include related messages from other folders (such as Sent Items) in addition to those in the current folder.

- **Show Senders Above The Subjects**   List all senders for the conversation above the subject line.

- **Always Expand Selected Conversation**   Select this option if you want Outlook to automatically expand a conversation when you select it. Outlook collapses the conversation when you select a different thread.

- **Use Classic Indented View**   Select this option if you want the messages in the conversation to be indented to visually show the order in which you received them.

Cleaning up conversations

Another benefit of the conversation features of Outlook 2013 is the capability to delete messages with duplicated content automatically. For example, assume that you send a message to someone, who sends a reply. You reply to that message, and then you receive another reply. So far, that's four messages. Each time there was a reply, the content of the original message and all the replies were duplicated. So, in reality, the last message contains not only the original message but all the replies. If all you need is the conversation and not the individual messages, why not just delete those first three messages and keep the fourth?

That's a simple scenario, but assume that you sent the message to 10 people, most replied to all at least once, and some messages bounced back and forth between people several times. At the end of the day, you have 30 messages on the same conversation, most of which are essentially duplicates of the others, but some have a little added content that the others don't have.

This is where the conversation cleanup in Outlook 2013 comes into play. It searches through the messages, finds the ones with duplicate content, and deletes them. The ones with unique content, it keeps. The result is that you have all the content from the conversation, but you have reduced the message count by a potentially significant amount, perhaps 50 percent or more. By default, when you run a cleanup, Outlook puts the duplicate messages in the Deleted Items folder of the account in which the messages are stored.

Chapter 9

You have three different levels at which you can run a cleanup: selected conversation, all conversations in the folder, and all conversations in the folder and all subfolders. To clean up a single item, click the conversation and then, on the Home tab of the ribbon, click the Clean Up button and choose Clean Up Conversation (see Figure 9-2). If you want to clean up the whole folder, choose Clean Up Folder or Clean Up Folder & Subfolders, depending on whether you want to get the subfolders, too.

Figure 9-2 Choose Clean Up Conversation to clean up the selected conversation.

Setting cleanup options

As you might have guessed, you have a handful of options that control how conversation cleanup works. To set these options, click File, Options, Mail, and scroll down to the Conversation Clean Up group (see Figure 9-3).

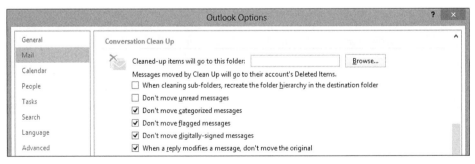

Figure 9-3 Set conversation cleanup options on the Mail page of the Outlook Options dialog box.

The options are generally self-explanatory. You can choose the folder in which to put the cleaned-up messages (by default, the Deleted Items folder), and you can specify whether Outlook will move unread, categorized, flagged, or digitally signed messages. You can also direct Outlook not to move the original message if a reply to that message modifies the original.

> **Note**
>
> Until you remove the messages permanently from the Deleted Items folder, you can recover them just as you would other deleted items. On a Microsoft Exchange Server mailbox, you can recover messages up until the point at which the retention period defined by the Exchange Server administrator causes the messages to be purged from your mailbox.

Ignoring a conversation

No doubt you've received messages that you didn't really need to be copied on or that you simply don't care about. Or, maybe you've received one of those messages where some hapless soul has sent a message to the entire company. Some of those people reply to all, and pretty soon there are people replying to all telling everyone not to reply to all! Don't you wish you could ignore those messages? Well, you can in Outlook 2013.

Click a conversation to select it and then click Ignore in the Delete group on the Home tab of the ribbon. After prompting you to confirm the action, Outlook moves all the current messages in the conversation to the Deleted Items folder (or another folder that you have designated in Outlook Options), and it also automatically moves all future messages in that conversation there as well.

Balancing cleanup against retention

I confess that I am an email pack rat. I have every message from my Exchange Server mailbox for the past several years. What isn't in my mailbox on the server is in one or more .pst files on my hard drive. Conversation cleanup is the middle ground between keeping all those messages and keeping none. You can keep the gist of all your email conversations without keeping every single message. That means potentially keeping your mailbox a more manageable size or having to archive less frequently. In either case, cleaning up the redundant messages reduces storage requirements on your server, your local computer, or both by reducing the sheer number of messages in your mail store.

If you have Exchange Server in your organization, you might already have an archiving solution in place like those from Microsoft, Mimosa Systems, EMC, or others. Generally, these solutions archive all messages that come into your mailbox, eliminating the need for you to archive items to a .pst on your local computer (and thereby avoiding the security risks associated with local .pst files). With an archiving solution in place, conversation cleanup makes even more sense, because all the messages in the conversation will be in your archive if you need them. Clean away!

Finding and organizing messages with Search Folders

The Outlook 2013 Search Folders are an extremely useful feature for finding and organizing messages. A Search Folder isn't really a folder; rather, it's a special view that functions much like a separate folder. In effect, a Search Folder is a saved search. You specify conditions for the folder, such as all messages from a specific sender or all messages received in the last day, and Outlook 2013 displays in that Search Folder view those messages that meet the specified conditions.

In a way, a Search Folder is like a rule that moves messages to a special folder. However, although the messages seem to exist in the Search Folder, they continue to reside in their respective folders. For example, a Search Folder might show all messages in the Inbox and Sent Items folders that were sent by Jim Boyce. Even though these messages appear in the Jim Boyce Search Folder (for example), they are actually still located in the Inbox and Sent Items folders.

Using Search Folders

It isn't difficult at all to use a Search Folder. The Folder List includes a Search Folders branch, as shown in Figure 9-4, that lists all the Search Folder contents. Simply click a Search Folder in the Folder List to view the headers for the messages it contains.

Figure 9-4 Search Folders appear under their own branch in the Folder List.

Customizing Search Folders

A new installation of Outlook 2013 includes a selection of Search Folders by default, which you can use as is or customize to suit your needs. The available Search Folders depend on the services available within your messaging system:

- **Call Logs**   This folder shows a log of incoming and outgoing calls (Exchange and Lync).

- **Fax**   If you are connected to an Exchange Server mailbox with unified messaging enabled, this Search Folder will enable you to see all received faxes in your mailbox.

- **Voice Mail**   If you are connected to an Exchange Server mailbox with unified messaging enabled, this Search Folder shows all received voice-mail messages.

- **Missed Calls**   This folder shows all missed voice calls (Exchange).

- **Missed Conversations**   This folder shows all missed IM conversations (Lync).

To customize an existing Search Folder, open the Folder List, right-click the folder, and then choose Customize This Search Folder to open the Custom Search Folder dialog box, similar to the one shown in Figure 9-5.

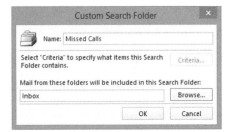

Figure 9-5 Modify a Search Folder using the Custom Search Folder dialog box.

You can change the name of the Search Folder in the Name box in the Custom Search Folder dialog box. To change the criteria for the Search Folder, click the Criteria button to display a dialog box that enables you to change your selection. The dialog box that appears depends on the criteria that you used when you created the folder. For example, if you are modifying a Search Folder that locates messages from a specific sender, Outlook 2013 displays the Select Names dialog box so that you can specify a different person (or additional people).

> **Note**
> You can't modify the criteria for the default Search Folders, but you can specify which folders are included.

To change which folders are included in the Search Folder, click Browse in the Custom Search Folder dialog box to open the Select Folder(s) dialog box. Select each folder that you want to include, or select the Personal Folders or Mailbox branch to include all folders in the mail store in the search. Select the Search Subfolders option to include all subfolders for a selected folder in the search. When you have finished selecting folders, click OK, and then click OK again to close the Custom Search Folder dialog box.

Creating a new Search Folder

If the default Search Folders don't suit your needs, you can create your own Search Folder with the criteria and included subfolders that locate the messages you want. To create a Search Folder, right-click the Search Folders branch, and then choose New Search Folder to open the New Search Folder dialog box, shown in Figure 9-6.

Figure 9-6 Create a new Search Folder with the New Search Folder dialog box.

The New Search Folder dialog box provides several predefined Search Folders, and you can create a custom Search Folder easily by choosing one from the list. If the Search Folder you select requires specifying additional criteria, click the Choose button to open a dialog box in which you specify the criteria. Then, in the New Search Folder dialog box, select an account in the Search Mail In drop-down list to search that account.

> **Note**
>
> The Choose button appears in the New Search Folder dialog box only if the selected Search Folder requires additional configuration, such as the sender's name.

If the predefined Search Folders won't do the trick, scroll to the bottom of the Select A Search Folder list, select Create A Custom Search Folder, and then click Choose to open the Custom Search Folder dialog box to specify a custom criterion for the Search Folder, a Search Folder name, and subfolders to include.

Flagging and monitoring messages and contacts

Outlook 2013 allows you to *flag* a message to draw your attention to the message and display an optional reminder when the follow-up action is due. The flag appears in the message header, as shown in Figure 9-7.

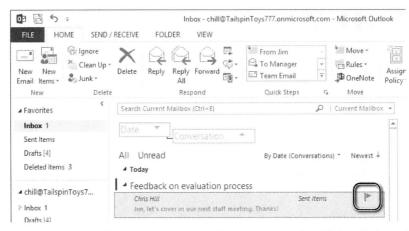

Figure 9-7 You can flag a message to highlight it or to include additional information.

Outlook 2003 offered six flag types, compared with just one in earlier versions. In Outlook 2007 and later (including Outlook 2013), colored flags are replaced by color categories, reducing follow-up flag colors to red and a few shades of pink. You can choose from one of five predefined flags or choose a custom flag. The predefined flags have date specifications of Today, Tomorrow, This Week, Next Week, and No Date. If you choose the custom flag option, you can specify any date you want. The predefined dates therefore give you a quick and easy way to assign a general follow-up date, while the custom option lets you specify a specific date.

See Chapter 5, "Creating and using categories," to learn more about color categories.

Flagging received and previously sent messages

You can flag messages that you've received from others, as well as those you've sent. This capability gives you a way to flag and follow up on messages from your end. You can flag messages in any message folder, including the Sent Items folder.

INSIDE OUT   Add notes to received messages

You can use flags to add notes to messages you receive from others, giving yourself a quick reminder of pending tasks or other pertinent information. Outlook 2013 can generate a reminder for you concerning the flagged item. To set up Outlook 2013 to do so, right-click the message, choose Follow Up, Add Reminder, and then set a due date and time.

Follow these steps to flag a message you have received (or a message that resides in the Sent Items folder):

1. Locate the message that you want to flag.

2. Right-click the message, choose Follow Up, and then select a follow-up period from the cascading menu (Today, Tomorrow, and so on). To specify a custom date, choose Custom.

3. If you chose Custom, enter the follow-up action text in the Flag To field or select an existing action from the drop-down list, and then specify a start date and an end date.

4. Click OK.

Flagging outgoing messages

You can also flag outgoing messages for follow-up for yourself, the recipient, or both. So, the capability to flag an outgoing message lets you set a reminder on the message to follow up on the message yourself. For example, you might send an email message to a coworker asking for information about a project. The follow-up flag could remind you in a week to follow up if you haven't had a response. You can also flag a message to generate a reminder on the recipient's computer.

Use the following steps to flag a message you send:

1. With the message form open prior to sending the message, on the Message tab on the ribbon, in the Tags group, click Follow Up, and then click Add Reminder to open the Custom dialog box, shown in Figure 9-8.

Figure 9-8 Select the flag text or type your own message in the Custom dialog box.

2. In the Flag To drop-down list, select the text you want to include with the flag, or type your own text in this box.

3. If you want to include a due date and a subsequent reminder, select the date in the Due Date drop-down list, which opens a calendar that you can use to select a date. Alternatively, you can enter a date, day, time, or other information as text in the Due Date box.

4. Click OK, and then send the message as you normally would.

Follow these steps to flag a message for follow-up on the recipient's computer:

1. With the message form open prior to sending the message, on the Message tab on the ribbon, in the Tags group, click Follow Up, and then click Add Reminder to open the Custom dialog box.

2. Select the Flag For Recipients option, and then select the follow-up action in the Flag To drop-down list.

3. Specify a reminder, and then click OK.

4. Complete the message, and then send it.

Viewing and responding to flagged messages

A flag icon appears next to the message header for flagged messages in the message folder. If you have configured Outlook 2013 to display the Reading Pane, the flag text appears in the InfoBar. The flag icons also help you to identify flagged messages regardless of whether the Reading Pane is displayed. You can sort the view in the folder using the Flag column, listing all flagged messages together to make them easier to locate. To view the flag text when the Reading Pane is turned off, simply open the message. The flag text appears in the message form's InfoBar.

Outlook 2013 has no special mechanism for processing flagged messages other than the reminders previously discussed. You simply call, email, or otherwise respond based on the flag message. To change the flag status, simply click the flag, or right-click a flagged message and then choose Mark Complete. To remove the flag from the message, right-click the message, and then choose Clear Flag.

Grouping messages by customizing the folder view

To help you organize information, Outlook 2013 allows you to customize various message folder views. By default, Outlook 2013 displays only a small selection of columns for messages, including the From, Subject, Received, Size, Flag, Attachment, and Importance columns.

You can sort messages easily using any of the column headers as your sort criterion. To view messages sorted alphabetically by sender, for example, click the column header of the From column (simple list views only). To sort messages by date received, click the column header of the Received column. Click the Attachment column header to view all messages with attachments.

In addition to managing your message view by controlling columns and sorting, you can *group* messages based on columns. Whereas sorting allows you to arrange messages in order using a single column as the sort criterion, grouping allows you to display the messages in groups based on one or more columns. For example, you might group messages based on sender, and then on date received, and finally on whether they have attachments. This method helps you locate messages more quickly than if you had to search through a message list sorted only by sender.

Chapter 9

Grouping messages in a message folder is a relatively simple process:

1. In Outlook 2013, open the folder that you want to organize.

2. Right-click the column header, and then choose Group By This Field if you want to group based only on the selected field. Choose Group By Box if you want to group based on multiple columns.

Filtering a view using categories

As explained in Chapter 5, color categories in Outlook 2013 make it very easy to identify specific messages or types of messages. For example, you might categorize messages you receive from specific people so that you can see at a glance that a message is from a particular person without grouping on the From field.

In some situations, you might want to customize a view so that you see only messages that fall into certain categories. For example, assume that you have categorized messages for two projects, each with a unique category. Now you want to view all messages from both projects. The easiest way to do that is to filter the view so that it shows only messages with those two categories assigned to them. You can do that using a custom view or a Search Folder. Both of these methods are explained in the section "Viewing selected categories only" in Chapter 5.

Managing email with folders

There are really two types of Outlook users: *searchers* and *filers* (and, of course, those people who are a hybrid of both types). Searchers tend to leave everything in their Inbox and just search for what they want. Filers organize their mailbox using folders, moving messages into various subfolders based on whatever criteria makes sense to them.

I'm a filer, so naturally I think that's the best method for organizing an otherwise chaotic mailbox. There are a couple of benefits to using folders to organize your mailbox. First, you can quickly find messages for specific projects, topics, and so on just by opening the folder where you've filed them. Second, you can still search for messages, even if you have filed them in different folders.

The first step is to create the new folders.

Creating folders

It's easy to create new mail folders:

1. Click the Mail icon in the Folder Pane to open your Inbox.

2. Click the Folder tab in the ribbon, and then click New Folder (see Figure 9-9).

3. In the Create New Folder dialog box (see Figure 9-10), type a name for the new folder in the Name field.

4. Click the folder that will be the root of the subfolder. For example, to create a folder under the Inbox, click the Inbox.

5. Make sure that Mail And Post Items is selected in the Folder Contains drop-down box, and then click OK.

Figure 9-9 Click New Folder in the ribbon to create a new email folder.

Figure 9-10 Use the Create New Folder dialog box to specify the folder name and location.

Chapter 9

Moving messages to other folders

After you create a folder, you're ready to move messages to that folder. The easiest method is to simply drag a message to the desired folder in the Folder List. You also have some other options:

- Select the message and then click Move on the Home tab of the ribbon. If the target folder is listed in the menu, just select it from the menu. Otherwise, click Other Folder and choose the target folder from the resulting dialog box.

- Right-click the message, choose Move, and then choose a folder from the menu or choose Other Folder and choose the target folder from the resulting dialog box.

> **Note**
> You can also copy messages to another folder. Just choose the Copy To Folder command from the Move menu.

Managing email effectively

Before offering tips on effective email management, I'll ask the question, "Why bother?" If you receive a large number of messages, the answer is probably staring you in the face—a chaotic Inbox full of messages. With a little bit of planning and effort, you can turn that Inbox into . . . well . . . an empty Inbox! When you leave the office at the end of the day with an empty Inbox, you'll be amazed at the sense of accomplishment you'll feel.

Here are some tips to help you get control of your mailbox:

- **Use Conversation view**   Take advantage of the new conversation features in Outlook 2013 to help you quickly organize messages by topic, clean up your Inbox, and ignore those inevitable message threads that are just not applicable or of interest to you.

- **Categorize, categorize, categorize**   Categorizing your messages offers several benefits. First, with color categories in Outlook 2013, assigning categories to messages will help you quickly identify specific types of messages. Second, you'll be able to search for messages by category with filtered views, Search Folders, and the search features built into Outlook 2013. You can assign categories manually or assign them automatically with rules. Whatever the case, the more diligent you are in assigning categories, the more useful they will be for finding messages and organizing your mailbox.

- **Organize with folders**   Although you could simply leave all messages in the Inbox, moving messages into other folders will unclutter your Inbox and help you locate messages when you need them. There is no right or wrong way to structure your message folders—use whatever structure and number of folders suits the way you work. What is important is that you organize in a way that suits you.

- **Organize with rules**   Use rules to move messages into other folders, assign categories, and otherwise process messages when they arrive in your Inbox. Rules enable you to organize your messages automatically, potentially saving you an enormous amount of time.

- **Let Search Folders organize for you**   Search Folders are an extremely useful feature in Outlook 2013. With a Search Folder, you can organize messages based on almost any criteria without actually moving the messages from their current locations. Search Folders take very little effort to set up and offer you the benefit of being able to search your entire mailbox for messages that fit the search criteria. You can bring together in one virtual folder all messages in your mail store that fit the search criteria.

Managing junk email

T IRED of wading through a bunch of junk email? Anyone with an email account these days is hard-pressed to avoid unsolicited ads, invitations to multilevel marketing schemes, or unwanted adult content messages. Fortunately, Microsoft Outlook 2013 offers several features to help you deal with all the junk email coming through your Inbox.

Outlook 2010 improved on the junk email and adult content filters in earlier versions of Outlook to provide much better anti-junk-mail features. Outlook 2013 retains those sophisticated filters. As in Outlook 2007, antiphishing measures scan email for suspicious content and automatically disable it. The Junk E-mail folder restricts certain email functionality, displaying email messages as plain text and preventing replies to messages contained in the folder, as well as blocking attachments and embedded links.

Outlook 2013 offers four levels of junk email protection, with Safe Senders and Safe Recipients lists to help you identify valid messages. It also provides a Blocked Senders list to help you identify email addresses and domains that send you junk email, which enables you to exclude those messages from your Inbox. Email can also be blocked based on the originating top-level domain or language encoding used.

How Outlook 2013 junk email filtering works

If you're familiar with the junk email filters in earlier versions of Outlook, you already know a little about how Outlook 2013 filters junk email. Before you start configuring Outlook 2013 to filter your junk email, you should have a better understanding of how it applies these filters.

As described earlier, Outlook 2013 provides four filter levels. To specify the filter level, click Junk in the Delete group of the Home tab of the ribbon, and click the Junk E-mail Options tab to display the Junk E-mail Options dialog box, shown in Figure 10-1. The following sections explain the four filter levels.

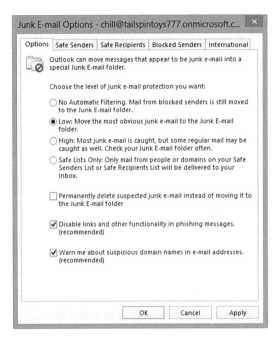

Figure 10-1 Use the Junk E-mail Options dialog box to configure Outlook 2013 to quickly filter unwanted messages.

No Automatic Filtering

This option protects only against mail from individuals and domains in your Blocked Senders list, moving it to the Junk E-mail folder. All other mail is delivered to your Inbox.

Low

This option functions essentially like the junk email and adult content filters in earlier versions of Outlook. Outlook 2013 uses a predefined filter to scan the body and subject of messages to identify likely spam.

You can't specify additional filter criteria for subject or content checking for this junk email filter, although you can create your own custom junk email rules to block messages using additional criteria.

High

This level uses the same filtering as the Low level, but it also uses additional message-scanning logic to determine whether a message is spam. Outlook 2013 scans the message body and message header for likely indications that the message is spam. You do not have any control over this scanning, other than to enable it by choosing the High scanning level.

If you choose the High option, you should not enable the option to delete junk email messages rather than move them to the Junk E-mail folder. Although Outlook 2013 will catch most spam, it will also generate false positives, blocking messages that you expect or want. You should review the Junk E-mail folder periodically and mark any valid messages as not being junk email.

For more information about marking messages in this way, see the section "Marking and unmarking junk email."

Safe Lists Only

This level provides the most extreme message blocking. Only messages originating from senders in your Safe Senders and Safe Recipients lists are treated as valid messages, and all others are treated as junk email.

Although this protection level offers the highest chance of blocking all your junk mail, it also offers the highest chance of blocking wanted messages. To use this level effectively, you should allow Outlook 2013 to place messages in the Junk E-mail folder and review the folder periodically for valid messages. When you find a valid message, add the sender to your Safe Senders list.

Understanding how Outlook 2013 uses the filter lists

Outlook 2013 maintains three lists: Safe Senders, Safe Recipients, and Blocked Senders. Figure 10-2 shows a Blocked Senders list, which blocks all messages from these senders. Messages originating from an address or a domain on the list are filtered out. Entering a domain in the Blocked Senders list blocks all messages from that domain, regardless of the sender. Add *wingtiptoys.com* to the list, for example, and Outlook 2013 will block messages from *joe@wingtiptoys.com, jane@wingtiptoys.com*, and all other email addresses ending in *@wingtiptoys.com*.

Chapter 10

Figure 10-2 Use the Blocked Senders list to block messages by address or domain.

The Safe Senders and Safe Recipients lists identify senders and domains that Outlook 2013 should not filter, regardless of subject or content. Use the Safe Senders list to identify valid messages by their originating address. Use the Safe Recipients list to identify valid messages by their target address. For example, if you participate in a mailing list, messages for that list are sometimes addressed to a mailing list address rather than your own address, such as *list@wingtiptoys.com* rather than *jim@wingtiptoys.com*. Add the mailing list address to the Safe Recipients list to prevent Outlook 2013 from treating the mailing list messages as junk email.

You have two options for adding entries to each of the three filter lists: specify an email address or specify a domain. As mentioned earlier, if you specify a domain, Outlook 2013 blocks or allows (depending on which list) all messages from that domain, regardless of sender. However, Outlook 2013 is rather selective in blocking. Specify *@wingtiptoys.com*, for example, and Outlook 2013 will block messages from *joe@wingtiptoys.com* and *jane@wingtiptoys.com* but will not block messages from *joe@sales.wingtiptoys.com*. You must specify the subdomain explicitly in a list to either accept or block that subdomain. For example, to block the subdomain *sales.wingtiptoys.com*, enter **sales.wingtiptoys.com** in the Blocked Senders list.

INSIDE OUT   Simplify management of filter lists

Outlook 2013 recognizes wildcard characters, so you can simply enter *.<*domain*> to block all messages from a domain and its subdomains. For example, use *.wingtiptoys.com to block *sales.wintiptoys.com*, *support.wingtiptoys.com*, and all other subdomains of *wingtiptoys.com*. You can import and export a filter list, which enables you to move a list between computers or share the list with others. The filter list is simply a text file with a single email address on each line, making it easy to create and manage the list.

Outlook 2013 also lets you specify a set of top-level domains and language encodings to block as part of its junk email filtering. You set these options on the International tab by selecting the desired domains and encodings from the provided lists.

Deleting instead of moving messages

Outlook 2013 by default moves junk email to the Junk E-mail folder, which it creates in your mailbox. The Junk E-mail folder gives you the ability to review your Junk E-mail messages before deleting them. If you prefer, you can configure Outlook 2013 to delete messages instead of placing them in the Junk E-mail folder. As a general rule, you should configure Outlook 2013 to delete messages automatically only after you have spent a month using the Junk E-mail folder, adding senders to your Safe Senders list and otherwise identifying to Outlook 2013 valid messages that have generated false positives.

How Outlook 2013 phishing protection works

Phishing is an attempt to obtain personal information fraudulently by luring you to a web-site and asking you to disclose data such as passwords, credit card numbers, and so on. This website is *spoofed*, or pretending to be a trusted site—sometimes remarkably well—when it is actually a fake site set up to help steal personal information. Phishing is often done by sending email that directs you to the spoofed site. With the widespread use of HTML email, it's easier to disguise the actual destination of a link, and accordingly, it is harder for you to detect the misdirection.

Fortunately, Outlook 2013 contains antiphishing features to help protect you from suspi-cious websites and email addresses. Email messages are evaluated as they arrive, and mes-sages that appear to be phishing are delivered to the Inbox, not the Junk E-mail folder, but are otherwise treated much like junk email, with a number of functions disabled.

Chapter 10

- **Disable Links And Other Functionality In Phishing Messages**   If Outlook 2013 determines that a message appears to be phishing, the message is delivered to the Inbox, but attachments and links in the message are blocked and the Reply and Reply All functions are disabled.

- **Warn Me About Suspicious Domain Names In E-mail Addresses**   This option warns you when the sender's email domain uses certain characters in an attempt to masquerade as a well-known, legitimate business. Leaving this functionality enabled protects you against phishing attacks using spoofed email addresses.

> **Note**
>
> Phishing protection can be functional even when the No Automatic Filtering option is selected and other junk email protection options are disabled.

Enabling and configuring junk email filtering

To begin filtering out unwanted messages, start Outlook 2013 and follow these steps:

1. Open the Inbox folder, and on the Home tab of the ribbon, click Junk and choose Junk E-mail Options to open the Junk E-mail Options dialog box (shown in Figure 10-1).

2. Choose a level of protection on the Options tab, as explained earlier.

3. If you want to delete messages rather than move them to the Junk E-mail folder, select the Permanently Delete Suspected Junk E-mail Instead Of Moving It To The Junk E-mail Folder check box.

4. Select the Disable Links And Other Functionality In Phishing Messages check box to protect against common phishing schemes.

5. If you want to be warned when a domain name appears to be spoofed, select Warn Me About Suspicious Domain Names In E-mail Addresses.

6. Click OK to apply the filter changes.

To configure the lists that Outlook 2013 uses in filtering junk email, start Outlook 2013 and follow these steps:

1. Open the Junk E-mail Options dialog box as described in the previous procedure.

2. Click the Safe Senders tab, and then click Add and enter the email address or domain of the sender that you want Outlook 2013 to deliver to your Inbox, regardless of content or subject. Click OK, and then repeat this procedure for each sender that you want to add.

3. On the Safe Senders tab, select the Also Trust E-mail From My Contacts check box if you want Outlook 2013 to always accept email from senders in your Contacts folder, regardless of content or subject. You can also choose to select the Automatically Add People I E-mail To The Safe Senders List check box.

4. Click the Safe Recipients tab, and add the target addresses or domains for which Outlook 2013 should allow messages (used typically to accept email sent to a mailing list).

5. Click the Blocked Senders tab, and add the addresses or domains of junk email senders whose messages you want Outlook 2013 to explicitly block.

6. Click the International tab, and select the top-level domains and types of language encoding that Outlook 2013 should always block.

7. Click OK to apply the filter changes.

Controlling automatic downloads

Images and other online content present another potential hazard in email because you usually, at minimum, confirm that your email address is valid when you download this content. Content from unknown sources can also be malicious, containing Trojan horses, viruses, and so on.

The Trust Center, shown in Figure 10-3, lets you decide when Outlook 2013 should download external content in email messages, Really Simple Syndication (RSS) items, and Microsoft SharePoint discussion boards. (To open the Trust Center, click File, Options, Trust Center, Trust Center Settings.) The Safe Senders and Safe Recipients lists can be used to determine downloading settings, as can Security Zones.

Chapter 10

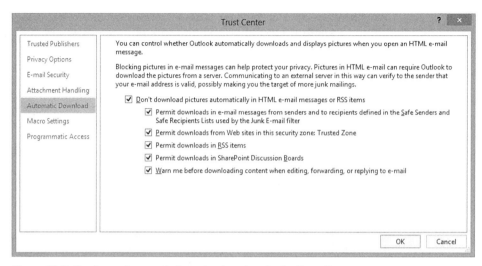

Figure 10-3 Configure Automatic Download options in the Trust Center.

The Automatic Download options are described in the following list:

- **Don't Download Pictures Automatically In HTML E-mail Messages Or RSS Items** This setting prevents images from downloading to your computer automatically, except as directed by additional settings on this page. Blocking automatic image downloads protects you from spammers who use your connection to their server to verify your identity as well as from malicious content (a Trojan horse disguised as an image, for example).

- **Permit Downloads In E-mail Messages From Senders And To Recipients Defined In The Safe Senders And Safe Recipients Lists Used By The Junk E-mail Filter** You can tell Outlook 2013 to use the safe lists that you have created to determine which images it will download automatically. This lets you see images from those sources that you have already decided you trust while blocking other images.

- **Permit Downloads From Web Sites In This Security Zone: Trusted Zone** Content that resides on a website included in the Trusted Zone is downloaded automatically when this setting is enabled. This lets you receive images and other content from trusted sources, such as corporate servers or partners, based on a common list, reducing the amount of configuration needed.

- **Permit Downloads In RSS Items** Control over images downloading in RSS feeds is configured separately, allowing you to block images in RSS feeds without affecting email messages.

- **Permit Downloads In SharePoint Discussion Boards**   You can configure whether to download content from SharePoint discussion boards separately, offering you greater control over the content that is downloaded to your computer.

- **Warn Me Before Downloading Content When Editing, Forwarding, Or Replying To E-mail**   If this setting is enabled, Outlook 2013 will warn you before downloading content in messages that you are replying to, forwarding, or editing. If you choose not to download the images and continue with your actions, Outlook 2013 will remove the images from the message, and the recipient will not be able to retrieve them.

Configuring automatic downloading of external content

To configure image downloading, start Outlook 2013, and then follow these steps:

1. Click File, Options, Trust Center, Trust Center Settings, and then select Automatic Download to view the options for handling image downloads (shown in Figure 10-3).

2. To stop Outlook 2013 from automatically downloading images, select the Don't Download Pictures Automatically In HTML E-mail Messages Or RSS Items check box.

> **CAUTION**
>
> If the Don't Download Pictures Automatically In HTML E-mail Messages Or RSS Items check box is not selected, all other options on this page will be unavailable, and all images will be displayed, creating potential security risks.

3. If you want to view images from sources that you trust, select the Permit Downloads In E-mail Messages From Senders And To Recipients Defined In The Safe Senders And Safe Recipients Lists Used By The Junk E-mail Filter check box.

4. To allow sites that you trust to download images, select Permit Downloads From Web Sites In This Security Zone: Trusted Zone.

5. If you want to view images in RSS feeds, select Permit Downloads In RSS Items.

6. To view images from SharePoint sites, select Permit Downloads In SharePoint Discussion Boards.

7. If you want Outlook 2013 to alert you that images are being downloaded when you take action on an email message, select Warn Me Before Downloading Content When Editing, Forwarding, Or Replying To E-mail.

8. Apply the changes by clicking OK.

Chapter 10

Marking and unmarking junk email

The junk email filters in Outlook 2013 might not catch all the messages that you consider to be junk. You can mark and unmark messages as junk mail easily without opening the Junk E-mail Options dialog box. When you receive a message that is junk but that Outlook 2013 does not place in the Junk E-mail folder (or delete), right-click the message, choose Junk, and then choose the list to which you want the sender added. You also can add the sender to the Blocked Senders list (choose Block Sender) if you want.

If Outlook 2013 marks a message as junk mail and moves it to the Junk E-mail folder but you don't want the message treated as junk mail, you can mark the message as not junk (essentially, unmark the message). Open the Junk E-mail folder, right-click the message, and choose Junk, Not Junk. Outlook 2013 displays a Mark As Not Junk dialog box. If you click OK without taking any other action, Outlook 2013 moves the message back to the Inbox. Select the Always Trust E-mail From option to also have the sender's email address added to the Safe Senders list. Any address that message was sent to can also be added to the Safe Recipients list.

> **Note**
> If the message is from a sender inside your organization, you do not have the option of adding that sender to the Safe Senders list, either from the shortcut menu or from the Mark As Not Junk dialog box, because that individual is already categorized as a safe sender.

Creating other junk email rules

Once you configure it and make adjustments for false positives, the filtering technology built into Outlook 2013 can be an effective tool for waging your daily fight against junk email. The filtering technology in Outlook 2013 isn't perfect, however, so you might need to handle junk email in other ways. One technique is to create your own rules to handle exceptions that the built-in filters can't adequately address.

You can create rules that look explicitly for keywords or phrases in the subject or body of a message or look for specific other criteria and then move those messages to the Junk E-mail folder (or delete them). See Chapter 11, "Using rules, alerts, and automatic responses," for details on creating and working with rules.

Reply or unsubscribe?

Although you might be tempted to have Outlook 2013 automatically send a nasty reply to every piece of spam you receive, resist the urge. In many cases, the spammer's only way of knowing whether a recipient address is valid is when a reply comes back from that address. You make your address that much more desirable to spammers when you reply, because they then know that there's a person at the address. The best course of action is to delete the message without looking at it.

In the past, many spammers also used unsubscribe messages to identify valid addresses, which made unsubscribing to a particular spammer a hit-or-miss proposition. In some cases, the spammer would delete your address, and in others, it would simply add your address to the good email address list. With state and federal laws like CAN-SPAM and individuals and companies becoming more litigious, spammers more often than not heed unsubscribe requests. Just a few years ago, I would have recommended that you not bother unsubscribing to spam. Today, you will likely have at least a little better luck unsubscribing to spam without generating a flood of new messages. However, you should still approach the problem with caution.

Other spam-filtering solutions

The spam-blocking features in Outlook 2013 can help considerably in blocking unwanted messages, but there are other options that you should consider in addition to the Outlook 2013 filtering technologies.

Filtering in Exchange Server

If your company or organization uses Microsoft Exchange Server, you can perform some spam-filtering tasks right at the server without adding third-party software. Exchange Server 2003 and later support domain filtering for virtual Simple Mail Transfer Protocol (SMTP) servers.

Exchange Server 2007 and 2010 offer some additional features not included in Exchange Server 2003, making them potentially more effective for blocking spam. One server in an organization is designated as the Edge Transport server and is responsible for mail flow and control between internal email servers and the Internet. By default, only unauthenticated, inbound email from the Internet is filtered, although internal email can also be filtered if desired.

Chapter 10

Exchange Server 2007 and 2010 can filter email based on a number of different criteria, including the following:

- **Content**   Email messages are examined to see whether they have characteristics of spam and are checked against a safe list aggregated from the Safe Senders lists of Outlook 2007 and 2010 users within the organization.

- **Attachment**   Attachments can be filtered based on either the Multipurpose Internet Mail Extensions (MIME) type of the file or the file name. Administrators can choose to strip the attachment and deliver the message or reject the message, either with a failure message to the sender or silently.

- **Connection**   Email is evaluated based on the Internet Protocol (IP) address of the server that is attempting to send the message using a variety of safe and blocked lists to determine whether the message should be delivered.

- **Recipient**   The addresses that the email is sent to are compared to a local directory and an administrator-managed blocked list to determine what to do with the email.

- **Sender**   Like the Recipient filter, this filter uses a locally maintained blocked list to block certain addresses from sending email to the organization.

- **Sender ID**   The sending system's Domain Name System (DNS) server is queried to determine whether the IP address of the system that originated the message is authorized to send email from that domain. This verification process protects you against spoofed email addresses, a ploy commonly used by spammers and phishers alike.

- **Sender Reputation**   This feature collects information about email senders and evaluates incoming email based on a number of characteristics to assign a Spam Confidence Level (SCL) rating. This rating determines whether the message is delivered, and the rating is passed to other computers running Exchange Server when the message is sent to them.

If you are responsible for administering a computer running Exchange Server, you will find additional information in the Help files provided with Exchange Server.

Using third-party filters

Several third-party antispam solutions are available that you can consider for your organization. For example, Symantec's Mail Security for Microsoft Exchange Server provides content scanning and filtering capabilities. Mail Security filters incoming messages for content, spyware, adware, and attachment file types (not just file name extensions).

Mail Security is available for Exchange Server, Domino, and SMTP servers. You'll find more information about Mail Security at *http://www.symantec.com/ mail-security-for-microsoft-exchange*.

Another product to consider is GFI MailEssentials (*http://www.gfi.com/exchange-server- antispam-antivirus*). MailEssentials provides several levels of content filtering with support for blocked lists, safe lists, and additional header-checking options that enable it to detect and block spam based on a broad range of criteria.

These are just a few of the solutions available for filtering and managing messages. Many mail servers offer their own filtering capabilities, and many other products provide filtering services for existing mail servers.

One of the most prevalent spam-filtering solutions is SpamAssassin, which is based on an open-source heuristic scanning application developed originally for UNIX-based servers. You can find information about open-source SpamAssassin at *http://spamassassin.apache.org*.

Managing junk email effectively

Email is a critical tool for most people, but it can also be a frustration when you feel overwhelmed by junk email. By using the features provided in Outlook 2013 and taking a few additional steps, you can greatly reduce the amount of junk email that you receive and the corresponding risks:

- **Use the Outlook 2013 junk email filters and phishing protection** The default option of Low on the Options tab in the Junk E-mail Options dialog box provides some protection, but it might not be enough. You may want to raise the level to High and check your Junk E-mail folder regularly to ensure that Outlook 2013 is not sending legitimate messages there. Use the International tab in the Junk E-mail Options dialog box to block top-level domains from which you never want to receive messages or to block messages in specific languages.

- **Use the Safe Senders and Blocked Senders lists** Building both your safe and blocked lists will make a considerable difference in how well Outlook 2013 can filter your email.

Chapter 10

- **Update the Outlook 2013 junk email filters regularly**   Updates for Outlook 2013 can be obtained by clicking File, Help, Check For Updates. You can also download updated filters from *http://office.microsoft.com/en-us/*.

- **Disable functionality that can confirm your identity inadvertently**   Features like read and delivery receipts and automatic acceptance of meeting requests can confirm your identity to a spammer. Outlook 2013 lets you configure receipt processing for Internet email differently from messages within your corporate network so that you can leave receipts on for your business contacts while disabling them for messages from outside the organization.

- **Guard your primary email address**   Many people have a secondary email address—often from a free public provider such as Outlook.com or Google mail—that they use when posting on message boards, newsgroups, and so on. Even so, you might want to change your email address when posting it in public by changing the @ symbol to *AT* or inserting extra characters (such as *chrisHillREMOVE@wingtiptoys.com*). This can help prevent automated gathering of your address by spammers' robots.

- **Don't reply to spam**   Even a seemingly simple unsubscribe message confirms that your email address is valid, so unless you know the sender, just delete the message.

- **Don't automatically download images and other online content**   Spammers can verify your email address when you connect to the server to download the external content in a message. Online content is blocked by default, and it's a good idea to leave it that way. You can download content for an individual message by right-clicking the message box telling you that the content has been blocked and then selecting Download Pictures.

- **Don't forward chain email**   These messages clutter up inboxes, expose email addresses, and are all too often hoaxes. If you absolutely must forward a message, send it to only the few people who will definitely be interested, and use the Bcc option for their email addresses.

- **Never provide personal information in email**   Even with a trusted correspondent, you should avoid sending critical data such as credit card or Social Security numbers in unencrypted email.

- **Don't provide personal information to links you get in email**   If you get email that appears to be from a company that you do business with, don't assume it actually is. Most email that provides a link and asks for personal data is spoofed in an attempt to get you to disclose this information. If you think the email might be valid, type the URL of the business into your browser rather than clicking the link in the email message to be sure you end up at the correct site.

- **Read each website's privacy policy**   Get in the habit of checking a website's privacy policy before providing your email address to the site. Sure, this can take a minute or two, but it takes longer than that to handle the spam that you will get if a site misuses or sells your email address. Most websites explain what they do with the information they collect; you might want to carefully consider whether to provide any information to those that do not.

- **Keep antivirus, spyware, and firewall protection up to date**   Outlook 2013 can help you avoid most junk email and the associated threats, but the most effective protection is a multilayered approach. You should also install firewall and antivirus software and make sure that it is kept up to date. You might also want to obtain utilities that protect against spyware and other malicious software.

Chapter 10

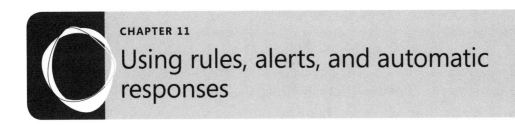

Using rules, alerts, and automatic responses

I F you receive a lot of messages, you might want to have the messages analyzed as they come in, to perform actions on them before you read them. For example, you can have all messages from a specific account sent to a specific folder. Perhaps you want messages that come from specific senders to be assigned high priority. Microsoft Outlook 2013 lets you manipulate your incoming messages to achieve the results that you want. This chapter shows you how to do this, starting with an overview of message rules and ending with an explanation of how to create automated alerts.

Understanding message rules

A *message rule* defines the actions that Outlook 2013 takes for a sent or received message if the message meets certain conditions specified by the rule. For example, you might create a rule that tells Outlook 2013 to move all messages from a specific sender or with a certain subject into a specified folder rather than leaving them in your default Inbox. Or you might want Outlook 2013 to place a copy of all outgoing high-priority messages in a special folder.

In Outlook 2013, you use one or more conditions for defining a message rule. These conditions can include the account from which the message was received, the message size, the sender or recipient, specific words in various fields or in the message itself, the priority assigned to the message, and a variety of other conditions. In addition, you can combine multiple actions to refine the rule and further control its function. For example, you might create a rule that moves all your incoming POP3 messages to a folder other than the Inbox and also deletes any messages that contain certain words in the Subject field. Although not a complete list, the following are some of the most common tasks you might perform with message rules:

- Organize messages based on sender, recipient, or subject.

- Copy or move messages from incoming or outgoing messages to a folder.

- Flag messages.

- Delete messages automatically.

- Reply to, forward, or redirect messages to individuals or distribution lists.

- Respond to messages with a specific reply.

- Monitor message importance (priority).

- Print a message.

- Play a sound.

- Execute a script or start an application.

For details on how to generate automatic replies to messages, see the sections "Creating automatic responses with Automatic Replies (Out of Office)" and "Creating automatic responses with custom rules."

Whatever your message-processing requirements, Outlook 2013 probably offers a solution through a message rule, based on either a single condition or multiple conditions. You also can create multiple rules that work together to process your mail. As you begin to create and use message rules, keep in mind that you can define a rule to function either when a message is received or when it is sent. When you create a rule, you specify the event to which the rule applies.

Rather than focusing on defining rules for specific tasks, this chapter explains the general process of creating rules. With an understanding of this process, you should have no problem setting up rules for a variety of situations.

Creating and using rules

In Outlook 2013, you can create either client-side or server-side rules. Outlook 2013 stores client-side rules locally on your computer and uses them to process messages that come to your local folders, although you also can use client-side rules to process messages on computers running Microsoft Exchange Server. A client-side rule is needed when you're moving messages to a local folder instead of to a folder on the computer running Exchange Server. For example, if messages from a specific sender that arrive in your Exchange Server Inbox must be moved to one of your personal folders, the rule must function as a client-side rule because the computer running Exchange Server is not able to access your personal folders (and your computer might not even be turned on when the message arrives in your mailbox on the server).

Server-side rules reside on the computer running Exchange Server instead of on your local computer, and they can usually process messages in your Exchange Server mailbox whether or not you're logged on and running Outlook 2013. The Automatic Replies feature (also called Out of Office Assistant) is a good example of how server-side rules can be used. It processes messages that come into your Inbox on the server even when your computer is turned off and you're a thousand miles away. So long as Exchange Server is up and functioning, the server-side rules can perform their intended function.

When you create a rule, Outlook 2013 examines the rule's logic to determine whether it can function as a server-side rule or a client-side rule. If it can function as a server-side rule, Outlook 2013 stores the rule on the computer running Exchange Server and treats it as a server-side rule. If the rule must function as a client-side rule, Outlook 2013 stores it locally and appends (client-only) after the rule name to designate it as a client-side rule. Figure 11-1 shows two rules in Outlook 2013, one that functions as a client-side rule and another that functions as a server-side rule.

> **Note**
> If you don't use an Exchange Server account, all rules that you create are client-side rules.

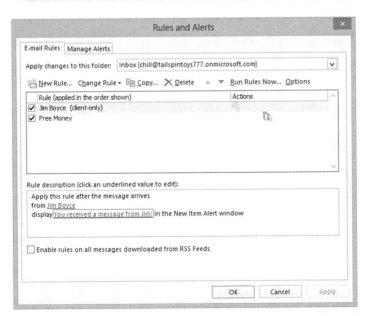

Figure 11-1 Outlook 2013 supports server-side rules as well as client-side rules.

Chapter 11

TROUBLESHOOTING

Your server-side rules don't execute

Server-side rules, which process messages arriving in your Exchange Server Inbox, usually can execute when Outlook 2013 isn't running. In some cases, however, server-side rules can't function unless Outlook 2013 is running and you're connected to the server.

When a server-side rule is unable to process a message because Outlook 2013 is offline (or for other reasons), the computer running Exchange Server generates a deferred action message (DAM), which it uses to process the message when Outlook 2013 comes back online. When Outlook 2013 goes online, it receives the DAM, performs the action, and deletes the DAM.

For information about how to apply client-side rules to specific folders or to all accounts, see the section "Applying rules to specific folders or all folders."

Creating new rules from existing items

Outlook 2013 offers a handful of ways to create a rule. For example, you can click a message, and on the Home tab, click Rules in the Move group. Outlook offers options to create rules based on the sender or recipient, and the number of options varies depending on the message itself (see Figure 11-2). Click an option to open the Rules And Alerts dialog box, choose a folder, and click OK. Outlook will create a rule to move messages based on your selections.

Figure 11-2 Use the options offered in the ribbon to create a rule based on the current message.

If you need to create a new rule for the currently selected message with different actions (such as creating a rule based on the subject of the message), click the message and, on the Home tab, click Rules in the Move group and choose Create Rule. Outlook displays the Create Rule dialog box shown in Figure 11-3.

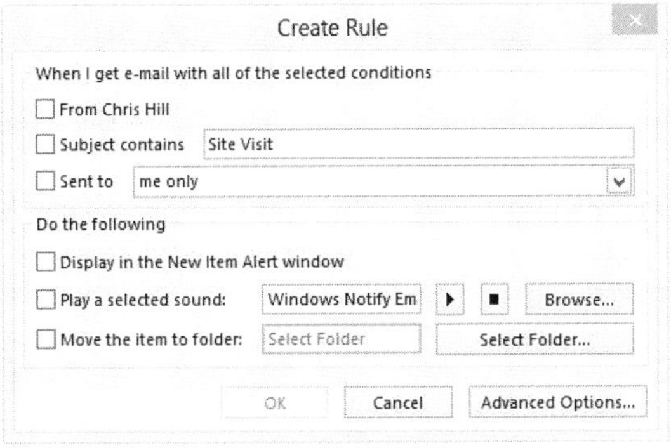

Figure 11-3 Use the Create Rule dialog box to create more complex rules.

The Create Rule dialog box offers properties based on the selected message, including sender, subject, and recipient. Choose the criteria for your rule using any combination of these three, and then choose an action from the Do The Following group of controls. Click OK to create the rule. Outlook names the rule according to the criteria you selected, such as the sender's name and the subject.

Create new rules using the Rules Wizard

When you need more complex rules, need to perform tasks other than moving messages, or want to create a rule that is not based on a specific message, you can turn to the Rules Wizard. You can open the Rules Wizard in a couple of ways:

- To create a rule based on a selected message, with a message selected, on the Home tab, click Rules in the Move group, and then click Create Rule.

- To create a general rule, on the Home tab, click Rules in the Move group and then choose Manage Rules & Alerts. In the Rules And Alerts dialog box, click New Rule.

You'll first see the Rules And Alerts dialog box, shown in Figure 11-1. The E-mail Rules tab contains all the existing rules that you have defined. Outlook 2013 applies the rules in the order in which they are listed, an important fact to consider when you're creating rules. You might use certain rules all the time and others only at special times. Each rule includes a check box beside it. Select this check box when you want to use the rule; clear it when you want to disable the rule.

> **Note**
> You can't open the Rules And Alerts dialog box if you are working offline with an Exchange Server account.

For more information about determining the order in which message rules execute, see the section "Setting rule order."

When you create a message rule using the Rules Wizard, you must first specify whether you want to create the rule from a predefined template or from scratch. Because the templates address common message processing tasks, using a template can save you a few steps. When you create a rule from scratch, you set up all the conditions for the rule as you create it. You can use many different conditions to define the actions the rule performs, all of which are available in the Rules Wizard. With or without a template, you have full control over the completed rule and can modify it to suit your needs. The Outlook 2013 templates are a great way to get started, however, if you're new to using Outlook 2013 or message rules.

Let's look first at the general procedure for creating rules and then at more specific steps. The general process is as follows:

1. Select the Inbox in which the rule will apply. For example, if you have an Exchange Server account and a Post Office Protocol (POP) account, you must choose the Inbox to which the rule will apply.

> **Note**
> The number of Inboxes offered in the Apply Changes To This Folder drop-down list on the E-mail Rules tab depends on the number of accounts in your Outlook profile and how they are configured to deliver mail. Accounts that use their own mail stores, such as Internet Message Access Protocol (IMAP) and Windows Live accounts, will have their own entries in this drop-down list.

2. Specify when the rule applies—that is, when a message is received or when it is sent.

3. Specify the conditions that define which messages are processed—for example, account, sender, priority, or content.

4. Specify the action to take for messages that meet the specified conditions—for example, move, copy, or delete the message; change its priority; flag it for follow-up; or generate a reply.

5. Create other message rules to accomplish other tasks as needed, including possibly working in conjunction with other rules.

6. Set the order of rules as needed.

> **Note**
> When you specify multiple conditions for a rule, the rule combines these conditions
> in a logical AND operation—that is, the message must meet all the conditions to be
> considered subject to the rule. You also can create rules that use a logical OR operation,
> meaning that the message is subject to the rule if it meets any one of the conditions. For
> details, see the section "Creating rules that use OR logic."

The following steps guide you through the more specific process of creating a
message rule:

1. On the Home tab, click Rules in the Move group and choose Manage Rules & Alerts
    to display the Rules And Alerts dialog box.

2. In the Apply Changes To This Folder drop-down list, select the folder to which
    you want to apply the rule. If you have only one Inbox, you don't need to make a
    selection (none is available).

3. Click New Rule to display the wizard page shown in Figure 11-4.

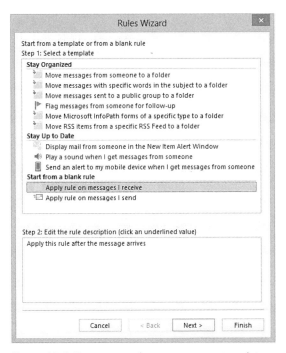

Figure 11-4 To create a rule, you can use a template or start from scratch.

4. If you want to use a template to create the rule, select the template from the list, and then click Next. To create a rule from scratch, choose Apply Rule On Messages I Receive or Apply Rule On Messages I Send, and then click Next.

5. In the Step 1: Select Condition(s) list in the top half of the wizard page shown in Figure 11-5, select the conditions that define the messages to which the rule should apply. For template-based rules, a condition is already selected, but you can change the condition and add others as necessary.

6. In the Step 2: Edit The Rule Description area of the wizard page (see Figure 11-5), click the underlined words that specify the data for the conditions. For example, if you're creating a rule to process messages from a specific account, click the word *specified*, which is underlined, and then select the account in the Account dialog box. Click OK, and then click Next.

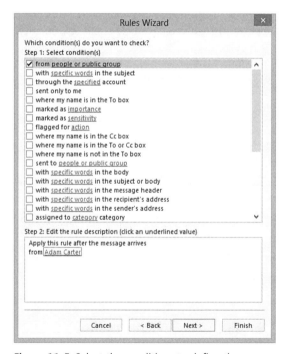

Figure 11-5 Select the conditions to define the messages to which the rule will apply.

7. In the Step 1: Select Action(s) area of the new wizard page, select the actions that you want Outlook 2013 to apply to messages that satisfy the specified conditions. For example, Figure 11-6 shows a rule that displays an alert for messages if they meet the rule's condition.

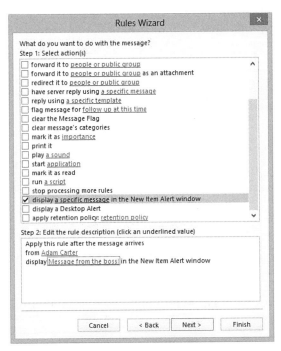

Figure 11-6 Select the actions that Outlook 2013 should take for messages that meet the rule's conditions.

8. In the Step 2: Edit The Rule Description area of the wizard page, click each underlined value needed to define the action, and then specify the data in the resulting dialog box. Click OK to close the dialog box, and then click Next.

9. In the Step 1: Select Exception(s) (If Necessary) area of the wizard page, select exceptions to the rule if needed, and specify the data for the exception conditions, as shown in Figure 11-7. Click Next.

Chapter 11

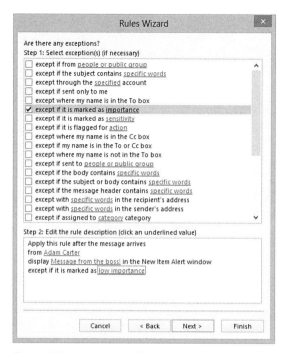

Figure 11-7 You can specify exceptions to the rule to fine-tune message processing.

10. On the final page of the Rules Wizard, shown in Figure 11-8, specify a name for the rule as you want it to appear in Outlook 2013.

Figure 11-8 Configure a name and options for the rule.

11. A message appears telling you that the rule will run only on the messages for the email Inbox you selected at the beginning of these steps. Select options according to the following list, and then click Finish:

○ **Run This Rule Now On Messages Already In "Inbox"** Select this check box if you want Outlook 2013 to apply the rule to messages that you have already received and that currently reside in the Inbox folder in which the rule applies. For example, if you have created a rule to delete messages from a specific recipient, any existing messages from the recipient are deleted after you select this check box and click Finish to create the rule.

○ **Turn On This Rule** Select this check box to begin applying the rule that you have created.

○ **Create This Rule On All Accounts** Select this check box to apply the rule to all applicable folders. For example, if you have three folders listed in the Apply Changes To This Folder drop-down list at the top of the initial Rules Wizard page, selecting this check box causes Outlook 2013 to apply the rule to all three folders instead of only the selected folder.

Chapter 11

For more details on using rules in various folders, see the following section, "Applying rules to specific folders or all folders."

> **Note**
>
> To create a rule that operates on all messages, don't specify a condition that Outlook 2013 must check. Outlook 2013 prompts you to verify that you want the rule applied to all messages.

Applying rules to specific folders or all folders

When you first open the Rules And Alerts dialog box, it displays the rules that have already been defined for your profile, both client-side and server-side, as shown earlier in Figure 11-1. You might recall that you use the Apply Changes To This Folder drop-down list at the top of the dialog box to select the folder for which you want to create or modify a rule. The rules that appear in the list depend on the folder that you select, showing only the rules that apply to the selected folder.

To apply a rule to a specific folder, select that folder in the Apply Changes To This Folder drop-down list when you begin creating the rule. To apply a rule to all folders, select the Create This Rule On All Accounts option at the completion of the wizard (as explained in the preceding section).

Copying rules to other folders

By default, Outlook 2013 doesn't create rules for all folders; instead, it creates the rule only for the selected folder. If you have created a rule for one folder but want to use it in a different folder, you can copy the rule to the other folder. Follow these steps to do so:

1. Choose Tools, Rules And Alerts to open the Rules And Alerts dialog box.

> **Note**
>
> If necessary, choose the target folder from the Apply Changes To This Folder list.

2. Select the rule that you want to copy, and then click Copy.

3. When you're prompted in the Copy Rules To dialog box, select the destination folder for the rule, and then click OK.

For details on sharing rules with other Outlook 2013 users, see the section "Sharing rules with others."

Creating rules that use OR logic

Up to now, you've explored relatively simple rules that function based on a single condition or on multiple AND conditions. In the latter case, the rule specifies multiple conditions and applies only to messages that meet all the conditions. If a rule is defined by three AND conditions, for example, Outlook 2013 uses it only on messages that meet condition 1, condition 2, and condition 3.

You also can create rules that follow OR logic. In this case, a rule specifies a single condition but multiple criteria for that condition. The rule will then act on any message that meets at least one of the criteria for the condition. For example, you might create a rule that deletes a message if the subject of the message contains any one of three words. If one of the conditions is met (that is, if the subject of a message contains at least one of the three words), Outlook 2013 deletes that message.

With Outlook 2013, you can create several rules that use OR logic within a single condition, but you can't create a single rule that uses OR logic on multiple conditions. For example, you might create a rule that deletes a message if the message contains the phrase "MLM," "Free Money," or "Guaranteed Results." However, you can't create a message rule that deletes the message if the subject of the message contains the words *Free Money* (condition 1), or if the message is from a specific sender (condition 2), or if the message is larger than a given size (condition 3). OR must operate within a single condition. When you create a rule with multiple conditions, Outlook 2013 always treats multiple conditions in the same rule using AND logic. You would have to create three separate rules to accommodate the latter example.

If you have a situation where you need to check for more than one piece of data in a single condition, you can do so easily enough; however, when you create the rule and define the condition, specify multiple items. For example, if you need a rule that processes messages based on three possible strings in the subject of the messages, click Specific Words in the rule description area of the Rules Wizard, where you specify rule conditions. In the Search Text dialog box, enter the strings separately. As you can see in Figure 11-9, the search list includes the word *or* to indicate that the rule applies if any one of the words appears in the subject.

Figure 11-9 Specify data separately to create a rule that uses OR logic.

Although you can't create a single rule with OR logic operating on multiple conditions in Outlook 2013, you can create rules that combine AND and OR logic. For example, you might create a rule that applies if the message arrives at a specific account and the subject contains the words *Free Money* or *Guaranteed Results*. Keep in mind that you must specify two conditions—not one—to build the rule. The first condition checks for the account, and the second checks for the words *Free Money* or *Guaranteed Results*.

Consider the following example:

1. On the Home tab, click Rules, Manage Rules & Alerts.

2. In the Rules And Alerts dialog box, click New Rule.

3. Click Apply Rule On Messages I Receive, and then click Next.

4. Select Through The Specified Account.

5. Select With Specific Words In The Subject.

6. At the bottom of the dialog box, click Specified, and then in the Account dialog box, select the email account and click OK.

7. Click Specific Words at the bottom of the dialog box to open the Search Text dialog box.

8. Type **Free Money**, and then click Add.

9. Type **Guaranteed Results**, click Add, and then click OK.

Look at the rule conditions in the Step 2 area of the dialog box. The rule indicates that it will act on messages that are from the specified account and that have the text *Free Money* or *Guaranteed Results* in the message.

Modifying rules

You can modify a rule at any time after you create it. Modifying a rule is much like creating one. To modify a rule, on the Home tab, click Tools, Manage Rules & Alerts to open the Rules And Alerts dialog box. Select the rule that you want to modify, and then click Change Rule to display a menu of editing options. If you choose Edit Rule Settings on the menu, Outlook 2013 presents the same options you saw when you created the rule, and you can work with them the same way. Click Rename Rule to change the name of the rule, or click an action to add the selected action to the rule (retaining any existing actions).

Controlling rules

Rules can be an effective tool for managing messages, but you also need to manage your rules to make them effective overall. For example, you need to consider the order in which rules run, control how and when rules run, and even disable or remove rules. The following sections explain how to control your rules.

Setting rule order

Outlook 2013 executes rules for incoming messages when they arrive in the Inbox, whether on the server or locally (depending on whether the rules are client side or server side). Outlook 2013 executes rules for outgoing messages when the messages arrive in the Sent Items folder.

As mentioned earlier, the order in which rules are listed in Outlook 2013 determines how Outlook 2013 applies them. In some situations, the sequence could be important. Perhaps you have one rule that moves high-priority messages to a separate folder and another rule that notifies you when high-priority messages arrive. For the latter rule to work properly, it needs to execute before the one that moves the messages, because the notification rule won't execute if the messages are no longer in the Inbox.

You can control the order of Outlook 2013 rules easily by taking the following steps:

1. On the Home tab, click Rules, Manage Rules & Alerts to open the Rules And Alerts dialog box.

2. Select a rule to be moved.

3. Use the Move Up and Move Down buttons to change the order in the list, as shown in Figure 11-10. Rules execute in the order listed, with the rule at the top executing first and the one at the bottom executing last.

Chapter 11

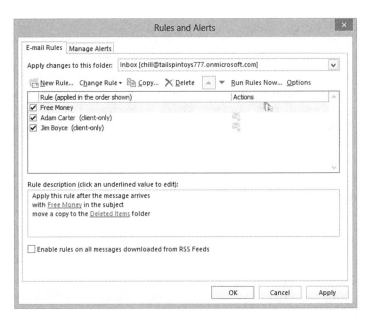

Figure 11-10 You can control execution order for rules by rearranging the rules list.

> **Note**
>
> The Rules And Alerts dialog box can show information and alerts if there are additional rules created with a different version of Outlook or with Outlook Web Access (OWA). For example, you may have a server-side mobile alert rule that sends an alert to your mobile phone when a message arrives with importance set to High. The mobile alert rules do not appear in the Rules And Alerts dialog box.

Stopping rules from being processed

In certain cases, you might want your message rules to stop being processed altogether. Perhaps someone has sent you a very large message that is causing your connection to time out or is taking a long time to download. You would like to create a rule to delete the message without downloading it, but you don't want any of your other rules to execute. In this case, you would place a new rule at the top of the list and define it so that the last action it takes is to stop processing any other rules. In effect, this allows you to bypass your other rules without going through the trouble of disabling them.

You can also use the Stop Processing More Rules action to control rule execution in other situations. To stop Outlook 2013 from executing other rules when a message meets a specific condition, include Stop Processing More Rules as the last action for the rule. You'll find this action in the What Do You Want To Do With The Message? list in the Rules Wizard.

Disabling and removing rules

In some cases, you might want to turn off message rules so that they don't execute. Perhaps you use a rule to do routine cleanup on your mail folders but don't want the rule to run automatically. Or perhaps you want to create a rule to use only once or twice but you would like to keep it in case you need it again later. In those cases, you can disable the rule. To do this, on the Home tab, click Rules, Manage Rules & Alerts, and then clear the check box for that rule in the list. Only those rules with check boxes that are selected will apply to incoming or outgoing messages.

If you don't plan to use a rule again, you can remove it by opening the Rules And Alerts dialog box, selecting the rule, and then clicking Delete.

Sharing rules with others

By default, Outlook 2013 stores server-side rules on the computer running Exchange Server and stores client-side rules on your local system. Regardless of where your message rules are stored, you can share them with others by exporting the rules to a file. You can then send the file as an email attachment or place it on a network share (or a local share) to allow other users to access it. You can also export the rules to create a backup of them for safekeeping or in case you need to move your Outlook 2013 rules to a new computer, as explained in the next section.

Follow these steps to export your message rules to a file:

1. On the Home tab, click Rules, Manage Rules & Alerts.

2. In the Rules And Alerts dialog box, click Options.

3. In the Options dialog box, shown in Figure 11-11, click Export Rules, and then select a path for the file in the resulting Save Exported Rules As dialog box (a standard file save dialog box).

Chapter 11

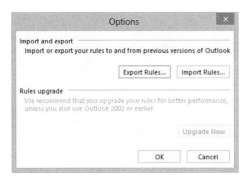

Figure 11-11 Use the Options dialog box to import and export rules.

4. To save the rules using Outlook 2002, Outlook 2000, or Outlook 98 format, select the appropriate format in the Save As Type drop-down list. Otherwise, leave the selection as Rules Wizard Rules.

5. Click Save.

You can export your rules in any of four formats, depending on the version of Outlook used by the people with whom you want to share your rules. If you need to share with various users, export using the earliest version of Outlook. Later versions will be able to import the rules because they are forward-compatible.

> **Note**
>
> If you are sharing rules with someone else, at this point, you have a rules file that you can send to the other person. The following section explains how to restore rules, which is the process that the other person would use to import your rules.

Backing up and restoring rules

Outlook 2013 stores server-side rules in your Exchange Server mailbox, so in principle, there is no reason to back up your server-side rules. I say "in principle" because that point of view assumes that the Exchange Server administrator is performing adequate backups of your mailbox so that you won't lose your messages or your rules. It's still a good idea to back up server-side rules just in case, using the method explained in the "Sharing rules with others" section.

Outlook 2013 stores client-side rules in the default mail store—that is, the .pst file defined in your Outlook 2013 profile as the location for incoming mail. Storing the rules in the .pst file simplifies moving your rules to another computer because you are also likely to move your .pst file to the other computer to retain all your Outlook 2013 items. To make this process work, however, you need to add the .pst file to the second computer in a certain way.

Outlook 2013 checks the default mail store .pst file for the rules, but it doesn't check any other .pst files that you might have added to your profile. Therefore, if you added an email account to the profile and then added the .pst file from your old system, you won't see your rules.

One of the easiest methods for making sure things get set up correctly is to add the .pst file to your profile before you add the email account. Then when you add the account, Outlook 2013 uses the existing .pst file as the default store. The result is that your rules will be available without any additional manipulation.

Here's how to make that happen:

1. Open the Mail item in Control Panel.

2. In the Mail Setup dialog box, click Show Profiles.

3. Click Add, type a name for the profile, and then click OK.

4. Click Cancel. When asked whether you want to create a profile with no email accounts, click OK.

5. Click Properties to open the newly created profile.

6. Click Data Files to display the Data Files tab in the Account Settings dialog box.

7. Click Add and in the Create Or Open Outlook Data File dialog box, browse to and select the .pst file that contains your rules, and then click OK.

8. In the Account Settings dialog box, click the newly added data file, and then click Set As Default.

9. Add your email accounts to the profile.

10. Click Close, click Close again, and then click OK to close the profile properties.

When you start Outlook 2013, you should now have access to the rules stored in the .pst file, plus all your existing Outlook 2013 items.

Chapter 11

Using rules to move messages between accounts

One common task that users often want to perform is to move messages between accounts. Assume that you have two accounts: an Exchange Server account for work and a POP3 account for personal messages. When certain messages come into your Exchange Server mailbox, you want them to be moved automatically to the .pst file for your other account. In this case, it's a simple matter to move the personal messages from the Exchange Server Inbox to the POP3 Inbox. Just create a rule that moves messages that meet the specified conditions to your POP3 Inbox.

> **Note**
> Before you run through these steps to create a rule for moving messages based on their account, create a folder to contain the messages.

Here's how to accomplish this:

1. On the Home tab, click Rules, Manage Rules & Alerts to open the Rules And Alerts dialog box.

2. Click New Rule, and in the Rules Wizard, select Apply Rule On Messages I Receive and then click Next.

3. Select Through The Specified Account. In the rule description area, click the underlined word *specified*, select your Exchange Server account, and then click OK.

4. Choose the other conditions that define the messages that you want moved between accounts, and click Next.

5. Select Move It To The Specified Folder, and then click the underlined word *specified* in the rule description area.

6. Select the folder in your .pst file to which the messages should be moved, and then click OK and Next.

7. Specify any exceptions to the rule, and then click Next again.

8. Specify a name for the rule and other options as needed, and then click Finish.

Running rules manually and in specific folders

Normally you use message rules to process messages when they arrive in your Inbox or are placed in the Sent Messages folder. However, you also can run rules manually at any time. Perhaps you have created a rule that you want to use periodically to clean out certain types of messages or move them to a specific folder. You don't want the rule to operate every time you check mail; instead, you want to execute it only when you think it's necessary. In this case, you can run the rule manually.

You might also want to run a rule manually when you need to run it in a folder other than the Inbox. For example, assume that you've deleted messages from a specific sender and now want to restore them, moving the messages from the Deleted Items folder back to your Inbox. In this situation, you could create the rule and then execute it manually in the Deleted Items folder.

It's easy to run a rule manually and in a specific folder by following these steps:

1. On the Home tab, click Rules, Manage Rules & Alerts.

2. Click Run Rules Now. Outlook 2013 displays the Run Rules Now dialog box.

3. Select the rule that you want to run in the list, as shown in Figure 11-12. By default, Outlook 2013 will run the rule in the Inbox unless you specify otherwise. Click Browse to browse for a different folder. If you also want to run the rule in subfolders of the selected folder, select the Include Subfolders check box.

Figure 11-12 Use the Run Rules Now dialog box to run a rule manually in a specified folder.

4. In the Apply Rules To drop-down list, select the type of messages on which you want to run the rule (All Messages, Read Messages, or Unread Messages).

5. Click Run Now to execute the rule, or click Close to cancel.

Creating and using Quick Steps

Quick Steps are a feature in Outlook 2013 that you can use to process messages automatically in a way similar to the way rules work. In fact, if you've read through the rest of this chapter, Quick Steps should make a lot of sense to you. If you have worked with rules much, you'll also quickly come to appreciate how easy it is to create and use Quick Steps. Let's start with an explanation of what they are.

Quick Steps overview

In a nutshell, Quick Steps are rules that you can apply to one or more messages whenever you need. Outlook 2013 includes several predefined Quick Steps, and you can also create your own. Unlike rules, Quick Steps don't have conditions. Instead, they contain one or more actions that are executed when you apply the Quick Step to one or more items.

For example, you might create a Quick Step to mark the selected message as read, send a predefined reply, set a category on the message, and then move it to a folder. Those actions are then performed on whatever message(s) you apply it to.

> **Note**
> Quick Steps are available only for email and other message types, like Really Simple Syndication (RSS) messages.

Using the default Quick Steps

To see the list of available Quick Steps, open a message folder and, on the Home tab of the ribbon, click the Manage Quick Steps button in the lower-right corner of the Quick Steps group. The default Quick Steps are shown in the Manage Quick Steps dialog box (see Figure 11-13). The Manage Quick Steps dialog box (explored in the next section) displays all the Quick Steps, including the following:

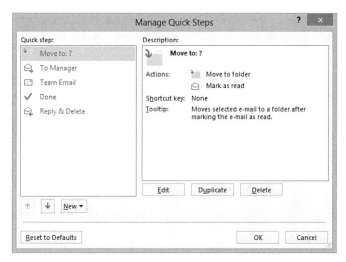

Figure 11-13 The Manage Quick Steps dialog box shows a list of predefined Quick Steps.

- **Move To: ?** Moves the selected message to a folder that you choose and then marks the message as read.

- **To Manager** Forwards the selected message to your manager. With Exchange Server accounts, Outlook automatically identifies your manager from the Manager field in Active Directory Domain Services (AD DS). If this field is incorrect, you can modify the Quick Step to specify the correct recipient address.

- **Team Email** Creates a new email addressed to everyone who reports to you. As with the To Manager Quick Step, this one uses the Manager field in AD DS to determine who reports to you. You can modify the recipient list if needed.

- **Done** Flags the message as complete, moves it to a folder that you choose, and marks the message as read.

- **Reply & Delete** Replies to the message and then deletes the original.

These default Quick Steps are not fully defined the first time you use them. The Move To: ? Quick Step, for example, prompts you to select a folder, specify the Inbox, or choose an option to always be prompted to select a folder. From that point on, the Quick Step retains those settings and you don't have to set them again (unless you want to modify the Quick Step). The name of the Move To: ? Quick Step changes to the name of the folder that you select (if you choose one rather than select the Inbox or have Outlook prompt you for a folder). Here's an example:

Chapter 11

1. Open the Inbox, click a message, and, on the Home tab of the ribbon, click Move To: ?. Outlook displays the First Time Setup dialog box (see Figure 11-14).

Figure 11-14 Configure the Quick Step using the First Time Setup dialog box.

2. In the Name text box, enter a new name for the Quick Step.

3. From the Move To Folder drop-down list, choose the desired destination for the message, or choose Always Ask For Folder if you want the Quick Step to prompt you to select the folder each time you use the Quick Step.

4. Click Save.

Your Quick Step is now customized, and the selected messages are moved and marked as read. If you want to reset the Quick Step to its default, on the Home tab, click the Manage Quick Steps button in the lower-right corner of the group. Then click Reset To Defaults. This will reset all changes you have made to the Quick Steps, including deleting new Quick Steps that you have created.

CAUTION

Click the Reset To Defaults button with care. You don't want to delete your custom Quick Steps accidentally.

Creating your own Quick Steps

As indicated in the previous section, you can modify the default Quick Steps as well as create your own. Modifying the existing ones uses much the same process as creating a new one, so let's take a look at that process.

Creating simple Quick Steps from predefined options

Outlook includes some partially defined Quick Steps to save a little time in creating your own. These include Quick Steps that perform the following actions on messages: move, categorize and move, flag and move, create a new message, forward a message, and create a meeting request. To create one of these Quick Steps, click the Manage Quick Steps button in the Quick Steps group on the ribbon to open the Manage Quick Steps dialog box shown earlier in Figure 11-13.

Click New, and then choose one of the predefined Quick Step types. Outlook displays the First Time Setup dialog box, similar to the one shown in Figure 11-14. Specify a name, make your selections, and click Finish.

Creating custom Quick Steps

You can also create custom Quick Steps that perform multiple actions that you specify. To create a new custom Quick Step, follow these steps:

1. On the Home tab, click the Create New option in the Quick Steps group. Outlook displays the Edit Quick Step dialog box shown in Figure 11-15.

Figure 11-15 Create or edit a Quick Step using the Edit Quick Step dialog box.

Chapter 11

2. In the Name field, type a name for the Quick Step. You can use a long name, but a short name will fit in the ribbon better.

3. From the drop-down list in the Actions group, choose the first action that you want the Quick Step to take.

4. If you want to add another action, click Add Action. Outlook adds another Choose An Action drop-down list to the Actions group. Choose the desired action, and then repeat the process to add any other actions as needed.

5. If you want to assign a shortcut key to the Quick Step so that you can start it from the keyboard, choose one from the Shortcut Key drop-down list.

6. If you want to add a tooltip that will appear when you pause the mouse over the Quick Step (to help you remember what it is for), type the text in the Tooltip Text field.

7. Click Finish.

Your new Quick Step should appear in the Quick Steps group on the ribbon. To use it, select one or more messages and then click the Quick Step on the ribbon.

Editing Quick Steps

Editing a Quick Step involves almost the same process as creating one. Click Manage Quick Steps in the Quick Steps group on the ribbon to open the Manage Quick Steps dialog box. Select the Quick Step you want to modify, and then click Edit. Outlook displays the Edit Quick Step dialog box, shown in Figure 11-15, which you can use to modify its settings as needed. Click Save when you are satisfied with your changes.

Copying Quick Steps

You can save some time creating a Quick Step by duplicating an existing one. Outlook copies all the settings to a new Quick Step, which you can customize as needed and save with a new name. To copy a Quick Step, click Manage Quick Steps on the ribbon, select the Quick Step that you want to copy, and click Duplicate. Outlook opens the Edit Quick Step dialog box with a copy of the Quick Step named Copy of *<original Quick Step name>*. Modify as needed and click Finish.

Using Quick Steps effectively

Quick Steps make common actions available at the click of a button. There is no right or wrong way to use them, and people will have a different set of Quick Steps that they use most often, depending on how they use Outlook, whether they use it at work or home, and other factors. To get the most out of this feature, take some time to think about the actions that you perform frequently in Outlook, and then create Quick Steps for those actions.

Here's a list of some common uses for Quick Steps to help stimulate your imagination:

- Move messages to a frequently used folder to organize your Inbox.

- Start a new message to your manager or to the people who work for you.

- Create a new meeting request to your team or manager.

- Categorize a message and move it to a folder.

- Set messages as read or unread.

- Flag a message for follow-up for a specific period of time.

- Create a task for yourself or assign a task based on the selected message.

- Create an appointment or meeting based on the selected message.

Creating automatic responses with Automatic Replies (Out of Office)

One of the key features in Outlook 2013 that makes it a great email client is the Automatic Replies (Out of Office) feature, formerly called the Out of Office Assistant, which lets you automatically generate replies to incoming messages when you aren't in the office. For example, if you're going on vacation for a couple of weeks and won't be checking your email, you might want to have the Automatic Replies (Out of Office) feature send an auto-matic reply to let senders know that you'll respond to their messages when you get back, or you might do something similar when you are traveling for the day.

The Automatic Replies (Out of Office) feature is a Microsoft Exchange Server feature. To learn how to create automatic responses with custom rules for use with other email servers, see the section "Creating automatic responses with custom rules" later in this chapter.

Before you start learning about the Automatic Replies (Out of Office) feature, take a few minutes to consider a few other issues that relate to managing email when you're out of the office.

Chapter 11

First, the Automatic Replies (Out of Office) feature is a server-side component for Exchange Server. This means that you can use it to process mail sent to your Exchange Server account but not your POP3, Internet Message Access Protocol (IMAP), or other email accounts, unless those accounts deliver incoming messages to your Exchange Server Inbox. You can create rules to process your other accounts and simulate the function of the Automatic Replies (Out of Office) feature, but you must do this by creating custom rules.

Second, because the Automatic Replies (Out of Office) feature functions as a server-side component, it processes your messages even when Outlook 2013 isn't running (a likely situation if you're scuba diving off the Great Barrier Reef for a couple of weeks). To process your other accounts with custom Automatic Replies (Out of Office) rules, Outlook 2013 must be running and checking your messages periodically. If you have a direct Internet connection, you can configure the rules, configure your send/receive groups to allow Outlook 2013 to check messages for non–Exchange Server accounts periodically, and leave Outlook 2013 running. If you have a dial-up connection to these accounts, you'll have to also configure Outlook 2013 to dial when needed and disconnect after each send/receive operation.

Understanding Automatic Replies (Out of Office) features

The features available in the Automatic Replies (Out of Office) feature depend on the version of Exchange Server that your account resides on. In Exchange Server 2003 and earlier, as soon as you turn on the Out of Office Assistant, Exchange Server responds to received messages by replying with your specified Out of Office reply. It continues to send Out of Office replies until you turn off the Out of Office Assistant. Exchange Server 2007, 2010, and 2013, on the other hand, let you specify the time period when you will be out. You don't have to turn on or turn off the assistant—just specify the start date and end date for the time you will be out of the office, and during that time, Exchange Server will respond with Out of Office replies.

Another difference in Exchange Server 2007, 2010, and 2013 is the capability to specify different behavior for external and internal Out of Office messages. For example, you might want to offer more information in the Out of Office message that you send to coworkers, such as who will be handling issues while you are gone, but omit that information from replies sent to people outside your organization. You or your Exchange Server administrator can control how replies are sent to specific external domains. For example, your organization might want to allow Out of Office replies to go to business partners in specific companies but not to other senders or specific domains, such as Microsoft Outlook.com, Yahoo!, and so on. The Automatic Replies (Out of Office) feature (or Out of Office Assistant) in Exchange Server 2007, 2010, and 2013 can also be configured not to send replies to junk mail. In addition, you can now use fonts, colors, and formatting in your replies.

> **Note**
>
> Because the Automatic Replies (Out of Office) feature is a server-side feature, you can take advantage of the Automatic Replies (Out of Office) feature (or Out of Office Assistant) in Exchange Server 2007, 2010, and 2013 from other versions of Outlook in addition to Outlook 2013.

Using the Automatic Replies (Out of Office) feature is easy. Here's the process in a nutshell:

1. Specify the text that you want Outlook 2013 to use for automatic replies when you're out of the office.

2. If necessary, create custom rules for the computer running Exchange Server to use to process incoming messages during your absence.

   For information about custom Out of Office rules, see the section "Creating custom Automatic Replies (Out of Office) rules" later in this chapter.

3. Turn on the Automatic Replies (Out of Office) feature, which causes the Automatic Replies (Out of Office) feature to start responding to incoming messages. Alternatively, if you are using an Exchange Server 2007, 2010, or 2013 account, you can specify the Automatic Replies (Out of Office) feature (or Out of Office Assistant) startup time, and Exchange Server will respond accordingly.

4. When you get back, turn off the Automatic Replies (Out of Office) feature so that it stops processing messages (unless you are using Exchange Server 2007 or later, where you can specify the end date for the Out of Office rule).

> **Note**
>
> When you start Outlook 2013, it checks to see whether the Automatic Replies (Out of Office) feature is turned on. If it is, Outlook 2013 displays a message below the ribbon indicating that Out of Office is turned on. After the Automatic Replies (Out of Office) feature is set up and functioning, messages that arrive in your Inbox receive an Out Of Office response with the message text that you've specified. Exchange Server keeps track of the send-to list and sends the Out of Office response the first time that a message comes from a given sender. When subsequent messages from that sender are sent to your Inbox, an Out of Office response is no longer sent. This procedure cuts down on the number of messages generated and keeps the senders from becoming annoyed by numerous Out of Office replies.

> **Note**
>
> Exchange Server deletes the send-to list for Out of Office responses when you turn off the Automatic Replies (Out of Office) feature from Outlook 2013.

Using the Out of Office Assistant with Exchange Server 2003 and earlier

Follow these steps to specify the text for automatic replies and to tell the computer running Exchange Server 2003 or earlier that you're out of the office:

1. In Outlook 2013, select the Exchange Server Inbox, and then click File, Automatic Replies.

2. In the Automatic Replies dialog box, shown in Figure 11-16, type the body of your automatic message reply in the AutoReply box. While the Out of Office Assistant is active, Exchange Server uses this message to reply to incoming messages.

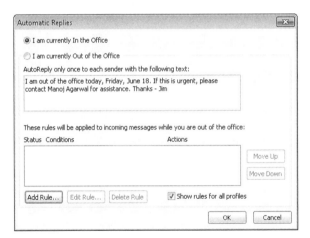

Figure 11-16 Use the Automatic Replies dialog box to specify your automatic message reply.

3. Select I Am Currently Out Of The Office, and then click OK.

Using the Automatic Replies (or Out of Office Assistant) feature for Exchange Server 2007, 2010, and 2013

Follow these steps to specify the text for automatic replies and to tell Exchange Server 2007 or later that you're out of the office:

1. In Outlook 2013, select the Exchange Server Inbox, and then click File, Automatic Replies.

2. In the Automatic Replies dialog box, shown in Figure 11-17, click Send Automatic Replies.

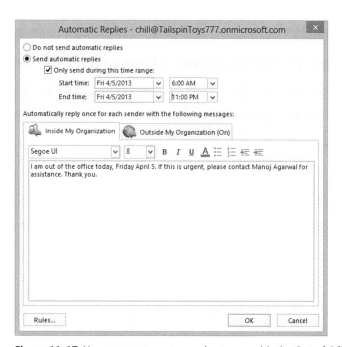

Figure 11-17 You can create custom rules to use with the Out of Office Assistant.

3. Choose Only Send During This Time Range and then use the Start Time drop-down list to specify the starting date and time when you will be out of the office.

4. Use the End Time drop-down list to specify the date and time that you will return to the office.

Chapter 11

5. Click in the Inside My Organization box, and then type your Out of Office reply. If you want to enhance your message, use fonts and other options from the formatting tools on the Out of Office toolbar.

6. Click the Outside My Organization tab, and then specify the message that you want sent to people outside your organization.

7. When you are satisfied with the message(s), click OK.

> **Note**
>
> If you want to turn off Out of Office replies, click File and click Turn Off in the Automatic Replies (Out of Office) area.

Creating custom Automatic Replies (Out of Office) rules

With the Automatic Replies (Out of Office) tool, you can create custom rules to use in addition to the basic automatic reply. To create a custom rule, open the Automatic Replies dialog box, click Rules, and then click Add Rule to display the Edit Rule dialog box, as shown in Figure 11-18.

Figure 11-18 You can create custom rules to use with the Automatic Replies (Out of Office) feature.

The options in the Edit Rule dialog box are straightforward, particularly if you're experienced at creating rules. Specify the conditions that the incoming messages should meet, and then specify the action that Exchange Server should perform if a message meets those conditions.

If you need more help creating and using rules, see the "Creating and using rules" section earlier in this chapter.

When you define the conditions, keep in mind that the Automatic Replies conditions can be met by either full or partial matches. For example, you could type **yce** in the Sent To box, and the rule would apply if the address contained Joyce, Boyce, or Cayce. If you want the condition to be met only if the full string is found, enclose the text in quotation marks—for example, type **"Boyce"**.

Creating automatic responses with custom rules

The Automatic Replies (Out of Office) feature is great for generating automatic replies to messages that arrive in your Inbox when you're out of the office. However, the Automatic Replies feature sends an Out of Office response only the first time a message arrives from a given sender. Subsequent messages go into the Inbox without generating an automatic response.

In some cases, you might want Outlook 2013 to generate automatic replies to messages at any time or for other types of accounts that do not use Exchange Server. Perhaps you've set up an Internet email account to take inquiries about a product or service that you're selling. You can create a rule to send a specific reply automatically to messages that come in to that account. Alternatively, you might want people to be able to request information about specific products or topics by sending a message containing a certain keyword in the subject line. In that case, you can create a rule to generate a reply based on the subject of the message.

> **Note**
> In web jargon, applications or rules that create automatic responses are often called *autoresponders*.

You create automatic responses such as these not by using the Automatic Replies feature, but by creating custom Outlook 2013 rules with the Rules Wizard. As with other rules, you specify conditions that incoming messages must meet to receive a specific reply. For

Chapter 11

example, you might specify that an incoming message must contain the text *Framistats* in its subject to generate a reply that provides pricing on your line of gold-plated framistats. (Note that the text need not be case sensitive.)

> **Note**
>
> You aren't limited to specifying conditions only for the subject of an incoming message. You can use any of the criteria supported by the Outlook 2013 rules to specify the conditions for an automatic response.

Setting up the reply

When you use a custom rule to create an automatic response, you don't define the reply text in the rule. Rather, you have two options: specifying a template on your local computer or setting up a specific message on the server. If you opt to use a template on your local computer, you create the message in Outlook 2013 and save it as a template file.

Follow these steps to create the template:

1. Begin a new message, and then enter the subject and body but leave the address boxes blank.

   > **Note**
   >
   > Include an address in the Bcc field if you want a copy of all automatic responses sent to you or to another specific address.

2. Click File, and then choose Save As.

3. In the Save As dialog box, specify a path and name for the file, select Outlook Template (*.oft) in the Save As Type drop-down list, and then click Save.

Using a template from your local system causes the rule to function as a client-side rule. As a result, Outlook 2013 can use the rule to process accounts other than your Exchange Server account (such as a POP3 account), but Exchange Server can't generate automatic responses when Outlook 2013 isn't running or is offline.

TROUBLESHOOTING

Your autoresponse rule executes only once

When you create a rule using the Reply Using A Specific Template rule action, Outlook 2013 executes the rule only once for a given sender in each Outlook 2013 session. Outlook 2013 keeps track of the senders in a list and checks incoming messages against the list. For the first message from a given sender that matches the rule conditions, Outlook 2013 generates the response; for subsequent messages, Outlook 2013 doesn't generate the response. This prevents Outlook 2013 from sending repetitive responses to a person who sends you multiple messages that satisfy the rule conditions. Closing and restarting Outlook 2013 refreshes the sender list, and the next message from that sender that meets the criteria generates a response. The Automatic Replies (Out of Office) feature uses the same process—and this behavior is by design.

If you create a server-side rule that uses Have Server Reply Using A Specific Message, Exchange Server creates an autoresponse for all messages that meet the specified conditions, regardless of whether the message is the first from a particular sender.

Creating automatic responses from local templates

Follow these steps to create a client-side rule that responds to incoming messages with a reply from a template stored locally on your computer:

1. Compose the reply message and save it as a template (.oft) file.

2. Click the Home tab, click Rules, and choose Manage Rules & Alerts to open the Rules And Alerts dialog box.

3. Click New Rule.

4. Select Apply Rule On Messages I Receive, and then click Next.

5. Specify the conditions for the rule (such as Sent Only To Me or Where My Name Is In The To Box), and then click Next.

6. Select Reply Using A Specific Template, and then, in the rule description area, click the A Specific Template link.

7. In the Select A Reply Template dialog box, shown in Figure 11-19, select the template that you want to use for the reply, and then click Open.

Chapter 11

> **Note**
> Use the Look In drop-down list to choose the location where the template is stored. You can open templates stored in Outlook or in the file system (including from a network file server).

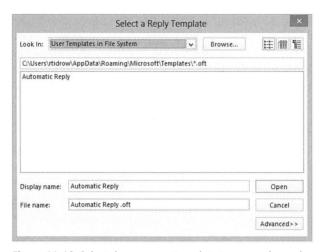

Figure 11-19 Select the message template to use as the reply.

8. Click Next, and then specify exceptions, if any, for the rule.

9. Click Next, specify final options for the rule, specify a name for the rule, and then click Finish.

> **Note**
> By default, Outlook turns on the rule. You can clear the Turn On Rule check box prior to clicking Finish if you don't want the rule enabled right away.

Creating automatic responses from the server

Follow these steps to create a server-side rule to generate automatic responses using a message stored on the server:

1. Click the Home tab, click Rules, and choose Manage Rules & Alerts to open the Rules And Alerts dialog box.

2. Click New Rule.

3. Select Apply Rule On Messages I Receive, and then click Next.

4. Specify the conditions for the rule, and then click Next.

5. Select Have Server Reply Using A Specific Message, and then, in the rule description area, click the A Specific Message link.

6. Create the message using the resulting message form, specifying the subject and text but no addresses (unless you want to copy the reply to a specific address), and then click Save & Close.

7. Click Next, and then specify exceptions, if any, for the rule.

8. Click Next, specify final options for the rule, and then click Finish.

Creating mobile alerts

You can configure Outlook 2013 to send alerts to your mobile device. For example, perhaps you want reminders and a calendar summary sent to your mobile device, or maybe you'll be out of the office for several hours and want your new messages redirected to your mobile device. You can accomplish both of these tasks with the Outlook Mobile Service account.

You have two options for sending alerts and forwarding messages to a mobile device. You can have Exchange Server 2010 or 2013 send the alerts with server-side rules, or you can have Outlook handle the alerts and forwarding using client-side rules. The former lets you receive alerts from your computer running Exchange Server even when Outlook isn't running; the latter lets you use alerts and forwarding if you don't have an Exchange Server account.

You configure server-side alerts and forwarding through Outlook Web App or an Office 365 account. The following sections explain how to configure server-side alerts.

> **Note**
> You can navigate directly to Outlook Web App or Office 365 to configure mobile notification settings rather than reach the settings through Outlook. After you log into Outlook Web App (or Office 365), click Options, Phone, and then Text Messaging.

Creating calendar alerts and summaries from Exchange Server

Outlook Mobile Service can forward reminders to your mobile device as well as a summary of your next day's calendar items. Follow these steps to configure forwarding of these items:

1. Click File, Account Settings, Manage Mobile Notifications to open a web browser for Outlook Web App.

2. Log in, and then click Options and then Phone in the left pane.

3. Click Text Messaging to show the Text Messaging options shown in Figure 11-20.

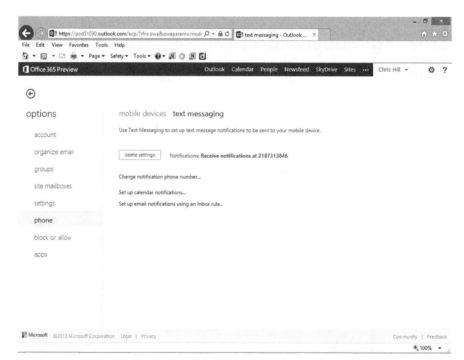

Figure 11-20 Use the Text Messaging page to configure the forwarding of reminders and calendar summaries.

> **Note**
> If you haven't set up your notification phone number yet, click the Change Notification Phone Number link shown in Figure 11-20 and configure your mobile number.

4.   Click Set Up Calendar Notifications to access the options shown in Figure 11-21. You can configure options to receive alerts when your calendar is updated, receive meeting reminders, and receive a daily calendar agenda.

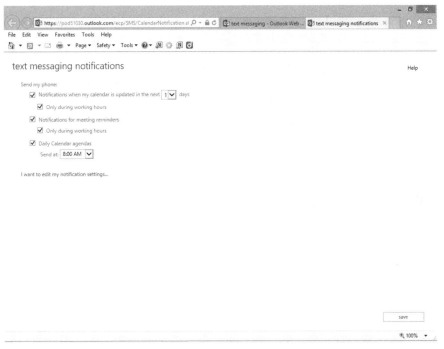

Figure 11-21 Use the Text Messaging Notifications window to configure options for receiving alerts.

5.   Click Save.

> **Note**
> To change your mobile number or other mobile settings, click the I Want To Edit My Notification Settings link on the Text Messaging Notifications page.

Forward email messages

You can configure Outlook Mobile Service to forward messages to your mobile phone based on conditions that you specify, including how your name appears in the message, the sender, words in the subject, and message importance. For example, you might configure it to forward messages you receive from your manager to your mobile device. Follow these steps to configure message forwarding to your mobile device:

Chapter 11

1. While in Outlook, click File, Account Settings, Manage Mobile Notifications, and log in when prompted.

2. Click Phone in the left pane.

3. Click Text Messaging, and then click Set Up E-mail Notifications to display the options shown in Figure 11-22.

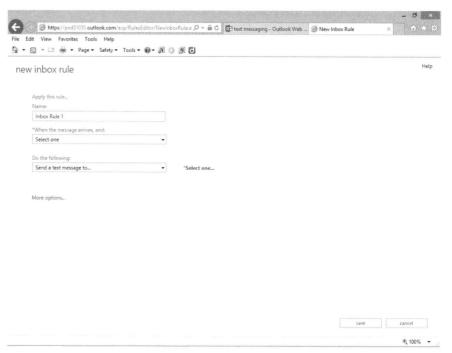

Figure 11-22 Use the New Inbox Rule page to configure message forwarding.

4. Enter a name for the rule in the Name field.

5. Select a condition for the rule from the When The Message Arrives, And drop-down list. For example, choose It Was Received From to have the message forwarded if it is from a specific sender. Another page will open, prompting you to provide more information. For instance, using the example previously described, you are prompted to choose a sender from the address book.

6. From the Do The Following drop-down list, choose Send A Text Message To.

7. Click Select One to choose the mobile device to which you want to send the alerts. If you have only one device configured, it is chosen by default.

8. If desired, click More Options to expand the page and add exceptions to the rule.

9. Click Save.

Creating message alerts

You don't need an Exchange Server account to forward messages to your mobile device. You can create client-side rules that use the Outlook Mobile Service to forward alerts and messages. However, Outlook must be running and have an Internet connection available for these features to work.

You create rules to forward messages to your mobile device by simply creating the rules yourself, just as you create any other rule. To do so, follow these steps:

1. Choose the Rules item on the Move area of the Home tab and click Manage Rules & Alerts. On the Rules And Alerts dialog box, start a new, blank rule using the Apply Rule On Messages I Receive option.

2. In the Rules Wizard, specify the conditions for the rule, such as received from a particular person, marked as high importance, with specific words in the subject, and so on.

3. Click Next, and in the second page of the wizard shown in Figure 11-23, choose the Forward It To People Or Public Group As An Attachment action.

Chapter 11

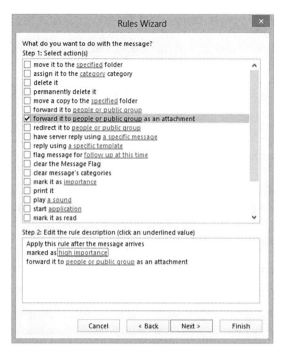

Figure 11-23 You can create a rule to forward messages to a mobile device.

4.   In the Edit The Rule Description area, click the People Or Public Group link.

5.   When the Rule Address dialog box opens, choose Contacts (Mobile) from the Address Book drop-down list.

6.   Choose the mobile device to which you want to send the message and then click OK.

7.   Specify other settings for the rule as desired and then click Finish.

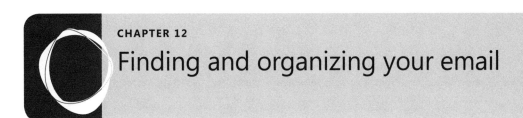

Finding and organizing your email

ALTHOUGH some people use Microsoft Outlook 2013 only for email, the majority of people use all the personal information manager (PIM) features the program has to offer. Because a PIM is only as good as its capability to help you search for and organize data, Outlook 2013 offers a solid selection of features to help you do just that.

This chapter shows you how to perform simple and advanced searches to locate data. You'll learn how to search using Instant Search as well as the Search People feature and Advanced Find. This chapter also explores various ways you can organize your Outlook 2013 data—for example, by creating additional folders for storing specific types of messages.

Using Instant Search

The Instant Search feature of the Microsoft Office system provides a simple, unified search interface that is the same across all the Outlook 2013 folders. Instant Search relies on the search subsystem built into Windows, which indexes Outlook 2013 mail folders to deliver search results faster.

Searching in Outlook 2013 is as simple as typing your search terms in the Instant Search box at the top of the Inbox. Outlook 2013 displays results as you type, automatically filtering out older results when there are a large number of items. To focus searches, Outlook 2013 searches only the folder that you have open, although you can easily choose to search all your folders instead.

When you start a search, you first determine the scope of your search. Outlook 2013 sets the search scope as the folder that is selected in the Navigation Pane. To change the search scope, you click a different folder in the Navigation Pane.

> **Note**
>
> If you prefer to use the tools provided in earlier versions of Outlook, you still can use the Advanced Find tool in the Search Tools group on the Search tab.

As you type text in the Instant Search box, the search results are displayed in the pane below the Instant Search box. To refine your search and get fewer results, type more text. To widen your search, delete some text. You can also build custom queries based on a wide range of criteria.

> **Note**
> Instant Search requires Windows Search, which is part of Microsoft Windows. For more information about Windows Search, you can visit the Windows Search site at *http://windows.microsoft.com/en-US/windows7/products/features/windows-search*.

Configuring Instant Search

While the default configuration of Instant Search should work in most circumstances, you might need to fine-tune the settings just a bit to optimize Instant Search for how you use Outlook 2013. Using Instant Search might require configuring a few different options, most of which are found in Outlook 2013, although a few options are set with Indexing Options in Control Panel.

Turning Instant Search on and off

Instant Search is enabled by default on computers running Windows 7 and Windows 8. If you have turned Instant Search off for Outlook, you can enable it again. Open the Indexing Options item from Control Panel or click it in the Instant Search box, and then, on the Search tab, click Search Tools, Search Options, Indexing Options. In the Indexing Options dialog box, click Modify, and then select the content that you want Instant Search to index and search, one of which is Microsoft Outlook. You must exit and restart Outlook 2013 for this change to take effect.

To turn on Instant Search if it is not currently enabled, click the Click Here To Enable Instant Search option under the Instant Search box.

To disable Instant Search, open the Indexing Options dialog box as described previously. Click Modify, and then clear the Microsoft Outlook option. You must exit and restart Outlook 2013 for this change to take effect.

Choosing search options

You can determine the initial scope of searches, as well as how Outlook 2013 handles results, in the Search Options dialog box.

To configure Instant Search, click File, Options, and then click Search in the left pane to display the Search page of the Outlook Options dialog box, shown in Figure 12-1. The following list explains the options available:

- To set the default scope of Instant Search, under Include Results Only From, choose either Current Folder or All Folders.

- If you want Outlook 2013 to search mail items that have been moved to the Deleted Items folder but not yet actually deleted, select Include Messages From The Deleted Items Folder In Each Data File When Searching In All Items.

- To have Outlook 2013 show you search results as you type, select When Possible, Display Results As The Query Is Typed. If this option is cleared, Outlook 2013 does not start searching until you click Search or press Enter.

- When your search has a large number of results, Outlook 2013 by default limits the number of items it displays by filtering for the most recent. To view all results of your searches, no matter the number, clear the Improve Search Speed By Limiting The Number Of Results Shown check box.

- To have Outlook 2013 highlight your search terms where they appear in the results, select Highlight Search Terms In The Results. You can also set the highlight color.

- The Notify Me When Results Might Be Limited Because Search Indexing Is Not Complete option sets Outlook to prompt you if the system is not done indexing your Outlook items when you want to perform a search.

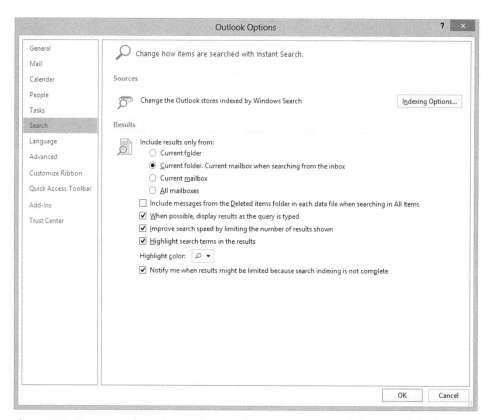

Figure 12-1 You can configure Instant Search using the Search page of the Outlook Options dialog box.

You can also specify which of your Outlook data files (if you have more than one) are indexed by Windows Search, as explained in the next section.

Controlling which data files are searched

If you have multiple Outlook 2013 data files, you can tell Outlook 2013 to include only specific data files in an Instant Search without removing them from the list of files that are indexed. This allows you to stop a file from being searched without having to re-create the index for the file when you want it included again—a much faster option. You might use this technique to segregate project or client files, or perhaps to exclude a large archive file from searches most of the time, yet be able to easily include the file when you need to.

To change which data files Outlook 2013 searches, follow these steps:

1. Click in the Instant Search box to open the Search tab, as shown in Figure 12-2.

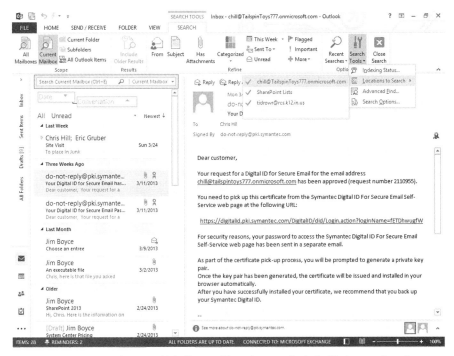

Figure 12-2 You can choose which files and locations are included in Instant Search.

2. Click Search Tools on the Search tab and choose Locations to Search.

3. Select the Outlook 2013 data files that you want included in searches by default. At least one data file must be selected, but you can choose additional files to search as well.

You can also specify whether your Outlook 2013 files are indexed in the Indexing Options item in Control Panel.

For information about using the Indexing Options item, see the section "Configuring indexing options."

Performing a search

Instant Search looks at most fields of Outlook 2013 items when performing searches, making it easy for you to find what you are looking for. This means that you can type almost anything that you think might be in the item you're looking for, even if the item is in an attachment. To search for a message or other Outlook 2013 item, follow these steps:

1.   Click in the Instant Search box (or press Ctrl+E), and then type your search text.

2.   Outlook 2013 will display the search results as you type, with the search terms highlighted. To narrow the search results, type more text. To widen the results, delete some text.

If you do not see the items you want, you can broaden your search scope by clicking the link Try Searching Again In All Mail Items (this link changes to reflect the current folder type) in the results pane.

If your search returns a large number of results, Outlook 2013 might display only the most recent results. You may see a message that says More at the bottom of the search results, as shown in Figure 12-3. Click it to see additional search items.

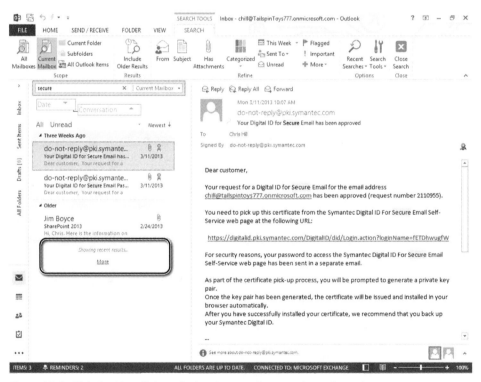

Figure 12-3 Click the More link to display the complete set of search results.

To clear the search and start over, click the *X* to the right of the Instant Search box.

To repeat a search that you have performed recently, click in the Instant Search box to display the Search tab, and then choose Recent Searches. Select the search that you want to repeat from the list.

> ## Note
> You might find that the results of some of your searches include an item that really doesn't seem to belong there and in which you can't find the words you searched for. This might be because the item has an attachment that contains the search term.

TROUBLESHOOTING

You don't get any search results

If you repeatedly get fewer results than you expect, or you get no results at all, you should try disabling Instant Search and repeating the search. If you do get results with Instant Search disabled, you might be having problems with Windows Desktop Search indexing.

Check your indexing status by clicking Search Tools on the Search tab and selecting Indexing Status. If a message appears stating that Outlook 2013 is currently indexing your files, note the number of items remaining to be indexed. Check back in a while to see whether the numbers are different. If the numbers are unchanged, you should rebuild the index. For information about rebuilding the index, see the section "Configuring indexing options."

Refining your search

The Refine group on the Search tab shows you a number of extra fields that you can search within to refine your search results. Each type of folder (Mail, Contacts, and so on) displays the most commonly used fields for that type of folder, so each one shows a different list of fields by default. You can also add fields, even those in custom forms, to support searches for exactly the data you want.

1. To display the Search tab, click in the Instant Search box.

2. Click an item in the Refine group, as shown in Figure 12-4, to add that field to the Instant Search box. Then type the criteria required by the added field, such as a name, a word, and so on.

3. To add other fields, click More to display the list shown in Figure 12-4.

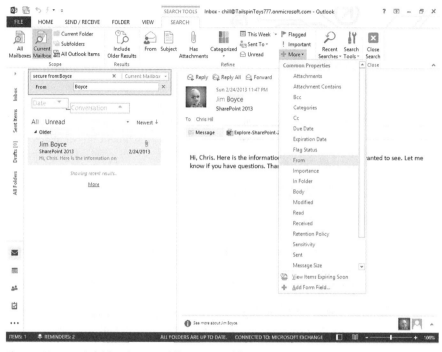

Figure 12-4 Each folder shows a different list of fields in the Refine group.

> **Note**
>
> Adding fields from the Refine group is a good way to learn about the search syntax that Windows Search uses. After you're familiar with the syntax, you can just type the search keywords yourself rather than pick them from the list. What's more, you can use the keywords outside Outlook to search for Outlook items. Just click Start and begin typing your search criteria. Windows Search will return results in the Start menu based on those criteria.

Making fields from custom forms available

To add a custom form to the Refine group More list, follow these steps:

1. Click in the Instant Search box.

2. Click More in the Refine group on the Search tab and choose Add Form Field.

3. In the Select Enterprise Forms For This Folder dialog box, choose the types of forms you want to select from.

4. In the list in the left pane, select the form you want to add, and then click Add. Repeat this process for each form you want to add. (To display form groups by category, select Show Categories.)

5. Click Close.

> **Note**
> If Windows Search is still building the search index, your search results will be incomplete. To check the status of indexing, click in the Instant Search field to open the Search tab, and then click Search Tools and choose Indexing Status.

Configuring indexing options

While indexing is generally self-maintaining, you can control some settings using the Indexing Options item in Control Panel. You can also display Indexing Options from Outlook. Click File, Options, Search, and then click Indexing Options.

To verify that your Outlook 2013 files are being indexed, follow these steps:

1. Click File, Options, Search.

2. Click Indexing Options. In the Indexing Options dialog box, shown in Figure 12-5, verify that your Outlook 2013 files are listed in the Included Locations list.

Figure 12-5 You can see the status of indexing across the entire system in the Indexing Options dialog box.

3. If your Outlook 2013 files are not listed, click Modify to display the Indexed Locations dialog box. Under Change Selected Locations, select the Microsoft Outlook check box to include the files in the locations that should be indexed. (Outlook 2013 files belonging to other users are also shown, but Outlook will return to you only results from your own data files.)

4. Click OK.

> **Note**
>
> Be patient after you click Modify. It can take quite a while for Windows to display the Indexed Locations dialog box.

TROUBLESHOOTING

You might need to troubleshoot indexing problems

Consider rebuilding the index due to problems such as empty search results when you know that there are items that match your search. Rebuilding an index takes a while, perhaps even several hours, and is significantly slower if you are also using the computer at the same time. Because of this, you will want to rebuild the index only when you are experiencing ongoing problems with Instant Search, and preferably when you will be away from the computer for a while.

You can rebuild the search index by opening the Indexing Options item in Control Panel and then clicking Advanced. Under Troubleshooting, click Rebuild. Once the index is rebuilt, restart Outlook 2013 to have it use the new index.

Finding messages with Windows 7 Search

You have some additional ways to search for messages outside of Outlook that can be very handy. To search for any item in Windows 7, whether in Outlook or not, click Start and start typing in the Search Programs And Files text box. As you type (assuming that indexing is enabled and has finished indexing the content on your computer), results that match your search appear above the text box. For example, Figure 12-6 shows a quick search for items related to Manoj Agarwal. In this example, Windows 7 found an Outlook profile, contacts, Really Simple Syndication (RSS) messages, and email.

Chapter 12

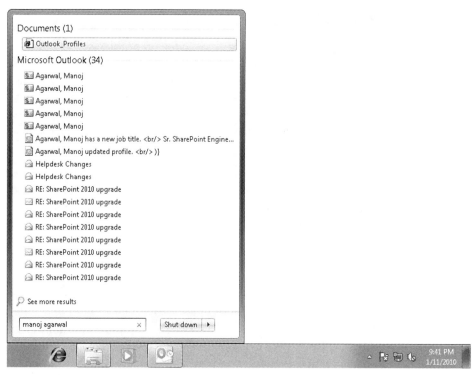

Figure 12-6 Windows 7 has returned several Outlook items related to Manoj Agarwal.

You can refine a search in Windows 7 further by using keywords. For example, to find messages with *SharePoint* in the subject, type the following in the Search Programs And Files text box:

Subject:SharePoint

This search term will return results for messages containing *SharePoint* in the subject, and it will also return other items, such as documents with *SharePoint* in the title. You can restrict your searches to Outlook items using a handful of keywords. Table 12-1 lists some useful, Outlook-related Windows search keywords to help you refine a search.

TABLE 12-1 Outlook-related Windows search keywords

Description	Keyword	Example
Email sender	from	from:Manoj Agarwal
Has an attachment	attachment	has:attachment
Is an attachment	attachment	is:attachment
Size of an item	size	size:>2MB
Date of an item	date	date:>2/15/13<=3/15/13
Is an email	kind	kind:email
Is a contact	kind	kind:contact
Is a meeting	kind	kind:meetings
Restrict search to Outlook	store	store:mapi
Search by subject	subject	subject:sharepoint
Sent to someone	to	to:Manoj Agarwal
Copied to someone	cc	cc:Manoj Agarwal
Has a specified category	category	category:Toy Show
From a specified person	from	from:manoj agarwal
Received on a certain date	received	received:yesterday
Sent on a certain date	sent	sent:today
Sent to a specific address	toaddress, to	toaddress:magarwal@tailspintoys.com
The item has been read	isread	isread:false

> **Note**
>
> Table 12-1 contains just some of the Outlook-related search terms that you can use to locate items. There are many others that are specific to the Outlook data types, including contacts, email messages, and calendar items. You'll find additional advanced tips for searching in Windows 7 at *http://windows.microsoft.com/en-us/windows7/advanced-tips-for-searching-in-windows*.

Keep in mind that you can limit your search to Outlook by using *store:mapi* in the search string. Also, you can use multiple search criteria to refine a search. For example, assume that you want to search only Outlook for email messages from Manoj Agarwal that have an attachment larger than 2 MB and were sent yesterday. Here's the search syntax to use:

store:mapi kind:email from:manoj agarwal hasattachment:true size:>2MB sent:yesterday

Searching for contacts

If you're like most Outlook 2013 users, your Contacts folder will grow to contain a lot of contact entries—typically, too many to allow you to browse through the folder when you need to find a particular contact quickly. You're also likely to encounter situations in which, for example, you need to locate contact information but can't remember the person's last name. Fortunately, Outlook 2013 makes it easy to locate contact data, providing two convenient ways to search contacts: Instant Search and the Search People box in the Find group on the Home tab on the ribbon.

Instant Search works the same way across all the Outlook 2013 folders, so to locate a contact, begin typing the contact's name in the Search Contacts box. You can use the buttons in the Refine group on the Search tab to add search criteria. If you want to add more fields, you can click More and then select the fields from the list.

You can also use the Search People box on the Home tab on the ribbon, shown in Figure 12-7, to search for contacts. Type the search criterion (such as a first name, last name, or company), and then press Enter.

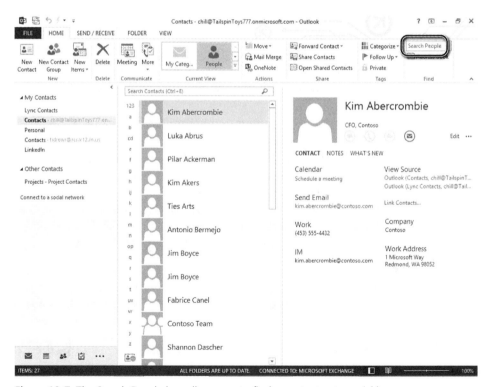

Figure 12-7 The Search People box allows you to find a contact entry quickly.

If Outlook 2013 finds only one contact that matches the search criteria, it opens the contact entry for that person. Otherwise, Outlook 2013 displays a results list, shown in Figure 12-8, from which you can select the contact entry to open.

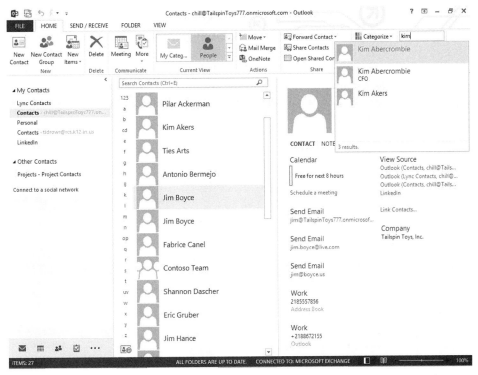

Figure 12-8 Select a contact when Outlook 2013 finds more than one that fits your search criteria.

> **Note**
>
> The results lists can be useful when you need to perform a quick search for a contact based on a limited amount of data. To locate contacts and other Outlook 2013 items based on multiple search conditions, use Instant Search or Advanced Find, as discussed in the next section.

Chapter 12

Using Advanced Find

In addition to Instant Search, Outlook 2013 still provides the Advanced Find feature for per-forming advanced searches that require specifying multiple search conditions.

The Advanced Find dialog box

To open the Advanced Find dialog box, shown in Figure 12-9, click in the Instant Search box, and then click Search Tools, Advanced Find or simply press Ctrl+Shift+F. You can use this dialog box to search for any type of Outlook 2013 item using multiple search conditions.

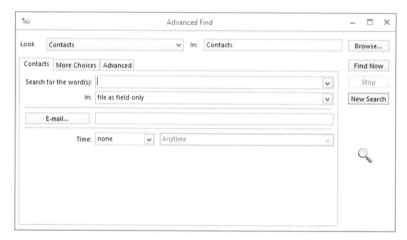

Figure 12-9 Use the Advanced Find dialog box when you need to search using multiple conditions.

The options provided in the Advanced Find dialog box change depending on the type of item that you select in the Look drop-down list. If you select Contacts, for example, the options change to provide specialized search criteria for contacts, such as restricting the search to a name, a company, or an address. Selecting Messages in the drop-down list changes the options so that you can search the subject field of messages, search the subject and message body, or specify other search criteria specific to messages.

> **Note**
>
> When you select a different item type in the Look drop-down list, Outlook 2013 clears the current search and starts a new one. Outlook 2013 does, however, prompt you to confirm that you want to clear the current search.

On the first tab in the Advanced Find dialog box (the title of which changes based on the type of item being searched—for example, Contacts in Figure 12-9), you specify the primary search criteria. The following list summarizes all the available options (although not all options appear at all times):

- **Search For The Word(s)**   Specify the word, words, or phrase for which you want to search. You can type words individually or include quotation marks around a phrase to search for the entire phrase. You also can select from a previous set of search words using the drop-down list.

- **In**   Specify the location in the Outlook 2013 item where you want to search, such as only the subject of a message. The options available in this list vary according to the type of item that you select in the Look drop-down list.

- **From**   Specify the name of the person who sent you the message. Type the name or click From to browse the address book for the name.

- **Sent To**   For messages, specify the recipients to whom the message was sent.

- **Attendees**   Specify the people scheduled to attend a meeting.

- **Organized By**   Specify the person who generated the meeting request.

- **E-mail**   Browse the address book to search for contacts by their email addresses.

- **Named**   Specify the file name of the item for which you're searching. You can specify a single file name or use wildcard characters to match multiple items. The Named box appears if you select Files or Files (Outlook/Exchange) in the Look drop-down list.

- **Of Type**   Choose the type of file for which to search when using the Files or Files (Outlook/Exchange) option.

- **Journal Entry Types**   Specify the journal entry type when searching the journal for items.

- **Contact**   Browse for a contact associated with an item for which you're searching.

- **Where I Am**   When searching for messages, specify that you are the only person in the To line, in the To line with others, or in the Cc line with others.

- **Status**   Search for tasks based on their status. You can select Doesn't Matter, Not Started, In Progress, Completed, Waiting On Someone Else, or Deferred.

- **Time**   Specify the creation or modification time, the start or end time, or other time properties specific to the type of item for which you are searching.

Chapter 12

Specifying advanced search criteria

You use the More Choices tab in the Advanced Find dialog box, shown in Figure 12-10, to specify additional search conditions to refine the search.

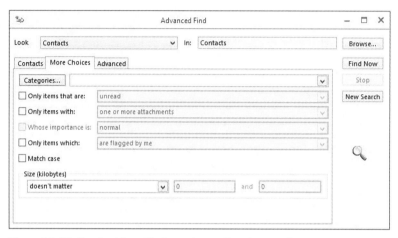

Figure 12-10 Use the More Choices tab to refine the search.

The following options are available on the More Choices tab:

- **Categories**   Specify the category or categories associated with the items for which you are searching. You can type the categories separated by commas, or you can click Categories to open the Categories dialog box and then select categories.

- **Only Items That Are**   Search for items by their read status (read or unread).

- **Only Items With**   Search for items by their attachment status (one or more attachments, or no attachments).

- **Whose Importance Is**   Specify the importance (High, Normal, or Low) of the items for which you are searching.

- **Only Items Which**   Specify the flag status of the items for which you are searching.

- **Match Case**   Direct Outlook 2013 to match the case of the text you entered as the search criterion. Clear this check box to make the search case-insensitive.

- **Size**   Specify the size criterion for the items in your search. You can select one of several options to define the size range in which the item must fall to match the search.

The More Choices tab is the same for all Outlook 2013 items except the Files search item. With Files selected in the Look drop-down list, the Only Items With option is not available.

You can use the Advanced tab in the Advanced Find dialog box, shown in Figure 12-11, to create more complex searches. On this tab, select the fields to include in the search, as well as the search conditions for each field. You can build a list of multiple fields.

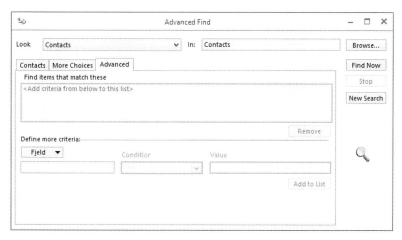

Figure 12-11 On the Advanced tab, select the fields to search and their search criteria.

Organizing data

Searching for data and organizing data usually go hand in hand. One of the main motivations for organizing your data is that you want to be able to find it easily. Even with perfect organization, however, you'll still need to perform searches now and then because of the sheer amount of data that might be involved. Outlook 2013 provides several ways to organize your data. Whereas other chapters in this book focus on specific ways to organize your Outlook 2013 items, this section provides an overview of ways that you can organize certain types of items and points you to the appropriate chapters for additional information.

Organizing your email

Email messages probably make up the bulk of your Outlook 2013 data. For that reason, organizing your messages can be a challenge. Outlook 2013 offers several features that will help you organize your messages so that you can find and work with them effectively and efficiently.

Search Folders

Search Folders are the best means in Outlook 2013 to organize messages quickly without moving them around to different folders. A Search Folder looks and acts like a folder, but it's really a special type of view that displays in a virtual folder view all messages that fit the search condition for the Search Folder. Search Folders offer two main benefits: They can search multiple folders, and they organize messages without requiring that the messages be moved from their current folder.

See the section "Finding and organizing messages with Search Folders" in Chapter 9, "Managing your email," to learn more about Search Folders.

Using folders

Another great way to organize your email messages is to separate them into different folders. For example, if you deal with several projects, consider creating a folder for each project and moving each message to its respective folder. You can create the folders as subfolders of your Inbox or place them elsewhere, depending on your preferences. You might even create a folder outside the Inbox named Projects and then create subfolders for each project under that folder.

For more information about creating and managing folders, see Chapter 9.

Using rules

Rules are one of the best tools you have in Outlook 2013 for organizing messages. You can apply rules to process messages selectively—moving, deleting, copying, and performing other actions on the messages based on the sender, the recipient, the account, and a host of other message properties. You can use rules in combination with folders to organize your email messages. For example, you might use rules to move messages for specific projects to their respective folders automatically. You can apply rules to messages when they arrive in the Inbox or any time you need to rearrange or organize.

For a detailed discussion of rules, see Chapter 11, "Using rules, alerts, and automatic responses."

Using color categories

Outlook 2013 uses color categories to help organize your email messages. If you create rules to apply certain color categories to specified email messages, the color can provide a visual indicator of the sender, the subject, the priority, or other properties of the message.

In this way, you can see at a glance whether a particular message meets certain criteria. You can also use automatic formatting in a view to apply color categories.

For more information about color categories, see Chapter 5, "Creating and using categories."

Using views

Views give you another important way to organize your Outlook 2013 data. The default views organize specific folders using the most common criteria. You can customize the Outlook Today view using HTML to provide different or additional levels of organization. You can also create custom views of any Outlook 2013 folder to organize your data to suit your preferences.

For more information about customizing views, see the sections "Customizing the Outlook Today view" and "Creating custom views," in Chapter 26, "Customizing the Outlook interface."

Organizing your calendar, contacts, tasks, and notes

As with mail folders, you can use categories to organize items in your other folders. For example, you might use categories to identify meetings for specific projects quickly. You can also use conditional formatting to display items in a certain color when those items match your conditional formatting condition. For contacts, you can use multiple folders to separate contacts, such as separating your business contacts from personal contacts.

Organizing your Outlook items effectively

It's far too easy to get swamped in email, but you can minimize this problem if you learn to use the options that Outlook 2013 offers to help you stay organized. Here are a few tips to get you started:

- **Clean out your Inbox every day**   There is a very real psychological boost when you can leave your office at the end of the day with your Inbox empty—and it's a pretty nice way to start your morning, too. A habitually empty Inbox also means that any mail that is in the Inbox is still unread, so it's easy to tell what you still need to read.

- **Handle each email message only once**   Many time management systems share a similar mantra: Open a message, read it, decide what you have to do about it, and then do it. Right now. For most people, a lot of their mail requires no action beyond reading it. If that's the case, delete (or file) mail items immediately. Move any items that require action to a folder other than the Inbox, assigning a color category to make it easier to locate, or set a follow-up flag to remind you of a deadline if needed.

- **Turn off the Reading Pane if you have a hard time emptying your Inbox** While the Reading Pane makes it easy to read a piece of mail quickly, the Reading Pane also makes it easy to read mail without dealing with it.

- **Use rules to sort mail that you don't need to read immediately into folders as it arrives** You can also assign categories using rules as messages arrive, providing additional information that you can use to locate those messages later.

- **Use a combination of folders and categories to manage your mail** Create folders to contain large groups of mail, and then categorize the messages to display a manageable subset of messages.

- **Use Search Folders to create customized views of your Outlook 2013 items** Search Folders automatically filter the contents of a list of folders that you specify based on the set of criteria found in the Advanced Find dialog box. This lets you see specific sets of messages by simply selecting a folder.

- **Create custom views of messages** Custom views that filter Outlook 2013 items are another powerful tool, letting you quickly switch between various subsets of messages. Because views can be used in multiple folders, you can create a view once and reuse it in many places.

- **If you have lots of email, consider using multiple .pst files to separate disparate information into discrete data stores** In addition to segregating data storage, this makes it easy to select specific data sets for Instant Search.

PART III

Working with contacts and address books

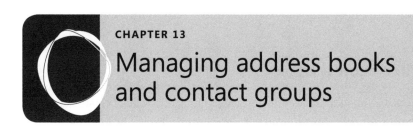

CHAPTER 13

Managing address books and contact groups

A N email program isn't very useful without the capability to store addresses. Microsoft Outlook 2013, like other email-enabled applications, has this storage capability. In fact, Outlook 2013 offers multiple address books that can not only help make sending messages easy and efficient, but also let you keep track of contact information for other purposes, such as postal mail, phone lists, and so on.

This chapter explores how Outlook 2013 stores addresses and explains how Outlook 2013 interacts with Microsoft Exchange Server (which has its own address lists) to provide addressing services. You'll learn how to store addresses in the Outlook 2013 Contacts folder and use them to address messages, meeting requests, appointments, and more. You'll also learn how to create distribution lists to broadcast messages and other items to groups of users and how to hide the details of the distribution list from recipients.

> ### Note
> Although this chapter discusses the Contacts folder in the context of address lists, it doesn't cover this folder in detail.

For a detailed discussion of using and managing the Contacts folder, see Chapter 14, "Working with contacts."

Understanding address books

As you begin working with addresses in Outlook 2013, you'll find that you can store them in multiple locations. For example, if you're using an Exchange Server account, you have a couple of locations from which to select addresses. Understanding where these address books reside is an important first step in putting them to work for you. The following sections describe the various address books in Outlook 2013 and how you can use them.

Outlook 2013 address book

On all installations, including those with no email accounts, Outlook 2013 creates a default Outlook Address Book (OAB). This address book consolidates all your Outlook 2013 Contacts folders. With a new installation of Outlook 2013, the OAB shows only one location for storing addresses: the default Contacts folder. As you add other Contacts folders, those additional folders appear in the OAB, as shown in Figure 13-1. As you'll learn in the section "Removing Contacts folders from the OAB" later in this chapter, you can configure additional Contacts folders so that they don't appear in the OAB.

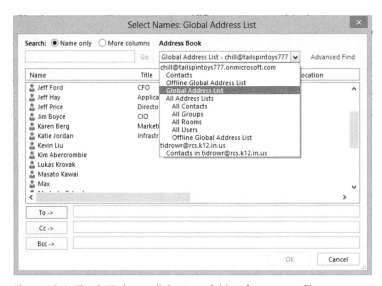

Figure 13-1 The OAB shows all Contacts folders for your profile.

For detailed information on creating and using additional Contacts folders, see the section "Creating other Contacts folders" in Chapter 14.

The OAB functions as a virtual address book collection instead of as an address book because Outlook 2013 doesn't store the OAB as a file separate from your data store. Instead, the OAB provides a view into your Contacts folders and other contact sources.

> **Note**
>
> Earlier versions of Outlook prior to 2007 enabled users to store addresses in Personal Address Books (PABs), which were kept in separate files from the personal data store. Although PABs are not available in Outlook 2013, you can import them into a Contacts folder, which is visible in the OAB.

Global Address List

When you use a profile that contains an Exchange Server account, you'll find one other address list in addition to the OAB: the Global Address List (GAL). This address list resides on the computer running Exchange Server and presents the list of mailboxes on the server as well as other address items created on the server, including distribution groups and external addresses (see Figure 13-2). However, users can't create address information in the GAL; only the Exchange Server system administrator can do this.

> ## Note
> An Exchange Server environment can and often does include more than one server. For the purposes of discussion in this book, the singular term *server* refers to the collection of computers running Exchange Server that make up your Exchange Server environment.

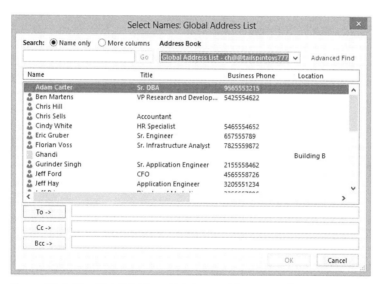

Figure 13-2 The Global Address List shows addresses on the computer running Exchange Server.

LDAP (Internet directory services)

Some email addresses are not available in the OAB or GAL but are available using the Lightweight Directory Access Protocol (LDAP). This requires network connectivity to the LDAP server. LDAP simply provides a mechanism for Outlook to query and obtain contact information from one or more servers that host LDAP data stores.

Other address lists

In addition to the OAB, GAL, and LDAP, you might see other address sources when you look for addresses in Outlook 2013. For example, in an organization with a large address list, the Exchange Server system administrator might create additional address lists to filter the view to show only a selection, such as contacts with last names starting with the letter *A* or contacts external to the organization. You might also see a list named All Address Lists. This list, which comes from Exchange Server, can be modified by the Exchange Server administrator to include additional address lists (see Figure 13-3). The list can also include Public Folders, which can store shared contacts. In addition, the list by default includes All Contacts, All Groups, All Rooms, and All Users, which sort addresses by type.

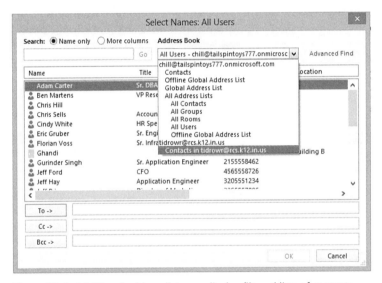

Figure 13-3 Additional address lists can display filtered lists of contacts.

Configuring address books and addressing options

Outlook 2013 offers a handful of settings that you can use to configure the way your address books display contacts and address information. You also can add other address books and choose which address book Outlook 2013 uses by default for opening and storing addresses and processing messages.

Setting the contacts display option for the OAB

You can set only one option for the OAB. This setting controls the order in which Outlook 2013 displays names from the OAB: either First Last or using the File As field (Last Name, First Name).

Follow these steps to set this display option:

1. If Outlook 2013 is open, click File, Account Settings, Account Settings, and then click the Address Books tab. If Outlook 2013 is not open, open the Mail item from Control Panel, click E-mail Accounts, and then select the Address Books tab.

2. Select Outlook Address Book and click Change to display the Microsoft Outlook Address Book dialog box, shown in Figure 13-4.

Figure 13-4 Select the display option for Outlook Address Book entries in the Microsoft Outlook Address Book dialog box.

3. In the Show Names By area, select the display format that you prefer. Click Close, and then click Close again.

Removing Contacts folders from the OAB

In most cases, you'll want all your Contacts folders to appear in the OAB. If you have several Contacts folders, however, you might prefer to limit how many folders appear in the OAB, or you might simply want to restrict the folders to ensure that specific addresses are used.

You can set the folder's properties to determine whether it appears in the OAB by following these steps:

1. Open Outlook 2013 and open the folders list (or click the Contacts button in the Navigation Pane). Then right-click the Contacts folder in question and choose Properties.

2. Click the Outlook Address Book tab and clear the Show This Folder As An E-mail Address Book option to prevent the folder from appearing in the OAB.

3. Change the folder name if necessary, and then click OK.

> **Note**
> You can't remove the default Contacts folder from the OAB.

Setting other addressing options

You can configure other addressing options to determine which address book Outlook 2013 displays by default for selecting addresses, which address book is used by default for storing new addresses, and the order in which address books are processed when Outlook 2013 checks names for sending messages. The following sections explain these options in detail.

Selecting the default address book for lookup

To suit your needs or preferences, you can have Outlook 2013 display a different address list by default. For example, for profiles that include Exchange Server accounts, Outlook 2013 displays the GAL by default. If you use the GAL infrequently and primarily use your Contacts folders for addressing, you might prefer to have Outlook 2013 show the OAB as the default address list instead of the GAL, or you might want to display a filtered address list other than the GAL on the server.

Follow these steps to specify the default address list:

1. In Outlook 2013, click Address Book in the Find group on the Home tab of the ribbon. Outlook 2013 displays the Address Book dialog box.

2. Choose Tools, Options.

3. In the Addressing dialog box, select the default address list from the When Opening The Address Book, Show This Address List First drop-down list (see Figure 13-5).

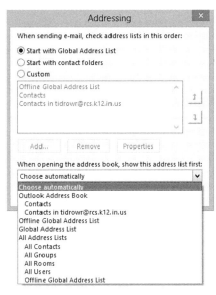

Figure 13-5 You can specify the default address list in the Addressing dialog box.

4. Click OK.

Creating address entries in a specific address book

Although you can't add addresses in the GAL or other server address books, you can store them in other, local address books. You can create addresses in the Outlook Address Book, and when you do so, Outlook 2013 suggests storing the entry in the address book that you have chosen as the default. If you want to store a particular address in a different address book, start by opening the Outlook Address Book as described in the previous section. Click File, New Entry to open the New Entry dialog box. Click the Put This Entry In option and select the address book from the drop-down list (see Figure 13-6). Click OK. Fill in the resulting Contact form and click Save & Close.

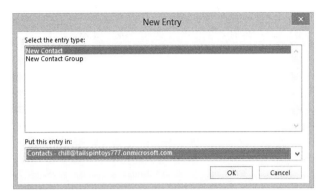

Figure 13-6 Use the New Entry dialog box to determine where to store a new address when you create it from the Outlook Address Book.

> **Note**
>
> Your local Contacts folder is the default location for storing new address book entries unless you set a different one as the default.

Specifying how names are checked

When you create a message, you can specify the recipient's name instead of specifying the address. Instead of typing **jim.boyce@tailspintoys777.onmicrosoft.com**, for example, you might type **Jim Boyce** and let Outlook 2013 convert the name to an email address for you. This saves you the time of opening the address book to look for the entry if you know the name under which it's stored. To have Outlook check the address, simply press Ctrl+K or click Check Names in the Names group on the ribbon.

Outlook 2013 checks the address books to determine the correct address based on the name you entered. Outlook 2013 checks names from multiple address books if they are defined in the current profile. For example, Outlook 2013 might process the address through the GAL first, then through your OAB, and then through the LDAP (assuming that all three are in the profile). If Outlook 2013 finds a match, it replaces the name in the message with the appropriate address. If it doesn't find a match or it finds more than one, it displays the Check Names dialog box, shown in Figure 13-7, in which you can select the correct address, create a new one, or open the address book to display more names and then select an address.

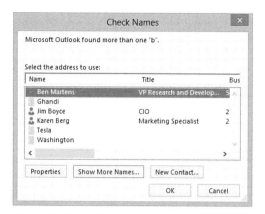

Figure 13-7 The Check Names dialog box helps you resolve address problems before you send a message.

Why change the order in which Outlook 2013 checks your address books? If most of your addresses are stored in an address book other than the one Outlook 2013 is currently checking first, changing the order can speed up name checking, particularly if the address book contains numerous entries.

Here's how to change the address book order:

1. In Outlook 2013, open the Address Book window from the Find group on the ribbon and choose Tools, Options.

2. Choose Custom, click an address book, and then click the up and down arrow buttons to rearrange the address book order in the list.

3. Click OK to close the dialog box.

Creating address book entries

To create a contact quickly while you're composing a message, type the email address in the To, Cc, or Bcc field, and then press Tab. The email address becomes underlined after a short delay. Right-click the email address and select Add To Outlook Contacts (see Figure 13-8). You can also create new contacts, contact groups, and other types of entries from any navigation pane. To do this, select the drop-down arrow next to the New Items button on the Home tab of the ribbon and choose the type of item to create.

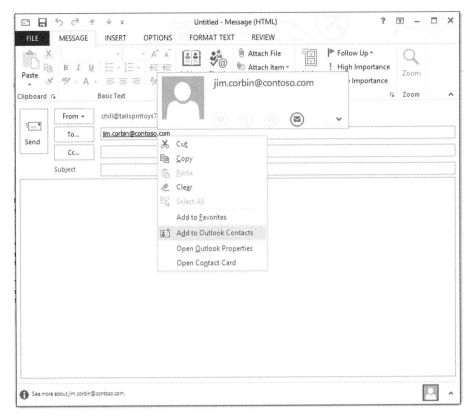

Figure 13-8 Right-clicking an email address gives you extra options.

Modifying addresses

You can modify any addresses stored in your own address books, as well as in the address books of other users for which you have the appropriate access. You can modify an address while working with an email message or while working directly in the address book. If you're using a message form, click To, Cc, or Bcc. Right-click the address you want to change and click Open Outlook Properties. If you're working in the address book instead, just right-click the address and choose Edit. Outlook 2013 displays a window in which you can change details about the contact. Make the changes you want and click Save.

Removing addresses

Removing a contact from the OAB is much easier than creating one. Open the OAB, double-click the address you want to delete, and press Delete.

Finding people in the address book

If your address book contains numerous addresses, as might be the case in a very large organization, it can be a chore to locate an address if you don't use it often. Outlook 2013 provides a search capability in the address book to overcome that problem, making it relatively easy to locate addresses based on several criteria.

> **Note**
>
> You can simply click in the text box at the top of the address book and type a name. Outlook 2013 locates the first name that matches the text you type. If you prefer to see only those items that match the text for which you are searching, you can use the Find dialog box, as described in the following procedure.

Follow these steps to locate an address in any address book:

1. Click the Address Book button on the ribbon to open the address book.

2. In the Address Book drop-down list, select the address book you want to search.

3. Click Advanced Find to display the Find dialog box shown in Figure 13-9 (for Exchange Server address lists) or Figure 13-10 (for the OAB).

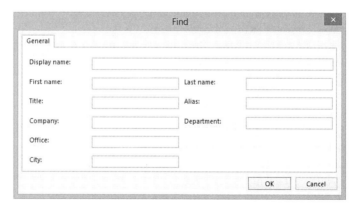

Figure 13-9 Use the Find dialog box to locate people in the Exchange Server GAL.

Figure 13-10 The Find dialog box offers only a single search field for OAB searches.

4. If you're searching an address list on the computer running Exchange Server, decide which criteria you want to use and enter data in the fields to define the search. If you're searching an OAB, specify the text to search for, which must be contained in the contact's name.

5. Click OK to perform the search.

6. When you click OK, Outlook 2013 performs a search in the selected address book based on your search criteria and displays the results in the Address Book window. You can revert to the full address book list by selecting the address book from the Address Book drop-down list. Select Search Results from the Address Book drop-down list to view the results of the last search.

INSIDE OUT Use a directory service

In addition to searching your address books, you can search a directory service for information about contacts. A *directory service* is a server that answers queries about data (typically contact information) stored on the server.

Using AutoComplete for addresses

If you have used versions of Outlook prior to Outlook 2010, you are probably familiar with Outlook's nickname cache, which stored the addresses that you typed in the address fields so that you would not have to type them again the next time you wanted to use them. Instead, you simply typed a few characters and Outlook suggested email addresses based on what you typed. In these previous versions of Outlook, these addresses were stored in a nickname file within your user profile.

Staring with Outlook 2010 and continuing with Outlook 2013, Outlook still automatically keeps track of addresses that you enter in the address fields, but it does away with the nickname cache file and instead stores them in the Suggested Contacts folder in Outlook. When you type an address in the To, Cc, or Bcc field, Outlook 2013 adds the address to the folder, which looks and functions much like your regular Outlook Contacts folder.

When you begin typing in any of these address fields, Outlook 2013 begins matching the typed characters against the entries in the Suggested Contacts folder. If it finds a match, it automatically completes the address. If there is more than one match in the folder, Outlook 2013 displays a drop-down list that contains the names for all the matching entries (see Figure 13-11). Use the arrow keys or mouse to select a name from the list and then press Enter or Tab to add the address to the field.

> **Note**
>
> AutoComplete doesn't check to see whether a particular contact has more than one email address. Instead, it uses whatever address it finds in the Suggested Contacts folder. If Outlook 2013 has cached one address, but you prefer that it cache a different one, delete the existing cache entry (as explained in the next section). Then, address a new message to the contact using the desired email address to cache that address. Or, as the following section explains, you can simply create a contact entry in the Suggested Contacts folder.

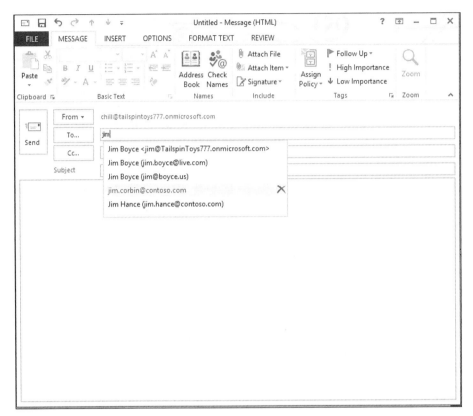

Figure 13-11 Select a name from the Suggested Contacts list offered by Outlook 2013.

You can turn AutoComplete on or off to suit your needs by following these steps:

1. Click File, choose Options, and click Mail in the left pane of the Outlook Options dialog box.

2. Scroll down to the Send Messages group of settings.

3. Select or clear the Use Auto-Complete List To Suggest Names When Typing In The To, Cc, And Bcc Lines check box to turn AutoComplete on or off, respectively.

> **Note**
>
> You can move your Suggested Contacts folder file from one computer to another by simply exporting the items and then importing them. You can also back it up so you can restore it in the event your computer crashes.

Deleting or adding entries in the Suggested Contacts folder

One common reason to delete a contact item from the Suggested Contacts folder is that you either don't use it very often or want to use a different email address for that contact.

It's easy to delete a name from the Suggested Contacts folder. One of the most direct ways is simply to open the Suggested Contacts folder, locate the item, and delete it. You can also get to it indirectly through the message form, which is often quicker than opening the folder and hunting for the item. To do this, perform the following steps:

1. Start a new email message and type the first few letters of the name.

2. When Outlook 2013 displays the shortcut menu with the matching entries, select the one you want to delete and then press Delete.

3. Repeat this process for any other cached addresses you want to delete.

As described in the previous section, you can add items to the Suggested Contacts folder simply by adding a new email address to one of the address fields on a message form and then sending the message. But because the Outlook 2013 Suggested Contacts folder acts just like your other Contacts folders, you can create items directly in the folder. In Outlook 2013, the Suggested Contacts folder has moved. To find it, click Contacts in the Navigation Pane, click the ellipsis button to show additional folders, and click Folders. In the list of folders, click Suggested Contacts. Click New Contact in the ribbon, fill in as much information as you like (or just add the email address), and click Save & Close.

Deleting the entire contents of the Suggested Contacts folder

On occasion, you might want to clear out your Suggested Contacts folder and let Outlook start fresh. Perhaps you have several hundred items in the folder or so many duplicates that you are getting too many off-target suggestions. You have two options for deleting all the items from the Suggested Contacts folder. One is simply to open the folder, press Ctrl+A to select all items in the folder, and then press Delete or click Delete in the ribbon. If you change your mind right after deleting something, immediately press Ctrl+Z to get it back.

You can also clear out the folder from the Outlook Options dialog box by doing the following:

1. Click File, Options to open the Outlook Options dialog box, and then click Mail in the left pane.

2. Scroll down to the Send Messages group and click Empty Auto-Complete List.

Using contact groups (distribution lists)

If you often send messages to groups of people, adding all their addresses to a message one at a time can be a real chore, particularly if you're sending the message to many recipients. Contact groups in Outlook 2013 help simplify the process, enabling you to send a message to a single address and have it broadcast to all recipients in the group. Instead of addressing a message to each individual user in the sales department, for example, you could address it to the sales contact group. Outlook 2013 (or Exchange Server) takes care of sending the message to all the members of the group.

> **Note**
>
> Versions of Outlook prior to Outlook 2010 refer to contact groups as distribution lists. Many corporate Outlook users still use that term to refer to contact groups. The terms *contact group* and *distribution list* are used synonymously in this book except where noted.

You can create contact groups in the OAB. You can't create contact groups in the GAL or other Exchange Server address lists—only the Exchange Server administrator can create the distribution lists on the server. However, you can modify distribution lists on the computer running Exchange Server if you're designated as the owner of the list.

Creating contact groups

Setting up a contact group in your OAB is a relatively simple procedure. You can create a contact group using addresses from multiple address books, which means, for example, that you might include addresses from the GAL on the computer running Exchange Server as well as personal addresses stored in your Contacts folder. You can also include addresses of different types (for example, Exchange Server addresses, Internet addresses, and X.400 addresses). In general, it's easiest to set up a contact group if all the addresses to be included already exist, but you can enter addresses on the fly if needed.

Follow these steps to create a contact group:

1. Open the Contacts folder.

2. Choose New Contact Group on the Home tab to display the Contact Group dialog box, as shown in Figure 13-12.

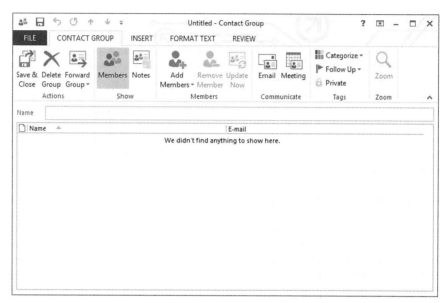

Figure 13-12 Use the Contact Group dialog box to create a contact group.

3. In the Name box, specify a name for the group. This is the contact group name that will appear in your address book.

4. Click Add Members, and then, if the contact already exists, choose From Outlook Contacts to add addresses from your Contacts folder, or choose From Address Book to add from other locations in the OAB (such as the Exchange Server GAL). In either case, the Select Members dialog box opens (see Figure 13-13).

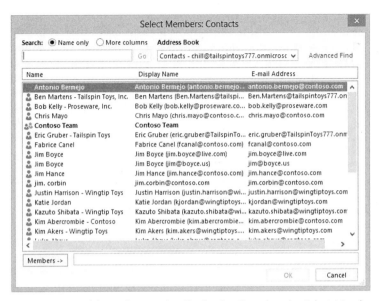

Figure 13-13 Add members to the distribution list using the Select Members dialog box.

5. Select the names of the contacts you want to be members of the new contact group. You can select one or more than one.

6. Click OK.

7. Set other options as needed for the distribution list—for example, you can assign categories to the list, mark it as private, or add notes to the group.

8. Click Save & Close in the Contact Group dialog box.

> **Note**
> Select the Advanced Find option in the Select Members dialog box to search all your address books for members. Enter a name or partial name to display all address book matches to find the desired contact.

Contact groups appear in the address book with a group icon and a boldface name to differentiate them from individual addresses (see Figure 13-14).

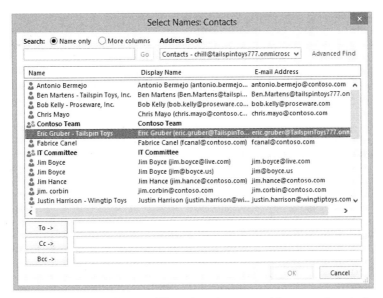

Figure 13-14 Outlook 2013 differentiates between addresses and contact groups in the address book.

INSIDE OUT   Identify address types

Outlook 2013 differentiates addresses in the Select Names dialog box as well as the Address Book. When you address an email message, you can tell which address is a fax number and which is an email address because Outlook displays those items separately in the list, even though they are stored in the same contact item. You can also easily differentiate personal addresses from work addresses in both the Select Names and Address Book dialog boxes.

Note

In a Contacts folder, contact groups look just like addresses, although Outlook 2013 displays a contact group in the address list with a group icon and with the contact group name in bold. The contact group also shows less information than a contact in the various Contacts folder views.

Modifying a contact group

Over time, you will add or remove names from your contact groups. To modify the contents of a group, locate the contact group in the address book or in your Contacts folder, open the group, and then use the Remove Members button to remove a member from the list. You can also remove members from the group by selecting the member and then pressing Delete on your keyboard.

Renaming a contact group

You can change the name of a contact group any time after you create it to reflect changes in the way you use the list, to correct spelling, or for any other reason. To rename a contact group, locate the list in the address book, open it, and then change the name in the Name box. Click Save & Close to apply the change.

Deleting a contact group

You can delete a contact group the same way you delete an address. Locate the contact group in the address book or Contacts folder, select it, and then click the Delete button on the ribbon or press Delete. Alternatively, you can right-click the group and choose Delete from its shortcut menu.

> **Note**
> Deleting a contact group doesn't delete the addresses associated with the group.

Hiding addresses when using a contact group

If you include a contact group in the To or Cc field of a message, all the recipients of your message—whether members of the group or not—can see the addresses of individuals in the group. Outlook 2013 doesn't retain the group name in the address field of the message but instead replaces it with the actual addresses from the group.

In some cases, you might not want to have their addresses made public, even to other members of the group. In these situations, add the contact group to the Bcc (blind carbon copy) field instead of the To or Cc field. The Bcc field sends copies of the email to all addresses and contact groups but keeps the addresses hidden from the other recipients.

Contact groups for multiple address fields

Regardless of where you create a contact group, you can't allocate some addresses in the group to the To field and other addresses to the Cc or Bcc field. You can, however, place the contact group address in either the Cc or Bcc field, if needed.

If you often need to separate addresses from contact groups into different address fields, you can use a couple of techniques to simplify the process. First, consider splitting the contact groups into two or three separate groups. This approach works well if the To, Cc, and Bcc fields generally receive the same addresses each time. A second approach is to create a template with the addresses already filled in, as follows:

1. Start a new mail message.

2. To view the Bcc field, click the Options tab on the ribbon and then click Bcc.

3. Fill in the addresses in the appropriate fields as needed.

4. Click File and choose Save As.

5. In the Save As dialog box, choose Outlook Template from the Save As Type drop-down list.

6. Specify a name and location for the template and click Save.

When you need to send a message using the template, browse to the folder in which the template is stored and double-click the file to open the message template. Add any additional addresses, text, or attachments, and then send the message as usual.

Using distribution lists with Exchange Server

You can use distribution lists with Exchange Server—which are set up by the Exchange Server administrator—in the same way that you use local contact groups to simplify broadcasting messages to multiple recipients. (As mentioned earlier, you can't create your own contact groups or distribution lists in the GAL or other Exchange Server address lists from Outlook 2013, although you can modify such a list if you are designated as the list owner.)

You can use a server-side distribution list in the same way that you use a local contact group. Select the list from the appropriate address list on the server. The list name is converted to addresses when you send the message, just as a local contact group is.

Adding a server-side distribution list to contacts

If you prefer working through your local address books instead of the server address lists, you might want to add a server-side distribution list to your local Contacts folder. You can do so easily through the address book or the list's dialog box. Open the address book, select the distribution list, and then choose File, Add To Contacts.

> **Note**
>
> If you have the list's dialog box open, click Add To Contacts on the General tab. Outlook 2013 then adds the list to your Contacts folder.

When Outlook 2013 displays the distribution list, you can then modify the group, assign categories, send a meeting request or email, mark it as private, or even use the Proof button to run the spelling checker or use the thesaurus (see Figure 13-15). Make any necessary changes to the distribution list and then click Save & Close.

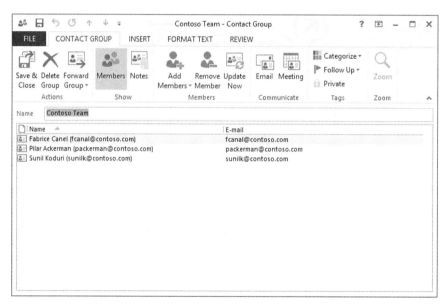

Figure 13-15 You can select various options for distribution lists you store in the Contacts folder.

Modifying a server-side distribution list

If you are an owner of a server-side distribution list, you can modify its members and other properties. For example, perhaps you manage a team of people and the team has a distribution list in Exchange Server. A new person joins your team, and you want to add that person to the list. To do so, open the address book and double-click the distribution list to open it (see Figure 13-16). You can add or remove members by clicking Modify Members.

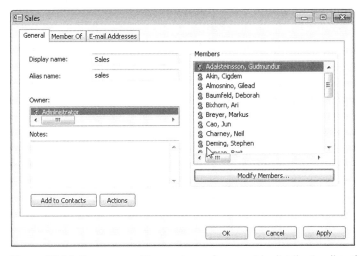

Figure 13-16 You can modify members of server-side distribution lists that you own.

Adding addresses to the address book automatically

When you receive a message from a sender whose address you want to save in your local Contacts folder, you can add the address manually. As it has in previous versions, however, Outlook 2013 also provides an easier method. With the message open, right-click the sender's address in the To field and choose Add To Outlook Contacts.

Outlook 2013 offers a new method for adding contacts from incoming email in the form of the Suggested Contacts folder. As new messages arrive, Outlook checks to see if the sender already exists in your Contacts folder. If not, Outlook adds the address to the Suggested Contacts folder. From there, you can drag the contact item to your regular Contacts folder, or you can copy and paste it from one folder to another. Outlook also adds the addresses of people to whom you have addressed email.

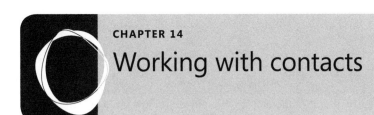

T HE Contacts folder in Microsoft Outlook 2013 is an electronic tool that can organize and store the thousands of details you need to know to communicate with people, businesses, and organizations. You can use the Contacts folder to store email addresses, street addresses, multiple phone numbers, and any other information that relates to a contact, such as a birthday or an anniversary date.

From a contact entry in your list of contacts, you can click a button or choose a command to have Outlook 2013 address a meeting request, an email message, a letter, or a task request to the contact. If you have a modem, Voice over Internet Protocol (VoIP) phone, Microsoft Lync, or other online conferencing application, you can have Outlook 2013 dial the contact's phone number. You can link any Outlook 2013 item or Microsoft Office 2013 system document to a contact to help you track activities associated with the contact.

Outlook 2013 allows you to customize the view in the Contacts folder to review and print your contact information. You can sort, group, or filter your contact list to better manage the information or to quickly find entries. You also can use Outlook contacts to create mail merges with other Office 2013 programs, such as Microsoft Word.

Outlook 2013 also supports the use of vCards, the Internet standard for creating and sharing virtual business cards. You can save a contact entry as a vCard and send it in an email message. You can also add a vCard to your email signature.

This chapter discusses contact management in Outlook 2013. The Outlook 2013 Contacts feature provides powerful tools to help you manage, organize, and find important contact information.

Working with the People Hub

The People Hub is a new feature in Outlook 2013. It provides a single place in Outlook to view, manage, and communicate with people in your contact list. The People Hub includes information about your contacts, including email information and social network information.

For detailed information about using Outlook and social media together, see Chapter 15, "Social networking and Outlook."

To use social network accounts in your People Hub, you must first enable social networking support in Outlook. To do so, follow these steps:

1. Click People on the Navigation Bar and then click the Connect To A Social Network link.

2. On the Connect Office To Your Social Networks screen, click Next.

3. On the Social Network Accounts screen, select the type of online social networks you want to set up, such as Facebook, LinkedIn, SharePoint, or More (see Figure 14-1).

4. For each social network you select in step 3, you are presented with user name and password fields to fill out. Do so for each social network you want to set up.

5. Click Finish.

6. Click Close.

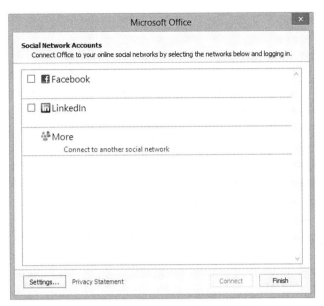

Figure 14-1 Use the Social Network Accounts window to set up the social network accounts you want to display in the People Hub.

When you click People on the Navigation Bar, you see a list of your contact folders, such as Contacts, Lync Contacts (if you have a Lync system), and so on. The Contacts folder is one of the Outlook 2013 default folders. This folder stores information such as name, physical address, phone number, social media links, and email address for each contact. You can use the People folder to address email messages, place phone calls, distribute bulk mailings through mail merge (in Microsoft Word 2013), and perform many other communication tasks quickly. The Contacts folder, however, is not the same as your address book. Your Outlook Address Book (OAB) lets you access the Contacts folder for addressing messages, but the OAB also lets you access addresses stored in other address lists.

For detailed information about working with address books in Outlook 2013, see Chapter 13, "Managing address books and contact groups."

You can open the Contacts folder by clicking the People button in the Navigation Pane. When you open the folder, you'll see its default view, People. This view displays the new Outlook 2013 Contact Card, which shows a photo (if available), a name, an address, a phone number, and a handful of other items for each contact, as shown in Figure 14-2. You also can initiate actions related to the contact. For example, you can click the email icon on the card to create a new email message with the selected contact as the recipient. Outlook 2013 provides several predefined views for the Contacts folder that offer different ways to display and sort the contact list.

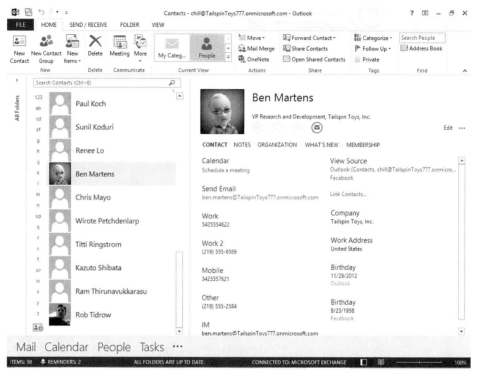

Figure 14-2 Use the Contacts folder to manage contact information such as address, phone number, and fax number for your business associates and friends.

For details about the available views in the Contacts folder and how to work with them, see the section "Viewing contacts."

> **Note**
>
> You can use the alphabet index on the left in the contact list window to jump quickly to a specific area in the Contacts folder. For example, click CD to jump to the list of contacts whose last names begin with C or D.

When you double-click an entry in the Contacts folder, Outlook 2013 opens a contact card similar to the one shown in Figure 14-3. This card lets you view and modify a wealth of information about the person. When you are done editing the card, click Save to return to the contact card view. You'll learn more about these tasks throughout the remainder of this chapter. The following section explains how to create a contact entry.

Figure 14-3 An open contact card shows an address, phone numbers, and other information about the contact.

Creating a contact entry

To create a contact entry, you can start from scratch, or you can base the new entry on a similar existing entry—for example, the entry for a contact from the same company.

You can open a contact form and create a new entry in any of the following ways:

- Click New Contact on the Home tab on the ribbon with the Contacts folder open.

- Right-click a blank area in the Contacts folder (not a contact entry), and then choose New Contact. This is available when Current View is set to Business Card or Card.

- With the Contacts folder open, press Ctrl+N.

- In any other folder view (such as Messages), click the arrow next to the New Items button on the ribbon, and then choose Contact.

Chapter 14

When the contact form opens (see Figure 14-4), type the contact's name in the Full Name box and enter the information that you want to include for the contact, switching between General and Details views (using the Show button) as needed. To save the entry, click Save & Close. To save this entry and continue to add contacts, click Save & New. To copy the company information to another new contact, click Save & New and then choose Contact From The Same Company.

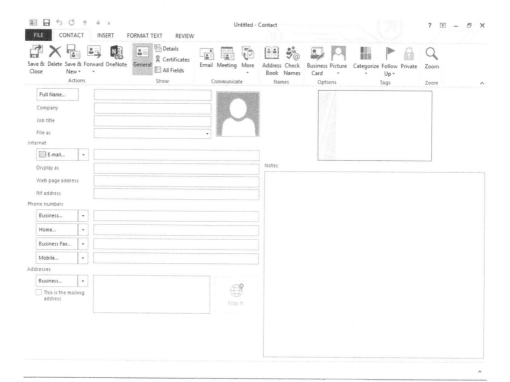

Figure 14-4 A new contact starts with a blank Untitled – Contact form.

Filling in the information on the contact form is straightforward. You might find a few of the features especially useful. For example, the File As drop-down list allows you to specify how you want the contact to be listed in the Contacts folder. You can choose to list the contact in either Last Name, First Name format or First Name, Last Name format; to list the contact by company name rather than personal name; or to use a combination of contact name and company name.

You can also store more phone numbers in the contact entry than the four that are displayed on the form. When you click the down arrow next to a phone number entry, you see a list of possible phone numbers from which you can select a number to view or modify;

the checked items on the list are those that currently contain information. When you select a number, Outlook 2013 shows it on the form.

In addition to storing multiple phone numbers for a contact, you also can store multiple physical addresses. Click the down arrow next to the Address button on the form to select a business, home, or other address. (By default, the button is labeled Business.) The E-mail box can also store multiple addresses; click the down arrow to choose one of three email addresses for the individual. For example, you might list both business and personal addresses for the contact. The Details page of the contact form, shown in Figure 14-5, lets you add other information, such as the contact's department, office number, birthday, and anniversary. To view Details, click Details in the Show group on the Contact tab. Internet Free/Busy is a feature of Outlook 2013 that allows you to see when others are free or busy so that you can schedule meetings efficiently. Outlook 2013 users have the option to publish their free/busy information to a user-specified URL file server, which you can enter in the Address box.

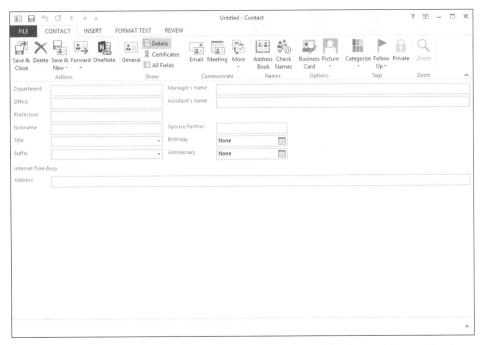

Figure 14-5 The Details page stores additional information—both business and personal—about the contact.

INSIDE OUT Add contacts quickly

When you use one of the table views (such as Phone List) to display your Contacts folder, you'll see a row at the top of the list labeled Click Here To Add A New Contact. This is a handy way to enter a contact's name and phone number quickly—simply type the information directly in the row, and Outlook 2013 adds the contact entry to the folder.

Creating contact entries from the same company

If you have several contacts who work for the same company, you can use an existing contact entry to create a new entry. Simply select the existing entry in Business Cards or Address Cards view, click New Items, and then choose Contact From Same Company. Outlook 2013 opens a new contact form with all the company information (name, address, and phone numbers) supplied—all you have to do is fill in the personal details for that individual.

Note

You can also use a template to create multiple contact entries that share common data such as company affiliation. For information about working with templates in Outlook 2013, see Chapter 25, "Creating and using templates."

Creating a contact entry from an email message

When you receive an email message from someone you'd like to add to your contact list, you can create a contact entry directly from the message. In the From line of the message form, right-click the name, and then choose Add To Outlook Contacts from the shortcut menu. Outlook 2013 opens a new contact form with the sender's name and email address already entered. Add any other necessary data for the contact, and then click Save to create the entry.

Copying an existing contact entry

In some cases, you might want to create a copy of a contact entry. For example, although you can keep both personal and business data in a single entry, you might want to store the data separately. You can save time by copying the existing entry rather than creating a new one from scratch.

To copy a contact entry in the Contacts folder, right-click and drag the entry to an empty spot in the folder, and then choose Copy. Outlook 2013 displays the Duplicate Contact Detected dialog box. Click Add New Contact, and then click Add to create a new entry containing all the same information as the original. You also can copy contact information to another folder. Open the folder where the contact entry is stored, and then locate the destination folder in the Navigation Pane or in the Folder List. Right-click and drag the contact entry to the destination folder, and then choose Copy on the shortcut menu.

Creating other contact folders

In addition to providing its default Contacts folder, Outlook 2013 allows you to use multiple contact folders to organize your contacts easily. For example, you might use a shared contact folder jointly with members of your workgroup for business contacts and keep your personal contacts in a separate folder, or you might prefer to keep contact information that you use infrequently in a separate folder to reduce the clutter in your main Contacts folder. The process of creating a contact entry in any contact folder is the same regardless of the folder's location—whether it is part of your Microsoft Exchange Server account or in a personal folder (.pst) file, for example.

To create a new folder for storing contacts, follow these steps:

1. Right-click Contacts in the Folder List and choose New Folder to open the Create New Folder dialog box, shown in Figure 14-6.

Figure 14-6 Use the Create New Folder dialog box to create new Outlook 2013 folders.

2. In the Name box, type a name for the folder. This is the folder name that will be displayed in Outlook 2013 (in the Navigation Pane and in the Folder List, for example).

3. Select Contact Items in the Folder Contains drop-down list.

4. In the Select Where To Place The Folder list, select the location for the new folder.

5. Click OK.

When you create a new contact folder using this method, Outlook 2013 sets up the folder using default properties for permissions, rules, descriptions, forms, and views.

Working with contacts

You can do much more with your Outlook 2013 contact list than just view address and phone information. Outlook 2013 provides a set of tools that make it easy to phone, write, email, or communicate with contacts in other ways. This section explains these tools.

Associating a contact with other items and documents

As you work with a contact, it's useful to have email messages, appointments, tasks, documents, or other items related to the contact at your fingertips. You can relate items to a contact by inserting one Outlook 2013 item in another. For example, if you create a task to call several of your contacts, you can use the Outlook Item button on the Insert tab to insert those contacts in the task. To do this, follow these steps:

1. With the task open, click Outlook Item on the Insert tab.

2. Select the contacts in the resulting Insert Item dialog box, shown in Figure 14-7.

3. Click OK to insert the item.

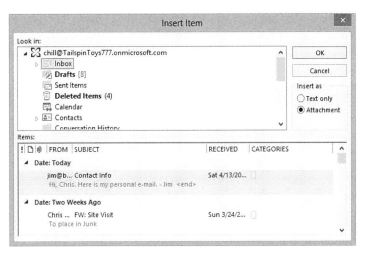

Figure 14-7 Use the Insert Item dialog box to associate contacts with a task.

For details on setting up tasks, see the section "Working with tasks in the Tasks folder" in Chapter 18, "Working with tasks."

Associating contacts and documents

In many cases, you might want to insert one or more documents in a contact. For example, assume that you manage contracts for several individuals or companies. You can insert a contract document into the contact that is covered by the contract to make it easier to open the document from the contact form. With this association, you don't need to remember the document name if you know the name of the contact with whom it is associated.

Follow these steps to insert a document in a contact:

1. Open the Contacts folder, change to Business Card or Card in the Current View group (or any view other than People), open the contact item, and then click the Insert tab.

2. Click Attach File.

3. Locate the files that you want to associate with the contact, and then click Insert.

4. The file now appears in the Notes area of the contact details.

5. Click the Contact tab, and then click Save & Close to create the link.

When you want to open the document, simply open the contact form and click the link in the Notes section.

In the preceding example, you actually insert the document in the contact item. An alternative is to insert a hyperlink to the document in the contact item. The advantage to this method is that you are not duplicating the document—it remains in its original location on disk. When you need to open the document, you can click the hyperlink in the contact item. Alternatively, you can open the document from its location on the disk. Another benefit of linking rather than embedding is that if the source document changes, you'll see the up-to-date copy when you open it from inside the contact item in Outlook. If you embed the document in the contact item instead, any changes to the original are not reflected in the copy stored in Outlook.

Linking a document in a contact is easy. In step 3 of the preceding procedure, rather than click Insert, click the down arrow next to the Insert button, and then select Insert As Hyperlink.

Removing a link

Occasionally, you'll want to remove a link between a contact and another item. For example, perhaps you've accidentally linked the wrong document to a contact.

To remove a link from a contact to an item, follow these steps:

1. Open the contact item, and then, on the Contact tab, in the Show group, click General.

2. In the Notes section of the contact form, select the item that you want to delete and press the Delete key.

3. Click Save.

Assigning categories to contacts

A *category* is a keyword or a phrase that helps you keep track of items so that you can find, sort, filter, or group them easily. Use categories to keep track of different types of items that are related but stored in different folders. For example, you can keep track of all the meetings, contacts, and messages for a specific project when you create a category named after the project and then assign items to it.

Categories also give you a way to keep track of contacts without putting them in separate folders. For example, you can keep business and personal contacts in the same contact folder and use the Business and Personal categories to sort the two sets of contacts into separate groups.

One quick way to assign categories to a contact is to right-click the contact item, choose Categorize, and then click a category. If the category you want doesn't appear in the category list, choose All Categories on the shortcut menu. Then, in the Color Categories dialog box, you can select the check boxes next to the categories that you want to assign to the contact. Alternatively, you can open the contact item, click the Categorize button on the contact form, and select a category, or click All Categories to open the Color Categories dialog box. This dialog box is useful not only for assigning categories, but also for reviewing the categories that you've already assigned to an item.

For more information about how to assign a category to a contact; how to use categories to sort, filter, and group contact items; and how to create your own categories, see Chapter 5, "Creating and using categories."

Resolving duplicate contacts

If you create a contact entry using the same name or email address as an entry that already exists in your Contacts folder, Outlook 2013 displays the Duplicate Contact Detected dialog box, in which you can choose to either add the new contact entry or update your existing entry with the new information, as shown in Figure 14-8.

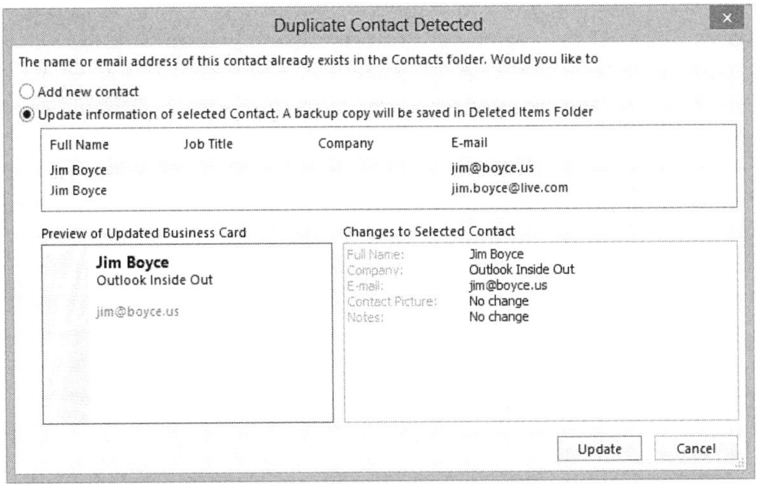

Figure 14-8 Use the Duplicate Contact Detected dialog box to tell Outlook 2013 how to handle a duplicate contact.

If you select the first option, Outlook 2013 adds the new contact to your Contacts folder, and you'll now have two entries listed under the same name or email address. In that case, you'll probably want to add some information to the contact forms—perhaps company affiliation or a middle initial—to distinguish the two entries.

If you select the second option, to update the existing entry with information from the new one, Outlook 2013 compares the fields containing data in both entries and copies the data from the new entry into any fields that have conflicting data. For example, if you have a contact named Chris Ashton whose phone number is 555-5655, and you create a new contact entry for Chris Ashton with a new phone number, Outlook 2013 copies the new number into the existing entry and leaves the other fields the same.

In case you need to revert to the information in the original contact entry, a copy of the original entry is stored in your Deleted Items folder whenever Outlook 2013 copies new data.

> ## Note
>
> **If you are adding many contacts, Outlook 2013 can save the information faster if you do not require the program to detect duplicates. To turn off duplicate detection, click File, Options. Click People, and then clear the Check For Duplicates When Saving New Contacts check box. Click OK.**

Phoning a contact

If you have a modem, VoIP phone, or voice conferencing software (such as Microsoft Lync), you can use Outlook 2013 to dial any phone number that you specify, including phone numbers for contacts in your contact list.

To make a phone call to a contact using Outlook 2013, follow these steps:

1. Open the Contacts folder.

2. If you are using the People view, click a contact and then click the arrow beside the Call button in the Reading Pane and choose a number. If you want to use a different number, choose Call New Number. Alternatively, you can change to Business Card or Card view, click a contact item, click More in the Communicate group on the Home tab, choose Call, and then choose a number to open the New Call dialog box with the contact's phone number already entered, as shown in Figure 14-9. If the contact form is open, in the Communicate group of the ribbon, click the More button and then choose Call.

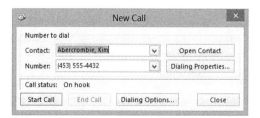

Figure 14-9 Select the number to call and other options in the New Call dialog box.

○ If you want Outlook 2013 to use a phone number associated with a different contact, type the contact's name in the Contact box, and then press Tab or click in the Number box. Alternatively, you can simply type the phone number in the Number box.

○ If the contact entry for the person you're calling already includes phone numbers, select the phone number in the Number box. If the contact entry doesn't specify a phone number, type the number in the Number box.

3. Click Start Call.

4. Pick up the phone handset, and click Talk to begin the call.

5. When you've finished the call, click End Call and hang up the phone.

> **Note**
>
> If you omit the country code and area code from a phone number, the automatic phone dialer uses settings from the Dialing Properties dialog box, which you can access through the Phone And Modem Options icon in Control Panel or by clicking Dialing Properties in the New Call dialog box. If you include letters in the phone number, the automatic phone dialer does not recognize them.

Sending an email message to a contact

If you're working in the Contacts folder, you can send an email message to one of your contacts without switching to the Inbox folder. This is a handy feature that can save a lot of time in an average workday.

Here's how to send a message from the Contacts folder:

1. In the Contacts folder, select the contact item, and then click the email icon. You also can click E-mail in the Communicate group on the Home tab. Finally, you can right-click the contact, click Create, and then click E-mail.

2. In the Subject box, type the subject of the message.

3. In the message body, type the message.

4. Click Send.

Connecting to a contact's website

It seems everyone has a website these days, whether it's a company site or a personal blog. If you have the URL for a contact's website recorded in the contact entry, you can connect to that site directly from Outlook 2013. This is particularly handy for linking to business sites from a company contact entry—for example, you might create a link to the company's support or sales page. Associating websites with contacts is often more meaningful than simply storing a URL in your Favorites folder.

With the contact item open, you can connect to the contact's website by clicking the URL in the Web Page Address field.

Scheduling appointments and meetings with contacts

Many Outlook 2013 users believe that the Calendar folder is the only place you can schedule a new appointment or meeting easily, but that's not the case. You can schedule an appointment or a meeting in any Outlook 2013 folder. The Contacts folder, however, is a logical place to create new appointments and meetings because those events are often associated with one or more contacts stored in the Contacts folder.

Scheduling a meeting with a contact

Meetings differ from appointments in that they are collaborative efforts that involve the schedules of all the attendees. When you set up a meeting, Outlook 2013 creates and sends meeting requests to the individuals you want to invite. You can create meeting requests for any number of contacts through the Contacts folder, saving the time of switching folders.

To send a meeting request to one or more of your contacts from the Contacts folder, follow these steps:

1. Open the Contacts folder, and then select the contact entries for those people you want to invite to the meeting. (To select multiple entries, hold down the Ctrl key and click the entries.)

2. Click Meeting in the Communicate group of the Home tab on the ribbon.

3. In the Subject box, type a description of the proposed meeting.

4. In the Location box, type the location.

5. Enter the proposed start and end times for the meeting.

6. Select any other options that you want.

7. Click Send.

For details about setting up meetings and sending meeting requests, see Chapter 17, "Scheduling meetings, rooms, and resources."

Assigning a task to a contact

The Tasks folder in Outlook 2013 offers a handy way to keep track of your work and the work that you delegate to others. For example, if you manage a group of people, you probably use the Tasks folder to assign tasks to the people who work for you. However, if you need to assign a job to one of your contacts, you can do this directly from the Contacts folder. Doing so adds the contact's name to the Contacts box in the task request.

Follow these steps to assign a task to a contact:

1. In the Contacts folder, select the contact, click More in the Communicate group on the Home tab of the ribbon, and choose Assign Task.

2. Outlook 2013 opens a new task form with the contact's email address in the To field. Enter other information as needed, such as start and stop dates for the task.

3. Click Send to send the task request.

Flagging a contact for follow-up

You can flag a contact item for follow-up to have Outlook 2013 remind you to call or email the contact. For example, suppose that you want to make a note to yourself to call a colleague at 10:00 A.M. tomorrow to ask about the status of a project. You could create a note in the Notes folder, create a task, or add an appointment to your schedule, but an easy way to create the reminder is to add a follow-up flag to the contact entry in the Contacts folder. Outlook 2013 adds the follow-up flag as text to the Card view, but there is no other visual indicator that contacts are flagged. However, you can click the To-Do Bar and see the contacts' names in the Daily Task List with a follow-up flag, as shown in Figure 14-10.

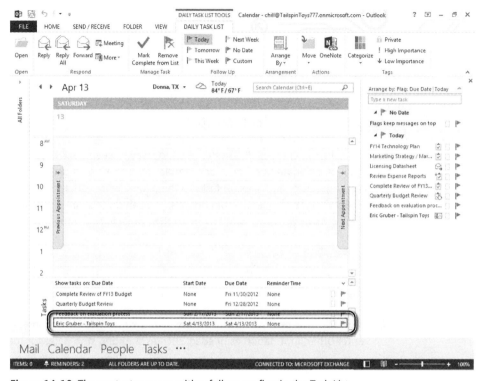

Figure 14-10 The contact appears with a follow-up flag in the Task List.

If you specify a particular date and time for follow-up when you add the flag, Outlook 2013 generates a reminder at the appointed time. Adding a reminder helps ensure that you don't forget to follow up with the contact at the appropriate time.

Follow these steps to flag a contact for follow-up:

1. In the Contacts folder, select the contact that you want to flag, and then in the Tags group on the Home tab on the ribbon, and click Follow Up. Alternatively, right-click the contact, and then choose Follow Up.

2. If one of the default follow-up time options suits you, click it. If not, click Custom to open the Custom dialog box.

3. In the Flag To box of the Custom dialog box, shown in Figure 14-11, select the flag text that you want Outlook 2013 to use or type your own flag text.

Figure 14-11 Use the Custom dialog box to specify the flag text and set an optional reminder.

4. Select a start date in the Start Date drop-down list, and then select a due date in the Due Date drop-down list.

5. If you want a reminder, select the Reminder option, choose a date, and then specify a time.

6. Click OK. Outlook 2013 adds the flag text to the contact item and adds an entry to your task list.

When you have completed your follow-up action, you can remove the flag from the contact item (clear the flag) or mark the follow-up as completed. If you clear the flag, Outlook 2013 removes it from the contact item and the Task List. If you prefer to have the flag remain, you can mark the follow-up as completed. In this case, the follow-up text remains, but the contact form includes a message indicating that the follow-up was accomplished (and the date). When you flag a contact as complete, the item disappears from the Task List.

Use one of the following methods to mark a follow-up flag as completed:

- Select the flagged contact item, click Follow Up on the Home tab, and then click Mark Complete.

- Right-click the contact item, click Follow Up, and then click Mark Complete.

Use one of the following methods to clear a flag, which removes it from the contact item:

- Select the contact item, click Follow Up, and then click Clear Flag.

- Right-click the contact item in the Contacts folder, click Follow Up, and then click Clear Flag.

Chapter 14

Finding contacts

If you store only a small list of contacts, finding a particular contact is usually not a problem. As the number of contacts grows, however, it becomes more and more difficult to
locate information, especially if you aren't sure about a name. For example, you might
remember that a person works for a certain company but can't recall the person's name.
Outlook 2013 provides features to help you quickly and easily locate contact information.

Perhaps the easiest method of locating a contact, if you know the name, is to type the
name in the Search Contacts box and then press Enter. Outlook 2013 locates the contact
and filters the view to display it. If more than one contact matches the data you've entered,
Outlook 2013 displays all of them, as shown in Figure 14-12.

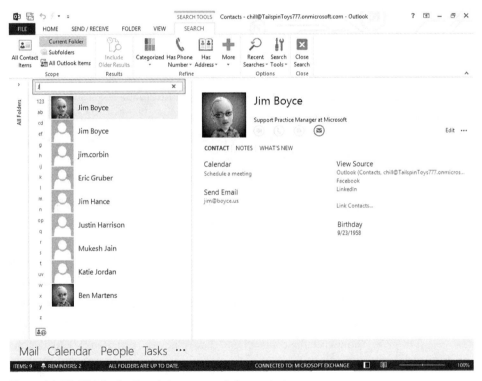

Figure 14-12 Click in the Search box to search for contacts.

The options on the Search tab can help you refine your search. For example, you can search
by email address, phone number, category, and more. Use the Scope group to specify
where to search, whether in the current folder, all subfolders, or all of Outlook.

Finally, if you need to perform an advanced search, click Search Tools and choose Advanced Find to open the Advanced Find dialog box, shown in Figure 14-13. You can use this dialog box to perform more complex searches based on multiple conditions, such as searching for both name and company.

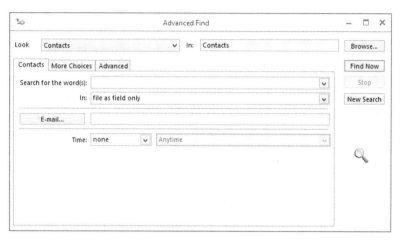

Figure 14-13 Use the Advanced Find dialog box to perform more complex searches using multiple conditions.

Viewing contacts

Outlook 2013 provides predefined views for reviewing your contact list in the Contacts folder. For example, the new Contact Card shows a photo of the contact, email information, social media connections, and other links. Card view displays names and addresses of contacts in blocks that look like address labels. This view is a convenient way to look up a contact's mailing address. In Phone view, Outlook 2013 displays contact entries in table rows with details such as phone, job title, and department name in columns. This view is helpful for quickly finding a contact's phone number or job title. You can customize the various standard views to control the amount of detail or to help you organize and analyze information.

Using standard views in the Contacts folder

The Contacts folder offers several standard formats for viewing contacts. To change views, select a view in the Navigation Pane or click View, Current View, and then select the view that you want to use. Three of the standard formats are card views, and the rest are table views, as described in the following list:

- **Contact Cards**   This view shows the contacts in the new Contacts Card view, which can be shown by double-clicking a contact, hovering over a contact, or clicking a contact. Figure 14-14, for example, shows how the new Contacts Card displays when you hover over the People link while viewing the Inbox folder (called People peek).

- **Business Cards**   This view shows the contacts in a business card format.

- **Card**   This view displays contact entries as individual cards with name, one mailing address, and business and home phone numbers.

- **Phone**   This table view displays a list with the contact's name, company name, business phone number, business fax number, home phone number, mobile phone number, categories, and a check box to enable or disable journaling for the contact.

- **List**   This view displays the items as a general list.

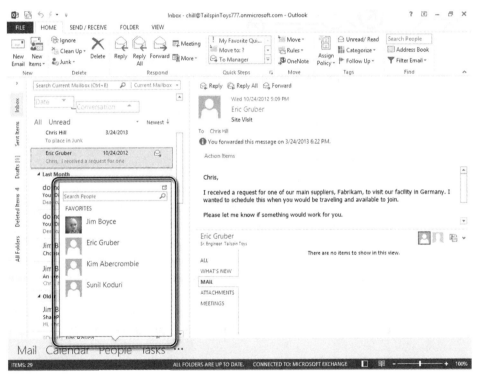

Figure 14-14 Hover over the People link to get a quick view (called People peek) of the last few contacts you opened.

> **Note**
> You can resize address cards easily by dragging the vertical separator between columns, which changes the width of all card columns.

Customizing Contacts view

The methods of customizing the view in Outlook 2013 folders are generally the same for all folders. This section examines some specific ways that you might customize the Contacts folder to make it easier to locate and work with contacts. For example, you might use a specific color for contacts who work for a particular company. You can also change the fonts used for the card headings and body, specify the card width and height, and automatically format contact entries based on rules.

Filtering Contacts view

You can filter the view in the Contacts folder to show only those contacts that meet the conditions that you specify in the filter. For example, you can use a filter to view only those contacts who work for a particular company or who live in a particular city.

Follow these steps to set up a view filter in the Contacts folder:

1. Click People to open the Contacts folder. Select the view you want to change, and then click View Settings on the View tab.

2. Click Filter in the Advanced View Settings dialog box.

3. In the Filter dialog box, specify the conditions for the filter. If you don't see the items that you need to specify for the condition, use the Field drop-down list on the Advanced tab to select the necessary field.

4. Click OK to close the Filter dialog box, and then click OK in the Advanced View Settings dialog box to apply the filter.

When you want to view the entire contents of the folder again, you can remove the filter using the procedure detailed here:

1. Select the view and click View Settings in the View tab on the ribbon.

2. Click Filter.

3. In the Filter dialog box, click Clear All, and then click OK.

4. Click OK to close the Advanced View Settings dialog box.

> **Note**
> If you want to reset the view to its default properties, click Reset Current View in the
> Advanced View Settings dialog box.

Configuring fonts and card dimensions

You can change the font used for card headings and the card body text. You can also change the font style, size, and script, but not the color. This does not work when the Current View option on the Home tab is set to People.

Follow these steps to change the font for card headings and body text:

1. Display the view that you want to modify and then click View Settings in the View tab on the ribbon.

2. In the Advanced View Settings dialog box, click Other Settings to display the Format Card View dialog box, shown in Figure 14-15.

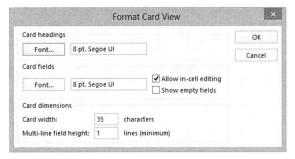

Figure 14-15 Use the Format Card View dialog box to specify the font for card headings and body text.

3. Click Font in the Card Headings or Card Fields area of the dialog box to open a standard Font dialog box in which you can select font characteristics.

4. Make your font selections, and then click OK.

5. Specify options according to the following list, and then click OK:

    ○ **Allow In-Cell Editing**   Select this check box if you want to modify contact data by clicking a field in the view without opening the contact form.

○ **Show Empty Fields**   Select this check box if you want to show all fields for all contacts, even if the fields are empty. Clear this check box to simplify the view of your Contacts folder. Note that when this check box is selected, Outlook 2013 displays all fields defined for the view, not all contact fields.

○ **Card Width**   Set the card width (in number of characters) using this option.

○ **Multi-Line Field Height**   Use this option to specify the number of lines that you want to display on the card for multiline fields.

6.   Click OK to close the Advanced View Settings dialog box.

Using automatic formatting

Outlook 2013 performs some limited automatic formatting of data in the Contacts folder. For example, it uses bold for contact group items, regular font for unread contacts, and red for overdue contacts (contact entries with an overdue follow-up flag). You can make changes to these automatic formatting rules, and you can even create your own rules. For example, you might want to display overdue contacts in blue rather than in red, or you might want to use a particular color for all contacts who work for a certain company. This does not work when the Current View option on the Home tab is set to People.

> **Note**
>
> Contacts can acquire an unread status when you copy a contact from a public folder to your local Outlook store. However, it's unlikely that you'll actually use or need the read or unread states for your contacts.

Follow these steps to modify the formatting for an existing rule or to create a new rule:

1.   Open the Contacts folder and display the view that you want to modify, and then click View Settings.

2.   Click Conditional Formatting in the Advanced View Settings dialog box to display the Conditional Formatting dialog box, shown in Figure 14-16.

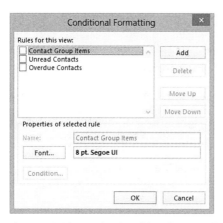

Figure 14-16 Use the Conditional Formatting dialog box to create custom rules that control how Outlook 2013 displays contacts.

3. If you want to modify an existing rule, select the rule, and then click Font to change the font characteristics or click Condition to modify the condition for the rule. If you are changing the condition, skip to step 6. Otherwise, skip to step 7.

> **Note**
> You can modify a rule condition only for rules that you have created. You cannot change the condition for the three predefined rules.

4. Click Add if you want to add a new rule. Outlook 2013 creates a new rule named Untitled.

5. Type a new name in the Name field, click Font and specify font characteristics, and then click Condition to open the Filter dialog box, shown in Figure 14-17.

Figure 14-17 You can specify complex conditions using the Filter dialog box.

6.   Specify the criteria to define the rule condition. For example, click Advanced, click Field, click Frequently Used Fields, and click Company. Then select Contains in the Condition drop-down list and type a company name in the Value box. This will format all contacts from the specified company automatically using the font properties you specify in the next step.

7.   Click OK to close the Filter dialog box, click Font in the Conditional Formatting dialog box, specify the font properties, and then click OK.

8.   Close the Conditional Formatting and Advanced View Settings dialog boxes to view the effects of the new rule.

> **Note**
>
> Automatic formatting rules follow the hierarchy in the list shown in the Automatic Formatting dialog box. Use the Move Up and Move Down buttons to change the order of rules in the lists and thereby change the order in which they are applied.

Filtering contacts with categories

Categorizing contacts allows you to organize your contacts into groups that you create. For example, categories provide an easy way to distinguish all your personal contacts from business contacts. Categorizing also gives you the ability to group people from different companies who are all involved in the same project. Outlook 2013 provides an easy way for you to categorize your contacts, using color coding to distinguish the categories from each other. You can also define custom labels for categories so that you can identify the category by both color and label.

You can define your categories either by using a color category for the first time or by using the Color Categories dialog box. Outlook 2013 offers a couple of ways to open the Color Categories dialog box:

- Click the Categorize button in the Tags group on the Home tab on the ribbon, and then click All Categories.

- Right-click any contact item, and then choose Categorize, All Categories.

> **Note**
>
> When you use a color category for the first time, Outlook 2013 displays a Rename Category dialog box that lets you change the text associated with the category.

To create a new category and assign a color to it, follow these steps:

1. In the Color Categories dialog box, click New.

2. Type an appropriate name for the category, and then select a color in the drop-down color palette.

3. Click OK.

> **Note**
>
> For quick category assignment, assign a unique shortcut key to each of the categories that you use most often. You can assign the shortcut key through the Color Categories dialog box.

You should now see the category that you just created in your category list. To assign these categories to your contacts, follow these steps:

1. In the Contacts folder, right-click any item in the contact list.

2. Click Categorize on the shortcut menu.

3. Select the category that you just added.

Now that you have categorized your contacts, it's time to view them. To do this, open any list view that includes the Categories column, right-click the Categories column, and choose Group By This Field.

For more information about categories, see Chapter 5.

Printing contacts

As an experienced user of Windows, you probably need little if any explanation of how to print. So rather than focusing on basic printing commands, this section offers some insight into why you might print from the Contacts folder and what your options are when you do print.

Why print? If you're like most people, you probably try to work from your computer as much as possible and reduce the amount of paper that you generate. The completely paperless office is still a distant goal for most people, however, and there will be times when you want to print your contact list. For example, you might need to take a copy of your contacts with you on a business trip, but you don't have a notebook computer. A hard copy of your contacts is the solution to this problem.

Outlook 2013 supports several predefined styles that allow you to print contact information using various formats, including preprinted sheets for several popular day planners. You can print a single contact entry, a selection of entries, or all entries. To print a selection (one or more), first select the contact entries to print by holding down the Ctrl key and clicking each one. If you want to print all contacts, first select all the contacts. Then choose File, Print to open the Print page, shown in Figure 14-18.

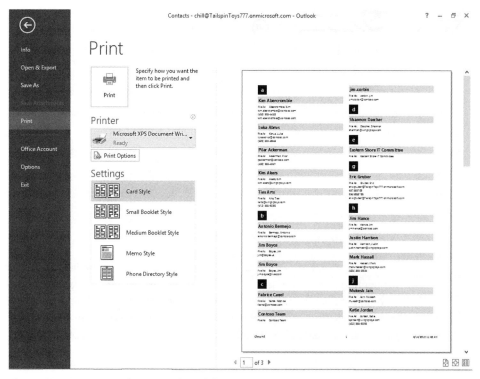

Figure 14-18 You can select several predefined styles on the Print page.

In the Settings area of the Print page, you can select one of five print styles (depending on the contact view that you selected before clicking File, Print), each of which results in a different printed layout. You can use the styles as listed, modify them, or create new styles. To modify an existing style, double-click the style to open the Page Setup dialog box, which resembles the one shown in Figure 14-19.

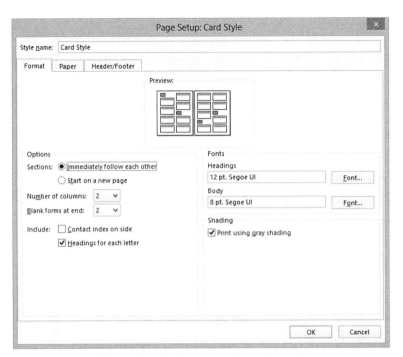

Figure 14-19 Modify a print style in the Page Setup dialog box.

Use the Format tab of this dialog box to specify fonts and shading and to set options such as printing a contact index on the side of each page, adding headings for each letter, and setting the number of columns. Use the Paper tab to select the type of paper, such as a pre-printed sheet for your day planner, as well as to set up margins, paper source, and orientation. Use the Header/Footer tab to add a header, a footer, or both to the printout.

Working with contact groups

A *contact group* (also called a *distribution list*) is a collection of contacts. It provides an easy way to send messages to a group of people. For example, if you frequently send messages to the marketing team, you can create a contact group named Marketing Team that contains the names of all members of this team. A message sent to this contact group goes to all recipients who belong to the group. Outlook 2013 converts the address list to individual addresses, so recipients see their own names and the names of all other recipients in the To box of the message instead of seeing the name of the contact group. You can use contact groups in messages, task requests, and meeting requests.

INSIDE OUT   Use nested contact groups

Contact groups can contain other contact groups as well as individual addresses. For example, you might create a contact group for each of seven departments and then create one contact group containing those seven others. You could use this second group when you need to send messages to all seven departments.

You can create contact groups in your Contacts folder using your contact list. You can store addresses from any available source, such as the Global Address List (GAL), a contact list, and so on. In general, you should create your contact groups in the location where you store the majority of your addresses.

Creating a personal contact group

Follow these steps to create a new contact group in the Contacts folder:

1. Click People on the Navigation Bar to open the Contacts folder. Click New Contact Group to open a contact group form, as shown in Figure 14-20.

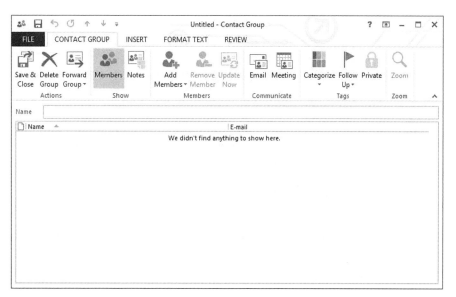

Figure 14-20 Add members to and remove members from a contact group on the contact group form.

2. Type the name for your contact group in the Name box. This is the list name that will appear in your Contacts folder. If you're creating a contact group for the marketing department, for example, use the name **Marketing**.

3. In the Members group, click Add Members and then choose From Address Book to open the Select Members dialog box, shown in Figure 14-21.

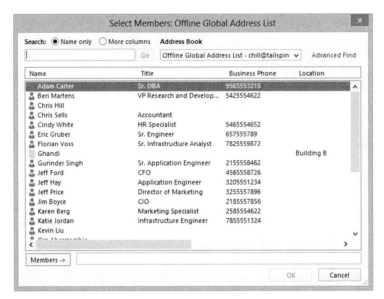

Figure 14-21 Use the Select Members dialog box to select addresses to include in the list.

4. In the Address Book drop-down list, select the location from which you want to select addresses (for example, the GAL or the Contacts folder).

5. In the Search box, type a name that you want to include, which locates the name in the list, or select the name from the Name list, and then click Members.

6. Repeat steps 4 and 5 to add all addressees to the list, and then click OK when you've finished.

7. If you want to add a longer description of the contact group, click Notes and type the text.

8. Click Save & Close. The new contact group is added to your contact list.

You probably realized that Outlook offers a couple of other options for adding members to a group. When you click Add Members, Outlook offers two additional options: From Outlook Contacts and New E-mail Contact. Choose the former if you want to add members from your Contacts folder. Choose the latter if you simply want to add an email address to the group.

Adding or deleting names in a contact group

You can add and delete names in a contact group easily. For example, perhaps your department has added a few new employees and you need to add their addresses to the department contact group.

Follow these steps to add or remove names in a contact group:

1. In your Contacts folder, open the contact group to display the contact group form.

2. Perform one or more of the following actions as desired:

   ○ To add an address from an address book or a contact folder, click Add Members, and then choose either From Outlook Contacts or From Address Book.

   ○ To add an address that is not in a contact folder or an address book, click Add Members, New E-mail Contact.

   ○ To delete a name, click the name and then click Remove Member.

3. Click Save & Close.

Chapter 14

INSIDE OUT   Fine-tune contact groups

You can assign categories to a contact group, mark it as private, or add notes to it by using the contact group form. You can also update addresses in a contact group if their source addresses have changed. For example, if you've changed a colleague's email address in the contact entry and now want to update the corresponding address in the contact group, you can open the contact group, select the address, and click Update Now on the contact group form.

Sharing contacts

Outlook 2013 lets you share contacts with others by sending vCards through email or by sharing your Contacts folder. The former method lets you share contacts with people who don't use Outlook 2013 or who don't have access to your network or to your computer running Exchange Server. The latter method—sharing your Contacts folder—is a good solution when you need to provide access to contacts for others on your network. This section explains how to share contacts through vCards, offers a brief overview of sharing the Contacts folder, and explains how to share contacts from a public folder.

> **Note**
>
> You can use SharePoint to share contacts and even integrate those contacts within Outlook 2013. See Chapter 20, "Sharing information between Outlook and SharePoint," to learn how to work with and share contacts from a SharePoint site.

Sharing your Contacts folders

If you're running Outlook 2013 with Exchange Server, you can assign permissions to a folder stored in your Exchange Server mailbox to give other users access to that folder. You can grant permissions on a group basis or a per-user basis. Outlook 2013 provides two groups by default—Anonymous and Default—that you can use to assign permissions on a global basis. You also can add individual users to the permissions list and use contact groups to assign permissions.

Follow these steps to set permissions on your Contacts folder to allow other users access to your contacts:

1. Open the Folder List, right-click the Contacts folder, and then choose Share, Folder Permissions to display the Contacts Properties dialog box for the folder (see Figure 14-22).

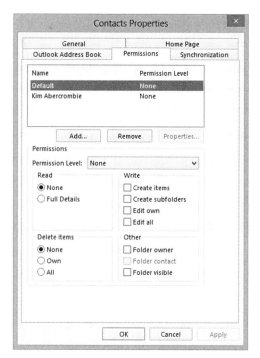

Figure 14-22 Configure permissions on the Permissions tab.

2.   Click Add to display the Add Users dialog box.

3.   Select the person for whom you want to configure permissions, and then click Add. Click OK to return to the Permissions tab.

4.   In the Name box, select the name of the person that you just added.

5.   In the Permission Level drop-down list, select a permissions level according to the tasks that the user should be able to perform with your Contacts folder. When you select a permissions level, Outlook 2013 selects one or more individual permissions in the Permissions area. You also can select or clear individual permissions as needed.

6.   Click OK to save the permission changes.

You can grant several permissions for a folder, and you can assign them in any combination you need. See Chapter 22, "Sharing calendars," to learn more about sharing permissions for Outlook folders.

For a complete explanation of permissions and folder sharing, see the section "Granting access to folders" in Chapter 21, "Delegating responsibilities to an assistant."

Sharing contacts with vCards

A vCard presents contact information as an electronic business card that can be sent through email. vCards are based on an open standard, allowing any application that supports vCards to share contact information. In addition to sending a vCard as an attachment, you can include it with your message signature.

When you receive a message with a vCard attached, a paper clip icon appears in the Reading Pane to indicate the attached vCard. Use one of the following methods to add the data in the vCard as a contact entry:

- In the Reading Pane, click the file name that appears.

- If you've opened the message, right-click the business card icon in the message, and then choose Open.

After you view the information sent in the vCard, click Save & Close to add the information to your contact list.

> **Note**
> You can drag a vCard from a message to your Contacts folder to add the contact information.

Creating a vCard from a contact entry

As mentioned earlier, one way to send contact information to someone else is to attach the contact entry to a message as a vCard. You can use this method to share your own contact information or to share one or more other contact entries with another person.

Follow these steps to attach a vCard to a message:

1. In the Contacts folder, select the contact item that you want to send as a vCard.

2. On the Home tab, click Forward Contact and choose As A Business Card. Outlook 2013 opens a new message form with the contact entry attached as a vCard.

3. Specify an address, complete the message as you would any other, and then click Send to send it.

Including a vCard with your signature

The second method of sharing a contact is useful when you want to share your own contact information. Rather than attaching it to a message, you can have Outlook 2013 send it along with your message signature, which ensures that the vCard is sent with all outgoing messages.

> **Note**
>
> You can attach text (such as a favorite quote) and graphics to each outgoing message as part of your signature. For complete details on using signatures with Outlook 2013, see the section "Using signatures" in Chapter 7, "Advanced email tasks."

Follow these steps to add your contact information as a vCard to your message signature:

1. Create your own contact entry if you have not already done so.

2. Click File, Options.

3. Click Mail, Signatures.

4. Click New.

5. Enter a name for your signature (such as vCard).

6. Click Business Card.

7. Browse to your own business card, and then click OK.

8. In the Signatures And Stationery dialog box, shown in Figure 14-23, add other information as needed.

Chapter 14

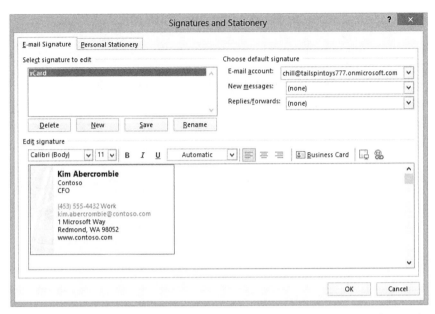

Figure 14-23 Use the Signatures And Stationery dialog box to add text, graphics, and a vCard to your outgoing messages automatically.

9. Click OK twice.

From now on, your contact information will be attached to outgoing messages.

> **Note**
>
> **To prevent signatures from being added to your outgoing messages, click File, Options; click Mail, Signatures; and then select None in the New Messages drop-down list.**

Saving a contact entry as a vCard

In addition to sending vCards as email attachments, Outlook 2013 allows you to save a contact entry to a file as a vCard. You might do this if you want to link to vCards on a website so that others can download the vCards directly rather than receiving a message with the vCards attached. Alternatively, perhaps you want to save a large number of contacts as vCards and send them to someone in a .zip file or on a CD.

Follow these steps to save a contact item as a vCard file:

1. Open the contact item that you want to save as a vCard.

2. Click File, Save As. In the Save As Type drop-down list, select vCard Files (*.vcf).

3. Type a name in the File Name box, and then click Save.

Saving a vCard attachment in your Contacts folder

When you receive a message containing a vCard attachment, you'll probably want to save the vCard as a contact item in your Contacts folder. Follow these steps to do so:

1. Open the message containing the attached vCard.

2. Double-click the attached vCard to open it.

3. In the open contact form, click Save & Close. The information in the vCard is saved in your Contacts folder by default.

Setting People options

Outlook 2013 provides several options that control how it stores and displays contacts. To view these options, click File, Options, and then click People in the left pane. On the People page of the Outlook Options dialog box, shown in Figure 14-24, you can configure the following options:

- **Default "Full Name" Order**   This option specifies how Outlook 2013 creates the Full Name field when you click Full Name in the new contact form and enter the contact's first, middle, and last name, along with suffix and title.

- **Default "File As" Order**   This option specifies the name that Outlook 2013 uses in the card title. Outlook 2013 uses the information that you specify for first, middle, and last name, as well as company, to create the card title.

- **Check For Duplicates When Saving New Contacts**   Select this check box if you want Outlook 2013 to check for duplicate contacts when you create new contacts.

- **Show An Additional Index**   Use this option to display a second index at the left edge of the Contacts folder in a different language.

- **Display Online Status Next To Name**   Select this option to show online presence information for the contact.

- **Show User Photographs When Available** Select this option to show photos for those users who have a photo associated in Outlook or through a social network connection.

- **Show Only Names In The People Peek** Select this option to show only a contact name when using the People peek option (hovering over the People link).

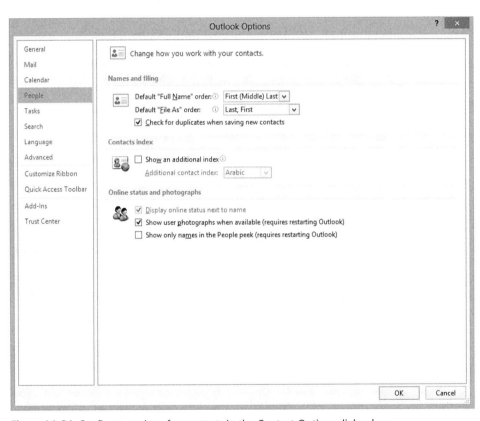

Figure 14-24 Configure options for contacts in the Contact Options dialog box.

Using contacts for a mail merge in Word

The Outlook 2013 People folder enables you to create contact entries to store information about a person, a group, or an organization. You can then use that contact data to create email messages, set up meetings or appointments, or complete other tasks associated with a contact. Your contact list can also be used as the data source to provide names, addresses, phone numbers, and other pertinent data to your mail merge documents.

You perform a *mail merge* in Word 2013 when you want to create multiple documents that are all based on the same letter or document but have different names, addresses, or other specific information (referred to as *merge data*). For instance, you might perform a mail merge operation when you want to do a mass mailing to your customers about a new product launch.

You begin by creating and saving a standard letter. Next, you place field codes where you want the recipient's address, the salutation, and other merge data to appear. *Field codes* are placeholders in documents where data will change. For instance, the name of the recipient should be a field code because it will change for each letter you send out.

You then create or assign a database to populate the field codes (that is, to insert the merge data). Word 2013 uses the database and contact information to create separate letters. You can then save these files or print each letter for your mass mailing.

> **Note**
> Before starting to set up a mail merge using your Outlook 2013 contact data, review your contact entries to make sure that the data is complete and current, and that you don't have duplicate entries.

To perform a mail merge using Word 2013, follow these steps:

1. Start Word 2013.

2. Click the Mailings tab on the ribbon.

3. Click Start Mail Merge.

4. Click Step By Step Mail Merge Wizard (see Figure 14-25).

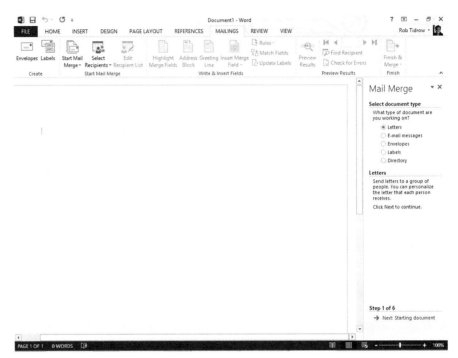

Figure 14-25 Start a mail merge by opening the Step By Step Mail Merge Wizard in Word 2013, which appears in the task pane on the right.

5. In the task pane, select the type of document to create, such as Letters, and then click Next: Starting Document at the bottom of the pane.

6. Select the document to use—for example, the current document. Click Next: Select Recipients.

7. Click Select From Outlook Contacts.

8. Select the Choose Contacts Folder option to open the Select Contacts dialog box (see Figure 14-26). (If you have configured Outlook 2013 to always prompt you for a profile and Outlook 2013 is not open, you are asked to select a profile.)

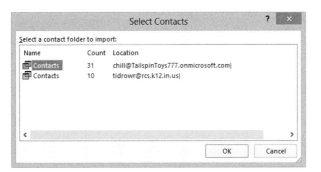

Figure 14-26 Select your Contacts folder here.

9. Select the folder that contains the contact list that you want to use, and then click OK to open the Mail Merge Recipients dialog box (see Figure 14-27).

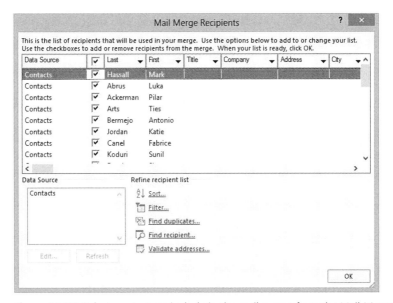

Figure 14-27 Select contacts to include in the mail merge from the Mail Merge Recipients dialog box.

10. Select the contacts that you want to use to populate the mail merge document. All the contacts are selected by default. You can use the following methods to modify the selected list of contacts:

  ❍ Select the check box beside the Data Source column to choose all the contacts in the list (the default), or clear the check box to clear all the contacts and then select individual contacts.

- ❍ Click Sort to sort the contact list.

- ❍ Click Filter to filter the list according to user-specified criteria.

- ❍ Click Find Duplicates to locate duplicate names to clear them from the mail merge list.

- ❍ Click Find Recipient to locate a specific name in your contact list.

- ❍ Click Validate Addresses to use an add-in tool to verify that the addresses are valid.

- ❍ Clear the check boxes next to the names of those contacts you do not want to include in the mail merge.

> **Note**
>
> **If you want to create a mailing list that is a subset of your Contacts folder, you can filter the contact list with a custom view and then use the custom view to perform a mail merge from Outlook 2013.**

For more information, see the section "Performing a mail merge from Outlook."

11. Click OK.

12. Click Next: Write Your Letter.

13. Click Address Block to open the Insert Address Block dialog box (see Figure 14-28).

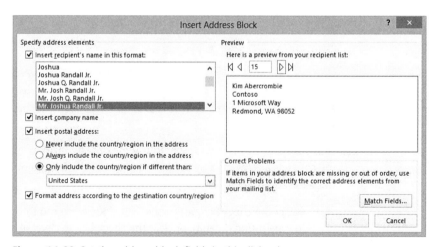

Figure 14-28 Set the address block fields in this dialog box.

14. Using the options in this dialog box, specify the address fields and format that you want to include in your letter. Click OK.

15. Press Enter and then click Greeting Line to insert and format a greeting line from your Contact information.

16. Click More Items to insert specific fields from your Contact information.

17. Write the body of your letter. When you finish, click Next: Preview Your Letters to see how the Outlook 2013 contact data looks in your letter.

> **Note**
> You will probably need to do some formatting of the mail merge fields, such as setting line spacing and spacing before or after paragraphs.

18. In the task pane, click Next: Complete The Merge to finish.

19. Finish editing your letter (or print it, if you want).

Filtering contacts in or out of the merge

When you perform a mail merge from Word 2013, you can use selection criteria to determine which of the contacts are included in the mail merge set. For example, assume that you want to send a letter to all your contacts who have addresses in California and whose last names begin with the letter *R*.

In the Mail Merge Recipients dialog box (see Figure 14-27), each data column includes a drop-down button next to the column heading. To specify selection criteria based on a particular column, click the drop-down button and choose one of the following commands:

- **All**   Do not filter based on the selected column.

- **Blanks**   Include only those contacts for whom the selected field is blank. For example, choose this option under the E-mail Address column to include all contacts who do not have an email address in their contact record.

- **Nonblanks**   Include only those contacts for whom the selected field is not blank. For example, select this option under the Last field to include only those contacts whose Last Name field is not blank.

- **Advanced**   Click this button to open the Filter And Sort dialog box, explained next.

If you click Advanced to open the Filter And Sort dialog box, shown in Figure 14-29, you can specify more-complex selection criteria. The following example includes those contacts whose last names start with *R* and whose state value equals CA:

1. In the Mail Merge Recipients dialog box, click the drop-down button beside the Last field. Click Advanced.

2. From the first Field drop-down list, choose Last, choose Greater Than from the Comparison drop-down list, and then enter **Q** in the Compare To field.

3. From the second Field drop-down list, choose Last, choose Less Than from the Comparison drop-down list, and then enter **S** in the Compare To field.

4. Select State from the third Field drop-down list, choose Equal To from the Comparison drop-down list, and enter **CA** in the Compare To field. The dialog box should look similar to the one shown in Figure 14-28.

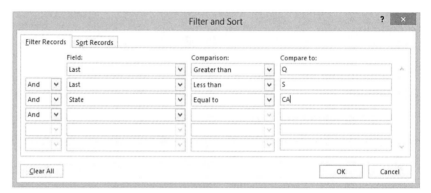

Figure 14-29 These settings select all contacts whose names start with *R* and whose addresses are in California.

5. Click OK to close the Filter And Sort dialog box. After a few moments, the Mail Merge Recipients list shows only those contacts whose last name begins with *R* and whose state value is listed as CA.

As you might have guessed from Figure 14-29, you can select *OR* instead of *AND* in the dialog box for a particular criterion. For example, you would use *OR* for the third crite-rion (step 4) to cause Outlook 2013 to include contacts in the mail merge if their name started with *R* or if they lived in California. A contact would also be included if both criteria were met.

Performing a mail merge from Outlook

As the previous sections illustrated, it's easy to perform a mail merge from Word 2013 and pull contact information from Outlook 2013. You can also filter the contacts to include only those that suit your needs.

You can also perform a mail merge from Outlook 2013. Starting from Outlook 2013 gives you a few advantages:

- **More control over contacts to be included**   You can merge all the contacts in the current view of the People folder or merge only those contacts you have selected in the folder.

- **Control over which fields to include**   You can include all contact fields or only those fields that are visible in the current folder view.

- **Capability to save the contacts for later use**   Outlook 2013 gives you the option of saving the contacts to a Word 2013 document to use for future reference or for future mail merges from Word 2013.

To begin a mail merge from Outlook 2013, select People in the Navigation Pane, and then click Mail Merge in the Actions group on the Home tab on the ribbon to open the Mail Merge Contacts dialog box. As Figure 14-30 illustrates, Outlook 2013 offers two options to control which contacts are included in the merge:

- **All Contacts In Current View**   Use this option to include all the contacts in the view, understanding that *all the contacts in the view* is not necessarily the same as *all contacts*. If you create a filtered view of the folder that excludes some of the contacts, those contacts will be excluded from the merge as well.

- **Only Selected Contacts**   Choose this option to include only those contacts that you selected in the Contacts folder prior to clicking Mail Merge. To include contacts selectively, in the Contacts folder, hold down the Ctrl key while clicking to select individual contacts, or Shift-click to select a range of contacts.

Chapter 14

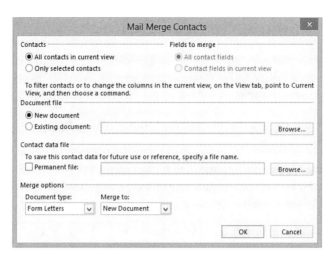

Figure 14-30 Use the Mail Merge Contacts dialog box to choose which contacts and fields to include in the merge.

In addition to specifying which contacts are included, you can control which fields are included, excluding those you don't need. The following two options determine which fields are included:

- **All Contact Fields**   Choose this option to include all the contact fields.

- **Contact Fields In Current View**   Choose this option to include only the fields displayed in the current view. You can customize the view prior to choosing Tools, Mail Merge to include only specific fields.

Creating custom views to filter items in a folder is covered in detail in the section "Creating and using custom views" in Chapter 26, "Customizing the Outlook interface."

You can merge the contacts to a new document if you want, or you can choose Existing Document to use a Word 2013 document that you have already created.

The merged contact information can be saved for later or repeated by selecting Permanent File under Contact Data File and specifying a file name.

You can choose from a variety of document types for your merged information: form letters, mailing labels, envelopes, and catalogs. The output of the mail merge can be saved as a Word 2013 document, sent directly to a printer, or sent as email to the contacts you have selected for the merge.

After you select your options in the Mail Merge Contacts dialog box and click OK, Outlook 2013 opens Word 2013, prepopulating the mail merge contact list and starting the document type that you have specified. The rest of the process depends on the type of document you have selected, as follows:

- **Form letters or catalogs**   To complete the mail merge for a form letter or catalog, click the Mailings tab, click Start Mail Merge, and select the Step By Step Mail Merge Wizard. The wizard opens at step 3, in which you choose the contacts to include in the letter. Because you have already generated a contact list, the Use An Existing List option is selected for you. You can then click Edit Recipient List to verify or fine-tune the list, or you can click Next: Write Your Letter to move to the next step.

- **Mailing labels or envelopes**   Select options in the Mail Merge Helper dialog box to complete the mail merge and create mailing labels or envelopes. You can change the type of document you are creating or click Setup to choose a specific type of mailing label or envelope size. The data source is already selected, but you can change or edit the data source.

See the section "Using contacts for a mail merge in Word" for detailed instructions on using the Mail Merge Wizard in Word 2013.

Using contacts effectively

Contacts can be a very powerful tool in Outlook 2013. As with any Outlook 2013 feature, you can use them in different ways to suit your needs, and how you use them might not be the most effective way for someone else. However, there are some things you can do to make contacts more useful:

- **Be complete**   The more information that you can include for each contact, the more useful your contacts will be. For example, fill in as many of the phone number fields as you can; this will give you more options when using Outlook 2013 to dial a contact.

- **Use categories to your advantage**   Assigning categories to your contacts will help you organize them more effectively—for example, keeping your personal contacts separated from your business contacts.

- **Enter the company name for your business contacts**   Entering the company name in the contact will enable you to group your contacts by company, making it easier not only to locate contacts, but also to modify contacts globally when a company change occurs (such as a phone number or company name change).

- **Work from the contact** If you work in the People folder a lot, keep in mind that you can initiate certain actions from the People folder, such as issuing a new meeting request, assigning a task, creating a new journal entry, or calling the contact. This can save you the trouble of switching to a different folder to initiate these actions.

- **Don't forget the picture** The capability to add a picture can be very useful. For example, if your organization is growing rapidly or is already large, providing pictures in contacts for employees can help your staff get to know each other.

Social networking and Outlook

O utLooK 2010 introduced a selection of social networking features, and Microsoft Outlook 2013 builds on that with improvements and additional features. The People Hub described in Chapter 14, "Working with contacts," is a good example— it integrates your contacts from social networking sites such as Facebook, LinkedIn, and SharePoint.

This chapter explores how to add and work with social networking contacts in Outlook, as well as the integration that Outlook 2013 provides for Skype. Let's start by adding some social networking contacts to Outlook.

Integrating social networking accounts in Outlook

Adding a social networking service doesn't mean that Outlook will automatically bring in all of your contacts from that service. That could result in several hundred contacts (or more) being added to Outlook, which could quickly become unmanageable.

Instead, Outlook adds the connection and then relies on you to add specific contacts. Outlook then determines whether to bring in content based on the email address of the contact. If the contact's email is associated with a Facebook contact, for example, then Outlook brings in the associated Facebook contact information for that contact.

Adding Facebook contacts

Adding Facebook as a social networking connection in Outlook enables you to integrate your Facebook contacts into the People Hub and view photos, updates, and other Facebook content associated with that contact in Outlook.

To add a Facebook account to Outlook, follow these steps:

1. Open the People Hub.

2. Click Connect To A Social Network (see Figure 15-1).

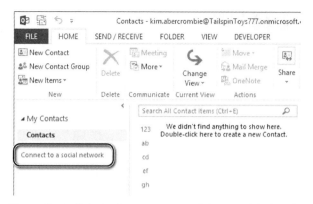

Figure 15-1 Click the Connect To A Social Network link in the People Hub to add social networking accounts.

3. In the resulting dialog box, click Facebook.

4. Enter your Facebook user name and password (see Figure 15-2).

Figure 15-2 Outlook offers three social network account types by default.

5. To have contact photos and other contact information automatically pulled in from Facebook for contacts that you add, select the check box labeled By Default, Show Photos And Information From This Network When Available.

6. Click Connect.

7. Click Finish.

At this point, as explained earlier in this section, Outlook does not go out to Facebook and grab all of your contacts. Instead, if you already have a contact entry with a matching email address, Outlook will download the photo and other relevant data from Facebook. If the contact doesn't exist yet, add it as you would any other contact. The next time Outlook syncs its contacts from Facebook, you'll see the user's Facebook account photo and other data in the contact record, as shown in Figure 15-3.

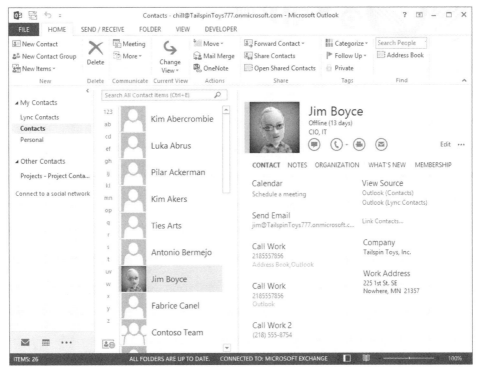

Figure 15-3 Outlook has downloaded information from Facebook for a selected contact.

Adding LinkedIn contacts

Another social networking service that Outlook supports is LinkedIn, enabling you to integrate your LinkedIn contacts' data in Outlook to view photos, social updates, and so on. To add a LinkedIn account to Outlook, follow these steps:

1. Open the People Hub.

2. Click Connect To A Social Network.

3. Click LinkedIn and enter your LinkedIn user name and password (see Figure 15-4).

Figure 15-4 Enter your LinkedIn user name and password to connect Outlook to LinkedIn.

4. Select the check box labeled By Default, Show Photos And Information From This Network When Available to pull profile photos and other data from LinkedIn when available.

5. Click Connect.

Adding SharePoint contacts

In addition to Facebook and LinkedIn accounts, you can add SharePoint as a connection in Outlook, enabling you to follow contact updates from SharePoint for your Outlook contacts. To add SharePoint, following these steps:

1. Open the People Hub.

2. Click Connect To A Social Network.

3. Click SharePoint.

4. Enter the URL for the SharePoint site (see Figure 15-5).

Figure 15-5 You can add SharePoint connections to Outlook to get social updates from SharePoint.

5. Select the check box labeled By Default, Show Photos And Information From This Network When Available to pull profile photos and other data from SharePoint when available.

6. Click Connect.

7. Enter the user name and password you use to connect to SharePoint (see Figure 15-6).

Figure 15-6 Enter the user name and password that you use to connect to SharePoint.

8. Click OK.

Linking contacts

After you connect Outlook to your social networking accounts, you can start using the associated social networking features in Outlook. For example, after adding a contact who is also a Facebook or LinkedIn contact, you'll see a photo appear beside that person's contact record in the People Hub, as shown in Figure 15-7.

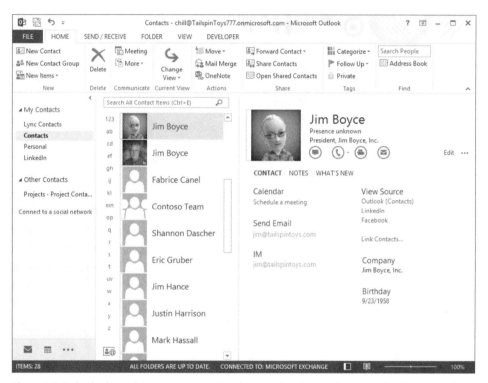

Figure 15-7 Outlook can integrate content (such as profile photos) from social networking sites into the People Hub.

In Figure 15-7, there are two contacts for Jim Boyce. The first has an email address that is associated with a Facebook and a LinkedIn account. The second is associated with a different LinkedIn account. In the first instance, Outlook is pulling the profile photo from Facebook. In the second, Outlook is pulling the profile photo from LinkedIn.

To view information from multiple sources, you can simply add multiple email addresses to the contact when you create it. Or, if the contacts are already created, you can link them to one another. Here's how:

1. In the People Hub, click the first contact that you want to link.

2. In the Reading Pane, click Link Contacts.

3. Type the contact's name and click the Search button.

4. Click the second contact (see Figure 15-8).

5. Click OK.

Figure 15-8 You can link multiple contacts in Outlook.

After you link contacts, Outlook combines them into a single contact in the People Hub. However, that doesn't mean that Outlook has merged those contact records. The individual contact items still exist and still appear in your Contacts folder (and in the People Hub).

With possibly multiple sources for profile photos for each contact, you might want to prioritize the service from which Outlook pulls the profile photo. For example, your contacts with LinkedIn accounts might be more likely to have a professional headshot in LinkedIn rather than a cartoon or unrelated image for the profile in Facebook. To specify which ser-vice has priority, open the People Hub and click Connect To A Social Network. Click the Edit button for the service that you want to have priority and then click Options. Place a check mark beside By Default, Show Photos And Information From This Network When Available. Then click OK and click Finish.

Viewing social updates

With social network connections added to Outlook, you can view social updates for your contacts in Outlook, rather than having to open the social networking site in a browser to see those updates. To view updates, first open the People Hub and select the contact. Then, in the Reading Pane, click the What's New link. Figure 15-9 shows updates from Facebook for the selected contact.

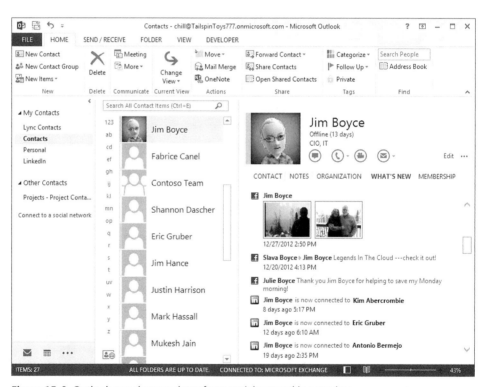

Figure 15-9 Outlook can show updates from social networking services.

Although Outlook can show updates from your social networking connections, that doesn't mean you can throw away your web browser and work with Facebook, LinkedIn, or other services solely from Outlook. You can, however, click names and photos in the What's New view to open a web browser session for that social networking service.

The People Hub isn't the only place you can access your contacts' social network feeds. The People Pane also gives you quick access to that information. Figure 15-10 shows the People Pane open in the Inbox, displaying the same updates previously shown in the People Hub in Figure 15-9.

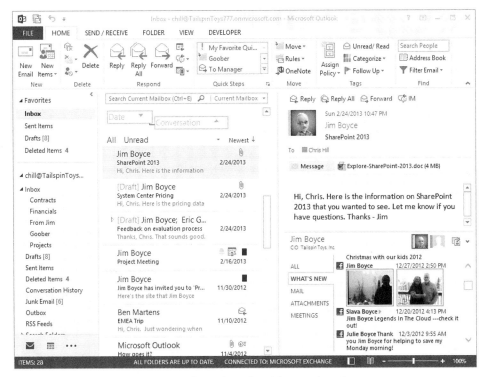

Figure 15-10 The People Pane provides a view of social network updates.

Using social networking add-on apps

The social networking features built into Outlook 2013 are handy, but they clearly don't provide all of the capabilities that many people might want. For example, perhaps you want tighter integration with LinkedIn or the capability to integrate Twitter in Outlook. Fortunately, Outlook's social networking features are extensible, and many developers have created apps for use with Outlook to extend the capabilities for several popular social networking services.

To access these apps, visit the Office Store at *http://office.microsoft.com/en-us/store/apps-for-outlook-FX102804983.aspx*. In addition to numerous other apps, you'll find a LinkedIn app that lets you view full LinkedIn profiles and connect to others, and a Twitter app that lets you tweet and access other Twitter features from within Outlook.

Using Outlook with Skype

If you are a Skype user and have Skype 6.1 for Windows Desktop (or later) installed on your PC, you can take advantage of some Outlook integration features built into Skype. For example, you can view contacts' online status, contact information, and mood message within Outlook. You can also send instant messages, start an audio or video call, or call a contact's phone through the Skype/Outlook integration. These integration features work with Outlook 2010 or later.

TROUBLESHOOTING

Skype and Outlook integration are not working

If you have Lync or Office Communicator installed on your PC, the integration features might not work for you. This is due to Lync or Communicator being designated in the Windows registry as the default instant message (IM) app on your PC. You can use the Registry Editor to change the value of HKCU\Software\IM Providers\DefaultIMApp to Skype and restart Outlook. Understand, however, that the integration features for Lync or Communicator will be replaced by Skype. So, for example, you will no longer be able to start a Lync IM conversation from someone's contact card in Outlook. You'll have to start the session from Lync instead.

Most important, as with any registry change, you should be very careful to make the correct change. Changing the registry incorrectly can result in Outlook not working and potentially cause problems with Windows itself.

The following sections explore the Skype and Outlook integration features and assume that you have installed Skype 6.1 for Windows Desktop (or later) on your PC and have a valid, active Skype account.

Sending an instant message

To send an instant message (IM) to a Skype user from Outlook, first open the user's contact card. Then hover the mouse pointer over the contact's email address, as shown in Figure 15-11. When the contact card appears, click the Send An IM button. Skype will open with the contact selected, and you can simply type your message and press Enter.

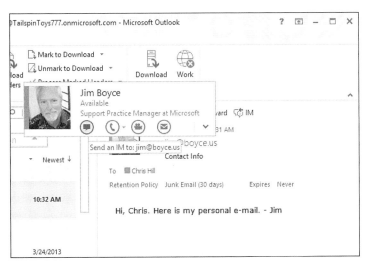

Figure 15-11 You can start a Skype IM session from the contact card in Outlook.

You can initiate an IM session anywhere you see the Send An IM button. For example, you can initiate an IM session from the People Hub, just as you can from an email.

Making audio or video calls

Just as you can initiate a Skype IM session with a contact from Outlook, you can also initiate audio and video calls from Outlook to other Skype users. To start an audio call, find the contact you want to call and open the contact card (for example, hover the mouse pointer over the contact's email address in the Inbox). Click the arrow beside the Call button and choose Call *<contact>*, where *<contact>* is the contact's name. Skype will open and initiate the call.

To start a video call, open the contact card and click the Start A Video Call button. Skype will open and initiate the video call.

Making phone calls

If you have a Skype credit or subscription, you can use Skype to call a contact's phone, whether a landline or cell phone. The process is very similar to calling the contact using Skype-to-Skype. To call a contact's phone, open the contact card in Outlook, click the arrow beside the Call button, and choose which phone number you want Skype to dial. Skype will open an initiate the call.

PART IV

Chapter 15

Managing your calendar and tasks

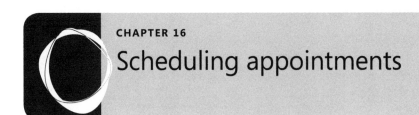

F OR most of us, a calendar is a basic tool for organizing our lives, both at work and at home. With the calendar in Microsoft Outlook 2013, you can schedule regular appointments, all-day and multiday events, and meetings. You can view your schedule almost any way you want. In addition, you can share your calendar with others, which is a big help when scheduling organizational activities.

This chapter first describes the calendar and explains how to work with the basic Calendar folder view. Then you'll learn how to schedule and work with appointments and events. You'll also learn about the more advanced view options for the calendar and about how to share your calendar and free/busy information and view different time zones.

Both this chapter and the next focus on the features available in the Outlook 2013 Calendar folder. This chapter covers appointments and events; Chapter 17, "Scheduling meetings, rooms, and resources," discusses how to handle meetings and resources.

Calendar basics

The Outlook 2013 Calendar folder provides a central location for storing vast amounts of information about your schedule. Figure 16-1 shows a basic one-day view of a calendar. You see this view when you click the Calendar icon in the Navigation Pane to open the folder and then click Day on the Home tab of the ribbon. This example calendar contains no appointments yet, and no tasks are listed in the Daily Task List.

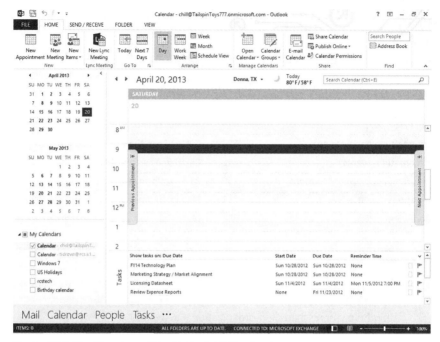

Figure 16-1 The Day view of the Outlook 2013 calendar.

Understanding calendar items

The Outlook 2013 calendar can contain three types of items: appointments, events, and meetings.

- An *appointment*, which is the default calendar item, involves only your schedule and time and does not require other attendees or resources. The calendar shows appointments in the time slots corresponding to their start and end times.

- When an appointment lasts longer than 24 hours, it becomes an *event*. An event is not marked on the calendar in a time slot, but rather in a banner at the top of the day on which it occurs.

- An appointment becomes a *meeting* when you invite other people, which requires coordinating their schedules, or when you must schedule resources. Meetings can be in-person meetings established through Outlook 2013 meeting requests.

For in-depth information about meetings initiated in Outlook 2013, see Chapter 17.

You can create an appointment in any of these ways:

- Click New Appointment on the Home tab.

- When any other Outlook 2013 folder is open, click the arrow next to New Items on the toolbar, and then choose Appointment.

- Click a time slot on the calendar (or drag to select a time range), and simply type the subject of the appointment in the time slot.

For detailed information about creating appointments and using the appointment form, see the section "Working with one-time appointments."

Using the time bar

When you choose a calendar display of seven or fewer days, the time bar appears, displaying 30-minute time increments by default. Figure 16-2 shows the time bar set to 30-minute increments, with a selection of appointments on the calendar, the shortest of which is 30 minutes.

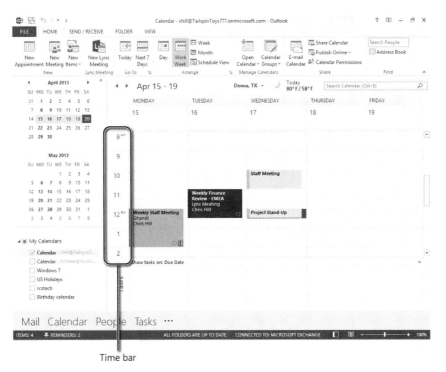

Time bar

Figure 16-2 By default, the time bar is set to display 30-minute increments.

You can set the time bar to display different time increments. To do so, begin by right-clicking the time bar to display the shortcut menu shown in Figure 16-3.

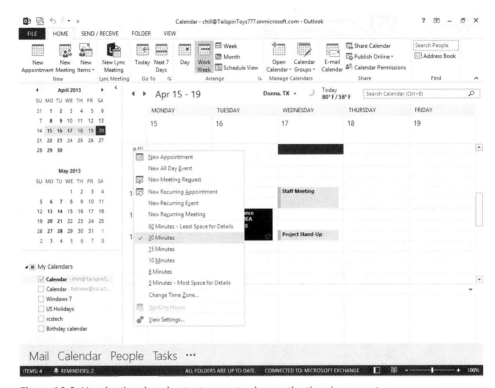

Figure 16-3 Use the time bar shortcut menu to change the time increment.

If you want to change the time scale to 10 minutes, select 10 Minutes; subsequently, the 30-minute appointment takes up three time intervals instead of one, as shown in Figure 16-4.

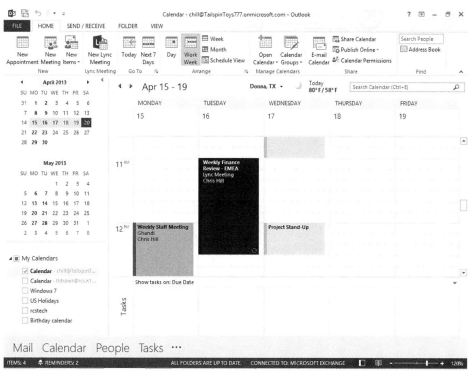

Figure 16-4 The time bar has been changed to display 10-minute increments.

To choose a 60-minute interval, right-click the time bar, and then select 60 Minutes; Figure 16-5 shows the result. Note that the scheduled time of the appointment is displayed as a ScreenTip when you hover the mouse pointer over the appointment subject on the calendar.

Chapter 16

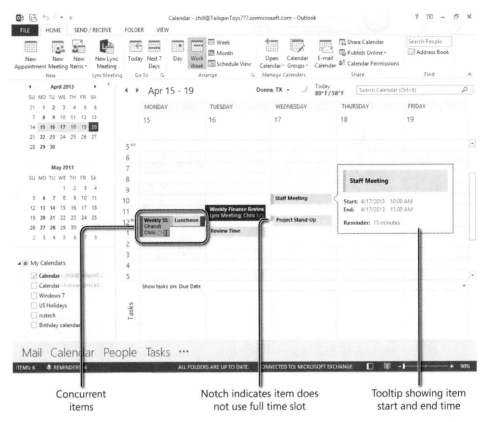

Concurrent
items

Notch indicates item does
not use full time slot

Tooltip showing item
start and end time

Figure 16-5 The time bar is set to 60-minute intervals and the time is displayed when you hover
the mouse pointer over the appointment.

Outlook 2013 places appointments side by side on the calendar when they are scheduled in
the same time interval (as shown in Figure 16-5). In addition, a notch at the left edge of an
item indicates that it does not consume the entire time slot.

Using the Date Navigator

The Date Navigator is shown as a small calendar at the top of the Navigation Pane. It has several important uses. For example, you can use it to select the day to view on the calendar—in effect, jumping from one date to another. When you click a day in the Date Navigator, Outlook 2013 displays that day according to how you have set the view (by using the Day, Work Week, or Week tab):

- In Day view, the selected day is displayed.

- In Work Week view (including five days by default—configurable by clicking File, Options, Calendar), Outlook 2013 displays the week containing the day that you clicked in the Date Navigator.

- In Week view (including seven days), the calendar displays the complete week containing the date you click.

By clicking the right and left arrows next to the month names in the Date Navigator, you can scroll forward and backward through the months.

For more information about the Day, Work Week, Week, and Month views, see the section "Setting the number of days displayed."

Another use of the Date Navigator is to denote days that contain scheduled items. Those days appear in bold type; days with no scheduled items appear as regular text. This allows you to assess your monthly schedule at a glance.

Finally, you can use the Date Navigator to view multiple days on the calendar. In the Date Navigator, simply drag across the range of days you want to view; those days will all appear on the calendar. For example, Figure 16-6 shows what happens when you drag across three days in the Date Navigator. You can also view multiple consecutive days by clicking the first day and then holding down the Shift key and clicking the last day. To view multiple nonconsecutive days, click the first day that you want to view and then hold down the Ctrl key and click each day that you want to add to the view.

Chapter 16

Figure 16-6 You can view multiple days by selecting them in the Date Navigator.

Using the To-Do Bar

The To-Do Bar offers an easy way of working with tasks from the Calendar folder. The To-Do Bar is not turned on by default, but it can be enabled using the To-Do Bar button in the Layout group on the View tab. The To-Do Bar displays existing tasks from the Tasks folder and also allows you to add new tasks. Adding a new task is as simple as clicking in the Task List area of the To-Do Bar and typing the task subject. Double-click the task item to open the task form if you'd like to add more details. When you create a task in the To-Do Bar, Outlook 2013 automatically adds it to the Tasks folder.

One of the main advantages of having the To-Do Bar in the Calendar folder is that it enables you to assess your schedule and fit in tasks where appropriate. When you drag a task from the Task List to the calendar, an appointment is added. When you double-click the appointment, the appointment form appears, with the task information filled in. You need only set the schedule information for the appointment and save it to the calendar (as explained in the section "Working with one-time appointments").

Setting the number of days displayed

You can set the number of days displayed in the calendar in several ways. One way is to use the Date Navigator, as discussed earlier. The easiest way, however, is to use the appropriate button in the Arrange group of the Home tab or the Arrangement group of the View tab. To select the number of days to view, click the Day, Work Week, Week, or Month button.

When the calendar displays seven or fewer days, the time bar shows the time of day. Figure 16-7 shows the calendar with seven days displayed.

Figure 16-7 The calendar display changes depending on the number of days you are viewing.

When you select more than seven days in the Date Navigator, the times are replaced by dates, as shown in Figure 16-8. The Date Navigator and the To-Do Bar can also appear in Month view, as shown in Figure 16-8.

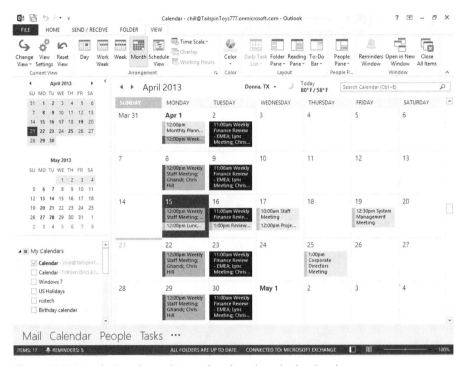

Figure 16-8 Month view shows dates rather than times in the time bar.

Selecting a date

You can select a date in two ways. The first is by using the Date Navigator, as described earlier. The second is by clicking the Today button on the Home tab on the ribbon; this action takes you to the current day using whatever view is currently shown.

Working with one-time appointments

The most basic calendar item is the one-time appointment. You can create a one-time appointment in several ways:

- If the Calendar folder is not open, click New Items on the Home tab on the ribbon, and then choose Appointment. The appointment defaults to the next full 30 minutes.

- If the Calendar folder is open, select a time in the calendar and then click New Appointment on the ribbon; alternatively, right-click the calendar and choose New Appointment. The appointment is scheduled for the time selected in the calendar.

- Right-click a date in Month view, and then choose New Appointment. The appointment defaults to your specified start-of-workday time and runs for 30 minutes.

When you take any of these actions, Outlook 2013 opens the appointment form, shown in Figure 16-9, where you can specify information for the new item.

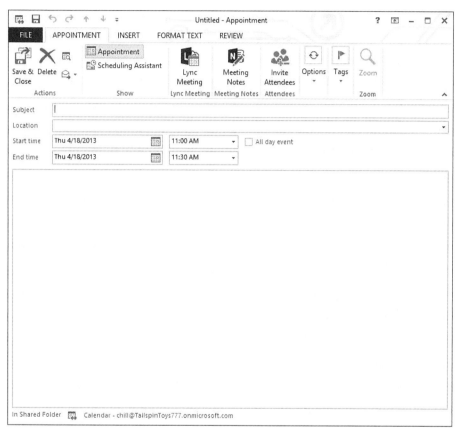

Figure 16-9 Use the appointment form to create a new appointment.

INSIDE OUT   Create an appointment quickly

To create an appointment quickly, you can click a blank time slot on the calendar and type the subject of the appointment. When you use this method, however, Outlook 2013 doesn't open a new appointment form automatically. To add details to the appointment, you must double-click the new appointment to open the form. Note that if you click a blank date in Month view and type a subject, Outlook 2013 creates an all-day event rather than an appointment.

Specifying the subject and location

Type the subject of an appointment in the Subject box at the top of the appointment form. Make the subject as descriptive as possible because it will appear on the calendar.

If you want, you can type a location for the appointment in the Location box. To view a list of all previously typed locations, click the Location drop-down arrow; you can select a location in this list. Outlook 2013 will display the location that you specify next to the appointment subject in Calendar view (and in parentheses next to the subject in ScreenTips when you hover the mouse pointer over the scheduled appointment).

Specifying start and end times

You set the start and end times of the appointment by typing the date and time in the Start Time and End Time boxes or by clicking the drop-down arrows beside each box. If you click a drop-down arrow for a date, a calendar appears. Click a drop-down arrow for time, and a list of potential start and end times in 30-minute increments appears. The End Time drop-down list shows how long the appointment will be for each given end time. You can also click in these fields and type a value. For example, you might use this method when you want to create a 15-minute appointment when Outlook 2013 is set to use a 30-minute default appointment duration.

Setting a reminder

You can set a reminder for an appointment by clicking the Reminder arrow in the Options group on the Appointment tab. In the Reminder drop-down list, you can specify when the reminder should appear; the default is 15 minutes before the appointment. By default, a reminder both plays a sound and displays a reminder window, as shown in Figure 16-10. If you don't want the reminder to play a sound, or if you want to use a different sound, click the Sound option at the bottom of the Reminder drop-down list to change the settings.

> **Note**
> To change the default behavior of appointment reminders, click File, Options, and then choose Calendar. In the Calendar Options area of the page, you can select (or clear) the default reminder and set the default reminder time.

Figure 16-10 You can dismiss a reminder by clicking Dismiss or postpone it by clicking Snooze.

Classifying an appointment

Outlook 2013 uses color and patterns to indicate free/busy information for appointments. In the calendar itself, Outlook 2013 does not show an indicator next to appointments marked Busy. It uses the following bars at the left edge of the appointment to indicate status:

- Free (white)

- Working Elsewhere (shaded with polka dots)

- Tentative (shaded with diagonal lines)

- Out Of Office (shaded dark purple)

> **Note**
> When you are scheduling a meeting or viewing a group schedule, Outlook 2013 shows busy time using a blue bar.

The indicator (a small bar to the left of the appointment) appears on your local calendar and is also displayed when other users view the free/busy times for that calendar. By default, the time occupied by an appointment is classified as Busy. To reclassify an appointment, select the indicator in the Show As drop-down list in the Options group, as shown in Figure 16-11.

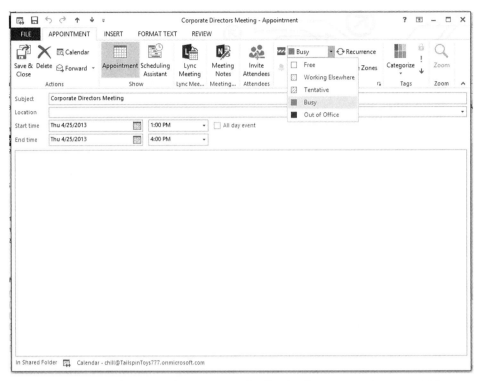

Figure 16-11 Use this drop-down list to select a classification for your appointment, which specifies how the appointment is displayed on your calendar.

Adding a note

Sometimes an appointment requires more detail. You might need to remind yourself about documents that you need to bring to the appointment, or perhaps you need to write down directions to an unfamiliar location. When that's the case, you can add a note by typing your text in the large text area of the form, as shown in Figure 16-12.

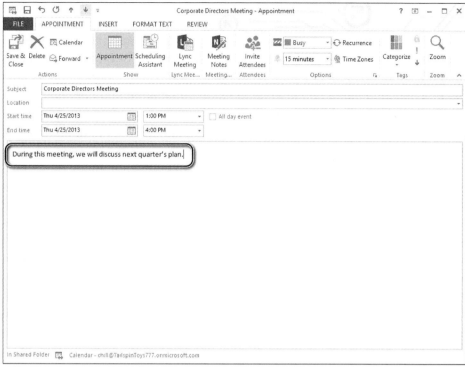

Figure 16-12 You can write a note on the appointment form.

Categorizing an appointment

Assigning a category to an appointment is simply another method of organizing your information. Outlook 2013 provides a number of default categories associated with colors, and you can customize the names for each category. The color association enables you to identify the categories of appointments more easily within your calendar. You can create additional categories as desired and associate each with a specific color. Outlook 2013 allows you to categorize your appointments so that you can then filter or sort them before viewing. In this way, you can get an overview of all Outlook 2013 items based on a particular category. For example, you could view all appointments, meetings, messages, contacts, and tasks that have been assigned the same category—perhaps all the items related to a specific work project or objective.

For more information about working with categories in Outlook 2013, see Chapter 5, "Creating and using categories."

To assign a category to an appointment, click Categorize in the Tags group of the appointment tab. To assign a single category to the appointment, simply select the category in the drop-down list, as shown in Figure 16-13. To select multiple categories, modify existing categories, or create new categories, select the All Categories option at the bottom of the drop-down list.

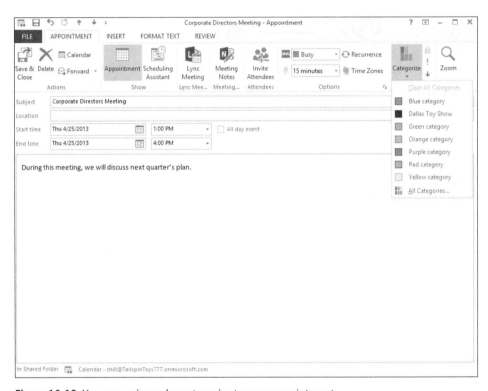

Figure 16-13 You can assign color categories to your appointment.

When you select All Categories, the Color Categories dialog box is displayed, as shown in Figure 16-14, enabling you to manage the categories. In this dialog box, you can select one or more categories and then click OK to assign them to the appointment. You can also rename or delete any of the existing categories and change the color association, as well as assign a shortcut key for each category.

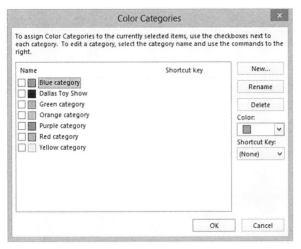

Figure 16-14 You can assign multiple categories to your appointment and configure a category label, color, and shortcut key.

Saving an appointment

You can save an appointment in several ways. The most basic method is to click the Save & Close button on the ribbon. This saves the appointment in the Calendar folder and closes the appointment form. If you want to save the appointment but keep the form open, click the Save button on the Quick Access Toolbar (or click File and then Save).

A more complex way to save appointments allows them to be transferred to other users (who may or may not use Outlook 2013) and opened in other applications. To save your appointments in any of a number of file formats, click File, and then choose Save As to display the Save As dialog box, shown in Figure 16-15.

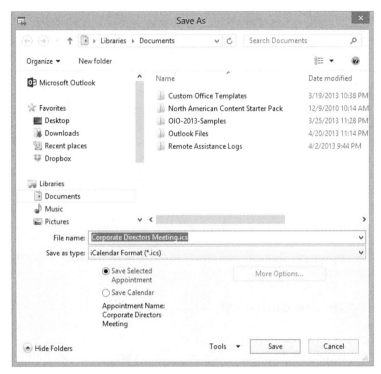

Figure 16-15 You can save your appointment in any of several formats so that the appointment can be opened with another application. You can also save the calendar or any date range portion of it.

The following formats are available:

- **Rich Text Format and Text Only**   These formats save the appointment in a file that text editors can read. Figure 16-16 shows an example of an appointment saved in Rich Text Format (RTF) and then opened in WordPad.

> **Note**
> You can create a new appointment from an Outlook 2013 template file by choosing File, New, Choose Form and then selecting User Templates In File System in the Look In list.

Figure 16-16 An appointment saved in Rich Text Format or Text Only can be displayed in any application that supports those file types.

● **Outlook Template**   This format allows you to save an appointment and use it later to create new appointments.

● **Outlook Message Format and Outlook Message Format – Unicode**   Saving an appointment in one of these formats is almost the same as saving an appointment to the calendar, except that the appointment is saved in a file in case you want to archive the file or move it to another installation of Outlook 2013. You can view the file in Outlook 2013, and the data appears as it would if you had opened the item from the calendar.

● **iCalendar Format and vCalendar Format**   These formats are used to share schedule items with people who use applications other than Outlook 2013.

Changing an appointment to an event

To change an appointment to an event, select the All Day Event check box on the appointment form. When an appointment is converted to an event, the start and end times are removed and only the start and end dates are left because events by definition last all day. The event appears in the banner area of the calendar.

Working with one-time events

An event is an appointment that lasts for one or more entire days. You can create an event by right-clicking the calendar and then choosing New All Day Event. Unlike appointments, events are not shown in time slots on the calendar. Instead, events are displayed as banners at the top of the calendar day. Figure 16-17 shows the calendar with a scheduled event—in this case, a trade show.

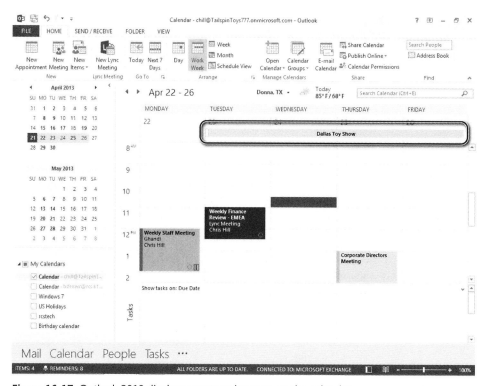

Figure 16-17 Outlook 2013 displays events as banners on the calendar.

INSIDE OUT Create an event quickly

A simple way to add an event is to click the banner area of the calendar and start typing the subject of the event. When you add an event this way, the event is automatically set to last for only the selected day. Alternatively, in Month view, click a date and then type the subject to create a one-time event on that date. To add details and change the duration of the event, you must use the event form.

Using the event form

You can use an event form in much the same way you use an appointment form, with a few exceptions:

- You can set the start and end times only as dates, not times. (If you select times, the form changes from an event form to an appointment form, and the All Day Event check box is cleared.)

- The default reminder is set to 12 hours.

- The time is shown by default as Free, as opposed to Busy.

The event form and the appointment form look the same except that the All Day Event check box is selected on the event form. You can open an event form by right-clicking the time in Calendar view and then choosing New All Day Event.

To create an event using the event form, type the subject, specify the start and end dates, add any optional information, and then click Save & Close in the Actions group. Figure 16-18 shows the event form for a trade show event.

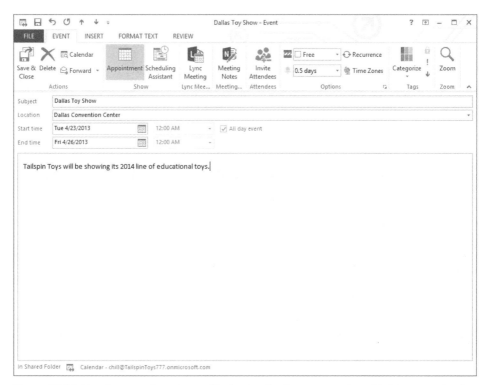

Figure 16-18 Use the event form to specify the details of an event to be added to your calendar.

Changing an event to an appointment

To change an event to an appointment, clear the All Day Event check box on the event form. The boxes for start and end times are re-enabled, and the event will now be displayed in time slots on the calendar, not in the banner area.

Creating a recurring appointment or event

When you create a recurring appointment or a recurring event, Outlook 2013 automatically displays the recurrences in the calendar. A recurring appointment could be something as simple as a reminder to feed your fish every day or pay your mortgage every month. You can create a recurring calendar item by right-clicking the calendar and then choosing New Recurring Appointment or New Recurring Event. Alternatively, you can open a normal (nonrecurring) item and then click the Recurrence button in the Options group. Either method displays the Appointment Recurrence dialog box, shown in Figure 16-19.

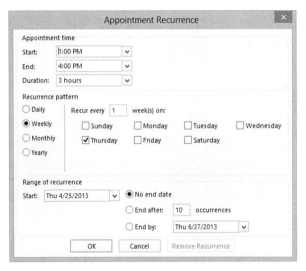

Figure 16-19 You can specify criteria that direct Outlook 2013 to display an appointment or event multiple times in the calendar.

In the Appointment Time area, you set the appointment time and duration. If you're creating the recurrence from an existing nonrecurring appointment, the time of that appointment is listed by default.

The Recurrence Pattern area changes depending on whether you select the Daily, Weekly, Monthly, or Yearly option, as follows:

- **Daily**   Specify the number of days or every weekday.

- **Weekly**   Specify the number of weeks and the day (or days) of the week.

- **Monthly**   Specify the number of months as well as the day of the month (such as 27) or the day and week of the month (such as the fourth Wednesday). Use the The Last Day Of Every 1 Month(s) option, rather than specifying 31 if you want the item to recur on the last day of each month (because not every month has 31 days).

- **Yearly**   Specify the date (such as December 27) or the day and week of the month (such as the fourth Wednesday of each December).

At the bottom of the Appointment Recurrence dialog box is the Range Of Recurrence area. By default, the start date is the current day, and the recurrence is set to No End Date. You can choose to have the appointment recur a specified number of times and then stop, or you can set it to recur until a specified date and then stop—either method has the same effect. For example, to set a recurring appointment that starts on the first Monday of a month and continues for four Mondays in that month, you could either set it to occur four times or set it to occur until the last day of the month.

Modifying an appointment or event

There are many reasons you might need to change a scheduled appointment or event—an event could be rescheduled, an appointment could be moved to a better time, or the topical focus could be added to or changed. In each case, you will need to modify the existing appointment or event, updating information or changing the date or time.

Changing an appointment or event

Modifying an existing appointment or event is easy. First, open the appointment or event by locating it in the calendar and then either double-clicking or right-clicking it and choosing Open. Make the necessary changes in the form, and then click Save & Close on the ribbon. The updated appointment or event is saved in the Calendar folder.

Chapter 16

Deleting an appointment or event

You can delete an appointment or event in several ways. To send the item to the Deleted Items folder, right-click the item and choose Delete, or select the item and press the Delete key. To permanently delete the item, hold down Shift while choosing Delete or pressing the Delete key.

> **CAUTION**
>
> You cannot recover an item that has been deleted using the Shift key unless you are using Microsoft Exchange Server and your administrator has configured the server for a retention period.

Using categories and colors

You can use color as a tool to identify appointments and events. The easiest way to assign color to an appointment is to use the Categorize drop-down list on the appointment form. You can also direct Outlook 2013 to assign color labels automatically via the Automatic Formatting option in Outlook 2013.

Assigning color categories to an appointment manually

The Categorize drop-down list on the appointment form shows the different color labels (associated with categories) that you can assign to an appointment as a visual cue to indicate the topic of the appointment. Categories can also reflect appointment importance or requirements. Simply select a color in the drop-down list when you fill in the appointment form. Figure 16-20 shows a business appointment, and it will be displayed on the calendar in the specified color. To set colors independent of categories, use the conditional formatting rules described in the next section.

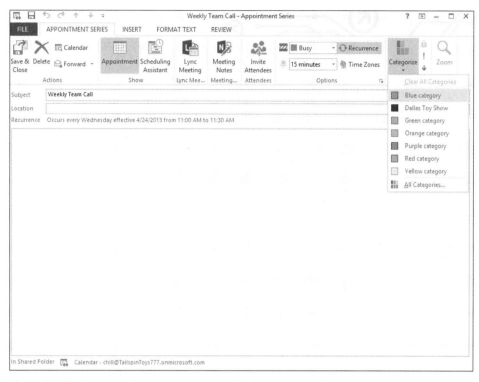

Figure 16-20 You can assign a color category label to your appointment.

You can assign a category to an appointment without associating a color with it by defining a category and selecting None for the color. Categories without colors will not provide the visual cue that enables you to identify the nature of an appointment quickly, but they are still useful—for example, when you filter your Calendar view by category.

> **Note**
> Manual color category settings always override automatic settings, even when the category color setting is set to None.

Assigning color to an appointment automatically

To have Outlook 2013 automatically assign a color label to an appointment, you can create conditional formatting rules.

To assign color automatically, do the following:

1. Click the View tab and click View Settings to display the Advanced View Settings dialog box. Then click Conditional Formatting.

2. Click Add to add a new rule.

3. Type a name and assign a label to the new rule. Figure 16-21 shows a rule to color all Important appointments automatically with red.

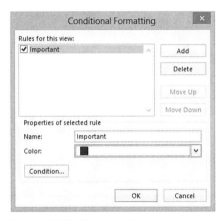

Figure 16-21 This new rule automatically assigns the red color to all appointments with high importance.

4. Click Condition to open the Filter dialog box, shown in Figure 16-22, where you specify the condition for the rule.

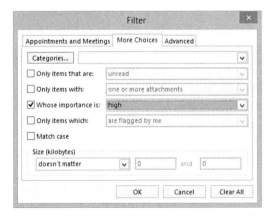

Figure 16-22 The Filter dialog box lets you set a filter that defines the condition on which the automatic color rule works.

For details about using filters, see the section "Customizing the current calendar view."

5. In this dialog box, assign a condition to the rule. For example, you might search for a word or phrase in all appointments, such as searching for the words *Phone Conference* in the Subject and Notes fields, and marking these appointments using the red color category if *Phone Conference* is found.

> **Note**
>
> The More Choices and Advanced tabs in the Filter dialog box enable you to select other criteria, such as categories, read status, attachments, size, or matching fields.

6. Click OK to assign the condition to the new rule.

7. Click OK twice, once to close the Conditional Formatting dialog box and again to close the Advanced View Settings dialog box.

Printing calendar items

You can print calendar items in two ways. The simplest method is to right-click the item and then choose Quick Print from the shortcut menu. This method prints the item using the default settings.

The other way to print an item is to first open it by double-clicking it. You can then click File, Print to display the Print dialog box.

You can make selections in the Print dialog box to change the target printer, the number of copies, and the print style, if necessary. The print style defines how the printed item will look. Click Print Options, Page Setup to change the options for the selected style. In the Page Setup dialog box, use the Format tab to set fonts and shading; the Paper tab to change the paper size, orientation, and margin settings; and the Header/Footer tab to add information to be printed at the top and bottom of the page.

Customizing the current calendar view

In addition to setting the number of days displayed, configuring the time bar, and color-coding your appointments, you can customize the standard view of the Calendar folder in other ways. You can redefine fields, set up filters that define which items are displayed on your calendar, and control fonts and other view settings. To configure the view, click View Settings on the View tab on the ribbon to open the Advanced View Settings dialog box, shown in Figure 16-23.

Chapter 16

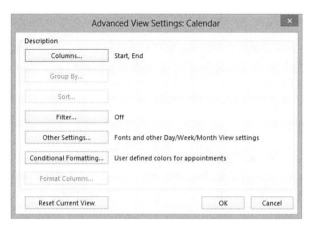

Figure 16-23 Use the Advanced View Settings dialog box to change view settings.

INSIDE OUT Customize additional views

You can also customize views other than the current one. To do so, click Change View, Manage Views. Select the view in the Manage All Views dialog box, and then click Modify. This displays the Advanced View Settings dialog box, where you can change the options for the selected view.

Redefining fields

Only two of the fields used for calendar items can be redefined: the Start and End fields. The values in these fields determine an item's precise location on the calendar—that is, where the item is displayed. By default, the value contained in the Start field is the start time of the appointment and the value contained in the End field is the end time of the appointment, which means that the item is displayed on the calendar in the time interval defined by the item's Start and End values.

To redefine either the Start or the End value, click Columns in the Advanced View Settings dialog box to open the Date/Time Fields dialog box. In the Available Date/Time Fields list, select the field that you want to use for the Start field, and then click Start. Click the End button to change the End field. For example, if you redefine the Start field to Recurrence Range Start and the End field to Recurrence Range End, all recurring calendar items will be displayed as a single item that starts on the date of the first occurrence and ends on the date of the last occurrence. This can be handy if you want to view the entire recurrence range for a given item graphically.

Filtering calendar items

You can filter calendar items based on their content, their assigned category, or other criteria. By filtering the current view, you can determine which calendar items are displayed
on your calendar—for example, all items related to one of your work projects, all items that
involve a specific coworker, or items with a particular importance level.

To filter calendar items, follow these steps:

1. On the View tab on the ribbon, click View Settings to open the Advanced View
    Settings dialog box.

2. Click Filter to open the Filter dialog box.

3. If the Appointments And Meetings tab isn't displayed, as shown in Figure 16-24, click
    it to bring it to the front.

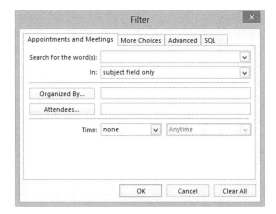

Figure 16-24 You can filter calendar items based on a specified word or phrase.

4. In the Search For The Word(s) box, type the word or phrase you want to use as the
    filter.

5. In the In drop-down list, select which areas of the calendar item to search—for
    example, you might have Outlook 2013 look only in the Subject field of your
    appointments.

6. Click OK. Outlook 2013 displays on your calendar only those calendar items that
    contain the specified word or phrase.

To set additional criteria, you can use the three other tabs in the Filter dialog box—More Choices, Advanced, and SQL—as follows:

- **More Choices**   On this tab, you can click Categories to select any number of categories. After you click OK, only calendar items belonging to the selected categories are displayed on the calendar. Using the check boxes on the More Choices tab, you can filter items based on whether they are read or unread, whether they have attachments, their flag status, or their importance setting. The final check box on the tab enables or disables case matching for the word or phrase specified on the Appointments And Meetings tab. You can also filter items depending on size.

- **Advanced**   This tab allows an even wider range of filter criteria. You can specify any field, adding a condition such as Contains or Is Not Empty or a value for conditions that require one. Clicking Add To List adds the criteria to the list of filters.

- **SQL**   This tab has two purposes. In most cases, it displays the Structured Query Language (SQL) code for the filter, based on the filter criteria you select on the other three tabs. If the Edit These Criteria Directly check box is selected, however, you can manually type the SQL code for filtering calendar items directly on the SQL tab. This flexibility allows you to fine-tune your filters with a great degree of precision.

Controlling fonts and other view settings

You can use the Advanced View Settings dialog box (previously shown in Figure 16-23) to make additional changes to the current view. In the Advanced View Settings dialog box, click Other Settings to display the Format Calendar dialog box, shown in Figure 16-25.

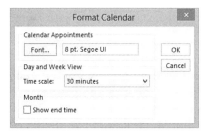

Figure 16-25 You can use the Format Calendar dialog box to set font preferences for the Calendar folder as well as other options.

In the Format Calendar dialog box, you can do the following:

- Set the fonts used in Calendar view.

- Set the calendar's time increments by selecting an option in the Time Scale drop-down list. This sets the amount of time represented by each interval in the time bar.

- Specify whether to show end times.

Creating a custom view

Up to now, we have looked only at the customization of existing views, but you can also create completely new views and copy and modify views. If your current view is one that you use often but nevertheless must change frequently to filter calendar items or modify fields, you might find it easier to create a new view.

To create a view or to see a list of already defined views, on the View tab, click Change View, Manage Views to open the Manage All Views dialog box, shown in Figure 16-26.

> **Note**
>
> To work with the Outlook 2013 calendar views, you must open the Calendar folder.

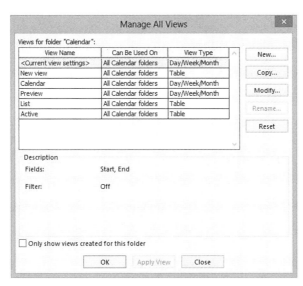

Figure 16-26 The Manage All Views dialog box allows you to see and work with the currently defined views as well as create new ones.

Creating a new view

To create a view, follow these steps:

1. Click New in the Manage All Views dialog box to open the Create A New View dialog box, shown in Figure 16-27.

Figure 16-27 You can use the Create A New View dialog box to specify a name, a view type, the folder to which the view applies, and who is allowed to see the view.

2. Name the new view, and then select a view type. In the Can Be Used On area, specify the folder to which the view applies and who is allowed to see the view. You can select one of the following options:

    ❍ **This Folder, Visible To Everyone**   Limits the view to the current folder and makes it available to any user

    ❍ **This Folder, Visible Only To Me**   Limits the view to the current folder, but makes it available only to the current user

    ❍ **All Calendar Folders**   Allows the view to be used in any Calendar folder by any user

3. Click OK to create the new view. The Customize View dialog box appears, in which you can set the options for the new view.

INSIDE OUT
Change the availability of an existing view

The Modify option in the Manage All Views dialog box does not let you change the availability of an existing view. To change the availability of an existing view or who is allowed to see a view, first copy the view and assign a name to the copy. (See the next section for more information about copying views.) Then select a new option in the Can Be Used On area. Last, delete the original view and rename the new view using the name of the deleted view.

For information about setting view options in the Customize View dialog box, see the section "Customizing the current calendar view."

Copying a view

If you want to modify an existing view but also want to keep the original, you can make a copy of the view. To copy a view, select it in the Manage All Views dialog box, and then click Copy. In the Copy View dialog box, you can specify the name of the new view, the folder to which the view will apply, and who is allowed to see the view. Click OK to create the copy, which is added to the list in the Manage All Views dialog box and the list on the Change View menu on the View tab.

Using overlay mode to view multiple calendars in one

There are times when you need to view and compare multiple schedules to identify related items, such as workflow dependencies within a project, as well as to find and alleviate scheduling conflicts. For example, you might want to view your personal calendar in contrast to your departmental calendar to compare scheduling and task overlaps, or perhaps you want to view calendars for multiple team members to identify a free slot for a meeting. Outlook 2013 enables you to view multiple calendars in overlay mode, as shown in Figure 16-28.

Chapter 16

Figure 16-28 You can overlay multiple calendars to view related or conflicting schedules.

To view multiple calendars in overlay mode:

1. Select multiple calendars by selecting the check boxes next to the calendars in the Navigation Pane.

2. Right-click one of the calendars in the Navigation Pane, and then choose Overlay.

> **Note**
>
> You can click the left arrow icon at the left edge of the calendar's name tab to overlay the calendar with the leftmost calendar. Click the right arrow icon to move the selected calendar out of overlay mode.

Backing up your schedule

To back up items in your Calendar folder, you must export the data to a personal folder (.pst) file. To do so, follow these steps:

1. Click File, Open & Export, Import/Export to start the Import And Export Wizard.

2. Click Export To A File, as shown in Figure 16-29, and then click Next.

Figure 16-29 To back up calendar items, start the Import And Export Wizard, and then select Export To A File.

3. On the Export To A File page, shown in Figure 16-30, select Outlook Data File (.pst), and then click Next.

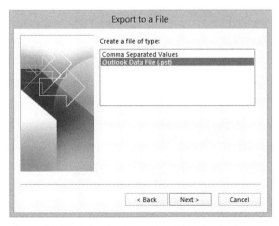

Figure 16-30 Calendar items should be backed up to a .pst file.

Chapter 16

4. In the Export Personal Folders dialog box, select the folder to export (the Calendar folder in the example shown in Figure 16-31). If you select the Include Subfolders check box, any subfolders of the selected folder are exported as well.

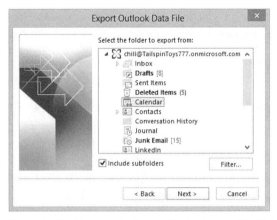

Figure 16-31 You use the Export Outlook Data File dialog box to specify the folder to export to a file.

5. Enter a name for the .pst file in the text box, or click Browse to select an existing .pst file.

6. Click Filter to open the Filter dialog box, in which you can specify the items to be exported. You can use the Filter dialog box if you want to export only specific items from your Calendar folder. If you choose not to use the Filter dialog box, all items will be exported. Click Next to continue.

   For details about using the Filter dialog box, see the section "Filtering calendar items."

7. Specify the exported file and the export options. The export options control how Outlook 2013 handles items that have duplicates in the target file. You can choose to overwrite duplicates, create duplicates in the file, or not export duplicate items.

8. Click Finish. If you did not select an existing .pst file, the Create Outlook Data File dialog box, shown in Figure 16-32, appears.

Figure 16-32 Type a password and verify the password before creating the .pst file.

9. Type password (optional) and click OK to create the file.

To restore data backed up to the .pst file, follow these steps:

1. Click File, Open & Export, Import/Export to start the Import And Export Wizard.

2. Select Import From Another Program Or File, and then click Next.

3. Select Outlook Data File (.pst), and then click Next.

4. On the Import Personal Folders page, specify the backup file and how Outlook 2013 should handle duplicate items. You can choose to overwrite duplicates, create duplicate items, or not import duplicates. Then click Next. If you assigned a password to the backup file, you will be prompted to enter it at this point.

5. Select the folder within the .pst file to be imported (the Calendar folder in this case), decide whether to include subfolders, and select the target folder. (By default, the target folder is the folder with the same name in the current mailbox, as shown in Figure 16-33.) You can also click Filter to specify in the Filter dialog box which items are to be imported.

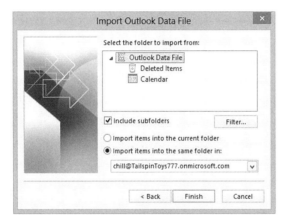

Figure 16-33 When you're importing items, you must select the folder to be imported from the .pst file, whether to include subfolders, and the target folder.

6. Click Finish to complete the import process.

Managing time zones

Outlook 2013 gives you a great deal of flexibility when it comes to time zones on your calendar. You can change time zones easily and even add a second time zone to the calendar. If you work for a corporation that has multiple offices in different time zones, being able to reference your calendar with various zones quickly can make scheduling simpler.

Changing the time zone

To work with time zones, use the Time Zones area on the Calendar page of the Outlook Options dialog box, as shown in Figure 16-34. To open this dialog box, right-click the time bar and choose Change Time Zone. (Alternatively, click File, Options, and then choose Calendar.)

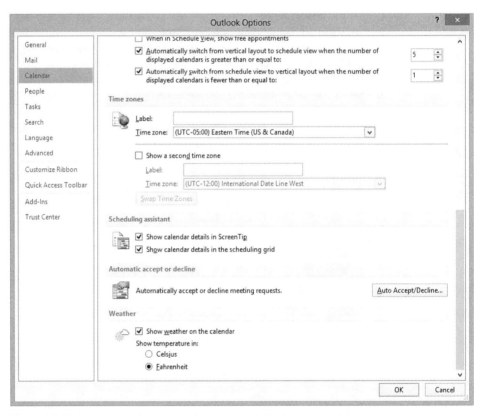

Figure 16-34 You can set the current time zone and display a second time zone.

In the Time Zone group, you can specify a label for the current time zone, which is displayed above the time bar on your calendar. You can also set the time zone that you want to use by selecting it in the Time Zone drop-down list, and you can also choose a second time zone to show.

> **Note**
> Changing the time zone in the Time Zones area of the Outlook Options dialog box
> has the same effect as changing the time zone by using the Date And Time dialog box
> through Control Panel.

When you change the time zone, the time of your appointments adjusts as well. Your appointments stay at their scheduled time in the original time zone but move to the appropriate time in the new time zone. For example, an appointment scheduled for 10:00 A.M. in the Central Time zone will move to 8:00 A.M. if the time zone is changed to Pacific Time. Appointments are scheduled in absolute time, regardless of the time zone.

Using two time zones

To add a second time zone to your calendar, follow these steps:

1. In the Time Zones group, select the Show A Second Time Zone check box.

2. Assign a label to the second time zone. This step is not necessary, but it can help to avoid confusion later on. (If your first time zone does not already have a label, adding one now will allow you to distinguish between the two easily.)

3. In the second Time Zone drop-down list, select the second time zone.

4. Click Swap Time Zones to swap the current time zone with the second time zone. This feature is useful if you travel between corporate offices in different time zones.

Figure 16-35 shows the calendar after these changes have been applied.

Chapter 16

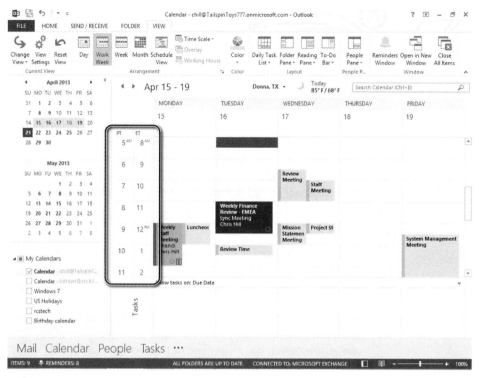

Figure 16-35 The calendar displays both time zones in the time bar under their respective labels.

Managing your calendar effectively

Your Outlook 2013 calendar can help you track your appointments and events and facilitate your collaboration with coworkers, vendors, and clients. To maximize the value of the Outlook 2013 calendar, you will want to provide as much detail in the information that you enter as you can. In addition to simply marking the dates and times of scheduled appointments and events, the calendar information will serve as a quick reference to key points in your workflow, projects, and goals. In addition, the interface features (such as categories and conditional formatting) can provide valuable visual and cognitive cues to the nature and importance of your calendar information, as follows:

- **Use color categories for quick identification**   Outlook 2013 has combined color and category labeling of appointments and events and allows you to define the name of each category and the color associated with it. By defining a set of categories that fits the categories of events, appointments, and information you will be storing in your calendar, you can make it easy to mark (and later identify) the nature and significance of items in your calendar at a glance. These user-defined color categories can provide you with visual cues that help you identify calendar items, tasks, and email that are related—such as a departmental project or role-based recurring activities. The color categories in Outlook 2013 are contained in your default data file; thus for users of Exchange Server, your color categories are available regardless of which computer you log on from.

- **Use conditional formatting to format items based on user-selectable criteria**
  In addition to color categories, you can use conditional formatting to assign a color to appointments, events, and so on in your calendar based on criteria that you define. This can be particularly useful in that you can provide specific words, phrases, or other criteria that Outlook 2013 will use to automatically tag the appointment or event with a specific color. You can use conditional formatting, for example, to find the phrase *Phone Conference* in the Subject or Notes field of appointments and automatically color all those items in your calendar (with a color you select) to provide you with visual cues that the item involves a phone conference.

  For specific information about how to assign colors automatically, see the section "Assigning color to an appointment automatically."

- **Delegate calendar update responsibilities**   In managing your calendar, scheduling appointments and events, and communicating your schedule information effectively, you can use the abilities to delegate access and degrees of editing and authoring control to team members, assistants, and key people involved in ongoing projects.

> **Note**
> To delegate control over your calendar (or other functions of Outlook 2013), you and the person you are delegating to must both be using Exchange Server for your mail servers.

  For network environments using Exchange Server, however, the ability to delegate differential levels of control can be a useful way to turn schedule management into a cooperative effort. Even without providing other users with the ability to send email messages as you, you can nevertheless enable them to read your schedule, create new items or subfolders, edit and delete their own additions to your schedule, and even edit all calendar content. When you are working closely with an associate or a team member on a mutual project, that person could add schedule items on your behalf that address his or her area (documentation, code development, marketing, and so on) of responsibility.

- **Share your calendar information**   In addition to those environments where you can delegate access to read information from and write information to your calendar directly, in all cases you can post your calendar information to the external or internal web servers so that management, team, and project members can view your

Chapter 16

schedule information. In some cases, you might want to publish only the free/busy portion of your schedule information—for example, when publishing your schedule on the Internet. But when publishing your schedule to internal corporate web servers, you will want to provide access to more detail so that coworkers and managers stay up to date. The calendar-sharing options let you specify the date range and level of detail published, determine access (everyone or just those you invite), and select calendar update frequency. You can also share your calendar via email with the selected group of email recipients for whom your calendar is relevant. This option also lets you choose the date range and level of detail sent so that you can control how much of your calendar information you are providing.

For detailed information about sharing calendars, see Chapter 22, "Sharing calendars."

- **Use views to manage your calendar** The various views of your calendar provide a built-in way for you to quickly assess your schedule—simply switching between the Day, Week, and Month tabs reminds you of your scheduled activities. Using the built-in views enables you to see your schedule laid out as a timeline (which you can view on a daily, weekly, or monthly basis). Other default views enable you to see all your scheduled items as a list that you can sort by date, type of appointment or event, subject, category, and a range of other criteria. Using these views can help you quickly find events and appointments of current topical interest and provide reminders of upcoming scheduled obligations. When specific view and filter criteria are particularly useful for you, creating a custom view using these criteria will provide you with an instant ability to see your schedule information in that format.

- **Use overlays to compare calendars** For everyone in a work environment, the scheduling of appointments and events has interdependencies with coworkers, teams, project groups, and departments. To avoid scheduling conflicts, it can be very helpful to align your schedule with schedules from other people or groups you are working with. Using Outlook 2013 to bring in additional calendars (from coworkers or groups) and review them in overlay mode greatly facilitates schedule comparison.

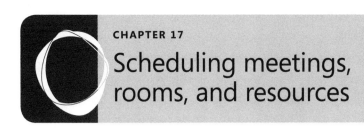

Scheduling meetings, rooms, and resources

B EFORE the introduction of workgroup software such as Microsoft Exchange Server and Microsoft Outlook 2013, scheduling a meeting could be a difficult task. Now all it takes is a few simple steps to avoid those endless email exchanges trying to find a suitable meeting time for all invitees. Outlook 2013 provides you with a single place to schedule both people and resources for meetings. You can take advantage of these features whether or not you use Exchange Server.

Chapter 16, "Scheduling appointments," tells you all about scheduling appointments. Meetings and appointments are similar, of course: Both types of items appear on your calendar, and you can create, view, and store them in your Calendar folder in Outlook 2013. An appointment, however, involves only your schedule and time, whereas a meeting involves inviting others and coordinating their schedules. Another difference is that a meeting often requires you to schedule resources, such as a conference room or an overhead projector.

You can schedule meetings with other Outlook 2013 users as well as those who use any email or collaboration application that supports the vCalendar or iCalendar standard. This chapter takes you through the process of scheduling meetings and lining up resources.

Sending a meeting request

To schedule a meeting, you begin by selecting your calendar in Outlook 2013 and sending a meeting request. Click New Meeting on the Home tab on the ribbon, or click New Items and choose Meeting. The meeting form opens, as shown in Figure 17-1.

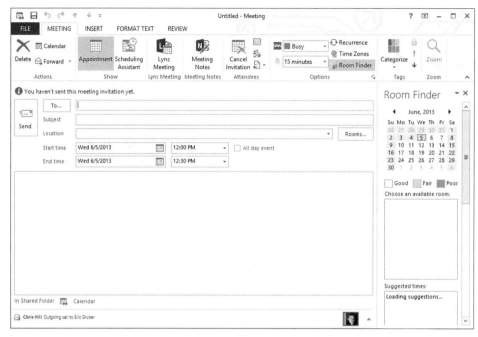

Figure 17-1 You use the meeting form to schedule meetings and send meeting requests.

A meeting request is like an appointment item, but with a few additional details, and you can work with it in much the same way you work with an appointment. This chapter describes only the parts of a meeting request that differ from an appointment.

> For details about creating and working with appointments in the Calendar folder in Outlook 2013, see Chapter 16.

Scheduling a meeting

To invite people to your meeting, start by selecting their names on the Meeting tab. You can type each name in the To box, separating the names with a semicolon. When you enter the names manually, Outlook 2013 considers each person a required attendee. Alternatively, you can click To to open the Select Attendees And Resources dialog box, shown in Figure 17-2. In this dialog box, select a name in the Name list, and then click Required or Optional to designate whether that person's attendance is critical. (This choice will be reflected in the meeting request that you send to these individuals.) After you have finished adding names, click OK to close the dialog box.

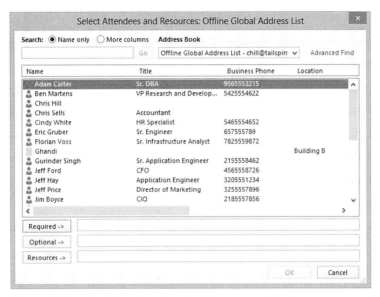

Figure 17-2 In the Select Attendees And Resources dialog box, you can add the names of the individuals you're inviting to your meeting.

> **Note**
>
> When using a non–Exchange Server account, the Show group on the Meeting tab of the ribbon contains a Scheduling button that opens the Scheduling page. With an Exchange Server account, the button is labeled Scheduling Assistant, and when clicked, the button opens the Scheduling Assistant. The two are nearly identical, but there are minor differences, such as the lack of the AutoPick feature in the Scheduling Assistant. See the section "Scheduling a meeting with the Scheduling Assistant" for more details.

Clicking Scheduling Assistant (or Scheduling if you are on a non–Exchange Server network) on the Meeting tab displays the Scheduling page, shown in Figure 17-3. You can click in the Click Here To Add A Name box in the All Attendees column and type a name or an email address. Alternatively, you can click Add Attendees to open the address book and choose attendees.

Chapter 17

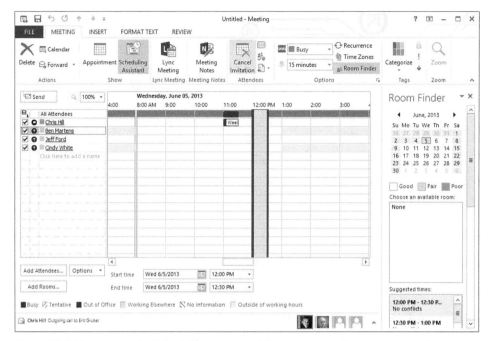

Figure 17-3 You can use the Scheduling page to add meeting attendees and view their schedules.

INSIDE OUT   Select the correct address list

Can't find the attendee you're looking for, and you know that attendee is in the address book? Make sure that the correct address list is selected in the Address Book drop-down list. By default, the Global Address List (GAL), which shows all names from your Exchange Server organization, is selected (if you're running Outlook 2013 with Exchange Server). It is possible to change the default address list, however, and yours could be set to something else.

After you have added the names of the individuals you want to invite, the Scheduling page on the meeting form displays free/busy information for all the people you selected (unless Outlook is unable to retrieve the free/busy information).

The icons you see beside each name have the meanings indicated in Table 17-1.

Table 17-1 Scheduling icons

Icon	Description
○	The magnifying glass icon indicates the meeting organizer.
○	The arrow icon indicates a required attendee.
○	The icon containing the letter *i* indicates an optional attendee.
○	The building icon indicates a scheduled resource.

INSIDE OUT   Specify free/busy server location

Outlook 2013 queries the free/busy time of each attendee based on the settings you have configured for that purpose. As you'll see in Chapter 22, "Sharing calendars," you can configure Outlook 2013 to check Microsoft Office Online, another globally specified free/busy server, and individual servers specified with each contact. These all work in conjunction with Exchange Server, if it is present.

After you have identified a time slot that fits everyone's schedule, you can schedule the meeting for a particular time slot using the Meeting Start Time and Meeting End Time drop-down lists.

If you want Outlook 2013 to fit the meeting into the next available time slot, click AutoPick Next. By default, AutoPick selects the next time slot in which all attendees and at least one resource are free.

Note

The AutoPick feature is not available in the Scheduling Assistant for Exchange Server accounts (as discussed in the "Scheduling a meeting with the Scheduling Assistant" section).

INSIDE OUT Configure the AutoPick feature

To change the default actions of AutoPick, click Options on the Scheduling page, and then make your choices on the AutoPick menu. You can set AutoPick to select the next time slot in which all attendees and all resources are free, the next time slot in which all attendees and at least one resource are free (the default), a time slot in which only required attendees are free, or a time slot in which required attendees and at least one resource are free. You can also choose an earlier time.

You can specify whether the display of free/busy information on the Scheduling page should show only working hours (the default) or the entire day. To define working hours for your calendar, click File, Options, and then click Calendar. To set displayed hours for a meeting, click the Options button on the Scheduling page and set or clear the Show Only My Working Hours option. Working hours are a way of displaying your time in the Calendar folder and controlling which hours are displayed on the Scheduling page. In most cases, including nonworking hours on the Scheduling page would become unmanageable.

After you have selected all the attendees, found an available time slot, and filled in all the necessary details on the message form, click Send on the form to send the meeting request to the attendees.

Scheduling a meeting from an email (Reply With Meeting)

Often, emails are the real source for meeting requests. For example, you might receive an email from someone asking for information about a project or task. Outlook 2013 makes it easy to reply to that message with a meeting request. To reply to a message using a meeting request, select the message in the Inbox or other message folder and click the Reply With Meeting button (which is just labeled Meeting) in the Respond group on the Home tab on the ribbon. Outlook displays a new meeting request form, automatically adds the message sender and recipient(s) to the meeting request, and adds the message contents to the notes section of the meeting invitation. Complete the invitation properties as you normally would and then click Send.

Scheduling a meeting from the Contacts folder

If it's more convenient, you can initiate meeting requests from the Contacts folder instead of the Calendar folder. Click the People item on the Navigation Bar, select one or more contacts in the Contacts folder, and click Meeting on the Home tab on the ribbon. Alternatively, right-click the contact entry for the person you want to invite to a meeting, and then choose Create, Meeting. The meeting form opens with the contact's name in the To box. From here, you can select more attendees and enter meeting details such as subject and location.

Changing a meeting

To change any part of a meeting request, including attendees, start and end times, or other information, first double-click the meeting item in the Calendar folder to open it, and then make your changes. Click the Save icon on the Quick Access Toolbar to save the changes to the Calendar folder, or click Send Update to send an updated meeting request to the attendees. If you make changes that affect the other attendees, such as adding or removing attendees or changing the time or location, you should click Send Update so that the attendees get the new information.

Scheduling a meeting with the Scheduling Assistant

When you are using Outlook 2013 with Exchange Server, you have an enhanced tool for scheduling meetings called the Scheduling Assistant. In most ways, scheduling a meeting with the Scheduling Assistant is the same as scheduling a meeting with other types of accounts. This section of the chapter focuses on the different options available in the Scheduling Assistant.

To schedule a meeting, you begin by sending a meeting request. Click New Meeting on the Home tab on the ribbon, or click New and choose Meeting. The meeting form opens, similar to the one shown previously in Figure 17-1. Select the attendees either on the Appointment page by clicking To and using the Select Attendees And Resources dialog box, or on the Scheduling Assistant page by clicking in the Click Here To Add A Name box and typing the name or address.

When you request a meeting (starting with Exchange Server 2010), you can select one or more rooms to reserve for the meeting by clicking the Rooms button to the right of the Location box, as shown in Figure 17-4. When you click Rooms, the Select Rooms dialog box is displayed, as shown in Figure 17-5. To select a room, click the room (or hold down the Ctrl key and click to select multiple rooms), click the Rooms button at the bottom of the dialog box to add the rooms to your meeting request, and then click OK.

Chapter 17

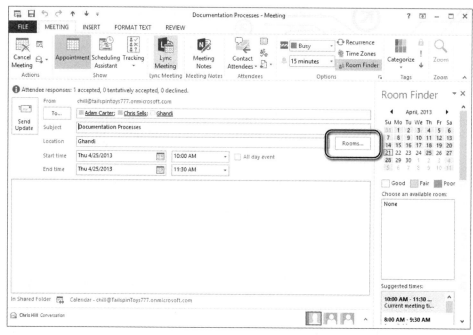

Figure 17-4 Click Rooms to select a room for the meeting.

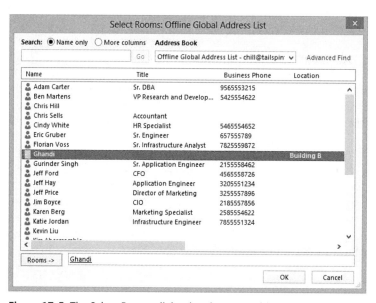

Figure 17-5 The Select Rooms dialog box lets you add one or more rooms to the meeting request.

As Figure 17-6 shows, the Scheduling Assistant page is slightly different from the Scheduling page for non–Exchange Server accounts. For example, the AutoPick option is not available, but the Add Rooms button is available. In addition, the Room Finder pane appears, enabling you to locate an available room for the meeting. Click the Room Finder button in the Options group of the Meeting tab to show or hide the Room Finder.

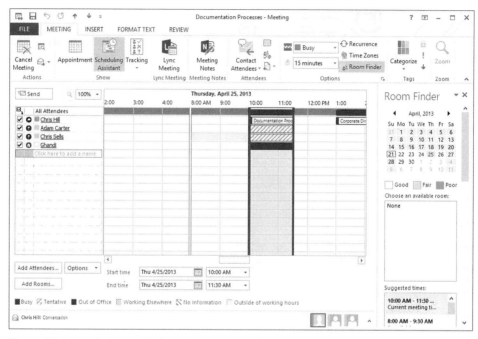

Figure 17-6 Use the Room Finder to locate a room for your meeting.

Responding to a meeting request

When you click Send on a meeting form, a meeting request email message is sent to the invited attendees. This message allows the attendees to accept, tentatively accept, or reject the meeting invitation; propose a new time for the meeting; and include a message in the reply.

Receiving a request for a meeting

The attendees you've invited to your meeting will receive a meeting request message similar to the one shown in Figure 17-7. The message includes a preview of the calendar, showing the requested meeting and any adjacent and conflicting calendar items.

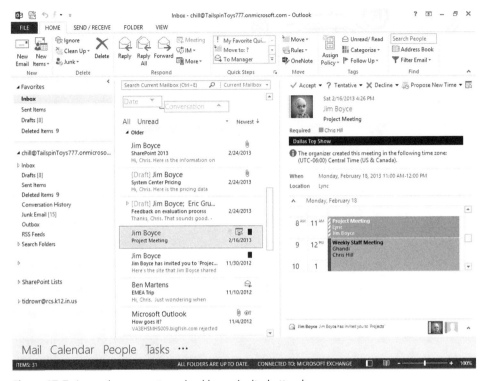

Figure 17-7 A meeting request received by an invited attendee.

An invited attendee has four options when replying to a meeting request:

● Accept the meeting outright.

● Accept the meeting tentatively.

● Decline the meeting.

● Propose a new time for the meeting.

When an attendee chooses to accept, tentatively accept, or decline a meeting request, the person is presented with three options: send the response now (which sends the default response), edit the response before sending (which allows the attendee to send a message with the response), or do not send a response. Each of these options is available in the meeting message header, as shown in Figure 17-8 (the Propose New Time option is not shown here, but it is available if the Reading Pane is wide enough). For example, if you want to accept a meeting invitation but add some notes to your response, click Accept and choose Edit The Response Before Sending. You can then type some notes in the response and click Send to send it.

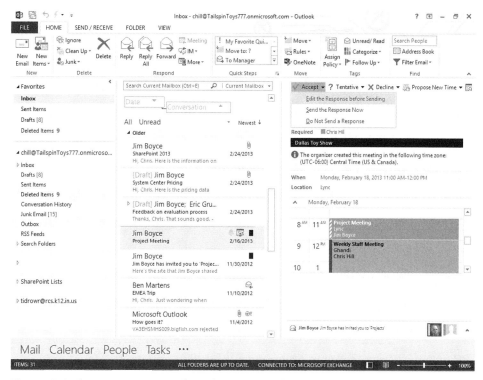

Figure 17-8 Choose your response from the options in the message header.

You can also propose a new meeting time for a meeting invitation that you have received. Click Propose New Time, and then choose Tentative And Propose New Time or Decline And Propose New Time (see Figure 17-9), depending on whether you want to accept or decline the invitation. The Propose New Time dialog box that appears is essentially the same as the Scheduling page of the meeting form (see Figure 17-10). From here, the attendee can select a new time for the meeting and propose it to the meeting organizer by clicking Propose Time.

Chapter 17

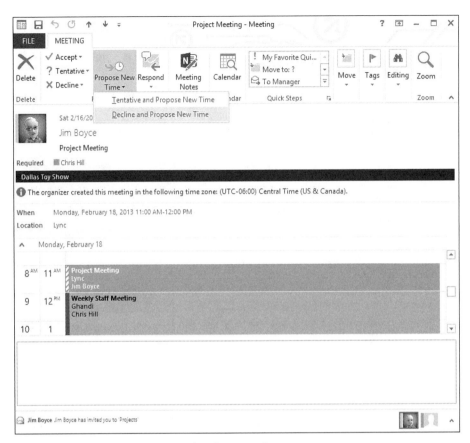

Figure 17-9 You can propose a new time for a meeting.

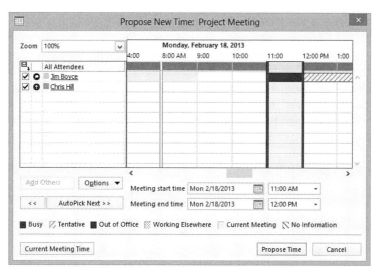

Figure 17-10 Choose a new time for the meeting and click Propose Time.

TROUBLESHOOTING

You've lost a meeting request

When you respond to a meeting request in email, the original request message is automatically deleted from your Inbox. Outlook 2013 automatically adds the meeting information to your Calendar folder when you receive the email message. If you respond to the meeting request from your calendar, however, the email message is not deleted from your Inbox.

If you need to retrieve any of the data in the email message, check your Deleted Items folder for the meeting request itself and your Calendar folder for the meeting information.

To have Outlook 2013 keep meeting request messages in your Inbox even after you've responded, follow these steps:

1. Click File, Options, and then click Mail.

2. Scroll down to locate the Send Messages group of settings.

3. Clear the Delete Meeting Request And Notifications From Inbox After Responding check box.

Receiving a response to your request

When an invited attendee responds to a meeting request, a message is returned to you, the meeting organizer. This message contains the response, including any message the attendee chose to include. In the meeting request response shown in Figure 17-11, the attendee has accepted the meeting and included a message. Notice that the response also lists the attendees who have accepted, tentatively accepted, and declined up to this point.

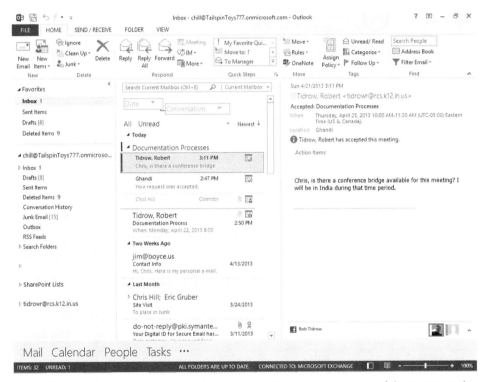

Figure 17-11 A response to a meeting request shows the acceptance status of the request and any message from the attendee.

Figure 17-12 shows a response in which the attendee has selected the Propose A New Time option on a meeting request.

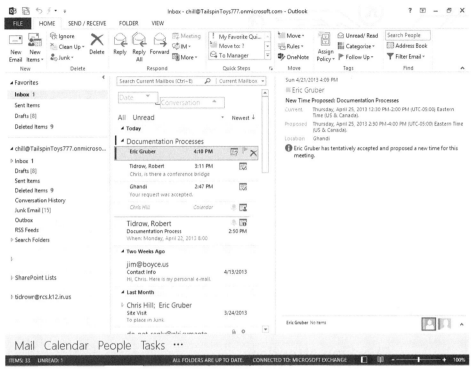

Figure 17-12 When an invited attendee proposes a new time for the meeting, the response to the meeting organizer looks like this.

When you receive a response proposing a new meeting time, you have two choices after you open the response:

- Click Accept Proposal to accept the new time and open the meeting form. Verify any changes, and then click Send Update to send the new proposed time to the attendees.

- Click View All Proposals to open the Scheduling page of the meeting form, which displays a list of all proposed new times for the meeting suggested by any of the attendees, as shown in Figure 17-13. You can select a new time from the list of proposed times and then click Send to send the new proposed time to the meeting attendees.

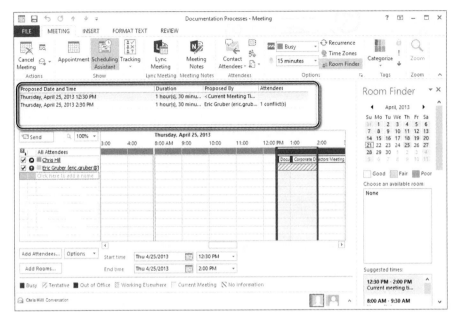

Figure 17-13 You can view the meeting times proposed by all attendees.

Checking attendees

After you send a meeting request, you can check which attendees have accepted or declined by opening the meeting form in the Calendar folder and clicking the form's Tracking button in the Show group on the Meeting tab, as shown in Figure 17-14. (The Tracking button is not displayed on the initial meeting form; Outlook 2013 adds it after the meeting request has been sent.) The Tracking button shows each invited attendee and indicates whether that person's attendance is required or optional and the status of the response. The meeting organizer is the only person who can view the status of attendees.

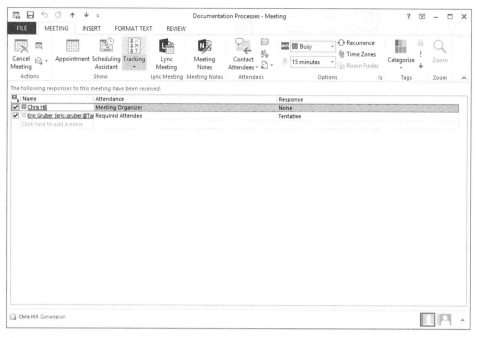

Figure 17-14 Only the person who scheduled the meeting can view the status of the attendees.

Scheduling resources

To plan and carry out a meeting successfully, you'll usually need to schedule resources as well as people. Resources are items (such as computers and projectors) or locations (such as a meeting room) that are required for a meeting. You select resources in much the same way you select attendees.

The ability to schedule resources is typically most useful when you need to set up a meeting, but you might find other occasions when this capability comes in handy. For example, you might want to schedule laptop computers for employees to take home for the weekend or schedule digital cameras to take to building sites.

Setting up resources for scheduling

You schedule a resource by sending a meeting request, adding the resource as a third type of attendee. (The other two types of attendees are Required and Optional, as previously mentioned; see the section "Scheduling a meeting.") Because a resource is scheduled as a type of attendee, it must have a mailbox and a method of accepting or rejecting meeting requests. When you use Outlook 2013 and Exchange Server, a resource is almost identical to any other Exchange Server user except that it is configured to allow another user (the resource administrator) full access to its mailbox. In Exchange Server 2007 or 2010, unlike user mailbox accounts, all resource mailbox accounts are disabled automatically (yet are still accessible as resources from within Outlook 2013).

The first step in setting up a resource for scheduling is to create (or have your system administrator create) a mailbox and an account for the resource. In many cases, resource account names are preceded by a symbol, such as # or &, so that the names, when alphabetized, appear as a group at the top or bottom of the GAL.

How resources are assigned on the mail server running Exchange Server depends on which version of Exchange Server you are using. When you set up resource accounts on a server running Exchange Server 2003, you have to go into Active Directory Users And Computers (within the domain in which the server running Exchange Server is operating) and create and configure user accounts and the subsequent mailboxes. You then have to modify the Mailbox Rights and assign Full Mailbox Access to the resource administrator. The resource administrator has to create a new profile and use the profile to access the mailbox and configure (using the Scheduling Resources option) the Automatically Accept Meeting Requests And Process Cancellations option, which allows the resource scheduling to work. To avoid schedule conflicts, it's also necessary to select Automatically Decline Conflicting Meeting Requests.

When you are using Exchange Server 2007 or 2010, you can schedule both room and equipment resources. Instead of using the Active Directory Users And Computers console to add users and their mail accounts, you use the Exchange Management Console. To add a user account and mailbox to Exchange Server 2010, you browse to the Recipients Configuration container and then select the New Mailbox link. The New Mailbox dialog box provides four options for mailbox creation:

- **User Mailbox**   In this option, the User mailbox is associated with a user account, enabling the user to send, receive, and store email messages, calendar items, tasks, and other Outlook 2013 items.

- **Room Mailbox**   In this option, the Room mailbox is reserved as a resource-type mailbox, and the associated account in Active Directory Domain Services (AD DS) is disabled.

- **Equipment Mailbox**   In this option, the Equipment mailbox is also reserved as a resource-type mailbox, and the associated account in AD DS is disabled.

- **Linked Mailbox**   In this option, the Linked mailbox is employed for users that will access the mailbox from a separate trusted forest.

To assign resources for use in Outlook 2013, you add a new mailbox, select the resource type (either Room or Equipment), and then complete the required information (which is essentially the same information that you would provide for any user account—name, logon name, password, and alias). After you have created a Room mailbox, for instance, when you click the Rooms button in an Outlook 2013 meeting form, all the rooms associated with Room mailboxes will be displayed. Equipment resources (as well as rooms) are displayed in the Select Attendees And Resources list and can be included in the meeting request by selecting the desired equipment and clicking Resources.

Using the configured resources

To schedule a resource after you have configured it, create a meeting request and fill in the details. When you add attendees to the meeting request using the Select Attendees And Resources dialog box, select the resource you want to add from the list and then click Resources, as shown in Figure 17-15. Resources are added to the Resources box instead of to the Required or Optional box. When you have finished adding resources, click OK. Then complete and send the meeting request as you normally would.

For details about creating and sending meeting requests, see the section "Sending a meeting request."

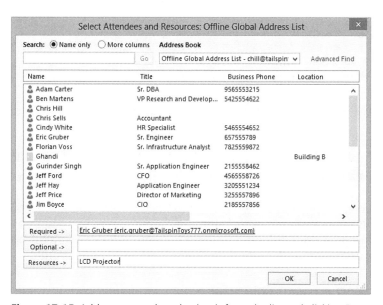

Figure 17-15 Add a resource by selecting it from the list and clicking Resources.

With Exchange Server 2007 and later, a resource's free/busy time appears in the Scheduling Assistant just like the free/busy time for a user. Therefore, you can tell at a glance when a resource is available, enabling you to schedule the meeting around the resource or the room's availability.

If the resource's mailbox is configured to use the Exchange Server Resource Booking Attendant, you will receive an automatic response to your meeting request from the Attendant, as shown in Figure 17-16. If the resource is managed manually, you will receive a response from the resource's delegate.

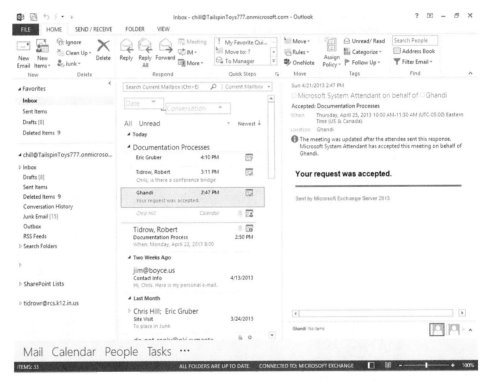

Figure 17-16 This response was generated by the Resource Booking Attendant.

In addition, depending on how the resource mailbox is configured, you might also be able to submit out-of-policy requests to the resource, such as booking a room outside its normally available hours. In these instances, a resource delegate will receive the request and process it.

Viewing a room calendar

The fact that rooms are treated as special mailboxes in Exchange Server made it possible for the Outlook development team to build in some special features for working with rooms. You've already seen that you can select a room with the Scheduling Assistant and view its availability in your meeting invitation before you send it. In addition, you can view room calendars within Outlook and, if needed, overlay them on your own calendar or over other people's calendars.

To view a room calendar, first open your Calendar folder. Then, in the Manage Calendars group on the Home tab on the ribbon, click Open Calendar and choose From Room List. Outlook displays the Select Room dialog box (shown in Figure 17-5), where you can choose the room whose calendar you want to view. Select one or more rooms, click Rooms, and then click OK. Outlook displays the room's calendar alongside your own, as shown in Figure 17-17.

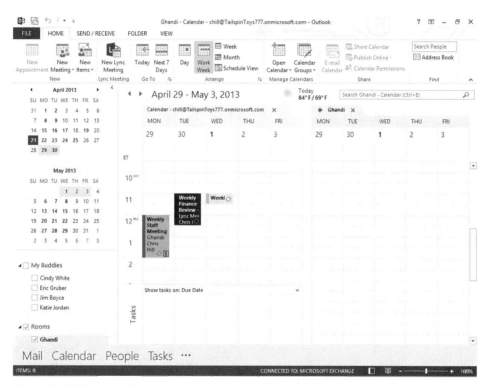

Figure 17-17 You can view room calendars alongside your own calendar.

The capability to view room free/busy information in Outlook means that you can determine ahead of time what rooms are most likely to be available before you even start booking your meeting. For example, if you want to book a meeting for your team, overlay all your team calendars with your own, and then open the desired room calendar and overlay that as well. You'll be able to tell at a glance what times match both your team's collective schedule and the room's availability.

Chapter 17

Managing meetings effectively

Meetings are an essential part of working in a corporate business environment. While necessary, they are not always the most effective use of your time. Using the scheduling tools in Outlook 2013 can help you expedite the scheduling of meetings, remind you in advance of upcoming meetings, and help you complete your meetings on time. Using the Outlook 2013 meeting scheduling capability can help improve the quality of your meetings as well. By planning the meeting and notifying all participants of the agenda (in the content of the meeting request), you give them (and yourself) time to prepare notes, documents, and other presentation materials ahead of time. This also allows participants an opportunity to present questions, concerns, and additions to the agenda prior to the meeting, thus ensuring a more comprehensive meeting that isn't distracted by unforeseen complications. You should also keep in mind the specific characteristics of the people invited to each meeting, anticipate aspects (people who show up late, are too verbose, or are distracted easily) that can impair meeting efficiency, and plan your meeting strategy to avoid such issues.

Finding the best time for the meeting

When you schedule a meeting in your Outlook 2013 calendar, you can use Outlook 2013 to review the free/busy time on the schedules of the other people you invite to the meeting, thus enabling you to pick times that are available for all attendees when you initially schedule the meeting. To view free/busy information when scheduling a meeting (adding a new meeting request), click Scheduling in the Show group on the Meeting tab. After you have added all attendees, their free/busy information will be retrieved and displayed in a timeline, showing the status of the schedules for each period in the timeline. In addition, resources (such as reserved rooms) will be displayed, showing you which times the resources are available for use. You can refresh the free/busy information by clicking Options and then selecting Refresh Free/Busy. You can also use AutoPick to select a meeting time. Outlook 2013 will select the next available meeting time based on your AutoPick criteria, such as All People, One Resource to pick the first time when all the attendees are free and one resource (such as a conference room) is available. The AutoPick criteria can be set on the Options, AutoPick menu, which lets you specify whether to require all or some attendees and whether one or more resources have to be available.

Using the Scheduling Assistant to help schedule meetings

If you have Outlook 2013 set up as a client to Exchange Server, the scheduling functionality is expanded—the Location box on the Appointment page on the Meeting tab has a Rooms button that facilitates meeting room selection, and the Scheduling Assistant page provides further capability to review free/busy information and find available meeting times. In addition to the Free/Busy grid displaying the available times for a meeting, the Suggested Times pane (on the right) shows the Date Navigator, with color-coded dates for possible meeting days (the darker the color, the lower the possibility of scheduling a meeting with the selected attendees). Below the Date Navigator is the selected Duration setting for the meeting, followed by a list of suggested times and showing how many of the requested attendees are free to attend.

Using these features, you can reliably schedule meetings where all people and resources are available, without a flurry of back-and-forth emails to determine availability for a particular date and time.

Setting a sufficient reminder to enable you to make meetings on time

Using the Outlook 2013 reminders can facilitate your getting to your meetings on time. You can assess your own work pattern and determine the best default time for Outlook 2013 to remind you of upcoming meetings. Click File, Options to open the Options dialog box, where you can set the default reminder time in the Calendar area to alert you at the best time prior to the meeting. You can also set reminders for specific meetings to provide an additional reminder (perhaps closer to the start of the meeting) by selecting the reminder time in the Options group on the Appointment page for each meeting.

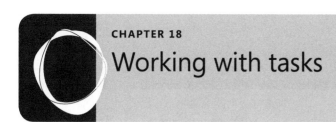

ICROSOFT Outlook 2013 offers a broad selection of tools to help you manage your workday, including techniques for handling email; a way to manage appointments, meetings, and events; a handy method of creating quick notes; and a journal for tracking projects, calls, and other items. All these tools are often related to creating and completing tasks. For example, writing this book was a long string of tasks to be completed: drawing up the outline, writing each chapter, and reviewing edits, for starters.

In your job, your tasks during the average day are no doubt different. Perhaps they include completing contracts, making sales calls, writing or reviewing documents, completing reports, creating websites, or writing program code. Some tasks take only a little time to complete, whereas others can take days, weeks, or even months.

Outlook 2013 provides the means not only to track your own tasks, but also to manage those tasks you need to assign to others. This feature is a much more efficient and effective way to manage tasks than using a notebook, sticky notes, or just your memory. You can set reminders and sort tasks according to category, priority, or status to help you view and manage them.

This chapter examines the Tasks folder and its related features. In addition to covering how to manage your own tasks, you'll learn to assign tasks to and manage tasks assigned to others.

Working with tasks in the Tasks folder

Outlook 2013 provides several ways for you to create and manage tasks. You can create one-time tasks or recurring tasks, set up reminders for tasks, and assign tasks to others. In this section, you'll see how to create tasks for yourself and how to use Outlook 2013 to manage those tasks effectively.

The default view in the Tasks folder is the To-Do List, shown in Figure 18-1, which organizes the tasks by Due Date. Depending on the amount of space available in the view,

Outlook 2013 shows additional columns in the To-Do List view, such as Start Date, Reminder Time, Due Date, the folder in which the tasks are located, and Categories.

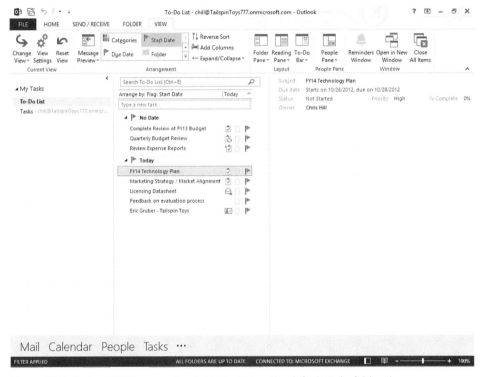

Figure 18-1 Outlook 2013 uses a simple To-Do List as the default Tasks folder view.

The group headers in the To-Do List include the following:

- **Task Subject** You can enter any text in the Subject column, but generally, this text should describe the task to be performed. You can also add notes to each task to identify further the purpose or goal of the task.

- **Icon** The Icon column indicates the type of task. For example, it can indicate either that the task is yours or that it's assigned to another person. The clipboard icon with a check mark indicates that the task is your own. The symbol with an arrow pointing to a small person indicates that the task is assigned to someone else. In addition, the icon can also be an envelope, indicating a message item for follow-up.

- **Start Date** This column indicates the start date for the task.

- **Reminder Time** This column shows the reminder for the task.

- **Due Date**   This column indicates the due date for the task and by default shows the day and date. You can specify different date formats if you want.

- **In Folder**   This column shows the folder in which the task is located.

- **Categories**   This column shows the categories, if any, assigned to the task.

- **Flag Status**   This column shows the task's current flag status, and you can use the column to mark the task as complete or right-click to choose other options.

For details on customizing the Tasks folder view, see the section "Viewing and customizing the Tasks folder." For additional information about features in Outlook 2013 that can help you use and manage views, see Chapter 4, "Working in and configuring Outlook."

Most details appear in the Reading Pane. You can also view all the details of a task by double-clicking the task item. Doing so opens the task form, the format of which varies depending on whether the task is yours or is assigned to someone else. Figure 18-2 shows the form for a task that belongs to you. Figure 18-3 shows the Task page of a form for a task assigned to someone else.

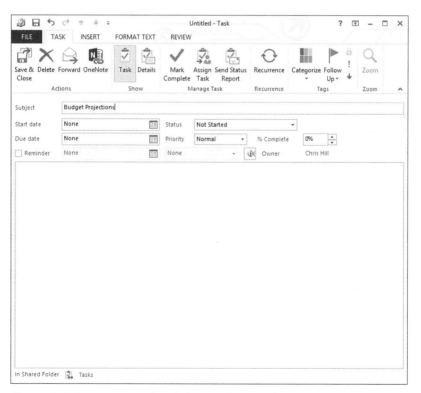

Figure 18-2 Create a new task with this standard task form.

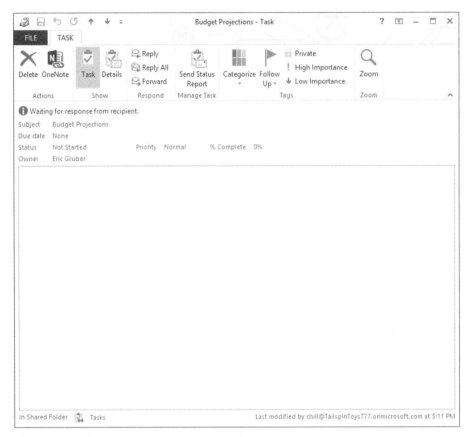

Figure 18-3 This task is assigned to someone else.

The Details page of the task form, shown in Figure 18-4, displays additional information about the task, such as the date completed, total work required, actual work performed, and related background information.

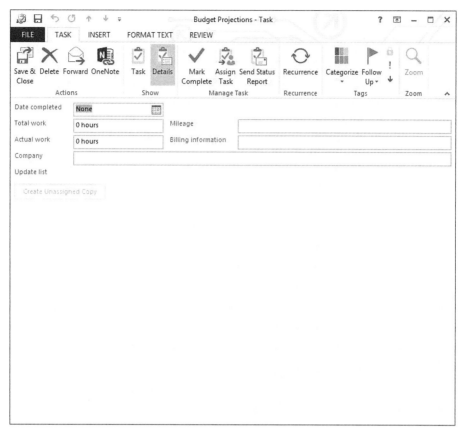

Figure 18-4 Use the Details page to view additional information about the task.

> **Note**
>
> Press Ctrl+Tab to switch between pages in any multipage dialog box or form, including the task form.

Browsing tasks quickly

Although you can open tasks by double-clicking them in the Tasks folder, you might prefer to cycle through your tasks right in the task form. For example, when you want to review several tasks, opening and closing them from the task list one after another is a waste of effort. Instead, you can use the Next Item and Previous Item buttons on the form's Quick Access Toolbar to display tasks in forward or reverse order (relative to the listed order in the Tasks folder). The list doesn't cycle from end to beginning or beginning to end, however, so clicking a button when you're at either of those points in the list closes the task form.

Creating a task

Creating a task is mechanically much the same as creating any item in Outlook 2013. Use any of the following methods to create a new task:

- Between the column header bar and the first task in the list is a new task entry line labeled Type A New Task. Click the line and start typing if you want to specify only the subject for the task, without initially adding details or selecting options. You can open the task at any time afterward to add other information.

- Double-click in an empty area of the task list.

- Right-click in an empty area of the task list, and then choose New Task.

- With the Tasks folder open, click New Task on the Home tab on the ribbon.

- With any Outlook 2013 folder open, click New Items, and then choose Task. This allows you to create a new task when another folder, such as the Inbox or the Calendar folder, is displayed.

The options on the task form are straightforward. Simply select the options that you want and set the task properties (such as start date and due date). Opening the Due Date or Start Date drop-down list displays a calendar that you can use to specify the month and date for the task. If no specific date is required for the task, you can leave the default value None selected. If you currently have a date selected and want to set the date to None, select None from the drop-down list.

INSIDE OUT Specify total work and actual work

As you'll learn a little later in this section, you can specify values for Total Work and Actual Work on the Details page of the task form. Total Work indicates the total number of hours (days, weeks, and so on) required for the task; Actual Work lets you record the amount of work performed to date on the task. Unfortunately, the % Complete value on the Task page is not tied to either of these numbers. Thus, if Total Work is set to 40 hours and Actual Work is set to 20 hours, the % Complete box doesn't show 50 percent complete. Instead, you must specify the value for % Complete manually.

Note

The % Complete value is tied to the Status field on the Task page. If you set % Complete to 100, Outlook 2013 sets the status to Completed. If you set % Complete to 0, Outlook 2013 sets the status to Not Started. Any value between 0 and 100 results in a status of In Progress. Selecting a value in the Status drop-down list has a similar effect on % Complete. Select Not Started, for example, and Outlook 2013 sets the % Complete value to 0.

In addition to entering information such as the percentage of work that's completed, the priority, and the status, you can also set a reminder for the task. As it does for other Outlook 2013 items, such as appointments, Outlook 2013 can display a reminder window and play a sound as a reminder to start or complete the task. You can set only one reminder per task, so it's up to you to decide when you want Outlook 2013 to remind you about the task. Click the speaker button on the task form to select the audio file that you want Outlook 2013 to use for the reminder.

One key task setting is the Owner setting. When you create a task, you own that task initially. Only the owner can modify a task. Task ownership is relevant only to assigned tasks—that is, tasks that you assign to others to perform.

For details about task ownership, see the section "Assigning tasks to others."

Other information that you can specify on the Task tab of the task form's ribbon includes categories and the private or nonprivate status of the task. The ability to assign categories to tasks can help you organize your tasks. You can assign multiple categories to each task as needed and view the Tasks folder sorted by category. For example, you might assign project categories to tasks to help you sort the tasks according to project, allowing you to focus on the tasks for a specific project.

Chapter 18

The private or nonprivate status of a task allows you to control whether others who have delegate access to your folders can see a specific task. Tasks marked as private aren't visible unless you explicitly grant permission to the delegate to view private items. To control the visibility of private items, click File, Account Settings, Delegate Access. Double-click a delegate, and in the Delegate Permissions dialog box, shown in Figure 18-5, select or clear the Delegate Can See My Private Items check box. Repeat the process for any other delegates as needed.

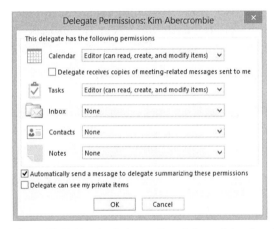

Figure 18-5 Use the Delegate Permissions dialog box to control the visibility of private items.

Note
The Delegates option is available only if you're using Microsoft Exchange Server.

The Details page of the task form (shown in Figure 18-4) allows you to specify additional information about the task. To view the Details page, click Details in the Show group of the ribbon. The options on the Details page include the following:

- **Date Completed**   Use this calendar to record the date that the task is completed. This is the actual completion date, not the projected completion date.

- **Total Work**   Specify the total amount of work required for the task. You can enter a value in minutes, hours, days, or weeks by entering a value followed by the unit, such as 3 days.

- **Actual Work**   Record the total amount of work performed on the task to date. You can enter the data using the same units as in the Total Work box.

- **Company**   List any companies associated with the task, such as suppliers, customers, or clients.

- **Mileage**   Record mileage associated with the task if mileage is reimbursable or a tax-deductible expense.

- **Billing Information**   Record information related to billing for the task, such as rate, person to bill, and billing address.

- **Update List**   This option applies to tasks assigned to others. It shows the person who originally sent the task request and the names of all others who received the task request, reassigned the task to someone else, or elected to keep an updated copy of the task on their task list. When you send a task status message, Outlook 2013 adds these people as recipients of the status message.

- **Create Unassigned Copy**   Use this button to create a copy of an assigned task that you can send to another person.

For details on working with the update list, assigned tasks, and unassigned copies, see the section "Assigning tasks to others."

TROUBLESHOOTING

Others can't see your tasks

For others to see your tasks, you must share your Tasks folder. If you're using Exchange Server as your mail server, you can also allow others to see your tasks by granting them delegate access to your Tasks folder. The two methods are similar with one major difference: Granting delegate access to others allows them to send messages on your behalf. Sharing a folder simply gives others access to it without granting send-on-behalf-of permission.

To share your Tasks folder without granting send-on-behalf-of permission, right-click the Tasks folder icon in the Folder List in the Navigation Pane, and then choose Properties. Click the Permissions tab, and then add or remove users and permissions as needed.

For additional details on sharing folders and setting permissions, see the section "Granting access to folders" in Chapter 21, "Delegating responsibilities to an assistant."

Chapter 18

Creating a recurring task

Earlier in this chapter, you learned several ways to create a task that occurs once. You can also use Outlook 2013 to create recurring tasks. For example, you might create a recurring task for reports that you have to submit on a weekly, monthly, or quarterly basis. Perhaps you perform backup operations once a week and want Outlook 2013 to remind you to do this.

You create a recurring task much the same way you create a single-instance task, except that when the task form is open, you click the Recurrence button on the Task tab of the ribbon to display the Task Recurrence dialog box, shown in Figure 18-6.

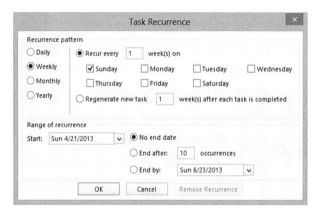

Figure 18-6 Create recurring tasks by using the Task Recurrence dialog box.

You can select daily, weekly, monthly, or yearly recurrence. Selecting one of these four options in the dialog box changes the options available in the dialog box, allowing you to select the recurrence pattern. For example, select Weekly, and then select the days of the week on which you want the task to occur.

When you create a recurring task, one of the decisions you must make is whether you want the task to recur at a specified period regardless of the task's completion status. You can also choose to regenerate a new task after the existing task is completed. For example, you can create a task that recurs every Friday. The task will recur whether or not you marked the previous instance as completed. If you need to complete the previous task before the next task is generated, however, you should configure the recurrence so that the new task is created only after the previous one is completed. For example, perhaps you run a series of reports, but each relies on the previous report being completed. In this situation, you would probably want to set up the task to regenerate only after the preceding one was completed.

The Regenerate New Task option in the Task Recurrence dialog box allows you to configure the recurrence so that the new task is generated a specified period of time after the previous task is completed. Select the Regenerate New Task option, and then specify the period of time that should pass after completion of the task before the task is regenerated.

Other options for a recurring task are the same as those for a one-time task. Specify subject, details, contacts, categories, and other information as needed. Remember to set up a reminder for the task if you want Outlook 2013 to remind you before the task's assigned completion time.

Adding a reminder

You can add a reminder to a task when you create the task or after you create it. As with reminders for appointments, you specify the date and time for the reminder as well as an optional sound that Outlook 2013 can play along with the reminder.

To add a reminder, follow these steps:

1. Open the task, and then select Reminder on the Task page.

2. Use the calendar in the drop-down list next to the Reminder check box to select the date, and then select a time for the reminder. You can select a time in half-hour increments in the drop-down list or specify your own value by typing it in the box.

3. Click the speaker button to open the Reminder Sound dialog box, in which you select a WAV file to assign to the reminder.

4. Click OK, and then close the task form.

> **Note**
> Outlook 2013 uses your workday start time as the default time for the reminder (if you change the default workday start time, the default task reminder time will update accordingly when you restart Outlook). You can change this default value by clicking File, Options, Tasks, and then setting the Default Reminder Time option.

Setting a task estimate

When you create a task, you might also want to estimate the time that it will take to complete the task. You can enter this estimate in the Total Work box on the Details page of the task form. As the task progresses, you can change the Total Work value to reflect your changing estimate or leave it at the original value to track time overruns and underruns for the task. For example, assume that you propose a 40-hour task to a client. As you work through the task, you continue to update the Actual Work box to reflect the number of hours you've worked on the task. You reach 40 hours of work on the task and haven't completed it. You then have to make a decision: Do you update the Total Work value to show a new estimate for completion and bill the client accordingly, or do you leave it as is and absorb the cost overrun?

Unfortunately, the Total Work and Actual Work fields are simple, nonreactive data fields. Outlook 2013 provides no interaction between the two to determine an actual % Complete value for the task. For that reason—and because Outlook 2013 can't calculate job costs based on charge rates and the amount of work completed—Outlook 2013 by itself generally isn't a complete job-tracking or billing application. You should investigate third-party applications to perform that task or develop your own applications using the Microsoft Office 2013 system as a development platform.

Marking a task as completed

Logically, the goal for most tasks is completion. At some point, therefore, you'll want to mark tasks as completed. When you mark a task as completed, Outlook 2013 strikes through the task in the task list to provide a visual cue that the task has been finished. The easiest way to mark a task as completed is to place a check in the Complete column, which by default is the first column from the left in the Detailed view. Alternatively, click the Mark Complete button on the ribbon. You can also mark a task as completed on the Task page simply by selecting Completed in the Status drop-down list or setting the % Complete box to 100.

Outlook 2013 by default sorts the task list by completion status. If you've changed the list to sort based on a different column, simply click that column header. For example, clicking the Complete column header sorts the task list by completion status. If you want to view only completed tasks, click Change View on the View tab on the ribbon and choose Completed. Viewing only incomplete tasks is just as easy: Click Change View and choose Active.

For additional details on customizing the Tasks folder view, see the section "Viewing and customizing the Tasks folder."

Assigning tasks to others

In addition to creating tasks for yourself in Outlook 2013, you can assign tasks to others. For example, you might manage a staff of several people and frequently need to assign projects or certain tasks in a project to them. The main benefit of using Outlook 2013 to assign those tasks is that you can receive status reports on assigned tasks and view these status reports in your Tasks folder. Outlook 2013 automates the process of sending task requests and processing responses to those requests. You'll learn more about assigning tasks in the sections that follow. First, however, you need to understand task ownership.

Understanding task ownership

When you create a task, you initially own that task. Only a task's owner can make changes to the task. This means that you can modify the properties (the percent complete, the status, the start date, and so on) of all tasks that you create and own. When you assign a task to someone else and that person accepts the task, the assignee becomes the owner of the task. You can then view the task's properties, but you can no longer change them. Similarly, you become the owner of tasks assigned to you when you accept them, and you can then make changes to those tasks.

A task's Owner property is a read-only value, which appears in the Owner box on the Task page. You can click the value, but you can't change it directly. The only way to change owners is to assign the task and have the assignee accept it.

Making or accepting an assignment

Assigning a task to someone else is a simple process. In general, you create the task, add details, and specify options for the task. Then you tell Outlook 2013 to whom you want to assign the task, and Outlook 2013 takes care of generating the task request and sending it to the assignee.

Follow these steps to assign a task to someone else:

1. In Outlook 2013, open the Tasks folder and create a new task.

2. Add information and set options for the task such as start date, due date, status, and priority.

3. On the Task tab, in the Manage Task group, click Assign Task. Outlook 2013 changes the form to include additional options, as shown in Figure 18-7.

Chapter 18

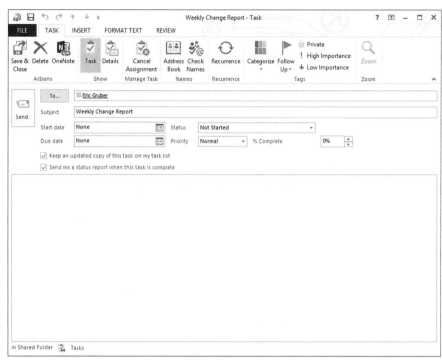

Figure 18-7 Outlook 2013 offers additional options when you assign a task to someone else.

4. In the To box, enter the address of the person to whom you're assigning the task, or click To to browse the address book for the person's address.

5. Outlook 2013 automatically selects the following two check boxes. Set them as you want, and then click Send to send the task request to the assignee.

- ○ **Keep An Updated Copy Of This Task On My Task List**   Select this check box if you want to keep a copy of the task in your own task list. You'll receive updates when the assignee makes changes to the task, such as a change in the % Complete status. If you clear this check box, you won't receive updates, nor will the task appear in your task list.

- ○ **Send Me A Status Report When This Task Is Complete**   Select this check box if you want to receive a status report on completion. The status report comes in the form of an email message that Outlook 2013 generates automatically on the assignee's system when the assignee marks the task as completed.

For information about task updates and status reports, see the section "Tracking the progress of a task."

> **Note**
> Click Cancel Assignment on the ribbon to cancel an assignment and restore the original task form.

When you click Send, Outlook 2013 creates a task request message and sends it to the assignee. If you open the task, you'll see a status message indicating that Outlook 2013 is waiting for a response from the assignee, as shown in Figure 18-8. This message changes after you receive a response and indicates whether the assignee accepted the task.

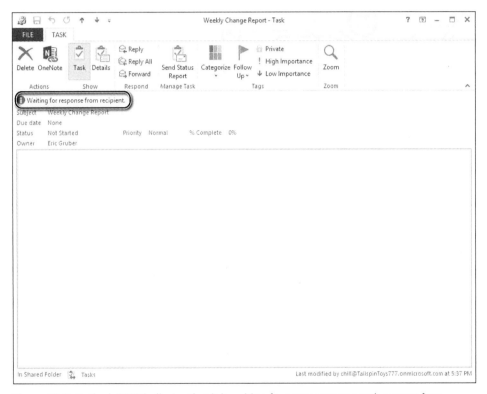

Figure 18-8 Outlook 2013 indicates that it is waiting for a response to a task request for a selected task.

When you receive a task request from someone who wants to assign a task to you, the message includes buttons that allow you to accept or decline the task. Figure 18-9 shows the buttons on the InfoBar when the Reading Pane is displayed.

Chapter 18

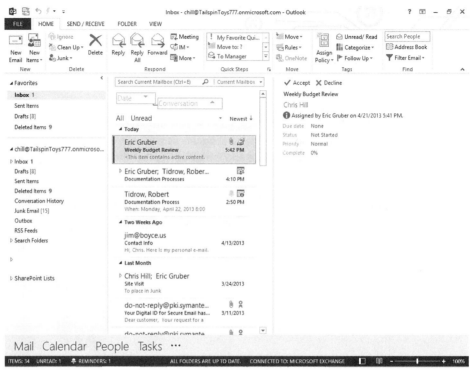

Figure 18-9 You can accept or decline a task request easily by clicking the Accept or Decline button on the InfoBar in the Reading Pane.

You can click either Accept or Decline to respond to the request. If the Reading Pane isn't visible, you can open the message and then click Accept or Decline in the Respond group on the message form's ribbon. When you do so, Outlook 2013 displays either an Accepting Task or a Declining Task dialog box, giving you the option of sending the accept or decline message as is or editing it. For example, you might want to add a note to the message that you'll have to change the due date for the task or that you need additional information about the task. Select Edit The Response Before Sending in the dialog box if you want to add your own comments; select Send The Response Now if you don't want to add comments. Then click OK to generate the message. The next time you synchronize your Outbox with the server, the message will be sent.

You have one more option in addition to accepting or declining a task request that's waiting for your response: You can assign the task to someone else. For example, assume that you manage a small group of people. Your supervisor assigns a task to you, and you want to assign it to one of the people under you. When you receive the task request, open it, click Assign Task, and then select the person to whom you want to assign the task. Outlook 2013 creates a task request and sends it to the assignee. When the assignee accepts the task, that person's copy of Outlook 2013 sends an acceptance notice to you and adds both the originator's address and your address to the update list on the Details page of the task form. This means that changes to the task by the assignee are updated to your copy of the task and to the originator's copy.

TROUBLESHOOTING

Task requests keep disappearing

After you accept or decline a task, Outlook 2013 automatically deletes the task request from your Inbox. Unlike meeting requests, task requests are always deleted—Outlook 2013 doesn't provide an option that allows you to control this behavior. Outlook 2013 does, however, keep a copy of the task request in the Sent Items folder. Outlook 2013 also deletes task update messages after you read them. These messages are generated automatically when someone modifies an assigned task. Outlook 2013 sends the task update message to the people listed in the update list on the Details page of the task form. Although you can move these update messages out of the Deleted Items folder manually, Outlook 2013 provides no way to prevent them from being deleted.

When a response to a task assignment reaches you, Outlook 2013 doesn't act automatically on the response. For example, if someone accepts a task that you assigned, Outlook 2013 doesn't consider the task accepted until you open the response. Until that point, the InfoBar in the Reading Pane still indicates that Outlook 2013 is waiting for a response. When you open the response, the InfoBar in the message form indicates whether the task has been accepted or declined, depending on the assignee's action. Outlook 2013 deletes the response when you close the message. You have no options for controlling this behavior—Outlook 2013 always deletes the response.

If an assignee declines your task request, you can assign the task to someone else (or reassign it to the same individual) easily. Open the response, and click Assign Task on the form's toolbar just as you would when assigning a new task.

Reclaiming ownership of a declined task

Your tasks won't always be accepted—you're bound to receive a rejection now and then. When you do, you have two choices: assign the task to someone else or reclaim ownership so that you can modify or complete the task yourself. To reclaim a task, open the message containing the declined task request and then click Return To Task List on the Task tab of the ribbon.

> **Note**
> When you assign a task, the assignee becomes the temporary owner until he or she accepts or rejects the task. Reclaiming the task restores your ownership so that you can modify the task.

Assigning tasks to multiple people

In some situations, you'll no doubt want to assign a task to more than one person. As a department manager, for example, you might need to assign a project to all the people in your department, or at least to a small group. Outlook 2013 is somewhat limited in task management: It can't track task status when you assign a task to more than one person. You can certainly assign the task, but you won't receive status reports.

What's the solution? You must change the way that you assign tasks, if only slightly. Rather than assigning the whole project as a single task, for example, break the project into separate tasks and assign each one individually, or break a specific task into multiple tasks. Use a similar name for each task to help you recognize that each one is really part of the same task. For example, you might use the names Quarterly Report: Joe and Quarterly Report: Jane to assign the preparation of a quarterly report to both Joe and Jane.

INSIDE OUT   Work around limitations

Although the Outlook 2013 task management features are certainly useful, a more comprehensive set of tools for distributing and managing tasks within a project would be a great addition to the program. For example, the ability to subdivide a task automatically would be helpful, as would the ability to assign a task to multiple people and still receive updates without having to subdivide the task. You can, however, work around this by adjusting the way that you assign and manage tasks.

Assigning multiple tasks through an assistant or a group leader

If you manage more than one group, task assignment becomes a little more complex because you probably have more than one group or department leader under you. Ideally, you would assign a task to a group leader, and the group leader would then delegate portions of the task to members of his or her group. How you accomplish that delegation depends on whether you want to receive status updates directly from group members or only from the group leader.

If you want to receive updates from group members, divide the overall task into subtasks and assign them to the group leader. The leader can then assign the tasks as needed to individuals in the group. Task updates are then sent to both you and the group leader. If you prefer to receive updates only from the group leader, create a single, all-encompassing task and assign it to the group leader, who can then divide the project into individual tasks to assign to group members as needed.

Tracking the progress of a task

When you assign a task, you can choose to keep an updated copy of the task in your task list. This copy allows you to track the status of the task. As the assignee adds or changes task information—such as changing the Total Work value—that assignee's copy of Outlook 2013 generates an update and sends it to the addresses listed in the task's update list (on the Details page of the task form). Typically, the update list includes only one name—the name of the person who assigned the task. If the task was delegated (passed from one person to another), the update list shows all persons in the assignment chain.

Note

If you assign a task to multiple people, Outlook 2013 can no longer track task status. This limitation is one reason to subdivide a task, as explained in the preceding section.

As mentioned, Outlook 2013 sends task status messages to the update list addresses when an assignee makes changes to a task. When you receive a status message, Outlook 2013 updates your copy of the task when you read the status message. Outlook 2013 then deletes the status message, with one exception: When the assignee marks the task as completed, Outlook 2013 sends a Task Completed message to the update list addresses. When you receive and read the message, Outlook 2013 marks your copy of the task as completed but does not delete the Task Completed message. Figure 18-10 shows a Task Completed message.

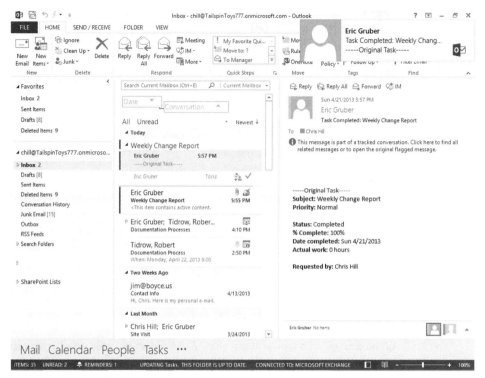

Figure 18-10 Outlook 2013 generates a Task Completed message when an assignee marks a task as completed.

Sending a task status report

As you work on an assigned task, you'll probably want to send status updates to the person who assigned the task to you. Sending task status reports is more than easy—it's automatic. Outlook 2013 generates the updates each time you modify the task, such as when you change the % Complete value.

You can also send an update manually, which is useful when you want to send an update without actually modifying the task. To send an update, open the task and then click the Send Status Report button in the Manage Task group of the Task tab. Outlook opens a new email message with the properties for the task in the body of the message, including Status, % Complete, and Actual Work. You can add your own notes and then click Send to send the message.

Creating an unassigned copy of an assigned task

Outlook 2013 allows you to create an unassigned copy of a task that you have assigned to someone else. This unassigned copy goes into your task list with you as the owner. You can then work on the task yourself or assign it to someone else. For example, suppose that you assigned a task to someone but you want to work on it too. You can create a copy and then work on the copy, changing its dates, completion status, and other information as you go.

Creating an unassigned copy has one drawback, however: You will no longer receive updates for the assigned task. This makes it more difficult to track the other person's progress on the assigned task.

Follow these steps to create an unassigned copy of a task:

1. In Outlook 2013, open the Tasks folder, and then open the assigned task.

2. Click the Task tab on the ribbon, click Details, and then click Create Unassigned Copy.

3. Outlook 2013 displays a warning that creating the copy will prevent you from receiving updates to the assigned task. Click OK to create the copy or Cancel to cancel the process.

4. Outlook 2013 replaces the existing task with a new one. The new task has the same name except that the word *copy* is appended to the name in the Subject box. Make changes as needed to the task, and then click Save & Close to save the changes.

Viewing and customizing the Tasks folder

As mentioned at the beginning of this chapter, Outlook 2013 uses the To-Do List view as the default Tasks folder view. Several other predefined views are also available, including those described in the following list. To use any of these views, click the View tab, click Change View, and then select the view you want.

- **Detailed**   Shows the same information as a simple list, along with the status, date completed, and modified date

- **Simple List**   Shows the task subject, due date, categories, folder, and whether the task is completed

- **To-Do List**   Shows the To-Do List

- **Prioritized**   Shows tasks in order of priority

Chapter 18

- **Active**   Shows tasks that are active (incomplete)

- **Completed Tasks**   Shows only completed tasks

- **Today**   Shows tasks due today

- **Next 7 Days**   Shows tasks for the next seven days

- **Overdue**   Shows incomplete tasks with due dates that have passed

- **Assigned**   Shows tasks assigned to specific people

- **Server Tasks**   Shows tasks stored on a server running Microsoft SharePoint

Outlook 2013 provides several ways to customize the view of the Tasks folder. These methods are the same as those for other Outlook 2013 folders.

For information about using filters to locate and display specific tasks, such as those with certain text, dates, or other properties, see the section "Using Advanced Find" in Chapter 12, "Finding and organizing your email."

You might also want to change the way Outlook 2013 displays certain items in the Tasks folder. For example, you could change the font or character size for the column names or change the color that Outlook 2013 uses to display overdue tasks (red by default). The following sections explain how to make these types of changes in the Tasks folder.

Changing fonts and table view settings

Outlook 2013 by default uses an 8-point Segoe UI font for column headings and row text. You can select a different font or different font characteristics (point size, italic, color, and so on). You also can change the style and color for the gridlines in list views and specify whether to show the Reading Pane.

Follow these steps to customize your view settings:

1.   Click View Settings on the View tab on the ribbon, or right-click the column header bar and then choose View Settings.

2.   In the Advanced View Settings dialog box, click Other Settings to display the Other Settings dialog box, shown in Figure 18-11.

Figure 18-11 Configure font properties for the Tasks folder in the Other Settings dialog box.

3. Click Column Font or Row Font in the Column Headings And Rows area of the dialog box to open a standard Font dialog box that you can use to configure font, size, and other settings for the specified text.

4. Use the options in the Grid Lines And Group Headings area to specify the line type and color that you want Outlook 2013 to use for list views.

5. Set the other options, using the following list as a guide:

    ○ **Automatic Column Sizing**   Select this option to size columns automatically and fit them to the display's width. Clear this check box to specify your own column width (by dragging each column's header) and use a scroll bar to view columns that don't fit the display.

    ○ **Allow In-Cell Editing**   This option allows you to click in a cell and modify the contents. If this check box is cleared, you must open the task to make changes.

    ○ **Show "New Item" Row**   Select this option to display a row at the top of the list for adding new tasks. The New Item row appears only if the Allow In-Cell Editing option is selected.

    ○ **Show Items in Groups**   This option groups items together (such as by date).

Chapter 18

○ **Reading Pane** The options in this area control the location of the Reading Pane. Click Off to hide the Reading Pane. You also can choose View, Reading Pane to select the location or turn the Reading Pane on or off.

○ **Other Options** These options control a handful of settings that determine view layout.

6. Click OK to close the Other Settings dialog box, and then click OK to close the Customize View dialog box.

Using conditional formatting

Outlook 2013 can perform conditional text formatting in the Tasks folder just as it can for other folders. For example, Outlook 2013 displays overdue tasks in red and uses gray strikethroughs for completed and read tasks. Outlook 2013 has five predefined conditional formatting rules, and you can create additional rules if you want to set up additional conditional formatting. For example, you might create a rule to show in red all tasks that haven't been started and are due within the next seven days.

To create conditional formatting rules, click View Settings, Conditional Formatting to display the Conditional Formatting dialog box, shown in Figure 18-12.

Figure 18-12 Modify or create custom automatic formatting rules in the Conditional Formatting dialog box.

Follow these steps to create a new rule:

1. In the Conditional Formatting dialog box, click Add. This creates a new rule named Untitled.

2. Type a title for the rule, and then click Font. Use the resulting Font dialog box to specify the font characteristics that you want Outlook 2013 to use for tasks that meet the rule's conditions. Click OK to close the Font dialog box.

3. Click Condition to open the Filter dialog box, shown in Figure 18-13. Specify the criteria for the condition. For example, select Due in the Time drop-down list, and then select In The Next 7 Days. This specifies that you want Outlook 2013 to use the font selections from step 2 to format any tasks that are due within the next seven days.

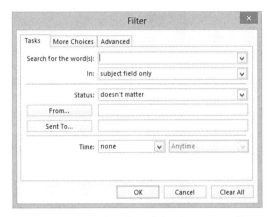

Figure 18-13 Use the Filter dialog box to specify conditions for the formatting rule.

4. Use the More Choices and Advanced tabs to set other conditions as needed, and then click OK.

5. Add other rules as needed. Click OK to close the Conditional Formatting dialog box, and then click OK to close the Advanced View Settings dialog box.

You can create fairly complex rules using the Filter dialog box, which can help you organize and identify specific types of tasks. Also note that you can change the order of the rules in the Automatic Formatting dialog box by using the Move Up and Move Down buttons. Outlook 2013 applies the rules in order from top to bottom, so it's possible for one rule to override another.

Chapter 18

Setting general task options

Outlook 2013 provides a few options that control the appearance of items in the Tasks folder, reminders, and other task-related elements. To set these options, click File, Options, Tasks. On the Tasks page of the Options dialog box, you'll find the following options:

- **Set Reminders On Tasks With Due Dates** Select this option to have Outlook 2013 set a reminder on tasks with due dates. Outlook 2013 bases the timer on the task's due date and the reminder time specified in the Options dialog box.

- **Default Reminder Time** Specifies the default reminder time for tasks. This option is set to 8:00 A.M. by default, but you can change the time if you want—perhaps you'd prefer to see reminders at 10:00 A.M. instead. Keep in mind that this setting is the default that Outlook 2013 uses for task reminders when you create a task, but you can change the reminder time for individual tasks as needed.

- **Keep My Task List Updated With Copies Of Tasks I Assign To Other People** Select this option to have Outlook 2013 keep copies of assigned tasks in your Tasks folder and update their status when assignees make changes to the tasks.

- **Send Status Reports When I Complete An Assigned Task** Select this option to have Outlook 2013 send status reports to you when you complete a task that was assigned to you.

- **Overdue Task Color** Select the color that you want Outlook 2013 to use to display overdue tasks.

- **Completed Task Color** Select the color that you want Outlook 2013 to use to display completed tasks.

- **Set Quick Click Flag** Use this option to specify the type of flag that shows when you single-click the Flags column to set a flag.

- **Task Working Hours Per Day** Use this option to set the number of hours in your workday.

- **Task Working Hours Per Week** Use this option to set the number of hours in the workweek.

Working with tasks in other ways

Outlook 2013 provides a few other ways to work with tasks in addition to the Tasks folder. The following sections explain how to set up and track tasks in the task list area of the To-Do Bar, in the Daily Task List, and in Outlook Today view.

Working with tasks in the To-Do Bar

The To-Do Bar is an interface feature that you can show or hide in Outlook 2013, and the task list is a component of the To-Do Bar. Figure 18-14 shows the To-Do Bar with the task list at the bottom.

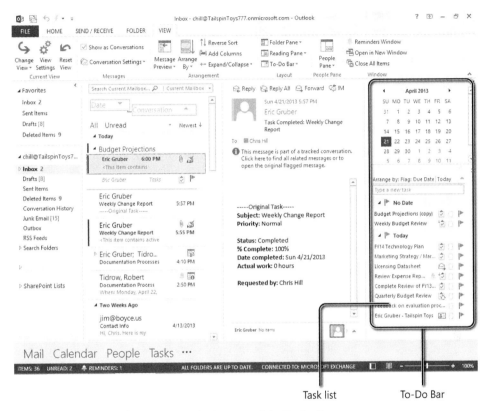

Task list   To-Do Bar

Figure 18-14 The task list appears at the bottom of the To-Do Bar.

By default, Outlook 2013 shows only the subject, the category color indicator, a reminder bell (if the task has a reminder set), and the flag status for each task in the task list, but as you expand the width of the To-Do Bar, other columns appear. You can add and remove columns as needed. To do so, right-click the column header bar above the task list, and then choose View Settings. In the Advanced View Settings dialog box, click Columns to open the Show Columns dialog box, where you can specify the columns to include in the view and their order.

You can modify tasks directly in the task list just as you can in the Tasks folder, depending on the view settings that you've specified. For example, if you've turned on in-cell editing, you can make changes to a task simply by clicking it and typing the needed changes. You can mark a task as completed, change the Actual Work value, change the due date, and so on. The task list is, in this respect, no different from the Tasks folder. The primary benefit of the task list is that it allows you to work with your tasks in a single window along with the other tools in the view.

INSIDE OUT Show and hide the task list

To show or hide the task list in the To-Do Bar, choose To-Do Bar from the Layout group of the View tab, and then choose Task List from the menu.

You can use the same methods that you use to create tasks in the Tasks folder to create a new task in the task list. Right-click in the empty area of the task list, and then choose New Task or New Task Request, depending on whether you're creating the task for yourself or assigning it to someone else. If both the Show New Item Row option and in-cell editing are enabled, you can click the Type A New Task row between the first task in the list and the column header to create a new task. Alternatively, you can click the arrow next to the New button on the Standard toolbar and then choose Task to create a new task.

Changing the task list view

Outlook 2013 offers six views for the task list, and you can create custom views as well. To change the view, right-click in an empty area of the task list, choose Arrange By, and then select a view. You can also click a column header in the task list and choose a view.

Working with tasks in Outlook Today

Chapter 26, "Customizing the Outlook interface," explains how Outlook Today gives you quick access to a useful selection of data. The Outlook Today view is shown in Figure 18-15. The Calendar area displays meetings and events scheduled for the current day (and for subsequent days, if space allows). The Messages area indicates the number of unread messages in your Inbox, messages in the Drafts folder, and unsent messages in the Outbox. The Tasks area lists your tasks.

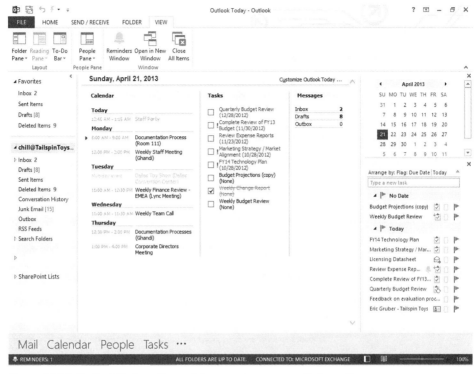

Figure 18-15 Outlook Today offers quick access to a range of information.

For more information about using Outlook Today, see the section "Customizing the Outlook Today view" in Chapter 26.

You can't create a task by clicking in the Tasks area of Outlook Today, but you can click the New Items button on the Home tab on the ribbon and then choose Task to create a new task. To modify a task, click the task's name in the list to open the task form. Mark a task as completed by selecting the check box next to its name.

Using the Daily Task List

Outlook 2013 enables you to manage tasks through the Daily Task List, which optionally appears at the bottom of the calendar, as shown in Figure 18-16. The Daily Task List shows the list of tasks that are due on the selected day. You can work with the tasks in the Daily Task List much as you can with the tasks in the To-Do Bar.

Chapter 18

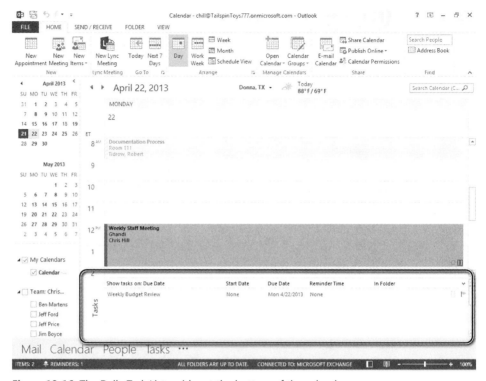

Figure 18-16 The Daily Task List resides at the bottom of the calendar.

When the Daily Task List is displayed, you can click the Minimize button at the far-right edge of the Daily Task List column bar to minimize it. Likewise, when the Daily Task List is minimized, click the Restore button to display it.

Managing tasks effectively

Tasks are one of the Outlook 2013 features that many people overlook, spending their time instead primarily in the Inbox, Contacts, and Calendar folders. Nevertheless, tasks can be extremely useful and a powerful productivity and workflow tool. If you haven't used tasks before, spend the time to become familiar with them. When you are comfortable using tasks, the following tips will help you make the most of them:

- **Really use them**   Tasks won't do you much good if you just put a few on your task list and then don't really use them. Instead, use tasks in Outlook 2013 for all of your daily, weekly, and monthly tasks. Make sure to set progress status as you go along and mark tasks as complete when you complete them.

- **Use task assignment**   Outlook 2013 tasks can be a great tool for helping you organize your day and get your job done. Task assignment extends that benefit across your team or workgroup. Get your group in the habit of using tasks, and then start using task assignment across the group to manage tasks.

- **Use realistic due dates**   Setting realistic due dates for your tasks and working on the tasks accordingly will help you integrate tasks into your daily work schedule. The keys to being successful using Outlook 2013 tasks are to be diligent about how you use them and to integrate them into your workday and workflow.

- **Use reminders**   By assigning reminders to your tasks, you'll be able to keep track of when the tasks are coming due. Assign a reminder period that is sufficiently long to enable you to complete the task by its due date.

- **Keep the tasks at hand**   Use the task list in the To-Do Bar and the Daily Task List in the Calendar folder to keep your tasks visible at all times so that you can work with them easily and see their status.

Using Outlook and Lync

I NSTANT messaging (IM) and desktop conferencing programs have been around for a long time. Microsoft's first foray into desktop conferencing came with Microsoft NetMeeting. Since then, their desktop conferencing products have changed and grown, including Office Communications Server, or OCS (formerly Live Communications Server), and the acquisition of Skype. Over the years, other companies have developed competing products, such as Google Hangouts, AOL Instant Messenger (AIM), Yahoo! Messenger, and others. These applications offer a range of features, from simple text-based IM (chat) to full-blown desktop conferencing complete with multiparty video conferencing, Voice over IP (VoIP) calling, desktop sharing, and more.

Today, Microsoft's flagship desktop conferencing solution is Microsoft Lync. Much like Microsoft Outlook is a client that connects to Microsoft Exchange Server, Lync is a client that connects to a Microsoft Lync Server or Microsoft Lync Online (web-based hosted solution) server. This chapter explores Lync and its integration with Outlook.

Overview of Lync and Outlook integration

Lync provides a wide range of communications features for text, voice, and video conferencing, along with media streaming and desktop application sharing. Figure 19-1 shows a desktop with the Lync client engaged in a video conversation with another Lync user. Lync integrates with Microsoft Outlook when you have a Lync Server or Microsoft Lync Online and have a Microsoft Exchange or Office 365 system.

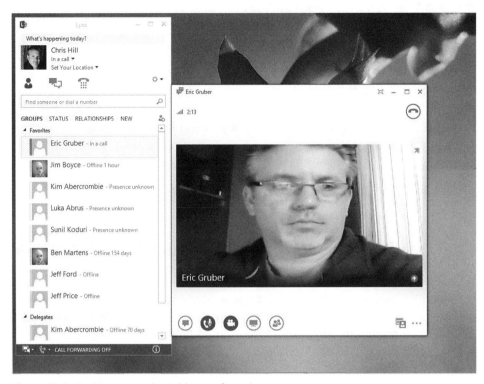

Figure 19-1 Use Lync to conduct video conferencing.

The main Lync window appears on the left side of the screen in Figure 19-1. This window shows contact names, status, and other information. You also can initiate calls, video conference sessions, and other Lync tasks from this window. By default, Lync runs as a background task even if you close or minimize this window.

The window on the right, as shown in Figure 19-1, is the Lync video conferencing window. This window displays a video of the user on the other end of the Lync session. You also can view a small window of your video by clicking the up arrow that appears in the lower-right corner of the video window. This shows your image to the other user.

Lync features include the following:

- **Voice** Lync Server provides the infrastructure needed to support software-based VoIP calling. Through the client-side application, Lync, users can initiate network-based voice calls through their computers, using either the microphone and speakers built into the computer or a VoIP phone connected to the computer. Microsoft Lync Server can integrate with the company's Private Branch Exchange (PBX) system to provide integrated calling, voicemail, and other features.

- **Audio/video conferencing** If you are familiar with desktop conferencing solutions from Cisco WebEx, GoToMeeting, and others, then you are already familiar with what Lync provides for audio/video conferencing. Users can participate in online voice conferences, video conferences, and share desktop applications.

- **Group IM** With Lync on the client side and Lync Server on the server side, you can initiate an IM session with multiple parties. Each participant can join in the online conversation, sending and receiving messages that all of the participants can see.

- **IM** In addition to multiparty IM, you can use Lync Server and Lync for user-to-user IM.

- **Presence** Lync Server and Lync work together to provide online status information for people in your organization, and you can view that status within Outlook, Lync, and Microsoft SharePoint.

- **Present features** With its present features, Lync enables you to share your desktop with other Lync participants so they can see what is on your screen, as well as take over that machine for support or training issues. Users can also share programs, PowerPoint presentations, whiteboard tasks, and online polls. Lync also lets you use Microsoft OneNote to share notes with other Lync users. The Attachment feature provides an easy way to share files with other users on a call.

Just as Outlook serves as the client-side application for Exchange Server, Lync serves as the client-side application for Lync Server. You can use Lync by itself to start IM sessions, voice calls, and video conferences, and to communicate in other ways. The following section explores Lync. Subsequent sections explore the Lync Server/Lync integration with Outlook.

This chapter does not discuss how to install and configure Lync. It assumes that Lync is installed on your computer and is operational. Once Lync is installed, you can join a Lync meeting by responding a call request when someone wants to connect. When a call comes in, Lync displays a small window on your screen that specifies the name and user picture of the person contacting you, as shown in Figure 19-2 in the bottom-right corner of the screen. Click anywhere on the small window to answer the call request.

Figure 19-2 A Lync call is coming in from Eric Gruber.

Once you accept the call, a larger window appears like the one shown in Figure 19-1.

Joining a Lync meeting

A Lync meeting is similar to a regular meeting in Outlook, except information on how to connect using the Lync interface is included in the meeting request. When it is time for the meeting to start, users can use the Lync meeting request information to call the host of the meeting.

To join a Lync meeting, you first need to receive a Lync meeting request via an email message. Figure 19-3 shows an example of a Lync meeting request. When you are ready to join the meeting, open the Lync meeting request and click the Join Lync Meeting link.

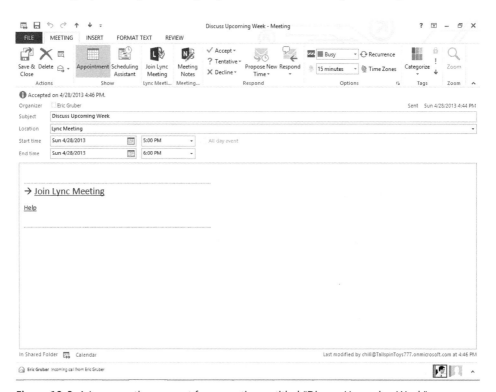

Figure 19-3 A Lync meeting request for a meeting entitled "Discuss Upcoming Week".

The Join Meeting Audio dialog box (see Figure 19-4) appears to let you set audio features for the call. You can choose from the following:

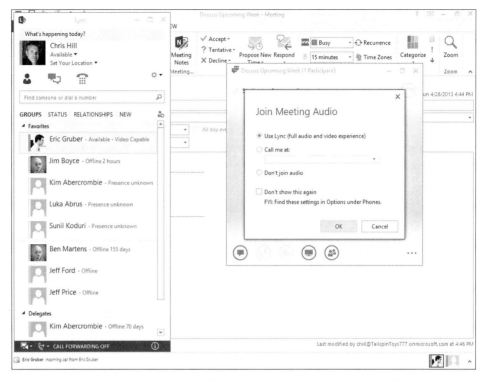

Figure 19-4 You can set audio features of Lync calls in the Join Meeting Audio dialog box.

- **Use Lync**   Use this option to use your computer's microphone to conduct the call.

- **Call Me At**   Use this option if you want the host to call you at a specific phone number.

- **Don't Join Audio**   Use this option if you plan not to use audio during the Lync meeting.

If you do not want to see these options for future Lync meetings, select the Don't Show This Again option. Although you may grow tired of seeing this dialog box, you may have a future meeting in which you will need to change an audio setting for a meeting. For this reason, you might consider leaving the Don't Show This Again option cleared. Click OK to save your settings.

When you close the Join Meeting Audio dialog box, Lync connects to the meeting. If you are the first one to join the meeting, you will see a screen similar to the one shown in Figure 19-5. It announces that you are the only one on the call at this time. As others arrive to the meeting, they appear in the Lync window. Depending on the setting options, you may have to wait in a "virtual lobby" until the host allows you in.

Figure 19-5 If you are the first to arrive on a Lync meeting, you will see a window similar to this one.

When all participants have joined, you can start the meeting. One task you may want to do right away is to unmute your microphone by clicking the microphone icon to remove the red line through the microphone.

Figure 19-6 shows an example of a Lync meeting with three participants: Eric Gruber (he sent out the original Lync message request), Katie Jordan, and Chris Hill. In this example, the meeting is shown on Chris Hill's computer, so his picture is smaller than those of the other two attendees.

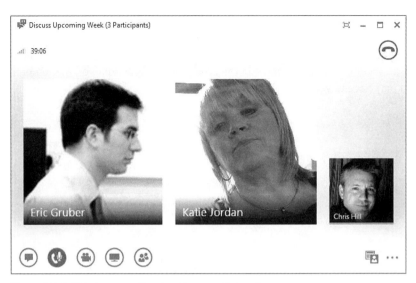

Figure 19-6 This Lync meeting has three participants.

When you finish with the meeting, click the red phone icon at the top-right corner of the Lync window. This disconnects you from the meeting.

Creating a Lync meeting

Now that you've seen how to join a Lync meeting, let's look at how you can use Outlook Calendar to set up a Lync meeting. When you set up meeting, keep in mind that the maximum number of participants is 250.

To set up a Lync meeting, use the following steps:

1. Start Microsoft Outlook and click Calendar in the Navigation Bar.

2. Find the date and time you want to start the meeting.

3. Click New Lync Meeting on the Home tab. A new blank meeting window appears. The top part of the window looks similar to a normal Outlook Meeting window. The bottom part, however, includes additional information for the Lync meeting details. Figure 19-7 shows an example of what you should see on your screen.

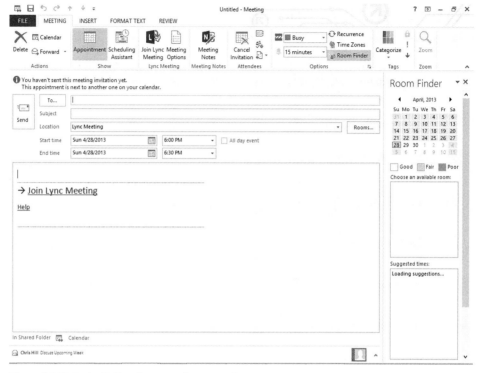

Figure 19-7 An invitation for a new Lync meeting.

4. Fill out the To, Subject, and Start and End Times fields. The Location field has Lync Meeting as the location. Keep this as is.

5. If you want to add something to the body of the message, enter it above or below the hash marks in the body area. This way, you do not modify or delete any of the Join Lync Meeting hyperlinks. If you do, your meeting recipients will not get the correct hyperlink information to connect to your Lync meeting.

6. Click Send.

Upon receipt of your Lync meeting request, the recipients can choose to accept or deny your request. If accepted, the meeting is placed on their calendar to be used to connect to the Lync meeting in the future.

Setting Lync meeting options

You just read how to set up a typical Lync meeting from within Outlook. The settings used were primarily default settings, which are typically sufficient for users who are part of your organization. What happens if you want to invite people from outside your company? For those cases, use the Lync Meeting Options dialog box settings.

To set Lync meeting options, use the following steps:

1.   Open Outlook.

2.   Locate the day and time you want to start your Lync meeting.

3.   Click New Lync Meeting on the Home tab. This displays a new Untitled – Meeting window.

4.   Click Meeting Options in the Lync Meeting area of the Meeting tab. The Lync Meeting Options dialog box appears (see Figure 19-8).

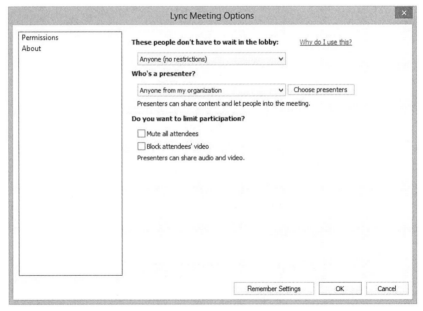

Figure 19-8 Use the Lync Meeting Options dialog box to set the options for a new Lync meeting.

5. Set the appropriate options for your meeting. The following list describes the options available:

    ○ **These People Don't Have To Wait In The Lobby**   You can choose to have all participants wait in a "virtual lobby" until you arrive as the host to allow them into the meeting area. You also have the choice to not require anyone to wait in the lobby (this is the default). Finally, you can set this option so anyone from within your organization or those you invite do not have to wait in the lobby.

    ○ **Who's A Presenter?**   Use these options to specify your presenters, such as anyone, only those you choose, anyone from your organization, or just you. When you choose People I Choose, click the Choose Presenters button to select presenters from the Meeting Options Presenters dialog box. This dialog box is populated by the names you specify in the To line of the Lync meeting request.

    ○ **Mute All Attendees**   This option enables you to mute all attendee microphones or phones when they connect.

    ○ **Block Attendees' Video**   This option enables you to block video connections from attendees when they connect.

6. Click OK, or optionally click Remember Settings (for future new Lync meetings) and then click OK.

7. Fill out the rest of your Lync meeting request.

8. Click Send.

Starting an IM conversation

Although you will often want to reply to an email with another email, there are times when a Lync IM might suffice as well or even better than the email. Outlook 2013 makes it easy to open an IM session with the sender of a message or with the entire group of people who are listed as recipients of the message.

In Outlook, select the message to which you want to reply with an IM. Then, in the Respond group of the Home tab, click IM and choose Reply With IM or Reply All With IM (see Figure 19-9). Use the former to open an IM session to only the sender. Choose the latter to open a group IM to the sender and all recipients.

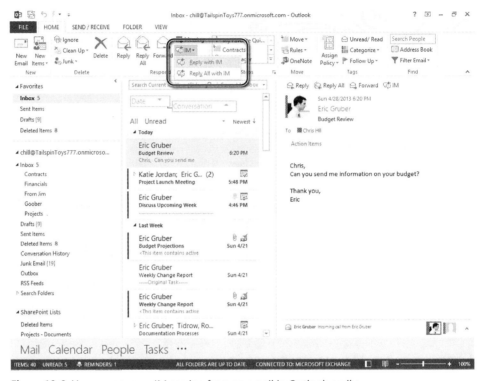

Figure 19-9 You can open an IM session from an email in Outlook easily.

When you choose one of these options, Lync opens and initiates an IM session with the specified user(s). If you choose Reply With IM, Lync opens an IM session with the sender. If you choose Reply All With IM, Lync opens a group IM session (see Figure 19-10). (Note that Lync includes all group members, even if their status is set to Offline.)

Figure 19-10 You can open a group IM session with everyone in an email conversation.

Note

If one or more of the people in the group are not available, the IM session will notify you of the individuals unavailable for the IM session.

A quick way to start an IM with just one contact of the message is to hover over the contact's photo at the bottom of the message and select Send An IM. Figure 19-11 shows an example of this tool.

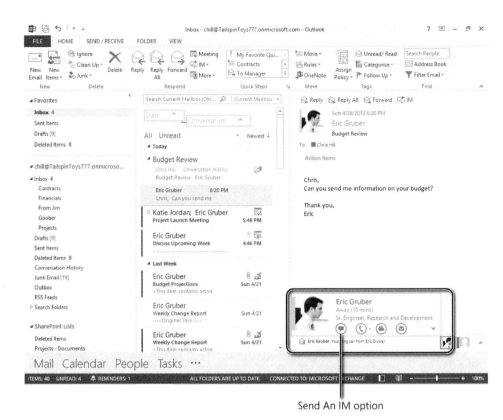

Send An IM option

Figure 19-11 You can quickly open a group IM session with one contact using the IM option icon.

Starting a voice call

In addition to starting IM sessions from Outlook, you can initiate voice calls with other Lync users. As with IM, you can start a call to just the sender of the message or open a call for everyone in the message.

To open a call, select the message whose sender you want to call. Then, in the Respond group of the Home tab, click More and choose Call. From the cascading menu, choose the sender's name to start a call to just that person, or choose Call All to open a call to everyone (see Figure 19-12). Lync opens and starts a voice conference session. After the other participants have answered, conduct the call as you would if you had initiated it from Lync. Click End Call when you are finished.

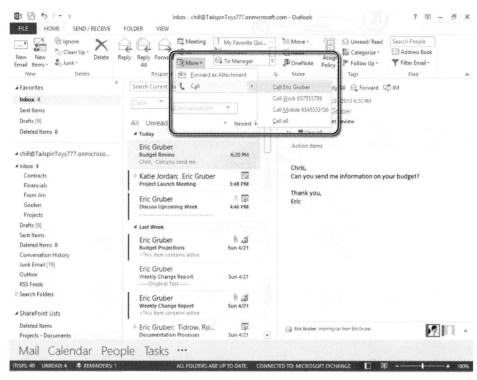

Figure 19-12 You can start a Lync call from within Outlook.

If you want to respond to only one person connected to the message, at the bottom of the message, hover over the photo of the person you want to call and click the Call icon. This starts a call with the contact.

Starting a video call

Much like responding to a contact via IM or call, you also can initiate a video call to a contact from within Outlook. To do this, open the message from the contact with whom you want to start a video call. At the bottom of the message, hover over the photo of the contact and choose Start Video Call from the pop-up window. This launches a Lync video call window and calls the contact. Figure 19-13 shows an example.

Figure 19-13 You can start a Lync video call from within Outlook.

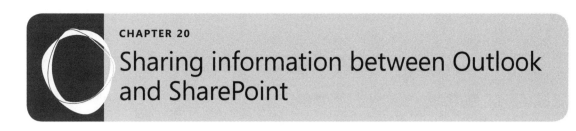

Sharing information between Outlook and SharePoint

MICROSOFT SharePoint is a set of technologies that form a rich collaboration framework for sharing documents, calendars, and other data. SharePoint is much more than just a tool for sharing documents or data, however. Its portal features enable organizations to create a rich portal experience for users, complete with audience targeting and personalization features. Over the years, SharePoint has grown in business use and importance. For example, the Business Data Catalog (BDC) and Business Connectivity Services (BCS) features, in SharePoint 2007 and SharePoint 2010 respectively, provide the tools needed to integrate SharePoint with back-end line-of-business solutions like SAP, Oracle, Structured Query Language (SQL), Business Objects, and many others. The Web 2.0 features of SharePoint, such as wikis and blogs, enable people to connect and share information in a wide variety of ways. With Office 365, the SharePoint model extends to a cloud-based presence where team sites, shared documents, shared contacts, and more are offered to businesses without the overhead of running an internal SharePoint infrastructure. These are just some of the features offered by SharePoint.

This chapter provides an overview of sharing information between SharePoint and Microsoft Outlook 2013. For example, you can share a SharePoint calendar or contact list with Outlook to make it easier to keep those items in sync. In addition, the new feature called site mailboxes is introduced in this chapter. Finally, details on how to set the online status option in Outlook are covered.

Overview of SharePoint

Over the years, SharePoint has come to encompass multiple services and components. For example, SharePoint 2007 relied on Windows SharePoint Services 3.0, while SharePoint Workspace 2010 uses the SharePoint Foundation 2010 to provide its core, foundational features. SharePoint 2013 builds on the past to offer Microsoft's most comprehensive web-based collaboration portal for all types of users, including mobile users. SharePoint delivers web content, document sharing, sharing of calendars and contacts, and workflows for automating processes such as document approvals, among other services.

The following list describes the key features of SharePoint:

- **Portals**   SharePoint enables you to create portals (webpages) for sharing informa-tion, whether for a typical intranet portal that serves relatively static pages, for con-tent that changes dynamically, or for collaboration features like document sharing. SharePoint provides several templates that make it a matter of a few clicks to create various types of websites, such as sites focused on team collaboration, document sharing, and other uses.

- **Document sharing**   Document sharing allows you to store documents on the SharePoint site, which can then be accessed by other team members. This is use-ful for sharing project-related documents, for example, or any other document that other team members might need access to. In addition to simple document storage, document sharing provides version-control tools such as document check-in and checkout so that a document is not accidentally modified by more than one user at a time. Support for metatags enables you to categorize documents for sorting and searching.

- **Picture libraries**   Picture libraries are similar to document libraries in that they store pictures that can be shared among team members. This is basically a web-based photo album.

- **Lists**   Lists are formatted collections of information. The list format can vary based on the type of information being stored. Several lists are predefined, such as Announcements, which are displayed on the main page of a team site by default; Cal-endar, which can contain events relating to your team or project; Links, which stores web links to pages that your team will find useful or interesting; and Tasks, which helps your team members keep track of work. You can also create your own lists and add new columns to existing lists.

- **Discussion boards**   Discussion boards allow team members to have threaded dis-cussions on specific subjects. Discussion boards are useful to replace email exchanges when more than two people are involved, as those involved can place comments and replies directly in the appropriate thread rather than exchanging a large number of email messages.

- **Surveys**   Surveys are simply a method of polling other team members for information.

- **Workflows**   SharePoint provides basic workflow capability to help you automate processes such as document approvals and movement of items between lists.

- **Search**   With the search functionality, you can locate documents, list items, and other information stored in your SharePoint environment quickly and easily.

Collaboration environments built on SharePoint can be very useful for sharing documents, calendars, and other information, and they are often used by large and small companies alike to enable collaboration among groups of people. SharePoint functionality can be extended in several ways:

- **Collaboration and social computing**   Features such as wikis and blogs enable people to share ideas and information in a variety of ways. My Sites adds the capability for users to have a personal site to share information with others as well as work with their own files, Microsoft Exchange Server mailbox, and other information within a SharePoint web interface. Support for Really Simple Syndication (RSS) feeds enables users to consume RSS content within SharePoint and subscribe to SharePoint content through RSS.

- **Portals**   Additional web parts and support for audience targeting and personalization enable you to tailor and deliver a broader range of information to your users, but in a more targeted fashion.

- **Enterprise content management (ECM)**   ECM encompasses a range of features, including additional capabilities for document management and sharing, and a publishing infrastructure to provide controlled deployment of content with various approval mechanisms.

- **Records management**   You can use SharePoint to store and manage records, such as email, in addition to documents. Versioning, expiration, and other features help you effectively manage the data.

- **Business processes and forms**   Enhanced workflow capabilities make it easier to use out-of-the-box SharePoint features for multiparty document approval and other business process automation.

- **Enterprise search**   Extend a search across your enterprise to include file servers, websites, line-of-business systems, and other data, making that data searchable and discoverable within SharePoint.

- **Business intelligence**   Use BDC or BCS to connect to back-end line-of-business systems to expose that data in SharePoint and provide a common interface for users to both consume and modify data stored in those back-end systems. Also use features such as Excel Services to create key progress indicator (KPI) reports, dashboards, and other portal elements that bubble up and organize data from a variety of sources.

As stated earlier, one of the key features of SharePoint is the ability to integrate with Microsoft Office applications. These features include document sharing, which can be done from almost any Office application; lists, which can be synchronized with Microsoft

Chapter 20

Excel or Microsoft Access files; and Calendar lists, contacts, and alerts, which can be linked to Outlook. In addition, Microsoft SharePoint Designer can be used to edit and customize SharePoint pages. This chapter focuses mainly on the integration of SharePoint and Outlook 2013 to help you consume SharePoint information in Outlook as well as publish your Outlook data to SharePoint.

> **Note**
>
> This chapter assumes you have a Microsoft SharePoint site set up and you have access to it. This chapter does not show how to set up or configure SharePoint sites or how to connect to SharePoint site. The examples in this chapter use SharePoint 2013, but many of the same steps can be used for previous versions of SharePoint. Contact your SharePoint administrator for specific instructions on how to connect to your SharePoint site.

Adding SharePoint calendars to Outlook

You can connect a SharePoint team site calendar list to Outlook 2013. SharePoint team site calendars are typically used to share schedules such as project timelines, vacation schedules, and so on. When you create a team site in SharePoint, the site includes a calendar by default. When you connect the SharePoint calendar to Outlook, the calendar looks and functions just like the calendars in your local Outlook data store(s). Subject to your permissions in the SharePoint calendar, you can modify the SharePoint calendar in Outlook and the changes are synchronized to SharePoint the next time a send/receive action takes place for the list.

> **Note**
>
> To ensure your team site calendar can be shared, be sure that Group Calendar Options is enabled. To do this, click the gear icon on the top-right side of the SharePoint window and click Site Settings. Click Site Libraries And List and click Customize "calendar_name", in which calendar_name is the actual name of the team site calendar you want to share. Click List Name, Description, Navigation. Click Yes under Use This Calendar To Share Member's Schedules and click Save. Wait a few minutes for the setting to be enabled and then follow the next steps to link your team site calendar to Outlook.

To link a team site calendar list to Outlook 2013, follow these steps:

1. Open your SharePoint site and navigate to the team site calendar you want to connect to Outlook. Figure 20-1 shows an example of a SharePoint team site calendar named Calendar – Hill Team 1.

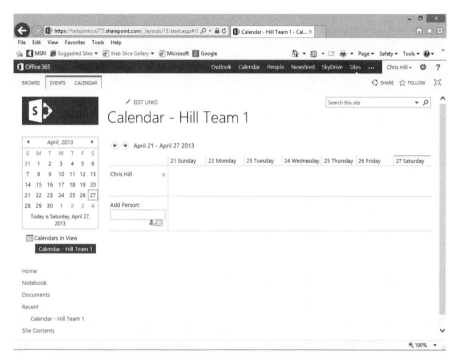

Figure 20-1 A SharePoint team site calendar.

2. Click the Calendar tab to show the Calendar ribbon, as shown in Figure 20-2.

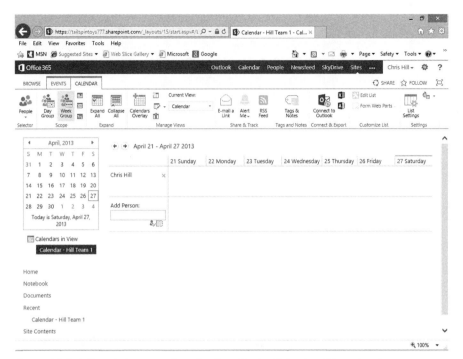

Figure 20-2 A SharePoint team site calendar with the Calendar ribbon showing.

3. Click the Connect To Outlook button in the Connect & Export group.

4. Click Allow when prompted if you want to allow this website to open a program on your computer. If Outlook is not opened, Windows will automatically open it and display the message Connect This SharePoint Calendar To Outlook? The connection may take a few moments depending on your Internet connection speed and the speed of your computer. Figure 20-3 shows what this message looks like. The name

of your SharePoint team site will be different from the one shown in this figure. The figure also shows Outlook displayed in the background, with the Calendar folder open.

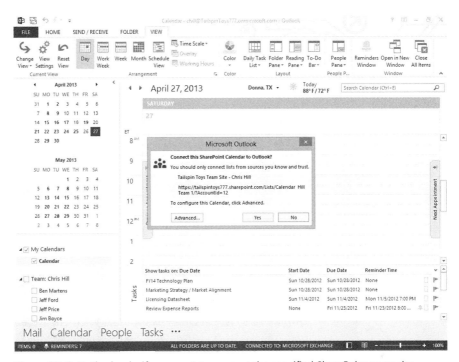

Figure 20-3 Outlook asks if you want to connect the specified SharePoint team site calendar with Outlook.

5. Click Advanced to open the SharePoint List Options dialog box (see Figure 20-4).

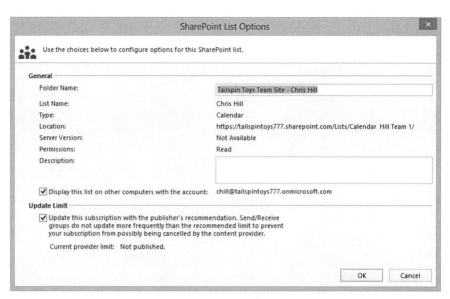

Figure 20-4 The SharePoint List Options dialog box is used to configure options for a SharePoint list.

6. Change the options as necessary, such as giving the calendar a new name or writing a description for the calendar. The following are two other options you can modify:

   ○ **Display This List On Other Computers With The Account** Choose this option to include the SharePoint list on other computers from which you use Outlook.

   ○ **Update This Subscription With The Publisher's Recommendation** If the SharePoint list is published through RSS, this setting determines how frequently the content is synchronized to Outlook based on the content's time to live (TTL) value. If no value is specified, the update defaults to 60 minutes. If you want to synchronize the content more frequently, clear this check box and create a custom send/receive group to update your SharePoint list(s).

7. Click OK to save your settings and return to the previous dialog box.

8. Click Yes to confirm that you want to connect this team site calendar to Outlook.

When the calendar is linked to Outlook 2013, it is displayed as shown in Figure 20-5. By default, the calendar will display alongside the currently displayed calendar. The name of the team site calendar (in this case, Tailspin Toys Team Site – Chris Hill) is at the top of the calendar. You can see the new calendar listed in the Navigation Pane on the left under the Other Calendars item. To view only the SharePoint team site calendar, click the Close button on the other calendar.

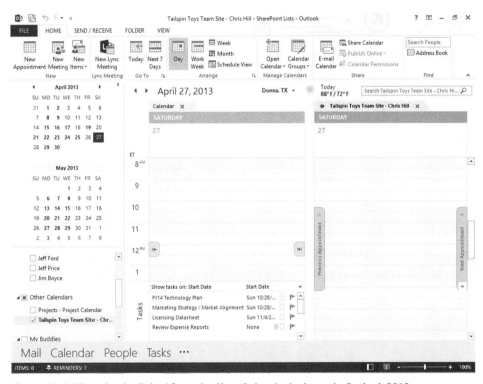

Figure 20-5 The calendar linked from the SharePoint site is shown in Outlook 2013.

You can modify the SharePoint calendar from within Outlook. Just click in or select a time slot and add appointments as you would for a local calendar. The next time a send/receive action occurs for the list, those changes are synchronized to the SharePoint list, where they will be visible by other SharePoint users. Figure 20-6, for example, shows a new meeting on the SharePoint team site set for Monday, April 29. This meeting was originally created in the Outlook calendar and then synced with the SharePoint site to show it to the shared team site calendar.

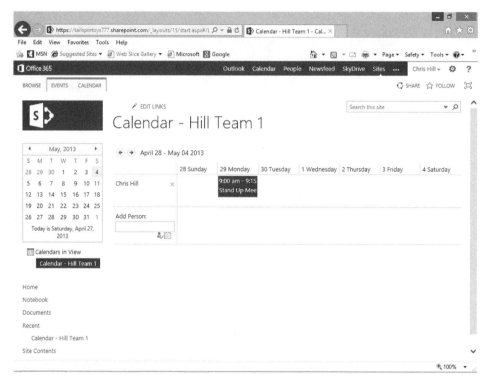

Figure 20-6   A new calendar item shared from Outlook to the SharePoint team site calendar.

You can add a new SharePoint team site calendar item by following these steps:

1.   Double-click a day or time on the SharePoint team site calendar. The New Item dialog box appears (see Figure 20-7).

2.   Fill out the New Item dialog box with details about the new calendar item.

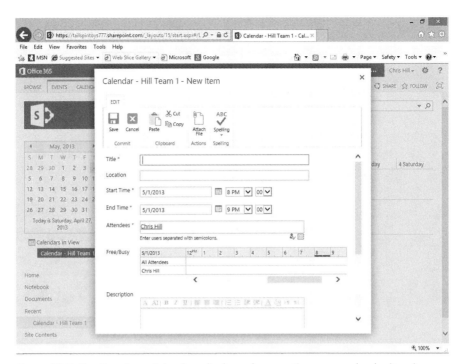

Figure 20-7 The New Item dialog box displays when creating a new calendar item in SharePoint.

3.   Click Save. The new item appears on the SharePoint team site calendar. In addition, when you display Outlook and a send/receive event occurs, the new SharePoint item will appear in Outlook on the team site calendar.

Because SharePoint calendars that are linked to Outlook function like Outlook calendars, you can use the same features for both. For example, you can overlay a SharePoint calendar on one or more of your local calendars for a combined view. Just select the calendars in the Navigation Pane to display them, and click the View In Overlay Mode button at the top of the calendar to overlay it with the others.

Using SharePoint contacts in Outlook

SharePoint provides lists that can be used to store, manage, and share a variety of information. One of the defined list types is contacts, which is used to store contact information in a way similar to the Contacts folder in Outlook. You can view these shared contacts within SharePoint or connect them to Outlook. This section explains how to use these shared contacts in Outlook.

Use the following steps to share team site contacts with Outlook:

1.   Start by connecting to a team site in SharePoint that has a shared contact list.

2.   Open that shared team site contact list.

3.   Click the List tab on the ribbon.

4.   Click Connect To Outlook (see Figure 20-8). You must have at least one contact in the contact list before the Connect To Outlook option is available.

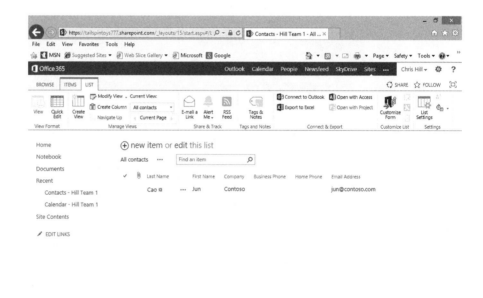

Figure 20-8 You can connect a shared contact list to Outlook.

5.   A dialog box opens, similar to the one shown in Figure 20-9, prompting you to allow the connection. The dialog box indicates the URL of the site and other information. Click Allow.

Figure 20-9 You are prompted to allow the connection to the SharePoint site.

6. Outlook then displays a dialog box that prompts you to confirm that you want to add the list to SharePoint. You can simply click Yes to add the list to Outlook without configuring any other settings. Alternatively, click Advanced to display the SharePoint List Options dialog box shown in Figure 20-10. In the SharePoint List Options dialog box, use these two options to control the connection (for explanations of the options, please see the section "Adding SharePoint calendars to Outlook"):

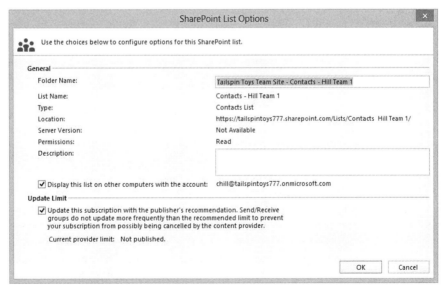

Figure 20-10 You can configure advanced settings for the connection to the list in the SharePoint List Options dialog box.

7. When you are satisfied with the settings, click OK, and then click Yes. The SharePoint list appears in the Navigation Pane when your People folder is open, and the contents of the SharePoint list appear in Outlook, as shown in Figure 20-11.

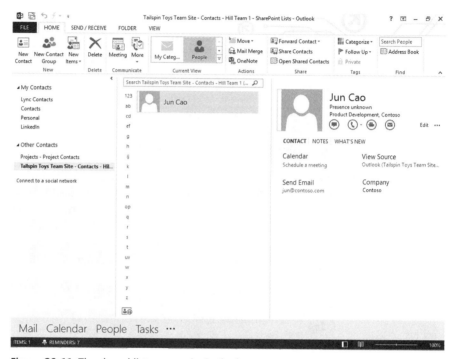

Figure 20-11 The shared list appears in Outlook.

With the list now connected to SharePoint, you can work with it just as you would a local Contacts folder. You can view individual items and even update items, subject to your permissions in SharePoint. Changes that you make in Outlook to the list are synchronized back to the SharePoint list the next time a send/receive action occurs for the list.

There is an easy way to add a contact from an existing contact folder (such as the contact list under My Contacts) to the SharePoint team site contact list. Open the contact list in Outlook and drag and drop the contact into the SharePoint team site contact list on the Navigation Pane. The team site contact list will appear under the Other Contacts heading in the Navigation Pane. After you drag and drop the contact, and after Outlook performs a send/receive action, the SharePoint team site contact list is updated with the new shared contact.

Using site mailboxes

Microsoft has introduced a new feature in Microsoft Exchange 2013 and SharePoint 2013 to help users in corporations who use email and who share documents. This new feature is called *site mailboxes*. Site mailboxes are mail-enabled document libraries. By using a SharePoint app (essentially a SharePoint add-in) designed for site mailboxes, a SharePoint site allows users to use one client interface for email and document sharing.

To configure a site mailbox, use the following steps:

1. Open the SharePoint site and click Sites at the top of the window (see Figure 20-12).

2. Click New Site.

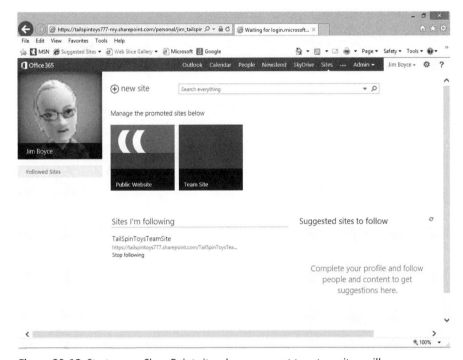

Figure 20-12 Start a new SharePoint site when you want to set up site mailboxes.

3. In the Start A New Site dialog box (see Figure 20-13), enter a new site name.

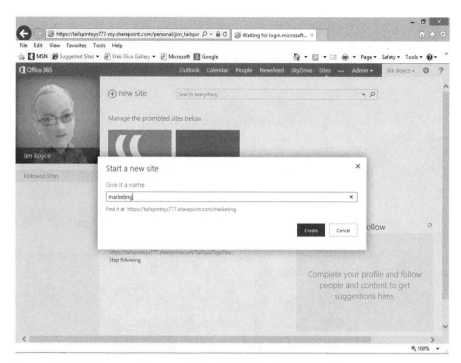

Figure 20-13 Add a new site name to the Start A New Site dialog box.

4. Click Create. A new site is created, as shown in Figure 20-14.

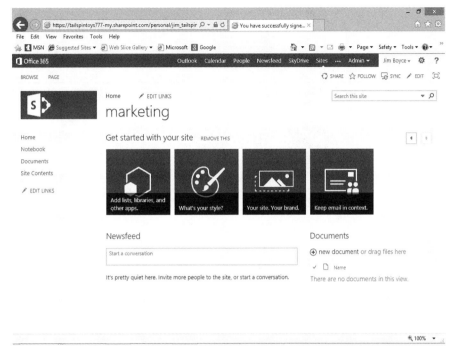

Figure 20-14 Click the Keep Email In Context button.

5. Click Keep Email In Context. You may need to scroll to the far right of the list items under the Get Started With Your Site label. The Site Mailbox window appears (see Figure 20-15).

Figure 20-15 Click the Add It button to create a site mailbox.

6. Click the Add It button. The Lists, Libraries, And Other Apps window appears (see Figure 20-16).

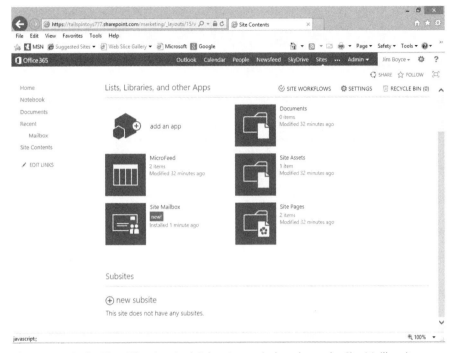

Figure 20-16 The Lists, Libraries, And Other Apps window shows the Site Mailbox item.

7. Click the Site Mailbox button. SharePoint starts setting up your new site mailbox feature. A screen appears showing you that it is being set up.

Once the site mailbox is created, a message appears telling you that it may take up to 30 minutes before you can access the site mailbox (see Figure 20-17). You will receive an email message when access to the site mailbox is available. In the meantime, you can continue by clicking the Go Back To The SharePoint Site For Now link. Under the Recent label on the left side of the screen, click Mailing. You can then choose your preferred language and time zone. Click Submit Query. If all is ready to go, you will see SharePoint with the Outlook window open displaying the newly created site mailbox (see Figure 20-18).

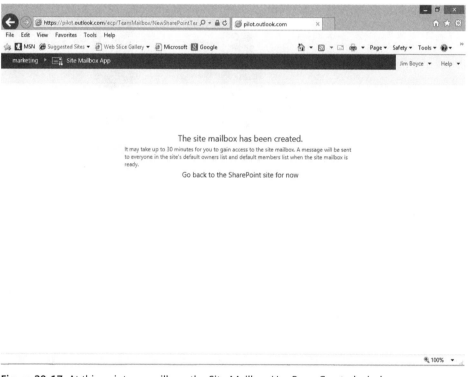

Figure 20-17 At this point, you will see the Site Mailbox Has Been Created window.

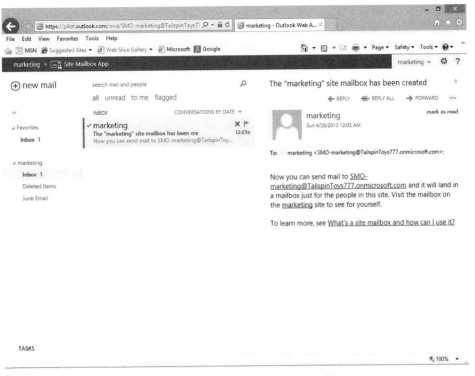

Figure 20-18 The new site mailbox has been created and is accessible.

In your Inbox, you will receive a message that lists the new email address for the site mailbox. For example, the email address for the site mailbox set up for these examples is as follows: *SMO-marketing@TailspinToys777.onmicrosoft.com*.

When you send email to this address, it will be delivered to the new site mailbox for all users set up to access this SharePoint site. To view the site mailbox, switch to the SharePoint site (in this example, it's called "marketing"). The email message contains a link that will help you find your way to your site if you are not sure which one it is.

Along with shared email, you can use the site mailbox to share documents with your team. Those documents can be stored on a SharePoint site or in Outlook. To begin, let's look at sharing documents that are stored in a SharePoint documents list. You will need to have some documents saved to a SharePoint documents list, as shown in Figure 20-19.

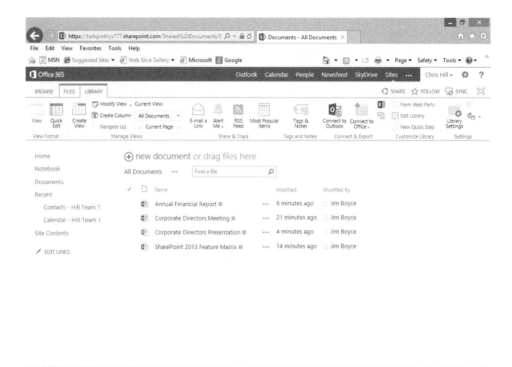

Figure 20-19 You can view documents in a SharePoint documents list.

> **Note**
>
> To store files in a SharePoint documents list, click the Documents link on the left side of your SharePoint page and click the New Document link. Click Upload Existing File, click Browse, and then select the file to upload. Click Open and then click OK. Alternatively, you can drag and drop files from your local computer (via Windows Explorer, for example) onto the part of the SharePoint documents list page labeled Or Drag Files Here. SharePoint uploads the documents to your documents list.

Those same documents appear in Outlook under the SharePoint Lists area. Figure 20-20, for example, shows the Tailspin Toys documents that were uploaded to the Tailspin Toys team site in SharePoint.

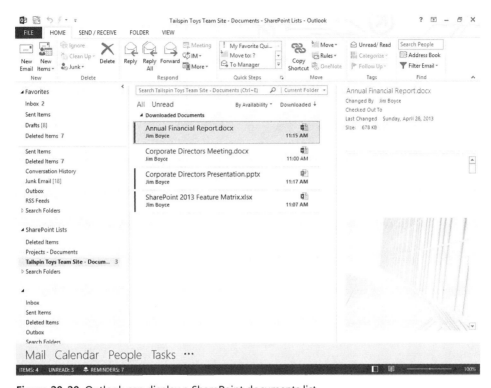

Figure 20-20 Outlook can display a SharePoint documents list.

Viewing online status

Outlook enables you to view the online status of other users. The information lets you know if a person is online, as well as if the person is busy or available. When the status shows as busy, the user is either at a meeting or appointment (based on Outlook Calendar information), away from his or her desk (based on if the computer screen is locked), or has set his or her status manually to Busy to avoid interruptions.

By default, status is enabled. However, you can turn it off or turn it on if has been disabled. To do so, use these steps:

1. Open Microsoft Outlook.

2. On the File tab, click Options to open the Outlook Options dialog box.

3. Click the People link.

4. Select the Display Online Status Next To Name option in the Online Status And Photographs section (see Figure 20-21).

5. Click OK.

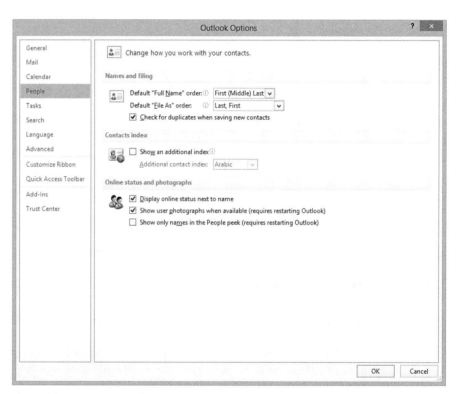

Figure 20-21 You can set the online status option in the Outlook Options dialog box.

Delegating responsibilities to an assistant

MICROSOFT Outlook 2013, when used with Microsoft Exchange Server, provides features that allow you to delegate certain responsibilities to an assistant. For example, you might want your assistant to manage your schedule, setting up appointments, meetings, and other events for you; or perhaps you want your assistant to send email messages on your behalf.

This chapter explains how to delegate access to your schedule, email messages, and other Outlook 2013 data, granting an assistant the ability to perform tasks in Outlook 2013 on your behalf. This chapter also explains how to access folders for which you've been granted delegate access.

Delegation overview

Why delegate? You could simply give your assistant your logon credentials and allow that person to access your Exchange Server mailbox through a separate profile on the assistant's system. The disadvantage to that approach, though, is that your assistant then has access to all your Outlook 2013 data. Plus, it surely violates at least one security policy at your company and gives your assistant access to everything else secured by your account, such as Microsoft SharePoint sites, line-of-business applications, and much more . . . clearly a horrible idea. By using the Outlook 2013 delegation features, however, you can restrict an assistant's access to your data selectively.

You have two ways of delegating access in Outlook 2013. First, you can specify individuals as delegates for your account, which gives them send-on-behalf-of privileges. This means that the delegated individuals can perform such tasks as sending email messages and meeting requests for you. When an assistant sends a meeting request on your behalf, the request appears to the recipients to have come from you. You can also specify that delegates should receive copies of meeting-related messages that are sent to you, such as meeting invitations. This is required if you want an assistant to be able to handle your calendar.

The second way that you can delegate access is to configure permissions for individual folders, granting various levels of access within the folders as needed. This does not give other users send-on-behalf-of privileges, but it does give them access to the folders and their contents. The tasks that they can perform in the folders are subject to the permission levels that you grant them.

> **Note**
>
> When a message is sent on your behalf, the recipient sees these words in the From box: *<delegate>* on behalf of *<owner>*, where *<delegate>* and *<owner>* are replaced by the appropriate names. This designation appears in the header of the message form when the recipient opens the message but doesn't appear in the header in the Inbox. The Inbox shows the message as coming from the owner, not the delegate.

Assigning delegates and working as an assistant

You can assign multiple delegates, so that more than one individual can access your data with send-on-behalf-of privileges. You might have an assistant who manages your schedule and therefore has delegate access to your calendar, and another delegate—your supervisor—who manages other aspects of your workday and therefore has access to your Tasks folder. In most cases, however, you'll probably want to assign only one delegate.

Adding and removing delegates

You can add, remove, and configure delegates for all your Outlook 2013 folders through the same interface.

Follow these steps to delegate access to one or more of your Outlook 2013 folders:

1. Click File, Account Settings.

2. Choose Delegate Access to open the Delegates dialog box, as shown in Figure 21-1.

Figure 21-1 The Delegates dialog box shows the current delegates, if any, and lets you add, remove, and configure delegates.

3. Click Add to open the Add Users dialog box.

4. Select one or more users, and then click Add.

5. Click OK. Outlook 2013 displays the Delegate Permissions dialog box, shown in Figure 21-2.

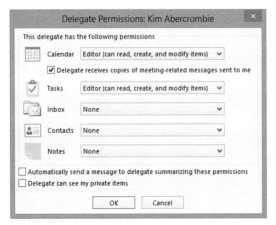

Figure 21-2 Configure delegate permissions in the Delegate Permissions dialog box.

6. For each folder, select the level of access that you want to give the delegate based on the following list:

- ○ **None** The delegate has no access to the selected folder.

- ○ **Reviewer** The delegate can read existing items in the folder but can't add, delete, or modify items. Essentially, this level gives the delegate read-only permission for the folder.

- ○ **Author** The delegate can read existing items and create new ones but can't modify or delete existing items.

- ○ **Editor** The delegate can read existing items, create new ones, and modify existing ones, including deleting them.

7. Set the other options in the dialog box using the following list as a guide:

- ○ **Automatically Send A Message To Delegate Summarizing These Permissions** This option sends an email message to the delegate informing that person of the access permissions that you've assigned in your Outlook 2013 folders, as shown in Figure 21-3.

- ○ **Delegate Can See My Private Items** This option allows the delegate to view items that you've marked as private. Clear this option to hide your private items.

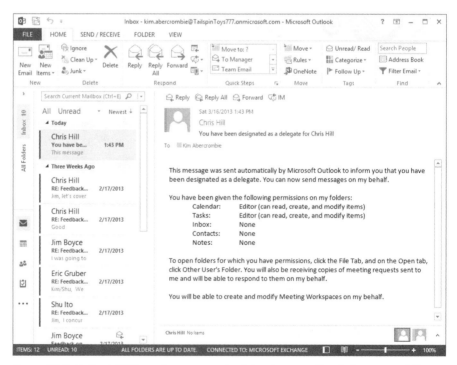

Figure 21-3 Outlook 2013 sends a message to delegates regarding their access privileges.

8. Click OK to close the Delegate Permissions dialog box.

9. Add and configure other delegates as you want, and then click OK.

If you need to modify the permissions for a delegate, open the Delegates dialog box, select the delegate in the list, and then click Permissions to open the Delegate Permissions dialog box. Change the settings as needed, just as you do when you add a delegate. If you need to remove a delegate, select the delegate on the Delegates tab, and then click Remove.

Taking yourself out of the meeting request loop

If your assistant has full responsibility for managing your calendar, you might want all meeting request messages to go to the assistant rather than to you. That way, meeting request messages won't clog your Inbox.

Taking yourself out of the request loop is easy. Here's how:

1. Click File, Account Settings, Delegate Access.

2. Select the My Delegates Only option, and click OK.

> **Note**
> The My Delegates Only option appears dimmed if you haven't assigned a delegate.

Opening folders delegated to you

If you are acting as a delegate for another person, you can open the folders to which you've been given delegate access and use them as if they were your own folders, subject to the permissions applied by the owner. For example, suppose that you've been given delegate access to your manager's schedule. You can open your manager's Calendar folder and create appointments, generate meeting requests, and perform the same tasks that you can perform in your own Calendar folder. However, you might find a few restrictions. For example, you won't be able to view the contents of personal items unless your manager has configured permissions to give you that ability.

Follow these steps to open another person's folder:

1. Start Outlook 2013 with your own profile.

2. Choose File, Open, Other User's Folder to display the Open Other User's Folder dialog box, as shown in Figure 21-4.

Figure 21-4 Use the Open Other User's Folder dialog box to open another person's Outlook 2013 folder.

3. Type the person's name in the dialog box, or click Name to browse the address list and then select a name.

4. In the Folder Type drop-down list, select the folder that you want to open, and then click OK. Outlook 2013 generates an error message if you don't have the necessary permissions for the folder; otherwise, the folder opens in a new window.

Depending on the permissions set for the other person's folder, you might be able to open the folder but not see anything in it. If someone grants you Folder Visible permission, you can open the folder but not necessarily view its contents. For example, if you are granted Folder Visible permission for a Calendar folder, you can view the other person's calendar. If you are granted Folder Visible permission for the Inbox folder, you can open the folder, but you can't see any headers. Obviously, this latter scenario isn't useful, so you might need to fine-tune the permissions to get the effect you need.

When you've finished working with another person's folder, close it as you would any other window.

Scheduling on behalf of another person

If you've been given delegate privileges for another person's calendar, you can schedule meetings and other appointments on behalf of that person.

To do so, follow these steps:

1. Start Outlook 2013 with your own profile.

2. Click File, Open & Export, and then select Other User's Folder. Type the user name into the text box, or click Name and select the user name from the Global Address List (GAL). From the Folder Type drop-down list, select Calendar, and then click OK.

3. In the other person's Calendar folder, create the meeting request, appointment, or other item as you normally would for your own calendar.

As mentioned earlier, a meeting request recipient sees the request as coming from the calendar's owner, not the delegate. When the recipient opens the message, however, the header indicates that the message was sent by the delegate on behalf of the owner. Responses to the meeting request come back to the delegate and a copy goes to the owner unless the owner has removed himself or herself from the meeting request loop.

For details about how to have meeting request messages go to the delegate rather than to the owner, see the section "Taking yourself out of the meeting request loop."

Sending email on behalf of another person

If you've been given Author or Editor permission for another person's Inbox, you can send messages on behalf of that person. For example, as someone's assistant, you might need to send notices, requests for comments, report reminders, or similar messages.

To send a message on behalf of another person, follow these steps:

1. Start Outlook 2013 with your own profile.

2. Start a new message.

3. Click From and choose Other Email Address to open the Send From Other Email Address dialog box.

4. In the From field, type the name of the person on whose behalf you're sending the message, or click From to select an address from the GAL. Then click OK.

5. Complete the message as you would any other, and then send it.

Granting access to folders

You can configure your folders to provide varying levels of access to other users according to the types of tasks that those users need to perform within the folders. For example, you might grant access to your Contacts folder to allow others to see and use your contacts list.

Granting permissions for folders is different from granting delegate access. Users with delegate access to your folders can send messages on your behalf, as explained in earlier sections of this chapter. Users with access permissions for your folders do not have that ability. Use access permissions for your folders when you want to grant others certain levels of access to your folders but not the ability to send messages on your behalf.

Configuring access permissions

Several levels of permissions control what a user can and cannot do in your folders. These permissions include the following:

- **Create Items**   Users can post items to the folder.

- **Create Subfolders**   Users can create additional folders inside the folder.

- **Edit Own**   Users can edit those items that they have created and own.

- **Edit All**   Users can edit all items, including those that they do not own.

- **Folder Owner**   The owner has all permissions for the folder.

- **Folder Contact**   The folder contact receives automated messages from the folder, such as replication conflict messages, requests from users for additional permissions, and other changes to the folder status.

- **Folder Visible**   Users can see the folder and its items.

- **Delete Items**   Depending on the setting that you choose, users can delete all items, only those items they own, or no items.

- **Free/Busy Time**   In the calendar, users can see your free/busy time.

- **Free/Busy Time, Subject, Location**   In the calendar, users can see your free/busy time, as well as the subject and location of calendar items.

- **Full Details**   In the calendar, users can see all details of items.

Outlook 2013 groups these permissions into several predefined levels, as follows:

- **Owner**   The Owner has all permissions and can edit and delete all items, including those that he or she doesn't own.

- **Publishing Editor**   The Publishing Editor has all permissions and can edit and delete all items but does not own the folder.

- **Editor**   Users are granted all permissions except the ability to create subfolders or act as the folder's Owner. Editors can edit and delete all items.

- **Publishing Author**   Users are granted all permissions except the ability to edit or delete items belonging to others and the ability to act as the folder's Owner.

- **Author**   This level is the same as the Publishing Author level, except that Authors can't create subfolders.

- **Nonediting Author**   Users can create and read items and delete items they own, but they can't delete others' items or create subfolders.

- **Reviewer**   Users can view items but can't modify or delete items or create subfolders.

- **Contributor**   Users can create items but can't view or modify existing items.

- **Free/Busy Time**   Users can see your free/busy time.

- **Free/Busy Time, Subject, Location**   Users can see your free/busy time, as well as the subject and location for items on your calendar.

- **None**   The folder is visible, but users can't read, create, or modify any items in the folder.

Follow these steps to grant permissions for a specific folder:

1.   Start Outlook 2013, open the Folder List, right-click the folder, and then choose Share, Folder Permissions to display the Permissions tab of the folder, shown in Figure 21-5.

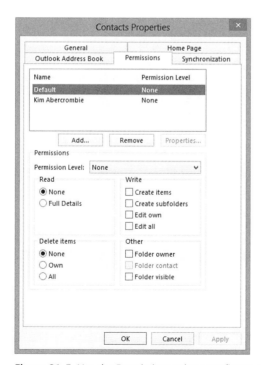

Figure 21-5 Use the Permissions tab to configure access permissions for the folder.

2. Select Default, and then set the permissions that you want users to have if they are not explicitly assigned permissions (that is, if their names don't appear in the Name list).

3. Click Add to add a user with explicit permissions. Select the name in the Add Users list, click Add, and then click OK.

4. From the Name list, select the user that you just added, and then set specific permissions for the user.

5. Click OK to close the folder's Contacts Properties dialog box.

As you can see in Figure 21-5, you can remove the explicit permissions you have given a user by simply removing the user. Just select the user, and then click Remove.

To view (but not modify) a user's address book properties, as shown in Figure 21-6, select the user, and then click Properties.

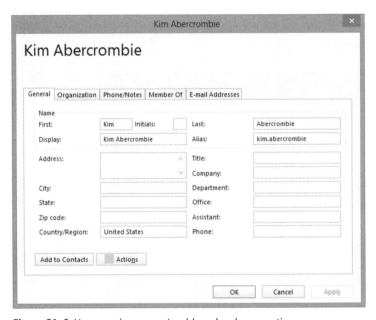

Figure 21-6 You can view a user's address book properties.

Accessing other users' folders

After you've been granted the necessary permissions for another user's folder, you can open the folder and perform actions according to your permissions. For example, if you have only read permission, you can read items but not add new ones. If you've been granted create permission, you can create items.

To open another user's folder, choose File, Open, and Other User's Folder. Type the user's name into the text box, or click Name, select the user in the GAL, and then click OK. Select the folder that you want to open in the Folder Type drop-down list, and then click OK.

For more information about opening and using another person's folder, see the section "Opening folders delegated to you."

Sharing folders with invitations

In addition to the method described in the previous section, you can use email invitations to suggest or request folder sharing. However, this option applies only to non–mail folders, including the Calendar, Tasks, Notes, Contacts, and Journal folders. You cannot share email folders using this method.

To share these types of folders using an email invitation, or to request access to someone else's folder, follow these steps:

1. Open the Folder List in the Folder Pane.

2. Right-click the folder that you want to share or request access to in the other person's mailbox, and choose Share, *<folder>*, where *<folder>* is the name of the folder. For example, choose Share, Calendar to share the Calendar folder.

3. Outlook opens a request form, as shown in Figure 21-7.

Chapter 21

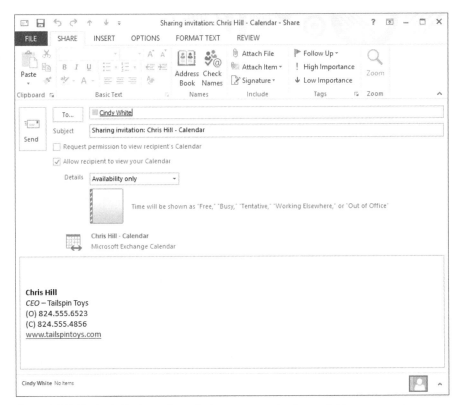

Figure 21-7 Outlook displays a form that you can use to share a folder or request access to one.

4. Enter an email address or click To and select one. This is the email address of the person with whom you are sharing your folder or for whose folder you want to request access.

5. Choose options based on the following list:

   ○ **Request Permission To View Recipient's Calendar**   Choose this item if you are requesting access to the other person's calendar.

   ○ **Allow Recipient To View Your Calendar**   Choose this option if you want to share your own calendar.

○ **Details**   This option applies only to Calendar folders. From the Details drop-down list, choose the level of access you want to grant to the other person to your Calendar folder. You can allow that person to see only your free/busy (availability) information, availability and item subjects, or all details.

6.   Click Send to send the request.

When you click Send, if you have specified that you are sharing your own folder, Outlook asks you to verify that you want to share it and then sends the message to the specified recipient. When the request arrives, the person receiving the request can click either Allow or Deny in the Respond group on the ribbon (or in the message header if the Reading Pane is open) to allow or deny the request. Figure 21-8 shows an example.

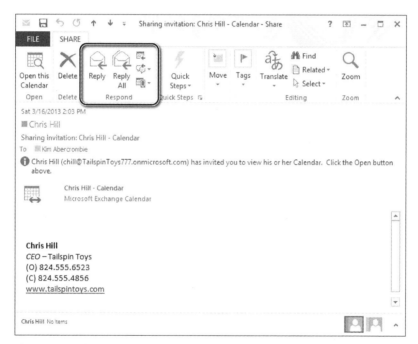

Figure 21-8 Click Allow or Deny in the Respond group to allow or deny an access request.

MICROSOFT Outlook 2013 provides a number of ways for you to share your calendar information with others. In addition to using Microsoft Exchange Server to share your calendar with other Exchange Server users, you can publish your calendar to the Internet and invite others to share access to it. You can publish your calendar to Microsoft Office Online or to any Web Distributed Authoring and Versioning (WebDAV) server. You can also send your calendar to someone else via email, save the calendar as a webpage and then send it, or post the calendar to a web server.

Sharing Exchange Server calendars

By default, if you're using Exchange Server, your free/busy information is shared automatically with all other users in your organization. For that reason, it isn't necessary to explicitly share your calendar just to enable others to see your free/busy information. However, in some situations you might want to share a calendar to enable others to manage it for you, or for a group to use a shared calendar. The following sections explain how to share a calendar.

Sharing your Exchange Server calendar

If you use Exchange Server, you can allow other users to access your entire calendar or selected calendar items. To share your calendar and its items, you must set permission levels for various users. In most cases, permissions are set by using built-in roles, as described in Table 22-1, but you can also set custom permissions for the rare cases when the built-in role does not fit the situation. Some permissions allow users only to view your calendar; others allow users to add or even edit items.

TABLE 22-1 Folder permissions

Permission	Description
Owner	The Owner role gives full control of the calendar. An Owner can create, modify, delete, and read folder items; create subfolders; and change permissions on the folder.
Publishing Editor	The Publishing Editor role has all rights granted to an Owner except the right to change permissions.
Editor	The Editor role has all rights granted to a Publishing Editor except the right to create subfolders.
Publishing Author	A Publishing Author can create and read folder items and create subfolders, but this role can modify and delete only folder items that he or she creates, not items created by other users.
Author	An Author has all rights granted to a Publishing Author but cannot create subfolders.
Nonediting Author	A Nonediting Author can create and read folder items but cannot modify or delete any items, including those that he or she creates.
Reviewer	A Reviewer can read folder items but nothing else.
Contributor	A Contributor can create folder items but cannot delete items.
Free/Busy Time, Subject, Location	A user with these access rights can view the free/busy information, as well as the subject and location.
Free/Busy Time	A user with these access rights can view only the free/busy information.
None	The None role has no rights to access to the folder.

The first step in sharing a calendar is to right-click it in the Folder Pane and then choose Share, Calendar Permissions. Figure 22-1 shows the Permissions tab with the Calendar folder's default permissions.

To allow all users to view details of the calendar, you need to assign Reviewer permission to the default user. A *default user* is any user who is logged in. Select Default in the Name column, and then change the permission level by selecting Reviewer in the Permission Level drop-down list.

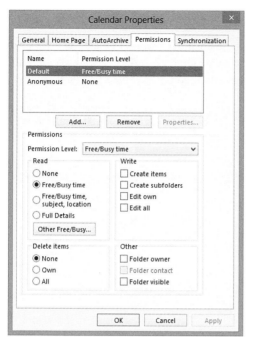

Figure 22-1 The default permissions for a calendar are set to Free/Busy Time.

INSIDE OUT   Share your calendar for review quickly

You can also right-click the calendar and then choose Share, Share Calendar. An email is generated that grants permission, and you can add people with whom you want to share the calendar to the To line. Reviewer (read-only) status is granted using this method. This approach not only shares the calendar but also automatically generates an email message to inform the recipients that you have made the calendar available to them.

You might assign a permission of Publishing Author to users if they are colleagues who need to be able to schedule items for you as well as view your calendar.

To give users Publishing Author access to the calendar, follow these steps:

1. On the Permissions tab in the Calendar Properties dialog box, click Add to open the Add Users dialog box, shown in Figure 22-2. Alternatively, you can right-click the calendar in the Folder Pane and then choose Share, Calendar Permissions.

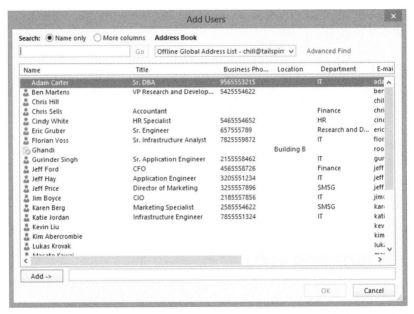

Figure 22-2 Add users to the Permissions tab so that you can specify their permissions for folder sharing.

2. Select a user or distribution list in the Add Users dialog box (hold down Shift and click to select a range of users, or hold down Ctrl and click to select multiple users), and then click Add. After you have selected all the users that you want to add, click OK.

3. By default, Outlook 2013 adds users to the Permissions tab with Free/Busy Time permission (see Figure 22-3). To change the permission of a newly added user to Publishing Author, select the user's name and then select the permission in the Permission Level drop-down list.

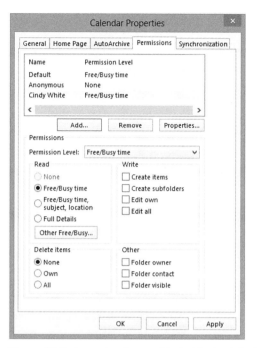

Figure 22-3 A user has been added with the default permission.

As you can see in Figure 22-3, the permissions granted to a user can be configured manually using the check boxes in the bottom half of the Permissions tab. However, this is usually unnecessary because you can set most combinations of settings using the Permission Level drop-down list.

You can configure your free/busy settings by clicking Other Free/Busy. The Free/Busy Options dialog box is displayed, as shown in Figure 22-4, allowing you to set the amount of free/busy information that you publish on the computer running Exchange Server and specify the frequency of updates. You can also configure your Internet free/busy publishing and search locations to set custom Internet addresses for your free/busy publishing and search locations.

Chapter 22

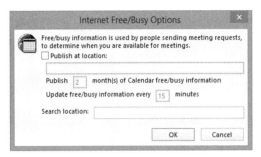

Figure 22-4 Configure your free/busy options for Exchange Server and Internet calendar publishing.

INSIDE OUT Permissions and delegation are different

Giving someone permission to view or modify your Calendar folder is not the same as assigning them to be a delegate. Delegate permission gives the person the ability to send and receive meeting notices on your behalf. See Chapter 21, "Delegating responsibilities to an assistant," for details on assigning delegate permissions.

Opening a shared Exchange Server calendar

After a calendar is shared, those who have permissions can open the calendar in Outlook and view it in much the same way they view their own calendars. To open a shared calendar, first open your own Calendar folder. Then, in the Manage Calendars group on the ribbon, click Open Calendar and choose Open Shared Calendar. In the resulting Open A Shared Calendar dialog box, click Name, select the calendar, and click OK. Then click OK again. The calendar will appear in Outlook as a separate folder.

Sharing non-Exchange Server calendars

The method you can use to publish your calendar depends on the type of account you have. Office 365 users can publish their calendars from Office 365. Outlook.com and Live.com users can share their calendars through those services. If you don't have these account types, you can publish your calendar to a WebDAV server.

> ## Note
> Previously, Microsoft provided a service enabling Outlook users to publish their calendars at Office.com. However, that service is being deprecated and is not available within Outlook 2013. Your alternatives are to switch to an Office 365 or Outlook.com account, or publish to a WebDAV service provided by your company or a third party.

The following sections explain how to publish to the different types of calendar servers.

Publishing your calendar on Office 365

If you have an Office 365 account, Outlook offers the option of publishing your calendar to Office 365, where others can access it by either subscribing to it or viewing it in a web browser. If you publish the calendar with public access, anyone can view the calendar at whatever detail you specify. For example, if you publish the calendar with Availability Only with a Public access level, anyone can view your availability as Free, Busy, Tentative, or Away. If you publish the calendar with Full Details, using the Public access level, everyone will be able to see all of your calendar details. In most cases, that's not a good idea. The exception is when you want to publish a public calendar of events or other calendar that doesn't contain personal items.

To publish your Office 365 calendar, follow these steps:

1. Open Outlook, and then open the Calendar folder.

2. On the Home tab of the ribbon, in the Share group, click Publish This Calendar. Outlook opens the webpage shown in Figure 22-5 (specify your Office 365 account login information if prompted for it).

Chapter 22

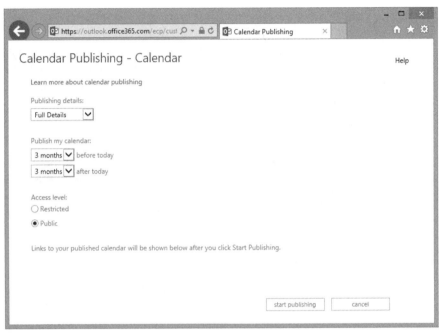

Figure 22-5 Office 365 allows you to share your calendar, enabling others to subscribe to it or view it in a web browser.

3. From the Publishing Details drop-down list, choose the level of detail you want to publish.

4. From the Publish My Calendar group, choose the range of dates you want to publish.

5. Choose Restricted if you want people to be able to access your calendar only if they receive a link to it. Choose Public if you want people to be able to search for and find your calendar on the Internet.

6. Click Start Publishing. The webpage changes to show the URLs for your calendar, as shown in Figure 22-6. You can click Copy Links To The Clipboard to copy the URLs to the Clipboard. From there, you can paste them into an email to send to your friends and colleagues whom you wish to have access to your calendar.

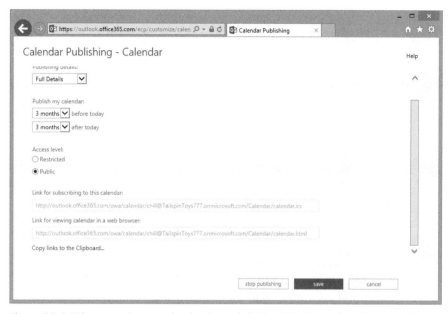

Figure 22-6 When you share a calendar through Office 365, the service gives you URLs for subscribing to and viewing the calendar.

It's important to note that publishing with the Restricted access level doesn't truly restrict who can access your calendar. The difference between the Restricted level and the Public level is that with Restricted, Office 365 obfuscates the URL for subscribing to and viewing your calendar, making it effectively undiscoverable through an Internet search. However, once someone has the URL, there is nothing to prevent that person from using the URL to view whatever level of information you have published.

Let's look at an example. The following URL is one created by Office 365 to view a calendar shared using the Restricted access level:

```
http://outlook.office365.com/owa/calendar/44306bfd7ba54675a232e0a1b86e67b1@Tailspin
Toys777.onmicrosoft.com/584c1c9889f54209a530bd1d114f63c116060447476368286888/
calendar.html
```

Sharing the same calendar with the Public access level results in the following URL:

```
http://outlook.office365.com/owa/calendar/chill@tailspintoys777.onmicrosoft.com/
calendar/calendar.html
```

Chapter 22

Any anonymous user who had either of those URLs could open the URL in a web browser. So, it might be more accurate to think of Restricted as "semihidden." If you send someone your calendar's URL, there is nothing to prevent the person from forwarding it to others, posting it on Facebook, and so on. Keep this in mind when deciding what level of information to publish.

Publishing your Outlook.com/Live.com calendar

When configured with an Outlook.com or Live.com account, Outlook doesn't give you the same level of automation for sharing a calendar as you have with an Office 365 account. With either type of account, Outlook offers the option of publishing to a WebDAV server. So, if you have either an Outlook.com or a Live.com account and you want to share your calendar, open the account in a web browser and then open the calendar, as shown in Figure 22-7. In the top menu bar, click Share and choose your calendar.

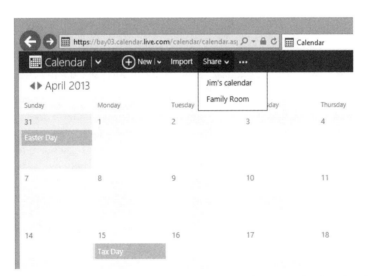

Figure 22-7 You can share your Outlook.com or Live.com calendar when logged on to your account from a web browser.

At this point, you have a handful of options for sharing your calendar (see Figure 22-8). You can enter the email addresses of people to have access to your calendar, specify what level of access people will have, or send people a view-only link to your calendar. If you choose the latter option, click Get Links to publish the calendar and view a list of links that you can give to others to enable them to view your calendar, subscribe to it, view it in an RSS feed, or embed it on your website.

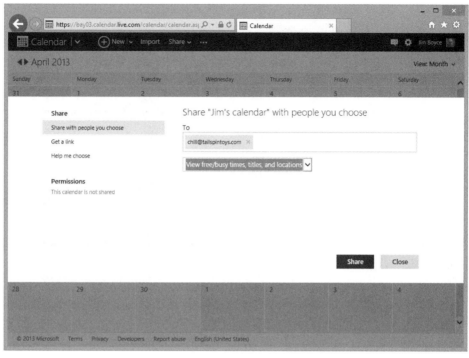

Figure 22-8 You have several options for sharing your Outlook.com or Live.com calendar.

Publishing your calendar to a WebDAV server

To publish your Calendar folder to a WebDAV service, open the Calendar folder and click Publish To WebDAV Server in the Share group on the Home tab on the ribbon. The Publish Calendar To Custom Server dialog box appears, as shown in Figure 22-9.

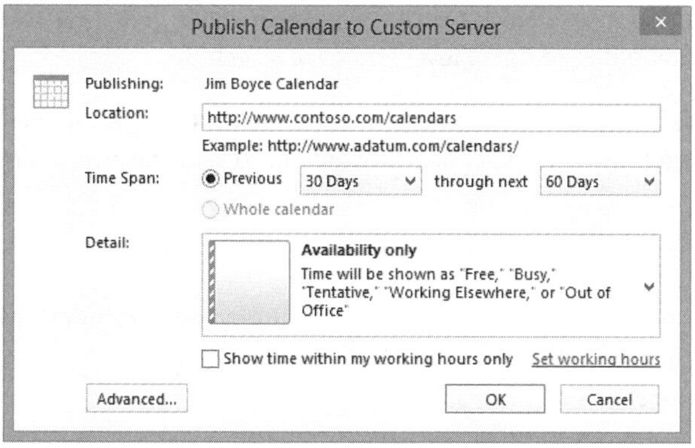

Figure 22-9 You can configure date range, details, access, and updates when publishing your calendar to a WebDAV server.

The Publish Calendar To Custom Server dialog box contains the following options:

- **Location**   In this field, specify the URL of the WebDAV server.

- **Time Span**   In this area, you can specify the range of calendar information by setting the Previous and Through Next options.

- **Detail**   In this area, you can select the level of information detail that will be displayed to users viewing your calendar:

  - **Availability Only**   Only the availability status of the time will be displayed, as Free, Busy, Tentative, or Out Of Office.

  - **Limited Details**   This option displays the availability status as well as the Subject line of calendar items.

  - **Full Details**   This option includes availability status and all information associated with the calendar items.

  - **Show Time Within My Working Hours Only**   You can limit the display of calendar information to only your working hours by selecting the Show Time Within My Working Hours Only check box. You can configure your working hours by clicking the Set Working Hours link.

- **Advanced**   Click to set the following options:

  - **Automatic Uploads**   This option enables the automatic updating of your published calendar.

  - **Single Upload**   This option enables the one-time publishing of your calendar with no further updates.

  - **Include Details Of Items Marked Private**   If this item is selected, Outlook will publish the details for items on your calendar that are marked private (depending on the detail level you have selected).

  - **Update Frequency**   Choose this option to update the calendar based on the server settings regardless of your configured send/receive settings.

Subscribing to a shared calendar

After a calendar is shared, others can access it from Outlook. For example, assume that one of your colleagues has shared his calendar. To subscribe to that calendar so you can see it in Outlook, follow these steps:

1. Open your Calendar folder.

2. In the Manage Calendars group on the ribbon, click Open Calendar and choose From Internet to open the New Internet Calendar Subscription dialog box, shown in Figure 22-10.

Figure 22-10 Specify the URL for the shared calendar.

3. Enter the URL for the shared calendar and click OK.

4. In the resulting dialog box, click Yes if you want to open the calendar with default settings, or click Advanced to open the Subscription Options dialog box shown in Figure 22-11.

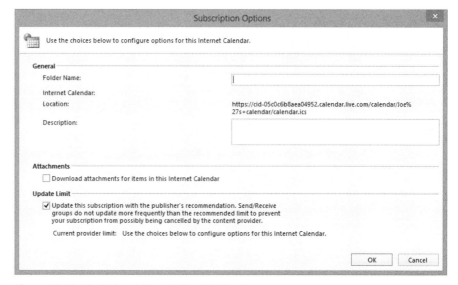

Figure 22-11 The Subscription Options dialog box.

5. In the Folder Name field, specify the name by which you want the shared calendar to appear in your calendar list.

6. If you want attachments in the shared calendar copied to your computer, select the Download Attachments For Items In This Internet Calendar check box.

7. Click OK.

Setting the search location for free/busy information

The Free/Busy Options dialog box includes a Search Location box that specifies where Outlook 2013 will search for free/busy information when you create group schedules or meeting requests. Specify the URL or file share where the group's calendars are published, and Outlook 2013 will search the specified URL for free/busy information. To access this setting, follow these steps:

1. Click File, Options, and click Calendar in the left pane.

2. In the Calendar Options group, click Free/Busy Options to open the Calendar Properties dialog box.

3. Click Other Free/Busy to open the Internet Free/Busy Options dialog box.

4. In the Search Location field, enter the URL of the additional free/busy server, and then click OK.

These global settings can work in conjunction with Exchange Server, providing a search location for calendars not stored in Exchange Server. In addition to these global settings, you can specify a search URL for individual contacts. You would specify the search URL in the contact if the contact's free/busy information is not stored on Exchange Server or another server specified in the Search Location box.

Follow these steps to set the free/busy search URL for a contact:

1. Open the contact. In the Show group on the Contact tab, click Details.

2. Click in the Address field in the Internet Free-Busy area, and then type the URL of the contact's free/busy information.

3. Click Save & Close.

Refreshing your schedule

Free/busy information is refreshed automatically at 15-minute intervals. You can refresh free/busy information manually as well. The command to do so does not by default appear in the ribbon, but you can add it. Right-click the ribbon and choose Customize The Ribbon.

From the Choose Commands From drop-down list, choose Commands Not In The Ribbon. Locate the Publish Internet Free/Busy command, add it to the ribbon, and then click OK. When you need to update your free/busy data, click Publish Internet Free/Busy on the ribbon.

Sharing your calendar via email

Outlook 2013 enables you to send your calendar to other people via email, either by clicking the E-mail Calendar button on the ribbon or by right-clicking the calendar and then choosing Share, E-mail Calendar. A new mail message form will open, and the Send A Calendar Via E-mail dialog box will display, as shown in Figure 22-12. In this dialog box, you can select the calendar to send and configure the date range and amount of detail that the calendar contains. When you click Show in the Advanced area, you can enable the display of information marked as private, include attachments in the calendar, and specify the layout of the calendar as either Daily Schedule or List Of Events. When you click OK, the calendar is written into the email message as text and as an attachment.

Figure 22-12 You can select a calendar and configure date range, details, and layout when emailing your calendar.

Sending a link to your Internet free/busy information through email

If you are using an Internet free/busy server to publish your availability, you can use email to send a vCard containing your free/busy URL to others who might need to see your availability. To email your free/busy information to others, you must first link that information to a vCard, as follows:

1. Open a contact item containing your own contact information.

2. In the Show group of the Contact tab, click Details. The Details page appears, as shown in Figure 22-13.

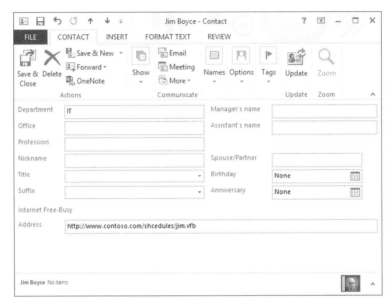

Figure 22-13 On the Details page of a contact form, you can specify the Internet free/busy server.

3. In the Address box in the Internet Free-Busy area, type the address of the server containing your free/busy information.

4. Click Save on the Quick Access Toolbar to save any changes, click File, Save As, and then select vCard Files from the Save As Type dialog box.

5. In the Save As dialog box, type the name of the file, and then select the location where you want to save the file.

6. Click Save to create the vCard.

You can now send the vCard to other users, and they can reference your free/busy information.

For more details about using vCards, see the section "Sharing contacts with vCards" in Chapter 14, "Working with contacts."

Changing the free/busy status of an item

You can change the free/busy status of an item easily. One method is to right-click the item, choose Show As, and then select Free, Busy, Tentative, or Out Of Office. The second method is to open the item (by double-clicking it, or right-clicking it and then choosing Open), and then select Free, Busy, Tentative, or Out Of Office from the Show As drop-down list in the Options group on the ribbon.

Using calendar groups and Schedule View

Outlook 2007 included a feature called Group Schedules that you could use to view the calendars of multiple people at one time, which was handy for seeing availability for a group of people at a glance. This feature was replaced in Outlook 2010 by calendar groups, and the feature has been carried over to Outlook 2013. Calendar groups offer the same capabilities as Group Schedules, but with the added benefit that some of your calendar groups get created automatically. These include two Team calendar groups, one that shows the schedules of everyone who reports to you, and another that shows the schedules of everyone who reports to your manager (your peers).

Using the built-in calendar groups

To view the default calendar groups, first open the Calendar folder. In the Folder Pane, you should see at least one Team. Place a check mark beside a group to view the calendars of the group members, as shown in Figure 22-14.

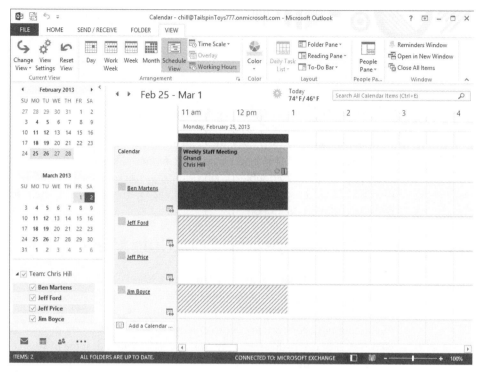

Figure 22-14 Outlook 2013 creates some calendar groups automatically.

As Figure 22-14 shows, the default view for a calendar group is Schedule View, which shows the individuals on the left and their schedules on the right. You can control whose calendars are shown by selecting or clearing the check boxes beside the names in the Folder Pane. To close the calendar group, clear the check box beside the group name.

In addition to giving you a quick, overall view of the group's availability, you can use calendar groups to schedule calendar items. For example, if you want to schedule a meeting with someone in a group, just double-click a time slot in someone's schedule. Outlook opens a new meeting request for the individual using the specified time slot. You can also right-click in a time slot and choose different types of calendar items from the menu, such as recurring events and appointments.

You can view the calendar group using the other standard calendar views, such as day or week. However, only the day view is really very useful (and then only if you have sufficient desktop space for Outlook) unless you overlay the calendars. To choose a different view for the calendar group, simply click a view on the Home tab.

> **Note**
> To turn off display of the Team calendar groups, on the Home tab of the ribbon, click Calendar Groups and choose Show Team Calendars to remove the check mark beside the command. Repeat the process to turn the display of calendar groups back on.

Creating a calendar group

The default calendar groups can be very useful, but you might want to create your own calendar groups. For example, maybe you have people working for you who don't report directly to you, and therefore their Active Directory Domain Services (AD DS) accounts don't reflect you as their manager. These people will not show up in your Team calendar. Alternatively, perhaps you are working on a major project and would like to see the calendars of the other people who are working on the project with you. Whatever the case, you can create your own calendar groups easily, as follows:

1. Open the Calendar folder, and then, on the Home tab on the ribbon, click Calendar Groups and choose Create New Calendar Group.

2. Outlook opens a dialog box to prompt for the name of the group (see Figure 22-15). Enter a name of your choice and click OK.

Figure 22-15 Enter a name for the calendar group.

3. In the Select Name dialog box, select the people whose calendars you want to view and then click Group Members.

4. Click OK.

The new calendar group appears in the Folder Pane, as shown in Figure 22-16. The calendar group is displayed along with any other individual calendars or groups that you have selected. Use the check boxes beside the groups and individual calendars to control which ones are displayed.

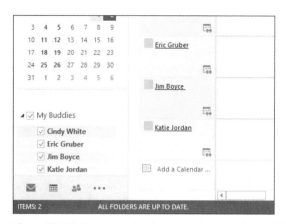

Figure 22-16 The new calendar group appears in the Folder Pane.

> **Note**
>
> You can change the order of calendar groups in the Folder Pane. To move a group up or down, right-click the group in the Folder Pane and choose Move Up or Move Down.

Creating a group from existing calendars

If you already have several calendars displayed in Outlook, but they are not part of a group, you can create a group containing those calendars easily. Place a check mark beside each of the calendars that you want in the group, and then click Calendar Groups on the ribbon and choose Save As New Calendar Group. Outlook moves the calendars to the group in the Folder Pane. If you later decide that you want to move some or all of the calendars to different groups, you can. The next section explains how.

Moving/removing calendars and groups

If you want to move a calendar from one group to another, just drag it to the desired group. Note that if you hold down the Ctrl key while dragging the calendar, Outlook displays a plus sign (+) beside the calendar, the standard sign that a program will copy the calendar rather than move it. This is a false indication, however, as the calendar is still moved and not copied. But this could be fixed in a subsequent hotfix or update.

It's easy to remove a calendar group. Just right-click the calendar group in the Folder Pane and choose Delete Group. Outlook displays a dialog box for confirmation. Click Yes to delete the group.

> **Note**
> Deleting a calendar group deletes the group only from Outlook. It does not delete the users' calendars or affect their accounts in any way.

PART VI

Security and backup

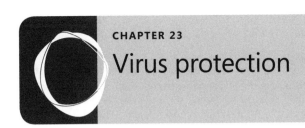

Virus protection

IF you use Microsoft Outlook 2013 on a daily basis to manage email, appointments, and contacts, losing the information that you've stored in Outlook 2013 would probably cause you significant problems. Outlook 2013 data can be lost in a number of ways, from accidental deletion to file corruption to hard disk failure. In addition, a user who purchases a new computer might leave behind information when transferring data to the new machine.

This chapter examines virus protection for both the server and workstation to help you understand how to protect yourself and your network from email-borne viruses. Outlook 2013 provides features to protect against viruses in attachments, and there are several steps you can and should take to add other forms of virus protection.

Providing virus protection

Hardware and software failures are by no means the only source of anguish for the average user or administrator. Viruses and worms have become major problems for system administrators and users alike. When a major virus or worm outbreak hits, companies grind to a halt, systems shut down, mail servers get overwhelmed, and general chaos ensues.

The effects of a particularly virulent virus or worm can be devastating for a company. A virus or worm can bring your mail servers to a quick halt because of the load that it imposes on them with the sheer amount of traffic it generates. Bandwidth, both local and across wide area network (WAN) links, is affected as multiple copies of infected messages flood the network. Files can become infected, rendering them unusable and subjecting users to reinfection. This means that you must recover the files from backups, making an adequate backup strategy even more important than usual.

One often-overlooked effect that viruses have on a company is the public relations nightmare that they can create. How would your customers react if they received a flood of infected messages from your company that brought their mail servers to a screeching halt and damaged their production files? Forget for a moment the ire of your customers' system administrators. Could your company survive the ill will generated by such a catastrophe?

At the least, your company would probably suffer serious consequences. Therefore, developing and implementing an effective virus protection strategy is as important as developing a backup strategy—perhaps even more so. When you examine your antivirus needs, approach the problem from two angles: protecting against outside infection and preventing an outgoing flood of infected messages. You can approach the former through either client-side or server-side solutions, but the latter typically requires a server-side solution.

Implementing server-side solutions

Your first line of defense against viruses and worms should lie between your local area network (LAN) and the Internet. Many antivirus solution vendors offer perimeter security products that monitor traffic coming from the Internet and detect and block viruses in real time. With perimeter protection in place, threats may never reach your network or servers at all.

Stopping viruses before they get into your LAN is a great goal, but even the best products sometimes miss. If your organization uses Microsoft Exchange Server, you should also consider installing an Exchange Server–based antivirus solution. All the major antivirus vendors offer Exchange Server solutions, as does Microsoft, with its cloud-based Exchange Online Protection service.

In addition to detecting and removing viruses from network and Exchange Server traffic, you should implement a solution that provides real-time virus detection for your network's file servers. These solutions scan the server for infected files as files are added or modified. For example, a remote user might upload a file containing a virus to your FTP server. If local users open the file, their systems become infected and the virus begins to spread across your LAN. Catching and removing the virus as soon as the file is uploaded to the FTP server is the ideal solution. Microsoft SharePoint is another application that should be protected at the application layer. Because documents are stored in Microsoft SQL Server rather than in a file system, the operating system–level antivirus products cannot detect or protect against threats in documents uploaded by users. So you should add a SharePoint antivirus solution in addition to your operating system protection on the servers themselves.

Consider all these points as you evaluate server-side antivirus products. Some might be more important to you than others, so prioritize them and then choose an antivirus suite that best suits your needs and priorities.

Implementing client-side solutions

In addition to blocking viruses and worms at the server, you should provide antivirus protection at each workstation, particularly if your server-side virus detection is limited. Even if you do provide a full suite of detection services at the server, client-side protection is a vital piece of any antivirus strategy. For example, suppose that your server provides virus filtering, scanning all email traffic coming from the Internet. Even so, the server might miss a new virus in a message with an attached file, perhaps because the virus definition file has not yet been updated. A user opens the infected file and it infects his or her system, and the worm begins replicating across the LAN. If the user has a client-side antivirus solution in place, the worm is blocked before it can do any damage.

Use the following criteria to evaluate client-side antivirus solutions:

- **Are frequent updates available?**   On any given day, several new viruses appear. Your antivirus solution is only as good as your virus definition files are current. Choose a solution that offers daily or (at least) weekly virus definition updates.

- **Can updates be scheduled for automatic execution?**   The average user doesn't back up documents on a regular basis, much less worry about whether antivirus definition files are up to date. For that reason, it's important that the client-side antivirus solution you choose provide automatic, scheduled updates.

- **Does the product scan a variety of file types?**   Make sure that the product you choose can scan not only executables and other application files, but also Microsoft Office system documents for macro viruses.

You'll find several client-side antivirus products on the market. Microsoft has two offerings that might be of interest: Microsoft Security Essentials includes antivirus protection in its suite of services for home and small business computer users, and Microsoft System Center Endpoint Protection offers similar protection for computers in an enterprise environment, although it *does not* scan email. Other popular products include Symantec Norton AntiVirus (*http://www.symantec.com*), McAfee VirusScan (*http://www.mcafee.com*), and Panda Antivirus for Servers and Desktops (*http://www.pandasecurity.com*). Many other products are available that offer comparable features.

Virus protection in Outlook

Virus protection is an important feature in Outlook 2013. You can configure Outlook 2013 to block specific types of attachments automatically, thus helping prevent virus infections. Outlook 2013 provides two levels of attachment protection, one for individual users and one for system administrators.

Outlook 2013 provides features to help protect your system against viruses and other malicious system attacks. For example, Outlook 2013 supports attachment virus protection, which helps protect against viruses you might receive through infected email attachments. Outlook 2013 offers protection against Office system macro viruses, letting you choose when macros run. Control over programmatic access is also configurable, allowing management of how applications interact with the security features in Outlook 2013 as well as their ability to send email.

> For information about protecting against malicious HTML-based messages, see the section "Configuring HTML message handling" in Chapter 8, "Security and data protection."

Protecting against viruses in attachments

In the computer dark ages, infected boot floppy disks were the most common way computer viruses were spread. Today, email is by far the most common infection mechanism. Viruses range from mostly harmless (but irritating) to severe, sometimes causing irreparable damage to your systems. Worms are a more recent variation, spreading across the Internet primarily through email and by exploited operating system flaws. Worms can bog down a system by consuming the majority of the system's resources, and they can cause the same types of damage as viruses.

Outlook 2013 provides protection against viruses and worms by letting you block certain types of attachments that are susceptible to infection. This prevents users from opening attached files that could infect their systems and execute malicious code to damage or steal data. Executable programs (.exe, .com, and .bat files) are also good examples of attachments that are primary delivery mechanisms for viruses. Many other document types are equally susceptible—HTML documents and scripts, for instance, have rapidly become favorite delivery tools for virus creators. Outlook 2013 provides two levels of protection for attachments: Level 1 and Level 2. The following sections explain these two levels, the file types assigned to each, and how to work with attachments.

Protected View

When you open an Office document that is attached to an email, the document's native application (such as Word) opens in a rights-limited sandbox instance. A banner just under the application's ribbon displays a message indicating that the file originated as an email attachment and might be unsafe. The banner also reminds you that the application is running in Protected View.

Limiting the rights that the sandbox application has limits the potential for a virus in the document to be able to "get outside" of the application and do any damage. If you feel comfortable that the document is safe, you can click Enable Editing to open the document in a normal instance and begin making changes, save it, and so on.

Level 1 attachments

Level 1 attachments are those that are common vectors for infection, such as executable (.exe) files. When you receive a message containing an attachment in the Level 1 group, Outlook 2013 displays the paper clip icon next to the message header, indicating that the message has an attachment, just as it does for other messages with attachments. When you click the message header, Outlook 2013 displays a message indicating that it has blocked the attachment.

You cannot open Level 1 attachments that are blocked by Outlook 2013. You can open and view the messages, but Outlook 2013 disables the interface elements that otherwise would allow you to open or save the attachments. Outlook 2013 displays a message in the InfoBar informing you that the attachment has been blocked and cannot be opened, as shown in Figure 23-1. If you forward a message with a blocked attachment, Outlook 2013 strips the attachment from the forwarded message.

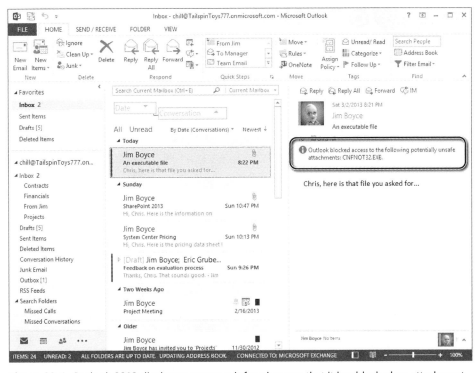

Figure 23-1 Outlook 2013 displays a message informing you that it has blocked an attachment.

Chapter 23

For details on how to open attachments that have been blocked by Outlook 2013, see the section "Opening blocked attachments."

Table 23-1 lists the file name extensions for Level 1 attachments. (Note that this list will change over time.)

TABLE 23-1 Level 1 attachments

File name extension	Description
.ade	Microsoft Access project extension
.adp	Access project
.app	Executable application
.asp	Active Server Page
.bas	BASIC source code
.bat	Batch processing
.cer	Internet security certificate file
.chm	Compiled HTML help
.cmd	DOS CP/M command file; command file for Windows NT
.cnt	Windows Help file
.com	Command
.cpl	Control Panel extension
.crt	Certificate file
.csh	csh script
.der	DER-encoded X509 certificate file
.exe	Executable file
.fxp	FoxPro compiled source
.gadget	Windows gadget file
.hlp	Windows Help file
.hta	Hypertext application
.inf	Information or setup file
.ins	Microsoft Internet Information Services (IIS) Internet communications settings
.isp	IIS Internet service provider (ISP) settings
.its	Internet document set; Internet translation
.js	JavaScript source code
.jse	JScript encoded script file
.ksh	UNIX shell script

File name extension	Description
.lnk	Windows shortcut file
.mad	Access module shortcut
.maf	Access file
.mag	Access diagram shortcut
.mam	Access macro shortcut
.maq	Access query shortcut
.mar	Access report shortcut
.mas	Access stored procedures
.mat	Access table shortcut
.mau	Media attachment unit
.mav	Access view shortcut
.maw	Access data access page
.mda	Access add-in; Microsoft MDA Access 2 workgroup
.mdb	Access application; Microsoft MDB Access database
.mde	Access MDE database file
.mdt	Access add-in data
.mdw	Access workgroup information
.mdz	Access wizard template
.msc	Microsoft Management Console (MMC) snap-in control file
.msh	Microsoft shell
.msh1	Microsoft shell
.msh2	Microsoft shell
.mshxml	Microsoft shell
.msh1xml	Microsoft shell
.msh2xml	Microsoft shell
.msi	Microsoft Windows Installer file
.msp	Microsoft Windows Installer update
.mst	Windows SDK setup transform script
.ops	Office system profile settings file
.pcd	Microsoft Visual Test
.pif	Windows program information file
.plg	Microsoft Developer Studio build log
.prf	Windows system file

File name extension	Description
.prg	Program file
.pst	Exchange Server address book file; Outlook personal folder file
.reg	Registration information/key for Windows 95 and Windows 98; registry data file
.scf	Windows Explorer command
.scr	Windows screen saver
.sct	Windows script component; FoxPro screen
.shb	Windows shortcut into a document
.shs	Shell scrap object file
.ps1	PowerShell
.ps1xml	PowerShell
.ps2	PowerShell
.ps2xml	PowerShell
.psc1	PowerShell
.psc2	PowerShell
.tmp	Temporary file/folder
.url	Internet location
.vb	Microsoft Visual Basic Scripting Edition (VBScript) file; any Visual Basic source
.vbe	VBScript encoded script file
.vbs	VBScript script file; Visual Basic for Applications (VBA) script
.vsmacros	Microsoft Visual Studio .NET binary-based macro project
.vsw	Microsoft Visio workspace file
.ws	Windows script file
.wsc	Windows script component
.wsf	Windows script file
.wsh	Windows script host settings file
.xnk	Exchange Server public folder shortcut

Level 2 attachments

Outlook 2013 also supports a second level of attachment blocking. Level 2 attachments are defined by the administrator at the server level and therefore apply only to Exchange Server accounts, not to POP3, IMAP, or other account types. Because the Level 2 list is empty by default, no attachments are blocked as Level 2 attachments unless the Exchange Server administrator has modified the Level 2 list.

You can't open Level 2 attachments directly in Outlook 2013, but Outlook 2013 does allow you to save them to disk, and you can open them from there.

Configuring blocked attachments

Attachment blocking is an important feature in Outlook 2013 to help prevent viruses from infecting systems. Although you can rely on the default Outlook 2013 attachment security, you can also choose a centrally managed method of customizing attachment handling for Outlook 2013. You can configure attachment blocking in three ways:

- **Using Group Policy**   With Outlook 2013, you can use Group Policy to control how Outlook 2013 handles security, including attachments and virus prevention features. The use of Group Policy also allows the application of these customized security settings in environments without public folders, such as a computer running Exchange Server without public folders deployed, or with clients running Outlook 2013 that are not using Exchange Server. Using Group Policy does, however, require that you use the Active Directory Domain Services (AD DS) to manage your network.

- **Using the Exchange Security Form**   Earlier versions of Outlook used the Exchange Security Form, which provides essentially the same options as the Group Policy settings now do. The Exchange Security Form relies on Exchange Server shared folders, however, which limits the use of these configuration options to organizations using Exchange Server. You can still use the Exchange Security Form with Exchange Server, for example, to support older Outlook clients.

- **At the user's workstation**   If neither of the preceding options is available to you, a limited amount of customization can be done on an individual workstation. For example, you can modify the client's registry to change the Level 1 list (as explained in the section "Configuring attachment blocking directly in Outlook"). These modifications also affect non–Exchange Server accounts.

Configuring attachment blocking centrally, either via Group Policy or on a computer running Exchange Server, is the most effective and efficient method; it gives you, as an administrator, control over attachment security. It also allows you to tailor security by groups within your Windows domains.

> **Note**
> Because this book focuses on Outlook 2013 used with Exchange Server 2013, the use of the Exchange Security Form is not covered.

In addition to specifying when Outlook 2013 blocks attachments, you can configure other aspects of Outlook 2013 security via Group Policy (or using the Exchange Security Form), letting you limit the behavior of custom forms and control programmatic access to Outlook 2013.

INSIDE OUT   Keep systems safe

Level 2 attachment filtering is really only effective if the user has a client-side antivirus solution in place that will scan the file automatically as soon as the user saves the file to disk. Alternatively, you could rely on the user to perform a virus check on the file manually. Neither of these scenarios is a sure bet by any means. Even if the user has antivirus software installed, it might be disabled or have an outdated virus definition file. That's why it's important to provide virus protection at the network and server levels to prevent viruses from reaching the user at all.

It's also important to educate users about the potential damage that can be caused by viruses and worms. Too often, these infect systems through user ignorance—users receive an attachment from a known recipient, assume that it's safe (if they even consider that the file could be infected), and open the file. The result is an infected system and potentially an infected network.

Configuring attachments in Exchange Server

Attachment blocking in Exchange Server can be configured in two ways:

- Group Policy is used by Exchange Server 2013, enabling the configuration of these settings without reliance on public folders, which are optional in Exchange Server 2013, or registry entries on each of the clients.

- The Exchange Security Form, which is configured via an administrative template stored in a public folder, is used in earlier versions of Exchange Server. While the Exchange Security Form can be used only in environments that have public folders, such as Exchange Server 2003 or 2007, it is still available for configurations, such as using down-level clients, where it is required.

The settings that are configurable in Group Policy and those set via the Exchange Security Form are largely the same. This chapter focuses on the use of Group Policy rather than the Exchange Security Form.

Using Outlook security settings

There are three categories of settings you can configure using Group Policy, controlling attachments, forms, and programmatic access to Outlook 2013. These settings are described in the following sections.

> **Note**
>
> This chapter covers the settings as described in Group Policy; settings in the Exchange Security Form are similar, even if worded slightly differently.
>
> To access these security settings, you must add the Office 2013 Group Policy Administrative Templates, which you can find at *http://www.microsoft.com/en-us/download/details.aspx?id=35554*.

Attachment security settings

Several options are available for customization of attachment handling, including making changes to the blocked attachment lists, specifying when prompts appear, and controlling users' ability to configure their own attachment management.

- **Display Level 1 Attachments** This option allows users of Outlook 2013 to see and open Level 1 attachments.

- **Allow Users To Demote Attachments To Level 2** Enabling this option allows users of Outlook 2013 to demote Level 1 attachments to Level 2, which lets a user save the attachments to disk and then open them.

- **Do Not Prompt About Level 1 Attachments When Sending An Item** This setting disables the warning that normally appears when a user tries to send a Level 1 attachment. The warning explains that the attachment could cause a virus infection and that the recipient might not receive the attachment (because of attachment blocking on the recipient's server).

- **Do Not Prompt About Level 1 Attachments When Closing An Item** You can disable the warning that normally appears when the user closes a message, an appointment, or another item that contains a Level 1 attachment.

Chapter 23

> **Note**
>
> Disabling warning prompts for Level 1 attachments does not change how Outlook 2013 deals with them. Even without a warning, users are not able to view or open Level 1 attachments in Outlook 2013 items when a setting that disables warning prompts is enabled.

- **Allow In-Place Activation Of Embedded OLE Objects**   This option allows users of Outlook 2013 to open embedded Object Linking and Embedding (OLE) objects (such as Microsoft Excel 2010 spreadsheets, Access 2010 databases, and other documents) by double-clicking the object's icon.

- **Display OLE Package Objects**   Enable this option to show embedded OLE objects in email messages. Hiding the objects prevents the user from opening them.

- **Add File Extensions To Block As Level 1**   Use this setting to modify the Level 1 attachment list. You can enter a list of file name extensions to add to the list.

- **Remove File Extensions Blocked As Level 1**   You can specify a list of file name extensions to remove from the Level 1 attachment list.

- **Add File Extensions To Block As Level 2**   Use this setting to modify the Level 2 attachment list. You can enter a list of file name extensions to add to the list.

- **Remove File Extensions Blocked As Level 2**   You can specify a list of file name extensions to remove from the Level 2 attachment list.

- **Prevent Users From Customizing Attachment Security Settings**   This Group Policy setting is used in earlier versions of Outlook to specify whether users can add files to (or remove files from) the Level 1 and Level 2 attachment lists that you have configured. This option overrides other settings; if it is enabled, users cannot configure the lists even if other settings would normally allow them to.

- **Allow Access To E-mail Attachments**   This setting also is for earlier versions of Outlook. You can create a list of file types that are to be removed from the default Level 1 attachment list. This is functionally equivalent to the Remove File Extensions Blocked As Level 1 setting, just for clients running previous versions of Outlook.

Custom form security settings

Several options control the actions that can be taken by scripts and controls in custom forms:

- **Allow Scripts In One-Off Outlook Forms**   Enabling this option allows scripts to be executed if the script and the form layout are contained in the message.

- **Set Outlook Object Model Custom Actions**   This setting determines the action Outlook 2013 takes if a program attempts to execute a task using the Outlook 2013 object model. For example, a virus could incorporate a script that uses the Outlook 2013 object model to reply to a message and attach itself to that message, bypassing the Outlook 2013 security safeguards. The policy setting Prompt User, which you can select from the Options drop-down list when configuring the policy, causes Outlook 2013 to prompt the user to allow or deny the action. Automatically Approve allows the program to execute the task without prompting the user. Automatically Deny prevents the program from executing the task without prompting the user. Prompt User Based On Computer Security uses the Outlook 2013 security settings.

- **Set Control ItemProperty Prompt**   This setting determines the action that Outlook 2013 takes if a user adds a control to a custom Outlook 2013 form and binds that control to any address information fields (To or From, for example). You can select Prompt User to have Outlook 2013 ask the user to allow or deny access to the address fields when the message is received, Automatically Approve to allow access without prompting the user, Automatically Deny to deny access without prompting the user, or Prompt User Based On Computer Security to use the Outlook 2013 security settings.

> **Note**
> You can control which applications can access Outlook 2013 programmatically, to send email or retrieve Outlook 2013 information, using Group Policy. For detailed information about how to do this, see the section "Enabling applications to send email with Outlook."

Configuring security using Group Policy

There are two steps involved in configuring Outlook 2013 attachment security using Group Policy. First, you configure the security settings for attachments and custom forms. Once you are satisfied with the configuration, you configure Group Policy as the method that Outlook 2013 uses to obtain security information.

> **Note**
>
> Security settings applied via Group Policy do not take effect immediately. Changes will
> be made after the computer receives a Group Policy update (usually at the next logon)
> and consequently starts Outlook 2013. Even when a computer receives refreshed Group
> Policy automatically, settings will not apply to Outlook 2013 until the next time it is
> started.

You manage Outlook 2013 attachment security using the Outlook 2013 administrative template and the Group Policy Editor.

For detailed information about using Group Policy Administrative Templates, and to access the download for the templates, go to *http://www.microsoft.com/en-us/download/details. aspx?id=35554*.

After you download the templates from the Microsoft website, run the download and extract the files to a folder. The Group Policy Administrative Templates for Office 2013 are in the XML format introduced with Windows Vista and Windows Server 2008. If you're familiar with using the previous ADM templates, note that there is a difference in how you add the templates to the Group Policy Management Editor (GPME).

To make the templates available, copy the desired .admx file (such as Outlk15.admx) from the folder where you extracted the template files to the folder *systemroot*\PolicyDefinitions. The default location is C:\Windows\PolicyDefinitions. Then, locate the corresponding .adml resource file (such as Outlk15.adml) in the appropriate language folder where you extracted the template files, and copy the file to the same language folder under *systemroot*\PolicyDefinitions.

For example, assume you extracted the template files to C:\GPTemplates and you are using U.S. English. Copy the file C:\GPTemplates\Outlk15.admx to C:\Windows\PolicyDefinitions. Then, copy C:\GPTemplates\en-us\Outlk15.adml to C:\Windows\PolicyDefinitions\en-us. The next time you open the GPME, you'll find the new Microsoft Outlook 2013 branch under User Configuration\Policies\Administrative Templates.

To configure the Outlook 2013 attachment security settings, follow these steps:

1. Open the Group Policy Management Console.

2. Browse to User Configuration\Administrative Templates\Microsoft Outlook 2013\ Security\Security Form Settings\Attachment Security.

3. Configure the settings, using the following list as a guide. The default setting is Not Configured for all items in this policy:

   ○ Enable Display Level 1 Attachments if you want to allow Outlook 2013 users to see and open Level 1 attachments, effectively setting the attachments to Level 2.

   ○ To allow Outlook 2013 users to change Level 1 attachments to Level 2, enable Allow Users To Demote Attachments To Level 2.

   ○ If you want to suppress the warning that usually appears when a Level 1 attachment is sent, enable Do Not Prompt About Level 1 Attachments When Sending An Item.

   ○ To disable the warning that normally appears when the user closes an item that contains a Level 1 attachment, enable Do Not Prompt About Level 1 Attachments When Closing An Item.

   ○ If you want to let Outlook 2013 users open embedded OLE objects (such as Microsoft Word 2013 documents, Excel 2013 spreadsheets, and other documents), enable Allow In-Place Activation Of Embedded OLE Objects.

   ○ Enable Display OLE Package Objects to show embedded OLE objects in email messages and allow users to open them.

   ○ You can block additional file types by enabling Add File Extensions To Block As Level 1. Specify a list of file name extensions, without periods and separated by semicolons (;), in the Additional Extensions field.

   ○ You can specify a list of file name extensions to remove from the Level 1 attachment list by enabling Remove File Extensions Blocked As Level 1 and entering the list in the Additional Extensions field.

   ○ To add file types to the Level 2 list, enable Add File Extensions To Block As Level 2, and then enter a list of extensions.

   ○ Enable Remove File Extensions Blocked As Level 2, and then specify a list of file name extensions to remove from the Level 2 attachment list.

To configure the Custom Form Security settings, follow these steps:

1. In Group Policy, go to User Configuration\Administrative Templates\Microsoft Outlook 2013\Security\Security Form Settings\Custom Form Security.

2. Select Allow Scripts In One-Off Outlook Forms if you want scripts to be executed when the script and the form layout are contained in the message.

Chapter 23

3. Set the Outlook object model Custom Actions execution prompt to specify the action that Outlook 2013 takes if a program attempts to execute a task using the Outlook 2013 object model. Select Prompt User to have Outlook 2013 prompt the user to allow or deny the action. Select Automatically Approve to allow the program to execute the task without prompting the user. Select Automatically Deny to prevent the program from executing the task without prompting the user. Select Prompt User Based On Computer Security to use the Outlook 2013 security settings.

4. You can select Set Control ItemProperty Prompt and then configure the action that Outlook 2013 takes if a user adds a control to a custom Outlook 2013 form and binds that control to an address information field (such as To or From). Select Prompt User to have Outlook 2013 ask the user to allow or deny access to the address fields when the message is received. Select Automatically Approve to allow access without prompting the user. Select Automatically Deny to deny access without prompting the user. Select Prompt User Based On Computer Security to use the Outlook 2013 security settings.

To configure older Outlook settings, follow these steps:

1. In Group Policy, go to User Configuration\Administrative Templates\Microsoft Outlook 2013\Security.

2. To force Outlook to use Protected View when opening attachments that were received from internal servers (for example, a message from another user of Exchange Server in the same Exchange Server environment), set the Use Protected View For Attachments Received From Internal Senders policy to Enabled.

3. If you do not want users to modify the Level 1 and Level 2 attachment lists, select Prevent Users From Customizing Attachment Security Settings.

Setting the Outlook security mode

After you have configured the Outlook 2013 security settings, you have to enable the use of those settings by enabling Exchange Server security and selecting the Outlook Security Mode. You do this using the same administrative template that you used to configure the security settings. To select the security mode for Outlook 2013, follow these steps:

1. Run Group Policy, and then open Outlk15.adm. Go to User Configuration\ Administrative Templates\Microsoft Outlook 2013\Security\Security Form Settings.

2. Double-click Outlook Security Mode, and then select Enabled. Select Use Outlook Security Group Policy from the drop-down list, and then click OK.

Configuring attachment blocking directly in Outlook

The preceding sections explained how to configure attachment blocking for Exchange Server users. Non–Exchange Server users can also control attachment blocking, although the method for modifying the attachment list is different. So if you use Outlook 2013 in a workgroup or on a stand-alone computer without Exchange Server, you can still control which attachments Outlook 2013 prevents you from opening. You simply have fewer options for controlling and applying security settings.

> **Note**
>
> If you modify the registry settings that affect the Level 1 list, you must restart Outlook 2013 for the changes to take effect.

Removing blocked file types from the Level 1 list

To change the Level 1 attachment list, you must modify a registry setting on your local computer. You can remove file types from the list as well as add them. To apply the changes across multiple computers, distribute a registry script file. You can distribute this file through a logon script, place it on a network share for users to access, or send users a message containing a shortcut to the file. (For information about how to deploy registry files using a logon script, see the Windows Server help file.)

Follow these steps to create the necessary registry settings and optionally export them as a .reg file for other users:

1. On a system with Outlook 2013 installed, choose Start, Run, and then type regedit in the Run dialog box.

2. In the Registry Editor, open the key HKEY_CURRENT_USER\Software\Microsoft\ Office\15.0\Outlook\Security.

3. In that key, type a string value named **Level1Remove**.

4. Set the value of Level1Remove to include the file name extensions of those files that you want removed from the Level 1 attachment list, without leading periods and separated by semicolons. The following example removes Microsoft Installer (.msi) files and Help (.hlp) files from the list:

   ```
   msi;hlp
   ```

5. If you want to share the customized registry with other users, choose File, Export Registry File. Select a location for the .reg file, and then click Save. You can then distribute the .reg file to the other users, as noted earlier.

Adding blocked file types to the Level 1 list

Outlook 2013 is aggressive about which attachments it blocks, but you might want to add other attachment types to the Level 1 list so that Outlook 2013 will block them. Using the same method as in the preceding procedure, add the registry value HKEY_CURRENT_USER\ Software\Microsoft\Office\15.0\Outlook\Security\Level1Add. Set the value of Level1Add to include the file name extensions that you want added to the Level 1 list. You can add multiple file types separated by semicolons. See the preceding section for options for propagating the change to other users.

Opening blocked attachments

Although it's useful to block attachments in general, there will undoubtedly still be the occasional legitimate attachment that ends up getting blocked by Outlook 2013. Fortunately, even though attachments are blocked, you can still access them using a few other approaches. The attachment file type (Level 1 or Level 2) and the other email programs available to you determine the best method for opening the file.

Allowing Level 1 attachments

You can configure Outlook 2013 to allow certain Level 1 attachments (essentially removing them from the Level 1 list) by modifying the registry. (See the section "Configuring attachment blocking directly in Outlook" for instructions.) You might want to do this if you find yourself repeatedly having to deal with the same type of blocked Level 1 attachment. If you are using Exchange Server, your ability to do this may be controlled by the administrator, as described in the section "Configuring blocked attachments."

Allowing Level 2 attachments

Outlook 2013 also uses a list of Level 2 attachments, which are defined by the administrator at the server level (and therefore apply to Exchange Server accounts). You can't open Level 2 attachments in Outlook 2013, but you can save them to disk and open them from there. To open a Level 2 attachment this way, follow these steps:

1. Right-click the attachment, either in the Reading Pane or in the message form, and choose Save As.

2. In the Save Attachment dialog box, specify the folder in which you want to save the file, and then click Save.

3. Outside Outlook 2013, browse to the folder where you saved the attachment, and then open the file.

Because the Level 2 list is empty by default, no attachments are blocked as Level 2 attachments unless the Exchange Server administrator has modified the Level 2 list.

For detailed information about configuring attachment blocking under Exchange Server, see the section "Configuring blocked attachments."

Protecting against Office macro viruses

Like other Office system applications, Outlook 2013 allows you to use macros to automate common tasks. Macros have become an increasingly popular infection mechanism for viruses because most inexperienced users don't expect to have their systems infected by the sort of Office documents they regularly work with. However, Office macros can contain viruses that cause just as much damage as any other virus. Protecting yourself against macro viruses is an important step in safeguarding your system overall.

You can guard against macro viruses by implementing a virus scanner on your computer that checks your documents for macro viruses, by installing an antivirus solution on your email servers or SharePoint farm, or by using both methods. Another line of protection is to control how and when macros are allowed to run. Outlook 2013 provides four security levels for macros that determine which macros can run on the system. To set the level in Outlook 2013, click File, Options, Trust Center, Trust Center Settings, Macro Settings, and then select one of these levels:

- **Disable All Macros Without Notification**   Macros are totally disabled, and Outlook 2013 does not display any warning that a macro is attempting to run.

- **Notifications For Digitally Signed Macros, All Other Macros Disabled**   Your system can run only macros that are digitally signed. This means that some macros— even benign and potentially useful ones—are not available.

- **Notifications For All Macros**   You will be prompted as to whether you want to run any macros.

- **Enable All Macros (Not Recommended; Potentially Dangerous Code Can Run)**   Macros run automatically, regardless of their signature. This is the most dangerous setting.

For additional information about configuring macro security and specifying trusted sources, see the section "Setting macro security" in Chapter 28, "Automating common tasks."

Chapter 23

Enabling applications to send email with Outlook

Some applications interact with Outlook 2013, most typically using the address book to address and send a message. In most cases, these applications will generate a security warning dialog box. The warning is built into Outlook 2013 to help you identify when unauthorized applications are attempting to access your Outlook 2013 data. For example, a worm that propagates itself by email would likely generate the warning.

The section "Configuring attachments in Exchange Server" explained how Exchange Server administrators can use Group Policy to configure security settings for Outlook 2013 users. That section covered how to configure attachment blocking. You can also use Group Policy to configure the behavior of specific types of applications in relation to the security features in Outlook 2013, as well as specify dynamic-link libraries (DLLs) that should be explicitly trusted and allowed to run without generating a security warning.

If you have not already configured Group Policy to manage security settings, see the section "Configuring attachments in Exchange Server."

Configuring programmatic access

Just as with the other security settings that can be configured in Exchange Server, you can control programmatic access to Outlook 2013 via either Group Policy or the Exchange Security Form.

Configuring programmatic access using Group Policy

To configure the settings that determine how Outlook 2013 security features handle various types of applications, follow these steps:

1. Run Group Policy, and then go to User Configuration\Administrative Templates\ Microsoft Outlook 2013\Security\Security Form Settings\Programmatic Security.

2. Configure the Outlook 2013 object model–related settings as desired. Each of these policy items has the same Guard behavior options. Select Prompt User to have Outlook 2013 prompt the user to allow or deny the action. Select Automatically Approve to allow the program to execute the task without prompting the user. Select Automatically Deny to prevent the program from executing the task without prompting the user. Select Prompt User Based On Computer Security to use the following Outlook 2013 security settings:

○ **Configure Outlook Object Model Prompt When Sending Mail**   Specifies the action that Outlook 2013 takes when an application tries to send mail programmatically with the Outlook 2013 object model.

○ **Configure Outlook Object Model Prompt When Accessing An Address Book**   Specifies the action that Outlook 2013 takes when an application tries to access an address book with the Outlook 2013 object model.

○ **Configure Outlook Object Model Prompt When Reading Address Information**   Specifies the action that Outlook 2013 takes when an application tries to access a recipient field, such as To or Cc, with the Outlook 2013 object model.

○ **Configure Outlook Object Model Prompt When Responding To Meeting And Task Requests**   Specifies the action that Outlook 2013 takes when an application tries to send mail programmatically by using the Respond method on task and meeting requests.

○ **Configure Outlook Object Model Prompt When Executing Save As**   Specifies the action that Outlook 2013 takes when an application tries to use the Save As command programmatically to save an item.

○ **Configure Outlook Object Model Prompt When Accessing The Formula Property Of A UserProperty Object**   Specifies the action that Outlook 2013 takes if a user has added a Combination or Formula custom field to a custom form and bound it to an Address Information field. Blocking access can prevent an application from indirectly retrieving the value of the Address Information field through its Value property.

3. When you have finished configuring programmatic settings, close Group Policy.

Part of the battle of getting an application past the Outlook 2013 security prompts is in understanding what method it is using to access your Outlook 2013 data. If you're not sure, you can simply change one setting, test, and if the change doesn't enable the application to bypass the security prompts, change a different setting. This trial-and-error method isn't the most direct, but it won't take much time to test each of the possibilities. Remember that you must refresh Group Policy and then start Outlook 2013 for these changes to be applied.

Chapter 23

Tips for securing your system

As you have seen, Outlook 2013 has several ways to help keep your system more secure, but there are additional steps you can take to further ensure that you don't fall victim to viruses or other malicious software.

- **Make sure that your antivirus protection is kept up to date** The threat from viruses changes on a daily basis, and virus definitions need updating just about as quickly. Set your antivirus software to check for updates automatically, and check it occasionally to make sure that it's doing so.

- **Create exceptions to the standard rules with discretion** Although there are several ways around the virus protection measures provided in Outlook 2013, you should be careful deciding when you use them. Just because you can demote all Level 1 attachments to Level 2 to get past the Outlook 2013 built-in filtering doesn't mean you should.

- **Get in the habit of storing attachment files in an archive, such as a compressed (zipped) folder, created using Windows Explorer (or a program such as WinZip) before sending** Since files with a .zip extension are not blocked by Outlook 2013, you can be sure that your attachment will arrive (unless the recipient server blocks it), allowing the recipient to save it and extract the contents.

If you have access to a location where you can upload files, such as a file server or a SharePoint site, upload your files there and send email with a link to the site rather than sending the file as an attachment. This method has advantages beyond avoiding unwanted attachment blocking: Mail files are smaller without large attachments, for example, and multiple people can download a file from a single location. Plus, you don't duplicate the file for multiple recipients, which adds to your storage requirements.

When it comes to computer security, a little common sense goes a long way. Pay attention to what you do in email. Don't open unexpected attachments or those from unknown sources.

Archiving and backing up your data

O VER time, your Microsoft Outlook 2013 data store can become overloaded with messages, contact information, appointments, and other data. If you can't manage all this data, you'll be lost each time you try to find a particular item. What's more, the more data in your data store, the larger your .pst file (if you're using one) or your Microsoft Exchange Server mailbox. Many companies impose mailbox size limits to help manage disk use on the servers, so the size of your mailbox can become a problem.

This chapter focuses on managing your Outlook 2013 folders and their contents. You'll learn how to archive your data, both manually and automatically, using AutoArchive. You'll also learn how to back up your data and recover it when needed.

Archiving items

Sooner or later, you will likely want to move some of your Outlook 2013 items to a separate location because you no longer need them but don't want to delete them. For example, perhaps you want to keep copies of all the messages in your Sent Items folder so that you can refer to them later if needed, but you don't want them to stay in Sent Items. In these situations, you can use the Outlook 2013 AutoArchive feature to move out those old items.

The Outlook 2013 AutoArchive feature archives data automatically according to settings that you configure for each folder or all your folders. There is no right or wrong time frame for AutoArchive; for some people, monthly is appropriate, and for others, weekly. It's mainly a factor of how much email you send and receive, although the other items in your mailbox also contribute to the overall space used.

> **Note**
>
> If your company uses Exchange Server, a better solution to users archiving their mailbox to a local .pst (which has negative security and backup implications) is to use a server-side archiving solution. Exchange Server 2013 includes an online archive option, which moves messages to a user's archive mailbox on the server based on retention criteria that you set. Or, you can choose a solution such as those from Barracuda, Mimosa Systems, GFI, and others. These archiving solutions not only help users keep their mailboxes trimmed down, but also can eliminate duplicate attachments, reduce storage requirements for Exchange Server, and facilitate discovery.

To set up a folder to archive automatically using the default AutoArchive settings, follow these steps:

1. Right-click a folder in the Folder List, choose Properties, and then, in the Properties dialog box, click the AutoArchive tab.

2. Select Archive Items In This Folder Using The Default Settings, as shown in Figure 24-1.

Figure 24-1 Use the AutoArchive feature to archive the data in your folders.

   3.   Click OK.

   4.   Repeat these steps for each folder that you want to archive.

By default, Outlook 2013 starts AutoArchive every 14 days and archives your data in the selected folder to the Archive.pst personal folders file.

For information about changing the default AutoArchive settings, see the section "Configuring automatic archiving."

You can also specify custom AutoArchive settings for a folder. Open the Properties dialog box for the folder, click the AutoArchive tab, and then select the Archive This Folder Using These Settings option. Then specify settings on the AutoArchive tab as desired for the folder. See the section "Configuring automatic archiving" for details about each of the available settings.

From this point on, the folder for which you have enabled automatic archiving will be archived when Outlook 2013 performs its next automatic archive operation. However, you can also initiate an archive operation any time you need. The next section explains how.

Archiving your data manually

You can archive data not only automatically but also manually—for example, before leaving on vacation, when your mailbox reaches its storage limit, or when you need to move your files to a new machine.

To archive data manually, perform these steps:

   1.   Choose File, Cleanup Tools, Archive.

   2.   In the Archive dialog box, shown in Figure 24-2, select one of the following options:

   ○   **Archive All Folders According To Their AutoArchive Settings**   Use this option to archive all folders using preset AutoArchive settings. When you select this option, the remaining options in this dialog box become unavailable. Go to step 7.

   ○   **Archive This Folder And All Subfolders**   Select this option if you want to archive individual folders and their subfolders. Go to step 3.

Chapter 24

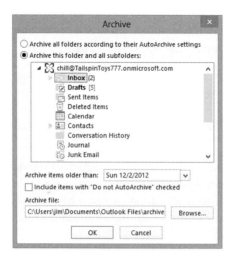

Figure 24-2 Select the way that you want to archive data in all or selected folders.

3. Select the folder you want to archive. If the folder includes subfolders, those folders are archived as well.

4. In the Archive Items Older Than drop-down list, specify the latest date from which Outlook 2013 should start archiving data. For instance, if you want to archive data older than today's date, select that date. Otherwise, all your data in the selected folder will not be archived.

5. If you have specified that items in a folder should not be archived automatically but you want to archive these items now, select the Include Items With "Do Not AutoArchive" Checked check box.

6. To change the personal folders file that will store your archive, click Browse, and then specify the file and folder where the archive will be stored. You also can type the path and file name in the Archive File box if you know this information.

7. Click OK.

Outlook 2013 begins archiving your data. If the folder contains a large amount of data, archiving might take several minutes (or longer, depending on the speed of your computer, network connection, and other factors). You can watch the status of the archiving by looking at the Outlook 2013 status bar. When the process has finished, the Archive.pst file (or whichever archive file that you specified in step 6) will contain the data that Outlook 2013 just archived.

Restoring data after a system failure or a reinstallation

Suppose that you've worked on a project for six months and you've been diligent about archiving messages and other items from the project. You come into work one day and find that your system has failed and all your data is lost. You need the archived data to get back all your lost information and continue working. How do you get it back?

You can restore data from an archive file in two ways: drag items from a .pst file to a folder, or import a .pst file.

Follow these steps to drag data from a .pst file:

1. After restoring your computer and, if necessary, reinstalling Outlook 2013, choose File, Open & Export, Open Outlook Data File to open the Open Outlook Data File dialog box, shown in Figure 24-3.

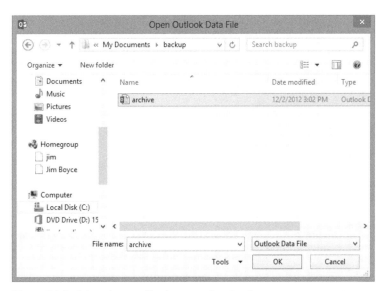

Figure 24-3 Select the .pst file that contains the data you want to restore.

2. Select the file that contains the archived items that you want to restore.

3. Click OK. The archive folder (named Archives by default) now appears in your folder list.

4. Click the plus sign (+) next to Archives (or the name you've given this folder) to expand the folder. Expand subsequent folders if necessary until your data is in the pane on the right.

5. Drag the folder or item to the original folder in which the data was stored.

6. Continue dragging items until all of them are restored. To drag multiple items at one time, hold down the Ctrl key, select the items, and then drag them to the destination.

To restore items by importing a .pst file, follow these steps:

1. Choose File, Open, Import to open the Import And Export Wizard.

2. Select Import From Another Program Or File, and then click Next.

3. Select Outlook Data File (.pst), and then click Next.

4. On the Import Outlook Data File page, shown in Figure 24-4, type the name of the file that you want to import in the File To Import box or click Browse to locate the file using the Open Personal Folders dialog box.

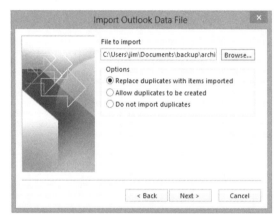

Figure 24-4 On the Import Outlook Data File page, specify the name of the file that you want to import.

5. Select one of the following import options pertaining to duplicate data:

   ○ **Replace Duplicates With Items Imported** This option has Outlook replace duplicate items that might be in your folders during import.

   ○ **Allow Duplicates To Be Created** This option lets Outlook 2013 create duplicates in the destination folders.

   ○ **Do Not Import Duplicates** Outlook 2013 will not create duplicate items.

6. Click Next.

7. Select the folder from which you want to import data.

8. If the archived folder includes subfolders that you want to import as well, select the Include Subfolders option.

9. To filter data, click Filter. You can filter by using search strings, Structured Query Language (SQL), and other advanced querying methods. Click OK after filling in your filter information.

10. Select one of the following destination options:

    ○ **Import Items Into The Current Folder**   Select this option to import data into the current folder—that is, the folder currently selected.

    ○ **Import Items Into The Same Folder In**   Choose this option to import data into the destination folder with the same name as the source folder (such as from the Inbox to the Inbox). Then, in the drop-down list under this last option, select the destination personal folders or mailbox.

11. Click Finish.

Outlook 2013 displays a window showing you the progress of the import process. The archive folder appears in the folder list (if the folder list is open), but it is removed when the operation is completed.

Configuring automatic archiving

Outlook 2013 provides several ways to configure and manage your data-archiving settings. For example, suppose that you want Outlook 2013 to run AutoArchive every day, but you want to be prompted before it starts. You can configure AutoArchive to do just that. In addition, you might want to delete old items after a specific date (say, after a message sits in the Inbox for six months). This section shows you how to configure AutoArchive to handle many of your archiving needs.

To set AutoArchive options, click File, Options, Advanced, and then click AutoArchive Settings to open the AutoArchive dialog box. The following sections explain the options that you'll find in the AutoArchive dialog box.

Run AutoArchive Every n Days

Outlook 2013 allows you to run AutoArchive on a per-day cycle. For example, if you want to run it each day, set it to run every 1 day. To archive every other day, set AutoArchive to run every 2 days, and so on.

Chapter 24

> **Note**
> Outlook 2013 has different aging periods for different types of items. Calendar, Notes, Drafts, and Inbox folders have a default of six months. The default for the Outbox folder is three months, and the default for Sent Items and Deleted Items is two months. Contacts folders do not have an AutoArchive option, so you must archive them manually.

To set the length of time between AutoArchive sessions, set the Run AutoArchive Every n Days option to the number of days you want between archiving sessions, as shown in Figure 24-5. The number that you enter must be between 1 and 60.

Figure 24-5 Set up Outlook 2013 to run AutoArchive at specified intervals.

Prompt Before AutoArchive Runs

You can have Outlook 2013 display a message before it starts an AutoArchive session. The message includes a Cancel button to let you cancel the AutoArchive session for that day.

To activate this option, select the Prompt Before AutoArchive Runs check box in the AutoArchive dialog box.

Delete Expired Items

In your message folders, AutoArchive can delete messages if they are older than a specified amount of time. To set this option, select the Delete Expired Items check box. Also make sure that the Archive Or Delete Old Items check box is selected.

In the Default Folder Settings For Archiving area, set the amount of time that you want to elapse before AutoArchive automatically deletes email messages. The default is 6 months, but you can set this to as high as 60 months or as low as 1 day.

Archive Or Delete Old Items

If you want AutoArchive to archive or delete old Outlook 2013 items, select the Archive Or Delete Old Items check box. Then set the amount of time that should elapse before old items are archived or deleted. Again, the default is 6 months, but you can set this to as high as 60 months or as low as 1 day.

> ### Note
> Archiving is based on an item's modified date, not the received date. For example, assume that you have an Outlook add-in that saves your attachments automatically to disk. When the add-in moves the attachment, it causes the Outlook item to be modified. If you run the add-in today on a message that you received a week ago, and then tell Outlook to archive items older than yesterday, that item will not be archived because it was modified today by the add-in.

Show Archive Folder In Folder List

If you want Outlook 2013 to display your archive folder in the Folder List, select the Show Archive Folder In Folder List check box. You might want to select this check box if you think you'd like to be able to see which items have been archived. Also, you might find that some items are removed from your working folders (such as Inbox or Calendar) before you want them removed. By showing the archive folder in the Folder List, you can move items back to a working folder quickly and easily.

Specifying how archived items are handled

In the Default Folder Settings For Archiving area, you can specify the number of days, weeks, or months that should elapse before email messages or other items are archived or deleted (as described in the preceding two sections).

In addition, this area includes options for the way old items are handled. With the Move Old Items To option, you can specify a .pst file to which Outlook 2013 should move archived items. Click Browse to identify a different location and the .pst file in which you want to store archives.

On the other hand, if you want to delete archived items, select Permanently Delete Old Items, and Outlook 2013 will delete items during the AutoArchive sessions. This option is probably not a good choice if you want to retain information for long periods of time.

Applying settings to all folders

If you want these AutoArchive settings to apply to all your folders, click Apply These Settings To All Folders Now. Any settings you establish for individual folders (see the next section) are not overridden by the default settings in the AutoArchive dialog box.

Using AutoArchive settings for individual folders

When you configure AutoArchive settings, you can use the default settings just described, or you can specify options for individual folders.

To take the latter approach, open the Properties dialog box for the folder, click the AutoArchive tab, and then click Archive This Folder Using These Settings. Then set the following options:

- **Do Not Archive Items In This Folder**   Select this option to specify that the current folder should not be archived.

- **Archive Items In This Folder Using The Default Settings**   Select this option to specify that the current folder should be archived using the default settings specified for the folder.

- **Archive This Folder Using These Settings**   This option directs Outlook 2013 to archive items in the folder based on the custom settings that you specify.

- **Clean Out Items Older Than n**   This option lets you specify the number of days, weeks, or months that should pass before AutoArchive removes items in the selected folder.

- **Move Old Items To Default Archive Folder**   You can have Outlook 2013 move old items to the folder specified for default AutoArchive settings.

- **Move Old Items To**   This option lets you specify a .pst file in which to archive old items. Click Browse to locate a file.

- **Permanently Delete Old Items**   You can direct Outlook 2013 to delete items in this folder during archiving.

Setting retention policy

Your system administrator might enforce company retention policies for your mailbox. If you are running Outlook 2013 with Exchange Server, your administrator can set retention polices that you can't override with AutoArchive settings. For example, your company might require that all email messages be saved and archived to backup tapes or disks and then retained for seven years. You can't change these settings without having the appropriate permissions.

Backing up your Outlook data

An important part of working with a computer system is ensuring that you protect any critical data against loss. You protect your data by making a backup, a copy of the information that you can store on another disk or on a backup tape. In the event of a critical failure, you can then use this copy to replace or restore any lost information.

Outlook 2013 stores information in two primary ways: in a set of personal folders or in an Exchange Server mailbox. With an Exchange Server mailbox, your message store is located on the server. The Exchange administrator is generally responsible for backing up the server, and with it, the Exchange Server data store that contains all the users' information.

If you don't use Exchange Server, Outlook 2013 stores your data in a .pst file, a set of personal folders. In this scenario, each user has his or her own .pst file or even multiple personal folder files. These .pst files can be located either on the local hard disk of your computer or in a home directory on the server. Although server-based .pst files and local .pst files are identical from a functional standpoint, they aren't identical from a backup perspective. Generally, the network administrator regularly backs up server-based user home directories, so if the .pst files are in your home directory, you shouldn't have to do backups on your own (although you can, of course).

With local message stores, however, normal network backup strategies do not apply. Most network administrators don't back up every hard disk on every machine. It simply isn't efficient. Similarly, if you're a home user, you probably don't have a server to which you can save data or a network administrator to watch over the server. In such cases, you need to take steps on your own to protect your data. Individual backup and restore scenarios apply to these kinds of cases.

Chapter 24

Backing up your Outlook data

Three primary options are available for backing up Outlook 2013 data:

- Exporting some or all information to a backup .pst file

- Copying the .pst file to another disk

- Using a backup program to save a copy of the .pst file to tape, another hard disk, or optical media such as CD-R/CD-RW or DVD-R/DVD-RW

Table 24-1 lists the features available in each backup option.

TABLE 24-1 Backup options in Outlook 2013

Backup type	Export	Copy	Backup
Complete backup	Yes	Yes	Yes
Partial backup	Yes	No	No
Automated backup	No	Yes	Yes

The following sections focus on the use of backup programs and .pst copies.

Backing up your personal folders

If you store your Outlook 2013 data in one or more sets of personal folders, the data resides in a .pst file. This file is usually located on your local hard disk, but it could also be stored on a shared network folder. The first step in backing up your personal folders is to determine where the .pst file is located.

If you are not sure whether you use an Exchange Server account, follow these steps to check your email settings:

1. Click the Mail icon in Control Panel.

2. In the Mail Setup dialog box, click Show Profiles, choose your profile, and then click Properties. Then click E-mail Accounts to open the E-mail Accounts dialog box.

If the E-mail Accounts list includes only Exchange Server, your Outlook 2013 data is stored in your Exchange Server mailbox on the server, and your Exchange Server administrator handles backups. However, you can export your data to an archive .pst to back up your mailbox locally.

If the E-mail Accounts list shows more than one email account, it's possible that your Outlook 2013 data is stored in more than one set of personal folders. For example, Internet Message Access Protocol (IMAP) and Hotmail/Live accounts store their data in their own .pst files. If you want to back up everything in this situation, you need to back up multiple .pst files.

To determine whether you are using more than one .pst file, click the Data Files tab of the Account Settings dialog box, shown in Figure 24-6. The path name and file name for the .pst are generally long, so it's unlikely that you'll be able to read the full name. Click the vertical bar at the right of the Location column and drag it to the right until you can view the entire path. Alternatively, simply click Open File Location, which opens the folder where the .pst file is stored and highlights the .pst file in the folder.

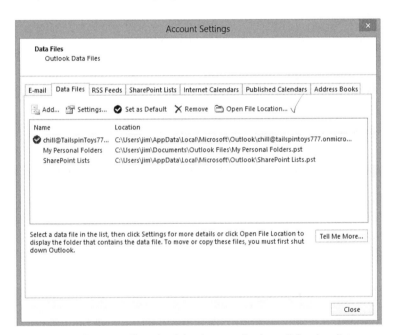

Figure 24-6 The Data Files tab of the Account Settings dialog box lists message stores in use.

After you have verified that the message store is not being backed up elsewhere and is stored in a .pst file, you need to choose which kind of backup to do. Both of the following methods work well, and each has its advantages. Back up each of the .pst files listed in the Data Files tab of the Account Settings dialog box using one of these methods.

Chapter 24

Backing up using file copy

Personal folders or archive files can be extremely large—often hundreds of megabytes or more—so you need to make sure that your backup method can accommodate the size of your .pst file(s). Any of the following options would be acceptable to use with a file backup method:

- Recordable (CD-R) or rewritable (CD-RW) CD drive

- Recordable (DVD-R) or rewritable (DVD-RW) DVD drive

- Flash drive or external universal serial bus (USB) drive

- Network server drive

- Drive on another computer on the network

- Separate hard disk in the machine where the .pst file is stored

INSIDE OUT   Check network backup policies

Be certain to check with your network administrator about the recommended policy for backing up .pst files in your organization. If, for example, .pst files are not allowed on your network because of resource allocation, you'll want to know this and choose another backup method rather than copying your .pst file to the network only to find it deleted the next week. Remember that whatever the merits of a particular backup method, it's critical that your IT staff support it.

If you are saving to a CD or DVD, you can probably use the software that was included with the drive to copy the file. If you're using a flash drive, USB drive, or a network location, simply drag the file to your chosen backup location. Just make sure to exit Outlook 2013 before starting the backup copy process.

INSIDE OUT   Don't move the .pst file

When copying, be careful not to move the .pst file instead by accident. If you move it, you'll find that you have no message store when you restart Outlook 2013. If you do move your .pst file accidentally, you simply need to copy the file back to the correct location. To avoid this potential problem, automate the copy.

Backing up using the Windows backup capability

Microsoft Windows 7 and Windows 8 both include backup capabilities that you can use to identify files for archiving. They offer the following enhancements over a standard file copy:

- Simple setup of a backup plan by using wizards

- Options for verifying the backup

- Built-in restore and scheduling options

In Windows 7, you'll find the Backup and Restore functions in Control Panel under the System And Security category. In Windows 8, you have two backup options. The Windows 7 File Recovery item in Control Panel lets you start and configure Windows Backup, where you can specify the backup location, which folders to back up, and so on. Windows 8 also provides a new backup feature called File History that builds on the Volume Shadow Copy feature that was first introduced in Windows Server 2003. File History is essentially a remake of the Previous Versions feature in Windows 7.

File History by default backs up your libraries, desktop, contacts (in the Windows Contacts folder, not Outlook), and favorites. So, as long as your .pst file(s) are located in a folder that isn't excluded from the list, they'll be backed up if you enable File History.

If you aren't familiar with either the Windows 7 or Windows 8 backup features, take some time to investigate and learn how they work. Both provide an acceptable backup strategy for your Outlook data.

Restoring your data

Anyone who works with computers long enough will eventually experience a critical error. A drive will become corrupted, a virus will get through your virus software's protection, or you'll accidentally delete something that you need. This is the point when all the time and trouble you've invested in backing up your data will pay dividends.

Depending on how you created your backup file, you will have one of two options: You can simply recopy your backup .pst file from the backup location where you copied it, or you can run the backup utility and use the Restore function to bring back the missing file or files. From there, you can select the backup file that contains the .pst file and then determine which files to restore and where to put them.

Chapter 24

> **Note**
>
> By default, the backup utility restores a file to its original location. This is generally the best choice because if the .pst file isn't restored to the proper location, Outlook 2013 won't be able to find it.

Whichever method you use, be certain to check the drive carefully for errors and viruses before you restore your data. You don't want to restore the file only to see it destroyed again a few hours later.

INSIDE OUT   Familiarize yourself with the restore process

It's important to be familiar with the restore process before a disaster recovery process is under way. You should occasionally try restoring your backed-up .pst file to another computer to verify that your backups work. This will help to ensure that the restore process will work and that you know how to perform the necessary tasks.

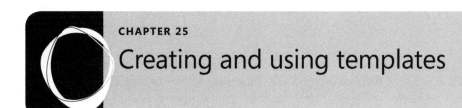

Creating and using templates

I F you use Microsoft Word frequently, you're probably familiar with templates. These useful tools can help you quickly and easily create documents that share standard elements—for example, boilerplate text, special font and paragraph formatting, and paragraph styles.

You can also use templates in Microsoft Outlook 2013 to streamline a variety of tasks. There is nothing magical about these templates; they are simply Outlook 2013 items that you use to create other Outlook 2013 items. For example, you might create an email template for preparing a weekly status report that you send to your staff or management. Perhaps you use email messages to submit expense reports and would like to use a template to simplify the process.

This chapter not only discusses email templates but also explores the use of templates for other Outlook 2013 items. For example, you'll learn how to use templates to create appointments, contact entries, task requests, and journal entries. The chapter also suggests some ways of sharing templates with others.

Working with email templates

An email template is really nothing more than a standard email message that you have saved as a template. Here are some suggested uses for email templates:

- Create an expense report form.

- Send product information to potential clients.

- Create status reports for ongoing projects.

- Send messages to specific groups of recipients.

- Create a form for information requests or product registration.

When you need to send similar messages on a regular basis, creating a message template can save you quite a bit of time, particularly if the message contains a great deal of frequently used text, graphics, or form elements. You also reduce potential errors by reusing the same message each time rather than creating multiple messages from scratch. You can use the template to provide the bulk of the message, filling in any additional information required in each particular instance.

Creating an email template

Creating an email template is as easy as creating an email message. You can start by opening a new message form, just as you would if you were sending a new message to a single recipient or group.

To create an email template from scratch, follow these steps:

1. With the Inbox folder open, click the New E-mail button on the toolbar to open a new mail message form. Enter the boilerplate text and any information that you want to include every time you send a message based on this template. For example, you can specify the subject, address, other headings, bullets, lists, and tables.

2. Click File, and then click Save As in the message form.

3. In the Save As dialog box, shown in Figure 25-1, specify a name for the file. Select Outlook Template (*.oft) in the Save As Type drop-down list. Outlook 2013 adds an .oft extension to the file name. You can specify a path if you want to save the file in a different location.

    The default location for user templates is the *<profile>*\AppData\Roaming\Microsoft\ Templates folder, where *<profile>* is your user profile folder. When you select Outlook Template as the file type, Outlook 2013 automatically switches to your Templates folder.

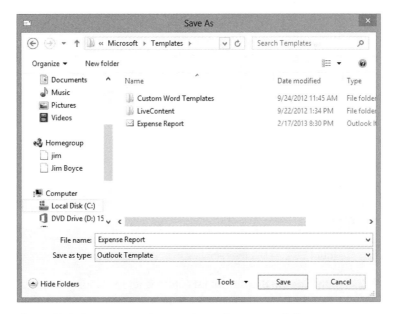

Figure 25-1 Save your newly created template as an .oft file.

4. Click Save to save the template. Close the message form, and then click No when asked whether you want to save the changes.

You can create as many email templates as you need, storing them on your local hard disk or on a network server. Placing templates on a network server allows other Outlook users to use them as well.

Using an email template

After you create an email template, it's a simple matter to use the template to create a message by following these steps:

1. In Outlook 2013, click New Items on the Home tab on the ribbon, and then click More Items, Choose Form. Outlook 2013 opens the Choose Form dialog box, as shown in Figure 25-2.

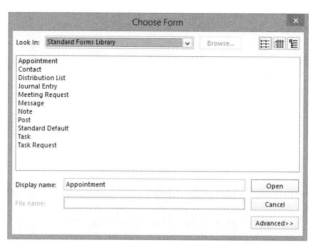

Figure 25-2 Select the template in the Choose Form dialog box.

2.   In the Look In drop-down list (which is set to Standard Forms Library by default), select the location where the template is stored. In this example, the template is stored in the user default template folder. To use this template, select User Templates In File System.

3.   Select the template from the list, and then click Open to display a message form based on the template data.

4.   Fill in the message form to include any additional or modified information, and then send the message as you would any other.

Using a template with a contact group

You can easily send messages to recipients in a contact group without using a template: Simply start a new message, select the contact group from the address book, and send the message. If the messages you send to the members of the list are different each time you use the list, you don't need a template. However, if the messages contain much the same information time after time, they're good candidates for templates. For example, you might need to submit weekly reports to a group of administrators or managers, send task lists to people who work for you, or broadcast regular updates about products or services.

You create a template for a contact group the same way that you create any other email template. The only difference is that you store the list of recipients within the template. To do so, simply select the contact group in the appropriate address box when you create the template. If you don't want the various members of the group to see the addresses of other members on the list, be sure to insert the distribution group in the Bcc box rather than in the To or Cc box.

For more information about working with contact groups, see Chapter 13, "Managing address books and contact groups."

Using other Outlook template types

Email messages are not the only Outlook 2013 item that you can create from a template. In fact, you can create a template for any type of Outlook 2013 item. This section of the chapter explores some common situations in which you might use specific types of templates.

Appointments and meetings

You might find it useful to create templates for setting up certain types of appointments and meetings. If you prefer to use a set of appointment properties that differ from the Outlook 2013 default properties, you can use a template that contains your preferred settings and then create each new appointment or meeting from that template. For example, if you have regular meetings with the same group of people, you can set up a template in which those individuals are already selected on the Scheduling page so that you don't have to assemble the list each time you schedule a meeting. Perhaps you prefer to have Outlook 2013 issue a reminder an hour before each appointment rather than the default of 15 minutes.

You can create templates for appointments and meetings the same way you create email templates. Open a new appointment form or meeting request, and then fill in all the data that will be standard each time you use the template. Then click File, Save As, and save the file as an Outlook Template. When you want to use the template, click New Items, More Items, Choose Form, and then follow the steps outlined in the section "Using an email template."

For more information about using appointment forms and their settings, see Chapter 16, "Scheduling appointments." For details about meeting requests, see Chapter 17, "Scheduling meetings, rooms, and resources."

Contacts

In your Contacts folder, you're likely to add contact entries for people who work in or belong to the same organization, business, department, or other entity. These contacts might share the same company name, address, or primary phone number. In such a case, why not create a template to save yourself the trouble of entering the information for each contact entry separately (and potentially getting it wrong)? Why not create a template that specifies the information, eliminating the chore of setting it each time you create a new contact?

As with other templates, you create a contact template by opening a new contact form and filling in the standard data. Then click File, Save As, and save the contact as an Outlook Template.

For more information about creating contact entries and working in the Contacts folder, see Chapter 14, "Working with contacts."

INSIDE OUT   Create contacts from the same company

You can create contact entries that share common company information by selecting a contact item and clicking New Items, Contact From Same Company. However, this might not give you the results you need in all cases. For example, the Contact From Same Company command uses the same address, company name, main business phone number, business fax number, and webpage address for the new contact as for the selected one. If you also want to use the same directory server, categories, notes, or other properties for the new contacts, it's best to create a contact entry, save it as a template, and then create other contact entries from the template.

Tasks and task requests

If you perform the same task frequently, you can create a basic task as a template and then modify it as needed for each occurrence of the task. You also can create a task template with a specific set of properties and then use it to create various tasks. For example, you could create all your tasks with the status specified as In Progress rather than the default Not Started, or perhaps you need to create many tasks with the same set of categories assigned to them.

In addition to creating task items from templates, you might want to use templates to create task requests. A task request template is handy if you manage a group of people to whom you need to assign similar or identical tasks. Set up a template that incorporates the common elements, and then create each task request from the template, filling in or modifying the unique elements and addressing the request to the specific person assigned to the task.

You use the same methods described earlier for email templates to create and open templates for tasks and task requests.

For more information about creating tasks and task requests, see Chapter 18, "Working with tasks."

Editing templates

Outlook 2013 stores templates as .oft files when you save them to disk. You can modify any template to make changes as needed.

To modify a template, follow these steps:

1. Click New Items, More Items, Choose Form.

2. Outlook 2013 displays the Choose Form dialog box (shown in Figure 25-2). In the Look In drop-down list, select the location where the template is stored.

3. Select the template, and then click Open.

4. Make changes as needed, and then choose Save & Close (or click File and then click Save) to save the changes.

> **Note**
> To find templates that you've created so that you can edit them, choose User Templates In File System from the Look In drop-down list in the Choose Form dialog box, and then browse to the folder where you saved the template.

Sharing templates

In some situations, you might find it useful to share templates with other users. For example, assume that you're responsible for managing several people who all submit the same type of report to you on a regular basis through email. In that situation, you might create an email template with the appropriate boilerplate information and your address in the To box and then have the staff use that template to generate the reports. This ensures that everyone is providing comparable information. In addition, whenever you need a different set of data from these employees, you need only modify the template or create a new one from it.

The easiest way to find the location where Outlook 2013 stores your templates is to save a template, or at least go through the motions of saving it. Open a form, click File, Save As, and then select Outlook Templates. Outlook 2013 displays the path to the folder.

Why do you need to know where Outlook 2013 stores your templates? To share a template, you need to share the template file. This means placing the template in a shared network folder, sharing your template folder, or sending the template file to other users (the least desirable option). For any of these options, you need to know the location of the template file that you want to share. After you locate the file, you can share the folder that contains it, copy the template to a network share, or forward it to other users as an attachment.

INSIDE OUT   Share a template using a network share

Probably the best option for sharing a template is to place it either on a network share or in a SharePoint document library. Set permissions on the share or library to control which users have the ability to edit the template.

Using templates effectively

The ability to use templates for Outlook 2013 email, meetings, appointments, tasks, and even journal entries provides you with the means to implement shortcuts in creating new items. Consider how much of your work involves repeatedly sending out email messages, meeting requests, and so on that have essentially the same information structure even though the details differ from day to day. Here are some guidelines for using templates:

- **Look at items you use repeatedly and create templates for them**   Imagine if every time you found yourself creating meetings, tasks, or email messages that contained common, repeated elements, instead of simply creating yet another individual meeting invitation (with your latest agenda and required materials), you created a template with only the common elements (meeting topic, agenda list, required materials, and meeting goals). Within a short time, you would have a catalog of templates available that corresponded to your specific Outlook 2013 items. Then when you needed to schedule such a meeting, you could use the template to shortcut the process of producing the meeting request. Examples could include the following:

  ○ Meeting templates for team meetings, general department meetings, budget meetings, and project meetings (a different one for each project)

  ○ Email templates for regular team notices (work schedules, weekly meetings, team building, and so on), travel or expense report submissions, project-related updates (a different one for each project), responses to information requests, and client/customer communications (a different one for each client)

  ○ Appointment templates for phone conferences, job interviews, client interviews, and off-site sales presentations

  ○ Task templates for weekly reports, weekly and monthly to-do lists, project tasks (a different template for each project), and quarterly and annual reports

Your own uses of templates will exceed and differ from those in the preceding list, and yet you can see how the use of templates can speed up many Outlook 2013 operations that you perform repeatedly.

- **Share your templates with others in your organization**   Each organization has many people who perform similar (if not the same) activities, tasks, and operations. Thus, it is likely that templates that you create to facilitate your own work will also be useful to your coworkers. Every team in your organization, for example, has (at least structurally) similar weekly/monthly status reports, and many employees have the same annual/semiannual review reporting requirements. As you create templates to ease your workflow, assess and identify the other people or groups within your organization that could benefit from each template (or a closely related derivation).

- **Store templates where they are easily accessible**   After you have created templates that are useful to other people in your organization, you need to store the templates in a location that is accessible to everyone who could use them. The default location for templates on your system is not the best place to share them from because your system might not be online at all times that others need access to the templates. You also might have templates in the default folder that you don't actually want to share.

Customizing the Outlook interface

MICROSOFT Outlook 2013 has an easy-to-use yet powerful interface that serves most users well right out of the box. However, you probably perform certain tasks that are not readily available through the standard Outlook 2013 interface. For example, perhaps you have a handful of macros you use often and you want quick access to them.

As all Microsoft Office 2013 applications do, Outlook 2013 provides a way to tailor the interface to your needs. You can customize the Folder Pane to add your own shortcuts, customize the To-Do Bar, customize the Outlook Today view and other standard views, customize the ribbon and Quick Access Toolbar, and customize the way Outlook 2013 displays your folders. You can also create custom views for each Outlook folder.

This chapter focuses on the various ways that you can fine-tune Outlook 2013 to the way you work. Some of the changes covered are minor; others are more significant. All of them can enhance your experience with Outlook 2013 and make it a more useful tool for bringing efficiency to your workday.

Customizing the Folder Pane

Most people browse through Outlook 2013 folders using the Folder Pane. This section explains how you can customize the Folder Pane to suit your preferences.

A quick tour of the Folder Pane

The Folder Pane, which appears on the left side of the Outlook 2013 window, was first introduced in Outlook 2003 to replace the Outlook Bar, which was a staple of the Outlook interface prior to Outlook 2003. From Outlook 2003 through Outlook 2010, the Folder Pane was called the Navigation Pane. Functionally, the Folder Pane is nearly identical to the Navigation Pane. The Folder Pane gives you quick access to all your Outlook 2013 folders. Outlook 2013 gives you the capability to minimize the Folder Pane to gain more window space for the current folder view but still open the Folder Pane quickly when you need it.

The Folder Pane contains buttons that serve as shortcuts to your Outlook 2013 folders, as shown in Figure 26-1. The Folder Pane also includes shortcuts to a few common items, including the Outlook Today view and the Microsoft Office Online website. You can access these shortcuts by clicking the Shortcuts icon in the Folder Pane.

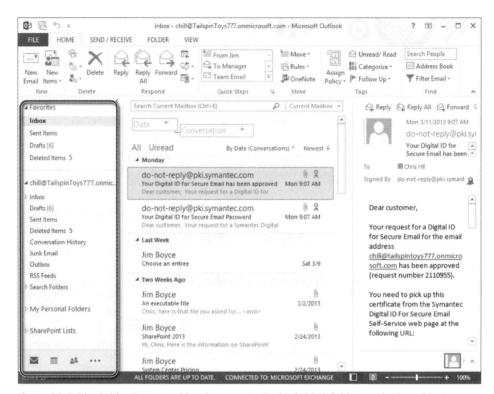

Figure 26-1 The Folder Pane provides shortcuts to Outlook 2013 folders and other objects.

You can make several changes to the Folder Pane, including adding and removing groups, adding and removing shortcuts, and changing the appearance of its icons. The following sections explain these changes.

> **Note**
> You can change the width of the Folder Pane by dragging its border.

Showing and hiding the Folder Pane

If you use the Folder Pane often, you'll probably want it to remain open all the time, but if you work with a particular Outlook 2013 folder most of the time, you might prefer to have the additional space for your favorite folder view or the Reading Pane. In Outlook 2013, you have the capability to minimize the Folder Pane to gain more window space but easily restore it when you need it, as shown in Figure 26-2. To minimize the Folder Pane, click the View tab, click Folder Pane, and then choose Minimize. Alternatively, simply click the left-facing arrow near the upper-right corner of the Folder Pane. When the Folder Pane is minimized, you'll find an Expand The Folder Pane button in the upper-right corner of the Folder Pane, as shown in Figure 26-2. Just click this button to expand the Folder Pane.

Click to Restore

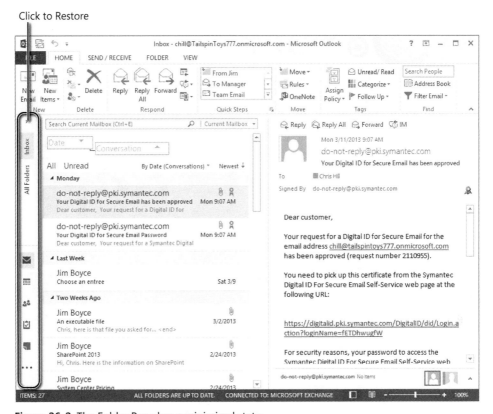

Figure 26-2 The Folder Pane has a minimized state.

Outlook 2013 also allows you to turn on or turn off the Folder Pane as needed. Click View, Folder Pane, and then choose Off to turn it off.

Changing the number of buttons on the Folder Pane

Outlook 2013 can display up to eight buttons in the bottom portion of the Folder Pane, and these include a button for each of the standard Outlook 2013 folders, the Folder List, and Shortcuts. The number of buttons displayed depends on the width of the Outlook 2013 window and how many buttons you choose to show.

Outlook 2013 offers two ways to view the Folder Pane: normal and compact navigation. Figures 26-1 and 26-2 both show the compact navigation mode. Figure 26-3 shows the normal mode, in which the Outlook folders are listed across the bottom of the Outlook window (the number shown depends on how you have configured the Folder Pane). You can show or hide buttons by clicking the ellipsis at the bottom of the Folder Pane and using the Maximum Number Of Visible Items control to choose how many items to show, as shown in Figure 26-3.

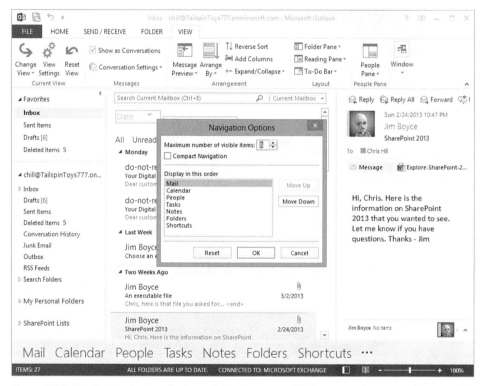

Figure 26-3 Use the Navigation Options dialog box to specify how many items are shown and in what order.

Outlook 2013 does not show all the available buttons in the Folder Pane by default. Unlike in previous versions of Outlook, you can configure Outlook 2013 to explicitly hide a particular item. For example, you can configure Outlook to never show the Notes folder icon. However, you can control which items are shown by controlling the number of items and their display order. So, if you never want to see the Notes folder icon, move it to the bottom of the priority list and configure Outlook to show a maximum of only six items. To configure these options, open the Navigation Options dialog box (see Figure 26-3) by clicking the ellipsis at the bottom of the Folder Pane.

Adding a shortcut to an Outlook folder or a public folder

The Folder Pane includes buttons for each of the built-in Outlook 2013 folders, and the Folder List provides quick access to all other Outlook 2013 folders and public folders (which are available only with Microsoft Exchange Server). You can add shortcuts to any folder easily by following these steps:

1. Click the ellipsis button at the bottom of the Folder Pane and then click Shortcuts to open the Shortcuts pane.

2. Right-click Shortcuts in the Folder Pane and choose New Shortcut to open the Add To Folder Pane dialog box, shown in Figure 26-4.

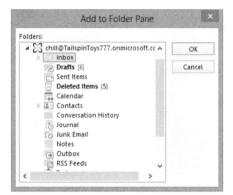

Figure 26-4 Select the folder for which you want to add a shortcut.

3. Select a folder in the list, and then click OK. Outlook 2013 adds the shortcut to the Shortcuts group.

4. Drag the shortcut to a different group, if desired.

Adding a file folder or document to the Folder Pane

You can create shortcuts to file system folders or Outlook 2013 folders and add them to existing Folder Pane groups or to new groups that you create. For example, if you use a particular document folder often, you might want to add that folder to one of your Folder Pane shortcut groups.

Chapter 26

The process is similar, regardless of the type of shortcut you're adding. Follow these steps:

1. In Outlook 2013, open the group in which you want to create the shortcut.

2. Click the Shortcuts button in the Folder Pane to open the Shortcuts pane.

3. In Microsoft Windows, open the folder containing the folder or file for which you want to create a shortcut, and then position the folder and the Outlook 2013 window so that you can see both, as shown in Figure 26-5.

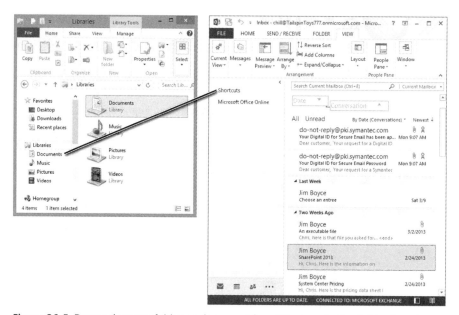

Figure 26-5 Drag a shortcut, folder, or document from Windows to the Folder Pane to create a shortcut.

4. Drag the folder or document from the folder window to the shortcut group name where you want to add it. Place it on the group header itself, not within the group.

> **Note**
> You can't drag a Windows library (such as the Documents library) to an Outlook shortcut group. However, you can open the library and drag a folder from the library, such as My Documents, to the shortcut. Figure 26-5 shows an example.

INSIDE OUT   Create shortcuts to network shares that you use often

You can specify Universal Naming Convention (UNC) paths in addition to mapped drives. A UNC path takes the form *<server>**<share>*, where *<server>* is the computer sharing the folder and *<share>* is the folder's share name. You can specify longer UNC paths, such as *<server>*\Documents\Contracts\Completed. To use network shortcuts in Outlook 2013, first create the shortcut on the desktop and then drag it to a shortcut group in the Folder Pane.

Adding a website to the Folder Pane

You can add shortcuts to websites to the Folder Pane, enabling you to quickly open a site from Outlook 2013 to do research, check stock quotes, view news, access documents in a SharePoint library, and so on. The website opens within the Outlook window.

To add a website shortcut to the Folder Pane, first create the shortcut on the desktop or in another folder. Open the Folder Pane shortcut group in which you want to place the shortcut, and then simply drag the existing shortcut to the Folder Pane and place it on the group header (such as Favorite Web Sites). You can also copy shortcuts from your Favorites menu easily. Open your web browser, open the Favorites menu, and then right-click the favorite and choose Copy. Right-click the desktop and choose Paste. Then drag the shortcut from the desktop to the shortcut group in the Folder Pane.

> **Note**
> You can create new web shortcuts on the desktop or in a file system folder (such as My Documents) by right-clicking the location and choosing New, Shortcut. On the first page of the Create Shortcut Wizard, type the URL for the webpage, File Transfer Protocol (FTP) site, or other Internet resource. Use *http://* as the URL prefix for webpages, use *ftp://* for FTP sites, and use *https://* for sites that use Secure Sockets Layer (SSL) for security.

INSIDE OUT   Troubleshoot errors in Outlook when viewing a webpage or removing a shortcut

There appears to be a bug in Outlook 2013 that causes it to generate script errors for certain sites when you view those sites in Outlook. If you experience this problem, open the site in Internet Explorer instead of Outlook. In addition, right-clicking a shortcut in Outlook 2013 can generate an OLE error. See the following section for a Note that explains how to remove a shortcut when this error occurs.

Removing a shortcut from the Folder Pane

If you decide that you no longer want a particular shortcut in the Folder Pane, you can remove it easily. Simply right-click the shortcut and choose Delete Shortcut. Click Yes to remove the shortcut or No to cancel the action.

> **Note**
>
> If you receive an OLE registration error when you right-click a shortcut in Outlook, you won't be able to open the context menu, which also means you can't delete the shortcut. To get around this problem, create a new shortcut group, move the problem shortcut to that group, and then delete the group. The OLE registration error appears to be a bug in Outlook 2013 as of this writing.

Renaming a shortcut in the Folder Pane

In some cases, you'll want to change the name that Outlook 2013 assigns to a shortcut in the Folder Pane. For example, when you add a website shortcut, its name is the URL, which typically doesn't fit very well in the Folder Pane. Perhaps you simply want to change the shortcut's name to something more descriptive and easier to remember.

To change the shortcut name, right-click the shortcut, and then choose Rename Shortcut. Type the new name, and then press Enter.

Working with groups in the Folder Pane

Outlook 2013 creates one group named Shortcuts in the Folder Pane by default. You can also add your own groups, remove groups, and rename them. This section explains these tasks.

Adding a group to the Folder Pane

At some point, you might want to add your own groups of shortcuts to the Folder Pane to help you reorganize existing shortcuts or organize new shortcuts. For example, you might want to create a group to contain all your web shortcuts.

Adding a new group is easy. Open the Shortcuts folder, right-click the Shortcuts group, and then click New Shortcut Group. Outlook 2013 adds a new group named New Group and highlights the group name so that you can change it, as shown in Figure 26-6. Type the group name, and then press Enter. Then begin adding shortcuts or moving shortcuts to the group from your other groups.

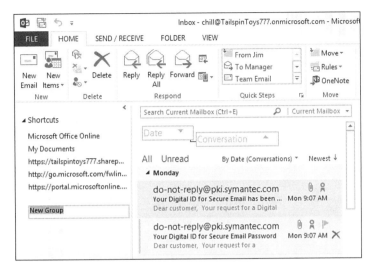

Figure 26-6 Type a name for the new group.

Renaming a group in the Folder Pane

You can rename a group as easily as you rename a shortcut. Start Outlook 2013, right-click the group name in the Folder Pane, and then choose Rename Group. Type a new name for the group, and then press Enter.

Removing a group from the Folder Pane

If you decide that you want to remove a group from the Folder Pane, you can do so at any time. Simply right-click the group name in the Folder Pane and then choose Delete Group. Click Yes to remove the group or No to cancel the action.

> **Note**
> If the group that you remove contains shortcuts that you've copied from other locations (such as the desktop), removing the group does not affect those shortcuts. Only the group is removed from the Folder Pane; the shortcuts remain in their other locations. Shortcuts that exist only in that group, however, are deleted.

Customizing the To-Do Bar

The To-Do Bar combines the Date Navigator, appointments, the task list, and the Quick Contacts list. The To-Do Bar sits at the right side of the Outlook 2013 window, as shown in Figure 26-7. As with the Folder Pane, you can minimize the To-Do Bar to make more window space available for your Outlook 2013 folders or for the Reading Pane, but you can still access the To-Do Bar quickly when you need it.

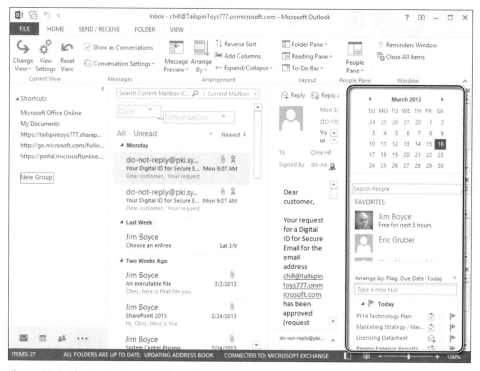

Figure 26-7 The To-Do Bar combines the Date Navigator, appointments, the task list, and contacts you've added to your Favorites list.

> **Note**
>
> To display the To-Do Bar, click View, To-Do Bar, and then choose which section of the To-Do Bar you want to display.

You can control which items appears in the To-Do Bar. To customize the To-Do Bar, choose To-Do Bar on the View tab, and then select or clear the Calendar, People, or Tasks options.

Customizing the ribbon

While the ribbon existed in only some parts of Outlook 2007, it became pervasive in Outlook 2010, and that trend continues in Outlook 2013. As you might expect, you have quite a bit of control over what appears in the Outlook ribbon. You can change the names of some items in the ribbon and even create your own tabs and option groups.

You manage the ribbon through the Outlook Options dialog box, as shown in Figure 26-8. To open these options, right-click the ribbon and choose Customize The Ribbon, or click File, choose Options, and then click Customize Ribbon in the left pane.

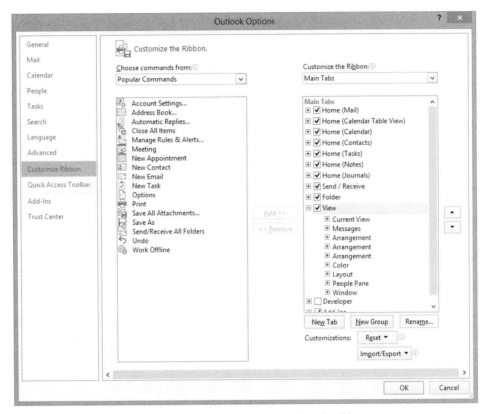

Figure 26-8 Use the Outlook Options dialog box to customize the ribbon.

Note

You can collapse the ribbon to gain more space for the rest of the Outlook interface when you aren't using the ribbon. Just click the Collapse The Ribbon button (an up-facing arrow in the bottom-right corner of the ribbon). The button changes to a down-facing arrow. Click any ribbon tab and then click the Pin The Ribbon button to restore it. You can also right-click any tab and choose Collapse The Ribbon to collapse or pin the ribbon.

Modifying existing items and tabs

As mentioned previously, you can make changes to existing items in the ribbon. Depending on the item, you might be able to remove it from the ribbon altogether. However, most of the items that appear in the ribbon by default cannot be removed. For example, in the Customize Ribbon page of the Outlook Options dialog box, expand the Home (Mail) group, expand Tags, and click the Follow Up branch. Note that the Remove button is dimmed, indicating that you can't remove this particular item. If the Remove button is not dimmed when you click an item, you can remove that item from the ribbon. Also, note that you can remove the default groups but not individual items in them. For example, you can remove the Tags group from the Home tab altogether, but you can't remove the Follow Up item individually.

If some of the group names on the ribbon don't make sense to you, or you feel you have a better, more descriptive name, you can rename the group. Just expand the list in the Outlook Options dialog box, click the group name, and then click Rename. Type a new name and click OK. (Note that some groups cannot be renamed.)

Adding new items

It's easy to add other items to the existing ribbon tabs, making those commands and options that you use most frequently readily available. You can't add new items to the default groups included with Outlook, but you can create your own groups to contain the items. Here's how:

1. Start by right-clicking the ribbon and choosing Customize The Ribbon to open the Customize The Ribbon page of the Outlook Options dialog box.

2. From the tabs list at the right of the dialog box, select the tab that you want to modify.

3. Click New Group to add a new group named New Group (Custom).

4. With the new group selected, click Rename, enter a name for the new group, and click OK.

5. In the Choose Commands From drop-down list shown in Figure 26-8, choose the types of commands that you want to add. For example, choose All Commands to show a list of all available commands.

6. Scroll through the list of commands and find the one that you want to add.

7. With the custom group selected in the list on the right, click Add to add the item to the group.

Creating your own ribbon tabs

While you might want to add some of your own groups to the existing ribbon tabs, more than likely you will want to add your own tabs and then add the commands that you use most often to the custom tabs. This is a great way to keep your customizations separate from the default tab sets.

Creating a new tab is easy. Just click New Tab on the Customize The Ribbon page of the Outlook Options dialog box. Outlook adds a new tab named New Tab (Custom). Select the newly created tab and click Rename to give it a more descriptive name of your choice. Figure 26-9 shows a new tab called My Stuff added to the ribbon, with just the default New Group and no commands or options.

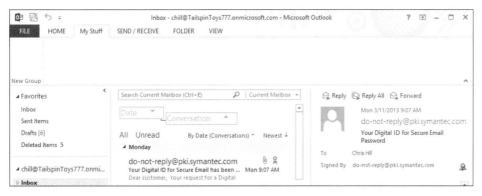

Figure 26-9 You can add a custom tab to the ribbon.

At this point, your new tab is a blank canvas. You can add groups as you see fit and add commands, macros, and so on to those groups. It doesn't matter if you already have a particular command on another tab. You can add it to your custom tab to make it readily available, along with all the other commands and options you use frequently. Use the process described previously in this chapter to add new groups and add items to the groups.

The next step is to organize the groups on your custom tab, placing individual items in the desired order as well as putting the groups themselves in the desired order. Here's how to rearrange items:

1. Right-click the ribbon and choose Customize The Ribbon to open the Customize The Ribbon page of the Outlook Options dialog box.

2. In the right half of the dialog box, expand the group whose items you want to rearrange.

3. To rearrange the items in a group, click the item you want to move. Use the Move Up and Move Down buttons highlighted in Figure 26-10 to move the item up and down.

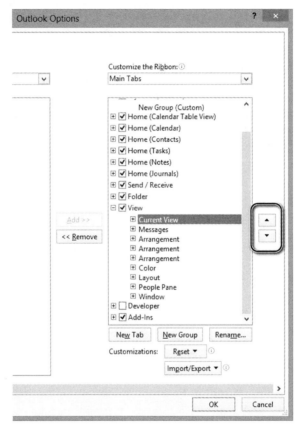

Figure 26-10 Use the Move Up and Move Down buttons to rearrange items, groups, and even tabs.

4. To rearrange the groups themselves, expand the tab containing the groups that you want to rearrange, and then use the Move Up and Move Down buttons to rearrange them.

5. To rearrange the order of the tabs on the ribbon, select a tab from the list and use the Move Up and Move Down buttons to rearrange it as desired.

6. Click OK when you are satisfied with the new ribbon arrangement.

Sharing your customized ribbon

If you have spent a lot of time customizing your ribbon and you want to share it with others who have the same general needs, you can export the customizations to a file so users can import it into their own copy of Outlook 2013. To export your ribbon customizations to a file, click File, Options, and click Customize Ribbon in the left pane. Click Import/Export and choose Export All Customizations. In the File Save dialog box, enter a name for the customization file and click Save. Then place the file on a network share or Microsoft SharePoint site, email it, or otherwise provide it to the others you want to have the same customizations. They can then click Import/Export on the Customize Ribbon page of the Outlook Options dialog box, choose Import Customization File, and import the file into Outlook.

Resetting customizations

If you decide you don't like the changes you've made to the ribbon, right-click the ribbon, choose Customize The Ribbon, and then click Reset. Choose Reset Only Selected Ribbon Tab to reset only the currently selected ribbon tab, or choose Reset All Customizations to return the ribbon to its default state.

Customizing the Quick Access Toolbar

The Quick Access Toolbar appears by default above the ribbon in the Outlook interface. It is a thin toolbar with small icons that you can customize to put frequently used commands close at hand (see Figure 26-11).

Figure 26-11 Use the Quick Access Toolbar to access frequently used commands.

By default, the Quick Access Toolbar contains only a very few items. However, you can add other items to the Quick Access Toolbar easily. In fact, Outlook provides a menu of preselected items that you can add. To add items from this list, click the Customize Quick

Access Toolbar button at the right edge of the Quick Access Toolbar to open the menu shown in Figure 26-12. Choose an item from the menu to either add it to or remove it from the Quick Access Toolbar.

Figure 26-12 You can add items to or remove items from the Quick Access Toolbar easily.

Note

You can move the Quick Access Toolbar under the ribbon if you prefer. Click the Customize Quick Access Toolbar button at the right edge of the toolbar and choose Show Below The Ribbon.

To add commands not shown in the menu, click the Customize Quick Access Toolbar button and choose More Commands from the menu. Outlook displays the Quick Access Toolbar page of the Outlook Options dialog box, shown in Figure 26-13.

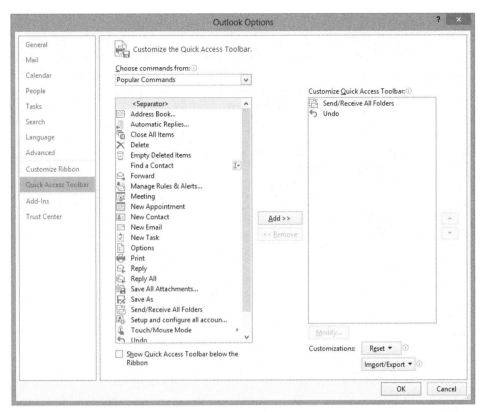

Figure 26-13 Use the Quick Access Toolbar page of the Outlook Options dialog box to add other items to the Quick Access Toolbar.

Adding items to the Quick Access Toolbar is easy. Just select an item and click Add. Click an item and click Remove to remove it from the toolbar. Use the Move Up and Move Down buttons to arrange items on the toolbar to your liking. Then click OK to save the changes.

> **Note**
>
> As you can with the ribbon customizations, you can export your Quick Access Toolbar customizations to a file that can be used by others to import those customizations into their own copy of Outlook. Use the Import/Export button on the Quick Access Toolbar page of the Outlook Options dialog box to export or import a customized Quick Access Toolbar.

Customizing the Outlook Today view

Outlook 2013 uses the Outlook Today view as its default view. Outlook Today combines your most commonly used Outlook 2013 data into a single view, summarizing your schedule, tasks, and key email folders for the current day, as shown in Figure 26-14. You can work with the view as is or modify it to suit your needs. This section explores how to customize the Outlook Today view.

For a basic description of how to use the Outlook Today view, see the next section, "Configuring Outlook Today."

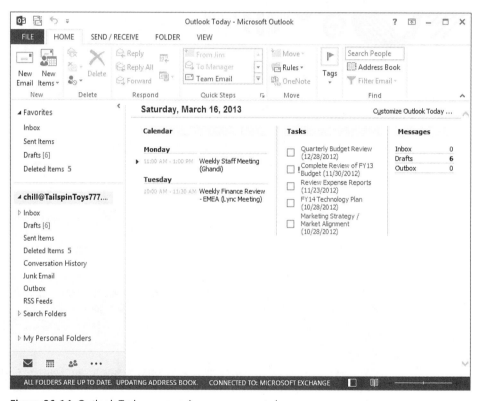

Figure 26-14 Outlook Today summarizes your current day.

Although Outlook Today presents useful information, it might not show all the information you want or need to really keep track of your workday. You can customize the Outlook Today view to show additional information and use HTML to present a truly customized interface. The following sections explain how.

Configuring Outlook Today

You can configure several options that control how this view looks, as well as the data that it displays. To configure the view, click the Customize Outlook Today link in Outlook Today view (in the upper-right corner of the view in all styles except Winter, where it appears in the lower-right area). The Customize Outlook Today page shown in Figure 26-15 appears.

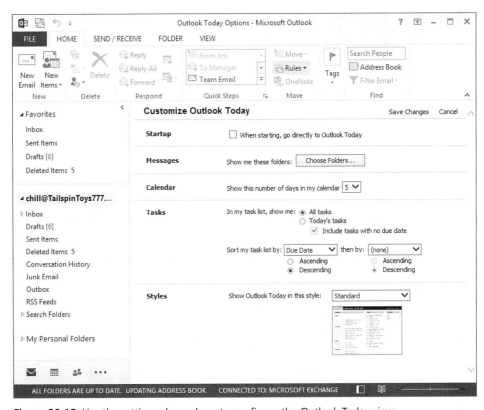

Figure 26-15 Use the settings shown here to configure the Outlook Today view.

The following sections explain the changes you can make to the Outlook Today view on this page. When you're satisfied with the changes, click Save Changes in the Customize Outlook Today title bar, or click Cancel to close the page without applying the changes.

Specifying the startup view

If you select the When Starting, Go Directly To Outlook Today check box, Outlook 2013 opens the Outlook Today view when you first start the program.

You also can specify the startup folder by using Outlook 2013 options, as explained here:

1. Click File, Options.

2. Click Advanced.

3. Beside the Start Outlook In This Folder box, click Browse.

4. Select the top level of your mailbox, indicated by the email address of the account.

5. Click OK twice to close the dialog boxes.

The Startup In This Folder drop-down list specifies the folder that Outlook 2013 will use by default when you start Outlook 2013. Choosing Outlook Today in the list has the same effect as selecting When Starting, Go Directly To Outlook Today in the Customize Outlook Today page.

> ### Note
> If Outlook Today is configured as the default view, and you clear the When Starting, Go Directly To Outlook Today check box without specifying a different startup folder in the Options dialog box, Outlook 2013 makes your Inbox the startup folder by default.

Specifying folders to show

The Outlook Today view shows the Drafts, Inbox, and Outbox folders. If you seldom use the Drafts folder, you might prefer to remove it from Outlook Today, or perhaps you want to add other folders to the view, such as Tasks and Contacts, to give you a quick way to open those folders without using the Folder Pane.

To configure the folders that Outlook Today displays, click Choose Folders on the Customize Outlook Today page to open the Select Folder dialog box, shown in Figure 26-16. Select each folder that you want to display, and then click OK.

Figure 26-16 Use the Select Folder dialog box to choose the folders that you want Outlook Today to display.

Setting calendar options

The Calendar portion of the Outlook Today view displays a certain number of days from your calendar based on the current date. You can specify the number of days displayed by using the Show This Number Of Days In My Calendar option. Select a number from 1 to 7.

Setting task options

The Tasks area of the Customize Outlook Today page lets you configure how Outlook Today displays your tasks. The following list summarizes these options:

- **All Tasks**   This option enables you to show all tasks regardless of the status or completion deadline.

- **Today's Tasks**   This option enables you to show overdue tasks and incomplete tasks that are due today.

- **Include Tasks With No Due Date**   You can include tasks to which you've assigned no due date with this option.

- **Sort My Task List By** *criteria* **Then By** *criteria*   You can sort your task list according to the task's importance, due date, creation time, and start date. You can specify two sort conditions and also choose between ascending or descending sort order for both conditions.

Chapter 26

Using styles

By default, Outlook Today displays its information using three columns on a white background. Outlook 2013 provides additional styles that you can select to change the overall appearance of the Outlook Today view. Use the Show Outlook Today In This Style drop-down list to select a style. The Customize Outlook Today page shows a sample of the style after you select it.

Customizing Outlook Today with HTML

Outlook Today is built on HTML that is contained in the dynamic-link library (DLL) file Outlwww.dll, located by default in C:\Program Files(x86)\Microsoft Office\Office15\1033. It's possible to extract the HTML code and graphics from the DLL file and use them as the basis for your own custom Outlook Today page. However, because Outlook Today is a deprecated feature, Microsoft doesn't recommend that developers spend time customizing it, because the feature at some point will go away (and all of your hard work will be for naught). But, if you're experienced in HTML and CSS and want to play around with customizing it, you certainly can. This tiny section of the chapter is for those brave souls who want to try customizing it.

But, again, because Outlook Today is a deprecated feature, I don't cover the topic in detail in this book! You can find several posts on the Internet that explain how to use resource URLs to extract the HTML code and graphics for Outlook.htm, Custom.htm, Gap.gif, and some of the other resources stored in the DLL file. Just do an Internet search with your favorite search engine on the phrase "customize Outlook Today." You can also get additional information from the Office 2000 Resource Kit, which you'll find at *http://www.microsoft.com/office/orkarchive/2000ddl.htm#outtoday*. There are two downloads available that include instructions and sample files.

> **Note**
>
> Several of the posts on the Internet have you open the exported HTML file in Internet Explorer and then try to right-click the Gap.gif file that separates the Calendar, Tasks, and Messages columns in the Outlook Today view. There's a much easier way to extract the image: Just open a Windows Explorer window and point it to res://C:\Program%20 Files%20(x86)\Microsoft%20Office\Office15\1033\outlwvw.dll/gap.gif. Then click File, Save As and save the image to the folder containing your other custom Outlook Today files.

Creating and using custom views

If the options for customizing existing Outlook 2013 views don't provide the information view that you need, you can create your own views. You have two options for doing this: modifying an existing view or creating a new view from scratch.

Basing a new view on an existing view

You can create a new, custom view from an existing view if the existing one offers most of the view elements that you need. This is usually the easiest method because it requires the least amount of work.

Follow these steps to create a new, custom view from an existing view:

1. Open the folder for which you want to modify the view, and then select the view to display it.

2. On the View tab, click Change View and choose Save Current View As A New View to open the Copy View dialog box, shown in Figure 26-17.

Figure 26-17 Use the Copy View dialog box to create a new view.

3. In the Copy View dialog box, type a name in the Name Of New View box, and then select one of the following options:

   ○ **This Folder, Visible To Everyone** Makes the view available only in the folder from which it was created. Anyone with access to the specified folder can use the view.

   ○ **This Folder, Visible Only To Me** Makes the view available only in the folder from which it was created. Only the person who created the view can use it.

○ **All Type Folders** Makes the view available in all folders that match the specified folder type. For example, when you create a custom view based on the Inbox, this option becomes All Mail And Post Folders, and Outlook 2013 makes the view available from the Inbox, Outbox, Drafts, Sent Items, and other message folders. If you base the new view on the Contacts folder, this option becomes All Contact Folders and makes the view available from all contact folders.

4. On the View tab, click View Settings to open the Advanced View Settings dialog box, as shown in Figure 26-18.

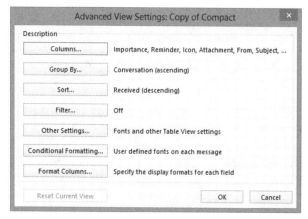

Figure 26-18 The Advanced View Settings dialog box lets you access the functions that you can use to define your custom view.

5. Use the options provided in the Advanced View Settings dialog box to customize the view.

   For details on all the options that you can configure in the Customize View dialog box, see the section "Customizing a view's settings."

6. After you've modified the settings as needed, click OK to close the Customize View dialog box and apply the view changes.

Creating a new view from scratch

You can create an Outlook 2013 view from scratch if the view you want doesn't have much in common with any of the existing views. For example, perhaps you want to create an Inbox view that displays your messages as icons rather than headers, as shown in Figure 26-19. You can't modify a standard message view to display messages as icons, so you need to create the view from scratch.

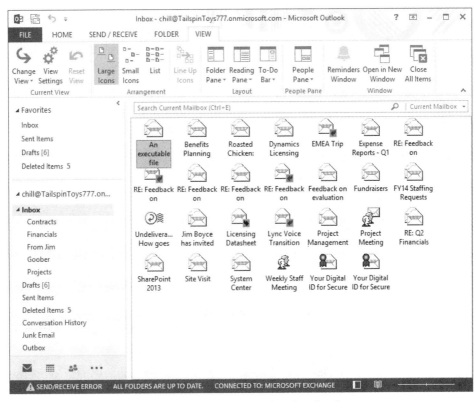

Figure 26-19 This Inbox view shows message icons rather than headers.

The process for creating a view from scratch is much like the process of modifying an existing view. When you create a new view, however, you have additional options for specifying the view.

Follow these steps to create a view from scratch:

1. Open the folder or folder type for which you want to create a custom view.

2. Click the View tab and then click Change View, Manage Views to open the Manage All Views dialog box.

3. Click New to open the Create A New View dialog box, shown in Figure 26-20.

Figure 26-20 You can create several types of new views.

4. In the Name Of New View box, type a name for your new view.

5. In the Type Of View list, select the type of view you want to create, as follows:

- ❍ **Table** Presents information in tabular form, with one item per row and columns laid out according to your selections. The default Inbox view is an example of a table view.

- ❍ **Timeline** Displays items on a timeline based on the item's creation date (such as the received date for a message or the event date for a meeting). You might find this view type most useful for the Calendar folder.

- ❍ **Card** Displays information using cards, as in Address Cards view (the default view in the Contacts folder).

- ❍ **Business Card** Displays information using customizable, graphical business cards, similar to Detailed Address Cards view.

- ❍ **People** Displays contacts using the view format of the People Hub (the default People view of the Contacts folder).

- ❍ **Day/Week/Month** Displays days in the left half of the window and monthly calendars in the right half. The actual view depends on the type of folder for which you create the view. Figure 26-21 shows a Day/Week/Month view created for the Inbox folder. The email messages appear in the calendar according to the day and time received.

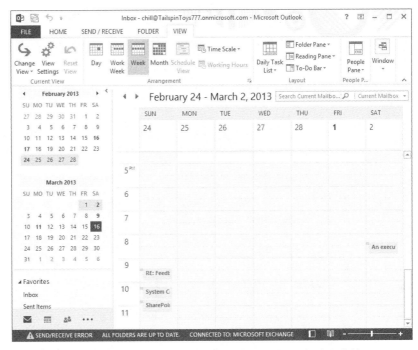

Figure 26-21 This Day/Week/Month view was created for the Inbox folder.

   ○   **Icon**   Displays the items as icons, much as a file system folder does.

6. In the Can Be Used On area, select an option as described in the preceding section, and then click OK. The Advanced View Settings dialog box opens.

7. Customize the view as needed, and then click OK.

8. Click Apply View to apply the view, or click Close to close the dialog box without applying the view.

For details on all the options you can configure in the Customize View dialog box, see the section "Customizing a view's settings."

Modifying, renaming, or deleting a view

You can easily modify, rename, and delete custom views. For example, perhaps you want to apply a filter to a view in the Contacts folder to show only those contacts who work for a particular company. Maybe you want to have Outlook 2013 apply a certain label to appointments that have specified text in the subject.

To modify, rename, or delete a view, follow these steps:

1. Click the View tab, and click Change View, Manage Views to open the Manage All Views dialog box.

2. In the Views For Folder list, select the view that you want to change, and then do one of the following:

   ○ To modify the view, click Modify. Use the options in the Customize View dialog box to apply changes to the view (as explained in the following section).

   ○ To rename the view, click Rename, and then type the new name.

   ○ To delete the view, click Delete. The Reset button changes to Delete if you select a custom view.

3. Click Close.

Customizing a view's settings

Outlook 2013 gives you considerable control over the appearance and contents of a view. When you define a new view or modify an existing view, you end up in the Advanced View Settings dialog box, shown in Figure 26-18. To open this dialog box, click the View tab and click View Settings in the Current View group.

The options available in the Advanced View Settings dialog box change according to the folder selected. For example, the options for the Contacts folder differ in some respects from the options for the Inbox. The same general concepts hold true for each type of folder, however. The following sections explain the various ways that you can use these dialog box options to customize a view.

Configuring columns

In most cases, clicking Columns in the Advanced View Settings dialog box opens the Show Columns dialog box, similar to the one shown in Figure 26-22, in which you can select the columns that you want to include in the view. (Exceptions to this behavior are discussed later in the section.) For example, you might use the dialog box to add the Cc or Sensitivity column to the view.

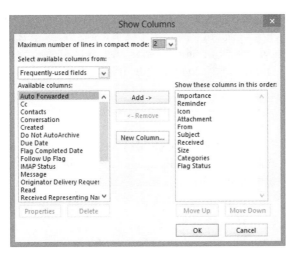

Figure 26-22 Use the Show Columns dialog box to add columns to or remove columns from the view.

Adding columns in the Show Columns dialog box is easy. The available columns (those not already in the view) appear in the list on the left, and the columns already displayed appear in the list on the right. Select a column in the Available Columns list, and then click Add to add it to the view. To remove a column from the view, select the field in the Show These Columns In This Order list, and then click Remove. Use the Move Up and Move Down buttons to rearrange the order in which the columns are displayed in the view.

TROUBLESHOOTING

You need to restore a view to its original settings

You've customized a view, and now you've decided that you need the old view back. (For the future, remember that rather than modifying an existing view, you can copy the view and then modify the copy. This way you'll still have the original view if you need it.)

It's easy to restore a standard view to its previous settings, however. Click View Settings on the View tab and then click Reset Current View. Click Yes when prompted to confirm the action.

Note

You can rearrange the order in which columns are displayed in a table view by dragging the column header for a column to a new location on the column header bar.

In some cases, clicking Columns in the Advanced View Settings dialog box opens a Date/Time Fields dialog box similar to the one shown in Figure 26-23. This occurs when you're working with a view that shows time duration, such as Day/Week/Month view in the Calendar folder or By Type view in the Journal folder—in effect, nontable views that show time duration graphically.

> **Note**
>
> You can click New Column in the Show Columns dialog box to create a custom column. For additional information about creating and using custom columns, see Chapter 27, "Designing and using custom forms."

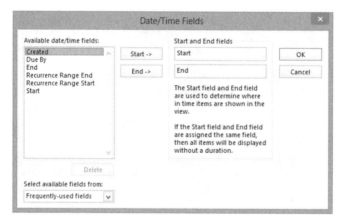

Figure 26-23 In the Date/Time Fields dialog box, specify the date fields used to show duration.

You use the Date/Time Fields dialog box to specify the fields that Outlook 2013 will use to show item duration in the view. The default settings vary but are typically either Start and End or Start Date and Due Date. As an example, you might use the Date/Time Fields dialog box to change the Task Timeline view in the Tasks folder to show the Date Completed field for the task's end rather than the Due Date field.

Grouping data

Sometimes it's helpful to be able to group items in an Outlook 2013 folder based on specific data fields. For example, you might want to group tasks by owner so that you can see at a glance the tasks assigned to specific people. Perhaps you want to organize contacts by country or region. In these and similar cases, you can modify an existing view or create a new one to organize the view based on the most pertinent data. To group data in a view, click Group By in the Advanced View Settings dialog box to open the Group By dialog box, shown in Figure 26-24.

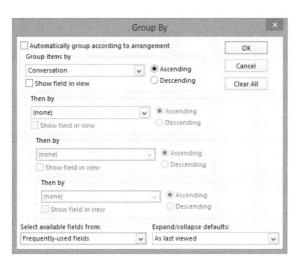

Figure 26-24 Use the Group By dialog box to specify criteria for grouping items in a view.

Follow these steps to group data in a view:

1. In the Group By dialog box, clear the Automatically Group According To Arrangement check box.

2. Select a field type in the Select Available Fields From drop-down list at the bottom of the dialog box. This selection controls the fields that appear in the Group Items By drop-down list.

3. Select a field in the Group Items By drop-down list, and then select either Ascending or Descending, depending on the sort order that you want to use. Select the Show Field In View check box to display the field in the view.

4. If you want to create subgroups under the main group, select a field in the Then By drop-down list. (The dialog box contains three such lists, providing three additional grouping levels.) For example, you might group tasks by Owner and then by Due Date.

5. After you've specified all the grouping levels that you need, use the Expand/Collapse Defaults drop-down list to specify how you want Outlook 2013 to treat the groups. Use the following list as a guide:

   ○ **As Last Viewed**   Collapses or expands the group according to its state in the previous session

   ○ **All Expanded**   Expands all items in all groups

   ○ **All Collapsed**   Collapses all items in all groups

6. When you're satisfied with the group settings, click OK to close the Group By dialog box. Then click OK to close the Advanced View Settings dialog box.

Sorting data

Sorting data in a view is different from grouping data. For example, you might group the Tasks folder by owner. Each group in the view will show the tasks assigned to a particular person. You can then sort the data within the group as needed. For example, Figure 26-25 shows the Tasks folder grouped by priority and sorted by due date.

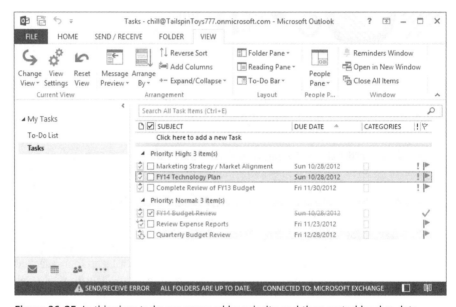

Figure 26-25 In this view, tasks are grouped by priority and then sorted by due date.

Sorting doesn't rely on grouping—you can sort a view whether or not it is grouped. For example, you might sort the Inbox based on the Received column to show messages in the order in which you received them.

INSIDE OUT Sort table views quickly

You can sort a table view quickly by clicking the column header for the column by which you want to sort the view. Click the header again to change between ascending and descending sort order.

To create a sort order when you customize or define a view, click Sort in the Advanced View Settings dialog box to open the Sort dialog box, shown in Figure 26-26.

Figure 26-26 Configure a sort order for the view in the Sort dialog box.

To configure sorting in the Sort dialog box, follow these steps:

1. In the Select Available Fields From drop-down list, select the type of field that the sort should be based on.

2. In the Sort Items By drop-down list, select the specific field by which you want to sort the view.

3. Select Ascending or Descending, depending on the type of sort you need.

4. Use the Then By lists to specify additional sort levels, if necessary.

5. Click OK to close the Sort dialog box, and then click OK to close the Customize View dialog box.

Applying filters to the view

In Outlook 2013, filtering a view is an extremely powerful feature that gives you considerable control over the data displayed in a given view. For example, you might have hundreds of messages in your Inbox and need to filter the view to show only those messages from a particular sender. You could simply sort the Inbox by the From field and scan the list of messages, but you might want to refine the search a little, perhaps viewing only messages from a specific sender that have an attachment and were sent within the previous week. Filters allow you to do just that.

To configure a filter, click Filter in the Advanced View Settings dialog box to open the Filter dialog box, shown in Figure 26-27. This multitabbed dialog box lets you specify multiple conditions to define which items will appear in the view.

Figure 26-27 Use the Filter dialog box to specify multiple conditions that determine the data that appears in the view.

Note that the first tab in the Filter dialog box varies according to the current folder type. For a contact folder, for example, the first tab is labeled Contacts and offers options for creating filter conditions that apply to contacts. For a message folder, the first tab is labeled Messages and provides options for creating filter conditions specific to messages.

The various tabs in the Filter dialog box include a broad range of options that let you specify multiple conditions for the filter. You can use conditions from more than one tab. For example, you might enter words to search for and a sender on the Messages tab, select categories on the More Choices tab, and specify a particular field and value on the Advanced tab.

> **Note**
>
> The Advanced tab of the Filter dialog box gives you access to all available fields and several criteria (Contains, Doesn't Contain, and Is Empty, for example), making it the place to go to configure conditions not available on the other tabs. To define filter criteria, select a field in the Field drop-down list, select an option in the Condition drop-down list, type a value, and then click Add. Use the SQL tab to perform Structured Query Language (SQL) queries to retrieve data from the folder to show in the custom view.

Configuring fonts and other general settings

When you click Other Settings in the Advanced View Settings dialog box, Outlook 2013 opens a dialog box that lets you configure some general settings for the custom view. These options vary from one folder type to another—for example, the Contacts folder, the Inbox, and the Calendar folder all use different options. You can change such properties as the font used for column headers and row text, the grid style and shading for table views, and a handful of other general options.

Creating rules for conditional formatting of text

Click Conditional Formatting in the Advanced View Settings dialog box to display the Conditional Formatting dialog box, similar to the one shown in Figure 26-28. This dialog box lets you create rules that cause Outlook 2013 to format data in the view automatically based on the criteria that you specify. For example, you might create an automatic conditional formatting rule that has Outlook 2013 display in blue all tasks that you own and display all other tasks in black. Or perhaps you may create a rule to display in green all contacts from a specific company.

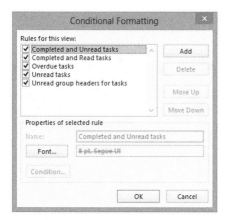

Figure 26-28 Use the Conditional Formatting dialog box to create rules that automatically format text in views based on the conditions that you specify.

As you're working in the Conditional Formatting dialog box, keep in mind that you can't create task-oriented rules, as you can with the Rules Wizard. For example, you can't create a rule in this dialog box that moves messages from one folder to another. The rules you create in the Conditional Formatting dialog box control only the appearance (color, font, and font styles) of data in the view.

For information about the Rules Wizard, see Chapter 11, "Using rules, alerts, and automatic responses."

Chapter 26

You can't modify the conditions for predefined rules, but you can specify the font characteristics to use for the rule. You can also create your own rules and change the order in which rules are applied to achieve the results you need.

To set up a conditional formatting rule for text, follow these steps:

1. Click Add in the Conditional Formatting dialog box to add a new rule named Untitled.

2. Click Font to open a standard Font dialog box, in which you specify the font, font style, and color that will apply to text that meets the rule's condition.

3. Close the Font dialog box, and then click Condition to open the Filter dialog box, shown in Figure 26-29. This dialog box offers three tabs that you can use to specify the condition for the rule. You can specify multiple conditions from multiple tabs, if needed.

Figure 26-29 Specify conditions for a rule in the Filter dialog box.

4. Click OK when you're satisfied with the filter condition.

TROUBLESHOOTING

You need to restrict the available views

In some situations, you might want to restrict the available views to only the custom views you've created, hiding the standard views that Outlook 2013 provides. For example, perhaps you created a custom calendar view that you want all employees to use instead of the standard calendar views because your custom view includes additional information that the standard views don't contain. When you restrict the Outlook 2013 views to only custom views, the standard views no longer appear on the View menu.

You must configure each folder separately. For example, you might restrict the Calendar folder views without restricting the Inbox folder views. This would give users the ability to choose one of the standard Outlook 2013 views in the Inbox folder but would limit their choices to only custom views in the Calendar folder.

Follow these steps to restrict the views that Outlook 2013 provides on the View menu:

1. In Outlook 2013, select the folder for which you want to restrict views.

2. Click View, Change View, Manage Views to open the Manage All Views dialog box.

3. Select the Only Show Views Created For This Folder check box, and then click Close.

4. Repeat steps 2 and 3 to restrict other folders as necessary.

Chapter 26

Designing and using custom forms

EVEN without any custom programming, Microsoft Outlook 2013 provides an excellent set of features. In fact, many organizations don't need anything beyond what Outlook 2013 offers right out of the box. Others, however, have special needs that Outlook 2013 does not address, perhaps because of the way these organizations do business or because of specific requirements in their particular industries. In such cases, you have ample opportunity to extend the functionality of Outlook 2013 through custom design and programming.

For example, you might need to add some fields to your message forms or your meeting request forms. Perhaps you need an easier way for users to perform mail merge operations with Microsoft Word 2013 and Outlook 2013 contact lists. Maybe you simply want to fine-tune your forms to add your company logo, special instructions, or warnings for users.

Whatever your situation, you can easily make changes to the existing Outlook 2013 forms, or you can even design new ones. The changes you make can be simple or complex: You might add one or two fields to the standard contact form, or you might add a considerable amount of program code to allow Outlook 2013 to perform custom tasks or interact with other Microsoft Office 2013 system applications. This chapter starts you on the right path by explaining how Outlook 2013 uses forms and how you can customize them to suit your needs. If you aren't comfortable programming with Microsoft Visual Basic for Applications (VBA), don't worry—you can accomplish a lot with custom forms without ever writing a single line of program code.

Forms are such a normal part of everything we do on computers that we sometimes take them for granted. It's still true, however, that a lot of programs used all over the world can be accessed only with screens that provide monochrome text and puzzling menus with strange codes and submission sequences. With their versatility and ease of use, forms offer a revolutionary approach, and you can unlock their power with several mouse clicks and some solid planning. This chapter discusses using Outlook 2013 forms as part of a software solution for individual computing needs. It also examines the types of forms that you can modify and create and how the forms are created, published, and stored.

With Outlook 2013, you can employ two basic strategies for form development. The first is to use or modify a standard form. The second is to create your own form from scratch. With either strategy, it's important to remember that you're programming events that are specifically associated with the item involved, not with the Outlook 2013 application generally. In other words, when you put code behind your form, you're dealing with events related to the item that's represented by the form. For example, if you were to design a form to create a custom email message, you'd probably program a common event named *Item_Send*, which occurs when the item (the message) is sent. You couldn't program the form to respond to an event that fires (that is, occurs or executes) when the item is specifically sent from the Outbox to another user's Inbox or when the user's view changes from one folder to another. This is because in form development, you can access only the events associated with the item in question.

Overview of standard forms, item types, and message classes

Outlook 2013 uses a combination of forms, item types, and message classes as its fundamental components. Although you don't need to understand much about any of these three components to use Outlook 2013, a developer must understand them reasonably well. Obviously, the more you know, the more powerful your Outlook 2013–based solution will be.

Outlook forms

Outlook 2013 provides numerous predefined forms that you can use as the foundation of your form-based solution. These standard forms include the following:

- Appointment form

- Contact form

- Distribution list form

- Meeting request form

- Message form

- Note form

- Post form

- RSS article form

- Task form

- Task request form

As this list of Outlook 2013 forms indicates, the basic item types available in a typical Outlook 2013 installation are each represented by a corresponding form. The Outlook 2013 forms in this list match the ones that you are used to working with on a daily basis, so you are not starting with a blank slate when you want to customize a form for your own use.

Each of these forms comes with built-in user interface elements and corresponding functionality. For example, the appointment form shown in Figure 27-1 has interface elements and functions that relate to setting appointments, such as generating reminders and controlling the calendar display. The contact form, in contrast, is designed to permit the addition or modification of contact information.

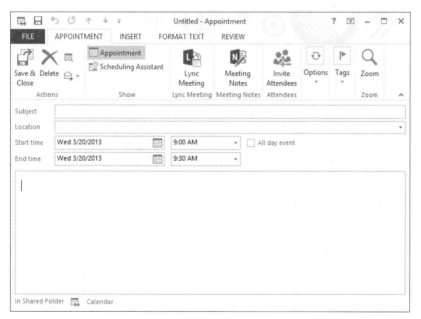

Figure 27-1 The appointment form is one of the standard forms that you can use in Outlook 2013.

Outlook item types

Several basic item types are part of an Outlook 2013 installation. Among the Office 2013 VBA item types that you can use are the following ones specific to Outlook 2013:

- MailItem

- ContactItem

- TaskItem

- AppointmentItem

- PostItem

- NoteItem

> **Note**
>
> Other item types are built into Outlook 2013, including the JournalItem and DistListItem types. This book does not cover these additional types, but you can find information about them by consulting the Microsoft MSDN website (*http://msdn.microsoft.com*) and searching for these item types.

These item types represent built-in functionality. If you have ever used Outlook 2013 to create an email message or to add an appointment to your calendar, you have benefited from this functionality. Of particular importance is the fact that this functionality is accessible to you as you develop custom solutions with Outlook 2013. Outlook 2013 provides corresponding forms for each of these item types, and these standard forms are designed with behaviors that directly relate to the item types that they represent. You can extend the behaviors of these forms and use all the functions and properties of the item types, some of which are not exposed in the standard forms. In addition, you can reach beyond Outlook 2013 to incorporate the functionality of other Microsoft Office applications such as Microsoft Word 2013, Microsoft Excel 2013, Microsoft InfoPath 2013, Microsoft PowerPoint 2013, Microsoft Project 2013, Microsoft Visio 2013, and any application or control that exposes a programmatic Component Object Model (COM) interface.

Outlook message classes

Although forms and item types are the basic elements you need to understand to create a custom Outlook 2013 solution, it's helpful to know what a message class is and how it relates to Outlook 2013 form development. A *message class* represents to Outlook 2013 internally what an item type represents to a user or developer externally. In other words, when a user opens an email message from the Inbox, that message is a MailItem. Internally, however, Outlook 2013 calls it by a different name: IPM.Note. IPM (which stands for *interpersonal message*) is a holdover from earlier generations of Microsoft's messaging systems. All messages in Outlook 2013 are representations of an IPM of some sort. An appointment calendar item, for example, is an IPM.Appointment. The list of default message classes includes the following:

- IPM.Note

- IPM.Contact

- IPM.DistList

- IPM.Appointment

- IPM.Task

- IPM.Post

- IPM.Activity

- IPM.Schedule.Meeting.Request

- IPM.StickyNote

- IPM.TaskRequest

Again, unless you're developing a fairly sophisticated collaborative solution, these message classes won't surface often. However, understanding what they mean to Outlook 2013 will help as you progress in your use of the program and in developing Outlook 2013 solutions.

Creating custom forms from standard forms

To begin working with the standard forms, first verify that you have added the Developer tab to the ribbon. If not, right-click the ribbon and choose Customize The Ribbon. Place a check beside Developer in the left list, and then click OK. Next, click the Developer tab in the ribbon, and then click Design A Form to display the Design Form dialog box, shown in Figure 27-2. You can simply select one of the standard forms listed in this dialog box and begin working with the form in design mode. Later sections in this chapter discuss how to save and publish the forms that you modify or create.

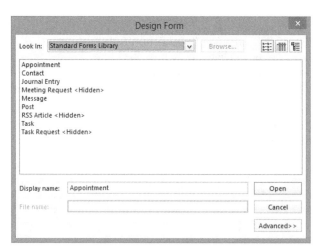

Figure 27-2 In the Design Form dialog box, you can choose the type of form you want to create.

INSIDE OUT Avoid scripts when opening forms for design purposes

When you choose to redesign an existing form, that form might have a script with event handlers that will fire when you open the form in design mode. Usually, however, you don't want to have code firing when you're trying to design a form. To keep this from happening, hold down the Shift key as you click the form to open it for design. The code will still be present and will run when you debug the form, but it will not run while you open, design, and save the form.

Compose vs. read

One of the most basic processes in Outlook 2013 is sending and receiving messages and documents. Although this is a fairly simple process, it requires a close look. In nearly all cases, the form that a sender employs to compose an email message is not the exact form that the receiver of that message uses to read the message. For example, the recipient of an email message can't modify the body of the message without replying to or forwarding the message. This is because the standard forms have Compose and Read areas.

Figure 27-3 shows a message being composed; Figure 27-4 shows the same message after it has been received.

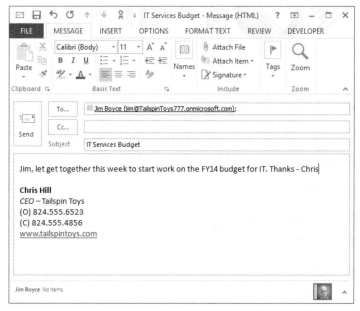

Figure 27-3 Compose a message using a standard message form.

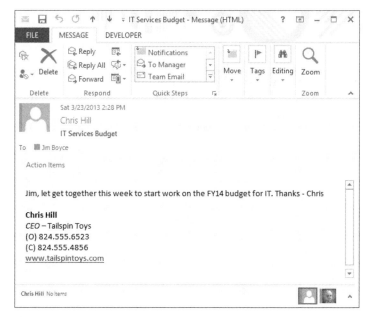

Figure 27-4 Here is the same message shown in Figure 27-3 after it has been received. Notice that some fields can no longer be modified.

Notice that some of the fields, such as Subject and To, can't be modified by the recipient in the Read version. It is, however, entirely possible to configure a form with identical Compose and Read areas. Whether this makes sense for your Outlook 2013 solution is up to you.

To work with a standard form, click Design A Form on the Developer tab to display the Design Form dialog box (shown in Figure 27-2), and then select a Message type form. When you're working with a standard form in design mode, you can switch between the Compose and Read pages by clicking the Page button in the Form group on the Developer tab and choosing Edit Compose Page or Edit Read Page. You can select these options by clicking Page, as shown in Figure 27-5, and then clicking the Edit Compose Page or Edit Read Page option.

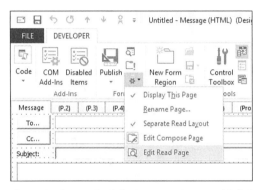

Figure 27-5 Use the Edit Compose Page and Edit Read Page options located in the Page menu to switch between compose and read views of the form.

In Figure 27-6, the Compose page of the standard message form is ready for editing. When you click Edit Read Page, the Read view of the form appears for editing, as shown in Figure 27-7.

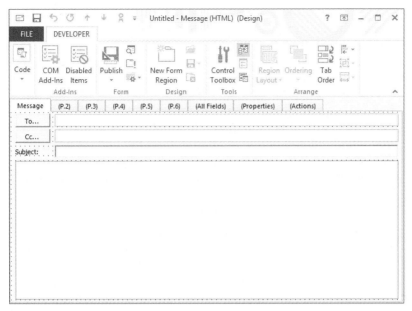

Figure 27-6 This standard Compose view is ready for editing.

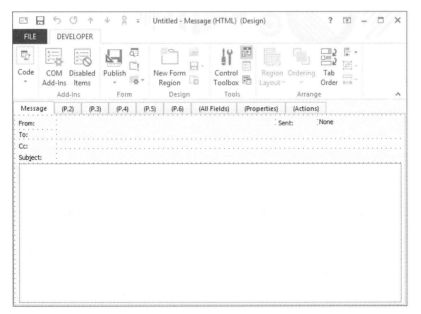

Figure 27-7 The Read view for a message item looks similar to the Compose view.

Because this is a standard form, a number of controls are already on the form. For example, the text box control for the body of the message is the largest element on the form. This control is bound to an Outlook 2013 field. The following section examines fields and what they mean to an Outlook 2013 solution; working with controls is discussed in the section "Adding and arranging controls."

Outlook fields

An Outlook 2013 field represents a discrete unit of information that is intelligible to Outlook 2013, such as the Bcc and To fields in an email message. You don't need to tell Outlook 2013 that email messages have these fields—they are already included in the standard form. Outlook 2013 provides a number of fields that you can use, and you can also add new fields. In theory, an unlimited number of fields are available, but the most common practice is to use a generous number of the built-in fields and a judicious number of new, user-defined properties. For now, this discussion focuses on the fields that are already available to you.

Because it provides so many built-in fields, Outlook 2013 groups them to make it easier to find the ones that you need. For example, some fields, such as To, From, Subject, Importance, Expires, Due By, Created, Size, and Attachment, are particular to email messages. Other fields, such as City, Children, and Birthday, are associated with Outlook 2013 contacts. You can, however, use fields from other forms to suit your needs on any form that you're designing—for example, Outlook 2013 doesn't prevent you from adding a Birthday field to an email form.

> **Note**
>
> You can find more information about user-defined fields in the Outlook 2013 Developer Reference at *http://msdn.microsoft.com/en-us/library/office/ee861520.aspx*.

When you work with a form, you can view the available fields in the Field Chooser, shown in Figure 27-8. To display the Field Chooser (if closed), click the Field Chooser button in the Tools group on the Developer tab; this button is a toggle that shows or hides the Field Chooser. In the Field Chooser, the fields are organized by categories and displayed in a list. You can choose a category in the drop-down list and then search in the body of the Field Chooser for the fields you need.

Figure 27-8 The Field Chooser allows you to view and choose the fields available for use.

Item types and fields

The scrollable list of fields shown in the Field Chooser in Figure 27-8 contains all the fields available for a form published in a certain folder. The standard item types come with a number of fields already defined. For example, a mail message comes with To, Subject, Body, and Sent fields already defined. Although you have the full range of fields available as you modify or create a form, you can speed up your development time and decrease your effort by carefully selecting a standard form that most closely corresponds to the solution you're developing. This way, you can use as many built-in fields as possible. You'll learn how to represent these fields on your form using controls in the section "Adding and arranging controls."

Creating custom forms from scratch

Working with standard forms is great if you want to build a solution that is directly related to one of the Outlook 2013 item types. However, you might need an Outlook 2013 form that isn't based on an item type at all. For example, you might want to create a form that allows users to report their work hours or initiate a purchase order. Although you could base these examples on a standard form, they could just as easily require a completely new form that you need to create.

The good news is that creating a completely new form is easier than it sounds. In fact, Outlook 2013 doesn't really permit you to create forms completely from scratch, although you can certainly achieve the same effect. You have two ways to create a form that doesn't contain any built-in form elements:

- Modify a standard form by deleting all built-in interface elements from the form and adding your own.

- Modify a standard form by hiding the page that contains built-in interface elements and showing a new page that contains elements that you add.

You'll learn how to add pages to forms in the next section. First let's look at how to break down a standard form to a blank form by removing built-in interface controls.

Follow these steps to turn a standard post form (a form that is used to post a note into a folder) into a blank form:

1. Click the Developer tab.

2. Click Design A Form.

3. Select the Post form, and then click Open. The form opens in design mode, with the Message page selected.

4. Click each control (TextBox, Label, Button, and so on) on the Message page and delete it.

5. With the Message page still selected, click Page in the Form group, and then select Rename Page.

6. Type a new name in the dialog box and then click OK.

Of course, you'll want to make the pages on this form useful, but for now, you at least have a blank form to work with. To have this blank form available as a template, click File, Save As, and then select Outlook Template from the Save As Type drop-down list.

Creating multipage forms

A multipage form allows you to fit a great deal of information on one form while also reducing confusion for the user. For example, you could create a form on which employees could both report their time for the week and report any expenses for which they need reimbursement. By using two pages, one form can serve both needs.

Any form can be a multipage form; all possible pages are already on the form that you create or modify. However, these pages are not visible automatically. If you look closely at the names on the page tabs shown previously in Figure 27-7, you'll see that except for the first name in the list, the name of each page is enclosed in parentheses, indicating that the page is not visible. To change the Visible property of a page, click its tab, click Page, and then select Display This Page.

> **Note**
>
> You can make all pages visible, but you cannot make all pages invisible. If you try to do so, Outlook 2013 tells you that at least one page must be visible on the form.

The first (default) page of a form, which is initially visible, has Compose and Read capabilities already available, as mentioned earlier. The additional pages on a form, which are initially invisible, don't have these capabilities until you add them. To do so, select one of these pages, click Page, and then choose Separate Read Layout, which activates the Edit Compose Page and Edit Read Page buttons.

Adding and arranging controls

The real power of forms comes from the controls that you place on them. To construct a robust Outlook 2013 forms solution, you need to plan carefully what the form is supposed to do; what pieces of information it will display, modify, save, or send; which controls will display these information units; and how the controls will be laid out. You can put two types of controls on a form: a control that is bound to an Outlook 2013 field and a control that is not. This section looks first at field-bound controls. Field-bound controls are bound to specific control types, such as drop-down lists, text boxes, command buttons, labels, or check boxes.

To display a field on your form, follow these steps:

1. Display the Field Chooser, and then select a field category in the drop-down list.

2. In the scrollable list in the Field Chooser, select the field that you want, and then drag it onto the form.

3. Format the control as needed.

INSIDE OUT   Work with the users of the form

You can place any number of controls on a form, but it's a good idea to plan your form with an eye toward usability. Work closely with those individuals who will be using the form to ensure that it corresponds to their real needs. Find out how the users want the forms to be laid out, and listen to their suggestions about how the information should flow. No matter how much work you put into your solution, it won't be useful unless people actually use it.

You can resize, move, or rename a control, and you can change a number of its properties. To resize the control, select the control by clicking it, and position the mouse pointer over one of the control handles, which are represented by small boxes. When a small arrow appears, you can drag the handles in the appropriate direction to resize the control.

To move a control to a new location, simply drag it. Notice that the form's canvas is covered with a grid. Each point on the grid is a possible location for a corner or other relevant point on a control. You can choose to have controls snap to the grid points by right-clicking the grid and selecting Snap To Grid. You can define the distances between the points on this grid. This is important because the greater the scale of the grid (the greater the distance between points on the grid), the fewer places you can locate a control on your form. Conversely, the smaller the scale, the more you can refine the positioning of your controls.

To change the grid, follow these steps:

1. In the Arrange group, click Align.

2. Click Set Grid Size.

3. Type a value (in pixels) for the height and width spacing.

4. Click OK.

The smaller the number that you use for spacing, the smaller the scale. This means that more points on the grid will appear, and you can have more control over where your objects fit on the grid. The default is 8, but 3 is a good number to choose for greater positioning control.

INSIDE OUT   Limit controls on your forms

When you're using controls on forms, you can be tempted to make one form do too much. Although there's no precise limit for the number of controls that can be included on one form, the recommendation is using fewer than 300. However, my experience with custom forms development suggests that even 100 is excessive. You should try to keep the number of controls down to a few dozen or so when possible. Forms that try to do too much usually become confusing to users, and these forms often do not perform well. Keeping your forms focused and giving them a crisp design makes them easier to code and debug, too. If you find that your form is overloaded, consider creating a COM add-in to allow a broader application context, or develop a stand-alone application that handles all your information needs.

Properties

Controls have a number of properties that you can view and modify. To find out what these properties are, right-click a control and then choose Properties on the shortcut menu to display the Properties dialog box. Figure 27-9 shows a Properties dialog box for a text box control.

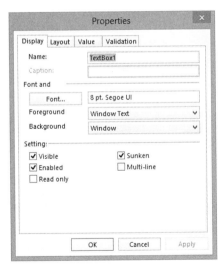

Figure 27-9 You can use the Properties dialog box to modify the properties of a control.

Display

The Display tab of a control's Properties dialog box (a text box example is shown in Figure 27-9) lists the most commonly used properties of the particular control. Changing the setting of a property in this dialog box enables the Apply button; clicking Apply or OK sets the value of that property for the selected control.

The default names of controls are rather generic, such as TextBox1 or CheckBox1. You'll want to change these to names that are more descriptive for your solution, such as txtFirstName or chkHasVacation.

You can learn more about naming conventions for controls by visiting the Microsoft MSDN website at *http://msdn.microsoft.com* and searching for "Visual Basic Coding Conventions Overview."

Layout

The Layout tab in the Properties dialog box lets you set the position of the field within the form. The position settings are set in pixels offset from the top and left side of the form. You can specify the height and width of the field as displayed in the form by setting the Height and Width values. You can also configure the field to resize itself automatically as the form size is being changed by selecting the Resize With Form check box in the Automatic Layout area, as shown in Figure 27-10.

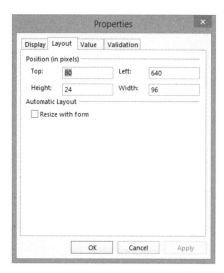

Figure 27-10 Use the Layout tab to set the position and size of a control.

Value

The Value tab in the Properties dialog box, shown in Figure 27-11, contains a number of settings that relate to the field value that the control represents. As mentioned, each control in the Field Chooser list is bound to an Outlook 2013 field. When you modify the properties of a control, you can change the field to which the control is bound.

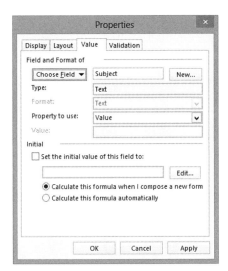

Figure 27-11 Use the options on the Value tab to set the field and format for a control.

To change the bound-field property, click Choose Field and then select the field to which you want to bind the control in the drop-down list. Make sure that the field value is bound to the correct property of your control. Normally, the field value is tied to the control's Value property; this is rarely changed. However, you can change this setting so that, for example, the value of a field is tied to your control's Enabled property. In this case, if the value of the field is True, the control is enabled; if the value is False, the control is not enabled.

You can also set the initial value of your control to display a default value. Set the Initial Value Of This Field To check box, and then type an initial value in the text box. This value doesn't have to be predetermined—you can have it correspond to a dynamic value, such as the current day or the concatenation of the Subject field and the current date. To make the initial value more dynamic, click Edit to open the Initial Value For dialog box; an example is shown in Figure 27-12.

Chapter 27

Figure 27-12 Use this dialog box to customize the initial value for a control.

In this dialog box, you establish a formula for the initial value of your control. For example, you can simply insert a built-in function, such as *Date( )*, for the formula.

To insert a built-in function—the *Date( )* function, in this example—follow these steps:

1. Click Function.

2. Click Date/Time, and then click Date( ).

3. The function appears in the Formula text box.

4. Click OK, and then click OK again to close the Properties dialog box.

When you run the form, the text box control will contain the current date as its initial value. Your users can always change the control's initial value unless you set the control to Read Only (on the Display tab).

Validation

The Validation tab in the Properties dialog box allows you to set certain properties that relate to how (or whether) the value of the control is validated. For example, if you create a form for a purchase order, you might want to ensure that users indicate the quantity of parts that they want to order. The order processing staff will send you many thanks for requiring certain values before the purchase order gets to them because it reduces the amount of information traffic and busywork needed to process an order.

Suppose that you've added a control to your form that requires a value for a text box, and that value is required to be less than or equal to 10 characters. If the user fails to enter a valid value, Outlook 2013 will display a message that prompts the user to enter a correct value.

To set the properties on the Validation tab that will be necessary for this example, as shown in Figure 27-13, follow these steps:

1. Display the Properties dialog box, and then click the Validation tab.

2. Select the A Value Is Required For This Field check box.

3. Select the Validate This Field Before Closing The Form check box.

4. Click the Edit button located to the right of the Validation Formula text box.

5. Click Function.

6. Click Text, Len(string), and then click OK. The Len(string) function appears in the Validation Formula text box.

7. In the Validation Formula text box, type **<=10** after the function, and then click OK.

8. In the Display This Message If The Validation Fails text box, type the following text (including the quotation marks):

    "Please enter a value between 1 and 10 characters in length."

    Alternatively, you can click Edit, type the message without quotation marks, and then click OK.

9. Click OK to close the Properties dialog box.

Figure 27-13 Use the Validation tab to require and verify the value entered in a control.

In the example exercise, when a user works with your form, the text box that requires validation must contain a value, and the value must be less than or equal to 10 characters. If the value the user enters is 11 characters or more, Outlook 2013 will display a message box containing the validation text that you provided when the user tries to send the form. The user can then make the appropriate changes to the text box value and attempt to resend the form.

Standard controls

This chapter has thus far concentrated on controls that are bound to Outlook 2013 fields and that appear in the Field Chooser. However, these aren't the only controls that you can add to a form. This section takes a brief look at some of the standard controls that are available in Outlook 2013, as well as controls that come as part of the Office system.

Controls appear in a Control Toolbox, which is a small, resizable window made visible when you click the button next to the Field Chooser button on the form. Figure 27-14 shows the Toolbox.

Figure 27-14 The Control Toolbox allows you to add controls to your form.

As you hold the mouse pointer over the control icons in the Toolbox, the name of each control appears. To add one of these controls to your form, drag the control icon onto the form. You can then resize and reposition the control or set its properties, as discussed earlier.

> **Note**
> Refer to the Outlook Developer Reference at *http://msdn.microsoft.com* to learn more about the properties, methods, events, and possible uses of the standard controls.

These standard controls are useful but limited. As your skills in developing Outlook 2013–based solutions progress, you'll find that you need functionality that transcends the abilities of the standard controls provided in the Toolbox. Fortunately, you can add other controls and make them accessible via the Toolbox window. For example, if you design a number of forms that need the Outlook Date Control to enable the user to pick a date, you can add that control to the Control Toolbox.

Follow these steps to add the Outlook Date control to the Toolbox:

1. Right-click an empty area of the Toolbox window.

2. Choose Custom Controls.

3. Scroll down the Available Controls list, and then click the box next to Microsoft Outlook Date Control.

4. Click OK. The control appears in the Toolbox.

You can now add this control to a form and work with its specific properties and behaviors just as you did for the standard controls.

Custom controls can make your Outlook 2013 solution extremely robust and powerful. However, be aware that the control you're using might not exist on the computer of the person receiving the message. In other words, although you might have a particular control on your computer, the person who uses your form to compose a message or receives a message composed on your form might not have that control installed. For your solution to work, you need to ensure that the custom controls you use are distributed to and installed on other users' computers properly.

> ### Note
> Methods of distributing custom controls vary widely. Some controls come without an installing package, many use Microsoft Installer, and others use a third-party installation mechanism. You should read the documentation that accompanies your custom control or consult the manufacturer to determine the best method for distributing your control.

After creating your form, you can test it to see what it looks like when it is run. With the new form open, choose Run This Form in the Form group. This won't cause the form to close or disappear; instead, Outlook 2013 produces a new form based on the form that you've just created. The newly created form is an actual running form that you can send and read, and any included functions or scripts are also run when the form is opened.

Adding graphics to forms

Although developing solutions in Outlook 2013 can require much thought and effort, users might not necessarily share your enthusiasm and excitement about the forms that you've created. One way to increase acceptance and usability is to add some pleasing graphics to the forms. These graphics can come in a variety of formats, such as JPEG, GIF, WMF, EMF, and ICO.

One way to add a graphic to your form is to use the image control from the Control Toolbox. Initially, the control will appear as a gray square. You can resize it, just as you can resize any of the standard controls, although it's a good idea to place the picture in the control before you resize it. Set the picture source for the image control by using the Properties dialog box, shown in Figure 27-15. Double-click the Picture property, and then select the desired picture in the Load Picture dialog box.

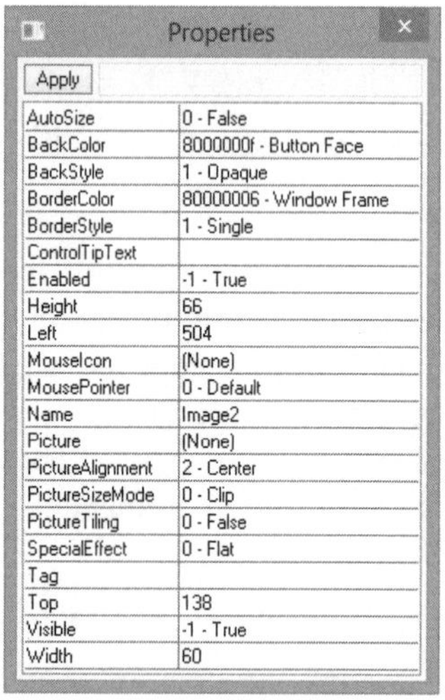

Figure 27-15 Use the Properties dialog box to select a picture to insert into the image control.

Follow these steps to insert a picture in your control:

1. Right-click the image control that you placed on your form.

2. Click Advanced Properties.

3. In the list of properties, scroll down to the Picture property.

4. Select the Picture property and then click the ellipsis button at the top of the form, or simply double-click the Picture property.

5. In the Load Picture dialog box, navigate to the picture that you want to appear in the image control, and then click Open.

6. Close the Advanced Properties dialog box, and then verify that the control now contains the picture you chose.

INSIDE OUT   Change your images at run time

As is the case with all the controls that you use on a custom form, you can change the values of many of their properties when the form is running. For example, you can create a form with an image that changes based on certain criteria. You can add code to your form that alters the setting of the control's Picture property and thus loads an image into the control that is different from the image you specified at design time.

Another way to make your forms more attractive and usable is to add an icon to buttons on the forms. You can configure the command button available in the Toolbox to display both a text caption and a graphic. For example, if your button sends a custom message to a recipient when clicked, you could add an envelope image to the button to convey the notion of sending a message. To have the button display an image, set the Picture property for the button just as you would for an image control. You can also set the Picture property for other controls, such as text boxes and labels.

In addition, you can display a custom icon in the form's title bar. Outlook 2013 always displays a default icon in the upper-left corner of a form that indicates whether it is a task form, an appointment form, and so on. You can change this icon by clicking the Properties tab of your form when you're working in design mode. Click Change Large Icon or Change Small Icon, and then navigate to the .ico file you want to use. The Large Icon setting tells Outlook 2013 which image to display when a user displays the properties of the form. The Small Icon setting specifies the title bar image and the image that is shown when the form is displayed in an Outlook 2013 folder.

Adding user-defined fields

There are times when the types of data that you need to share, gather, or track with forms exceed the Outlook 2013 default field definitions. You might want to have your contact form display the hire date and review date, for example, but these fields don't exist in the Outlook 2013 field list.

You can define new fields that contain information that is relevant to your use of Outlook 2013. These user-defined fields can be bound to a control in the same way that you bind a preexisting field to controls in Outlook 2013 forms.

When you want to implement a new field in a form, start by opening the Design Form dialog box. To create a new form field, you can either open the Field Chooser and click New or click the All Fields tab and then click New.

The New Column dialog box will prompt you for the field name, data type, and display format for the new field. In the Name box, type the name of the new field, such as **Hire Date**, and then select the data type for the field in the Type drop-down list—in this case, Date/Time. In the Format drop-down list, select the display format for the date (or day, time, and date) layout that you want for the field.

The new field is added to the Select From drop-down list, and you can find the new field in the User Defined Fields In Inbox item. The field can be selected in the Field Chooser and on the All Fields tab. To use your new field, drag it onto your form. You will need to remember to add the field to both the Compose Page and the Read Page, and commonly you will want to set the properties of the field in the Read Page to read-only (on the Display tab).

Publishing and sharing forms

After you create your form and define its behaviors, properties, and settings, you'll want to make it available to users. First, however, you'll need to preserve your form in one of these two ways:

- Save the form as a file.

- Publish the form to a folder or other location.

Saving forms

You can save a form by clicking File and then clicking Save As. In the Save As dialog box, enter the file name and select the location. The form file is saved as an Outlook Template file (.oft).

Publishing forms

Publishing a form is a lot like saving the form. When you finish your form, you can publish it to a specific folder location. You can publish it to your Inbox or another folder in your mailbox, a public folder, the Organizational Forms Library (with Microsoft Exchange Server), or your Personal Forms Library.

Follow these steps to publish a form to a folder or forms library:

1. Click Design A Form on the Developer tab.

2. In the Design Form dialog box, select the location (such as User Templates In File System) containing the form that you want to publish.

3. Select the form that you want to publish, and then click Open.

4. In the Form group, click Publish, and then click Publish Form As to open the Publish Form As dialog box. (The first time you use the Publish button, the Publish Form As dialog box will be displayed, but after a form has been saved once, the Publish button will simply save the existing form, overwriting the previous version.)

5. In the Look In drop-down list, select the folder or forms library where you want to publish the form. (The default is the Personal Forms Library.)

6. Type the display name and the form name.

7. Click Publish in the Publish Form As dialog box to save the form in the selected location.

INSIDE OUT   Create a staging area for your forms

When you're creating a form, it's a good idea to keep the production version of the form separate from the development version. Create a staging folder where you publish the forms that you're working on. When you complete a form design, publish your form in this staging folder at regular intervals so that you don't lose the modifications you've made to the form. Only people designing and testing forms for your organization should have access to this folder.

After you publish a form, the folder in which you publish it contains the form itself and all the underlying information that another person's instance of Outlook 2013 needs to understand the form.

Choosing forms

After you have created a custom form and saved or published it for common use, you will need to select the form to use it. Custom forms are normally stored in a location related to their expected use. Custom forms intended for common use, for example, are usually stored in an accessible network location. If you have a custom form intended for your own use, however, you would store it in the Personal Forms Library. Alternatively, if you want to use a form that you have saved to a folder on your local hard disk, you would store it using the User Templates In File System location.

In each of these cases, to locate your custom form, select the appropriate location in the Look In drop-down list of the Choose Form dialog box, shown in Figure 27-16.

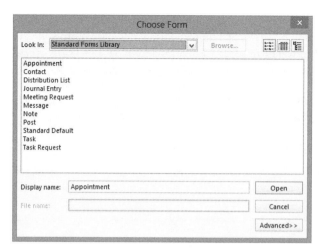

Figure 27-16   Select a custom form in the Choose Form dialog box by first selecting its location.

To use a custom form from these (or any other) locations, follow these steps:

1. Click Choose Form on the Developer tab.

2. In the Choose Form dialog box, select the location in which your custom form is stored (such as the Personal Forms Library).

3. Select the custom form that you want to use.

4. Click Open.

Using forms effectively

Each of the forms in Outlook 2013 serves the same purpose—to present information in a specific format. Outlook 2013 forms provide access to all Outlook 2013 items (messages, notes, meetings, tasks, journal entries, and so on) and enable you to create custom forms using any of the available fields. By creating custom forms that align with your workflow, you can ease the communication of information as well as the transfer of data important to your business.

In creating custom forms, you begin by selecting a default form that most closely resembles the form and function that you want for your new forms. You can then choose to add or delete fields on the default page and/or create additional pages containing fields to display or gather further information. Here are some pointers about using forms:

- **Know when not to create forms**   Outlook 2013 form creation can give you the ability to customize email messages, meeting requests, and other Outlook 2013 items, but if existing forms provide the functionality you need, it is easier and more effective to use the existing forms. When you consider creating a new form, start by asking, "Is the functionality I need already present in an existing form?" Consider that in addition to the time needed to create a custom form, there are distribution logistics (how you get the form to all who would need it), as well as training needed to enable people to effectively use the new form.

- **Keep forms simple but comprehensive**   Once you have decided that a new form is necessary, evaluate the information that you need the form to display, transmit, or gather, and then limit the form information to the minimum data required to fulfill your operational or organizational needs. You can create a custom form with multiple pages containing an exhaustive array of fields, yet the complexity of using such a form could easily outweigh any hoped-for benefits. Keep in mind that each custom form that you create is intended to facilitate the communication of information. The easier it is for people to use the custom form to exchange information, the more likely it is that people will use the form, and thus the more value it will have for your organization.

  Consider a custom form created to enhance customer relationship management by including 15 fields of concise contact information, key project assessment, and a project status summary versus a custom form that includes 5 pages containing 200 fields of exhaustive contact information, step-by-step project notes, milestones and time-lines, equipment reserved, travel time, technical assessments, customer evaluation, and so on. The first option with 15 fields is much more likely to be used. When you actually have a need to gather 200 fields' worth of information, you'll want to consider subdividing the data into related sets and then creating separate forms for each set. (Or in this case, use an existing solution like Microsoft Dynamics CRM.)

- **Use user-defined fields to store information not included by default in Outlook**   Although Outlook 2013 contains fields for the data it uses in contacts, email, meeting requests, tasks, and so on, there are invariably additional pieces of information that your organization could benefit by having included that are not part of the Outlook 2013 default field set. Consider additions to the meeting form that could be useful when you're scheduling meetings with coworkers. For example, to identify who will be leading the meeting, you could add a Presenter field to the custom meeting request form. Likewise, you might consider adding Food Preferences and Food Allergies fields to a custom appointment form for those appointments with clients or staff that involve dining out or food being brought into the event.

Chapter 27

You might want to add information in your contact list that isn't shared, but that assists you in working with others or relating to their personal interests. You could, for example, create a custom contact form to enable you to track the specialized knowledge or favorite sports of each of the people in your contact list. Then, for example, when you want to find a coworker who just happens to know how IPv6 actually works, you can search on "IPv6" and display the names of every person in your contact list who is fluent in IPv6. (Searching for user-defined fields requires you to select the Query Builder and then add your custom form and fields to the query criteria.)

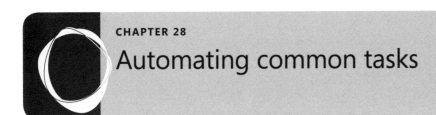

CHAPTER 28

Automating common tasks

MICROSOFT Outlook 2013 is a feature-rich product and, as such, it has an option, a wizard, or a graphical tool for accomplishing nearly anything that you require from a personal information manager (PIM). If something does come up that the folks at Microsoft haven't planned for, however, you also have the option of customizing Outlook 2013 by using its built-in support for Microsoft Visual Basic code additions. Through the use of flexible Microsoft Visual Basic for Applications (VBA) scripting options and built-in security controls, you can simplify and automate common tasks.

In this chapter, you'll learn how to create and use macros, including how to create a macro, step through a macro to test it, and delete any macros you no longer need. In addition, you'll find out about implementing security options for macros.

See Chapter 11, "Using rules, alerts, and automatic responses," for a discussion of Quick Steps, which enable you to process messages automatically.

Understanding automation options

Outlook 2013 has a number of built-in automation options that allow the application to perform certain tasks for you. For example, the Rules Wizard lets you build rules to automatically move, copy, and forward email messages. The Out of Office Assistant sends automatic replies when you're away.

For information about these examples of built-in automation options, see Chapter 11 and the section "Creating automatic responses with Automatic Replies (Out of Office)."

If a built-in option can accomplish the automated task that you require, it should be your first choice. By using a built-in option instead of a custom one, you minimize problems that can occur if you need to reinstall Outlook 2013 or use Outlook 2013 on multiple machines. Using standardized options also guards against compatibility problems with upgrades to Outlook 2013.

If none of the automation options does the trick, however, you can accomplish just about any customization by using VBA. This chapter focuses on the use of VBA procedures known as macros to automate common tasks.

Understanding macros

So just what is a macro? In general terms, a *macro* is a number of commands grouped together to execute a particular task. Macros are like small programs that operate within other programs. Macros have been around for a long time, and all Microsoft Office 2013 products support them at some level. In Outlook 2013, macros are implemented as VBA procedures that are not linked to a particular form and are available from anywhere in Outlook 2013. In Outlook 2013, you manage macros by using commands in the Code area on the Developer tab. To display the Developer tab, right-click the ribbon and choose Customize The Ribbon. In the Outlook Options dialog box, place a check beside Developer in the tab list on the right and click OK.

Using macros

Macros are most useful for tasks that must be performed repeatedly without change. Even so, because a macro contains Visual Basic code, it can be flexible and can respond to variables or user input. With the power of scripting, a macro can accomplish a task in the most efficient way in response to specific conditions.

> **CAUTION**
>
> Macros can be extremely powerful. This power can be a great asset for you, but it can also mean that any problems can become serious ones. Like many other things, macros can be dangerous when used improperly. Inexperienced programmers should take great care when writing and using macros in Outlook 2013.

The following are the three basic programming elements you can work with in an Outlook 2013 macro:

- **Object** An object is a particular part of a form, such as a button, a menu item, or a text field. Objects make up any element of Outlook 2013 that you can see or work with. An object has properties, and how you set these properties determines how the object functions.

- **Property** Any descriptor of an object—its color, its width, and its value—is part of the set of attributes that make up its properties.

- **Method** A method is a task that an object carries out, such as showing a form or reading file information. Methods can be modified based on user input or the value of certain properties.

> **Note**
>
> Before you can work with macros, you might need to configure macro security set-tings. For information about configuring macro security, see the section "Setting macro security."

In general, a VBA macro either determines or modifies the value of an object property or calls a method. Macros, then, are nothing more than simple programs that use VBA to access or modify Outlook 2013 information.

> **Note**
>
> In Microsoft Excel 2013 and Microsoft Word 2013, you can simply record your mouse movements and keystrokes using the Macro Recorder, and the computer plays them back when you execute the macro. Outlook 2013 doesn't include a macro recorder, so you have to create macros by writing the macro code yourself. Therefore, users familiar with programming basics and VBA will have a head start in learning to create Outlook 2013 macros.

Creating a macro from scratch

The process for creating an Outlook 2013 macro is simple. The process for creating a useful macro, on the other hand, is more complex. In this chapter, we'll fall back on the most basic of functions, the "Hello World" message box macro. This macro creates a function that dis-plays a message box containing the text *Hello World*. Clicking OK (the only button) closes the message box and ends the macro.

To create this macro, follow these steps:

1. Click the Developer tab, click Macros, and choose Macros to open the Macros dialog box.

2. In the Macro Name box, type a descriptive name for your new macro (no spaces are allowed). In Figure 28-1, the macro is titled HelloWorldMsgBox.

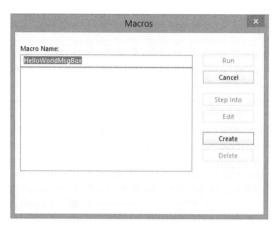

Figure 28-1 Enter the name for a new macro in the Macro Name box.

3. Click Create. Visual Basic starts, which allows you to add functionality to your macro. If you are not a programmer, creating VBA code might seem daunting, but simple tasks are actually quite easy to write code for. (Note that if you have macros, they will be displayed in this window, each in its own section of the project file.)

4. The first line of the macro starts with *Sub* and contains the macro name—in this case, HelloWorldMsgBox. On the next line, type the following, as shown in Figure 28-2:

```
MsgBox ("Hello World")
```

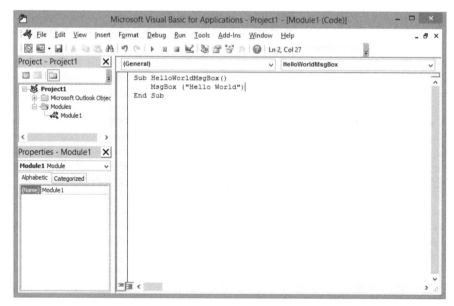

Figure 28-2 You add code between the first and last lines of a macro.

5. To test the code, choose Run, Run Sub/UserForm, or click the Run Sub/UserForm button on the toolbar (or press F5). The message box shown in Figure 28-3 appears.

Figure 28-3 The Hello World message box appears when you run the macro.

> **Note**
>
> If you get a message saying macros are not enabled, you should check your macro security settings. To learn how to configure macro security, see the section "Setting macro security."

6. Choose File, Save. (The file name, which cannot be changed here, is VbaProject.OTM.)

7. Close the Visual Basic Editor.

Running a macro

After you save a macro, it is available for use. Click the Developer tab, click Macros, and then select the HelloWorldMsgBox macro. The message box appears, just as it did when you tested the macro in the Visual Basic Editor.

Although macros are available from the Developer tab, in some cases you might want to add a macro to the ribbon or Quick Access Toolbar to make it readily available when you need it. To add the macro to a tab in the Outlook 2013 ribbon, follow these steps:

1. Right-click the ribbon and choose Customize The Ribbon.

2. In the Choose Commands From list, select Macros. The HelloWorldMsgBox macro appears on the left, as shown in Figure 28-4.

Figure 28-4 Locate the macro and then add it to the desired tab.

3. Select a custom group in which to place the macro (you can't add the macro to any of the default groups).

4. Click Add to add the HelloWorldMsgBox macro to the group. Clicking the button in the group will run the macro.

To add the macro to the Quick Access Toolbar, follow these steps:

1. Click Customize Quick Access Toolbar, and then choose More Commands to open the Editor Options dialog box.

2. In the Choose Commands From drop-down list, select Macros. The HelloWorldMsgBox macro appears in the list below, as shown in Figure 28-5.

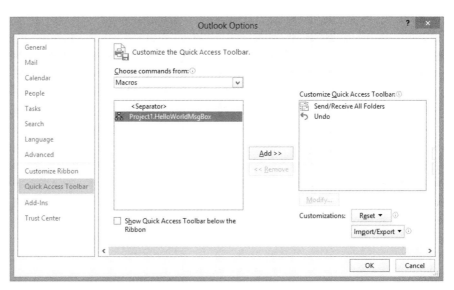

Figure 28-5 Add a button for the macro to the Quick Access Toolbar.

3. Click Add to add the HelloWorldMsgBox macro button to the Quick Access Toolbar.

4. Click OK to close the Outlook Options dialog box.

Editing a macro

After you create a macro, you can edit it by returning to the Macros dialog box as follows:

1. Open the Macros dialog box from the Developer tab, select the HelloWorldMsgBox macro, and click Edit. The Visual Basic Editor starts and displays the selected macro.

2. Modify the macro so that it matches the following:

```
Sub HelloWorldMsgBox()
MsgBox ("Click OK to create a new message")
Set newMsg = Application.CreateItem(0)
    newMsg.Subject = "Sample Message from a Macro"
    newMsg.Body = "You can even add text automatically."
    newMsg.Display
End Sub
```

Chapter 28

3. Verify that the changed macro works properly by clicking the Run Sub/UserForm button on the Microsoft Visual Basic toolbar. Instead of showing a simple message box as before, the macro should now present you with an email message window. (This window might be hidden behind the Microsoft Visual Basic for Applications window.) The message should have information automatically filled in the subject and body fields, as shown in Figure 28-6.

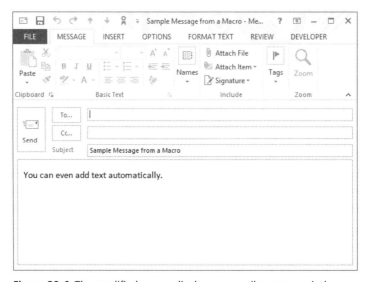

Figure 28-6 The modified macro displays an email message window.

4. Save the changes to your Visual Basic project, and then close the Microsoft Visual Basic for Applications window. Close the email message that you created.

5. When you return to the Macros dialog box, select the modified macro, and then click Run. You should see the same email message as shown in Figure 28-6. Close the email message.

Note

When you edit a macro, you'll eventually want to save it and test the changes. To ensure that you can return to the original macro in case of trouble, first export the project so that you can retrieve it later. For more information about exporting, see the section "Sharing macros with others."

Stepping through a macro

When you're creating a macro, it's often helpful to step through the code, which allows you to watch each line as it is being processed and see problems as they occur. To do this, open the HelloWorldMsgBox macro for editing (as described in the preceding section), and then press F8. Alternatively, open the Macros dialog box, select the macro, and then choose Step Into. The first line of the macro is highlighted, and its code is processed. To process the next line, press F8 again.

Step through the rest of the macro using the F8 key. Notice that clicking OK merely closes the message box rather than creating the email message. This is because later steps are not followed automatically. The new email message is created only after you press F8 through the line of the subprocedure that displays it—in this case, the last line of the macro.

> **Note**
> You can step through a macro only when it is being edited. When macros are executed from within Outlook 2013, they automatically move through all procedures.

TROUBLESHOOTING

Your macro doesn't run properly

If you are having problems getting a macro to run properly, you can try several approaches to determine the source of the problem. The most common problem is incorrect syntax in your code. Finding errors in code can be a vexing job, but using the step-through process generally helps to find the line that is causing you problems.

If your syntax is correct, the problem might have to do with the way you're running the macro. Among the problems you should check for are the security settings on the macro and the security settings on the computer. Also, if the macro has been deleted but a toolbar button still remains, you might be trying to run a macro that no longer exists.

Deleting a macro

Sometimes a macro outlives its usefulness. To delete a macro that you no longer need, click the Developer tab, click Macros, and choose Macros. In the Macros dialog box, select the macro that you want to remove, and then click Delete. When you're prompted to verify that you want to delete the macro permanently, click Yes to remove the macro from the list, making its code unavailable to Outlook 2013.

> **Note**
> If you have created a toolbar button for a macro that you subsequently delete, you must locate the button and remove it in a separate operation.

Sharing macros with others

If you're creating macros for use by a group of people, or even an entire organization, the macros must be installed separately for each user. Unfortunately, although the Macros dialog box has options for creating and deleting macros, it has no option for adding macros from other places. You can't share macros in the same way you can share files. Instead, sharing macros with other users is generally a two-step process: the user who creates the macro must export the macro code, and the other user must import the code. To share a macro, follow these steps:

1. On the Developer tab, click Visual Basic in the Code group.

2. In Visual Basic, choose File, Export File to open the Export File dialog box, shown in Figure 28-7.

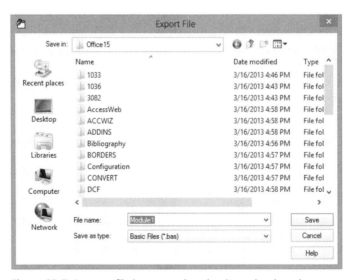

Figure 28-7 A macro file is exported so that it can be shared.

3. In the Save As Type box, save the project as a .bas file. (By doing so, you can then email the file to another user or make it available on your network.)

Once another user has access to the .bas file, that user can install the macro by following these steps:

1. On the Developer tab, click Visual Basic.

2. In the Visual Basic Editor, choose File, Import File.

3. Browse to the file, open it, and then save it.

The user can now access the macro through the Macros dialog box.

Setting macro security

Macros have several advantages, including their power, their flexibility, and their ability to run automatically, even without your knowledge. These advantages have a dark side, however, and poorly written or malicious macros can do significant damage to an Outlook 2013 message store. Because of the potential danger that macros pose, the Outlook 2013 Trust Center offers four security levels for Outlook 2013 macros:

- **Disable All Macros Without Notification**   Macros are totally disabled, and Outlook 2013 does not display any warning that a macro is attempting to run.

- **Notifications For Digitally Signed Macros, All Other Macros Disabled**   Your system can run only macros that are signed digitally. This means that some macros—even benign and potentially useful ones—are not available unless they are signed.

- **Notifications For All Macros**   You will be prompted as to whether you want to run any macros.

- **Enable All Macros (Not Recommended)**   Macros run automatically, regardless of their signature. This is the most dangerous setting.

To view or change the security level, on the Developer tab, click Macro Security to open the Macro Settings page of the Trust Center, as shown in Figure 28-8. (You can also access the Trust Center by opening an Outlook 2013 item and, on the Developer tab, in the Code group, clicking Macro Security.) The default setting is Notifications For Digitally Signed Macros, All Other Macros Disabled, which is probably the best choice for most users.

Chapter 28

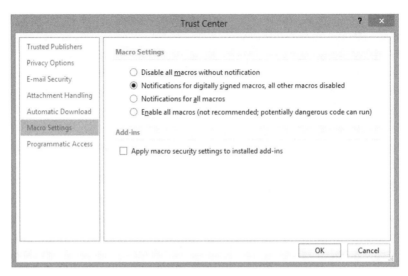

Figure 28-8 You can set the security level for macros in the Trust Center.

INSIDE OUT   Understand security and user-created macros

When you create your own macros, they are not controlled by the security settings. User-created macros do not need to be signed and will run regardless of the security setting that you have selected—even if you choose the Disable All Macros Without Notification option! This is nice for purposes of design and editing, but it assumes that you realize exactly what a macro will do. Moreover, it means that when you want to test macro security settings, you must run Outlook 2013 using a different user account.

Specifying trusted sources

To reduce the number of times you're prompted about whether to run a macro (if you've set the security level to Notifications For Digitally Signed Macros, All Other Macros Disabled) or to be able to run macros at all (if you've set the security level to Notifications For All Macros), you can specify a trusted source.

When a digitally signed macro runs, Outlook 2013 displays the certificate attached to the macro. In addition to choosing whether to run the macro, you're given the choice of adding the certificate holder (the organization or individual who created the macro) to your list of trusted sources. Once the holder of the certificate is trusted, any macros signed with that certificate run without prompting at the Notifications For Digitally Signed Macros, All Other Macros Disabled security setting. To view the list of trusted certificates or to remove a trusted source, click File, Options, Trust Center, Trust Center Settings. Click Trusted Publishers to view the sources. To remove a trusted source, select the source and then click Remove.

Using Group Policy and custom installations

I F you are charged with administering Microsoft Office or Outlook in your environment, you're likely interested in methods you can use to control how office apps like Outlook function in your environment. For example, you might be interested in deploying Outlook with specific settings already configured for your users, certain features locked down, or customizations in place.

Fortunately, you can control a broad range of features and behaviors in Office apps and Outlook in particular through the use of Group Policy. This chapter provides an overview of Group Policy and explores the tools and methods you have available to control Outlook through Group Policy. The chapter also explores your options for customizing Outlook deployment. Because these are large, complex topics, it isn't practical to cover every aspect in this chapter (each could encompass a book on its own). Instead, this chapter serves as an overview and resource guide to help put you on the right path to understanding these topics.

Overview of Group Policy

Group Policy is an aspect of Active Directory (directory services) in Microsoft Windows Server. Group Policy enables you to specify managed configurations for users and computers, and have those configurations applied to the users' accounts and computers at boot and when they log on (as well as at other times). Group Policy therefore gives you a mechanism to configure the operating system, applications, and the behaviors of both, all automatically.

Group Policy settings are contained in a Group Policy Object (GPO). You create and edit GPOs using the Group Policy Management Console (GPMC). Within the GPMC, you associate a selected GPO with an Active Directory site, domain, or organizational unit (OU). The capability to apply GPOs at these various levels in Active Directory gives you relative granularity to apply policies where needed. For example, to apply a Group Policy to every computer or user in your organization, you would likely link the GPO to the site or domain level. If you need to apply policies to only a subset of users, you would link the GPO to an OU or security group that is applicable to that subset of users.

Let's explore an example and how Group Policy can be used to resolve a potential configuration challenge. Assume that you, as an administrator for your organization, want to disable the Weather Bar in Outlook. The behavior is controlled by the registry setting HKCU\Software\Policies\Microsoft\Office\15.0\Outlook\Options\Calendar\DisableWeather. You could set that registry value manually for each user, but that's generally very impractical. Instead, you can push out the change using Group Policy.

Configuring something as relatively trivial as the Weather Bar is just one aspect of Outlook's look and behavior that you can control through Group Policy. There are numerous settings for Outlook as well as the other Office apps. But as you might have already guessed, these Group Policy settings are not included in the base set of policies inherent in Active Directory. Instead, you can use the Office Administrative Templates, explained in the following section, to configure Office and Outlook Group Policy settings.

> **Note**
>
> As previously mentioned, Group Policy and Active Directory are topics that could fill multiple books. TechNet and other Microsoft online resources—not to mention other resources on the Internet—contain thousands of documents that explain various aspects of Group Policy. For a solid overview, navigate to *http://technet.microsoft.com* and search on the phrase "Group Policy overview."

Using the Office Administrative Templates

Group Policy is extensible, meaning a core set of functionality is built into Group Policy as it exists within Microsoft Windows Server, but additional policies can be easily added. With Office apps, these Group Policy settings are configured using the Office Administrative Templates. These templates are part of the Office 2013 Resource Kit, which you'll find at *http://technet.microsoft.com/en-us/library/cc303401.aspx*. For the templates themselves, visit *http://technet.microsoft.com/en-us/library/cc178992.aspx*.

After you download the templates from the TechNet website, run the download and extract the files to a folder. The administrative templates for Office 2013 Group Policy are in the XML format introduced with Microsoft Windows Vista and Windows Server 2008. If you're familiar with using the previous ADM templates, note that there is a difference in how you add the templates to the Group Policy Management Editor (GPME).

To make the templates available, copy the desired .admx file (such as Outlk15.admx) from the folder where you extracted the template files to the folder systemroot\PolicyDefinitions. The default location is C:\Windows\PolicyDefinitions. Then locate the corresponding .adml resource file (such as Outlk15.adml) in the appropriate language folder where you extracted

the template files, and copy the file to the same language folder under systemroot\
PolicyDefinitions.

For example, assume you extracted the template files to C:\GPTemplates and are using U.S.
English. Copy the file C:\GPTemplates\Outlk15.admx to C:\Windows\PolicyDefinitions. Then
copy C:\GPTemplates\en-us\Outlk15.adml to C:\Windows\PolicyDefinitions\en-us. The next
time you open the GPME, you'll find the new Microsoft Outlook 2013 branch under User
Configuration\Policies\Administrative Templates.

Now that you have added the Outlook template, it's relatively easy to add and configure settings to control the behavior of Outlook 2013. Keep in mind that where you link
the GPO in which you configure the settings determines which users will come under the
scope of the policy. So, the first step is deciding at what level you want to apply the settings. Next, open the Group Policy Management console from the Administrative Tools
folder in Control Panel. Locate the GPO where you want to apply the settings, right-click
the GPO, and choose Edit to open the GPME. Open the branch User Configuration\Policies\
Administrative Templates\Microsoft Outlook 2013, as shown in Figure 29-1.

Figure 29-1 Configure Outlook 2013 Group Policy settings through the Administrative Templates branch of the Group Policy Management Editor (GPME).

Do you remember the Weather Bar example cited at the beginning of this chapter? Let's navigate through the Group Policy settings to locate the one that enables or disables the Weather Bar. With the GPME open, navigate to User Configuration\Policies\Administrative Templates\Microsoft Outlook 2013\Outlook Options\Preferences\Calendar Options. In the right pane (see Figure 29-2), double-click Disable Weather Bar. After you double-click the policy setting, a policy dialog box opens that is similar to the one shown in Figure 29-3. Set the policy as desired and then click OK.

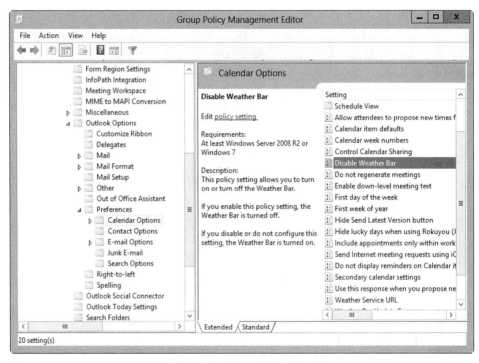

Figure 29-2 The Disable Weather Bar policy selected in the GPME.

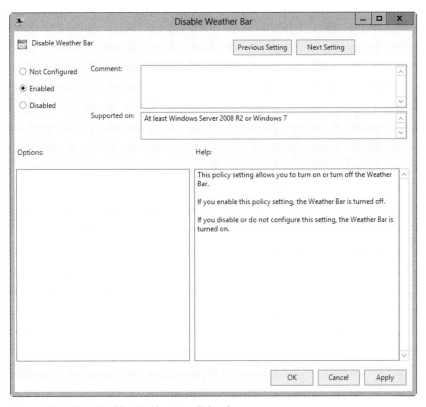

Figure 29-3 The Disable Weather Bar dialog box.

Although the Office Administrative Templates download includes an Excel file that describes each policy covered by the templates, a good way to get familiar with the settings you can configure via Group Policy is to simply walk through the settings in the GPME. When you click a setting in the right pane, you'll see an explanation in the left half of the right pane (assuming you have clicked the Extended tab). You can also double-click a policy setting to open the setting's dialog box and view a description of the policy in the dialog box.

Customizing Outlook deployment

Microsoft provides a second tool in addition to Group Policy that enables you to customize the setup for Outlook 2013 (and other Office apps). The Office Customization Tool (OCT) enables you to create a Setup customization (.msp) file that configures Office apps when a user installs Office. You can also use the OCT to create a Setup customization file to use to modify an existing Office installation.

The .msp file created by the OCT is a Windows Installer package. As such, you can apply the file to a user's computer in the same way you apply a software update. For example, a user can run the update file simply by double-clicking the .msp file. Alternatively, you can push out the update using System Center Configuration Manager or Windows Server Update Services.

Although you can configure a broad range of settings for Office and specific Office apps through the OCT, this section of the chapter focuses on customizing Outlook. Also, because TechNet offers several detailed explanations of the OCT and how to use it, this chapter provides an only an overview of the tool and process to get you started. To learn how to customize Setup before installing Office 2013, see *http://technet.microsoft.com/en-us/library/cc179121.aspx*. To learn how to customize Office after it has been installed, see *http://technet.microsoft.com/en-us/library/cc179141.aspx*.

What can you customize?

The Outlook section of the OCT enables you to configure several aspects of Outlook 2013. The following list summarizes the items you can configure through the OCT:

- **Outlook profile**   You can specify that the installation use an existing profile on the user's system or prompt the user to create a profile the first time Outlook starts. You can also specify modifications to a profile, create a new profile, and apply a .prf file to define a new profile or update an existing one. The .prf file (which you create with the OCT) contains settings that define the profile.

- **Exchange options**   Use these options to specify an account name, user name, initial Exchange Server, Cached Exchange Mode settings, and Outlook Anywhere settings.

- **Send/receive groups**   Create send/receive groups and related send/receive settings.

- **Address book settings**   Specify settings to define the default way in which Outlook updates the Offline Address Book from Exchange Server.

As with the Group Policy settings for configuring Office 2013, the best way to learn about the settings you can configure with the OCT is to run through a sample. Spend some time reading the resources listed at the beginning of this section, and then download the OCT and run through a sample deployment to explore its capabilities.

Accessing your mailboxes without Outlook

M ICROSOFT first introduced Microsoft Outlook Web Access (OWA) in Microsoft Exchange Server 5.0 so that clients could access their Exchange Server mailboxes through a web browser. Microsoft has made significant improvements in OWA in each new version of Exchange Server to provide support for a larger number of users, better performance, and improved functionality for clients. The latest version of this feature in Exchange Server 2013, called Outlook Web App, provides most of the functionality of the Microsoft Outlook 2013 client.

This chapter explores Outlook Web App to help you learn why it can be an important feature to implement and how best to put it to work for you, and also to help you put it to work as an alternative or complement to Outlook 2013. This chapter also looks at two other options you have for accessing your mailboxes without Outlook: the Windows 8 Mail app and Windows Phone.

Overview of Outlook Web App

With Outlook Web App and a web browser, users can send and receive messages, view and modify their calendars, and perform most of the other tasks available through Outlook 2013. The features and appearance of Outlook Web App (or Outlook Web Access) depend on the version of Exchange Server that is hosting it. Each successive version of Exchange Server adds a new look and new capabilities.

Outlook 2013 provides full access to an Exchange Server mailbox. Although Outlook Web App isn't intended as a complete replacement for Outlook 2013, it is useful for roaming users who want to access the most common mailbox features when they don't have access to their personal Outlook 2013 installation. Linux, UNIX, and Macintosh users can also benefit from Outlook Web App by being able to access Exchange Server mailboxes and participate in workgroup messaging and scheduling. In addition, Outlook Web App can save the administrative overhead and support associated with deploying Outlook 2013 to users who don't need everything that Outlook 2013 has to offer. These users can use a free web browser to access many functions provided by Exchange Server. However, you must still purchase a Client Access License (CAL) for each user or device that accesses the server running Exchange Server, even if the users do not use Outlook to connect to the server.

Outlook Web App features

Because email is the primary function of Exchange Server and Outlook 2013, Outlook Web App supports email access. Users can view message headers and read messages (see Figure 30-1) as well as send, reply to, forward, and delete messages. This last capability—deleting messages—might seem commonplace, but it is a useful feature. If your mailbox contains a very large attachment or a corrupted message that is preventing you from viewing your messages in Outlook 2013, you can use Outlook Web App to delete the message without downloading or reading it. Just open your mailbox in your web browser, select the message header, and delete the message.

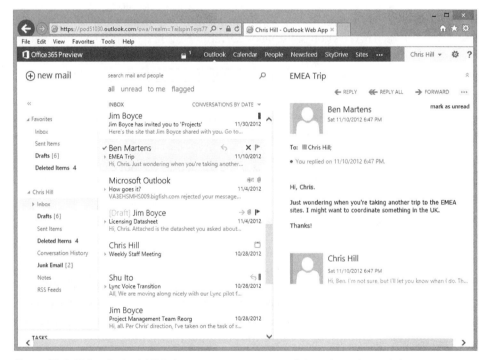

Figure 30-1 Using Outlook Web App, you can access your Inbox through a web browser.

> **Note**
>
> This chapter uses Office 365 as the back-end mail service for all examples. While the menu across the top of the interface is somewhat different (the title at the left is Office 365 Preview rather than Outlook Web App, for example), the available features are the same whether you are accessing an Office 365 mailbox or an on-premise Exchange account.

As mentioned earlier, you're not limited to just messaging—you can also access your Calendar folder through Outlook Web App. You can view and modify existing items and create appointments (see Figure 30-2). You can't perform all the same scheduling tasks through Outlook Web App that you can with Outlook 2013, but the ability to view your schedule and add appointments is useful, particularly when you're working from a remote location or on a system without Outlook 2013 installed.

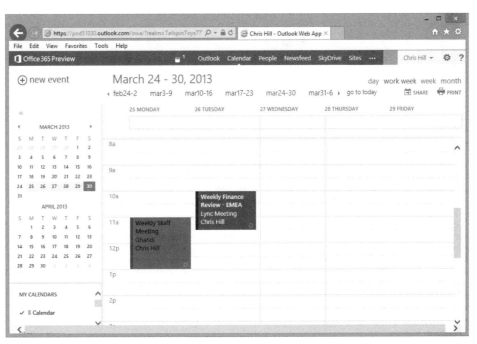

Figure 30-2 Use Outlook Web App to manage your schedule as well as your email messages.

Contacts are another type of item that you can manage through Outlook Web App. You can view and modify existing contact items and add new ones (see Figure 30-3).

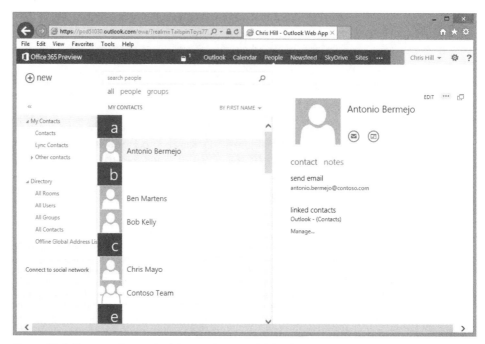

Figure 30-3 You can also work with your Contacts folder through Outlook Web App.

Each successive release of Exchange Server has incorporated changes to Outlook Web Access. These changes have included an interface to match the Outlook interface more closely, the addition of a spelling checker, access to task lists, Secure/Multipurpose Internet Mail Extensions (S/MIME) support, HTML content blocking, scheduling and control of Out of Office messages, the addition of the Scheduling Assistant, access to Microsoft SharePoint documents, Really Simple Syndication (RSS) subscriptions, support for rights management, and many other features. The end result is that Outlook Web App in Exchange Server 2013 provides most of the features offered by the native Outlook client.

Web browser options

The following are the requirements to access your mailbox through the latest release of Outlook Web App on a computer running Windows 2003 or later:

- Internet Explorer 7 and later versions

- Firefox 3.0.1 and later versions

- Chrome 3.0.195.27 and later versions

On a computer running Mac OS X 10.5 and later versions, you can use the following:

- Safari 3.1 and later versions

- Firefox 3.0.1 and later versions

On a computer running Linux, you can use the following:

- Firefox 3.0.1 and later versions

In addition to these requirements, you need to enable session cookies in the browser, enable JavaScript, and allow pop-ups for the site hosting OWA.

> **Note**
> If your browser doesn't meet the requirements previously listed, the light version of OWA opens. The light version doesn't provide all of the same functionality as the standard version, but it can perform faster than the standard version in some situations.

Authentication options

Outlook Web App offers several options for authentication:

- **Basic Authentication**   This option uses clear text and simple challenge/response to authenticate access. This option offers the broadest client support, but it also offers the least security because passwords are transmitted as clear text.

- **Integrated Windows Authentication**   This option uses the native Windows authentication method for the client's operating system. Integrated Windows authentication provides better security than basic authentication because passwords are encrypted. The client doesn't need to enter authentication credentials because the browser uses the client's Windows logon credentials to authenticate on the Outlook Web App server.

- **Digest Authentication**   This authentication method works only with Active Directory Domain Services (AD DS) accounts. It offers the benefit of sending passwords as a hash rather than in plain text. However, to use digest authentication, you must configure AD DS to allow reversible encryption, which reduces security.

In addition to these authentication methods, Outlook Web App supports the use of Secure Sockets Layer (SSL) to provide additional security for remote connections.

Using Outlook Web App

After your Exchange Server administrators install and configure Outlook Web App on the server(s), users can begin accessing their mailboxes through their web browsers rather than (or in conjunction with) Outlook 2013. This section explains how to connect to the computer running Exchange Server and use Outlook Web App to access your mailbox.

> **Note**
>
> This section assumes that you are connecting to Exchange Server 2013 with Outlook Web App. If you have an earlier version of Exchange Server, the features available to you are slightly different, and the look and feel are also different.

Connecting to the server

Typically, you connect to the computer running Exchange Server through the URL *http://<server>/exchange*, where *<server>* is the Domain Name System (DNS) name, Internet Protocol (IP) address, or NetBIOS name of the server. An example is *https://owa.tailspintoys.com/exchange*. This URL isn't set in stone. The system administrator might have changed the virtual directory name for security purposes. Check with the system administrator if you're not sure what URL to use to connect to the computer running Exchange Server.

> **Note**
>
> Windows Internet Name Service (WINS) maps NetBIOS names (computer names) to IP addresses, performing a service similar to that provided by DNS (although DNS maps host names, not NetBIOS names). You can use an Lmhosts file to perform NetBIOS name-to-address mapping without a WINS server, just as you can use a Hosts file to perform host name-to-address mapping without a DNS server.

Depending on the server's authentication settings, you might be prompted to log on. Enter your user name and password for the Exchange Server account. If the account resides in a different domain from the one in which the server resides, enter the account name in the form *<domain>\<account>*, where *<domain>* is the logon domain and *<account>* is the user account.

When you connect to your mailbox, you should see a page similar to the one shown previously in Figure 30-1. Earlier versions of Exchange Server show a somewhat different interface (Outlook Web Access 5.5, not shown, is considerably different). Outlook Web App opens your Inbox by default, but you can switch to other folders as needed.

The left pane functions much as the Folder Pane does in Outlook 2013, and you can select folders from it. (Throughout this chapter, I'll refer to the left pane as the Folder Pane for simplicity.) The right pane changes to show the folder's contents.

Sending and receiving messages

Outlook Web App automatically shows your current messages when you connect. You can preview messages in the Reading Pane. To read a message in a separate pane, double-click its header to display a window similar to the one shown in Figure 30-4.

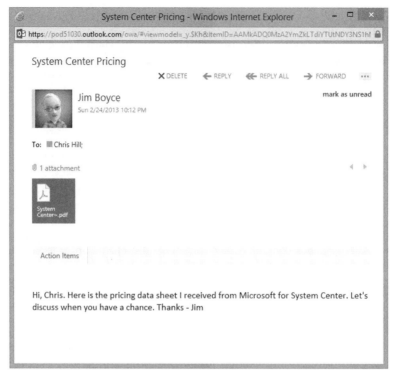

Figure 30-4 Outlook Web App can display messages in a separate window.

As in Outlook 2013, you can reply to or forward email messages. Simply click Reply or Reply All to reply to a message, or click Forward to forward a message. Outlook Web App opens a form similar to the one shown in Figure 30-5. Add addresses as needed and type your text. If you want to add an attachment, click the Insert button on the toolbar at the top of the form and choose Attachment from the resulting menu. Outlook Web App opens the window shown in Figure 30-6 so that you can add one or more attachments to the message.

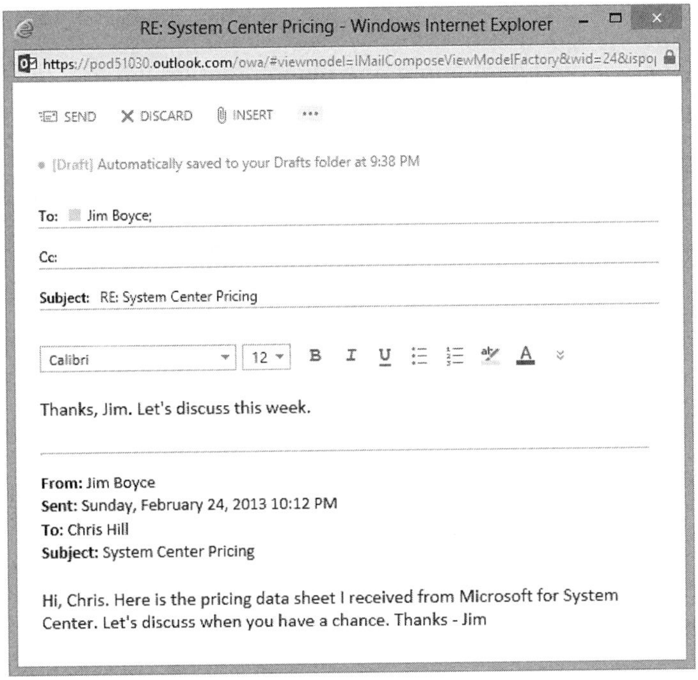

Figure 30-5 This is the Outlook Web App form generated for a reply.

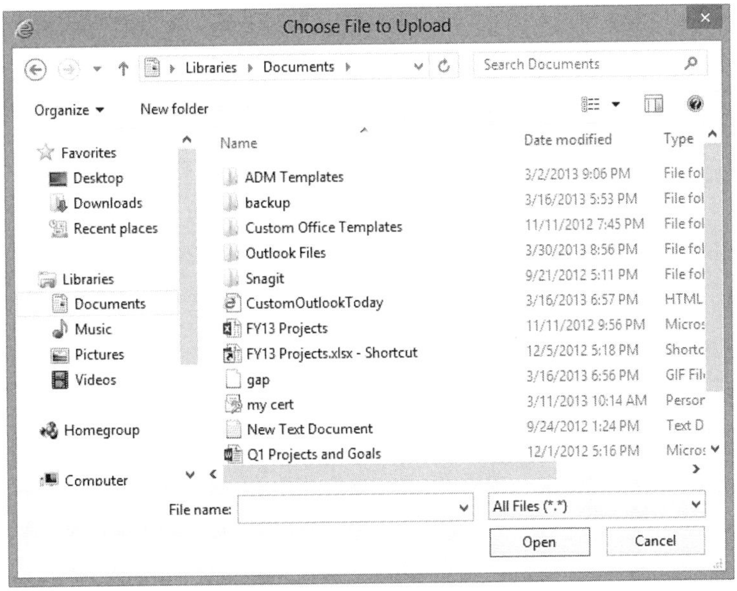

Figure 30-6 Outlook Web App enables you to add attachments to email messages.

When you want to create a message, click the New Mail button near the upper-left corner of the OWA window (refer to Figure 30-1). Outlook Web App opens a new message within the OWA window, as shown in Figure 30-7. You can specify addresses, attachments, body text, and other message properties. Click Send when you're ready to send the message.

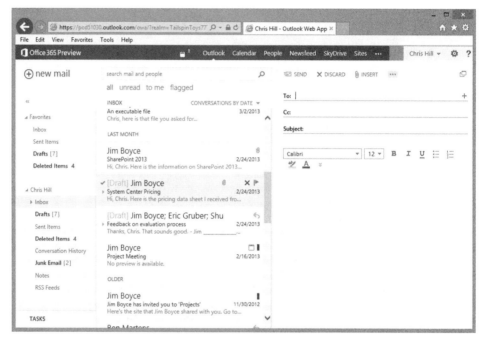

Figure 30-7 Outlook Web App uses in-pane editing for new messages.

> **Note**
>
> **Click Discard if you want to discard the new email.**

You can set a handful of options for a new message by clicking Options with the new message form open. These options correspond to some of the options available in Outlook 2013 (see Figure 30-8).

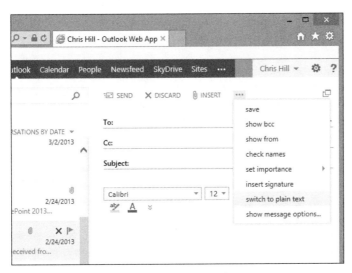

Figure 30-8 Configure message options such as Importance.

Sorting messages

By default, Outlook Web App displays messages sorted by date and time received in multi-line view. You can sort the messages by other properties as well. To do so, select the drop-down menu beside Conversations By Date and choose the field by which you want to sort messages (see Figure 30-9).

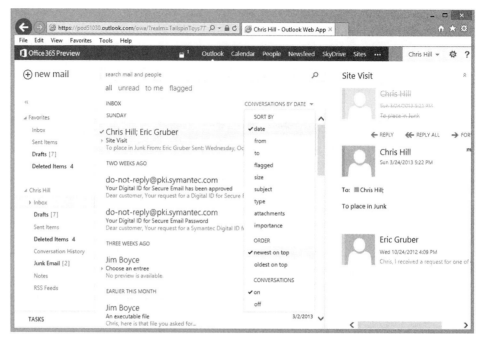

Figure 30-9 You can sort messages by one of several fields.

Copying and moving messages

You can copy and move messages by dragging in Outlook Web App. Open the folder containing the messages that you want to copy or move. If the target folder is hidden, scroll and expand folders as needed in the Folder Pane to display the folder in the Folder List. To move messages, drag them from the right pane to the destination folder in the Folder List. If you want to copy the messages instead of moving them, hold down the Ctrl key while dragging.

Deleting messages

Deleting messages in Outlook Web App is a good way to clean out your mailbox when you don't have Outlook 2013 handy. It's also particularly useful for deleting large or corrupted messages that would otherwise prevent Outlook 2013 from downloading your messages normally.

To delete messages in Outlook Web App, just select the messages and press the Delete key on the keyboard. Outlook Web App moves the messages to the Deleted Items folder. You can also right-click a message and choose Delete from the context menu.

Working with other folders

Outlook Web App does not limit you to working only with your Inbox. You can work with your Mail, Calendar, Contacts, and Tasks folders as well. You can also work with SharePoint libraries and file servers configured on the computer running Exchange Server by the Exchange Server administrator(s). When you select a different folder in the Folder Pane, Outlook Web App 2013 displays the contents of the selected folder in the right pane.

Renaming and deleting folders

While in Outlook Web App 2013, you can rename and delete folders in the Exchange Server mailbox that you have created—but note that you cannot rename or delete the default Outlook 2013 folders. To perform either of the first two actions, display the folder in the Folder Pane, right-click that folder, and then choose either Rename or Delete.

Working with the calendar, contacts, and other items

In addition to working with the Inbox or other message folders, you can manage your schedule, tasks, and contact list on Exchange Server through Outlook Web App.

Calendar folder

To manage your schedule, click the Calendar link at the top of the OWA window. Outlook Web App then displays your Calendar folder. Click the toolbar buttons to choose among the Day, Work Week, Week, and Month views. The page also includes a Date Navigator similar to the one in Outlook 2013, which you can use to select dates (see Figure 30-10).

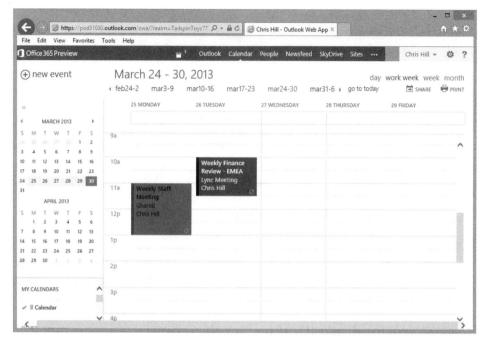

Figure 30-10 You can view and modify your schedule in Outlook Web App.

Click New Event to display an appointment form similar to the one in Outlook 2013. Use the appointment form to specify the title, the time, and other properties for an appointment, just as you would in Outlook 2013.

Contacts folder (People)

You can also view and manage contacts in Outlook Web App. Click People in the Navigation Bar to display the Contacts folder (see Figure 30-11).

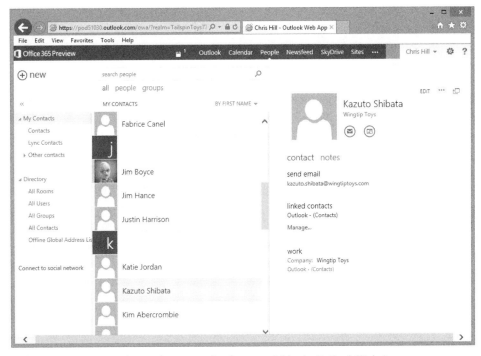

Figure 30-11 You can view and manage the Contacts folder in Outlook Web App.

Simply double-click a contact entry in the list to open a form that contains detailed information for that contact. Click New and choose Create Contact to open the form shown in Figure 30-12, which you can use to create new contact entries. Click Save & Close to save a new contact entry or to save changes to an existing contact entry.

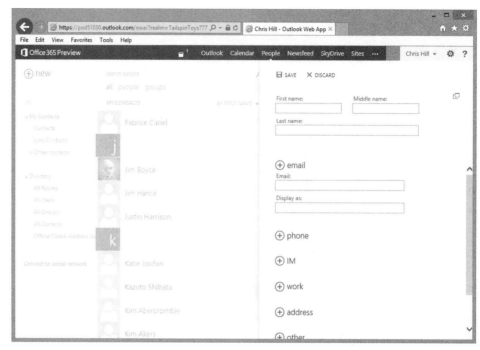

Figure 30-12 The form for creating contact entries in Outlook Web App is similar to the contact form in Outlook 2013.

As when you are working with your mail folders, you can click the drop-down button beside By First Name to choose a different field for sorting contacts. To locate a contact, click in the Search People text field, type a name, and click the magnifying glass icon. Click the X to clear the search results.

Configuring the Out of Office Assistant in Outlook Web App

The Out of Office Assistant automatically responds to messages when you are out of the office. The Out of Office Assistant functions essentially as a server-side rule, replying to messages as they arrive in your Inbox. Although you usually configure the Out of Office Assistant in Outlook 2013, you can also configure it in Outlook Web App.

For details on using the Out of Office Assistant, see the section "Creating Automatic Responses with Automatic Replies (Out of Office)" in Chapter 11, "Using rules, alerts, and automatic responses."

To configure the Out of Office Assistant in Outlook Web App, connect to the server using your web browser and click the gear button (beside the question mark in the upper right) and choose Options to view the Options page. Then click Organize Email, Automatic

Replies to view the Out of Office Assistant (Automatic Replies) properties. To turn on the Out of Office Assistant, select Send Automatic Replies. Outlook Web App 2013 enables you to specify two different replies: one for people inside your organization and one for people outside your organization. When you are satisfied with the autoreply text, click Save to save the changes. When you want to turn off the Out of Office Assistant, open the Options page again and select Don't Send Automatic Replies.

Configuring other options for Outlook Web App

You can use the Outlook Web App Options page (see Figure 30-13) to set general options for your account. Click Settings to configure many other options for Outlook Web App (see Figure 30-14). You can configure date and time options, calendar options, and contact options, and you can also change your password. You can configure reminders, set up a signature for outgoing messages, set spelling options, and configure many additional options, all of which are essentially the same as those available in Outlook 2013 and covered elsewhere in this book.

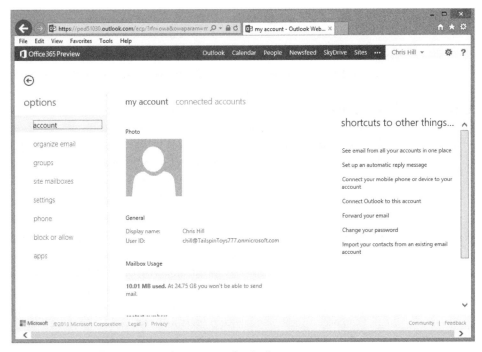

Figure 30-13 Configure options for OWA on the Options page.

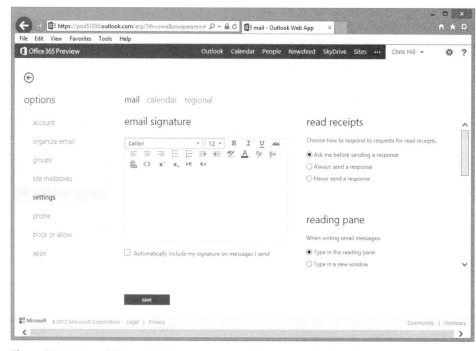

Figure 30-14 Use additional Options pages to configure more Outlook Web App options.

Using Windows 8 Mail

Another alternative to using Outlook or OWA to access your mailbox, whether Exchange Server or other, is the Windows 8 Mail app. This streamlined email application is included with Windows 8 and gives you the ability to connect to mailboxes on a variety of mail services including Live.com, MSN, Exchange, Outlook.com, Office 365, Google, AOL, Yahoo!, and accounts on IMAP mail servers.

I spend a good portion of my day in Outlook. However, I travel fairly regularly and don't always want to lug along my laptop. Instead, I rely on the Mail app running on a Microsoft Surface tablet to access my Exchange mailbox. While the Mail app doesn't give me all the same features as Outlook, I can read, reply to, and forward messages, accomplishing most of what I need to do. For anything the Mail app can't handle, I can fall back on OWA. Best of all, I can access multiple mailboxes (personal and work) within the same app, switching easily between them as needed.

Figure 30-15 shows the Mail app with a selection of accounts added.

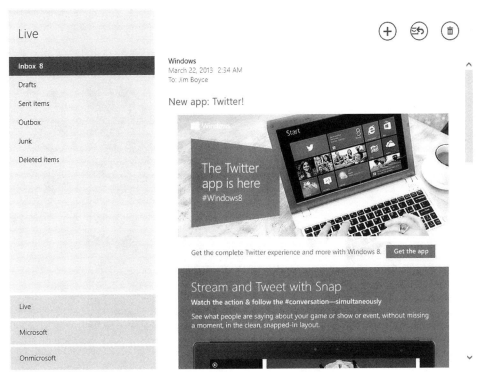

Figure 30-15 The Windows 8 Mail app configured with four mail accounts.

To add an email account to the Windows 8 Mail app, first open the Mail app. Then, open the charms and click Settings to open the Settings page. Click Accounts, and then click Add An Account to access the options shown in Figure 30-16.

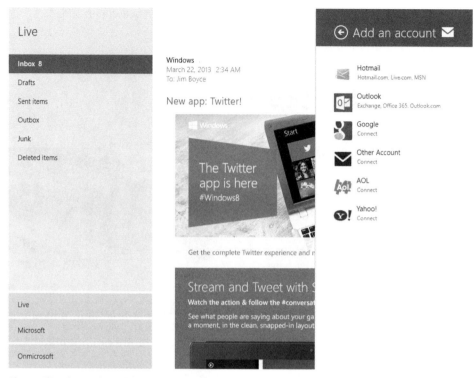

Figure 30-16 Use the Add An Account page to add an email account to the Windows 8 Mail app.

If you are connecting to an Exchange Server account, click the Outlook option in the right pane. The app then prompts you for your email address and password. In most cases, you can enter those two pieces of information and click or tap Connect, and the app will use AutoDiscover to determine the appropriate settings to use for the account. If not, you can click Show More Details and enter the server address, domain, and user name.

> **Note**
>
> Usually, the Mail app will be able to identify your appropriate email server settings based on a minimum of information, such as your email address, user name, and password, regardless of the account type. Just click or tap the account type, enter the information, and click or tap Connect to add the account.

Regardless of the type of account you're using in the Mail app, you can configure various settings to control how the Mail app handles mail for the selected account. For example, with an Exchange Server or Office 365 account, you might want to download only a few weeks' worth of mail, rather than everything in your mailbox. To configure account settings such as these, open the Mail app, then open the charms. Click or tap Settings, click or tap Accounts, and click or tap the account you want to configure. Figure 30-17 shows the settings for an Office 365 account.

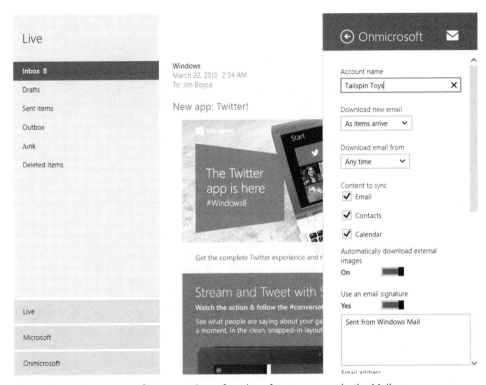

Figure 30-17 You can configure a variety of settings for an account in the Mail app.

Configure the settings as needed, and then simply click or tap any other area of the Mail app to close the settings pane.

Using Windows Phone

While Microsoft's Windows Phone currently has a relatively small market share compared to iOS and Android devices, Windows Phone bears mentioning here as an alternative to Outlook for accessing your mailbox, particularly if that mailbox is on Exchange Server or a related service such as Office 365. Windows Phone provides a solid platform for accessing not only these email services, but also your POP, IMAP, or other email accounts.

Adding an account is easy. The following steps assume you are running Windows Phone 8, but the process should be similar if you are running a different version:

Chapter 30

1. Open Settings, and then open Email+Accounts.

2. Tap Add An Account.

3. Tap Outlook.

4. Enter the email address and password (see Figure 30-18) and then tap Sign In.

Figure 30-18 Enter the email address and password to add an Exchange or Office 365 account in Windows Phone.

5.   Windows Phone automatically adds the new account to your Start screen, as shown
     in Figure 30-19.

Figure 30-19 The new account is added to the Start screen automatically.

Assuming Windows Phone is able to identify the appropriate email server and other set-tings based on the information you've provided, you'll be able to access your email from your phone, as shown in Figure 30-20.

Figure 30-20 You can access your email from a variety of mail servers on a Windows Phone device.

Index

Symbols

% Complete value, 501

A

Accept button, InfoBar, 510
Accepting Task dialog box, 510
Accept Proposal option, 485
Access file extensions (Level 1 attachments), 613–614
access permissions to folders, 576–578
accounts
  AD DS, 748
  data storage for, 31–33
  Exchange ActiveSync, 41
  Exchange Server
    adding, 50–53
    advanced properties for, 53–54
    connection properties for, 55–57
    general properties for, 53
    overview, 41
    security properties for, 54–55
    testing connection, 58–59
    verifying connection status for, 57–58
  Hotmail, 59
  IMAP
    adding, 49–50
    overview, 40–41
  Office 365, 59
  Outlook.com, 59
  POP3
    adding, 41–46
    advanced settings for, 48–49
    general settings for, 46
    outgoing server settings for, 47–48
    overview, 40
  profiles
    choosing, 38–39
    copying, 36
    creating, 35–36
    modifying, 37
    overview, 33–35
    removing, 37
    setting default, 37–38
  SMTP, 39
Active Directory Domain Services (AD DS), 228, 297, 488, 601, 748
Active Server Page, 612

ActiveSync. *See* Exchange ActiveSync
Active view, View tab, 516
Activity class, 699
Actual Work option, Details page, 502
Add An Account page, 762
Add A Timestamp To The Data option, 230
Add Digital Signature To This Message option, 217
Add File Extensions To Block As Level 1 setting, 618
Add File Extensions To Block As Level 2 setting, 618
Add From Store option, 229
Add New Account Wizard, 36
Add New Category dialog box, 79
add-on apps for social networking, 423
Address Book dialog box, 345
address books
  AutoComplete, using for addresses
    deleting entire contents of Suggested Contacts folder, 355
    deleting or adding entries in Suggested Contacts folder, 355
    overview, 353–354
  configuring
    creating address book entries, 349–350
    creating address entries in specific address book, 347–348
    default address book for lookup, 346–347
    how names are checked, 348–349
    modifying addresses, 350
    overview, 344
    removing addresses, 350
    removing Contacts folders from OAB, 345–346
    setting contacts display option for OAB, 345
  contact groups
    creating, 356–359
    deleting, 360
    hiding addresses when using, 360
    modifying, 360
    for multiple address fields, 361
    overview, 356
    renaming, 360
    using with Exchange Server, 361–362
  finding contacts in, 351–352
  Global Address List, 343
  LDAP (Internet directory services), 343
  other address lists, 344
  Outlook 2013 address book, 342

767

About the author

Jim Boyce has authored and coauthored nearly 60 books on computers and technology over the past 20 years, covering operating systems, applications, and programming topics. He has been a frequent contributor to Microsoft.com, TechRepublic.com, and other online publications. Jim has also written for a number of print publications over the years, including *Windows IT Pro, WINDOWS Magazine, InfoWorld*, and others, and was a contributing editor to *WINDOWS Magazine*. He is a former Microsoft MVP.

Jim has been involved with IT in various capacities for nearly 30 years. He has been a CAD system administrator and trainer, college instructor, IT consultant, ISP owner, and practice director for managed services in a global IT services organization. Today, Jim is a support practice manager for Microsoft in its Premier Services organization.

How To Download Your eBook

Thank you for purchasing this Microsoft Press® title. Your companion PDF eBook is ready to download from O'Reilly Media, official distributor of Microsoft Press titles.

To download your eBook, go to

http://aka.ms/PressEbook

and follow the instructions.

Please note: You will be asked to create a free online account and enter the access code below.

Your access code:

> ## LJGBJZN

Microsoft® Outlook® 2013 Inside Out

Your PDF eBook allows you to:

- Search the full text
- Print
- Copy and paste

Best yet, you will be notified about free updates to your eBook.

If you ever lose your eBook file, you can download it again just by logging in to your account.

Need help? Please contact:
mspbooksupport@oreilly.com
or call 800-889-8969.

Now that you've read the book...

Tell us what you think!

Was it useful?
Did it teach you what you wanted to learn?
Was there room for improvement?

Let us know at http://aka.ms/tellpress

Your feedback goes directly to the staff at Microsoft Press,
and we read every one of your responses. Thanks in advance!